Advice from a Pro

Decision-Making Worksheets

personal finance

personal finance

ninth edition

E. Thomas Garman
Virginia Tech University, Professor Emeritus

Raymond E. Forgue
University of Kentucky

Houghton Mifflin Company

Boston   New York

Executive Publisher	George Hoffman
Executive Editor	Lise Johnson
Sponsoring Editor	Mike Schenk
Senior Marketing Manager	Nicole Moore
Senior Project Editor	Margaret Park Bridges
Cover Design Manager	Anne S. Katzeff
Senior Photo Editor	Jennifer Meyer Dare
Senior Composition Buyer	Chuck Dutton
New Title Project Manager	James Lonergan
Editorial Assistant	Katilyn Crowley

Cover image: © Image Source, Getty Images

© Mick Broughton/Alamy; 3, 26: © Gary Conner/PhotoEdit; 11: © REUTERS/HO/Landov; 23: © Mike Watson Images/Corbis; 31, 45: © Kayte M. Deioma/PhotoEdit; 36: © Left Lane Productions/CORBIS; 43: © Dennis Flaherty/Getty Images; 59, 90: © Tara Moore/Getty Images; 70: © Jürg Carstensen/dpa/Corbis; 87: © Michael Newman/PhotoEdit; 95: © Jim Wileman/ Alamy; 97, 126: © Austin MacRae; 108: © Robert Brenner/PhotoEdit; 125: © David Young-Wolff/PhotoEdit; 131, 154: © Antonio Mo/Getty Images; 136: © PM Images/Getty Images; 153: © Michael Newman/PhotoEdit; 159, 179: © Comstock Images/PictureQuest; 166: © Jose Luis Pelaez/Getty Images; 171: TransUnion and the "T" logo are registered or unregistered; copyrighted works, service marks or trademarks of TransUnion LLC. All Rights Reserved. 183, 202: © David Young-Wolff/PhotoEdit; 189: © Joel Gordon; 196: © Digital Vision/Getty Images; 207, 227: © Don Mason/Corbis; 210: © 2007 by Consumers Union of U.S., Inc. Yonkers, NY 10703-1057, a nonprofit organization. Reprinted with permission from ConsumerReports.org for educational purposes only. No commercial use or reproduction permitted. www.ConsumerReports.org. 221: © Bob Daemmrich/The Image Works; 231, 260: © Jason Bye/Alamy; 234: © Andrea Rugg/Beateworks/ Corbis; 258: © Corbis; 265, 294: © Comstock/PictureQuest; 267: © Joel Gordon; 271: © Tom Carter/PhotoEdit; 286: © Ashley Cooper/CORBIS; 299, 316: © Joel Gordon; 302: © Bill Aron/ PhotoEdit; 312: © FURGOLLE/Image Point FR/Corbis; 321, 347: © BananaStock/PictureQuest; 323: © Leslye Borden/PhotoEdit; 341: © Roy Botterell/Corbis; 351: © Spencer Grant/PhotoEdit; 353, 380: © Joel Gordon; 361: © Brian Leng/CORBIS; 369: © Juan Silva/Getty Images; 385, 427: © AP/Wide World Photos; 394: © Motley Fool; 402: © Rachel Epstein/PhotoEdit; 433, 456: © Joel Gordon; 449: © AP/Wide World Photos; 454: © David Young-Wolff/PhotoEdit; 461: © Michael Newman/PhotoEdit; 468: © Fotopic/Index Stock Imagery; 474: © Tim Street-Porter/ Beateworks/Corbis; 485: © Peter M. Fisher/CORBIS; 487, 516: © Kaluzny-Thatcher/Getty Images; 490: © Colin Young-Wolff/PhotoEdit; 496: © Fabio Cardoso/zefa/Corbis; 521, 535: © Joel Gordon; 526: © Jim Arbogast/ Getty Images; 531: © Gabe Palmer/CORBIS

Printed in the U.S.A.

Library of Congress Control Number: 2007921600

ISBN-10: 0-618-93873-7
ISBN-13: 978-0-618-93873-5

1 2 3 4 5 6 7 8 9-DOW-11 10 09 08 07

Brief Contents

Contents

PART 3

Income and Asset Protection   265

10 Managing Property and Liability Risk   266

11 Managing Health Expenses   298

A Note to the Student

Within ten years of graduation, the typical college graduate will purchase three vehicles for more than $25,000 each; spend several thousand dollars on furniture and other household items; shell out a few thousand dollars in interest on credit cards; pay thousands of dollars to the Internal Revenue Service in income and Social Security taxes; buy a life insurance policy; contribute $2000 to $4000 annually to an employer-sponsored tax-sheltered retirement plan; and make a $15,000 to $30,000 down payment to purchase a home valued at more than $200,000. Though this book will give you the skills you need to balance your checkbook and balance your personal budget so that you can perform each of these financial tasks, it is also our hope that it will assist you in making sound financial decisions that will positively affect the balance of your life. Our goal as authors is to give you the knowledge, tools, attitudes, and skills you need to be financially sound and strike your own personal balance. Along with the text, we have developed a full, rich student website that you can use to learn as much as possible from your efforts and, perhaps more importantly, develop your own financial plans.

To the Instructor

This ninth edition of *Personal Finance* appropriately balances *all* the pieces of financial planning. It provides your students with the tools and knowledge they need for their short- and long-term financial success. In addition to updating and enhancing the quality of the content, this edition truly stimulates student interest in a half dozen new ways.

What is the greatest challenge in teaching personal finance? Instructors tell us "to connect all the pieces in a comprehensive manner," "to cover all the material in one course," "to accommodate different learning styles," "to show students the relevancy of the topics," "to visualize real-life examples," "to get students to do a reality check on their own finances," "to make topics interesting that are important later in life," "to teach the time value of money with lots of Excel spreadsheet exercises," "to deliver an effective e-package (including self-tests and decision-making worksheets)," and "to stimulate student interest such that the instructor receives verbal and nonverbal feedback in class." We have listened and responded. The ninth edition addresses those needs precisely. We have made many changes . . . for the better.

Topical Coverage of the Ninth Edition

We have carefully constructed the ninth edition to address instructors' concerns about getting through all the necessary material for this course. The new, streamlined table of contents consists of 18 chapters total broken into 5 Parts: Financial Planning, Money Management, Income and Asset Protection, Investments, and Retirement and Estate Planning. A **new** chapter on Career Planning provides students with the steps they need for successful career planning.

Features

We have carefully designed pedagogical features to strengthen learning opportunities for students. Each feature is designed to communicate vital information meaningfully and to maintain student interest. The following features support student understanding and retention.

CHAPTER 7

Credit Cards and Consumer Loans

⁉ You Must Be Kidding, Right?

College students who have a credit card in their own name (and most do) have an average debt of $2700 at graduation. If they maintain that level of debt for ten years (because their payments equal the charges they make plus interest), how much total interest will they pay?

A. $1200

B. $1800

C. $2700

D. $4860

The answer is D. A credit card with an 18 percent APR (typical for college students) translates to a 1.5 percent rate per month (18% ÷ 12). The $2700 debt multiplied by this rate equals $40.50 ($2700 × 0.015) per month in interest. And $40.50 multiplied by 120 months equals $4860. You must pay more than the amount you charge plus any interest owed for each month in order to reduce your credit card debt and avoid paying many thousands of dollars in interest over the years. Otherwise, you will be in debt forever!

New to this edition, "You Must Be Kidding, Right?" Instructor alert! If you typically skip the opening case, now is the time to change your ways. This feature opens every chapter with a short narrative about a financial topic and a question with four possible answers. The often surprising answers provide an excellent opportunity to engage students in the chapter concepts.

What Do You Recommend?

Darrell Cochrane, a 31-year-old optician in Tampa, Florida, made $42,000 last year. Darrell avoided using credit and credit cards until he was 28 years old, when he missed three months of work due to a water-skiing accident. He made ends meet by obtaining two bank credit cards that, because of his lack of a credit history, carry 19.6 and 24 percent annual percentage rates (APRs). Darrell now has 11 credit card accounts open: five bank cards and six retail store cards. He uses them regularly, presenting whatever card a store will honor. He owes $13,000 on the 24 percent APR card and $4400 on the 19.6 percent APR card. His other three bank cards carry APRs of 11 percent, 12 percent, and 15 percent, and he owes $500 to $700 on each one. For the past year, Darrell has been making only the minimum payments on his bank cards. His retail cards all carry APRs in excess of 21 percent. Although he has managed to keep from running a balance on those cards during most months, occasionally these accounts have balances as well.

What would you recommend to Darrell on the subject of credit cards and consumer loans regarding:

1. His approach to using credit cards, including the number of cards he has?

2. Estimating the credit card interest charges he is paying each month?

3. How he might lower his interest expense each month?

4. Consolidating his credit card debts into one installment loan?

Pretest/Posttest Chapter Opening Case: "What Do You Recommend?" These concise, realistic cases are presented at the beginning of each chapter and are followed by leading questions tying the most important fundamental concepts in the chapter. The case acts as a pretest because students will be able to offer only simplistic, experience-based opinions and suggestions to respond to the questions. This will communicate to students how much they have to learn from reading the chapter. "What Would You Recommend Now?" appears as part of the end-of-chapter pedagogy. At that point, student responses should be informed, practical, and action oriented.

Good Money Habits in Building and Maintaining Good Credit

Make the following your money habits for building and maintaining good credit:

1. Protect your credit reputation just as you would guard your personal reputation.

2. Calculate your own debt limits before taking on any credit.

3. Obtain copies of your credit bureau reports regularly, and challenge all errors or omissions on them.

4. Never cosign a loan for anyone, including relatives.

5. Always repay your debts in a timely manner.

New to this edition, "Good Money Habits in Personal Finance" boxes concisely list the "right kind of advice" for readers desiring success in their personal finances throughout their lives.

Instant Message

Closing Accounts Does Not Help Your Credit Score

Many people think that closing credit card accounts will help a credit score. This is not the case. Credit scores are higher when accounts have been open for longer periods of time. Only when individuals have ten or more cards should they consider closing some accounts and, even then, they should close their newest accounts, not the oldest.

New to this edition, "Instant Messages" provide quick, practical information on a variety of financial issues and opportunities.

"Decision-Making Worksheets" guide students to their best personal finance decisions following a step-by-step process.

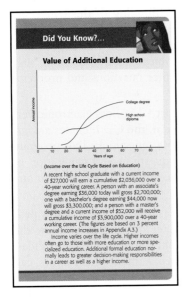

Did You Know?...

Value of Additional Education

(Income over the Life Cycle Based on Education)

A recent high school graduate with a current income of $27,000 will earn a cumulative $2,036,000 over a 40-year working career. A person with an associate's degree earning $36,000 today will gross $2,700,000; one with a bachelor's degree earning $44,000 now will gross $3,300,000; and a person with a master's degree and a current income of $52,000 will receive a cumulative income of $3,900,000 over a 40-year working career. (The figures are based on 3 percent annual income increases in Appendix A.3.)

Income varies over the life cycle. Higher incomes often go to those with more education or more specialized education. Additional formal education normally leads to greater decision-making responsibilities in a career as well as a higher income.

"Did You Know?..." boxes have interesting, catchy titles that encourage students to actually read the information, and research demonstrates this technique works.

"Advice from a Pro" boxes, written by some of the nation's very best personal finance experts, offer expert, real-world advice on getting out of credit card debt, making purchases online, buying a used car, and paying for retirement on the layaway plan plus many other topics.

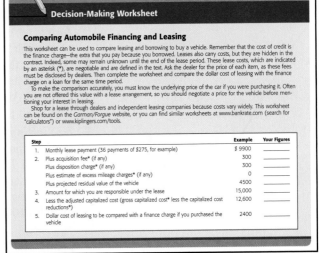

Decision-Making Worksheet

Comparing Automobile Financing and Leasing

This worksheet can be used to compare leasing and borrowing to buy a vehicle. Remember that the cost of credit is the finance charge—the extra that you pay because you borrowed. Leases also carry costs, but they are hidden in the contract. Indeed, some may remain unknown until the end of the lease period. These lease costs, which are indicated by an asterisk (*), are negotiable and are defined in the text. Ask the dealer for the price of each item, as these fees must be disclosed by dealers. Then complete the worksheet and compare the dollar cost of leasing with the finance charge on a loan for the same time period.

To make the comparison accurately, you must know the underlying price of the car if you were purchasing it. Often you are not offered this value with a lease arrangement, so you should negotiate a price for the vehicle before mentioning your interest in leasing.

Shop for a lease through dealers and independent leasing companies because costs vary widely. This worksheet can be found on the *Garman/Forgue* website, or you can find similar worksheets at www.bankrate.com (search for "calculators") or www.kiplingers.com/tools.

Step		Example	Your Figures
1.	Monthly lease payment (36 payments of $275, for example)	$ 9900	_____
2.	Plus acquisition fee* (if any)	300	_____
	Plus disposition charge* (if any)	300	_____
	Plus estimate of excess mileage charges* (if any)	0	_____
	Plus projected residual value of the vehicle	4500	_____
3.	Amount for which you are responsible under the lease	15,000	_____
4.	Less the adjusted capitalized cost (gross capitalized cost* less the capitalized cost reductions*)	12,600	_____
5.	Dollar cost of leasing to be compared with a finance charge if you purchased the vehicle	2400	_____

End-of-Chapter Pedagogy. The end-of-chapter pedagogy carefully directs student learning of the concepts and principles key to success in personal finance.

What Do You Recommend Now? The same leading questions pertaining to the case at the beginning of the chapter are repeated in this section. At this point, however, instructors can anticipate higher-quality responses and a deeper level of understanding because students have read the chapter. Suggested answers appear in the *Instructor's Resource Manual.*

What Do You Recommend Now?

Now that you have read the chapter on buying housing, what do you recommend to Libby Clark regarding:

1. Buying or renting housing in the Denver area?
2. Steps she should take prior to actively looking at homes?
3. Finding a home and negotiating the purchase?
4. The closing process in home buying?
5. Selecting the type of mortgage to fit her needs?
6. Things to consider regarding the sale of her home should she ultimately be promoted to a position in another of the four regions?

Big Picture Summary of Learning Objectives. Three to four sentences review the chapter content following each of the chapter learning objectives.

Let's Talk About It. Students are given an opportunity to converse about their personal experiences related to the chapter by addressing these questions.

Do the Numbers. These questions apply the relevant quantitative mathematical calculations utilized in personal finance decision making. The student website includes calculators for these exercises.

Financial Planning Cases. Students must apply key concepts when analyzing typical personal financial problems, dilemmas, and challenges that face individuals and couples. Because the cases are designed to be both continuous *and* independent of the other chapters' cases, each case can be analyzed by itself. The series of case questions requires data analysis and critical thinking, and this effort reinforces mastery of chapter concepts.

On the 'Net. This end-of-chapter feature offers two or three Internet-based exercises, activities, and focused questions that expand the student's learning in a guided manner, allowing the student to research and apply chapter concepts while finding the answers.

New to this edition, Glossary. A comprehensive end-of-text glossary that includes detailed definitions of all key terms and concepts.

Complete Instructor Support

- **Instructor's Resource Manual.** Written by Karin Bonding of the University of Virginia, this ancillary includes a variety of useful components: suggested course outlines to emphasize a general, insurance, or investments approach to personal finance; a summary overview; learning objectives; and teaching suggestions. Answers and solutions to all end-of-chapter questions and problems have been provided by Raymond Forgue.

- **HMTesting Instructor CD.** This instructor support CD offers electronic versions of the IRM and PowerPoint slides. In addition, the CD includes a computerized *Test Bank*, which contains more than 2500 questions. This program is very user friendly and permits editing of test questions and generation of class exams. The test bank is offered in a Printable Diploma-based format and includes 100 to 200 questions per chapter.

Are You Ready to Invest?

- You balance your budget.
- You are able to save regularly.
- You use credit wisely.
- You carry adequate insurance.

- **PowerPoint slides.** Two sets of downloadable slides are available for this program. The Basic PowerPoint slides contain chapter outlines that follow the text. The Premium slides include all of the content found in the Basic slides, along with supplemental art questions and video content. Instructors can select which set best suits their in-classroom presentation needs. In addition, Classroom Response System ("Clicker") slides with question-and-answer PPT slides for in-class drill and knowledge testing are a new option available to instructors with the ninth edition of the text.

- **Instructor website.** The instructor website that accompanies *Personal Finance* provides a wealth of supplemental materials to enhance learning and aid in course management. Features of the site include Basic and Premium PowerPoint slides, downloadable *Instructor Resource Manual* files, an Updated Content section that highlights changes in personal finance, personal finance online calculators and Web links, and much more.

- **EduSpace powered by Blackboard/WebCT.** EduSpace allows flexible, efficient, and creative ways to present learning materials and opportunities. In addition to course management benefits, instructors may make use of an electronic grade book, receive papers from students enrolled in the course via the Internet, and track student use of communication and collaboration functions.

- **New to this edition,** *Instructor DVD—featuring personal finance tips from The Kiplinger Co.* This Instructor DVD features video discussions with numerous personal finance professionals from The Kiplinger Co. These discussions contain personal finance tips illustrating and explaining pertinent topics such as job searching, income taxes, student loans, mortgage shopping, and more. The video clips from the DVD will also be available as streaming content in EduSpace.

Kiplinger

Complete Student Support

My Personal Financial Planner is a handbook for students to use in planning and organizing their personal finances. This booklet contains worksheets, schedules, and planners for financial planning. Some of the worksheets mimic the calculations and planning exercises covered in the book, others are for your use in developing your own financial plans and activities.

Student website with *Your Guide to an A*. The student website accompanying *Personal Finance* contains many useful study aids and resources:

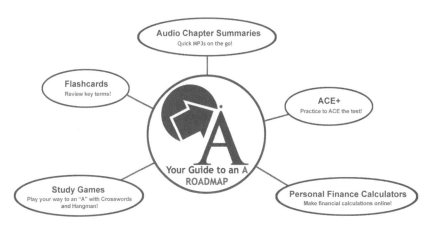

The free open-access student website includes an *ACE Practice* Test for each chapter, online versions of several in-text features, a full glossary, a list of updated content, and more. A selection of the worksheets from the *My Personal Financial Planner* workbook are also available online. These can be copied and printed for students to turn in, as assigned, to their instructor.

The password-protected *Your Guide to an A* student website includes additional premium content. This site includes all the open-access resources **plus** *ACE Plus Tests* (two 25-question tests per chapter); audio chapter reviews; hangman, crossword, and drill flashcard games for each chapter; and a new set of Excel spreadsheet calculators to assist students in decision making and problem solving.

New to this edition, Excel spreadsheet calculators. Over 50 Excel calculators prepared by the authors are on the student website. Most of the "Decision-Making Worksheets" from the book have been included, as well as all the major formulas from the text. You can use these materials to complete class assignments and end-of-chapter *Do the Numbers* and *Financial Planning Cases* AND to create key parts of your own personal financial plan.

CHAPTER 1

Understanding Personal Finance

You Must Be Kidding, Right?

Se Ri Pak invests $250 a month, or $3000 a year, in her 401(k) retirement account, which earns an 8 percent annual return. After 35 years, how much money will she have in the account over and above the amounts she will contribute through the years?

A. $105,000

B. $210,000

C. $471,000

D. $576,000

The answer is D, $471,000 ($576,000 − $105,000). Se Ri will contribute $105,000 ($3000 × 35). Se Ri makes the big money ($471,000) off "the compounding money," not on the amount of money ($105,000) she put into her retirement plan. It's all about the magic of compound interest!

LEARNING OBJECTIVES

After reading this chapter, you should be able to:

1 **Use** the building blocks to achieving financial success.

2 **Understand** how the economy affects your personal financial success.

3 **Apply** economic principles when making financial decisions.

4 **Perform** time value of money calculations in personal financial decision making.

5 **Make** smart decisions about your employee benefits.

6 **Identify** the professional qualifications of providers of financial advice.

What Do You Recommend?

Lauren Crawford, age 23, recently graduated with her bachelor's degree in library and information sciences. She is about to take her first professional position as an archivist with a civil engineering firm in a rapidly expanding area in the U.S. Southwest. While in school, Lauren worked part time, earning about $8000 per year. For the past two years, she has managed to put $1000 each year into an individual retirement account (IRA). Lauren owes $15,000 in student loans on which she is obliged now to begin making payments. Her new job will pay $45,000. Lauren may begin participating in her employer's 401(k) retirement plan immediately, and she can contribute up to 6 percent of her salary to the plan.

What do you recommend to Lauren on the importance of personal finance regarding:

1. Participating in her employer's 401(k) retirement plan?

2. Understanding the effects of income taxes on her decision to participate in her employer's 401(k) plan?

3. Factoring the current state of the economy into her personal financial planning?

4. Using time value of money considerations to project what her IRA might be worth at age 63?

5. Using time value of money considerations to project what her 401(k) plan might be worth when she is age 63 if she were to participate fully?

FOR HELP with studying this chapter, visit the Online Student Center:

www.college.hmco.com/pic/garman9e

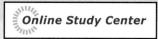

Good Money Habits in Personal Finance

Make the following your money habits in understanding personal finance:

1. Spend significantly less than you make and save using a pay-yourself-first approach.

2. Stay up-to-date with current economic conditions and the knowledge to manage your personal finances.

3. When making financial decisions, use marginal and opportunity costs and time value of money calculations.

4. Establish financial goals and take actions to achieve them.

5. Take advantage of tax sheltering through your employer's benefits program.

6. Believe in compounding by allowing your money to work for you over time by earning interest on top of the principal and other accrued interest.

7. Keep debt under control.

8. Take responsibility for managing your own financial success.

financial literacy Knowledge of facts, concepts, principles, and technological tools that are fundamental to being smart about money.

personal finance The study of personal and family resources considered important in achieving financial success; it involves how people spend, save, protect, and invest their financial resources.

financial responsibility Means that you are accountable for your future financial well-being and that you strive to make wise personal financial decisions.

1 LEARNING OBJECTIVE

Use the building blocks to achieving financial success.

trade-off Giving up one thing for another.

Your **financial literacy** is your knowledge of facts, concepts, principles, and technological tools that are fundamental to being smart about money. Financial literacy empowers you. It improves your ability to handle day-to-day financial matters, helps you avoid the consequences of poor financial decisions that could take years to overcome, and helps you make informed and confident personal money decisions.

Personal finance is the study of personal and family resources considered important in achieving financial success; it involves how people spend, save, protect, and invest their financial resources. Topics in personal finance include financial and career planning, budgeting, tax management, cash management, credit cards, borrowing, major expenditures, risk management, investments, retirement planning, and estate planning. A solid understanding of personal finance topics offers you a better chance of success in facing the financial challenges, responsibilities, and opportunities of life. Such successes might include paying minimal credit costs, not paying too much in income taxes, purchasing automobiles at low prices, financing housing on excellent terms, buying appropriate and fairly priced insurance, selecting successful investments that match your needs, planning for a comfortable retirement, and passing on your estate with minimal transfer costs.

Financial responsibility means that you are accountable for your future financial well-being and that you strive to make good decisions in personal finance. Studying personal finance will help you avoid financial mistakes and show you how to take advantage of financial opportunities. At the beginning of each chapter, we provide a short case vignette titled "What Do You Recommend?" Each case focuses on the financial challenges that can be experienced by someone who has not learned about the material in that chapter. You will be asked to think about what advice you might give the person as you study the chapter. Then at the end of each chapter, you will again be asked to provide more informed advice based on what you have learned. You will be smarter then!

The goal of this book is to provide you access to up-to-date information and rational suggestions to empower you to be able to make informed decisions about spending, managing money, maintaining creditworthiness, purchasing insurance, and saving and investing. Good decision making means you will control your personal financial destiny.

The Building Blocks to Achieving Personal Financial Success

Today's marketplace provides a constant barrage of messages suggesting that you can spend and borrow your way to financial success, security, and wealth. These messages are very enticing for those starting out in their financial lives. In truth, overspending and overuse of consumer credit actually *impede* financial success!

Many people think that being wealthy is a function of how much you earn or inherit. In reality, it is much more closely related to your ability to understand the trade-offs and decisions that generate wealth for you. A **trade-off** is giving up one thing for another. For example, it is wise to give up some current spending in order to enjoy a financially comfortable retirement.

You have to do only a *few* things right in personal finance during your lifetime, as long as you don't do too many things wrong. Personal finance is not rocket science. You can succeed very well in your personal finances by making appropriate plans and taking actions to implement those plans.

Spend Less to Save and Invest

First, recognize that financial objectives are rarely achieved without forgoing or sacrificing current *consumption* (spending on goods and services). This restraint is accomplished by putting money into **savings** (income not spent on current consumption) for use in achieving future goals. Some savings are actually **investments** (assets purchased with the goal of providing additional income from the asset itself). By saving and investing, people are much more likely to have funds available for future consumption.

Effective financial management often separates the haves from the have-nots. The haves, observes Virginia Tech professor Celia Hayhoe, are those people who learn to live on less than they earn and are the savers and investors of society. The have-nots are the spenders who live paycheck to paycheck, usually with high consumer debt. In short, follow the adage to "Spend some and save some."

Saving for future consumption represents a good illustration of the human desire to achieve a certain **standard of living.** This standard is what an individual or group earnestly desires and seeks to attain, to maintain if attained, to preserve if threatened, and to regain if lost. At any particular time, individuals actually experience their **standard of living.** In essence, your **level of living** is where you would like to be, and your level of living is where you actually are.

Financial Success and Happiness

Financial success is the achievement of financial aspirations that are desired, planned, or attempted. Success is defined by the person that seeks it. Some define financial success as being able to actually live according to one's standard of living. Many seek financial security, which provides the comfortable feeling that your financial resources will be adequate to fulfill any needs you have as well as most of your wants. Others want to be wealthy and have an abundance of money, property, investments, and other resources. A fundamental truth of personal finance is that you cannot build financial security or wealth unless you spend less than you earn. As a result, you cannot reach your standard of living without somewhat restricting your level of living as you save and invest. That's the trade-off.

Financial happiness encompasses a lot more than just making money. It is the satisfaction you feel about money matters. People who are happy about their finances are likely to be in control of their money, and this happiness spills over in a positive way to feelings about their overall enjoyment of life. Financial happiness is in part a result of practicing *good financial behaviors*—the subject of this book. Examples of such behaviors include paying bills on time, spending less than you earn, knowing where your money goes, and investing some money for the future. The more good financial behaviors you practice, the greater your financial happiness. In fact, just making progress toward achieving financial goals contributes to financial happiness.

Using the Building Blocks

Bridging the gap between one's level of living and one's desired standard of living involves learning about how to achieve financial success. Figure 1.1 shows how the building blocks of a financially

savings Income not spent on current consumption.

investments Assets purchased with the goal of providing additional income from the asset itself.

standard of living Material well-being and peace of mind that individuals or groups earnestly desire and seek to attain, to maintain if attained, to preserve if threatened, and to regain if lost.

Instant Message

Buy Happiness With Money

Twenty-five percent of Americans believe that you can buy happiness with money.

Instant Message

Frequently Heard Advice

The most frequently heard advice from financial advisers is to reduce your debts so you can save more.

Figure 1.1

The Building Blocks of Your Financial Success

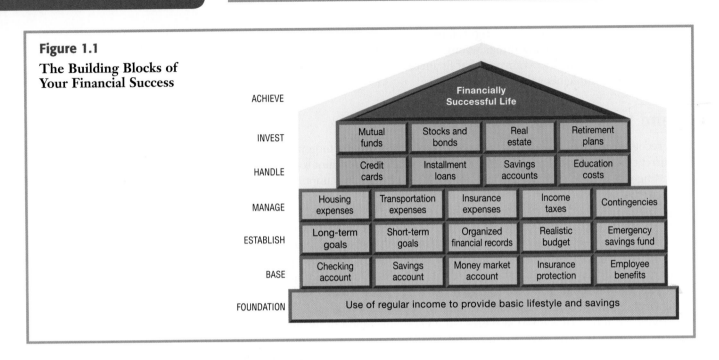

ACHIEVE		**Financially Successful Life**	
INVEST	Mutual funds	Stocks and bonds	Real estate	Retirement plans
HANDLE	Credit cards	Installment loans	Savings accounts	Education costs
MANAGE	Housing expenses	Transportation expenses	Insurance expenses	Income taxes	Contingencies
ESTABLISH	Long-term goals	Short-term goals	Organized financial records	Realistic budget	Emergency savings fund
BASE	Checking account	Savings account	Money market account	Insurance protection	Employee benefits
FOUNDATION	Use of regular income to provide basic lifestyle and savings			

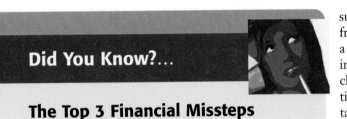

Did You Know?...

The Top 3 Financial Missteps in Personal Finance

People slip up in personal finance when they do the following:

1. Only think about money matters when they have a financial problem
2. Spend more than they earn
3. Get financial advice from amateurs

successful life fit together. Financial success and happiness come from using the building blocks of personal finance, such as having a foundation of regular income to provide basic lifestyle and savings, and establishing a financial base using employee benefits and checking and savings accounts. Other building blocks include setting financial goals, controlling expenditures, managing income taxes, handling credit cards, and investing in mutual funds and retirement plans. All of these factors are examined in the remaining chapters of the text.

✓ CONCEPT CHECK 1.1

1. Describe financial success.
2. What is financial happiness?
3. What are the building blocks to achieving financial success?

The Economy Affects Your Personal Financial Success

2 LEARNING OBJECTIVE

Understand how the economy affects your personal financial success.

Your success in personal finance depends in part on how well you understand the economic environment; the current stage of the business cycle; and the future direction of the economy, inflation, and interest rates.

Where Are We in the Business Cycle?

economic growth A condition of increasing production (business spending) and consumption (consumer spending) in the economy and hence increasing national income.

An **economy** is a system of managing the productive and employment resources of a country, state, or community. The U.S. federal government attempts to regulate the country's overall economy to maintain stable prices (low inflation) and stable levels of employment (low unemployment). In this way, the government seeks to achieve sustained **economic growth**, which is a condition of increasing production (business spending) and consumption (consumer spending) in the economy—and hence increasing national income. Government policies also affect the economy. For example, tax cuts put money into consumers' pockets, which they are then likely to spend. Tax increases, in contrast, depress consumer demand.

Growth in the U.S. economy varies over time. The **business cycle** (also called the **economic cycle**) is a process by which the economy grows and contracts over time, and it can be depicted as a wavelike pattern of rising and falling economic activity in which the same pattern occurs again and again over time. As illustrated in Figure 1.2, the phases of the business cycle are *expansion* (when the economy is increasing), *peak* (the end of an expansion and the beginning of a contraction), *contraction* (when the economy is falling), and *trough* (the end of a contraction and beginning of an expansion).

The preferred stage of the economic cycle is the expansion phase, where production is at high capacity, unemployment is low, retail sales are high, and prices and interest rates are low or falling. Under these conditions, consumers find it easier to buy homes, cars, and expensive goods on credit, and businesses are encouraged to borrow to expand production to meet the increased consumer demand. The stock market also rises because investors expect higher profits.

As the demand for credit increases, short-term interest rates rise because more borrowers want money. Consumers and businesses purchase more goods, exerting upward pressure on prices. Eventually, prices and interest rates climb high enough to stifle consumer and business borrowing, send stock prices down, and choke off the expansion. The result is a period of negligible economic growth or even a decline in economic activity.

In such situations, the economy often contracts and moves toward a **recession.** The federal government's Business Cycle Dating Committee officially defines a recession as "a recurring period of decline in total output, income, employment and trade, usually lasting from six months to a year and marked by widespread contractions in many sectors of the economy." During recessions, consumers become pessimistic about their future buying plans. The typical U.S. recession is marked by an average economic decline of 2 percent that lasts for ten months with an average unemployment rate exceeding 6 percent. There have been three recessions in the past 25 years.

Did You Know?...

How to Be Financially Literate

The financially illiterate easily incur excessive levels of consumer debt, pay too much interest on debt, spend money unconsciously or frivolously, delay saving for retirement, fall prey to investment scams, buy the wrong kind of life insurance, and ultimately are unable to reach their financial objectives. They may not even have any financial goals. It is not fun going through life mired in financial problems and "learning from bad experiences."

Financial literacy is not widespread. Obstacles to financial literacy include a lack of knowledge about personal finance, the complexity of financial decisions, and the lack of time to learn about personal finance. People today face the challenge of saving, investing, and managing their own retirement funds, so it is no wonder that many feel less than competent, a bit confused, and a little anxious about financial matters.

But we are not talking about you! You are taking a course in personal finance, so you are already ahead in your money matters. So keep reading and studying. You will be financially literate!

business cycle/economic cycle Business cycles can be depicted as a wavelike pattern of rising and falling economic activity; the phases of the business cycle include expansion, peak, contraction (which may turn into recession), and trough.

recession A recurring period of decline in total output, income, employment and trade, usually lasting from six months to a year and marked by widespread contractions in many sectors of the economy.

Figure 1.2
Business Cycle Phases

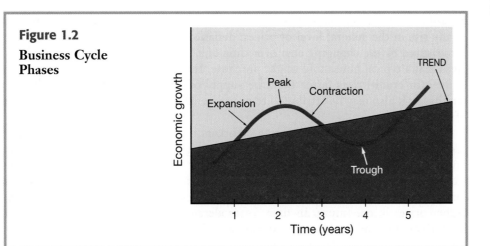

Eventually the economic contraction ends, and consumers and businesses become more optimistic. The economy then moves beyond the trough toward expansion, where levels of production, employment, and retail sales begin to improve (usually rapidly), allowing the overall economy to experience some growth from its previously weakened state. The entire business cycle may take four to five years.

What Is the Future Direction of the Economy?

To make sound financial decisions, you need to know both the current state of the business cycle and the direction in which it may be headed in the next few years. For example, when the economy begins to show clear signs of a slowdown, it may be a good time to invest in fixed-interest securities because interest rates are sure to fall as the government lowers its own interest rates to boost the economy. A point at which the economy is in the trough of a recession may be an excellent time to invest in stocks because the economy will soon expand and stock prices will rise. Using your knowledge of where we are in the business cycle and tracking a few economic statistics will guide you to make modest adjustment in your long-term financial strategy.

gross domestic product (GDP)
The nation's broadest measure of economic health, it reports how much economic activity (all goods and services) has occurred within the U.S. borders during a given period.

Track the Gross Domestic Product The **gross domestic product (GDP)** is the broadest measure of the economic health of the nation because it reports how much economic activity (all goods and services) has occurred within the U.S. borders. The government regularly announces the rate at which the GDP has grown during the previous three months (www.bea.gov/newsreleases/rels.htm). An annual rate of less than 2 percent is considered low growth; 4 percent or more is considered vigorous growth.

Track the Employment Report The federal government's *Employment Report* tracks the number of jobs created every month (www.bls.gov/ces). More new jobs means more consumer spending.

index of leading economic indicators (LEI) A composite index reported monthly by the Conference Board that collects relevant economic data for business, governments, and individuals' use.

Track the Index of Leading Economic Indicators The **index of leading economic indicators (LEI)** is a composite index, reported monthly by the Conference Board, that suggests the future direction of the U.S. economy (www.conference-board .org). The LEI averages 21 components of growth from different segments of the economy, such as building permits, factory orders, and new private housing starts.

Track the Consumer Confidence Index The *consumer confidence index* gives a sense of consumers' willingness to spend, which spurs the economy (www .conference-board.org). Growing confidence suggests increased consumer spending.

What Is the Future Direction of Inflation, Prices, and Interest Rates?

inflation A steady and sustained rise in general price levels across economic sectors; measured by the changing cost over time of a "market basket" of goods and services that a typical household might purchase.

Inflation and interest rates typically move in the same direction. **Inflation** is a steady rise in the general level of prices; deflation involves falling prices. Inflation is measured by the changing cost over time of a "market basket" of goods and services that a typical household might purchase. Inflation occurs when the supply of money (or credit) rises faster than the supply of goods and services available for purchases. It also may be attributed to excessive demand or sharply increasing costs of production.

Inflation can be self-perpetuating. Workers may ask for higher wages, thereby adding to the cost of production. In response to the increases in the costs of labor and raw materials, manufacturers will charge more for their products. Lenders, in turn, will require higher interest rates to offset the lost purchasing power of the loaned funds. Consumers will lessen their resistance to price increases because they fear even higher prices in the future. In times of moderate to high inflation, buying power declines rapidly, and people on fixed incomes suffer the most.

How Inflation Affects Income and Consumption

When prices are rising, an individual's income must rise at the same rate to maintain its **purchasing power,** which is a measure of the goods and services that one's income will buy. From an income point of view, inflation has significant effects. Consider the case of Scott Marshall of Chicago, a single man who took a job in retail management three years ago at a salary of $32,000 per year. Since that time, Scott has received annual raises of $800, $900, and $1000, but he still cannot make ends meet because of inflation. Although Scott received raises, his current income of $34,700 ($32,000 + $800 + $900 + $1000) did not keep pace with the annual inflation rate of 4.0 percent ($32,000 × 1.04 = $33,280; $33,280 × 1.04 = $34,611; $34,611 × 1.04 = $35,996). If Scott's cost of living rose at the same rate as the general price level, in the third year he would be $1296 ($35,996 − $34,700) short of keeping up with inflation. He would need $1296 more in the third year to maintain the same purchasing power that he enjoyed in the first year.

Personal incomes rarely keep up in times of high inflation. Your **real income** (income measured in constant prices relative to some base time period) is the more important number. It reflects the actual buying power of the **nominal income** (also called **money income**) that you have to spend as measured in current dollars. Rising nominal income during times of inflation creates the illusion that you are making more money, when in actuality that may not be true.

To compare your annual wage increase with the rate of inflation for the same time period, you first convert your dollar raise into a percentage, as follows:

$$\text{Percentage change} = \frac{\text{nominal income after raise} - \text{nominal income last year}}{\text{nominal income last year}} \times 100 \quad (1.1)$$

For example, imagine that John Bedoin, a single parent and assistant manager of a convenience store in Columbia, Missouri, received a $1600 raise to push his $37,000 annual salary to $38,600. Using Equation (1.1), John calculated his percentage change in personal income as follows:

$$\frac{(\$38,600 - \$37,000)}{\$37,000} = 0.043 \times 100 = 4.3\%^*$$

After a year during which inflation was 4.0 percent, he did better than the inflation rate because his raise amounted to 4.3 percent. Measured in real terms, John's raise was 0.3 percent (4.3 − 4.0). In dollars, his real income after the raise can be calculated by dividing his new nominal income by 1.0 plus the previous year's inflation rate (expressed as a decimal):

$$\text{Real income} = \frac{\text{nominal income after raise}}{1.0 + \text{previous inflation rate}} \quad (1.2)$$

$$\frac{\$38,600}{1 + 0.040} = \$37,115$$

Clearly, a large part of the $1600 raise John received was eaten up by inflation. To John, only $115 ($37,115 − $37,000) represents real economic progress, while $1485 ($1600 − $115) was used to pay the inflated prices on goods and services. The $115 real raise is equivalent to 0.31 percent ($115 ÷ $37,000) of his previous income, reflecting the difference between John's percentage raise in nominal dollars and the inflation rate.

How Inflation Is Measured

The U.S. Bureau of Labor Statistics measures inflation on a monthly basis using the **consumer price index (CPI).** The CPI is a broad measure of changes in the prices of all goods and services purchased for

---

purchasing power Measure of the goods and services that one's income will buy.

real income Income measured in constant prices relative to some base time period. It reflects the actual buying power of the money you have as measured in constant dollars.

nominal income Also called money income, it is income that has not been adjusted for inflation and decreasing purchasing power.

consumer price index (CPI) A broad measure of changes in the prices of all goods and services purchased for consumption by urban households.

---

*This equation shows how the percentage change is calculated for any difference between two measurements. Divide the difference between measurement 1 and measurement 2 by the value of measurement 1. For example, a stock selling for $65 per share on January 1 and for $76 on December 31 of the same year would have risen 16.92 percent during the year: ($76 − $65) ÷ $65 = 0.1692 or 16.92%.

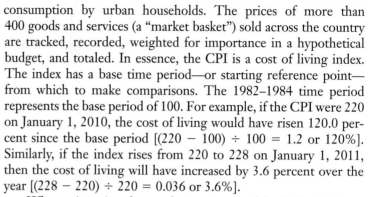

Advice from a Pro...

Seven Money Mantras for a Richer Life

1. It's not an asset if you are wearing it!
2. Is this a need or is it a want?
3. Sweat the small stuff.
4. Cash is better than credit.
5. Keep it simple.
6. Priorities lead to prosperity.
7. Enough is enough!

Michelle Singletary
Nationally syndicated Washington Post *columnist ("The Color of Money") and author of 7* Money Mantras for a Richer Life: How to Live Well with the Money You Have

Reprinted with permission of the author.

consumption by urban households. The prices of more than 400 goods and services (a "market basket") sold across the country are tracked, recorded, weighted for importance in a hypothetical budget, and totaled. In essence, the CPI is a cost of living index. The index has a base time period—or starting reference point— from which to make comparisons. The 1982–1984 time period represents the base period of 100. For example, if the CPI were 220 on January 1, 2010, the cost of living would have risen 120.0 percent since the base period [(220 − 100) ÷ 100 = 1.2 or 120%]. Similarly, if the index rises from 220 to 228 on January 1, 2011, then the cost of living will have increased by 3.6 percent over the year [(228 − 220) ÷ 220 = 0.036 or 3.6%].

When prices rise, the purchasing power of the dollar declines, but not by the same percentage. Instead, it falls by the *reciprocal amount* of the price increase (the counterpart ratio quantity needed to produce unity). In the preceding illustration where prices increase between 2010 and 2011, prices rose 3.6 percent, whereas the purchasing power of the dollar declined 3.5 percent over the same period. [The previous year base of 220 divided by the index of 228 equals 0.965; the reciprocal is 0.035 (1 − 0.965), or 3.5%]

Inflation pushes up the costs of the products and services we consume. If automobile prices rose 20 percent over the past five years, for example, then it will take $28,800 now to buy a car that once sold for $24,000. Conversely, the purchasing power of the car-buying dollar has fallen to 83.3 percent of its original power ($24,000 ÷ $28,800) five years ago. If your market basket of goods and services differs from that used to calculate the CPI, you might have a very different *personal inflation* rate (the rate of increase in prices of items purchased by a particular person). Inflation pushes up the cost of borrowing, so monthly car payments and home mortgage rates increase when inflation rises.

federal funds rate The rate that banks charge one another for overnight loans; set by the Federal Reserve Board.

Track the Federal Funds Rate to Forecast Inflation
You can forecast interest rates by paying attention to changes in the **federal funds rate,** which is the rate that banks charge one another on overnight loans. Because it is set by the **Federal Reserve Board** (an agency of the federal government commonly referred to as the **Fed**) and regularly reported by the news media, the federal funds rate provides an early indication of Fed policy and trends for longer-term interest rates. When the Fed believes the economy is growing too fast, it raises the rate and in turn lenders raise their rates for short-term loans, thereby making it more costly to borrow and spend. As a result, spending in the economy slows.

interest The price of borrowing money.

How Inflation Affects Borrowing, Saving, and Investing
Interest is the price of money. During times of high inflation, interest rates on new loans for cars, homes, and credit cards rise. Even though nominal interest rates for savers rise as well, the increases do not provide "real" gains if the inflation rate is higher than the interest rate on savings accounts or certificates of deposit.

Smart investors recognize that the degree of inflation risk is higher for long-term lending (5 or 20 years, for example) than for short-term lending (such as a year) because the likelihood of error when estimating inflation increases when lots of time is involved. Therefore, long-term interest rates are generally higher than short-term interest rates. Similarly, stock market investors are negatively affected when inflation causes businesses to pay more when they borrow, thereby reducing their profits, and depressing stock prices. Throughout your financial life, you will want to factor the impact of inflation into your financial decisions so as to avoid its negative effects.

The Fed meets regularly to discuss the economy and review federal interest rates.

CONCEPT CHECK 1.2

1. Summarize the phases of the business cycle.
2. Describe two statistics that help predict the future direction of the economy.
3. Give an example of how inflation affects income and consumption.
4. Explain how the federal government measures inflation.

Think Like an Economist When Making Financial Decisions

Understanding and applying basic economic principles will affect your financial success. The most important of these are opportunity costs, marginal utility and costs, and marginal income tax rate.

3 LEARNING OBJECTIVE
Apply economic principles when making financial decisions.

Opportunity Costs in Decision Making

The **opportunity cost** of a decision is the value of the next best alternative that must be forgone. Examples of personal opportunity costs are time, effort, and health, and examples of financial opportunity costs are interest, safety, and liquidity. Using the concept of opportunity costs allows you to address the personal consequences of choices because every decision inevitably involves trade-offs. For example, suppose that instead of reading this book you could have gone to a movie or watched television, but mainly you wanted to sleep. The lost benefit of that sleep—the next best alternative—is the opportunity cost when you choose to read. Knowing the opportunity cost of alternatives aids decision making because it indicates whether the decision made is truly the best option.

In personal finance, opportunity cost reflects the best alternative of what one could have done instead of choosing to spend, save, or invest money. For example, by decid-

opportunity cost The opportunity cost of any decision is the value of the next best alternative that must be forgone.

ing to put $2000 into a stock mutual fund for retirement rather than keeping the funds readily available in a savings account, you are giving up the option of using the money for a down payment on a new automobile. Keeping the money in a savings account has the opportunity cost of the higher return on investment that the stock mutual fund might pay. This opportunity to earn a higher rate of return is a primary consideration when making low-risk investment decisions.

Other challenging opportunity cost decisions are renting versus buying housing, buying a new or used car, buying or leasing a vehicle, working or borrowing to pay for college, purchasing life insurance or not, and starting early or late to save and invest for retirement. Another opportunity cost decision often is returning to college for a graduate degree.

If these costs are underestimated, then decisions will be based on faulty information, and judgments may prove wrong. Properly valuing the costs and benefits of alternatives represents a key step in rational decision making. The opportunity cost mathematics of the rent versus buy decision is illustrated later in Chapter 9.

Marginal Utility and Costs in Decision Making

Utility is the ability of a good or service to satisfy a human want. A key task in personal finance is to determine how much utility you will gain from a particular decision. For example, if you decide to spend $70 on a ticket to a concert, you might begin by thinking about what you might gain from the expenditure. Perhaps you'll enjoy a nice evening, good music, and so on. **Marginal utility** is the extra satisfaction derived from having one more incremental unit of a product or service. **Marginal cost** is the additional (marginal) cost of one more incremental unit of some item. When known, this cost can be compared with the marginal utility received. Thinking about marginal utility and marginal cost can help in decision making because it reminds us to compare only the most important variables. It requires that we examine what we will really gain if we also experience a certain extra cost.

To illustrate this idea, assume that you consider spending $150 instead of $90 (an additional $60) for a front-row seat at the concert. What marginal utility will you gain from that decision? Perhaps an ability to see and hear more or the satisfaction of having one of the best seats in the facility. You would then ask yourself whether those extra benefits are worth 60 extra dollars. In practice, people are inclined to seek additional utility as long as the marginal utility exceeds the marginal cost.

In another example, imagine that two new automobiles are available on a dealership lot in Ferndale, Michigan, where retired engineer Charlene Hicks is trying to make a purchase decision. Both vehicles are similar models, but one is a Mercury and the other is a Ford. The Mercury, with a sticker price of $29,100, has a moderate number of options; the Ford, with a sticker price of $30,800, has numerous options. Marginal analysis suggests that Charlene does not need to consider all of the options when comparing the vehicles. Instead, the concept of marginal cost says to compare the benefits of the additional options with the additional costs—$1700 in this instance ($30,800 − $29,100). Charlene need decide only whether the additional options are worth $1700.

Marginal Income Tax Rate in Decision Making

When making financial decisions, consider the economic effects of paying income taxes. Of particular importance is the **marginal tax rate,** which is the tax rate at which your last dollar earned is taxed. As income rises, taxpayers pay progressively higher marginal income tax rates. Financially successful people often pay U.S. federal income taxes at the 25 percent, or higher, marginal tax rate. For example, if Juanita Martinez, an unmarried office manager working in Atlanta, Georgia, has a taxable income of

Instant Message

Save $4.66 for Every $1 Not Saved Earlier

If you want to retire at age 63, you will have to save about $4.66 beginning at age 40 to make up for every dollar you did not save at age 20.

marginal utility The extra satisfaction derived from gaining one more incremental unit of a product or service.

marginal cost The additional (marginal) cost of one more incremental unit of some item.

marginal tax rate The tax rate at which your last dollar earned is taxed.

$66,000 and receives a $1000 bonus from her employer, she has to pay an extra $250 in taxes on the bonus income ($1000 × 0.25 = $250). Juanita also has to pay state income taxes of 6 percent, or $60 ($1000 × 0.06 = $60), and Social Security taxes of 7.65 percent, or $76.50 ($1000 × 0.0765 = $76.50). Therefore, Juanita pays an **effective marginal tax rate** of nearly 40 percent (25% + 6% + 7.65% = 38.65%), or $386.50, on the extra $1000 of earned income.

People who pay high marginal tax rates can do better by making tax-exempt investments, such as buying bonds issued by various agencies of states and municipalities. For example, Serena Miller, a married chiropractor with two children from Cleveland, Ohio, currently has $5000 in utility stocks earning 5 percent, or $250 ($5000 × 0.05), annually. She pays $62.50 in federal income tax on that income at her 25 percent marginal tax rate ($250 × 0.25), leaving her with $187.50 after taxes. Alternatively, a tax-exempt $5000 state bond paying 4 percent will provide Serena with a better after-tax return, $200.00 instead of $187.50. That is, she would receive $200.00 tax free from the state bond ($5000 × 0.04) compared with $187.50 ($250 − $62.50) after taxes on the income from the stocks.

The Very Best Kind of Income Is Tax-Exempt Income

The very best kind of income, as this discussion implies, is **tax-exempt income,** which is income that is totally and permanently free of taxes. By legally avoiding paying one dollar in income taxes, you gain by not paying that dollar in taxes and, therefore, you receive the alternative use for that dollar. You also benefit by not having to earn another dollar to replace the one that might have been paid in taxes.

tax-exempt income Income that is totally and permanently free of taxes.

The Second Best Kind of Income Is Tax-Sheltered Income

The second-best kind of income for individuals is **tax-sheltered (or tax-deferred) income**—that is, income that is exempt from income taxes in the current year but that will be subject to taxation in a later tax year. Figure 1.3 shows that tax-sheltered returns on savings and investments provide much greater returns than returns on which income taxes have to be paid because more money remains available to be invested. In addition, tax-sheltered funds grow more rapidly because compounding (the subject of the next section in this chapter) is enhanced when larger dollar amounts

tax-sheltered income Income exempt from income taxes in the current year but that will be subject to taxation in a later tax year.

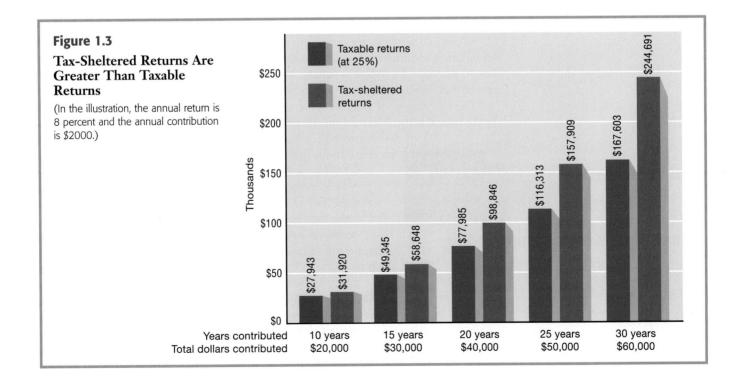

Figure 1.3

Tax-Sheltered Returns Are Greater Than Taxable Returns

(In the illustration, the annual return is 8 percent and the annual contribution is $2000.)

Legend: Taxable returns (at 25%); Tax-sheltered returns

Years contributed	10 years	15 years	20 years	25 years	30 years
Total dollars contributed	$20,000	$30,000	$40,000	$50,000	$60,000
Taxable returns (at 25%)	$27,943	$49,345	$77,985	$116,313	$167,603
Tax-sheltered returns	$31,920	$58,648	$98,846	$157,909	$244,691

grow during the last years of an investment. Realize that eventually one must pay income taxes on the income deferred.

CONCEPT CHECK 1.3

1. Define *opportunity cost* and give an example of how opportunity costs might affect your financial decision making.
2. Explain and give an example of how marginal analysis makes some financial decisions easier.
3. Describe and give an example of how income taxes can affect financial decision making.

The Time Value of Money: Setting Dollar Values on Financial Goals

4 LEARNING OBJECTIVE

Perform time value of money calculations in personal financial decision making.

time value of money (TVM)
A method by which one can compare cash flows across time, either as what a future cash flow is worth today (present value) or what an investment made today will be worth in the future (future value).

A dollar in your pocket today is worth more than a dollar received five years from now. Why? Time is money.

The **time value of money** is perhaps the single most important concept in personal finance. It adjusts for the fact that dollars to be received or paid out in the future are not equivalent to those received or paid out today. It is easy to understand that a dollar received today is worth more than a dollar received five years from now because today's dollar can be saved or invested and in five years you expect it to be worth more than a dollar. The time value of money involves two components: future value and present value.

Two Common Questions in Personal Finance To illustrate the time value of money, two questions in personal finance are commonly asked:

1. What will an investment (or a series of investments) be worth after a period of time? This question asks for a future value.
2. How much has to be put away today (or as a series of investments) to provide some dollar amount in the future? This question asks for a present value.

As you can see from these two questions, comparisons between time periods cannot be made without making adjustments to money values. Accordingly, time value of money calculations compare future and present values by taking into account the interest rate (or investment rate of return) and the time period involved.

principal The original amount invested.

The calculation of interest involves (1) the dollar amount, called the **principal,** (2) the rate of interest earned on the principal, and (3) the amount of time the princi-pal is invested. One way of calculating interest is called **simple interest** and is illustrated by the **simple interest formula** where

$$i = prt \text{ where} \tag{1.3}$$

p = the *principal* set aside
r = the *rate* of interest
t = the *time* in years that the funds are left on deposit

If someone saved or invested $1000 at 8 percent for four years, he would receive $320 in interest ($1000 × 0.08 × 4) over the four years.

Compounding But something is missing here. The simple interest formula assumes that the interest is withdrawn each year and only the $1000 stays on deposit for the entire four years. Most people do *not* invest this way. Instead, they leave the interest earned in the account so that it will earn additional interest. This

Instant Message

Reinvesting Means Compounding

If you earn 6 percent on a $1000 bond and spend your $60 annual interest every year for 20 years, you will have received $1200. But if you can reinvest your interest at 6 percent, you would net $2,262. Aha, the power of compounding.

earning of interest on interest is referred to as compound interest. And compound interest is always assumed in time value of money calculations.

Earning compound interest (or **compounding**) is the best way to build investment values over time. Because of compound interest, money grows much faster when the income from an investment is left in the account. In fact, the deposit of $1000 in our example would grow to $4,661 after 20 years (the calculation is described in the following paragraph). Many of the techniques for building wealth that we describe in this book are based on compounding. The way to build wealth is to make money on your money, not simply to put money away. Yes, you need to put money away first. But compounding over time is what really builds wealth.

Compounding serves as the basis of all time value of money considerations. To see how this works, let us look again at our example in which $1000 is invested at 8 percent for four years. Here is how the amount invested (or principal) would grow using compounding:

At the end of year 1, the $1000 would have grown to $1080 [$1000 + ($1000 × 0.08)].

At the end of year 2, the $1080 would have grown to $1166.40 [$1080 + ($1080 × 0.08)].

At the end of year 3, the $1166.40 would have grown to $1259.71 [$1166.40 + ($1166.40 × 0.08)].

At the end of year 4, the $1259.71 would have grown to $1360.49 [$1259.71 + ($1259.71 × 0.08)].

Due to the effects of compounding, this investor would have earned an additional $40.49 ($360.49 − $320). While this amount might not seem like much, realize that a $1000 investment for a longer period—say, 40 years—earning 8 percent interest would grow to $21,724.52, providing $20,724.52 in interest over that time period. Simple interest would have resulted in only $3200 in interest ($1000 × 0.08 × 40). The benefit of compounding over that time period is an additional $17,524.52 in interest ($20,724.52 − $3200).

The results are even more dramatic if $1000 is invested at the end of each year for 40 years. The total at the end of 40 years would be $259,056, with $219,056 representing the interest on the invested funds. This illustration suggests one of the cardinal rules of personal financial planning: Getting rich is not a function of investing a lot of money. It is the result of investing regularly for long periods of time.

Two Types of Time Value of Money Calculations

Essentially there are two types of time value of money calculations: (1) converting present values to future values (as illustrated in the preceding example) and (2) converting future values to present values. Within each type, the calculations differ slightly depending on whether a lump sum is involved or whether a series of payments (an annuity) is involved.

Calculating Future Values

Future value (FV) is the valuation of an asset projected to the end of a particular time period in the future. You can calculate the future value of a lump sum or the future value of a series of deposits.

compounding When interest on an investment itself earns interest.

Did You Know?...

State Lotteries Use Time Value of Money Calculations

How often have you heard or seen reports of lottery jackpots reaching extremely high amounts? Does the lottery actually pay out these amounts? Not really. Let's assume a lucky ticket holder wins a jackpot of $100 million. The announced jackpot is based on the assumption that the winner will receive the amount in a series of 20 annual payments of $5 million each, adding up to the $100 million advertised total. In fact, the lottery will invest a lump sum right away to fund the annual payments made over the 20 years. It needs to invest only $57,349,500 at 6 percent to fund the stream of $5 million payments ($5 million × 11.4699 from the 6 percent column and 20-year row of Appendix Table A.4). Alternatively, lottery winners may be permitted to take a "cash option" instead of the annual payments. In this case, a winner of a $100 million jackpot who chooses the cash option would receive only $57,349,500. The winner would also have to pay federal taxes, and perhaps state and city income taxes on this amount, resulting in an after-tax jackpot of closer to $35 million.

Instant Message

Compound Your Way to Wealth

One of the greatest investment strategies is compounding. Only through compounding will you attain the serious growth of your wealth over time.

future value The valuation of an asset projected to the end of a particular time period in the future.

Table 1.1   Future Value of $1 After a Given Number of Periods

Periods	1%	2%	3%	4%	5%	6%	7%	8%	9%	10%
1	1.0100	1.0200	1.0300	1.0400	1.0500	1.0600	1.0700	1.0800	1.0900	1.1000
2	1.0201	1.0404	1.0609	1.0816	1.1025	1.1236	1.1449	1.1664	1.1881	1.2100
3	1.0303	1.0612	1.0927	1.1249	1.1576	1.1910	1.2250	1.2597	1.2950	1.3310
4	1.0406	1.0824	1.1255	1.1699	1.2155	1.2625	1.3108	1.3605	1.4116	1.4641
5	1.0510	1.1041	1.1593	1.2167	1.2763	1.3382	1.4026	1.4693	1.5386	1.6105
6	1.0615	1.1262	1.1941	1.2653	1.3401	1.4185	1.5007	1.5869	1.6771	1.7716
7	1.0721	1.1487	1.2299	1.3159	1.4071	1.5036	1.6058	1.7138	1.8280	1.9487
8	1.0829	1.1717	1.2668	1.3686	1.4775	1.5938	1.7182	1.8509	1.9926	2.1436
9	1.0937	1.1951	1.3048	1.4233	1.5513	1.6895	1.8385	1.9990	2.1719	2.3579
10	1.1046	1.2190	1.3439	1.4802	1.6289	1.7908	1.9672	2.1589	2.3674	2.5937

Future Value of a Lump Sum Equation (1.4) can be used to calculate the future value of a lump sum:

$$FV = (\text{Present value of sum of money}) \, (i + 1.0)^n \qquad (1.4)$$

where i represents the interest rate and n represents the number of time periods. Applying this formula to our earlier example of investing $1000 at 8 percent for four years, we obtain

$$\$1360.49 = (\$1000) \, (1 + 0.08)^4$$

or

$$\$1360.49 = (\$1000)(1.08)(1.08)(1.08)(1.08)$$

While mathematically correct, these calculations can be cumbersome when using long time periods. Table 1.1 provides a quick and easy way to determine the future dollar value of an investment. For the preceding example, use the table in the following manner: Go across the top row to the 8 percent column. Read down the 8 percent column to the row for four years to locate the factor 1.3605 (at the intersection of the green column and row). Multiply that factor by the present value of the cash asset ($1000) to arrive at the future value ($1360.50).

Appendix Table A.1 provides an even more complete table for calculating the future value of lump-sum amounts. Figure 1.4 demonstrates the effects of various com-

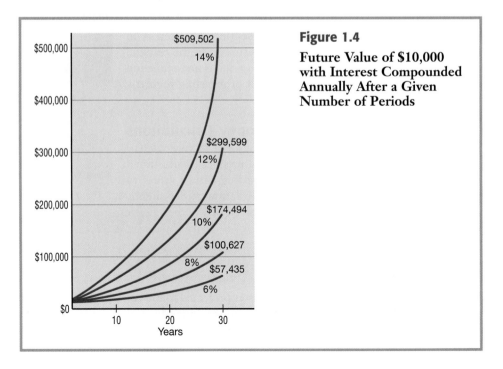

Figure 1.4

Future Value of $10,000 with Interest Compounded Annually After a Given Number of Periods

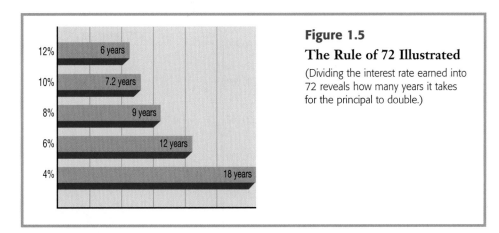

Figure 1.5

The Rule of 72 Illustrated

(Dividing the interest rate earned into 72 reveals how many years it takes for the principal to double.)

pounded returns on a $10,000 investment. The $10,000 will grow to $57,435 in 30 years with an interest rate of 6 percent. Compounding $10,000 at 10 percent yields $174,494 over the same time period; at 14 percent, it yields a whopping $509,502! For practice you might want to confirm these results using Appendix Table A.1.

Rule of 72 Reveals Number of Years for Principal to Double The **rule of 72** is a handy formula for figuring the number of years it takes to double the principal using compound interest. You simply divide the interest rate that the money will earn *into* the number 72. For example, if interest is compounded at a rate of 7 percent per year, your principal will double in 10.3 years (72 ÷ 7); if the rate is 6 percent, it will take 12 years (72 ÷ 6). The rule of 72 (see Figure 1.5) also works for determining how long it would take for the price of something to double given a rate of increase in the price. For example, if college tuition costs were rising 8 percent per year, the cost of a college education would double in just over nine years. In addition, the rule of 72 can be used to calculate the number of years before prices will double given a certain inflation rate. Just divide the inflation rate into 72.

rule of 72 A formula for figuring the number of years it takes to double the principal using compound interest; simply divide the interest rate that the money will earn *into* the number 72.

Future Value of an Annuity People often save for long-term goals by putting away a series of payments. Appendix Table A.3 provides a complete table for calculating the future value of a stream of deposited amounts, referred to as an annuity. Figure 1.6 graphically demonstrates the effects of various compounded returns on a $2000 annual investment made at the end of each year. The $2000 will grow to $91,524 in 20 years (read across the interest rate row in Appendix Table A.3 to 8 percent and then down the column to 20 years to obtain the factor of 45.762 to multiply by $2000) and to $226,566 in 30 years at an 8 percent rate. Compounding $2000 at 10 percent yields $114,550 in 20 years and $328,988 over 30 years; at 14 percent, it becomes $713,574 after 30 years! For practice you might want to confirm these results using Appendix Table A.3.

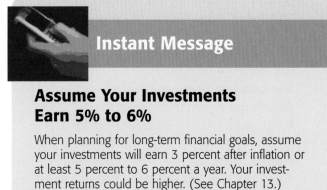

Instant Message

Assume Your Investments Earn 5% to 6%

When planning for long-term financial goals, assume your investments will earn 3 percent after inflation or at least 5 percent to 6 percent a year. Your investment returns could be higher. (See Chapter 13.)

Calculating Present Values

Present value (or **discounted value**) is the current value of an asset (or stream of assets) that will be received in the future. You can calculate the present value of a lump sum to be received in the future or the present value of a series of payments to be received in the future.

present value The current value of an asset (or stream of assets) that will be received in the future; also known as discounted value.

Present Value of a Lump Sum The present value of a lump sum is the current worth of an asset to be received in the future. Alternatively, it can be thought of as the amount you would need to set aside today at a given rate of inter-

Figure 1.6

Future Value of $2000 Annual Investments

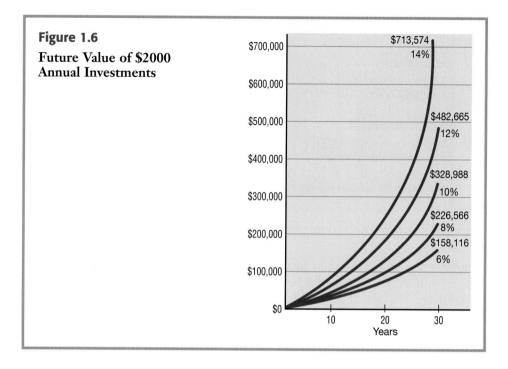

Instant Message

Web Calculators

Present and future value calculations can be readily performed on the Internet. Among the best calculators are those found at the following websites:

USA Today (www.usatoday.com/money/perfi/ calculators/calculator.htm)

Financial Calculators (www.fincalc.com/)

KJE (www.dinkytown.net/)

Bankrate.com (www.bankrate.com)

CNNMoney (cgi.money.cnn.com/tools/)

Fool.com (www.fool.com/calcs/calculators .htm?source=LN)

Fidelity (www.moneychimp.com/calculator/ compound_interest_calculator.htm)

annuity A stream of payments to be received in the future.

est for a given time period so as to have some desired amount in the future. Suppose you want to have $20,000 for the down payment on a new home in ten years. What would you need to set aside today to reach this goal if you could invest your money and receive a 7 percent return? Using Appendix Table A.2 you could look across the interest rate rows to 7 percent and then down to ten years to obtain the factor of 0.5083. Multiplying $20,000 by this factor reveals that $10,166 set aside today would allow you to reach your goal. (Note the connection here to the rule of 72: 7 percent divided into 72 is approximately 10.28, meaning that the investment would double in about 10.28 years. Indeed, $10,166 would approximately double to $20,000 in ten years.)

Present Value of an Annuity The present value of an **annuity** is the current worth of a stream of payments to be received in the future. Alternatively, it can be thought of as the amount you would need to set aside today at a given rate of interest for a given time period so as to receive that stream of payments. Suppose you want to have $30,000 per year for 20 years during your retirement. What amount would you need to have invested at retirement to reach this goal if you could invest your money and receive a 7 percent return? Using Appendix Table A.4 you could look across the interest rate rows to 7 percent and then down to 20 years to obtain the factor of 10.5940. Multiplying $30,000 by this factor reveals that $317,820 (10.5940 × $30,000) set aside at retirement would fund this stream of payments. Note the beauty of compound interest in this result. It takes only $317,820—not $600,000—to fund a $30,000 per year retirement for 20 years if you can earn 7 percent on your financial nest egg.*

*If you are using a financial calculator for time value of money calculations, see "How to Use a Financial Calculator" on the *Garman/Forgue* website, or you can use the present and future value calculators found on the *Garman/Forgue* website, college.hmco.com/business.students.

✔ **CONCEPT CHECK 1.4**

1. Explain the difference between simple interest and compound interest, and describe why that difference is critical.

2. What are the two components used when figuring the time value of money?

3. Use Table 1.1 to calculate the future value of [a] $2000 at 5 percent for four years, [b] $4500 at 9 percent for eight years, and [c] $10,000 at 6 percent for ten years.

Make Smart Money Decisions at Work

Smart decisions about your employee benefits can increase your actual income by thousands of dollars each year. To do so wisely, select among employer-sponsored plans for health care, out-of-pocket spending for health and dependent care, life insurance, disability, long-term care, and retirement. These decisions often require you to calculate the tax-sheltered aspects of the employee benefits. Your benefits package might also include dental and vision care, child care, elder care, subsidized food services, and an educational assistance program.

An **employee benefit** is compensation for employment that does not take the form of wages, salaries, commissions, or other cash payments. Examples include paid holidays, health insurance, and a retirement plan. The value of employee benefits often amounts to 30 percent or more of one's salary. Some employee benefits are tax sheltered, such as flexible spending accounts and retirement plans. Tax sheltered in this situation means that the employee avoids paying current income taxes on the value of the benefits received from the employer. The taxes may be postponed, or deferred, until a later date (usually a good idea)—perhaps until retirement, when the individual's income tax rate might be lower.

5 LEARNING OBJECTIVE
Make smart decisions about your employee benefits.

employee benefit Compensation for employment that does not take the form of wages, salaries, commissions, or other cash payments.

Flexible Benefit Plans Offer Tax-Free Money

A **flexible benefit plan,** also known as a **cafeteria plan,** is an employer-sponsored plan that gives the employee a choice of selecting either cash or one or more qualifying nontaxable benefits. For example, an employer might offer $2500 annually to each employee to spend on one or more benefits, and you pay no income taxes on the value of the benefits. A flexible benefits plan might offer dependent care, adoption assistance, medical expense reimbursements, insurance, or transportation benefits. Employees select the benefits they want. Employees working for employers that offer a cafeteria plan avoid having to pay out-of-pocket money for certain expenses.

flexible benefit plan An employer-sponsored plan that gives the employee a choice of selecting either cash or one or more qualifying nontaxable benefits; also known as a cafeteria plan.

Making Decisions About Employer-Sponsored Health Care Plans

Many employers offer: employees a choice of **health care plans.** Employees usually can make a decision to change health plans once a year as well as when one's family situation changes, such as marriage. The premium for an unmarried employee could be $5000 or more annually depending upon the amount of coverage provided. Fortunately, the premiums for employees are either paid for entirely or subsidized by the employer. Some employers pay perhaps the first $3000 of annual premiums for employee health care coverage and require that employees pay the remainder.

Partly because of soaring costs of health care coverage, employers often offer multiple policies. These can range from an expensive plan, perhaps with a $6600 premium,

health care plan An employee benefit designed to pay all or part of the employee's medical expenses.

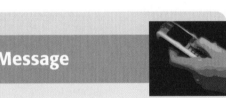

Instant Message

Don't Pay Extra Taxes

Contributing $1000 to a tax-advantaged employee benefit plan saves a worker as much as $400 that does not have to be paid to the government in taxes.

that offers comprehensive coverage requiring little out-of-pocket spending by the employee to an inexpensive **high-deductible health care plan,** perhaps with a $3100 premium, requiring larger out-of-pocket health care spending by the employee. The **deductible** is the amount paid to cover expenses before benefits begin. Employees, especially healthy ones, hope to save money on premiums by choosing these policies.

Younger employers, particularly those who are typically healthy, often select high-deductible plans to save on the cost of premiums. For example, if an employer pays only the first $3000 in health care premiums for employees, an employee selecting the high-cost plan described previously has to pay $3600 ($6600 − $3000) annually, or $300 a month in premiums. This contrasts with a $100 annual premium for employees who select the high-deductible plan ($3100 − $3000). If the person experiences lots of health care expenses, he/she will have to pay additional costs.

Some employers also offer **health savings accounts (HSAs).** This special savings account is intended for people who have a high-deductible health care plan (with annual deductibles of at least $1000 for individuals and $2000 for families). Employees make tax-deductible contributions to a savings account to be used for eligible expenses. Employers may also contribute. The employee invests HSA funds and the money in the account grows tax free. Withdrawals are made to pay for medical expenses. The limits on contributions to an HSA savings account are $2900 per year for individuals and $5800 for families. The money in the account does not vanish if you don't spend it within a certain time period.

The tax-advantaged aspect of making a health care plan choice adds another dimension to making the best personal financial decision. Because many workers have an effective marginal tax rate (discussed earlier in the chapter) of nearly 40 percent, that same percentage can be *saved* or not spent by giving it to the government in taxes. The worker who contributes $3000, for example, to a health savings account saves approximately $1200 ($3000 × 0.40), further reducing his or her health care expenses.

Making Decisions About Employer's Flexible Spending Accounts

A **flexible spending account (FSA)** is an employer-sponsored account that allows employee-paid expenses for medical or dependent care to be paid with an employee's pretax dollars rather than after-tax income. Under a typical FSA, the employee agrees to have a certain amount deducted from each paycheck, and that amount is then deposited in a separate account called a flexible spending account. As eligible expenses are incurred, the employee requests and receives reimbursements from the account.

Funds in a **dependent care FSA account** may be used to pay for the care of a dependent younger than age 13 or the care of another dependent who is physically or mentally incapable of caring for himself or herself and who resides in the taxpayer's home. Funds in a **health care FSA account** may be used to pay for qualified, unreimbursed out-of-pocket expenses for health care.

The tax advantage of an FSA occurs because the amounts deducted from the employee's salary avoid federal income tax, Social Security taxes, and, in most states, state income taxes, thereby allowing selected personal expenses to be paid with pretax (rather than after-tax) income. Paying the expenses with **pretax dollars** (money income that has not been taxed by the government) lowers taxable income, decreases take-home pay, and increases effective take-home pay because of the reimbursements. The maximum annual contribution limits are usually $5000 for dependent care FSA and $2000 to $3000 for medical care FSA.

Younger workers who anticipate few medical costs usually do not sign up for a medical FSA, although FSAs do pay for eyeglasses, contacts, copayments, and some over-the-counter medications. Workers with children or others to take care of financially, such as elderly or disabled parents, often sign up for dependent care FSA. Only 20 percent of eligible employees participate in flexible spending accounts even though doing so saves money.

Before enrolling in an FSA, you need to estimate your expenses carefully so that the amount in the FSA does not exceed anticipated expenses. According to Internal Revenue Service (IRS) regulations, unused amounts are forfeited and are not returned to the employee—a condition called the "use it or lose it" rule. However, employers may offer a 2½-month grace period during which time you can continue to spend the previous year's FSA money. Many employers offer debit cards that withdraw money directly from an employee's FSA.

Making Decisions About Participating in Employer Life, Disability, and Long-Term Care Insurance Plans

Life, disability, and long-term care insurance coverage is often available through employers. While the premiums charged for the group of employees for life insurance are not as low as those available in the general marketplace, some employers pay for part or all of employees' premiums. Coverage is typically one or two times the employee's salary. So sign up for free or subsidized life insurance at work. The premiums for disability and long-term care insurance are often less expensive when purchased through one's employer. See Chapters 10, 11, and 12 to begin to purchase any needed insurance coverage.

Making Decisions About Participating in Your Employer's Retirement Plan

More than half of all workers are covered by an employer-sponsored, defined-contribution **retirement plan,** also called a **tax-sheltered retirement plan.** These include 401(k) plans and similar 403(b) and 457 plans. Employer-sponsored retirement plans provide four distinct advantages.

First Advantage: Tax-Deductible Contributions
Tax-sheltered retirement plans provide tremendous tax benefits compared with ordinary savings and investment plans. Because pretax contributions to qualified plans reduce income, the current year's tax liability is lowered. The money saved in taxes can then be used to partially fund a larger contribution, which creates even greater returns. The 401(k) plan lets the IRS help employees finance their retirement plans because of the income taxes saved.

As Table 1.2 illustrates, you can save substantial sums for retirement with minimal effects on your monthly take-home pay. For example, a single person with a monthly taxable income of $4000 in the 25 percent marginal tax bracket who forgoes consumption and instead places $500 into a tax-sheltered retirement plan every month reduces monthly take-home pay from $3175 to $2800, or $375—that is certainly not an enormous amount. The net effect is that it costs that person only $375 to put away that $500 per month into a retirement plan. The

tax-sheltered retirement plan Employer-sponsored, defined-contribution retirement plans including 401(k) plans and similar 403(b) and 457 plans.

Instant Message

Living More Years Than Working

You will likely work full time for 45 years, from ages 22 to 67, so saving for retirement during those years is critical since you are likely to live 20 more years during retirement.

Table 1.2 It Costs Only $375 a Month to Save $6000 a Year for Retirement

Monthly salary	$4000	Monthly salary	$4000
Pretax retirement plan contribution	0	Pretax retirement plan contribution	500
Taxable income	4000	Taxable income	3500
Federal taxes*	825	Federal taxes*	700
Monthly take-home pay	3175	Monthly take-home pay	2800
You put away for retirement	0	Cost to put away $500 per month ($3175 − $2800)	375
		You put away for retirement	6000

*From Chapter 4; 25 percent income tax rate, single.

immediate "return on investment" equals a fantastic 25 percent ($125 ÷ $500). In essence, the taxpayer puts $375 into his or her retirement plan and the government contributes $125. (Without the plan, the taxpayer would pay the $125 directly to the government.) A taxpayer paying a higher marginal tax rate realizes even greater gains. Because a substantial part of your contributions to a tax-sheltered retirement plan comes from money that you would have paid in income taxes, it costs you less to save more.

Second Advantage: Employer's Matching Contributions To encourage saving for retirement, many employers "match" all or part of their employees' contributions, perhaps up to 6 percent of salary. An employee who saves $375 might receive an additional $375 a month from his/her employer. That's a 100 percent return on the employee's $375!

Third Advantage: Tax-Deferred Growth Because interest, dividends, and capital gains from qualified plans are taxed only after funds are withdrawn from the plan, investments in tax-sheltered retirement plans grow tax free. The benefits of tax deferral can be substantial.

For example, if a person in the 25 percent tax bracket invests $2000 at the beginning of every year for 30 years and the investment earns an 8 percent taxable return compounded annually, the fund will grow to $167,603 at the end of the 30-year period. If the same $2000 invested annually was instead compounded at 8 percent within a tax-sheltered program, it would grow to $244,691! The higher amount results from compounding at the full 8 percent and not paying any income taxes. (Figure 1.3 on page 13 illustrates these differences in returns.) Indeed, when the funds are finally taxed upon their withdrawal some years later, the taxpayer may be in a lower marginal tax bracket.

Fourth Advantage: Starting Early Really Pays Off Big Recall the rule of 72, which can be used to calculate the number of years it would take for a lump-sum investment to double. A 9 percent rate of return doubles an investment every eight years. Waiting eight years to begin saving results in the loss of one doubling. Unfortunately, it is the *last* doubling that is lost, as illustrated in Table 1.3. In that example, $48,000 ($96,000 − $48,000) is lost due to a hesitancy to invest $3000. This is a tremendous opportunity cost for waiting eight years to start.

The gains are awesome when the one starts early and makes regular, continuing investments instead of delaying. For example, a worker who starts saving $25 per week in a qualified retirement plan at age 23 will have about $616,390 by age 65, assuming

Instant Message

Income Does Not Create Wealth

People do not get wealthy by earning an income. Real wealth comes from increases in the value of assets over time, such as their home or the growth of their investments within a 401(k) retirement program.

Careful planning can result in a much more comfortable lifestyle when you retire.

Table 1.3 Starting to Save Early Versus Starting Late

Starting Earlier		Starting Later	
Age	**$ Value**	**Age**	**$ Value**
23	$ 3,000	23	$ 0
31	6,000	31	3,000
39	12,000	39	6,000
47	24,000	47	12,000
55	48,000	55	24,000
63	$96,000	63	$48,000

Starting to save $3000 eight years earlier (age 23 instead of 31) earns the investor an extra $48,000 ($96,000 − $48,000) assuming a compound growth rate of 9 percent.

an annual rate of return of 9 percent. Waiting until age 33 to start saving, instead of beginning at age 23, results in a retirement fund of *only* about $242,230. The benefit of starting to invest early is about $374,000 ($616,390 − $242,230). And the total extra dollars invested over the ten years was a mere $13,000. Putting in $13,000 early results in an extra $374,000. This effect occurs because most of the power of compounding appears in the last years of growth.

 CONCEPT CHECK 1.5

1. Summarize the benefits of participating in a high-deductible health care plan at work.

2. Show a math example of why many employees participate in a tax-sheltered employee benefit plan, such as an HSA or 401(k) plan.

3. List two ways you can maximize the benefits from a tax-sheltered retirement program.

Did You Know?...

Examples of Poor Financial Behaviors

Poor financial behaviors to avoid include the following:

1. Purchasing something expensive that was wanted but not needed
2. Reaching the maximum limit on credit card
3. Spending more money than available
4. Making credit purchase after running out of money
5. Obtaining cash advance on a credit card after running out of money
6. Using cash advance on a credit card to pay another
7. Receiving an overdue notice from a creditor
8. Paying credit card bill late
9. Paying service charge for paying a utility bill late
10. Making vehicle loan/lease payment late
11. Paying rent/mortgage late
12. Borrowing money from a coworker
13. Obtaining cash advance from employer
14. Borrowing from 401(k) retirement plan at work
15. Taking old employer's 401(k) money in cash when changing jobs
16. Writing a check with insufficient funds ("bounce" a check)

Where to Seek Expert Financial Advice

6 LEARNING OBJECTIVE

Identify the professional qualifications of providers of financial advice.

financial planner An investment professional who evaluates the personal finances of an individual or family and recommends strategies to set and achieve long-term financial goals.

At various points in their lives, many people rely on the advice of a professional to make financial plans and decisions. Often this consultation is focused on a narrow area of their finances. Professional financial advisers, such as a family lawyer, tax preparer, insurance agent, credit counselor, or stockbroker, can be helpful. Too often these people are not impartial because they are salespeople for specific financial services. They typically want to sell you something rather than have your best interests at heart. People often find it helpful to obtain the services of more broadly qualified financial experts.

A **financial planner** is an investment professional who evaluates the personal finances of an individual or family and recommends strategies to set and achieve long-term financial goals. A good financial planner should be able to analyze a family's total needs in such areas as investments, taxes, insurance, education goals, and retirement and pull all of the information together into a cohesive plan. The planner may help a client select and prioritize goals and then rearrange assets and liabilities to fit the client's lifestyle, stage in the life cycle, and financial goals. When appropriate, planners should make referrals to outside advisers, such as attorneys, accountants, trust officers, real estate brokers, stockbrokers, and insurance agents. Effective financial advice helps you make better day-to-day financial decisions so you have more to spend, save, invest, and donate.

You can check the background of the planner you are considering. Self-regulatory organizations and government agencies are available to help.

- The Certified Financial Planner Board of Standards [(888) 237-6275; www.cfp.net] assists those searching for a CFP as well as accepts complaints.
- The National Association of Insurance Commissioners [(816) 842-3600; www.naic .org] directs inquiries to the appropriate state agency where you can check on planners who also sell insurance products.
- Financial Industry Regulatory Authority (FINRA) [(800) 289-9999; www .finra.org] oversees securities brokers.

Advice from a Pro...

Choosing a Financial Planner

When interviewing financial planners, ask them these questions:

1. Am I permitted a no-cost, initial consultation, and how much time is allowed?

2. What education, formal training, and credentials do you have to practice financial planning, is this your primary activity, and how long have you been in financial planning?

3. Are you licensed as an investment or life insurance broker?

4. How long have you resided in the community, and who can vouch for your professional reputation?

5. Will you provide references that I can contact from three or more clients you have counseled for at least two years?

6. Will you or an associate be involved in evaluating and updating the plan you suggest, and how often are formal reviews held with the client?

7. What process do you follow to identify a client's financial goals?

8. How do you evaluate investment performance, and how often?

9. May I see representative examples of financial plans, monitoring reports, and portfolios or actual case studies of your clients?

10. How are you personally compensated, and if you earn commissions, how are they earned and from whom?

11. May I have a copy of the contract you use with clients?

12. To whom do I take a complaint, if I had one?

Joan Koonce
University of Georgia

- The Securities and Exchange Commission [(800) 732-0330; www.sec.gov] regulates investment advisers and all securities dealers.

How Financial Planners Are Compensated

Financial planners earn their income in one of four ways:

1. **Commission-only financial planners/brokers** live solely on the commissions they receive on the financial products (such as investments or insurance) they sell to their clients. In this case, the plan will be "free," but a commission will be paid to the adviser by the source of the financial product, such as an insurance company or mutual fund. Advantage: Save money if you make only a few transactions.

2. **Fee-based financial planner/brokers** charge an up-front fee for providing services and charge a commission on any securities trades or insurance purchases that they conduct on your behalf. Advantage: Unlimited consultations with broker.

3. **Fee-offset financial planners/brokers** charge an annual or hourly fee. That fee will be reduced by any commissions earned off the purchase of financial products sold to the client. Advantage: Fee will be reduced as you trade investments.

4. **Fee-only financial planners** earn no commissions and work solely on a fee-for-service basis—that is, they charge a specified fee (typically $50 to $200 per hour or 1 percent of the client's assets annually) for the services provided. They usually need five or more one-hour appointments to analyze a client's financial situation and to present a thorough plan. Fee-only planners do not sell financial products, such as

Instant Message

Paying for Financial Advice

One way or another, you will pay to get financial advice—commissions, fees, both, your mistakes—so assess the total costs up front as well as the opportunity costs.

2. Rachael Berry, a freshman horticulture major at the University of Minnesota, has some financial questions for the next three years of school and beyond. Answers to these questions can be obtained by using Appendix Table A or the *Garman/Forgue* website.

   (a) If Rachael's tuition, fees, and expenditures for books this year total $12,000, what will they be during her senior year (three years from now), assuming costs rise 6 percent annually? (Hint: Use Appendix Table A.1 or the *Garman/Forgue* website.)

   (b) Rachael is applying for a scholarship currently valued at $5000. If she is awarded it at the end of next year, how much is the scholarship worth in today's dollars, assuming inflation of 5 percent? (Hint: Use Appendix Table A.2 or the *Garman/Forgue* website.)

   (c) Rachael is already looking ahead to graduation and a job, and she wants to buy a new car not long after her graduation. If after graduation she begins a savings program of $2400 per year in an investment yielding 6 percent, what will be the value of the fund after three years? (Hint: Use Appendix Table A.3 or the *Garman/Forgue* website.)

   (d) Rachael's Aunt Karroll told her that she would give Kathryn $1000 at the end of each year for the next three years to help with her college expenses. Assuming an annual interest rate of 6 percent, what is the present value of that stream of payments? (Hint: Use Appendix Table A.4 or the *Garman/Forgue* website.)

3. Using the present and future value tables in Appendix A, the appropriate calculations on the *Garman/Forgue* website, or a financial calculator, calculate the following:

   (a) The future value of $400 in two years that earns 5 percent.

   (b) The future value of $1200 saved each year for ten years that earns 7 percent.

   (c) The amount a person would need to deposit today with a 5 percent interest rate to have $2000 in three years.

   (d) The amount a person would need to deposit today to be able to withdraw $6000 each year for ten years from an account earning 6 percent.

   (e) A person is offered a gift of $5000 now or $8000 five years from now. If such funds could be expected to earn 8 percent over the next five years, which is the better choice?

   (f) A person wants to have $3000 available to spend on an overseas trip four years from now. If such funds could be expected to earn 7 percent, how much should be invested in a lump sum to realize the $3000 when needed?

   (g) A person who invests $1200 each year finds one choice that is expected to pay 9 percent per year and another choice that may pay 10 percent. What is the difference in return if the investment is made for 15 years?

   (h) A person invests $50,000 in an investment that earns 6 percent. If $6000 is withdrawn each year, how many years will it take for the fund to run out?

4. You win a contest. The prize is cash, and you are offered several alternative payment plans. Which plan should you choose? Assume you can earn 5 percent on your money and ignore inflation.

   (a) $30,000 today

   (b) $40,000 in five years

   (c) $10,000 one year from today and $25,000 two years later

   (d) $4000 per year starting today for the next ten years

5. Using the rule of 72, calculate how quickly $1000 will double to $2000 at interest rates of 2 percent, 4 percent, 6 percent, 8 percent, and 10 percent.

Financial Planning Cases

Case 1
Reasons to Study Personal Finance

Lindsey Beliveau Bailey of Redding, California, is a senior in college, majoring in sociology. She anticipates getting married a year or so after graduation. Lindsey has only one elective course remaining and is going to choose between another advanced class in sociology and one in personal finance. As Lindsey's friend, you want to persuade her to take personal finance. Give some examples of how Lindsey might benefit from the study of personal finance.

Case 2
A Closer Look at Lifetime Financial Objectives

You have been asked to give a brief speech on how to achieve financial success. Define financial success and financial happiness, and summarize the building blocks to achieving financial success.

On the 'Net

Go to the Web pages indicated to complete these exercises. You can also go to the *Garman/Forgue* website at college .hmco.com/business/students for an expanded list of exercises. Under General Business, select the title of this text. Click on the Internet Exercises link for this chapter.

1. Visit the Bureau of Labor Statistics Consumer Price Index homepage at http://www.bls.gov/cpi/ and link to information for various areas of the country and metropolitan areas of various sizes. Describe how prices have been changing for your area and city size during the past year.

2. Visit the Conference Board website, http://www .conference-board.org/economics/consumer Confidence.cfm/, for the latest information on the consumer confidence index and the index of leading economic indicators. What do the indexes say about the direction of the economy over the next six months to one year?

3. Visit the website of the Financial Planning Association at http://www.fpanet.org/member/about/principles/ ethics.cfm. Read through the code of ethics for members of the organization. What does the code tell you about the members?

Visit the Garman/Forgue website ...

@college.hmco.com/business/students

Under General Business, select *Personal Finance 9e.* There, among other valuable resources, you will find a complete glossary, ACE questions, links to help you complete the chapter exercises, and links to other personal finance sites.

CHAPTER 2

Career Planning

You Must Be Kidding, Right?

Jessica Springsteen is contemplating going to graduate school at night for a master's degree so she can advance her career and earn more than her current $44,000 salary income. She is a sales account manager for a health care organization, and she has a small online business selling gourmet foods. How much more income can Jessica expect over an anticipated 40-year career if she obtains the advanced degree?

A. $100,000

B. $300,000

C. $600,000

D. $900,000

The answer is C, $600,000. Over a 40-year working career, a person with a postgraduate degree can expect to earn more than $3 million, and this is about $600,000 more than a person with a bachelor's degree will earn. Getting an advanced degree is no guarantee of a bigger income, but the likelihood of such a reality is high!

LEARNING OBJECTIVES

After reading this chapter, you should be able to:

1 Identify the key steps in successful career planning.

2 Clarify your work-style personality.

3 Analyze the financial and legal aspects of employment.

4 Practice effective employment search strategies.

What Do You Recommend?

Arthur Linkletter, age 21, expects to graduate next spring with a bachelor's degree in business administration. Arthur's grades are mostly Cs and Bs, and he has worked part time throughout his college career. Arthur is vice president of the Student Marketing Association on his campus. He would like to work in management or marketing for a medium-to large-size employer. Because he loves the outdoors, Arthur thinks he would prefer a job in the Northwest, perhaps in northern California, Oregon, or Washington.

What would you recommend to Arthur on the importance of career planning regarding:

1. Clarifying his values and lifestyle trade-offs?

2. Enhancing his career-related experiences before graduation?

3. Creating career plans and goals?

4. Understanding his work-style personality?

5. Identifying job opportunities?

FOR HELP with studying this chapter, visit the Online Student Center:

www.college.hmco.com/pic/garman9e

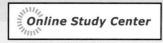

career The lifework chosen by a person to use personal talent, education, and training.

Career planning in the twenty-first century is an absolute necessity. Going from job to job may be okay for American teenagers and college students. And working for $12, $15, or $20 an hour and changing jobs for a $2-per-hour raise might be okay for a couple of years. But for many working adults, that's not an agreeable job advancement pattern. A **career** is the lifework chosen by a person to use personal talent, education, and training, and the general progression of one's career may include a number of related jobs.

You *can* control much of your financial future with effective career planning. Moving through the years in a career of your choice not only translates into jobs that are personally satisfying but also improves your level of living. A career translates into a base of income, employee benefits, additional educational experiences, advancement opportunities, and confidence in a secure financial future. Treat your career as a high priority, do-it-yourself project, and take control of where you are going and how you are going to get there.

Key Steps in Successful Career Planning

1 LEARNING OBJECTIVE

Identify the key steps in successful career planning.

Career planning can help you identify an employment pathway that aligns your interests and abilities with the tasks expected and one that supports your preferred lifestyle. You might take a job primarily to earn income. When you start looking for employment positions in your career path, you consider income, of course, but you also keep in mind opportunities for continued training, personal growth, and advancement. A career that suits you will give you opportunities to display your abilities in jobs you find satisfying while providing balance between work and your personal life.

Career planning and financial planning go hand in hand. You can't advance very far in planning your financial life without also planning a career that will pay you adequately. We include a chapter on career planning quite early in this book so that the principles and other information in the remaining chapters are relevant to you personally and to the way you want to make your living.

Career planning doesn't stop when you take your first career job. Rather, career planning is a vibrant process that lasts throughout your life. Every time your life circumstances change, you will likely reconsider your career. But first you have to start. As you plan your career, you need to perform several steps, and you should take care to carry each step out to the best of your ability. Why? Because your actions and the impression you make upon prospective employers will affect the probability of getting a good job in your field that satisfies your interests and provides an income to meet your financial needs. The time and effort you put into your career planning effort will affect how much income you earn and how far you advance in your career. First, let's take a look at the key steps to successful career planning.

career planning Finding employment that will use your interests and abilities and that will support you financially.

Figure 2.1
Steps in Career Planning

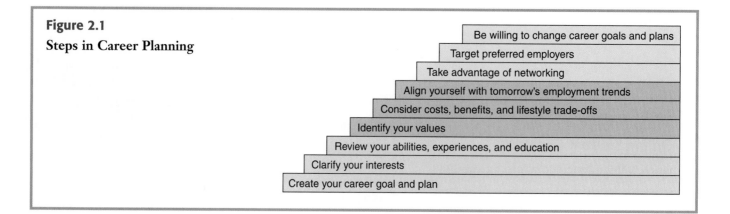

Be willing to change career goals and plans
Target preferred employers
Take advantage of networking
Align yourself with tomorrow's employment trends
Consider costs, benefits, and lifestyle trade-offs
Identify your values
Review your abilities, experiences, and education
Clarify your interests
Create your career goal and plan

Create Your Career Goal and Plan

The workplace has changed dramatically. People used to take a single job and remain at the same company until they retired. Now, people change jobs five to ten times during their working years. You are not likely to remain with one employer a lifetime let alone ten years. You probably will completely change careers two or three times.

Thinking about a career goal helps you focus on what you want to do for a living. A **career goal** can be a specific job (e.g., cost accountant, teacher, human resources manager) or a particular field of work (e.g., health care, communications, construction). It helps guide you to do the kind of work you want in life rather than drift from job to job. Formulating a career goal requires thinking about your interests, skills, and experiences and learning about different careers and employment trends. The process of establishing a career goal motivates you to consider career possibilities that you may not have thought of otherwise.

To create a career goal, explore the jobs, careers, and trends in the employment marketplace that fit your interests and skills. Ask people about careers. Search websites such as those for the *Occupational Outlook Handbook* (www.bls.gov/oco/) and the *Occupational Outlook Quarterly* (www.bls.gov/opub/ooq/ooqhome.htm). Research the education requirements.

A *career plan* identifies employment that interests you; fits your abilities, skills, work style, and lifestyle; and provides strategic guidance to help you reach your career goal. It includes short-, medium-, longer-, and long-term goals as well as future education and work-related experiences that will serve to advance your career interests. Figure 2.2 provides an illustrative career plan.

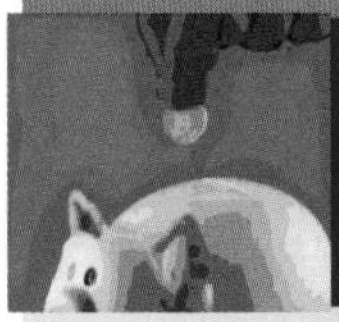

Good Money Habits in Understanding Career Planning

Make the following your money habits in career planning:

1. Take the time to plan and make the effort required to obtain employment in your career.

2. Identify your career planning values and live them in your selection of jobs and in your performance at work.

3. Do not miss an opportunity to continually enhance your education and professional training.

4. Understand your preferred work-style personality.

5. Practice effective employment search strategies, especially interviewing skills.

career goal Identifying what you want to do for a living, whether a specific job or field of employment

---

Harry Johnson began his working career following graduation from college by obtaining employment with a small commercial interior design firm. He has an undergraduate degree from a university accredited by the American Society of Interior Designers. He is happy that his first professional job is in his major field of interest.

Initial career goal: To become an interior designer. To design, plan, and supervise commercial/contract design projects.

Long-term career goal (20-plus years): Own or become a partner in a medium- to large-size commercial/contract interior design firm.

Short-term plans and goals in career establishment stage (3 to 6 years): Gain work experience in current job; receive employer compliments on quality of work; obtain continuing education credits for professional growth and development; secure higher-level design responsibilities, such as lead professional design team; volunteer for committee responsibilities in local and state professional associations; obtain substantial increases in income; receive promotions; learn operational aspects and marketing of the company.

Medium-term plans and goals in professional growth stage (7 to 12 years): Be promoted to the level of senior designer; consider going to work for another employer as a senior designer and, if necessary, move to another community; volunteer for higher-level service in professional associations; obtain a master of fine arts degree in interior design; become assistant to the firm's general manager.

Longer-term plans and goals in advancement stage (13 to 20 years): Become general manager of commercial design firm; seek out potential partners and sufficient financing to either buy out or start up a medium-size design firm.

Figure 2.2

Career Goals and Plans for Harry Johnson

The Top 3 Financial Missteps in Career Planning

People slip up in career planning when they do the following:

1. Don't learn as much as possible about a company before going for an interview

2. Change jobs and cash out all the money in their employer-sponsored retirement savings plan instead of leaving it there, transferring it to their new employer's 401(k) plan, or moving it to a rollover IRA account

3. Fail to use the COBRA law (Consolidated Omnibus Budget Reconciliation Act) to elect to continue participating in their old employer's medical health plan benefits for up to 18 months

---

interests Long-standing topics and activities that engage your attention.

interest inventories Scaled surveys that assess career interests and activities.

professional abilities Job-related activities that you can perform physically, mentally, artistically, mechanically, and financially.

aptitudes The natural abilities and talents that individuals possess.

Clarify Your Interests

Your **interests** are topics and activities about which you have feelings of curiosity or concern. Interests engage or arouse your attention. They reflect what you like to do. Interests, including occupational interests, are likely to vary over time.

You might consider making a list of your top ten interests. On that list will probably be some things you enjoy but have not done recently. Because of conflicting interests and alternative claims on your time, you cannot pursue all your interests. It is important in career planning to evaluate your interests; if you plan your career with your interests in mind, you will increase the likelihood of career satisfaction.

Interest inventories are measures that assist people in assessing and profiling the interests and activities that give them satisfaction. They compare how your interests are similar or dissimilar to the interests of people successfully employed in various occupations; the theory behind these interest inventories is that individuals with similar interests are often attracted to the same kind of work. These inventories can help you identify possible career goals that match your strongest personal interests.

The Strong Interest Inventory assessment is considered by many to be the gold standard of career exploration tools. The opportunity to take one or more interest inventory assessments, usually for free or at a nominal cost, is available at most colleges and state-supported career counseling facilities. These assessments can also be completed online for a fee. (See, for example, www.discoveryourpersonality .com/Strong.html and www.careercc.com/career_assessment.shtml.)

Review Your Abilities, Experiences, and Education

Reviewing your abilities, aptitudes, experiences, and education is a key step in career planning. The purpose is to see how well they match up with your career-related interests.

Abilities Your professional **abilities** are the qualities that allow you to perform physically, mentally, artistically, mechanically, or financially job-related tasks. Most of us think of *ability* as a word describing how well we do something, a proficiency, dexterity, or technique, particularly one requiring use of the mind, hands, or body. Other examples of abilities include being skilled in working with people, being able to easily meet the public, and being good at persuading people. Employer surveys indicate that the single most important ability needed for career success in the twenty-first century is computer skills. Also very highly ranked are communication skills and honesty/integrity. Consider making a list of your top ten abilities.

Aptitudes are the natural abilities and talents that people possess. Aptitudes suggest that you have a tendency or inclination to learn and develop certain skills or abilities. Are you good with numbers? Do you find public speaking easy to do? Do you enjoy solving problems? What are your natural talents? Consider making a list of your top ten aptitudes.

Experiences College graduates have much more going for them than a degree and a string of part-time job experiences. Reviewing your experiences is a step in career planning. Evaluate what you have been doing in your life, including jobs and internships; participation in student organizations and community and church groups; leadership on school projects; and volunteer activities.

Those still in college can enhance their résumés by learning as much as possible in school, participating in clubs and other student organizations (including volunteering for committees and campus projects), getting involved in a faculty research project, and attending off-campus professional meetings in their major. Academic advisers can provide suggestions. Employers want workers with good writing and public speaking talents, strong computer skills, fluency in a second language, and an understanding of global commerce and industry. Experiences that use and develop these traits are a big plus for job seekers.

Education and Professional Training Going to college is excellent preparation for your career and your life. But college may not have provided you with all the skills and abilities to be successfully employed. A review of your abilities, experiences, and education may suggest you need to seek additional education and professional training.

Identify Your Values

Thinking about and discovering what you want out of life gives you guidance for what to do to lead a satisfying life. Understanding yourself enables you to select a career path that best suits you. This is a key step in career planning.

Values are the principles, standards, or qualities considered worthwhile or desirable. Values provide a basis for decisions about how to live, serving as guides we can use to direct our actions. For something to be a value, it must be prized, publicly affirmed, chosen from alternatives, and acted upon repeatedly and consistently. Values are not right or wrong, or true or false; they are personal preferences.

People may place value on family, friends, helping others, religious commitment, security, honesty, pleasure, good health, material possessions, financial achievement, and a satisfying career. Examples of conflicting values are family versus friends, stability versus adventure, religious beliefs versus actions, and work versus leisure. When you make important decisions, you might be wise to think carefully to clarify your values before taking action. Consider making a list of your ten most important values.

Consider Costs, Benefits, and Lifestyle Trade-offs

Selecting a career involves making decisions about costs and benefits and **lifestyle trade-offs.**

Costs and Benefits When making career choices, you must weigh the benefits against the costs. The benefits could include a big salary, likelihood of personal growth and job advancements, and high job satisfaction. For some, the pluses might include the psychic benefit of a prestigious job with a high income. The costs might include living in a less desirable geographic area and climate, being too far from friends and family, sitting at a desk all day, working long hours, and doing too much travel.

Lifestyle Trade-offs When considering any career, think about what lifestyle or social and cultural factors are important to you. For example, if access to big-name live entertainment, museums, and artistic activities is important, then working and living in a rural area may not be appropriate. If you like to visit new places, you may choose a career that involves frequent travel.

Consider the following lifestyle options in your decision making:
- Urban/rural setting
- Close/far from work
- Own/rent housing

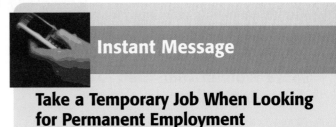

Instant Message

Education and Earnings

Adults with a bachelor's degree earn an average of $55,000 compared with $33,000 for high school graduates and $81,000 for those with advanced degrees, reports the U.S. Census Bureau.

values The principles, standards, or qualities that you consider desirable.

lifestyle trade-offs Weighing the demands of particular jobs with your social and cultural preferences.

Instant Message

Take a Temporary Job When Looking for Permanent Employment

Accepting a temporary job eases the pressure of taking the first decent real job opportunity offered. It also gives you a chance to network, develop new skills, and perhaps convert the temporary job into a full-time position. The downside is that you have to conduct your full-time job search activities after working hours.

Career planning should take lifestyle preferences into consideration.

- City/suburban life
- Warm/cold climate
- Near/far from relatives
- Constant/variable climate

In addition, employers in certain careers provide more support for working parents. Employer-subsidized child care as well as flexible work hours might be available at a "family-friendly" workplace.

These are all quality-of-life issues, your quality of life. The challenges are greater for dual-career couples because they must communicate effectively when considering the impact of one person's career decisions on the other. (Chapter 5 offers some tips on communication skills.) Remember, you always have the freedom to change your life and career objectives as you learn more about yourself and the world of work.

Instant Message

More Women Than Men Are Attending College

More women than men are going to college. Statistics show that nearly six in ten college students are women, and that proportion is expected to continue to increase.

Align Yourself with Tomorrow's Employment Trends

Right now, you may be focused on school—graduating and getting a good job. But you also need to find out where the jobs will be in the future. The job market today is rapidly changing—a result of economic downturns, corporate restructuring, downsizing, and globalization—and the career path you are considering now may not continue to be a good choice in the years ahead.

What, then, are the trends in employment? The aging U.S. population will create jobs in the service industries of finance, insurance, health care, recreation, and travel. Jobs are gravitating to existing population centers, particularly in warmer climates that have superior transportation systems. Jobs in manufacturing are largely going overseas to Mexico, Asia, Europe, and other countries, with the U.S. job market primarily demanding highly skilled workers in the service industries. Strong job growth is projected for the twenty-first century in computer technology, busi-

Advice from a Pro

Competencies of Successful People

People who are successful in their chosen careers, with their finances, and/or in life in general often possess and exhibit certain competencies.

1. Set goals in the various aspects of life and track progress toward attaining goals.

2. Use organizational tools such as lists as well as time management techniques.

3. Exhibit integrity.

4. Understand their motives and behave ethically.

5. Make a quality effort every time.

6. Accept accountability for their decisions and actions.

7. Exhibit good written and oral communication skills.

8. Demonstrate strong computer skills.

9. Open to new ideas.

10. Adapt easily to change.

11. Share knowledge to assist and mentor others.

12. Acquire advanced education and technical training and are life-long learners.

13. Take on new assignments and capitalize on the new skills learned.

14. Anticipate problems and work proactively to implement solutions.

15. Work well in teams and know when to lead and when to follow.

16. Project an image consistent with organizational values.

17. Understand operations, structure and culture of organization.

18. Loyal to and supportive of company and boss.

Caroline S. Fulmer
The University of Alabama
Certified Leadership Trainer for the Achieve Global Corporation

ness services, social services, child care, wholesale and retail sales, food services, hospitality, retirement facilities, travel, and human resources. All require good communication skills. High-demand occupations tend to pay high salaries and offer career advancement opportunities. They often require good computer skills. Table 2.1 shows the projected job growth in high-wage, high-growth occupations in the United States.

Take Advantage of Networking

Professional networking is the process of making and using contacts, such as individuals, groups, or institutions, to obtain and exchange information in career planning. Every person you know or meet is a possible useful contact. Networking requires that you make a conscious effort to use people you know and meet to maximize your job search process. Networking involves utilizing your social contacts, taking advantage of casual meetings, and asking for personal referrals. Most of your contacts will not be able to hire you, but they could refer you to the person who can, or they may be able to give you useful information about a potential employer.

professional networking Making and using contacts with individuals, groups, and other firms to exchange career information.

Maintain a continually growing list of people who are family, neighbors, friends, college associates, coworkers, previous supervisors, teachers, professors, alumni, business contacts, and others you know through civic and community organizations such as churches and business and social groups. Take note of where your contacts work and what types of jobs they have. Ask these people for 10 to 20 minutes of their time so you can seek information and suggestions from them. Perhaps meet at their workplaces (where you might meet other potential networking contacts), and afterward send them thank-you notes.

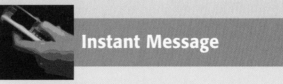

Instant Message

Network Your Way into a Company

The best way to find work at a company is to try to network your way in. Find someone you know who knows someone else in the company and can arrange an introduction.

Table 2.1 Projected High-Wage, High-Growth Occupations*

Job Title	Employment in 2014	Median Annual Income
General and operations managers	2,100,000	$115,000
Property association managers	454,000	60,000
Business operations specialists	396,000	79,000
Computer system analysts	640,000	100,000
Sales managers	403,000	122,000
Medical/health service managers	305,000	102,000
Training and development specialists	261,000	74,000
Marketing managers	228,000	153,000
Industrial engineers	205,000	98,000
Compensation benefits managers	70,000	100,000
Technical writers	62,000	81,000
Human resource managers	72,000	122,000
Media and communications	46,000	61,000
Air traffic controllers	28,000	153,000
Accountants/auditors	1,440,000	76,000
Child and social workers	324,000	51,000
Public relations specialists	231,000	66,000
Market research analysts	227,000	81,000
Advertising promotions managers	77,000	95,000

*Source: Bureau of Labor Statistics, Table I5, High-wage, high-growth occupations, by educational attainment cluster and earnings; authors' income projections to 2014.

As many as three-quarters of all job openings may never be listed in want ads, so the people in your network become a vital source of information about employment opportunities. For this reason, expanding the number of people in your network is advantageous; some of the people you know will also likely share their networking contacts. Networking is the number one way people are successful in their job search.

Target Preferred Employers

preferred employer Identifying employers that would suit you best.

Answering classified job advertisements probably is not the best way to start a career, unless you are lucky and the job listed is actually in your field of interest. A key step in the career search process is to think about both the industries in which you would prefer employment and which employers might be best for you.

If, for example, you want to work in the health care industry, you must research it. Get on the Internet. Go to the library. Visit the websites of health trade associations. Learn as much as you can about the health care industry. How broad is the industry? What types of companies are at the retail level? At the wholesale level? What kinds of firms provide services to the industry? Which companies are the largest? Which have the fastest growth rates? Which employers have employment facilities in geographic areas that are of interest to you? What are the leading companies? Which are the "employers of choice" that are family friendly or offer especially good benefits? What are the employee benefits at different companies? Knowing the industry and specific employers of interest to you tells you whom to target for employment in your career path.

Be Willing to Change Career Goals and Plans

Your career plan should be realistic and flexible. Your career interests and goals will change over time, especially as you continue your education, gain work experience, and see how your friends fare with their jobs and avocations. Teaching music education might be your first career, but you may eventually realize that the accompanying small income could keep you on a tight financial budget forever. This issue might encourage you to consider a total career change—perhaps to sales in the music industry or a related field, where incomes are higher.

Some people go the other way. For example, after some years in the field of accounting, you might change career goals and go to work in your longtime interest area of horticulture, which pays less. Your interests might evolve over time as well. For example, a person with a full-time job in retail store management might decide to turn a hobby of gun collecting into selling guns as an online business. Staying in a career path but changing jobs occurs, too. For example, some hospital nurses decide after a few years that they have made a wrong career choice. While the job pays well, it involves shift work and very long days. Those who want to remain in the nursing profession may decide to leave the hospital setting and go to work for a nursing home or college health facility.

Assessing yourself and your career plans every few years is important to achieving success in your working life. What do you find satisfying and not so satisfying? Honest answers will help you, particularly as your interests evolve. Your work experiences should hone your abilities and skills. Learning new skills on the job is common, and if that is not happening in a job, move on and change employers and perhaps careers.

CONCEPT CHECK 2.1

1. Distinguish between a job and a career.
2. How do your values affect your trade-offs in career planning?
3. What can be done to enhance your abilities and experiences without working in a job situation?
4. What are the components of career plans and goals?

Know Your Preferred Work-Style Personality

Every job requires the worker to function in relation to data, people, and things in differing work environments and corporate cultures. Your **work-style personality** is a unique set of ways of working with and responding to your job requirements, surroundings, and associates. When making a career selection, you must balance your work-style personality against the demands of the work environment.

You can begin by rating each work value as shown in the "Decision-Making Worksheet: What Is Your Work-Style Personality." Next, go back to the list and circle the activities that you prefer to do "most often." Armed with this information, you can now more clearly decide on careers that are most suitable for you.

2 LEARNING OBJECTIVE
Clarify your work-style personality.

work-style personality Your own ways of working with and responding to job requirements surroundings, and associates.

CONCEPT CHECK 2.2

1. Summarize the three major parts of your work-style personality.

Decision-Making Worksheet

What Is Your Work-Style Personality?

It would be useful for you to consider a number of work values critical to the process of career selection, particularly in the areas of work conditions, work purposes, and work relationships. Rate how you value the following work values as either very important in my choice of career (VI), somewhat important in my choice of career (SI), or unimportant in my choice of career (UI).

Work-Style Factor	Your Rating of Importance		
	VI	SI	UI
1. Work Conditions			
Independence and autonomy			
Time flexibility			
Change and variety			
Change and risk			
Stability and security			
Physical challenge			
Physical demands			
Mental challenge			
Pressure and time deadlines			
Precise work			
Decision making			
2. Work Purposes			
Truth and knowledge			
Expertise and authority			
Esthetic appreciation			
Social conditions			
Material gain			
Achievement and recognition			
Ethical and moral			
Spiritual and transpersonal			
3. Work Relationships			
Working alone			
Public contact			
Close friendships			
Group membership			
Helping others			
Influencing others			
Supervising others			
Controlling others			

For additional values clarification, go back to the list and *circle the activities* that you want to do more often. The goal is to match your highest work-style values to career choices with similar work-style requirements.

Source: Adapted from D. C. Borchard, J. J. Kelly, and N. P. K. Weaver, *Your Career: Choices, Chances, Changes* (Dubuque, IA: Kendall/Hunt, 1990), Chapter 11.

Financial and Legal Aspects of Employment

This section examines financial and legal aspects of employment to consider when analyzing your career plans, and it includes the Decision Making Worksheet: Assessing the Value of a Second Income.

3 LEARNING OBJECTIVE
Analyze the financial and legal aspects of employment.

Compare Salary and Living Costs in Different Cities

Incomes range by geographic region, community, and size of employer. Median household income is lowest in the South, a little higher in the Midwest, higher still in the West, and highest in the Northeast. These regional differences reflect the industrial base, unemployment rates, general economic conditions, costs of living (especially for housing and transportation), and the supply and demand for skilled workers. Incomes in rural areas are usually much lower than in urban areas. The highest incomes are paid in metropolitan areas exceeding 1 million in population. Higher salaries are paid in the largest communities for the reasons just mentioned but also because employers compete for the most skilled workers since so many people often live in these communities. Employers with fewer than 100 employees typically pay lower salaries for comparable positions than do larger employers.

Compare Using City Indexes Comparing salary offers from employers located in different cities can be tricky without sufficient information on the approximate cost of living in each community. Sometimes those costs vary drastically. Information from the Internet reveals, for example, that life in a high-cost city such as Seattle is more expensive than life in a lower-cost city such as Portland, Oregon. The data are reported in index form, with the "average cost" community being given a rating of 100.

The following example demonstrates how to compare salary offers in two cities. Assume the Seattle (city 1) index is 138, and Portland's (city 2) is 114. You want to compare the buying power of a salary offer of $52,000 in Portland with a $65,000 offer in Seattle. The costs can be compared using Equations (2.1) and (2.2).

$$\text{Salary in city 1} \times \frac{\text{index city 2}}{\text{index city 1}} = \text{equivalent salary in city 2} \qquad 2.1$$

$$\text{Seattle salary of \$65,000} \times \frac{114}{138} = \$53,696 \text{ in buying power in Portland}$$

Thus, the $65,000 Seattle salary offer would buy $53,695 of goods and services in Portland, an amount more than the Portland offer of $52,000. All things being equal (and they are both nice cities), the Seattle offer is slightly better ($53,696 − $52,000 = $1,695).

To compare the buying power of salaries in the other direction, reverse the formula:

$$\text{Salary in city 2} \times \frac{\text{index city 1}}{\text{index city 2}} = \text{equivalent salary in city 1} \qquad 2.2$$

$$\text{Portland salary of \$52,000} \times \frac{138}{114} = \$62,947 \text{ in buying power in Seattle}$$

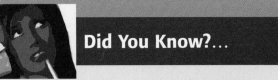

Did You Know?...

How to Work at Home Online

Technology has made it possible for many people to work at home online, as 1 in 15 workers has such an alternative work arrangement. Some people work off site for an employer, telecommuting (or teleworking) and perhaps spending one day every two weeks at the company office. Other people are self-employed entrepreneurs who run microbusinesses. A good computer and software make it possible.

Lots of scams exist in the work-at-home industry, especially selling overpriced products and services that people don't need or want. See scam information at the National Fraud Information Center (www.fraud.org/tips/internet/workathome.htm).

Many excellent legitimate job opportunities exist. Examples of online employment are Web hosting, desktop publishing, information processing, database administration, researcher, public relations, employee assistance counseling, telemarketing, personal care services, data entry, accounting, consulting, technical writing, editing, debt counseling, and project management. For ideas on working at home, see the Small Business Administration (www.sba.gov), National Association for the Self-Employed (www.nase.org), and Service Corps of Retired Executives (www.score.org).

city indexes Comparing wages and cost of living for various employment locations.

Value of Additional Education

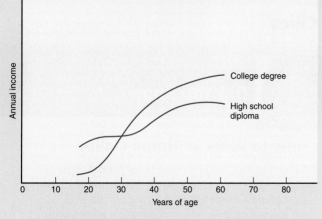

(Income over the Life Cycle Based on Education)

A recent high school graduate with a current income of $27,000 will earn a cumulative $2,036,000 over a 40-year working career. A person with an associate's degree earning $36,000 today will gross $2,700,000; one with a bachelor's degree earning $44,000 now will gross $3,300,000; and a person with a master's degree and a current income of $52,000 will receive a cumulative income of $3,900,000 over a 40-year working career. (The figures are based on 3 percent annual income increases in Appendix A.3.)

Income varies over the life cycle. Higher incomes often go to those with more education or more specialized education. Additional formal education normally leads to greater decision-making responsibilities in a career as well as a higher income.

nonsalary benefits Forms of remuneration provided by employers to employees that result in the employee not having to pay out-of-pocket money for certain expenses; also known as employee benefits.

Thus, the $52,000 Portland offer can buy only $62,947 of goods and services in Seattle—an amount less than the $65,000 Seattle salary offer. All things being equal, the Seattle offer is still better. For fairer comparisons, add the value of employee benefits and redo the calculations.

Compare Salaries and Living Costs on the 'Net You may compare salary figures and the cost of living in different communities at the following websites:

- CityRating.com (http://www.cityrating.com/costofliving.asp)
- CNNMoney.com (http://cgi.money.cnn.com/tools/costofliving/costofliving.html)
- Moving.com (http://www.moving.com/find_a_place/relosmart/rs.asp)
- Salary.com (http://swz.salary.com/costoflivingwizard/layoutscripts/coll_start.asp)

Place Values on Employee Benefits

Employee benefits are tremendously important to employees, especially when comparing the benefits provided by one employer with another. **Nonsalary benefits** (or **employee benefits**) are forms of remuneration provided by employers to employees that result in the employee not having to pay out-of-pocket money for certain expenses. Examples include paid vacations, health care, paid sick leave, child care, tuition reimbursement, and financial planning services.

The topic of "making smart money decisions at work" was examined in Chapter 1, which provided details on selecting among employer benefits such as health care plans (including health savings accounts), flexible spending plans (such as dependent and health care FSA accounts), insurance (such as life, disability, and long-term care), and employer retirement plans.

You can place a monetary value on each employee benefit that is available. Some nonsalary benefits might not be applicable, such as child care if you are single. Others are supervaluable, such as a health plan, since a policy purchased in the private market for a single person might have a premium of $5000 a year. To put monetary values on employee benefits, you may (1) place a market value on the benefit or (2) calculate the future value of the benefit. See www.salary.com to calculate the value of your employee benefits.

Place a Market Value on the Benefit If instead of enjoying a certain employee benefit, you had to pay out-of-pocket dollars for it, you can easily determine its market value. Private child care might cost $300 a week in your community; thus, when provided free from your employer, that is a whopping $15,000 ($300 × 50 weeks) saved annually. Actually, it is more because you would likely have to earn perhaps $22,000 to have $15,000 left over after paying $7000 in income and Social Security taxes. An employer-provided paid-for life insurance policy with a face value of $50,000 might cost $600 if you had to buy it yourself.

Calculate the Future Value of the Benefit The best income is income that is never taxed, called tax-exempt income. Chapter 1 examined this topic. Many employee benefits are of this type and that's great from your personal finance per-

Seattle has a lot to offer, but it comes at a price.

spective. Future value calculations come into play when you are trying to place a value on an employee benefit that is tax sheltered. Such income is exempt from income taxes in the current year but is subject to taxation in a later tax year. An employer that provides a 401(k) retirement plan offers a valuable benefit. If an employer provides a match of $1200 a year to the regular contributions of the employee, for example, those $1200 contributions will eventually be the worker's money. And it will grow free of income taxes until the funds are withdrawn. Over 20 years, the annual employer contributions of $1200 grow to more than $44,000 (using Appendix A.3) at 6 percent annual return. That's a good employee benefit!

Know Your Legal Employment Rights

You have legal rights both during the hiring process and after you are hired. When selecting employees, employers may not discriminate based on gender, race, color, national origin, age, marital status, pregnancy, or mental or physical disabilities (if the person can perform the essential job tasks). Laws in many states and cities also prohibit discrimination against gays and lesbians in the hiring process.

Once hired, you have many rights. Employers must do the following:

- Pay the minimum wage established by federal, state, or local laws
- Provide unemployment insurance
- Provide workers' compensation benefits to any employee who is injured or becomes ill on the job
- Pay Social Security taxes to the government, which are then credited to the employee's lifetime earnings account maintained by the Social Security Administration

Once hired, the law requires that hourly employees be paid overtime for extra work hours put in beyond the standard 40-hour workweek. (Salaried employees are not paid overtime, and the vast majority of college graduates have salaried jobs.) In addition, a woman cannot be forced to go on maternity leave before she wants to do so if she does choose to take leave. You have the rights not to be unfairly discriminated against or harassed and to be employed in a safe workplace.

Decision-Making Worksheet

Assessing the Benefits of a Second Income

A second income might add surprisingly little to your total earnings because of all the costs associated with earning it. In this example, a nonworking spouse is considering a job that pays $30,000 annually. The accurate net amount of the extra $30,000 income is a mere $9,205, thus adding only $767 a month to total earnings.

1. Second Income

Annual earnings	$30,000
Value of benefits (life insurance)	300
Total 1	$30,300

2. Expenses

Federal income taxes (25% rate × $30,000)	$ 7,500
State/local income taxes (6% rate × $30,000)	1,800
Social Security taxes (7.65% × $30,000)	2,295
Transportation and commuting (50 weeks @$40)	2,000
Child care (8 months after-school only)	3,200
Lunches out (50 weeks, twice a week at $10)	1,000
Work wardrobe (including dry cleaning)	1,200
Other work-related expenses (magazines, dues, gifts)	300
Take-out food for supper (too tired to cook; $100 month)	1,200
Guilt complex purchases (to make up for time lost with others)	600
Total 2	$21,095

3. Net Value of Second Income

Total of 1 from above	$30,300
Subtract total of 2 from above	21,095
Accurate net amount of second income	$ 9,205

You have the right to take leave for personal or family medical problems, pregnancy, or adoption. You also have the right to privacy in such personal matters. When you leave an employer, you have the right to continue your health insurance coverage, perhaps for as long as 18 months, by paying the premiums yourself. If you believe you have been wronged, you can assert your legal rights.

✓ CONCEPT CHECK 2.3

1. Summarize how education level and age affect income.

2. Explain how to compare salary and living costs in different cities.

3. What two techniques can be used to place monetary values on employee benefits?

4. Choose three career advancement tips and explain how each one might apply in someone's personal situation.

Advice from a Pro

Career Advancement Tips

The essence of career advancement is to build your job-related knowledge and skills for the future by learning. You do not want to fall behind your coworkers and those who work for other employers, as they may be your future job market competitors. To advance in your career, consider the following:

1. Ask one or two people to serve as your mentors, people with whom you can regularly discuss your career progress. A **mentor** is an experienced person, often a senior coworker, who offers friendly career-related advice, guidance, and coaching to a less experienced person.

2. Volunteer for new assignments.

3. Sign up for employer-sponsored seminars and training opportunities.

4. Attend meetings and conferences in your field.

5. Complete certification programs offered by professional associations.

6. Take advanced college courses and complete a graduate degree.

7. Stay alert to what is happening in your career field by reading professional and trade publications.

8. Be up-to-date on current events and business and economic news by reviewing websites and reading newspapers, news magazines, and business periodicals.

9. Be actively involved in something besides work, such as coaching children's athletics, playing softball, singing in a choral group, or teaching reading to illiterate adults.

10. Change jobs when appropriate to obtain a different or better position that advances your career, or when deemed necessary to entirely alter your career.

Dana Wolff
Southeast Technical Institute

Did You Know?...

What You Give Up When Cashing Out Your 401(k) Account

When changing jobs, nearly half of workers unwisely cash out all the money in their employer-sponsored retirement plan instead of leaving it with the old employer, transferring it to a new employer's 401(k) plan, or moving it to an IRA rollover account. If an individual has $50,000 in a 401(k) account and cashes it out, that person gives up $233,000 in future dollars over the following 20 years.

	If you cash out $50,000:	If you roll over $50,000:
20% federal income tax withholding	−$10,000	
5% additional tax (in 25% tax bracket)	−2,500	
10% early-withdrawal penalty	−5,000	
5% state/local income tax	−2,500	
Total withdrawn	−$20,000	+$50,000
Money spent on new car, TV, home repair, vacation, etc.	−$30,000	Money invested in another tax-deferred retirement account that earns 8 percent annually
Total	−$50,000	+$50,000
Additional investment actions taken	None	None
Investment balance after 20 years	$0	$233,050

Effective Employment Search Strategies

4 LEARNING OBJECTIVE
Practice effective employment search strategies.

Once you have undertaken some career planning, you will want to get a job in your preferred career field. This is a process that takes much effort. A successful job search might require 25 to 30 hours per week of your time. Effective search strategies follow.

Assemble a Résumé

résumé Summary record of your education, training, experience, and other qualifications.

chronological format Résumé that provides your information in reverse order, with most recent first.

skills format Résumé that emphasizes your aptitudes and qualities.

functional format Résumé that emphasizes career-related experiences.

The Internet is a valuable resource for you in all aspects of career planning, including preparing a résumé. A **résumé** is a summary record of your education, training, experience, and other qualifications. It is often submitted with a job application. Your résumé, usually one or two pages in length, should be carefully written and contain zero errors or inconsistencies in message, content, and appearance.

Its primary function is to provide a basis for screening people out of contention for jobs. When you supply a résumé, you are providing documentation for some kind of subjective evaluation against unknown criteria. Large employers, recruiters, and local and national websites screen résumés, and computer software is frequently used to scan them instead of humans. Use key buzzwords from the job description such as "Microsoft Office" so the scanning process picks them up.

When it is necessary to technically fulfill a requirement in the employment process, tailor a special edition of your résumé to fit that special set of circumstances. Résumés are usually presented in a **chronological format** (information in reverse order with most recent first), **skills format** (aptitudes and qualities), or **functional format** (career-related experiences). See Figures 2.3, 2.4, and 2.5 for sample résumés. Colleges have career centers with sample résumés and professional staff who can offer personal advice. You can also find examples of résumés on the Internet.

Monster.com has 500,000 online résumés and ResumeMailman .com forwards résumés to recruiters. Simply posting your résumé on an Internet site or sending out résumés is not conducting a significant job search. Realize, of course, that your current employer can view your résumé if it is posted on the Internet.

Did You Know?...

Résumé Buzzwords for Skills, Traits, and Technical Expertise

When preparing your résumé, it is important to include buzzwords for skills, traits, and technical expertise that a potential employer will identify as desirable. This is especially important when computer software is used to scan résumés. Following are examples of good buzzwords:

- Attributes: honesty, integrity
- Skills: oral, written, editing, mediating
- Interests: fun, avocations, volunteer efforts
- Teamwork: coordinated, designed, developed, led, researched
- Computer literacy and expertise: list programs and applications
- Job responsibilities: initiated, managed, monitored, planned, trained, supervised
- Job accomplishments: achieved, administered, built, created, designed, implemented, organized, produced

Identify Job Opportunities

The next step is to identify job opportunities that fit your skill set and provide opportunities for advancement in your career. Use the following resources, and keep track of your job search progress using the Decision-Making Worksheet.

Career Fairs **Career fairs** are university-, community-, and employer-sponsored opportunities for job seekers to meet with perhaps hundreds or even thousands of potential employers over one or more days. Here you can schedule brief screening interviews with a dozen or more employers in a single day. Career fairs are advertised in local newspapers, on television, and on the Internet. Seearch "career fairs" on the Internet as well as at CareerBuilder.com and NationalCareerFairs.com.

Classified Advertisements Advertisements in newspapers and professional and trade publications—as well as their Internet equivalents—are an excellent starting place in the job search process. Larger newspapers, such as the *Atlanta Constitution* and *Chicago Daily News* advertise jobs in large geographic areas. Others such as the

Decision-Making Worksheet

Keeping Track of Your Job Search Progress

The job search process involves a tremendous number of details. Below is a list of task areas in worksheet format that you can use to help keep track of your job search progress. Create lots of columns to the right so you can input important information, such as dates.

1. Identify your values.

2. Decide on economic, psychic, and lifestyle trade-offs.

3. Clarify career-related interests.

4. Review abilities, experiences, and education.

5. Identify employment trends.

6. Create career goals and plans.

7. Target preferred employers.

8. Analyze your work-style personality.

9. Compare salary and living costs in different cities.

10. Place values on employee benefits.

11. Create an expanding list of networking contacts.

12. Obtain excellent letters of reference.

13. Compile revealing personal stories.

14. Assemble a résumé.

15. Assemble a cover letter.

16. Identify job opportunities:

    a. Career fairs.

    b. Classified advertisements.

    c. Employment agencies.

    d. Internet.

17. Interviewing

    Research the company.

    Create responses for anticipated interview questions.

    Create positive responses to list of negative questions.

    Evaluate your interview performance.

18. Send a thank-you note.

19. Accept the job.

Instant Message

"Blink" Is Important in Interviewing

Malcolm Gladwell, author of *Blink*, argues that when you meet someone for the first time, "your mind takes about two seconds to jump to a series of conclusions." It is not intuition or a snap judgment; it is rapid rational thinking. Your appearance, smile, handshake, first few sentences, and tone of voice send critically important information to the interviewer. Practice and make your blink the best you can communicate. (See www.gladwell.com/blink/.)

Instant Message

Only 20% Prepare for Interviews

Professional recruiters estimate that perhaps only 20 percent of college seniors adequately prepare for their campus interviews.

Instant Message

Personality Tests

One-third of employers give job candidates personality tests assessing team orientation, strengths important to a job, emotional intelligence, motivation, and true work-style inclinations. Don't try to game the employer by telling them what they want to hear—the "right" answer. Being honest confirms what the prospective employer already knows about you.

Prepare Responses for Anticipated Interview Questions Your responsibilities during the interview are to remain calm, reveal your personality, be honest, convey your best characteristics, handle questions well, and communicate your enthusiasm about the job. Always answer in a controlled manner. During the interview, be confident that you are the best person for the job and project yourself accordingly.

Job interviewers seem to ask similar questions, so prepare some articulate responses to the following inquiries:

1. Tell me about yourself.

2. How would your instructors and previous employers describe you?

3. What did you like the most about college, and the least?

4. Tell me what you know about our company.

5. Why are you interested in working for this company?

6. What unique abilities and experiences qualify you for the job?

7. Describe some of your strengths and weaknesses.

8. What experiences have you had working with teams and coordinating such efforts?

9. Give an example of an ethical challenge you faced and tell how you handled it.

10. Relate a time when you were faced with a very difficult problem and how you handled it.

11. Describe the supervisors who motivated you to do your best work.

12. What were some of the best and worst aspects of your last job?

13. What do you do in your leisure time?

14. Describe your career plans for five and ten years from now.

Create Positive Responses to Negative Questions

Be prepared to "turn any negative into a positive" when asked such questions. One popular negative question, of course, is, "What are your weaknesses?" Interviewers who ask these types of questions want to determine whether the applicant possesses certain qualities such as honesty, self-awareness, humility, sincerity, zest, and skill in managing shortcomings and mistakes. Denying weakness or being evasive means you don't get the job.

Beforehand, practice your interview skills. Practice your responses, especially to negative questions. Perhaps make a videotape of a mock interview, and after evaluating your performance do it again.

Be Ready for Telephone Interviews Present yourself in a professional manner when returning a telephone call or engaging in an interview. Have a pen or pencil and paper handy. Be aware of distractions in your surroundings, such as traffic

Did You Know?...

How to Interview over a Meal

More people lose a job interview over lunch than during the formal interview because they fail to realize that going to lunch is a continuation of the interview rather than a social situation. Employers want to hire people with some degree of refinement, people who will mix well with clients and executives. It is smart to engage in conversation over a meal, of course, but let the boss do most of the talking. Good etiquette tips include the following:

- Order a meal less expensive than the host.
- Keep your elbows off the table.
- Break (don't cut) your bread or roll before buttering.
- Use the bread knife (the small knife to the left of your plate).
- Use the small fork outermost from the plate for the first course.
- Don't salt and pepper your meal before tasting.

- Cut your meat one bite at a time.
- Don't talk with food in your mouth.
- Don't order beer, wine, or liquor.
- Avoid ordering soup or pastas because they can be too messy.
- Be extremely polite and respectful of the servers.
- Never complain about a meal.
- Leave it to your host to signal the server.
- If confused, be patient and follow the lead of the host.
- Leave your napkin on your chair when excusing yourself.
- When the meal is over, thank the host and state that you want the job.
- When appropriate, shake hands and say goodbye.

noise. If needed, arrange to call the interviewer back when you find a quiet place. Speak clearly, and eliminate the "uhs" and "ums." The interviewer will notice if you take a sip of coffee or a bite out of a bagel. Try to eliminate as many annoyances as possible to improve your chances of getting the job.

After the Interview, Evaluate It and Send a Thank-You Note After a job interview, take a few minutes to objectively evaluate your performance. Write down any questions you were asked that were different from what you expected and make some notes about ways to improve in your next interview. The more interviews you have, the better you will be able to present yourself. Also, immediately mail a thank-you note (don't e-mail it) expressing your appreciation for the opportunity to interview and restate your interest in the position.

Instant Message

Common Job Interview Mistakes

1. Displayed little knowledge of employer
2. Unprepared to discuss abilities, skills, and experience
3. Unable to discuss career plans and goals
4. Demonstrated little enthusiasm
5. Exhibited poor eye contact

Negotiate and Accept the Job

Wait until after the job has been firmly offered to discuss salary. Do not be the first to give a definitive dollar amount. Ask for the salary range for the position. Your objective in negotiating is to obtain a salary 20 percent above the highest figure because you are an exceptional candidate and you will perform at the highest level anticipated. Don't sell yourself short.

Did You Know?...

How to Deal with Rejection

The job search process is filled with rejections. Before you land a job, you might have 5 or even 50 potential employers say "No!" Don't let employment rejections strip you of your self-esteem or you will begin to falsely think that there is something wrong with you. A rejection is simply an indicator that there is an inadequate match between your qualities and the employer's needs as perceived in the interview.

After a turndown, when possible ask the company for a review of the strengths and weaknesses of your interview. Make an effort to improve for the next interview. Then, forget the disappointment and move on with your job search.

Did You Know?...

How to Get a Raise

The first step in getting a raise is to talk with your boss and write down well-defined, achievable, and measurable goals that you can work toward. This may occur during a formal annual review. Throughout the year, perhaps on a quarterly basis, discuss these with your boss. Do so not in hallway conversations but in brief sit-down meetings. Document your accomplishments in writing and keep records. Find out what people in your field earn by talking with others, reviewing trade publications, and checking online at sites such as Salary.com and Yahoo's HotJobs.com. Schedule a meeting with your boss before the scheduled time for the annual personnel review. Avoid mentioning how much you need a big raise (because bosses may not care and you might imply you are a poor money manager) and focus on your performance. If the boss cannot give you all the money you deserve, ask for a bigger bonus, enhanced health or retirement benefits, a more flexible work schedule, a change in work hours, permission to occasionally telecommute, or more vacation time.

Be comfortable with silence, and wait for a response. If the offer is less than what you were expecting, explain that point. Be firm but amicable. This will enhance the employer's respect for you. Tell the employer that you are not willing to start at the bottom or middle of the salary ladder. Reiterate your two or three strongest selling points. Be certain to make a short list of these points beforehand. If the employer states that the offer is final, reply that you need a day or two to think it over. Never turn down an offer until you are absolutely positive you must do so.

If the terms are right, accept the job. Give your new employer your acceptance orally as well as in writing. Obtain a letter confirming your acceptance of the job at the agreed-upon salary with benefits such as moving expenses, flexible hours, and extra vacation days.

✓ **CONCEPT CHECK 2.4**

1. Explain how networking can be used to one's advantage in career planning.
2. Offer suggestions on correctly assembling a résumé and cover letter, and explain how the two documents differ.
3. Summarize the best methods to identify job opportunities.
4. List five suggestions for interviewing with success.

What Do You Recommend Now?

Now that you have read the chapter on the importance of career planning, what do you recommend to Arthur in the case at the beginning of the chapter regarding:

1. Clarifying his values and life-style trade-offs in career planning?
2. Enhancing his career-related experiences before graduation?
3. Creating career plans and goals?
4. Understanding his work-style personality?
5. Identifying job opportunities?

Big Picture Summary of Learning Objectives

1 Identify the key steps in successful career planning.

Career planning is identifying an employment pathway that aligns with your interests and abilities and that is expected to provide the lifestyle and work style you find enjoyable and satisfying. It includes defining your values, making lifestyle trade-offs, clarifying career-related interests, reviewing your talents, understanding employment trends, creating career goals, and targeting preferred employers.

2 Clarify your work-style personality.

Your work-style personality is a unique set of ways of working with and responding to one's job requirements, surroundings, and associates.

3 Analyze the financial and legal aspects of employment.

The financial side of career planning includes comparing salary and living costs in different cities and placing values on employee benefits.

4 Practice effective employment search strategies.

Smart job search strategies include networking, obtaining excellent reference letters, compiling revealing stories, assembling a résumé and cover letter, identifying job opportunities, and interviewing for success.

Let's Talk About It

1. Thinking about some common mistakes that people make in job interviews, which five are the worst? Make a list of ten things people should do to improve success in an interview.

2. People regularly make decisions in career planning that have trade-offs. List three career decisions that people are likely to face, and identify some economic, psychic, and lifestyle trade-offs for each.

3. Review the task areas in the "Decision-Making Worksheet: Keeping Track of Your Job Search Progress," and identify what you think are the five that likely are the most difficult for people to accomplish. For each of the five, offer a suggestion that might help people accomplish the task.

Do the Numbers

1. Delores Springsteen hopes to earn an extra $600,000 over her remaining 40-year working career by going to night school to obtain a master's degree. If her income projection is correct, that's an average of $15,000 more income a year. Delores's employer is willing to pay $45,000 toward the $60,000 schooling costs, so she must pay out $15,000 of her own money.

   (a) What is the forgone lost future value of her $15,000 over the 40 years at 6 percent? (Hint: See Appendix A.1.)

   (b) What would be the forgone lost future value of $60,000 over 40 years if Delores had to pay all the costs for her master's degree? (Hint: See Appendix A.1.)

2. Using Equation (2.1) or (2.2), if the cost-of-living index was 132 for Chicago and 114 for San Antonio, compare the buying power of a $50,000 salary in Chicago with a $47,000 offer in San Antonio.

3. Johann Winkle's employer makes a matching contributing of $1200 a year to his 401(k) retirement account at work. If the employer's match increases 4 percent annually, how much will the employer contribute to the plan in the 20th year from now? (Hint: See Appendix A.1.)

4. Betty Amarrada has accepted a new job and is thinking about cashing out the $30,000 she has built up in her employer's 401(k) plan to use to buy a new car. If, instead, she left the funds in the plan and they earn 7 percent annually for the next 20 years, how much would Betty have in her plan? (Hint: See Appendix A.1.)

Financial Planning Cases

Case 1
Matching Yourself with a Job

After completing his associate of arts degree four months ago from a community college in Birmingham, Alabama, Jimmy Jackson has answered more than a dozen advertisements and interviewed several times in his effort to get a sales job, but he has had no success. Jimmy has never done sales work before, but he did take some business classes in college, including "Personal Selling." After some of the interviews, Jimmy telephoned some of those potential employers only to find that even though they liked him, they said they typically hired only those people with previous sales experience or who seemed to possess terrific potential.

(a) If Jimmy actually was well suited for sales, which work values and work-style factors do you think he would rate as "very important"?

(b) What would you recommend to Jimmy regarding how to find out about the depth of his interest in a sales career?

(c) Assuming Jimmy has appropriate personal qualities and academic strengths to be successful in a sales career, what additional strategies should he consider to better market himself?

Case 2
Career Promotion Opportunity

Nina and Ting Guo of Des Plaines, Illinois, have been together for eight years, having married just after completing college. Nina has been working as an insurance salesperson ever since. Ting began working as a family counselor for the state of Illinois last year after completing his master's degree in counseling. Recently Nina's boss commented confidentially that he was going to recommend Nina to be the next person to be promoted, given a raise of about $15,000, and relocated to the home office in St. Louis, Missouri. Nina thinks that if offered the opportunity she would like to take it, even if it means that Ting will have to resign his new job.

(a) What suggestions can you offer Nina when she gets home from work and wants to discuss with her husband her likely career promotion?

(b) What lifestyle factors and costs and benefits issues should Nina and Ting probably discuss?

Case 3
Victor and Maria Hernandez

Throughout this book, we will present a continuing narrative about Victor and Maria Hernandez. Following is a brief description of the lives of this couple.

Victor and Maria, both in their late 30s, have two children: John, age 13, and Joseph, age 15. Victor has had a long sales career with a retail appliance store. Maria works part time as a dental hygienist. Victor is somewhat satisfied with his career but has always wondered about a career as a teacher in a public school. He would have to take a year off work to go to college to obtain his teaching certificate, and that would mean giving up his $43,000 salary. Victor expects that he could earn about the same income as an inner-city teacher.

(a) What is the future value of $43,000 over 20 years at six percent? (Hint: Use Appendix A.1.)

(b) What if Victor could earn $4000 each year teaching in the summers? What is the future value of earning those annual amounts over 20 years at six percent? (Hint: Use Appendix A.3.)

Case 4
Harry and Belinda Johnson

Throughout this book, we will present a continuing narrative about Harry and Belinda Johnson. Following is a brief description of the lives of this couple.

Harry graduated with a bachelor's degree in interior design last spring from a large Midwestern university near his hometown. Belinda has a degree in business finance from a university on the West Coast. Harry and Belinda both worked on their school's student newspapers and met at a conference during their junior year in college. They were married last June and live in an apartment in Kansas City.

(a) Harry receives $3000 in interest income annually from a trust fund set up by his deceased father's estate. The amount will never change. What will be the buying power of $3000 in ten years if inflation rises at 3 percent a year? (Hint: Use Appendix A.2.)

(b) Belinda and Harry have discussed starting a family but decided to wait for perhaps five years in order to get their careers off to a good start and organize their personal finances. They also know that having children is expensive. They figure that the extra expense of a child would be about $5000 annually until high school graduation. How much money will they likely cumulatively spend on a child over 18 years? (Hint: Use Appendix A.3.)

On the 'Net

Go to the Web pages indicated to complete these exercises. You can also go to the *Garman/Forgue* website at college.hmco.com/business/students for an expanded list of exercises. Under General Business, select the title of this text. Click on the Internet Exercises link for this chapter.

1. Go to the website for the *Occupational Outlook Handbook* at http://www.bls.gov/oco/home.htm. Select two occupational areas that are of interest to you and for each determine the likely starting salary, career path, future salary expectations, and demand for people with the skills appropriate for the occupation.

2. Go to the website for the Bureau of Labor Statistics' assessment of the labor outlook in the United States

at http://www.bls.gov/bls/employment.htm. Browse through the information provided to determine the current national unemployment rate for the nation as a whole and for a city/area of interest to you. Compare current statistics with those of one year ago and with projections for five and ten years in the future.

Visit the Garman/Forgue website...

@college.hmco.com/business/students

Under General Business, select *Personal Finance 9e*. There, among other valuable resources, you will find a complete glossary, ACE questions, links to help you complete the chapter exercises, and links to other personal finance sites.

CHAPTER 3

Financial Statements, Tools, and Budgets

You Must Be Kidding, Right?

The median net worth of American families is $93,000, and the mean amount is $448,000. (Those with high net worth pull the mean above the median.) What are the median and mean figures for families headed by a person less than 35 years of age?

A. $17,000 and $88,000

B. $30,000 and $128,000

C. $47,000 and $178,000

D. $60,000 and $198,000

The answer is A, $17,000 median and $88,000 mean. Median net worth goes up with age. It is $83,000 for families ages 35 to 44, $174,000 for ages 45 to 54, and $298,000 for ages 55 to 64. It all about saving money and building wealth over time!

LEARNING OBJECTIVES

After reading this chapter, you should be able to:

1 **Identify** your financial values, goals, and strategies.

2 **Use** balance sheets and cash-flow statements to measure your financial health and progress, just as businesses do.

3 **Evaluate** your financial strength and progress using financial ratios.

4 **Maintain** the financial records necessary for managing your personal finances.

5 **Outline** and work toward achieving your financial goals through budgeting.

What Do You Recommend?

Robert and Nicole Patterson, both age 26, have been married for four years and have no children. Robert is a licensed electrician earning $46,000 per year, and Nicole earns $41,000 annually as a middle-school teacher. Robert would like to go to half time on his job and return to school on a part-time basis; he is one year short of finishing his bachelor's degree in engineering. His education expenses would be about $10,000 per year, which could be partially covered by student loans. He has not yet discussed his plans with Nicole.

Robert and Nicole have recently started saving for retirement through their employment and have set aside some savings for emergencies. They have substantial credit card debt and are still paying off their student loans. The couple rents a two-bedroom apartment. Robert always thought it smart to save all of their receipts, bank statements, and other financial documents. His system for organizing their records is very simple; each month he puts everything in a manila envelope and then puts the 12 envelopes into a box at the end of the year.

Robert knows that his educational plans will have financial implications for the couple. He wants to factor these financial issues into his discussion with Nicole about his plans. To this point, they have never developed financial statements or explicit financial goals.

What do you recommend to Robert for his talk with Nicole on the subject of financial planning regarding:

1. Determining what they own and owe?

2. Better understanding their patterns of family income and expenditure?

3. Using the information in Robert's newly prepared financial statements to summarize the family's financial situation?

4. Evaluating their financial progress?

5. Setting up a record-keeping system to better serve their needs?

6. Starting a budgeting process to guide saving and spending?

FOR HELP with studying this chapter, visit the Online Student Center:

www.college.hmco.com/pic/garman9e

- Housing (rent, mortgage, loan payment)
- Automobile (installment payment, lease)
- Insurance (life, health, liability, disability, renter's, homeowner's, automobile)
- Installment loan payments (appliances, furniture)
- Taxes (federal income, state income, local income, real estate, Social Security, personal property)

Variable Expenses

- Meals (at home and away)
- Utilities (electricity, water, gas, telephone)
- Transportation (gasoline and maintenance, licenses, registration, public transportation, tolls)
- Medical expenses
- Child care (nursery, baby-sitting)
- Clothing and accessories (jewelry, shoes, handbags, briefcases)
- Snacks (candy, soft drinks, other beverages)
- Education (tuition, fees, books, supplies)
- Household furnishings (furniture, appliances, curtains)
- Cable television (beyond basic services)
- Personal care (beauty shop, barbershop, cosmetics, dry cleaner)
- Entertainment and recreation (hobbies, socializing, health club, tapes/CDs, videotape/DVD rentals, movies)
- Charitable contributions (gifts, church, school, charity)
- Magazine subscriptions
- Vacations and long weekends
- Credit card payments
- Savings and investments
- Miscellaneous (postage, books, magazines, newspapers, personal allowances, domestic help, membership fees)

There is no rigid list of categories to be used in the expenses section, but you do need to classify all of your expenditures in some way. Rather than just use fixed and

Lattes are a variable expense that can add up quickly.

variable expenses categories, you might also separate expenditures into savings/investments, debts, insurance, taxes, and household expenses. The more specific your categories, the deeper your understanding of your outlays.

Cash Surplus (or Cash Deficit)   The surplus (deficit) section shows the amount of cash remaining after you have itemized income and subtracted expenditures from income, as illustrated by the following calculations using Equation (3.2), *the surplus/deficit formula*. (A business would call this amount its net profit or net loss.)

$$\text{Surplus (deficit)} = \text{total income} - \text{total expenses} \qquad (3.2)$$

or $1100 \text{ surplus} = \$12,500 - \$11,400$

($800 \text{ deficit}) = \$14,900 - \$15,700$

A surplus demonstrates that you are managing your financial resources successfully and do not have to use savings or borrow money to make financial ends meet. When the calculation shows a surplus, that amount is then available (in your checking and savings accounts) to spend, save, invest, or donate. A surplus is not really cash lying around on the kitchen table; it is the cash value reflected in the accounts on your balance sheet. Figure 3.3 shows the typical personal financial situation over the life cycle in present value dollars, from the wealth accumulation years through retirement.

Sample Cash-Flow Statements   Table 3.4 and Table 3.5 show the cash-flow statements for a college student and a couple with two children, respectively. Table 3.5 vividly highlights the additional income needed to rear children and shows the increased variety of expenditures that characterize a family's

Instant Message

Take the Wheel of Your Personal Finances

Financial expert Angie Hollerich says that it is easy to be a passenger, but it takes courage to take the wheel and control of your own personal finances.

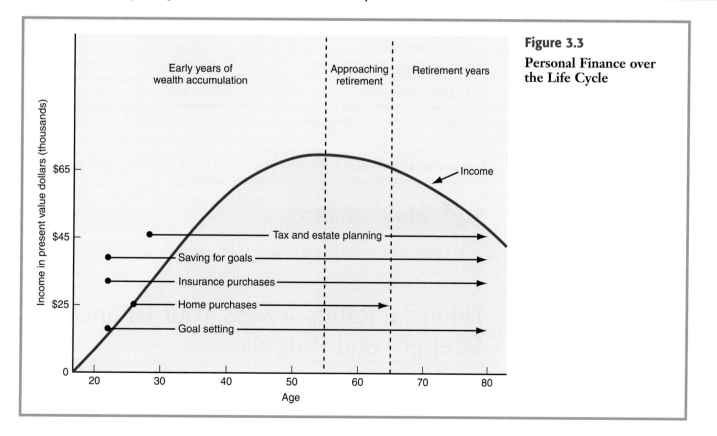

Figure 3.3

Personal Finance over the Life Cycle

Table 3.4 Cash-Flow Statement for a College Student—William Soshnik,
January 1–December 31, 2008

	Dollars	Percent
INCOME		
Wages (after withholding)	$ 4,650	39.71
Scholarship	1,750	14.94
Government grant	2,500	21.35
Government loan*	2,600	22.20
Tax refund	210	1.79
Total Income	**$11,710**	**100.00**
EXPENSES		
Room rent (includes utilities)	$ 1,500	12.81
Laundry	216	1.84
Food	1,346	11.49
Automobile loan payments	1,292	11.03
Automobile insurance	778	6.64
Books and supplies	932	7.96
Tuition	3,160	26.99
Telephone	282	2.41
Clothing	475	4.06
Gifts	300	2.56
Automobile expenses	600	5.12
Health insurance	102	0.87
Recreation and entertainment	360	3.07
Personal expenses	300	2.56
Total Expenses	**$11,643**	**99.43**
Surplus (deficit)	**$ 67**	**0.57**

*Technically, loans are not income. William plans to be a teacher, and his loan will be forgiven if he goes into teaching and remains in the profession for five years.

(rather than an individual's) lifestyle. As a person earns more income, the cash-flow statement usually becomes more involved and detailed.

CONCEPT CHECK 3.2

1. Distinguish between the balance sheet and cash-flow statement.

Financial Ratios Assess Your Financial Strength and Progress

3 **LEARNING OBJECTIVE**
Evaluate your financial strength and progress using financial ratios.

Financial ratios are numerical calculations designed to simplify the process of evaluating your financial strength and the progress of your financial condition. Ratios serve as tools or yardsticks to develop saving, spending, and credit-use pat-

Table 3.5 Cash-Flow Statement for a Couple with Two Children—Victor and Maria Hernandez, January 1, 2008–December 31, 2008

	Dollars	Percent
INCOME		
Victor's gross salary	$43,180	65.42
Maria's salary (part time)	12,500	18.94
Interest and dividends	1,800	2.73
Bonus	600	0.91
Tax refunds	200	0.30
Net rental income	7,720	11.70
Total Income	**$66,000**	100.00
EXPENSES		
Fixed Expenses		
Mortgage loan payments	$12,000	18.18
Real estate taxes	2,400	3.64
Homeowner's insurance	760	1.15
Automobile loan payment	4,400	6.67
Automobile insurance and registration	1,191	1.80
Life insurance premiums	1,200	1.82
Medical insurance (employee portion)	2,980 ✓	4.52
Savings at credit union	1,260	1.91
Federal income taxes	6,800 ✓	10.30
State income taxes	3,100 ✓	4.70
City income taxes	720 ✓	1.09
Social Security taxes	4,260 ✓	6.45
Personal property taxes	950 ✓	1.44
Retirement IRAs	4,000	6.06
Total Fixed Expenses	**$46,021**	69.73
Variable Expenses		
Food	$ 4,900	7.42
Utilities	2,100	3.18
Gasoline, oil, maintenance	3,100	4.70
Medical expenses	1,245	1.89
Medicines	750	1.14
Clothing and upkeep	1,950	2.95
Church	1,200	1.82
Gifts	900	1.36
Personal allowances	1,160	1.76
Children's allowances	960	1.45
Miscellaneous	500	0.76
Total variable expenses	**$18,765**	28.43
Total Expenses	**$64,786**	98.16
Surplus (deficit)	1,214	1.84

$$\text{Investment assets-to-total assets ratio} = \frac{\text{investment assets}}{\text{total assets}} \qquad (3.7)$$
$$= \frac{\$109,000}{\$309,920}$$
$$= 0.352$$

Other Ways to Assess Financial Progress

You can use other data from your balance sheet and cash-flow statement to help analyze your finances. Consider the assets listed on the balance sheet for Victor and Maria Hernandez in Table 3.3. Do they have too few monetary assets compared with tangible and investment assets? Experts recommend that 15 to 20 percent of your assets be in monetary form and that this proportion increase as you near retirement. Do you have too much invested in one asset, or have you diversified, like the Hernandezes? Have your balance sheet figures changed in a favorable direction since last year? Is a growing proportion of your income coming from your investments? Are you making progress toward your financial goals? If not, ask: "Am I spending money where I really want to?" "In which categories can I reduce expenses?" "Could I increase income?"

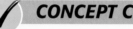 **CONCEPT CHECK 3.2**

1. Distinguish between the basic liquidity ratio and debt-service-to-income ratio.

Financial Record Keeping Saves Time and Makes You Money

4   LEARNING OBJECTIVE
Maintain the financial records necessary for managing your personal finances.

financial records Documents that evidence financial transactions.

Financial records are documents that evidence financial transactions, such as bills, receipts, credit card receipts and statements, bank records, tax returns, brokerage statements, and paycheck stubs. Your financial records will help determine where you are, where you have been, and where you are going financially. They also help you save money as well as make money. Good records enable you to review the results of financial transactions as well as permit other family members to find them in an emergency. Organized records help you take advantage of all available tax deductions when filing income taxes and provide you with more dollars to spend, save, invest, or donate. Table 3.6 shows categories of financial records and the contents that might be included in each.

Some records may be safely stored at home in a fire-resistant file cabinet or a safe. Other records should be kept in a **safe-deposit box.** Safe-deposit boxes are secured lock boxes available for rent ($50 to $250 per year) in banks. Two keys are used to open such a box. The customer keeps one key, and the bank holds the other. Many people keep duplicates of important records at their workplace or with relatives because the likelihood of records at both locations being stolen or destroyed simultaneously is very small. You can purge or shred some of your records when you no longer need them, such as non-tax-related checks and credit card receipts more than a year old, expired insurance policies, and financial reports when supplanted with updated summary information.

 **CONCEPT CHECK 3.2**

1. List some advantages of keeping good financial records.
2. Name three financial records that might best be kept in a safe-deposit box.

Table 3.6   Financial Records: What to Keep and Where

Category	Contents	
	In Home Files and Fireproof Home Safe	**In Safe-Deposit Box**
Financial plans/ budgeting	Financial plans Balance sheets and cash-flow statements Current budget List of safe-deposit box contents Names and contact information for financial advisers	Names and contact information for financial advisers Copy of written financial plans, goals, and budgets
Career and employment	Current résumé College transcripts Letters of recommendation Employee benefits descriptions Written career plans	
Banking and financial services	Checkbook, unused checks, and canceled checks List of locations and account numbers for all bank accounts Checking and savings account statements Locations and access numbers for safe-deposit boxes Account transaction receipts	List of financial institutions and account numbers for all financial services accounts Certificates of deposit
Taxes	Copies of all income tax returns, both state and federal, for the past three years, including all supporting documentation Receipts for all donations of cash or property Log of volunteer expenses Receipts for property taxes paid	Copies of all income tax filings, both state and federal, for the past three years Records of securities purchased and sold
Credit	Utility and telephone bills Monthly credit card statements Receipts of credit payments List of credit accounts and telephone numbers to report lost/ stolen cards Unused credit cards Credit reports and scores	List of credit accounts and telephone numbers to report lost/stolen cards
Housing, vehicles, and consumer purchases	Copies of legal documents (leases, mortgage, deeds, titles) Property appraisals and inspection reports Home repair/home improvement receipts Warranties Owners manuals for purchases Auto registration records Vehicle service and repair receipts Receipts for important purchases	Original legal documents (leases, mortgage, deeds, titles) Copies of property appraisals Vehicle purchase contracts (until vehicle is sold) Photographs or videos of valuable possessions
Insurance	Original insurance policies List of insurance policies with premium amounts and due dates Premium payment receipts Calculation of life insurance needs Insurance claims forms and reports Medical records for family, including immunization records and list of prescription drugs	List of all insurance policies with company and agent names and addresses and policy numbers Listing with photographs or videotape of personal property
Investments	Records of stock, bond, and mutual fund transactions and certificate numbers Mutual fund statements Statements from brokers Reports from financial planner Company annual reports Retirement plan quarterly and annual reports Documents on business interests Written investment philosophy Written investment strategies	Contact information for all investment needs Stock and bond certificates Rare coins, stamps, and other collectibles

Continued

Figure 3.5

Goals Worksheet for Harry and Belinda Johnson

Date worksheet prepared _Feb. 20, 2008_

1	2	3	4	5	6
LONG-TERM GOALS	AMOUNT NEEDED	MONTH & YEAR NEEDED*	MONTHS TO SAVE	DATE START SAVING	MONTHLY AMOUNT TO SAVE (2 ÷ 4)
European vacation	$3,000	Aug. 2010	30	Feb. '08	$100
Down payment on new auto	5,000	Oct. 2011	45	Jan. '08	111

Date worksheet prepared _Feb. 20, 2008_

1	2	3	4	5	6
INTERMEDIATE-TERM GOALS	AMOUNT NEEDED	MONTH & YEAR NEEDED*	MONTHS TO SAVE	DATE START SAVING	MONTHLY AMOUNT TO SAVE (2 ÷ 4)
Down payment on home	$26,078	Dec. 2013	60	Jan. '08	$435

Date worksheet prepared _Feb. 20, 2008_

1	2	3	4	5	6
SHORT-TERM GOALS	AMOUNT NEEDED	MONTH & YEAR NEEDED*	MONTHS TO SAVE	DATE START SAVING	MONTHLY AMOUNT TO SAVE (2 ÷ 4)
Partial down payment on new auto	$1,332	Dec. '08	12	Jan. '08	$111
House fund	4,815	Dec. '08	12	Jan. '08	401
Christmas vacation	700	Dec. '08	12	Jan. '08	58
Summer vacation	600	Aug. '08	6	Mar. '08	100
Anniversary party	250	June '08	5	Feb. '08	50

*Goals requiring five years or more to achieve require consideration of investment return and after-tax yield, which will be presented in Chapter 4.

Action Before: Make and Reconcile Budget Estimates

Before the month begins, you make and reconcile budget estimates of income and expenditures. Here you resolve conflicting needs and wants by revising estimates as necessary. You can't have everything in life—especially this month—even though you might want it.

budget estimates Projected dollar amounts to receive or spend in a budgeting period.

take-home pay/disposable income Pay received after employer withholdings for taxes, insurance, and union dues.

discretionary income Money left over after necessities such as housing and food are paid for.

Make Budget Estimates **Budget estimates** are the projected dollar amounts in a budget that one plans to receive or spend during the period covered by the budget. Begin by estimating total gross income from all sources, and review take-home pay and then discretionary income. For example, Jonny Deppe's annual gross income is $60,000 and after employer withholdings for taxes, insurance, and union dues, his **take-home pay** (also called **disposable income**) is $48,000. This is the money available for spending, saving, investing, and donating. Focus also on your **discretionary income.** This is the money left over once the necessities of living are covered, such as paying for housing, food, and other necessities. It is usually the money that is really "controllable" and often makes up the bulk of your variable expenses. After Jonny pays his rent, food, utilities, and car payment, his discretionary income is $18,000.

Table 3.7 presents budget estimates for a college student, a single working person, a young married couple, a married couple with two young children, and a married couple with two college-age children. The college student's budget requires monthly withdrawals of previously deposited savings to make ends meet. The single working person's budget allows for an automobile loan, but not much else. The young married couple's budget permits one automobile loan, an investment program, contributions to individual retirement accounts, and significant spending on food and entertainment. The budget of the married couple with two young children allows for only an inexpensive automobile loan payment even though one spouse has a part-time job to help with the finances. The budget of the married couple with two college-age children permits a home mortgage payment, ownership of two paid-for automobiles, savings and investment programs, and a substantial contribution for college expenses.

It is essential to make reasonable budget estimates. If you have seven Christmas gifts to buy and expect to spend $50 for each, it's easy to make an estimate of $350. If you want to go out to dinner once each week at $50 per meal, estimate an expense of $200 per month. Avoid using unrealistically low figures by simply being fair and honest in your estimates. Then add up your totals.

Revise Budget Estimates Sometimes the math is alarming! When initial expense estimates exceed income estimates, three choices are available: (1) earn more income, (2) cut back on expenses, or (3) try a combination of more income and fewer expenses. The process of reconciling needs and wants is a healthy exercise. It helps identify your priorities by telling you what is important in your life at the current time, and it identifies areas of sacrifice that you might make. Revising your short-term financial goals may also be required.

You have no choice: You must reconcile conflicting wants to revise your budget until total expenses do not exceed income. Perhaps you can change some "must have" items to "maybe next year" purchases. Perhaps you can keep some quality items but reduce their quantity. For example, instead of $200 for four meals at restaurants each month, consider dining out twice each month at $60 per meal. You'll save $40 and still have two really nice meals. Your actions on money matters override your words, so act accordingly.

Table 3.8 presents the annual budget for Harry and Belinda Johnson and reflects their efforts to reconcile their budget estimates until the total planned expenses fall below the total planned income. Harry and Belinda are "paying themselves first," in the amount of $400 per month, to save to buy their own home. The Johnsons have a little way to go to fully reconcile their annual budget estimates.

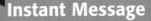

Action Before: Plan Cash Flows

Before the month begins, you plan your cash flows. Income usually remains somewhat constant month after month, but expenses do rise and fall sharply. As a result, people occasionally complain that they are "broke, out of money, and sick of budgeting." This challenge can be anticipated by using a cash-flow calendar and eliminated with a revolving savings fund.

The budget estimates for monthly income and expenses in Table 3.8 have been recast in summary form in Table 3.9, providing a **cash-flow calendar** for the Johnsons. This is a very useful budgeting tool. Annual estimated income and expenses are recorded in this calendar for each budgeting time period in an effort to identify surplus or deficit situations. In the Johnsons' case, planned annual income exceeds

cash-flow calendar Budget estimates for monthly income and expenses.

Table 3.9   Cash-Flow Calendar for Harry and Belinda Johnson

Month	1 Estimated Income	2 Estimated Expenses	3 Surplus/Deficit (1 − 2)	4 Cumulative Surplus/Deficit
January	$ 5,524	$ 5,524	$ 0	$ 0
February	5,524	5,524	0	0
March	5,824	5,824	0	0
April	5,825	5,825	0	0
May	5,826	5,826	0	0
June	5,827	6,527	−700	−700
July	5,902	5,902	0	−700
August	5,903	6,153	−250	−950
September	8,905	8,905	0	−950
October	5,906	5,906	0	−950
November	5,908	6,113	−205	−1,155
December	5,908	7,158	−1,250	−2,405
Total	**$72,782**	**$75,187**	**−2,405**	

revolving savings fund Variable budgeting tool that places funds in savings to cover large irregular or higher-than-usual expenses.

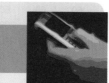
expenses. The couple starts out the year with many expenses, resulting in deficits for the next six months. Later in the year, income usually exceeds expenses, but they are still faced with a deficit at year's end.

Effective management of cash flow can involve curtailing expenses during months with financial deficits, increasing income, using savings, or borrowing. If you borrow money and pay finance charges, the credit costs will further increase your monthly expenses.

For this reason alone, it is smart to "borrow from yourself" by using a **revolving savings fund.** This is a variable expense classification budgeting tool into which funds are allocated in an effort to create savings that can be used to balance the budget later so as to avoid running out of money. Establishing such a fund involves planning ahead—much like a college student does when saving money all summer (creating a revolving savings fund) to draw on during the school months. You establish a revolving savings fund for two purposes: (1) to accumulate funds for large irregular expenses, such as automobile insurance premiums, medical costs, Christmas gifts, and vacations, and (2) to meet occasional deficits due to income fluctuations.

Table 3.10 shows the Johnsons' revolving savings fund. When preparing their budget, the Johnsons realized that in June, August, November, and December they were going to have significant deficits. They decided to begin setting aside $140 per month to cover the June deficit. To do so, they decided to wait to start building their emergency fund. By June they had $700 in their revolving savings fund to cover the June deficit. Continued use of the revolving savings fund helped them meet the August and November deficits as well.

The Johnsons will still be $1050 short in December. Lacking that much money, the couple has three alternatives: (1) use some of Harry's trust fund money to cover the deficit, (2) dip into their

Table 3.10 Revolving Savings Fund for Harry and Belinda Johnson

Month	Large Expenses	Amount Needed	Deposit into Fund	Withdrawal from Fund	Fund Balance
January		$ 0	$ 140	$ 0	$ 140
February		0	140	0	280
March		0	140	0	420
April		0	140	0	560
May		0	140	0	700
June	Party and insurance	700	0	700	0
July		0	250	0	250
August	Vacation	250	0	250	0
September		0	215	0	215
October		0	190	0	405
November	Holiday gifts	205	0	205	200
December	Holiday gifts and vacation	1250	0	200	0
Total		**$2405**	**$1355**	**$1355**	**−$1050**

emergency savings in December, or (3) cut back on their expenses enough throughout the year to create sufficient surpluses. Ideally, the Johnsons want to have sufficient emergency funds by the end of the year to establish their revolving savings fund for the following year. Cutting back on expenses may be their best option.

Action During Budgeting Period: Control Spending

Budget controls are techniques to maintain control over personal spending so that planned amounts are not exceeded. They give feedback on whether spending is on target and provide information on overspending, errors, emergencies, and exceptions or omissions. Following are examples of budget controls:

Monitor Unexpended Balances to Control Overspending The number one method to control overspending is to monitor unexpended balances in each of your budget classifications. You can accomplish this task by using a budget design that keeps a declining balance, as illustrated by parts (a) and (b) of Figure 3.6 (page 89). Other budget designs, such as those shown in parts (c) and (d) of Figure 3.6, need to be monitored differently. As illustrated in parts (c) and (d) of the figure, simply calculate subtotals every week or so, as needed, during a monthly budgeting period.

Budget for Shopping Trips Set a budget for every shopping trip, and don't spend a penny more.

Use a Subordinate Budget A **subordinate budget** is a detailed listing of planned expenses within a single budgeting classification. For example, an estimate of $1200 for a vacation could be supported by a subordinate budget as follows: motel, $700; restaurants, $300; and entertainment, $200.

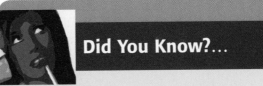

Did You Know?...

The Top 3 Financial Missteps in Budget Planning

People slip up in budget planning when they do the following:

1. Fail to plan for occasional, nonmonthly expenditures
2. Underestimate how much they spend each month
3. Use credit cards to "balance" their budget

subordinate budget Detailed listing of planned expenses within a single budgeting classification.

Pay by Check to Record the Purpose of Expenditures Each check contains a space to record the purpose. The check stub or register also provides a place to record explanations of expenditures. If you use automatic teller machines (ATMs) to withdraw cash or use debit cards to pay for day-to-day expenditures, record these withdrawals in the check register *immediately.* Retain the paperwork and write the purpose of each expense on the back of each. Deposit all checks received to your checking account without receiving a portion in cash; if you need cash, write a check or make an ATM withdrawal.

Keep Track of Credit Transactions Some people do not record their credit transactions until they receive a statement. It is easy to continue buying on credit without recognizing the amount of indebtedness until the statement arrives. Record each credit transaction when it occurs; if you misplace a receipt, you still have a record available for verification.

budget exceptions When budget estimates differ from actual expenditures.

Justify Exceptions to Avoid Lying to Yourself **Budget exceptions** occur when budget estimates in various classifications differ from actual expenditures. Exceptions usually take the form of overexpenditures, but can also occur in the over- or underreceipt of earnings. Simply spending extra income instead of recording it is not being honest with yourself. Recording the truth—by writing a few words to explain the exception—gives you the information to control your finances. If the exception is an expenditure, then immediately determine how to make up for the overexpenditure by reducing other expenses in your spending plan.

envelope system Placing exact amounts into envelopes for each budgetary purpose.

For the Strongest Control, Use the Envelope System The **envelope system** of budgeting entails placing exact amounts of money into envelopes for purposes of strict budgetary control. Here you place money equal to the budget estimate for the various expenditure classifications in envelopes at the start of a budgeting period and write the classification name and the budget amount on the outside of each envelope. As expenditures are made, record them on the appropriate envelope and remove the proper amounts of cash. When an envelope is empty, funds are exhausted for that classification.

Action After: Evaluate Budgeting Progress

budget variance Difference between amount budgeted and actual amount spent or received.

Evaluation occurs at the end of each budgeting cycle. The purpose is to determine whether the earlier steps in your budgeting efforts have worked, and it gives you feedback to use for the next budget cycle. You review by comparing actual amounts with budgeted amounts, evaluating whether your objectives were met, and assessing the success of the overall process as well as your progress toward your short- and long-term goals.

In some budget expenditure classifications, the budget estimates rarely agree with the actual expenditures—particularly in variable expenses. A **budget variance** is the difference between the amount budgeted and the actual amount spent or received. The remarks column, as illustrated in parts (c) and (d) of Figure 3.6 (page 89), can help clarify why variances occurred. Overages on a few expenditures may cause little concern. If excessive variances have prevented you from achieving your objectives or making the budget balance, then take some action. Serious budget controls might have to be instituted or current controls tightened.

Whatever your goals, it feels good when you make progress toward them, and it is thrilling to achieve them. If you did not achieve some of your objectives, you can determine why and then adjust your budget and objectives accordingly. It is "okay" to revise your plans. Suppose the Johnsons find that they are unable to set aside the

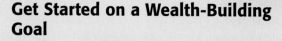

Instant Message

Get Started on a Wealth-Building Goal

Set a wealth-building goal and strategy that will allow you to achieve the goal, such as building a retirement fund by contributing to a 401(k) retirement plan or saving for the down payment on a home. Find the money to save by reducing expenses or earning extra income.

Keep to a budget when shopping, and use checks to keep track of purchases.

planned $400 for their new home. By evaluating their budget, they find that unexpected medical expenses and an out-of-state trip to visit a sick relative led them to dip into their savings. Because they understand why the objective was not achieved, they can set their sights on reaching the goal during the next budgeting time period.

Financial Software and Planning Tools Make Managing Your Money a Snap

Financial software and planning tools, including many on the Internet, make managing your money—including record keeping—a snap. Financial software offers many benefits. Laborious calculations are sharply reduced, banking transactions can be performed with automatic updating of financial records, the balance sheet and cash-flow statements are automatically updated when transactions occur, and your financial plans can be developed.

Quicken and Microsoft Money are the two most popular user-friendly brands of personal finance software. Both provide complete financial planning systems. Several other programs focus primarily on income tax preparation, including TurboTax, which works with your day-to-day financial software to help you do your taxes. Many companies have financial planning tools and calculators on their websites, including CNNmoney.com, Fool.com, Kiplinger.com, USAToday.com, and Yahoo.com.

Record Keeping In the process of budgeting, **record keeping** is the process of recording the sources and amounts of dollars earned and spent. Recording the estimated and actual amounts for both income and expenditures helps you monitor your money flow. Keeping track of income and expenses is the only way to collect sufficient information to evaluate how close you are to achieving your financial objectives. For those who keep records on paper, Figure 3.6 shows four samples of self-prepared record-keeping formats that vary in complexity. Most people record earnings and expenditures when they occur. When writing in the "activity" and "remarks" columns in your record, be descriptive because you may need the information later.

Instant Message

Manage Your Finances Using Web Portals

Some comprehensive Web portals on personal finances are Yahoo! Finance (finance.yahoo.com), MSN Money Central (moneycentral.com), and Quicken.com (quicken.com). You will find all kinds of easy-to-use financial tools, including bill paying, banking, vehicle loan rate comparisons, mortgage shopping, online tax preparation, stock screening, stock quotes, online brokers, retirement calculators, and breaking news stories.

record keeping Recording sources and amounts of dollars earned and spent.

Advice from a Pro

Crisis Steps to Take If Budget Deficits Occur Repeatedly

If you always run out of money before the month is over, you may need to take some drastic steps to get your finances under control. Consider the following:

1. Stop using credit cards.

2. Spend only cash or money that you have, and leave debit and credit cards at home.

3. Stop making ATM withdrawals and getting cash back from purchases to use for pocket money.

4. Reduce or stop spending on luxuries such as eating out, clothing, movies, entertainment, memberships, hobbies, clothing, CDs, DVDs, and expanded cable channels.

5. Drop landline telephone service and use only a cell phone.

6. Use a list when shopping, and stick to it.

7. Avoid shopping malls and discount stores.

8. Sell an asset, especially one that requires additional expenses, such as a second car.

9. Move to lower-cost housing.

10. Increase income by working overtime or finding a second job.

Alena C. Johnson
Utah State University

Adding Up Actual Income and Expenditures After the budgeting period has ended—usually at the beginning of a new month—you need to add up the actual income received and expenditures made during that period. You can perform this calculation on a form for each budget classification, as shown in parts (a) and (b) of Figure 3.6 or on a form with all income and expenditure classifications, as in parts (c) and (d) of Figure 3.6. Such calculations indicate where you may have overspent within your budget categories. If you are new at budgeting, do not be too concerned about overspending; it occurs in some classifications almost always, only to be balanced by underspending in other categories. Use such information to refine your budget estimates in the future. In three or four months, you will be able to estimate your expenses much more accurately. The *Garman/Forgue* website provides budgeting software as well as numerous other templates, calculators, and worksheets that you can use in your own personal financial planning.

Instant Message

Instant Budget Analyses on the Internet

To compare your spending with that of people like you, describe your situation on the CNNMoney website at cgi.money.cnn.com/tools/instantbudget/instantbudget_101.jsp.

What to Do with Budgeted Money Left Over at the End of the Month At the end of the budgeting time period, some budget classifications may still have a positive balance. For example, perhaps you estimated the electric bill at $100, but it was only $80. You may then ask, "What do I do with the $20 surplus?" You also may ask, "What happens to budget classifications that were overspent?"

People handle the **net surplus** (the amount remaining after all budget classification deficits are subtracted from those with surpluses) in any of the following ways:

- Carry the surpluses forward
- Put into a revolving savings fund
- Build a cash reserve by depositing in a savings account
- Pay down credit card debt
- Put toward a mortgage or other loan
- Invest in a retirement account
- Spend like "mad money"

net surplus Amount remaining after all budget classification deficits are subtracted from those with surpluses.

Figure 3.6
Record-Keeping Formats

(a)

Food Budget: $90			
DATE	ACTIVITY	AMOUNT	BALANCE
2-6	Groceries	$20	$70
2-9	Dinner out	18	52
2-14	Groceries	11	

(b)

DATE	ACTIVITY	AMOUNT BUDGETED	EXPENDITURES	BALANCE
2-1	Budget estimate	$90		$90
2-6	Groceries		$20	70
2-9	Dinner out		18	52
2-14	Groceries		11	41
2-20	Groceries		25	16
2-28	February Totals	$90	$74	$16

(c)

DATE	ACTIVITY	Food Budget: $90	Clothing Budget: $30	Auto Budget: $60	Rent Budget: $275	Savings Budget: $60	Utilities Budget: $40	TOTAL Budget: $680	REMARKS
				EXPENDITURES					
2-1	Gasoline			10				10	
2-6	Groceries	20						20	Had friends over
2-8	Gasoline			17				17	Good price
2-9	Dinner out	18						18	
2-14	Groceries	11						11	Pepsi on sale
2-15	Subtotals	/49		/27				/76	

(d)

			INCOME			EXPENDITURES							REMARKS
			Salary	Other	TOTAL	Food	Clothing	Auto	Rent	Savings	Utilities	TOTAL	
Estimates			700	40	740	90	30	60	275	60	40	680	
Balance forwarded from January			—	—	—	6	—	14	—	—	2	28	
Sum			700	40	740	96	30	74	275	60	42	708	
DATE	ACTIVITY	CASH IN	Salary	Other	TOTAL	Food	Clothing	Auto	Rent	Savings	Utilities	TOTAL	
2-1	Paycheck	700	700										
2-1	Texaco-gasoline							10				10	
2-6	Safeway-groceries					20						20	Had friends over
2-8	7/11-gasoline							17				17	Good price
2-9	Dinner out-pizza					18						18	
2-14	Giant-groceries					11						11	Pepsi on sale
2-15	Subtotals	/700				/49		/27				/76	
2-16	Cell phone										41	41	
2-28	Totals	700		40	740	83	28	27	275	60	41	660	Good month

The budgeting form in part (d) of Figure 3.6 allows for carrying balances forward to the next period. Some people carry forward deficits, with the hope that having less available in a budgeted classification the following month will motivate them to keep expenditures low. Because variable expense estimates are usually averages, it is best not to change the estimate based on a variation that occurs over just one or two months. If estimates are too high or low for a longer period, you will want to make adjustments.

Using financial software for budgeting takes the drudgery out of making and using a spending plan. And it gets to be easy after a few months. Budgeting can help you succeed financially.

✔ CONCEPT CHECK 3.5

1. List two actions that should be performed before establishing a budget.
2. What are budget estimates and offer some suggestions on how to go about making budget estimates for various types of expenses.
3. Distinguish between a cash flow calendar and a revolving savings fund, and tell why each is important.
4. Offer three suggestions for effective budget controls.

What Do You Recommend Now?

Now that you have read the chapter on financial planning, what do you recommend to Robert for his talk with Nicole on the subject of financial planning regarding:

1. Determining what they own and owe?
2. Better understanding their patterns of family income and expenditure?
3. Using the information in Robert's newly prepared financial statements to summarize the family's financial situation?
4. Evaluating their financial progress?
5. Setting up a record-keeping system to better serve their needs?
6. Starting a budgeting process to guide saving and spending?

Big Picture Summary of Learning Objectives

1 Identify your financial values, goals, and strategies.

By identifying your financial values, goals, and strategies, you can always keep a balance between spending and saving and stay committed to your financial success. You may create financial plans in three broad areas: plans for spending, plans for risk management, and plans for capital accumulation.

2 Use balance sheets and cash-flow statements to measure your financial health and progress.

Financial statements are compilations of personal financial data designed to furnish information on money matters. The balance sheet provides information on what you own, what you owe, and what the net result would be if you paid off all your debts. The cash-flow statement lists income and expenditures over a specific period of time, such as the previous month or year.

3 Evaluate your financial strength and progress using financial ratios.

Financial ratios are numerical calculations designed to simplify the process of evaluating your financial strength and the progress of your financial condition. Ratios serve as tools or yardsticks to develop saving, spending, and credit-use patterns consistent with your goals.

4 Maintain the financial records necessary for managing your personal finances.

Your financial records will help determine where you are, where you have been, and where you are going financially. They also help you make money.

5 Achieve your financial goals through budgeting.

Budgeting is all about logical thinking about your finances. Budgeting forces you to consider what is important in your life, what things you want to own, how you want to live, what it will take to do that, and, more generally, what you want to achieve in life. A budget is a process used to record both projected and actual income and expenditures over a period of time, and it represents the major mechanism through which your financial plans are carried out and goals are achieved.

Let's Talk About It

1. What are your three most important personal values? Give an example of how each of those values might influence your financial plans.

2. College students often have little income and many expenses. Does this reduce or increase the importance of completing a cash-flow statement on a monthly basis? Why?

3. Of the financial ratios described in this chapter, which two might be most revealing for the typical college student? Which two are the most revealing for a retiree?

4. Do you have a budget? Why or why not? What do you think are the major reasons why people do not make formal budgets?

5. What is the biggest budget-related mistake that you have made? What would you do differently?

Do the Numbers

1. Review the financial statements of Victor and Maria Hernandez (Table 3.3 and Table 3.5) and respond to the following questions:

   (a) Using the data in the Hernandezes' balance sheet, calculate an investment assets-to-net worth ratio. How would you interpret the ratio? The Hernandez family appears to have too few monetary assets compared with tangible and investment assets. How would you suggest that they remedy that situation over the next few years?

   (b) Comment on the couple's diversification of their investment assets.

   (c) Calculate the asset-to-debt ratio for Victor and Maria. How does this information help you understand their financial situation? How do their total assets compare with their total liabilities?

   (d) The Hernandezes seem to receive most of their income from labor rather than investments. What actions would you recommend for them to remedy that imbalance over the next few years?

   (e) The Hernandezes want to take a two-week vacation next summer, and they have only eight months to save the necessary $2400. What reasonable changes in expenses and income might they consider to increase net income and make the needed $200 per month?

2. John Green has been a retail salesclerk for six years. At age 35, he is divorced with one child, Amanda, age 7. John's salary is $36,000 per year. He regularly receives $250 per month for child support from Amanda's mother. John invests $100 each month ($50 in his mutual fund and $50 in U.S. savings bonds). Using the following information, construct a balance sheet and a cash-flow statement for John.

ASSETS	Amount
Vested retirement benefits (no employee contribution)	$3000
Money market account (includes $150 of interest earned last year)	5000
Mutual fund (includes $200 of reinvested dividend income from last year)	4000
Checking account	1000
Personal property	5000
Automobile	3000
U.S. savings bonds	3000

LIABILITIES	Outstanding Balance
Dental bill (pays $25 per month and is included in uninsured medical/dental)	$ 450
Visa (pays $100 per month)	1500
Student loan (pays $100 per month)	7500

ANNUAL EXPENSES	Amount
Auto insurance	$ 780
Rent	9100
Utilities	1200
Phone	680
Cable	360
Food	3000
Uninsured medical/dental	1000
Dry cleaning	480
Personal care	420
Gas, maintenance, license	2120
Clothes	500
Entertainment	1700
Vacations/visitation travel	1300
Child care	3820
Gifts	400
Miscellaneous	300
Taxes	6400
Health insurance	2440

3. Sharon and Dick DeVaney of West Lafayette, Indiana, have decided to start a family next year, so they are looking over their budget (illustrated in Table 3.7 as the "young married couple"). Sharon thinks that she can go on half-salary ($1050 instead of $2100 per month) in her job as a graduate assistant for about 18

Tangible Assets		
Automobile (3-year-old Toyota)	$ 11,000	51.13
Personal property	2,300	10.69
Furniture	1,700	7.90
Total tangible assets	**$15,000**	69.72
Investment Assets		
Harry's retirement account	$ 1,425	6.62
Belinda's retirement account	1,550	7.20
Total investment assets	**$ 2,975**	13.83
Total Assets	**$21,515**	100.00

LIABILITIES

Short-Term Liabilities

Visa credit card	$ 390	1.81
Sears card	45	0.21
Dental bill	400	1.86
Total short-term liabilities	**$ 835**	3.88
Long-Term Liabilities		
Student loan (Belinda)	$ 3,800	17.66
Automobile loan (First Federal Bank)	8,200	38.11
Total long-term liabilities	$ 12,000	55.78
Total Liabilities	**$ 12,835**	59.66
Net Worth	**$ 8,680**	40.34
Total Liabilities and Net Worth	**$ 21,515**	100.00

Cash-Flow Statement for Harry and Belinda Johnson
July 1–December 31, 2007 (First Six Months of Marriage)

	Dollars	Percent
INCOME		
Harry's gross income ($2500 × 6)	$ 15,000	41.64
Belinda's gross income ($3000 × 6)	18,000	49.97
Interest on savings account	24	0.07
Harry's trust fund	3,000	8.33
Total Income	**$36,024**	100.00
EXPENSES		
Fixed Expenses		
Rent	$ 5,400	14.99
Renter's insurance	220	0.61
Automobile loan payment	1,710	4.75
Automobile insurance	420	1.17
Medical insurance (withheld from salary)	750	2.08
Student loan payments	870	2.42
Life insurance (withheld from salary)	54	0.15
Cable television	540	1.50
Health club	300	0.83
Savings (withheld from salary)	900	2.50
Harry's retirement plan (6% of salary)	900	2.50
Belinda's retirement plan (4% of salary)	720	2.00
Federal income taxes (withheld from salary)	4,600	12.77
State income taxes (withheld from salary)	1,600	4.44
Social Security (withheld from salary)	2,520	7.00
Automobile registration	90	0.25
Total fixed expenses	**$21,594**	59.94

Variable Expenses		
Food	$ 2,300	6.38
Utilities	750	2.08
Telephone	420	1.17
Gasoline, oil, maintenance	700	1.94
Doctor's and dentist's bills	710	1.97
Medicines	345	0.96
Clothing and upkeep	1,900	5.27
Church and charity	800	2.22
Gifts	720	2.00
Christmas gifts	350	0.97
Public transportation	720	2.00
Personal allowances	1,040	2.89
Entertainment	980	2.72
Vacation (holiday)	700	1.94
Vacation (summer)	600	1.67
Miscellaneous	545	1.51
Total variable expenses	**$13,580**	37.70
Total Expenses	**$35,174**	97.64
Surplus (deficit)	**$ 850**	2.36

On the 'Net

Go to the Web pages indicated to complete these exercises. You can also go to the *Garman/Forgue* website at college.hmco.com/business/students for an expanded list of exercises. Under General Business, select the title of this text. Click on the Internet Exercises link for this chapter.

1. Visit *Kiplinger's Personal Finance Magazine* website at http://www.kiplinger.com/tools/. There you will find a link to a long list of calculators that can be used in various present and future value calculations. Select four that you believe would be particularly useful in the aspects of personal financial planning that were discussed in this chapter.

2. Visit the website for SRI Consulting at http://www.sric-bi.com/VALS/presurvey.shtml where you will find the VALS questionnaire. This short questionnaire will help you identify your values in the context of the values of other members of American society.

3. Visit the website for the Economic Policy Institute at http://www.epi.org/content.cfm/datazone_fambud_budget where you can find an example of a family budget for many areas of the United States. Calculate the budget for an area of interest to you. How useful do you think such a calculator would be for a family interested in developing its own budget?

Visit the Garman/Forgue website...

@college.hmco.com/business/students

Under General Business, select *Personal Finance 9e*. There, among other valuable resources, you will find a complete glossary, ACE questions, links to help you complete the chapter exercises, and links to other personal finance sites.

PART 2

CHAPTER 4

Managing Income Taxes

! ? You Must Be Kidding, Right?

Bharat Persaud's employer gave him a $2000 bonus last year, and when Bharat was filling out his federal income tax form, he discovered that $1000 of it moved him from the 15 percent marginal tax rate to 25 percent. How much tax will Bharat pay on the $1000?

A. $150

B. $180

C. $250

D. $380

The answer is C. The federal marginal tax rate is applied to your last dollar of earnings. The first $1000 of Bharat's bonus is taxed at the marginal tax rate of 15 percent ($150), but the second $1000 is taxed at 25 percent ($250). Be aware of your marginal tax rate!

LEARNING OBJECTIVES

After reading this chapter, you should be able to:

1 **Explain** the nature of progressive income taxes and the marginal tax rate.

2 **Differentiate** among the eight steps involved in calculating your federal income taxes.

3 **Use appropriate strategies** to avoid overpayment of income taxes.

What Do You Recommend?

Jeffrey Hutchinson and Amber Martin plan to get married in two years. Jeffrey earns $44,000 per year managing a fast-food restaurant. He also earns about $10,000 per year selling jewelry that he designs at craft shows held monthly in various nearby cities. Right after they get married, Jeffrey plans to go back to college full time to finish the last year of his undergraduate degree. Amber earns $58,000 annually working as an institutional sales representative for an insurance company. Both Jeffrey and Amber each contribute $100 per month to their employer-sponsored 401(k) retirement accounts. Jeffrey has little additional savings, but Amber has accumulated $18,000 that she wants to use for a down payment on a home. Amber also owns 300 shares of stock in an oil company that she inherited four years ago when the price was $90 per share; now the stock is worth $130 per share. Jeffrey and Amber live in a state where the state income tax is 6 percent.

What would you recommend to Jeffrey and Amber on the subject of managing income taxes regarding:

1. Using tax credits to help pay for Jeffrey's college expenses?

2. Determining how much money Amber will realize if she sells the stocks, assuming she pays federal income taxes at the 25 percent rate?

3. Buying a home?

4. Increasing contributions to their employer-sponsored retirement plans?

5. Establishing a sideline business for Jeffrey's jewelry operation?

FOR HELP with studying this chapter, visit the Online Student Center:

www.college.hmco.com/pic/garman9e

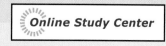

Good Money Habits in Managing Income Taxes

Make the following your money habits in managing your income taxes:

1. Reduce your income taxes by signing up for tax-advantaged employee benefits at your workplace.

2. Contribute to your employer-sponsored 401(k) retirement plan at least up to the amount of the employer's matching contribution.

3. Buy a home to reduce income taxes.

4. Do your own tax return so you can learn how to reduce your income tax liability.

5. Maintain good tax records.

Managing your money effectively includes efforts to avoid paying unnecessary sums to the government in taxes. You should pay your income tax liabilities in full, but that's all—there is no need to pay a dime extra. To achieve this goal, you need to adopt a **tax planning** perspective designed to reduce, defer, or eliminate some income taxes. To get started, you should recognize that you pay personal income taxes only on your **taxable income.** This amount is determined by subtracting your allowable exclusions, adjustments, exemptions, and deductions from your gross income, with the result being the income upon which the tax is actually calculated. Details for these calculations are provided later. For now, simply remember that the main idea in managing income taxes is to reduce your taxable income as much as possible, which, in turn, reduces your tax liability. By carefully analyzing and managing the subject of income taxes to your advantage, you can avoid overpayment of income taxes. Then you will have more money available every year to manage, spend, save, invest, and donate—activities that are the focus of the remainder of this book.

tax planning Seeking legal ways to reduce, eliminate, or defer income taxes.

taxable income Income upon which income taxes are levied.

Progressive Income Taxes and the Marginal Tax Rate

1 LEARNING OBJECTIVE

Explain the nature of progressive income taxes and the marginal tax rate.

taxes Compulsory government-imposed charges levied on citizens and their property.

progressive income tax Tax rate increases as taxable income increases.

Taxes are compulsory charges imposed by a government on its citizens and their property. The U.S. **Internal Revenue Service (IRS)** is the agency charged with the responsibility for collecting federal income taxes based on the legal provisions in the **Internal Revenue Code.**

The Progressive Nature of the Federal Income Tax

Taxes can be classified as progressive or regressive. The federal personal income tax is a **progressive tax** because the tax rate increases as a taxpayer's taxable income increases. A higher income implies a greater ability to pay. As Table 4.1 shows, the higher portions of a taxpayer's taxable income are taxed at increasingly higher rates under the federal income tax.* A **regressive tax** operates in the opposite way. That is, as income rises, the tax demands a decreasing proportion of a person's income. An example is a state sales tax, since a rate of perhaps 5 percent might have to be paid by everyone regardless of income.

The Marginal Tax Rate Is Applied to the Last Dollar Earned

marginal tax bracket (MTB)/marginal tax rate One of six income-range segments at which income is taxed at increasing rates.

The **marginal tax bracket (MTB)** is one of the six income-range segments that are taxed at increasing rates as income goes up. This is also called the **marginal tax rate.** Recall from Chapter 1 that the marginal tax rate is applied to your last dollar of earnings. Depending on their income, taxpayers fit into one of the six tax brackets (as shown in Table 4.1) and, accordingly, pay at one of those marginal tax rates: 10 percent, 15 percent, 25 percent, 28 percent, 33 percent, or 35 percent. Each year the taxable income levels for

IRS tax table Used to figure income tax for taxable incomes up to $100,000.

tax rate schedules Equations to figure taxes for returns with taxable incomes above $100,000.

*All tax rates cited in this chapter are for income tax returns filed in 2008. The mathematics shown in Figure 4.1 is based on the Internal Revenue Service's **tax table** (used for returns with taxable incomes up to $100,000) and **tax-rate schedules** (used for returns with taxable incomes above $100,000). Figures in the chapter may vary due to adjustments for inflation and tax law changes.

Table 4.1 The Progressive Nature of the Federal Income Tax (Taxable Income Brackets)

Segment of Taxable Income	Marginal Tax Rate*
First $7,825	10%
Over $7,825 but not over $31,850	15%
Over $31,850 but not over $77,100	25%
Over $77,100 but not over $160,850	28%
Over $160,850 but not over $349,700	33%
Over $349,700	35%

*Tax rates for single taxpayer.

the tax brackets are adjusted to reduce the effects of inflation, a process called **indexing**. Indexing keeps taxpayers from being unfairly forced to pay more taxes as they receive raises simply to keep up with inflation.

Your marginal tax rate is perhaps the single most important concept in personal finance. It tells you the portion of any extra taxable earnings—from a raise, investment income, or money from a second job—you must pay in income taxes. Correspondingly, it measures the tax reduction benefits of a tax-deductible expense that allows you to reduce your taxable income.

Consider this example of how the marginal tax rate might apply. Susan Bassett is from Syracuse, New York (see Figure 4.1). Part of her $60,000 gross income ($3400 + $5350) is not taxed, the next $7825 is taxed at 10 percent, the next $24,025 is taxed at 15 percent, and the remaining $19,400 of Susan's $60,000 taxable income is taxed at 25 percent. Thus, Susan is in the 25 percent marginal tax bracket because the *last* dollar that she earned is taxed at that level.

indexing Yearly adjustments to tax brackets that reduce inflation's effects on tax brackets.

The Marginal Tax Rate Affects Your Financial Decisions

The marginal tax rate can affect many financial decisions that you make. Consider, for example, what happens if you are in the 25 percent marginal tax bracket and you make a $100 tax-deductible contribution to a charity. The charity receives the $100, and you deduct the $100 from your taxable income. This deduction results in a $25 reduction in your federal income tax ($100 × 0.25). In effect, you give $75 and the government "gives" $25 to the charity.

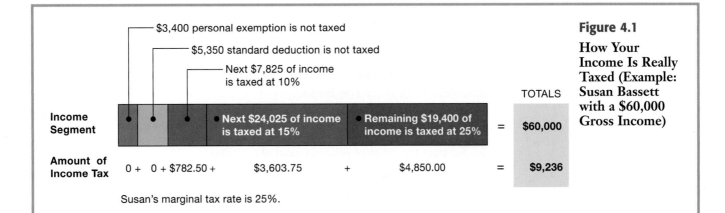

Figure 4.1

How Your Income Is Really Taxed (Example: Susan Bassett with a $60,000 Gross Income)

How to Determine Your Marginal Tax Rate

You can determine your marginal tax rate by following this example.

1. Robert Heatherton is single and has a taxable income of $27,825, and looking at the illustrated tax table (Table 4.3 on page 111) he finds his tax on that amount of income ($3783).

2. Add $100 to that income for a total of $27,925, and find the tax on that amount ($3798).

3. Calculate the difference between the two tax amounts ($3798 − $3783). The extra $15 in taxes from a $100 increase in income reflects a federal marginal tax rate of 15 percent.

effective marginal tax rate The total marginal rate reflects all taxes on a person's income, including federal, state, and local income taxes as well as Social Security and Medicare taxes.

average tax rate Proportion of total income paid in income taxes.

Your Effective Marginal Tax Rate Is Probably 43 Percent

The **effective marginal tax rate** describes a person's total marginal tax rate on income after including federal, state, and local income taxes as well as Social Security and Medicare taxes. To determine your effective marginal tax rate on income, add all of these other taxes to your federal marginal tax rate. For example, a taxpayer might have a federal marginal income tax rate of 25 percent, a combined Social Security and Medicare tax rate of 7.65 percent, a state income tax rate of 6 percent, and a city income tax rate of 4 percent. These taxes result in an effective marginal tax rate of 43 percent (25 + 7.65 + 6 + 4 = 42.65, rounded to 43). Many employed taxpayers pay an effective marginal tax rate of 43 percent or higher!

Your Average Tax Rate Is Lower

Many people wonder what proportion of their total income they pay in income taxes.

Your **average tax rate** gives the answer to this question. For example, the average tax rate on Susan Bassett's total income (the illustration in Figure 4.1) is 15.39 percent ($9236 ÷ $60,000), about the same for all U.S. taxpayers. Because total income is not fully taxed by the federal government, the average tax rate is always less than the marginal tax rate. But it is the marginal tax bracket that is most important because knowing what that rate is helps you make better financial decisions.

✓ CONCEPT CHECK 4.1

1. Distinguish between a progressive and a regressive tax.
2. What is a marginal tax bracket, and how does it affect taxpayers?
3. Explain why many taxpayers have a marginal tax rate as high as 43 percent.

2 LEARNING OBJECTIVE
Differentiate among the eight steps involved in calculating federal income taxes.

Eight Steps in Calculating Your Income Taxes

There are eight basic steps in calculating federal income taxes:

1. Determine your total income.
2. Determine and report your gross income after subtracting exclusions.
3. Subtract adjustments to income.
4. Subtract either the IRS's standard deduction amount for your tax status or your itemized deductions.
5. Subtract the value of your personal exemptions.
6. Determine your preliminary tax liability.
7. Subtract tax credits for which you qualify.
8. Calculate the balance due the IRS or the amount of your refund.

Did You Know?...

Determine Whether You Should File an Income Tax Return

Citizens and residents of the United States and Puerto Rico must file federal income tax returns if they have sufficient **earned income** (compensation for performing personal services, such as salaries, wages, tips, and net earnings from self-employment). To **file** simply means to report formally to the IRS income earned and your tax liability for the year. The minimum levels of income that require filing a return are $8750 for single individuals and $17,500 for married people filing jointly. These numbers represent the sum of the value of the personal exemption and the standard deduction for taxpayers of the appropriate filing status (discussed later).

The law also requires you to file a return (even if you owe no taxes) when someone (such as your parent) can claim you as a dependent and you have **unearned income** (investment returns in the form of rents, dividends, capital gains, interest, or royalties) exceeding $1700, or if you have earned income greater than $5350 (the value of a standard deduction). There are several other cases in which it is wise to file a tax return, even though it is not required:

1. **To get a refund of any federal income taxes withheld.** People who have had federal income taxes withheld from paychecks but who did not receive enough income to be required to file must submit a return to obtain a refund. If you moved and never received a filed-for, deserved refund, submit IRS Form 8822, the official change-of-address notification, and the agency will forward you a check.

2. **To get a refund if you neglected to file for refunds in the past.** If you have neglected to file for refunds in the past, you can complete the appropriate tax form for the year in question: 1040EZ (which the IRS calls its "very short form"), 1040A (short form), or 1040 (the long form).

3. **To get a refund if you overpaid your taxes in the past three years.** You may file an amended return for a refund on Form 1040X to correct returns filed in error during the past three years. For example, you might have overpaid your tax on your original return because you neglected to take all allowable deductions or credits (details are given later in this chapter), or you might need to correct a mistake on an original or previously amended return.

4. **To get a refund if you can qualify for a refundable tax credit.** You also may qualify for the earned income credit or child tax credit. Claiming a credit may allow you to get money from the government even though you owed no income taxes for the year. (More information about credits is found on pages 111–113).

Figure 4.2 (page 102) graphically depicts these eight steps in the overall process of federal income tax calculation. The idea is to reduce your income so that you pay the smallest amount possible in income taxes. You do so by reducing total income by removing nontaxable income and then subtracting exclusions, deductions, exemptions, and tax credits, as indicated in the unshaded boxes in Figure 4.2.

1. Determine Your Total Income

Practically everything you receive in return for your work or services and any profit from the sale of assets is considered income, whether the compensation is paid in cash, property, or services. Listing these earnings will reveal your **total income**—compensation from all sources—and much of it, but not all, will be subject to income taxes.

total income Compensation from all sources.

Income to Include For most people, earned income is reported to them annually on a Form W-2, Wage and Tax Statement. Employers must provide W-2 information (see Figure 4.3) by January 31 of the next year. If you receive income from interest or dividends or other sources, those sources may send you a Form 1099. All this information is provided to the IRS.

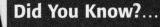

Did You Know?...

Ways to Pay Income Taxes

The federal income tax is a "pay as you go" tax. Through **payroll withholding,** an employer takes a certain amount from an employee's income as a prepayment of an individual's tax liability for the year and sends that amount to the IRS, where it is credited to that particular taxpayer's account. The amount withheld is based on the amount of income earned, the number of exemptions reported to the employer by the employee on Form W-4 (the Employee's Withholding Allowance Certificate), and other factors.

You may be exempt from payroll withholding (for example, if you are a student who works only summers) if you meet three tests:

1. You had no income tax liability last year and were entitled to a full refund of any tax withheld.

2. You expect to owe no tax in the current year on an income of no more than $850 and investment income of no more than $300.

3. You are not claimed as an exemption on another person's tax return.

If you satisfy these criteria, request a Form W-4 from your employer and write the word *exempt* in the appropriate place. If you do not satisfy all three tests, you must file a tax return after the end of the year to obtain a refund of the money withheld. Withholding for Social Security and Medicare taxes occurs regardless of whether you are exempt from income tax withholding.

People who are self-employed or receive substantial income from an employer that is not required to practice payroll withholding, such as lawyers, accountants, consultants, and owners of rental property, must pay estimated taxes. They are required to estimate their tax liability and pay their **estimated taxes** in advance in quarterly installments on April 15, June 15, September 15, and the following January 15.

Figure 4.2

The Process of Income Tax Calculation

Step 1 Total income

Step 2 Gross income | Subtract exclusions (tax-exempt income)

Step 3 Adjusted gross income | Subtract adjustments to income

Step 4 Subtotal | Subtract standard deduction or total itemized deductions

Step 5 Taxable income | Subtract value of exemptions

Step 6 Apply tax table or tax-rate schedule to determine tax liability

Step 7 Final tax liability | Subtract tax credits

Step 8 Calculate balance owed or refund

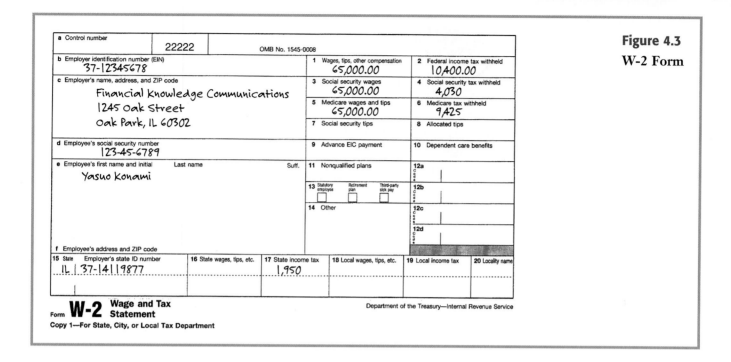

Figure 4.3

W-2 Form

The following types of income are included when you report your income to the IRS:

- Wages and salaries
- Commissions
- Bonuses
- Professional fees earned
- Income from stock options
- Tips earned
- Fair value of anything received in a barter arrangement
- Alimony received
- Scholarship and fellowship income spent on room, board, and other living expenses
- Grants and the value of tuition reductions that pay for teaching or other services
- Annuity and pension income received
- Withdrawals and disbursements from retirement accounts, such as an individual retirement account (IRA) or 401(k) retirement plan (discussed in Chapter 17, "Retirement Planning")
- Withdrawals from retirement accounts and tax-deferred annuities
- Military retirement income
- Social Security income (a portion is taxed above certain income thresholds)
- Disability payments received if you did not pay the premiums
- Damage payments from personal injury lawsuits (punitive damages only)
- Value of personal use of employer-provided car
- State and local income tax refunds (only if the taxpayer itemized deductions during the previous year)
- Employee productivity awards
- Awards for artistic, scientific, and charitable achievements unless assigned to a charity
- Prizes, contest winnings, and rewards
- Gambling and lottery winnings
- All kinds of illegal income
- Fees for serving as a juror or election worker
- Unemployment benefits

- Partnership income or share of profits
- Net rental income
- Royalties
- Investment, business, and farm profits
- Interest income (this includes credit union dividends)
- Dividends from mutual funds (including capital gains distributions even though they are reinvested)
- Dividend income

Include Capital Gains and Losses in Total Income An **asset** is property owned by a taxpayer for personal use or as an investment that has monetary value. Examples of assets include stocks, mutual funds, bonds, land, art, gems, stamps, coins, vehicles, and homes. The net income received from the sale of an asset above the costs incurred to purchase and sell it is a **capital gain.** A **capital loss** results when the sale of an asset brings less income than the costs of purchasing and selling the asset. Capital gains and losses on investments must be reported on your tax return. Capital gains from the sale or exchange of property held for personal use, such as on a vehicle or vacation home, must be reported as income, but losses on such property are not deductible. There is no tax liability on any capital gain until the stock, bond, mutual fund, real estate, or other investment is sold.

A **short-term gain** (or **loss**) occurs when you sell an asset that you have owned for one year or less; it is taxed at the same rates as ordinary income. A **long-term gain** (or **loss**) occurs when you sell an asset that you have owned for more than one year (at least a year and a day), and it is taxed at special low rates. Long-term capital gains are taxed at a maximum rate of 15 percent, and the rate is only 5 percent for taxpayers in the lower two brackets (15 and 10 percent).

Capital losses may be used first to offset capital gains. If there are no capital gains, or if the capital losses are larger than the capital gains, you can deduct the capital loss against your other income, but only up to a limit of $3000 in one year. If your net capital loss is more than $3000, the excess carries forward to the next tax year, up to an annual $3000 maximum.

asset Property owned by a taxpayer for personal use or as an investment that has monetary value.

capital gain Net income received from sale of an asset above its purchase price.

short-term gain/loss A profit or loss on the sale of an asset that has been held for one year or less.

long-term gain/or loss A profit or loss on the sale of an asset that has been held for more than a year.

2. Determine and Report Your Gross Income After Subtracting Exclusions

Gross income consists of all income (both earned and unearned) received in the form of money, goods, services, and property that a taxpayer is required to report to the IRS. To determine gross income, you need to determine which kinds of income are not subject to federal taxation and, therefore, need not be reported as part of gross income. These amounts are called **exclusions.**

gross income All income in the form of money, goods, services, and/or property.

exclusions Income not subject to federal taxation.

Income to Exclude The more common exclusions (some are subject to limits) are as follows:
- Gifts
- Inherited money or property
- Income from a carpool
- Income from items sold at a garage sale for a sum less than what you paid
- Cash rebates on purchases of new cars and other products
- Tuition reduction, if not received as compensation for teaching or service
- Federal income tax refunds
- State and local income tax refunds for a year in which you claimed the standard deduction
- Scholarship and fellowship income spent on course-required tuition, fees, books, supplies, and equipment (degree candidates only)

- Withdrawals from state-sponsored Section 529 plans (prepaid tuition and savings) used for education
- Prizes and awards made primarily to recognize artistic, civic, charitable, educational, and similar achievements
- Return of money loaned
- Withdrawals from medical savings accounts used for qualified expenses
- Earnings accumulating within annuities, cash-value life insurance policies, Series EE bonds, and qualified retirement accounts
- Interest income received on tax-exempt government bonds issued by states, counties, cities, and districts
- Life insurance benefits received
- Combat zone pay for military personnel
- Welfare, black lung, workers' compensation, and veterans' benefits
- Value of food stamps
- First $500,000 ($250,000 if single) gain on the sale of a principal residence
- Disability insurance benefits if you paid the insurance premiums
- Social Security benefits (except for high-income taxpayers)
- Rental income from a vacation home if not rented for more than 14 days
- First $5000 of death benefits paid by an employer to a worker's beneficiary
- Travel and mileage expenses reimbursed by an employer (if not previously deducted by the taxpayer)
- Employer-provided per diem allowance covering only meals and incidentals
- Amounts paid by employers for premiums for medical insurance, workers' compensation, and health and long-term care insurance
- Moving expense reimbursements received from an employer (if not previously deducted by the taxpayer)
- Employer-provided commuter highway vehicle transportation and transit passes (up to $110 per month for both) and parking (up to $215 per month)
- Value of premiums for first $50,000 worth of group-term life insurance provided by an employer
- Employer payments (up to $5000) for dependent care assistance (for children and parents)
- Benefits from employers that are impractical to tax because they are so modest, such as occasional supper money and taxi fares for overtime work, company parties, holiday gifts (not cash), and occasional theater or sporting events
- Employee contributions to flexible spending accounts
- Reimbursements from flexible spending accounts
- Reimbursements for medical expenses from health reimbursement accounts funded solely by employer contributions
- Employer-provided educational assistance payments for undergraduate and graduate classes (up to $5250 annually)
- Interest received on Series EE and Series I bonds used for college tuition and fees
- Child support payments received
- Property settlement in a divorce
- Compensatory damages in physical injury cases

Instant Message

Tax-Free Employee Benefits

Many employers offer tax-free benefits to employees, including company car, chauffeur services, transit passes, van pooling, parking, cell phone, company eating facility, business subscriptions, membership dues in professional associations, product testing, education assistance, job placement services, and meals and lodging as a condition of employment.

3. Subtract Adjustments to Income

In the process of determining your taxable income, you make **adjustments to income** (or **adjustments**). These allowable subtractions from gross income include items such as moving expenses to a new job location (including college graduates who move to take their first job); higher-education expenses for tuition and fees (up to $4000); student loan interest for higher education ($2500 maximum); reservists' travel expenses (for more than 100 miles); contributions to qualified personal retirement accounts [IRA and 401(k)

adjustments to income Allowable subtractions from gross income.

Table 4.2 Tax-Rate Schedules

SINGLE

If taxable income is over-	But not over-	The tax is:
$0	$7,825	10% of the amount over $0
$7,825	$31,850	$7,825.00 plus 15% of the amount over $7,825
$31,850	$77,100	$4,386.25 plus 25% of the amount over $31,850
$77,100	$160,850	$15,698.75 plus 28% of the amount over $77,100
$160,850	$349,700	$39,148.75 plus 33% of the amount over $160,850
$349,700	No limit	$101,469.25 plus 35% of the amount over $349,700

MARRIED FILING JOINTLY

If taxable income is over-	But not over-	The tax is:
$0	$15,650	10% of the amount over $0
$15,650	$63,700	$1,565.00 plus 15% of the amount over $15,650
$63,700	$128,500	$8,772.50 plus 28% of the amount over $63,700
$128,500	$195,850	$24,972.50 plus 28% of the amount over $128,500
$195,850	$349,700	$43,830.50 plus 33% of the amount over $195,850
$349,700	No limit	$94,601.00 plus 35% of the amount over $349,700

adjusted gross income (AGI) Gross income less any exclusions and adjustments.

qualified retirement accounts IRS-approved retirement savings programs.

above-the-line deductions Adjustments subtracted from gross income whether taxpayer itemizes deductions or not.

accounts] and health savings accounts; alimony payments; interest penalties for early withdrawal of savings certificates of deposit; business expenses; net operating losses; capital losses (up to $3000); and certain expenses of self-employed people (such as health insurance premiums). Adjustments are subtracted from gross income to determine **adjusted gross income (AGI).** Subtracting adjustments to income from gross income results in a subtotal.

To illustrate the value of adjustments to income, consider a person with a gross income of $41,000 who contributes $1000 to certain types of **qualified retirement accounts** (plans that the IRS has approved to encourage saving for retirement). The adjustment reduces gross income to $40,000 and, therefore, saves $250 in income taxes (calculated using Table 4.2). (Contributions to retirement plans are covered later in this chapter and in Chapter 17.)

Adjustments are called **above-the-line deductions** because they may be subtracted from gross income even if itemized deductions are not claimed. Adjustments may be taken regardless of whether the taxpayer itemizes deductions or takes the standard deduction amount (discussed next).

4. Subtract Either the IRS's Standard Deduction for Your Tax Status or Your Itemized Deductions

standard deduction Fixed amount that all taxpayers may subtract from their adjusted gross income if they do not itemize their deductions.

Taxpayers may reduce income further by the amount of the standard deduction. Or they can list, or itemize their deductions. They can use either method, but not both. You would want to use the larger of the two. The **standard deduction** is a fixed

Advice from a Pro

A Sideline Business Can Reduce Your Income Taxes

A sideline business can open many doors to tax deductions. We would never recommend spending money for a tax deduction; however, if you're going to spend the money anyway, you should do everything you can to make it tax deductible.

By having your own business, every dollar you spend attempting to make a profit becomes tax deductible. You can deduct expenses for auto, travel, office, office equipment (e.g., desk, chair, computer), contributions to self-funded retirement accounts, health insurance premiums, educational expenses, entertainment, business gifts, and more. You can deduct salaries of employees, even if they are your children, other relatives, or friends.

The business does not have to be your primary employment. If you lose money in the business, you can deduct those losses from your other income. The IRS says that you must do what a "reasonable business person" would do to make a profit. If you do not meet that test, the IRS will classify the operation as a hobby business, require you to report the income, and disallow the deductions.

Anthony J. Campolo
Columbus State Community College

amount that all taxpayers (except some dependents) who do not choose to itemize deductions may subtract from their adjusted gross income. In effect, it consists of the government's permissible estimate of any likely tax-deductible expenses these taxpayers might have.

The standard deduction amount depends upon **filing status,** a description of your marital status on the last day of the year. A return can be filed with a status of a single person, a married person (filing separately or jointly), or a head of household. For example, the standard deduction amounts are $5350 for single individuals and twice as much, $10,700, for married people filing jointly. Those who are age 65 or older and/or blind may claim an extra amount for their standard deduction.

Taxpayers whose tax-deductible expenses, called **itemized deductions,** exceed the standard deduction amount may deduct the larger amount instead of taking the standard deduction. For example, single people might list all of their possible tax deductions and find that they total $6000, which is more than the standard deduction amount of $5350 permitted for single taxpayers. The tax form lists the following six classifications of itemized deductions:

filing status Description of a taxpayer's marital status on last day of tax year (December 31).

itemized deductions Tax-deductible expenses.

1. Medical and Dental Expenses

2. Taxes You Paid

3. Interest You Paid

4. Gifts to Charity

5. Casualty and Theft Losses

6. Job Expenses and Most Other Miscellaneous Deductions

Examples of deductions in each of these categories follow.

1. Medical and Dental Expenses (Not Paid by Insurance) in Excess of 7.5 Percent of Adjusted Gross Income
- Medicine and drugs
- Insurance premiums for medical, long-term care and contact lenses
- Medical services (doctors, dentists, nurses, hospitals, long-term health care)

Charitable contributions are typically tax deductible.

- Sterilizations and prescription contraceptives
- Costs of a physician-prescribed course of treatment for obesity
- Expenses for prescription drugs/programs to quit smoking
- Medical equipment and aids (contact lenses, eyeglasses, hearing devices, orthopedic shoes, false teeth, wheelchair lifts)
- Fees for childbirth preparation classes
- Costs of sending a mentally or physically challenged person to a special school
- Home improvements made for the physically disabled (ramps, railings, widening doors)
- Travel and conference registration fees for a parent to learn about a child's disease
- Transportation costs to and from locations where medical services are obtained, using a standard flat mileage allowance

2. Taxes You Paid
- Real estate property taxes (such as on a home or land)
- Personal property taxes (such as on an automobile or boat when any part of the tax is based on the value of the asset)
- State, local, and foreign income taxes
- State and local sales taxes (instead of state and local income taxes)

3. Interest You Paid
- Interest paid on home mortgage loans
- "Points" treated as a type of prepaid interest on the purchase of a principal residence
- Interest paid on home-equity loans
- Interest paid on loans used for investments
- Mortgage insurance premiums on new loans after January 1, 2007 (this is not interest)

4. Gifts to Charity
- Cash contributions to qualified organizations such as churches, schools, and charities (receipt required for $250 or more)

- Noncash contributions at **fair market value** (what a willing buyer would pay to a willing seller); IRS says that personal property must be in "good used condition or better" to qualify
- Mileage allowance for travel and out-of-pocket expenses for volunteer charitable work
- Charitable contributions made through payroll deduction

fair market value Amount a willing buyer would pay to a willing seller for a charitable item.

5. Casualty and Theft Losses (Not Paid by Insurance) in Excess of 10 Percent of Adjusted Gross Income

- Casualty losses (such as from storms, vandalism, and fires) in excess of $100
- Theft of money or property in excess of $100
- Mislaid or lost property if the loss results from an identifiable event that is unexpected or unusual (such as catching a diamond ring in a car door and losing the stone)

6. Job Expenses and Most Other Miscellaneous Deductions in Excess of 2 Percent of Adjusted Gross Income (Partial Listing)

- Union or professional association dues and membership fees
- Subscriptions to magazines, journals, and newspapers used for business or professional purposes
- Books, software, tools, and supplies used in a business or profession
- Tools and supplies for use in a profession
- Cost of computers and cell phones required as a condition of your job
- Clothing and uniforms not suitable for off-the-job usage as ordinary wearing apparel (protective shoes, hats, safety goggles, gloves, uniforms), laundering and cleaning
- Unreimbursed employee business expenses (but only a portion of the cost of meals and entertainment), including long-distance telephone calls, cleaning and laundry, and car washes (of business vehicle)
- Investment-related expenses (e.g., computer software, fees for online trading, adviser fees, investment club expenses, IRA fees, safe-deposit box rental, subscriptions to investment magazines and newsletters, tax preparation fees)
- Legal fees that pertain to tax advice in a divorce or alimony payments
- Travel costs between two jobs, using a flat mileage allowance
- Job-related car expenses (but not commuting to a regular job), using a flat mileage allowance or actual expenses
- Commuting costs to a temporary workplace
- Commuting costs that qualify as a business or education expense
- Medical examinations required (but not paid for) by an employer to obtain or keep a job
- Appraisal fees for charitable donations or casualty losses
- Education expenses if required to keep your job or improve your job or professional skills (but not if the training readies you for a new career)
- Job-hunting expenses for typing, printing, résumé advice, career counseling, want ads, telephone calls, employment agency fees, mailing costs, and travel for seeking a job in your current career field
- Transportation, food, and entertainment costs for job hunting (which does not have to be successful) in your current career

Other Miscellaneous Deductions Allowed at 100 Percent

- Gambling losses (but only to offset reported gambling income)
- Business expenses for workers with disabilities

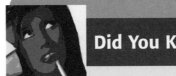

Did You Know?...

Keep Your Tax Records a Long Time

You should never discard records relating to home purchases, contributions to retirement accounts, and investments. Because you have the burden of proving that the numbers you provided to the IRS are accurate, when in doubt about keeping a tax record, do not throw it out. Record keeping is fundamental in tax matters, and being able to prove your deductions is crucial to keeping more of your money.

Given the considerable number of deductions listed here and numerous others for which you might qualify, it makes sense to take time to estimate how much you can count up in possible itemized deductible expenses. If the amount exceeds the standard deduction amount or is even close, go back and carefully itemize deductions and deduct the larger amount.

5. Subtract the Value of Your Personal Exemptions

exemption (or personal exemption)
Legally permitted amount deducted from AGI based on number of people that taxpayer's income supports.

An **exemption** (or **personal exemption**) is a legally permitted amount deducted from adjusted gross income based on the number of people supported by the taxpayer's income. An exemption may be claimed for the taxpayer and qualifying dependents, such as a spouse (if filing jointly), children, parents, and other dependents earning less than a specific income and for whom the taxpayer provides more than half of their financial support. For example, a husband and wife with two young children would have four exemptions.

A person can serve as an exemption on only one tax return—his or her own or another person's (usually a parent). Each exemption reduces taxable income by $3400. The value of an exemption is phased out for higher-income taxpayers.

Claiming Another Person as an Exemption To claim someone else as a dependent for tax purposes and, therefore, that person's exemption value, the dependent must meet five criteria:

1. The dependent must be a relative or, if unrelated, must have resided in your home as a member of your household.

2. If the person was younger than age 19 or was a full-time student younger than age 24, his or her income does not matter. A person not meeting this age and student status requirement must have received less than $3400 in gross income for the year to be claimed as a dependent.

3. You must have provided more than half of the dependent's total support. (Exceptions include children of divorced parents, who generally can be claimed only by the custodial parent.)

4. The dependent must be a U.S. citizen or a legal resident of the United States, Canada, or Mexico.

5. The dependent must not have filed a joint return with his or her spouse. If the person and the person's spouse file a joint return only to obtain a refund, you may claim him or her if the other criteria apply.

What If You Are Claimed as an Exemption? If you are claimed as a dependent on someone else's return or are eligible to be claimed, you may not claim a personal exemption for yourself, as only one person receives the exemption.

6. Determine Your Preliminary Tax Liability

The steps detailed to this point have explained how to determine your taxable income. Taxable income is calculated by taking the taxpayer's gross income, subtracting the adjustments to income, subtracting the amount permitted for the number of exemptions allowed, and subtracting either the standard deduction or total itemized deductions.

The amount of taxable income is then used to determine taxpayers' preliminary tax liability via the tax tables or tax-rate schedules for their filing status (such as single or married filing jointly).* The following examples illustrate how to determine tax liability. Table 4.3 shows segments of the tax table.

1. A married couple filing jointly has a gross income of $47,675, adjustments of $5350, two exemptions ($3400 each), and itemized deductions of $8285. They take the standard deduction of $10,700 because their itemized deductions do not exceed that amount.

Gross income	$47,675
Less adjustments to income	− 5,000
Adjusted gross income	41,675
Less standard deduction for married couple	− 10,700
Subtotal	30,975
Less value of two exemptions	− 6,800
Taxable income	24,175
Tax liability (from Table 4.3)	$ 2,844

2. A single person has a gross income of $47,300, adjustments of $5220, one exemption, and itemized deductions of $8400. She subtracts her itemized deductions because the amount exceeds the $5350 standard deduction value.

Gross income	$47,300
Less adjustments to income	− 5,220
Adjusted gross income	42,080
Less itemized deductions	− 8,400
Subtotal	33,680
Less value of one exemption	− 3,400
Taxable income	30,280
Tax liability (from Table 4.3)	$ 4,150

3. A married couple with a gross income of $137,000 has adjustments of $4400, two exemptions, and itemized deductions of $9800. The standard deduction value for a married couple is taken because it exceeds the itemized deductions.

Gross income	$ 137,000
Less adjustments to income	− 4,400
Adjusted gross income	132,600
Less itemized deductions	− 10,700
Subtotal	121,900
Less value of two exemptions	− 6,800
Taxable income	115,100
Tax liability (from Table 4.2)†	$21,622.59

Table 4.3 Tax Table*

If Taxable Income Is		Your Tax Is	
At Least	But Less Than	Single	Married Filing Jointly
20,200	20,250	2,643	2,251
20,250	20,300	2,650	2,259
24,150	24,200	3,235	2,844
24,200	24,250	3,243	2,851
26,050	26,100	3,520	3,129
26,100	26,150	3,528	3,136
27,400	27,450	3,723	3,331
27,450	27,500	3,730	3,339
27,800	27,850	3,783	3,391
27,850	27,900	3,790	3,399
27,900	27,950	3,798	3,406
27,950	28,000	3,805	3,414
30,250	30,300	4,150	3,759
30,300	30,350	4,158	3,766
33,950	34,000	4,918	4,314
34,000	34,050	4,930	4,321
42,550	42,600	7,068	5,604
42,600	42,650	7,080	5,611
49,700	49,750	8,855	6,676
49,750	49,800	8,668	6,684
53,000	53,050	9,680	7,171
53,050	53,100	9,693	7,179
53,100	53,150	9,705	7,186
53,150	53,200	9,718	7,194
58,050	58,100	10,943	7,929
58,100	58,150	10,955	7,936
71,950	72,000	14,418	10,841
72,000	72,050	14,430	10,854
74,100	74,150	14,955	11,379
74,150	74,200	14,968	11,391
90,200	90,250	18,980	15,404
90,250	90,300	18,993	15,416

*These segments of the tax table are derived from IRS tax-rate schedules.

7. Subtract Tax Credits for Which You Qualify

You may be able to lower your preliminary tax liability through tax credits. **Tax credits** provide bigger tax breaks than deductions because they represent a dollar-for-dollar subtraction from your tax liability. A credit directly reduces your tax liability, as opposed to deductions that reduce the income subject to tax. A $1000 deduction saves $250 in

tax credit Dollar-for-dollar decrease in tax liability; also known as credit.

*Instead of paying income taxes at the standard tax rates, about 3 million high-income taxpayers must pay a **higher alternative minimum tax (AMT).** The AMT rate (26 or 28 percent) is triggered for people with excessive deductions. Examples include taxpayers who have several children and income from tax-exempt sources. When the value of those benefits is added back to your income, it results in an AMT amount that may exceed your regular tax.

†The tax liability is calculated from the tax-rate schedules in Table 4.2 because the taxable income exceeds $100,000. The tax liability is computed on taxable income as follows: $8,772.50 + 0.25 × over $63,700, or $8,772.50 + 0.25 × $51,400 ($115,100 − $63,700) = $8,772.50 + $12,850 = $21,622,50.

alternative minimum tax (AMT) Tax rate (26 or 28 percent) triggered for people with excessive deductions.

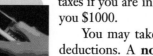
refundable tax credit Credit that reduces taxes to below zero and the excess is refunded to taxpayer.

taxes if you are in the 25 percent bracket. A $1000 tax credit saves you $1000.

You may take tax credits regardless of whether you itemize deductions. A **nonrefundable tax credit** may reduce your tax liability only to zero; if the credit is more than your tax, the excess is not refunded to you. A **refundable tax credit** can reduce your taxes to below zero and the excess will be refunded to the taxpayer. Credits are often subject to income limits, meaning that high-income taxpayers may not be eligible for a particular credit.

Hope Scholarship Credit The **Hope Scholarship credit** is $1650 per eligible student. The money must have been spent for qualified tuition and expenses for books, supplies, equipment, and student activity fees if required as a condition of enrollment. The credit can be claimed in two taxable years (but not beyond the year when the student completes the first two years of college) for individuals enrolled on at least a half-time basis during any part of the year. The Hope Scholarship credit is nonrefundable.

Lifetime Learning Credit The **lifetime learning credit** (nonrefundable) may be claimed every year for tuition and related expenses paid for all years of postsecondary education undertaken to acquire or improve job skills. The expenses for one or more courses may be for yourself, your spouse, or your dependents. The student need not be pursuing a degree or other recognized credential. This credit amounts to 20 percent of the first $10,000 paid, for a maximum of $2000 for all eligible students in a family. There is no limit on the number of years the credit may be taken for the student. The lifetime learning and Hope Scholarship credits may not be claimed for the same student expenses for the same tax year.

Earned Income Credit The **earned income credit (EIC)** is refundable, and it may be claimed not only by workers with a qualifying child but also, in certain cases, by childless workers. This credit (or a portion of it) is available for joint filers whose earned income and adjusted gross income are less than about $40,000. The maximum credit is about $4700 for a family with two children, about $2900 for a family with one child, and about $420 for a single person with no qualifying children. The greatest EIC credits go to those with the lowest taxable incomes.

Child Tax Credit You may claim a refundable $1000 child tax credit for each qualifying child younger than age 17 claimed as a dependent.

Child and Dependent Care Credit The **child and dependent care credit** (nonrefundable) may be claimed by workers who pay employment-related expenses for care of a child or other dependent if that care gives them the freedom to work, seek work, or attend school full time. Depending on your income, the maximum credit is 35 percent of qualifying care expenses up to a $1050 maximum credit ($3000 in expenses × 0.35) for one dependent and a maximum credit of $2100 for two or more dependents. Taxpayers may claim both a dependent care tax credit and a child tax credit.

Adoption Credit An **adoption tax credit** (nonrefundable) of up to $11,390 is available for the qualifying costs of an adoption.

Mortgage Interest Credit A **mortgage interest tax credit** (nonrefundable) of up to $2000 for mortgage interest paid may be claimed under special state and local government programs that provide a "mortgage credit certificate" for people who purchase a principal residence or borrow funds for certain home improvements. The home must not cost more than 90 to 110 percent of the average area purchase price.

Retirement Savings Contribution Credit A credit of 50 percent of the amount contributed to a qualified retirement plan applies if adjusted gross income does not exceed $31,000 on a joint return or $15,500 for singles. A 20 percent credit applies if AGI is $31,001 to $34,000 on a joint return and $15,001 to $17,000 for singles. A 10 percent credit applies if AGI is from $34,001 to $52,000 on a joint return and $17,001 to $26,000 for singles. The retirement savings contribution credit (also known as a **saver credit**) is nonrefundable.

Elderly or Disabled Tax Credit Individuals who are age 65 or older or who are permanently and totally disabled may claim a nonrefundable federal tax credit that can be as much as $1125.

Energy-Savings Tax Credit Congress keeps changing the laws on these types of credits. If you placed an energy-savings vehicle (such as a hybrid car) in service during the year or upgraded heating and cooling equipment, windows, solar panels, solar water heaters, and fuel cell equipment, you may qualify for a refundable credit.

8. Calculate the Balance Due the IRS or the Amount of Your Refund

If the amount withheld (shown on your W-2 form) plus any estimated tax payments you made is greater than your final tax liability, then you are entitled to receive a **tax refund.** If the amount is less than your final tax liability, then you have a **tax balance due.** If you owe money, you pay by check, money order, or credit card. The IRS imposes a convenience fee of 2.5 percent of the amount charged on a credit card.

Taxpayers may file their returns by mail or online; visit www .irs.gov and click on Free File link. You should file your return on time to avoid a penalty. If you owe the IRS and you are broke, you can borrow to pay the taxes or contact the IRS about setting up an installment plan that will repay the debt within three years. Taxpayers hear from the IRS within three weeks if they have failed to sign the return, neglected to attach a copy of the Form W-2, made an error in arithmetic, or figured the tax incorrectly. Figure 4.4 shows a completed 1040 Form for a taxpayer.

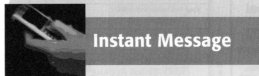

Instant Message

File 1040X to Obtain Refunds for Previous Years

Anyone who was eligible for a refundable tax credit may file to receive it retroactively for the previous three tax years using Form 1040X. Use this easy-to-complete form to obtain a refund when correcting any tax filing mistakes.

Instant Message

Invest Your Tax Refund into Your IRA

Taxpayers may direct the IRS to split their refund into various checking, saving, or investment accounts. Thus, you may earmark all or part of it into a new or existing individual retirement account (IRA) online with a financial institution or mutual fund. An IRA can be opened online in minutes without making an initial deposit.

tax refund Amount the IRS sends back to taxpayer if withholding and estimated payments exceed tax liability.

tax balance due Money you must pay to the IRS if withholding and quarterly payments are insufficient to cover tax liability.

✓ CONCEPT CHECK 4.2

1. Give five examples of income that must be included in income reported to the Internal Revenue Service.
2. How are long-term and short-term capital gains treated differently for income tax purposes?
3. Give five examples of income that is excluded from IRS reporting.
4. List three examples of adjustments to income.
5. Distinguish between a standard deduction and a personal exemption.
6. What advice on filing a Form 1040X can you offer someone who did not file a federal income tax return last year or in any one of the past three years?
7. List five examples of tax credits.

Avoid Taxes Through Proper Planning

3 LEARNING OBJECTIVE
Use appropriate strategies to avoid overpayment of income taxes.

While the U.S. tax laws are strict and punitive about compliance (although the IRS audits less than 0.5 percent of all returns), they remain neutral about whether the taxpayer should take advantage of every "break" and opportunity possible. Economist John Maynard Keynes said, "The avoidance of taxes is the only intellectual pursuit that carries any reward." The strategies described here will enable you to reduce your tax liability.

Practice Legal Tax Avoidance, Not Tax Evasion

Tax evasion involves deliberately and willfully hiding income, falsely claiming deductions, or otherwise cheating the government out of taxes owed. It is illegal. A waiter who does not report tips received and a baby-sitter who does not report income are both evading taxes, as is a person who deducts $150 in charitable contributions but who fails to actually make the donations.

tax avoidance Reducing tax liability through legal techniques.

    Tax avoidance means reducing tax liability through legal techniques. It involves applying knowledge of the tax code and regulations to personal income tax planning. Tax evasion results in penalties, fines, interest charges, and a possible jail sentence. In contrast, tax avoidance boosts your income because you pay less in taxes; as a result, you will have more money available for spending, saving, investing, and donating.

A Dollar Saved from Taxes Is Really Two Dollars— or More

These three reasons ought to motivate you to find legal ways to reduce your tax liability.

opportunity cost Most valuable alternative that must be sacrificed to satisfy a want or need.

1. **The opportunity cost.** As noted in Chapter 1, the most valuable alternative that must be sacrificed to satisfy a want is called an opportunity cost. An opportunity cost is measured in terms of the value of this forgone option, and it is reflected by the cost of what one must do without or what one could have bought instead. By paying $1 in taxes, you lose the alternative use of that dollar.

2. **Earning another dollar to replace one given to the IRS.** If you pay a dollar too much in taxes, you may need to earn another dollar to replace it. A dollar saved in taxes, therefore, may be viewed as two dollars in your pocket.

3. **Earnings on a dollar not given to the IRS.** If the two dollars saved are invested, the earnings from that investment further expand your savings.

Strategy: Reduce Taxable Income via Your Employer

It may seem illogical to suggest that to lower your tax liability you should reduce your income. The objective is to reduce *taxable* income. Reducing your federal taxable income also will reduce the personal income taxes imposed by state and local governments. Three useful ways of reducing taxable income are premium-only plans, dependent care flexible spending accounts, and defined-contribution retirement plans. Employees often are already paying for these expenses out of their own pockets with after-tax dollars, thus these plans allow people to reduce taxes on money they are already spending.

    Contributions to these employer-sponsored plans are entirely free of federal, state, and Social Security and Medicare taxes. The amount withheld to pay for the benefit is deducted from a worker's salary before taxes are calculated. In effect, the IRS subsidizes or helps pay for part of your planned expenses. If your effective marginal tax rate is 43 percent, that is how much savings you obtain by participating. So if you contribute $5000 in pretax income per year to one or more employer-sponsored plans, you immediately save $2150 because you do not have to pay that amount to the IRS.

Premium-Only Plan Many large employers offer a **premium-only plan (POP)** that allows employees to withhold a portion of their pretax salary to pay their premium contributions for employer-provided health benefits. Benefits could include health, dental, vision, and disability insurance. Amounts withheld are not reported to the IRS as taxable income. For example, if Nhon Ngo, a restaurant manager in Dallas, has $40 per month ($480 annually) withheld through his employer to pay for his share of the employer-sponsored health insurance premium, he saves $206 [$480 × 0.43 (effective marginal tax rate)] a year because he does not have to send that amount to the government in taxes.

Transportation Reimbursement Plan A transportation reimbursement plan is a similar pretax program. This employer plan allows you the opportunity to save money by using payroll deduction with pretax salary dollars to pay for work-related transportation expenses, such as transit passes, vanpool commuting, and qualified parking. If Nhon contributes $600 in pretax income to his employer's transportation plan, he saves $258 ($600 × 0.43).

Dependent Care Flexible Spending Account An attractive benefit for employees who pay for child care or provide care for a parent is a salary reduction plan known as a **flexible spending account (FSA).** This is also called an **expense reimbursement account.** An FSA allows an employee to fund qualified medical expenses on a pretax basis through salary reduction to pay for out-of-pocket unreimbursed expenses for health care (usually a maximum of $3000 annually) and dependent care (maximum $5000 annually) that are not covered by insurance. Examples are annual deductibles, office copayments, over-the-counter drugs, prescriptions, and orthodontia. The salary reductions are not included in the individual's taxable earnings reported on Form W-2, and reimbursements from an FSA account are tax free.

Suppose Nhon in the preceding example has $1200 annually withheld through his employer to be used to pay out-of-pocket medical expenses (e.g., eyeglasses, chiropractors, physician copayments) plus another $3000 to pay out-of-pocket expenses for dependent care of his child. Nhon's $4200 ($1200 + $3000) in FSA withholdings reduces his costs by $1806 ($4200 × 0.43).

FSAs are subject to a **use-it-or-lose-it rule,** which means that any unspent dollars in the account at the end of the year are forfeited and not returned to the employee. The IRS allows a 2½-month additional "grace period" if your employer provides this extension. As a result, you should make conservative estimates of your expenses when you elect your choices. For example, if you had $1000 withheld for medical expenses but spent only $700 over the year, the balance of $300 goes back to your employer, not to you.

Defined-Contribution Retirement Plan Contributing money to a qualified employer-sponsored retirement plan reduces income taxes. A **defined-contribution retirement plan** (described in Chapters 1 and 17) is an IRS-approved retirement plan sponsored by an employer to which employees may make pretax contributions that lower their tax liability. The most popular plan is known as a **401(k) retirement plan,** although other variations exist as well.

Did You Know?...

Cafeteria Plans Offer Tax-Free Employee Benefits

Employers often offer some benefits via a **cafeteria plan.** This is a program in which the employer gives the employee a specified number of credits that the employee can "spend" on different employee benefit plans or contribute to a flexible spending account. A cafeteria plan might offer tax-free benefits such as accident and health insurance, group life insurance, long-term disability insurance, dependent care, adoption assistance, medical expense reimbursements, or transportation benefits. For example, an employer might offer $4000 annually to each employee to spend on these benefits. The employee is not taxed on the value of the benefits.

Typically, there are sufficient employer credits for employees to choose a low-cost medical plan and a small amount of life insurance coverage without having to contribute their own money. If employees choose more costly benefits, they will have to make contributions out of their own money. Some plans give the employee a choice of selecting either cash or the benefits. Employees working for employers that offer a cafeteria plan avoid having to pay out-of-pocket money for certain expenses.

flexible spending account (FSA) or expense reimbursement account Allows employees to fund qualified medical or dependent expenses on pretax basis by reducing take-home salary.

use-it-or-lose-it rule An IRS regulation requiring that unspent dollars in a flexible spending account at the end of a calendar year be forfeited, unless the employer allows a three-month grace period for spending the funds.

defined-contribution retirement plan IRS-approved retirement plan sponsored by employers that allows employees to make pretax contributions that lower their tax liability.

The amount of money that an employee contributes to his or her individual account is not taxable income to the employee. For example, if you contribute $2000 to your employer's retirement plan, this immediately saves you $500 that you will not have to pay in taxes, assuming you pay taxes at the 25 percent marginalized tax rate.

An extra benefit of a defined-contribution retirement plan is that employers often offer full or partial **matching contributions** to employees' accounts up to a certain proportion and/or limit of the contributions made by the employee participant. For example, if you invest $2000 into your 401(k) plan and your employer matches half of what you contribute, that is an immediate return of 50 percent ($1000 ÷ $2000) on your investment! The employer's "match" is essentially free money.

matching contributions Employer programs that match employees' 401(k) contributions up to a particular percentage.

All of the dollars in a qualified retirement plan are likely to be invested in alternatives such as stocks and stock mutual funds, where they will grow free of income taxes. Income taxes must be paid when withdrawals are made, presumably during retirement.

Strategy: Make Tax-Sheltered Investments

Investments are often made with **after-tax dollars,** which means that the individual earned the money and paid income taxes on it. They take their after-tax money and invest it. (Investment alternatives are examined in Chapters 13 through 16.) The returns earned from these investments usually result in taxable income.

Tax laws encourage certain types of investments or other taxpayer behaviors by giving them special tax advantages over other activities. As a result, numerous **tax-sheltered investments** exist. The tax laws allow certain income to be exempt from income taxes in the current year or permit an adjustment, reduction, deferral, or elimination of income tax liability. When making investment decisions, investors should consider tax-sheltered investments.

Some of the best tax-sheltering opportunities are offered to people who wish to save and invest for their retirement. Retirement accounts are not investments themselves but rather the "housing" for tax-advantaged investments. Several additional tax-sheltered opportunities exist that can help reduce one's tax liability.

after-tax dollars Money on which employee has already paid taxes.

tax-sheltered investments Investments that yield returns that are tax advantaged.

pretax income Income before taxes are calculated.

Investing with Pretax Income

Making an investment contribution with **pretax income** means that you do not have to pay taxes this year on the income. For example, Britney Speigel made a $1000 contribution into an IRA that qualified as an adjustment to income. Britney's $1000 will not count as taxable income this year. This will save her $250 ($1000 × 0.25), assuming she pays income taxes at the 25 percent rate. Instead of paying the $250 in taxes on the $1000 in income, she can invest the $1000 in a stock mutual fund (discussed in Chapter 15) within her IRA account. Britney's $1000 includes $250 that otherwise would have gone to the government in taxes. This tax shelter is available with most retirement accounts. In effect, investing with pretax income is an interest-free deferral of taxes, $250 in this case, to fund one's investment.

tax deferred Interest, dividends, or capital gains that are allowed to grow without taxes until distributions are taken.

Tax-Deferred Investment Growth

When interest, dividends, or capital gains are **tax deferred,** the investor does not pay the current-year tax liability. For example, if Adam Reynolds received $2000 in interest from his investments, he would owe $500 in income taxes this year assuming he pays at the 25 percent marginal tax rate. If his investments were either in tax-deferred alternatives or made within tax-deferred accounts, the law allows the taxes to be paid sometime in the future (or perhaps never at all). This benefit is substantial. Investments can grow faster because the money that would have gone to the government in taxes every year can remain in the investment to accumulate. The tax-free growth of such investments is called **tax-deferred compounding.**

tax-deferred compounding Tax-free growth of tax-deferred investments.

Assume that Kyle Broflosken, who pays combined federal and state income taxes at the 30 percent rate, opens two mutual fund accounts: a regular taxable investment account and a tax-sheltered IRA investment account. Kyle puts $1000 into each account. One year later, each account is worth $1090. The extra $90 in each case represents investment growth derived from interest, dividends, and capital gains. The $90 increase in the regular taxable account is considered taxable income. If Kyle took out $27 to pay the tax liability, that would leave a net amount of $1063 in the account. In contrast, the whole $90 increase in the tax-sheltered account can stay there and continue to grow at a pretax annual rate of return rather than an after-tax rate. This means that the extra $27 in the tax-sheltered account is an asset that Kyle can keep out of Uncle Sam's reach for years and years; it can be invested and reinvested again and again. By the time income taxes must finally be paid—probably during retirement—Kyle might be in a lower tax bracket. In effect, the government "loans" tax-free money to Kyle to help fund his retirement plan.

IRA The amount contributed (up to $5000 annually) to an **individual retirement account (IRA)** is considered an adjustment to income, which reduces your current-year income tax liability. Investments inside the IRA (such as stocks and stock mutual funds) accumulate tax free. Income taxes are owed on any eventual withdrawals, likely during retirement. This type of IRA is also known as a **traditional individual retirement account.**

(traditional) individual retirement account (IRA) Investment accounts that reduce current year income and that are allowed to accumulate tax free.

Roth IRA Contributions (up to $4000 annually) to a **Roth IRA** accumulate tax free and withdrawals are tax free. There is no tax break on contributions, as they are made with after-tax money. This is an excellent investment vehicle for people with a long-term investment horizon. IRAs are examined in Chapter 17.

Roth individual retirement accounts Investments made with after-tax money; the interest on such accounts is allowed to grow tax free, and withdrawals are also tax free.

Coverdell Education Savings Account Contributions of up to $2000 per year of after-tax money may be made to a **Coverdell education savings account** (also known as an **education savings account** and formerly known as an **education IRA**) to pay the future education costs for a child younger than age 18. Earnings accumulate tax free and withdrawals for qualified expenses are tax free. The money can be used to pay for public, private, or religious school expenses, from kindergarten through trade school or college, including tuition, fees, room and board, tutoring, uniforms, home computers, Internet access and related technology, transportation, and extended day care.

Qualified Tuition (Section 529) Programs There are two types of **qualified tuition (Section 529) programs**. Under the **prepaid educational service plan,** an individual purchases tuition credits today for use in the future. Also known as a **state-sponsored prepaid tuition plan,** this program allows parents, relatives, and friends to purchase a child's future college education at today's prices by guaranteeing that amounts prepaid will be used for the future tuition at an approved institution of higher education in a particular state. The funds may be used to pay for tuition only—not room, board, or supplies.

prepaid educational service plan Type of qualified tuition program that allows purchase of a child's future college education at today's prices, locking in tuition prices.

The second qualified (Section 529) tuition program, called a **college savings plan,** is set up for a designated beneficiary. You may contribute up to $12,000 per year per child of after-tax money to a 529 college savings plan. Withdrawals are tax free if made for qualified education expenses such as tuition, room, and board. If one child does not go to college, the funds may be transferred to another relative. One may contribute to both a Section 529 plan and an education IRA for the same beneficiary in the same year.

Government Savings Bonds **Series EE** and **Series I** government savings bonds are promissory notes issued by the federal government. The income is exempt from state and local taxes. You may defer the income tax until final maturity (30 years) or report the

Did You Know?...

Consider the Tax Consequences of Managing Income Taxes

This is an example of how one couple—model taxpayers—took numerous tax deductions to reduce their income taxes. Ron and Marilyn West of Longmont, Colorado, have a complex income return because they have both made it a habit to learn about tax-saving strategies and to take advantage of them whenever possible. The Wests have a son in elementary school and a daughter in college; Ron's disabled mother, who requires in-home nursing care, lives in their home as well. Because Marilyn went to work immediately after high school, she only recently started taking college classes at night. Last year, she spent $1000 on night-school tuition.

Part of the Wests' income comes from tax-exempt sources. The table shows their total income and demonstrates how they arrived at a very low final tax liability. The couple has taken advantage of applicable exclusions, adjustments, deductions, exemptions, and credits. Their deductions and tax credits, typical for a couple with three dependents, result in a tax liability of only $3044. The marginal tax rate for the West family is 15 percent. Their average tax rate for all income is 3.0 percent ($3044 ÷ $100,550). For a family with such a substantial income, they have been quite successful in lowering their tax liability.

Total Income		
Ron's salary (self-employed)	$ 54,200	
Marilyn's salary	35,570	
Marilyn's year-end bonus	1,000	
State income tax refund (itemized last year)	180	
Interest on savings account	350	
Interest on tax-exempt state bonds	2,000*	
Gift from Marilyn's mother	2,500*	
Carpool income (Ron's van pool)	250*	
Reimbursements from flexible spending accounts	4,500*	
Total all income		$100,550
Minus* Excludable Income		
($2,000 + $2500 + $250 + $4,500 from above)		− $ 9,250
Gross Income		$91,300
Adjustments to Income		
Contribution—Ron's retirement account	$ 4,000	
Contribution—Marilyn's IRA	2,500	
Flexible spending account for health care	500	
Flexible spending account for dependent care	4,000	
College tuition and fees (daughter)	3,000	
Minus Adjustments to Income		−14,000
Adjusted Gross Income (AGI)		$77,300
Deductions		
Medical expenses (includes long-term care premiums)	$ 6,900	
Exclusion (7.5% of AGI)	− 5,798	
Total net medical expenses	$1,102	

Taxes

Real property	$2,800
Personal property (vehicles)	210
Total deductible taxes	$3,010

Interest Expenses

Home mortgage interest	$10,800
Home-equity loan interest	460
Total deductible interest expenses	$11,260

Contributions

Church	$1,200
Other qualified charities	240
Charitable travel	90
Total deductible contributions	$1,530

Casualty or Theft

Lost diamond ring (uninsured)	$8,100
Insurance reimbursement	− 0
Reduction	− 100
Exclusion (10% of AGI)	− 7,730
Total deductible casualty loss	$ 270

Miscellaneous

Union dues (Ron)	$480
Safe-deposit box	30
Unreimbursed job expenses	460
Cost of Ron looking for a new job	900
Investment publications	60
Financial planning tax advice	150
Tax publications	40
Subtotal	2,120
Less 2% of AGI	− 1,546
Total net miscellaneous deductions	$574

Total Itemized Deductions		− 17,746
Minus Exemptions (5 @$3400)		− 17,000
Taxable Income		$42,554
Tax Liability (from Table 4.3)	$5,604	

Tax Credits

Hope Scholarship credit (Marilyn)	−1,000	
Dependent care credit (Ron's mother)	− 960	
Child tax credit (son)	− 600	
Minus total tax credits		−2,560
Final Tax Liability		$3,044

interest annually. Reporting the interest in a child's name is advisable when it can be offset totally by the child's standard deduction. You may exclude accumulated interest from bonds from income tax in the year you redeem the bonds to pay qualified educational expenses. (See Chapter 14 for more information on these and similar bonds.)

municipal bonds (munis) Long-term debt issued by state and local governments and their agencies to finance public improvement projects; usually tax-free interest to buyer.

Municipal Bonds Municipal bonds (also called **munis**) are long-term debts issued by local governments and their agencies used to finance public improvement projects. Interest is free from federal and state taxes if the bond is purchased in one's state of residence. Taxpayers in higher-income brackets (28 percent or more) often take advantage of these kinds of investments. (See Chapter 14.) Smart investors choose the bonds that pay the better return after payment of income taxes. The formula to decide whether a taxable investment or nontaxable investment is better for you appears in the box "Compare Taxable and After-Tax Yields."

Did You Know?...

How to Compare Taxable and After-Tax Yields

Investors may choose to put their money into vehicles that provide taxable income, such as stocks, corporate bonds, and stock mutual funds. Taxpayers also have the opportunity to lower their income tax liabilities by investing in tax-exempt municipal bonds, money market funds that invest in municipal bonds, and other tax-exempt ventures. (These investment alternatives are discussed in Chapter 14.)

Because of their tax-exempt status, these investments offer lower nominal returns than taxable alternatives. But after considering the effects of taxes, the actual return to an investor on a tax-exempt investment may be higher than the after-tax yield on a taxable corporate bond.

To find out whether a taxable investment pays a higher after-tax yield than a tax-exempt alternative, the investor must determine the after-tax yield of each alternative. The **after-tax yield** is the percentage yield on a taxable investment after subtracting the effect of federal income taxes that will need to be paid on the investment. The after-tax yield on a tax-exempt investment is the same as the nominal yield because you do not have to pay income taxes on income from this kind of investment. So the question is, "How does the investor calculate the after-tax yield on a taxable investment?"

When you know the taxable yield, use Equation (4.1) to determine the equivalent after-tax yield on a taxable investment. Only then can you decide which investment is better. For example, suppose Bobby Bigbucks pays income taxes at the 35 percent combined federal and

state marginal tax rate and is considering buying either a municipal bond that pays a 3.5 percent yield or a taxable corporate bond that pays a 5.7 percent yield. Equation (4.1) calculates the equivalent after-tax yield on the corporate bond:*

$$
\begin{aligned}
\text{After-tax yield} &= \text{taxable yield} \times \\
&\quad (1 - \text{federal marginal tax rate}) \\
&= 5.7 \times (1.00 - 0.35) \\
&= 5.7 \times 0.65 \qquad\qquad (4.1) \\
&= 3.71
\end{aligned}
$$

The answer is 3.71 percent. Thus, a 5.7 percent taxable yield is equivalent to an after-tax yield of 3.71 percent. Eureka! Now Bobby knows that he should buy the corporate bond paying 5.7 percent because its after-tax yield of 3.71 percent is higher than the 3.5 percent paid by the municipal bond. These differences may look small, and they are, but over time they add up. For example, the extra 0.21 percent (3.71 − 3.50) yield on a $20,000 bond investment for 20 years amounts to $840 [$20,000 × 0.0021 × 20 (bond interest is not compounded)]. That's real money!†

The higher your federal tax rate, the more favorable tax-exempt municipal bonds become as an investment compared with taxable bonds. The tax-exempt status of municipal bonds does not apply to capital gains. When you sell an investment for more than what you paid for it, you will owe federal income taxes on the capital gain.

*This and similar equations can be found and used on the *Garman/Forgue* website.
†The formula can be reversed to solve for the equivalent taxable yield when one knows the tax-exempt yield. To continue the example, the return for Bobby on a 3.71 percent tax-exempt bond is equivalent to a taxable yield of 5.7 percent [3.71 ÷ (1.00 − 0.35)]. If Bobby finds a tax-exempt bond paying more than 3.71 percent, he should consider buying it.

Advice from a Pro

Buy a Home to Reduce Taxes

Hanna Pallagrosi of Rome, New York, took a sales position at a retail chain store two years ago, where she earned a gross income of $46,736. Hanna wisely made a $1000 contribution to her IRA. Her itemized deductions came to only $3800, so she took the standard deduction and personal exemption amounts. The result was a tax liability of $6046. Hanna was not happy about paying what she thought was a large tax bill that year.

Gross income	$46,736
Less adjustment to income	− 1,000
Adjusted gross income	45,736
Less value of one exemption (old figure)	− 3,200
Subtotal	42,536
Less standard deduction (old figure)	− 5,000
Taxable income	37,536
Tax liability (from old tax table not shown)	$ 6,046

Last year Hanna did not receive a raise. Nonetheless, Hanna continued to contribute $1000 into her IRA. To reduce her federal income taxes, she also became a homeowner after using some inheritance money to make the down payment on a condominium. During the year, she paid out $9126 in mortgage interest expenses

and $1995 in real estate taxes. After studying various tax publications, Hanna determined that she had $3814 in other itemized deductions that, when combined with the interest and real estate taxes, totaled $14,935. These deductions reduced Hanna's tax liability dramatically.

Gross income	$46,736
Less adjustment to income	− 1,000
Adjusted gross income	45,736
Less itemized deductions	−14,935
Subtotal	30,801
Less value of one exemption	− 3,400
Taxable income	27,401
Tax liability (from Table 4.3)	$ 3,723

Hanna correctly concluded that the IRS "paid" $2323 ($6046 − $3723) toward the purchase of her condominium and her living costs because she did not have to forward those dollars to the government. An additional benefit for Hanna is that she now owns a home whose value could appreciate in the future. The best advice is to buy a home to reduce income taxes.

Frances C. Lawrence
Louisiana State University

Here is an example to illustrate the benefits of municipal bonds. Assume that Lauren Rider, a retiree living in Lincoln, Nebraska, currently has $100,000 in a certificate of deposit earning 4.5 percent, or $4500 annually ($100,000 × 0.045). She pays $1125 in tax on this income at her 25 percent federal marginal tax rate ($4500 × 0.25), leaving her a net after-tax return of $3375. Investing in a tax-exempt $100,000 municipal bond paying 3.9 percent would provide Lauren with a better after-tax return. She would receive $3900 ($100,000 × 0.039) tax free from a municipal bond, compared with $3375 ($4500 − $1125) after taxes on the certificate of deposit. The increase in her after-tax income would be $525 ($3900 − $3375).

Capital Gains on Housing A big tax shelter is available to homeowners when they sell their homes. Those with appreciated principal residences are allowed to avoid taxes on capital gains of up to $500,000 if married and filing jointly and on gains up to $250,000 if single. The home must have been owned and used as the taxpayer's private residence for two out of the past five years prior to the date of the sale.

Strategy: Postpone Income

Another way to reduce income tax liability is to postpone income. This goal is achieved by purposefully making arrangements to receive some of this year's income in the next year, when your marginal tax rate might be lower, perhaps only 25 percent rather than

Did You Know?...

Top 3 Financial Missteps in Managing Income Taxes

People slip up in managing income taxes when they do the following:

1. Turn all your income tax planning over to someone else
2. Overwithhold too much income to receive a refund next year
3. Ignore the impact of income taxes in your personal financial planning

What Do You Recommend Now?

Now that you have read the chapter on managing income taxes, what advice can you offer Jeffrey Hutchinson and Amber Martin in the case at the beginning of the chapter regarding:

1. Using tax credits to help pay for Jeffrey's college expenses?

2. Determining how much money Amber will realize if she sells the stocks, assuming she pays federal income taxes at the 25 percent rate?

3. Buying a home?

4. Increasing contributions to their employer-sponsored retirement plans?

5. Establishing a sideline business for Jeffrey's jewelry operation?

Big Picture Summary of Learning Objectives

1 Explain the nature of progressive income taxes and the marginal tax rate.

The federal personal income tax is a progressive tax because the tax rate increases as a taxpayer's taxable income increases. The marginal tax rate is applied to your last dollar of earnings. Your effective marginal tax rate is probably 43 percent.

2 Differentiate among the eight steps involved in calculating your federal income taxes.

There are eight steps in calculating your income taxes. Certain types of income may be excluded. Regulations permit you to subtract adjustments to income, exemptions, deductions, and tax credits before determining your final tax liability.

3 Use appropriate strategies to avoid overpayment of income taxes.

You can reduce your tax liability by following certain tax avoidance strategies, such as putting your money in tax-

sheltered investments, reducing taxable income via your employer, and investing pretax money for tax-deferred compounding. Other strategies are to postpone income, bunch deductions, take all your legal deductions, and buy and manage a real estate investment.

Let's Talk About It

1. Many college students choose not to file a federal income tax return, assuming that the income taxes withheld by employers "probably" will cover their tax liability. Is such an assumption correct? What are the negatives of this practice if the employers withheld too much in income taxes? What are the negatives if the employers did not withhold enough in income taxes?

2. Long-term capital gains are taxed at a rate of 15 or 5 percent. What is your opinion on the fairness of these lower capital gains tax rates as compared with the marginal rates applied to income earned from employment that range as high as 35 percent?

3. Some college students earn money that is paid to them in cash and then do not include this as income when they file their tax returns. What are the pros and cons of this practice?

4. Identify two possible sideline businesses that you might engage in to reduce your income tax liability.

5. Name three tax credits that a college student might take advantage of while still in college or during the first few years after graduation.

6. Identify five strategies to reduce income tax liability that you will likely take advantage of in the future.

Do the Numbers

1. What would be the tax liability for a single taxpayer who has a gross income of $33,975? (Hint: Use Table 4.3, and don't forget to first subtract the value of a standard deduction and one exemption.)

2. What would be the marginal tax rate for a single person who has a taxable income of (a) $20,210, (b) $27,800, (c) $26,055, and (d) $90,230? (Hint: Use Table 4.3.)

3. Find the tax liabilities based on the taxable income of the following people: (a) married couple, $74,125; (b) married couple, $53,077; (c) single person, $27,880; (d) single person, $53,000. (Hint: Use Table 4.3.)

4. Joseph Addai determined the following tax information: gross salary, $59,400; interest earned, $90; IRA contribution, $1000; personal exemption, $3400; and itemized deductions, $3950. Calculate Joseph's taxable income and tax liability. (Hint: Use Table 4.3.)

5. Brandon and Rachael Timmerman determined the following tax information: gross salaries, $234,000 and $222,000, respectively; interest earned, $11,000; qualified retirement plan contributions, $60,000; personal exemptions, $6800; and itemized deductions, $26,000. Calculate the Timmermans' taxable income and tax liability. (Hint: Use Table 4.2.)

6. Anthony Clark determined the following tax information: salary, $144,000; interest earned, $2000; personal exemption, $3400; itemized deductions, $9000; qualified retirement plan contribution, $7000. Calculate Anthony's taxable income and tax liability. (Hint: Use Table 4.2.)

Financial Planning Cases

Case 1
A New Family Calculates Income and Tax Liability

Stephanie Nichols and her two children, Austin and Alexandra, moved into the home of her new husband, Glenn Sandler, in Ames, Iowa. Stephanie is employed as a union organizer, and her husband manages a vegetar-

ian food store. The Nichols-Sandler family income consists of the following: $40,000 from Stephanie's salary; $42,000 from Glenn's salary; $10,000 in life insurance proceeds from a deceased aunt; $140 in interest savings; $4380 in alimony from Stephanie's ex-husband; $14,200 in child support from her ex-husband; $500 cash as a Christmas gift from Glenn's parents; $90 from a friend who rides to work in Stephanie's vehicle; $60 in lottery winnings gained from playing the lottery at $5 every week; $170 worth of dental services traded for a quilt Stephanie gave to the dentist; and a $1600 tuition-and-books scholarship Stephanie received to go to college part time last year.

(a) What is the total of the Nichols-Sandler reportable gross income?

(b) After putting $2800 into qualified retirement plan accounts last year, what is their adjusted gross income?

(c) How many exemptions can the family claim, and how much is the total value allowed the household?

(d) How much is the allowable standard deduction for the household?

(e) Their itemized deductions are $12,200, so should they itemize or take the standard deduction?

(f) What is their taxable income for a joint return, and what is their marginal tax rate?

(g) What is their final federal income tax liability? (Hint: Use Table 4.3.)

(h) If Stephanie's and Glenn's employers withheld $6000 for income taxes, does the couple owe money to the government or do they get a refund? How much?

Case 2
Taxable Versus Tax-Exempt Bonds

Art Williams, radio station manager in Franklin County, New Jersey, is in the 25 percent federal marginal tax bracket and pays an additional 5 percent in taxes to the state of New Jersey. Art currently has more than $20,000 invested in corporate bonds bought at various times that are earning differing amounts of taxable interest: $10,000 in ABC earning 5.9 percent; $5000 in DEF earning 5.5 percent; $3000 in GHI earning 5.8 percent; and $2000 in JKL earning 5.4 percent. What is the after-tax return of each investment? To calculate your answers, use the after-tax yield formula (or the reversed formula) on page 122, or the *Garman/Forgue* website.

CHAPTER 5

Managing Checking and Savings Accounts

! ? You Must Be Kidding, Right?

Patti Patterson realized about two weeks ago that she had misplaced her ATM card. At first she was not worried because she reasoned that it had to be somewhere in the house. Last week she received her savings account statement. She looked at her statement today and found that $200 had been illegally withdrawn from her account on five different occasions ($1000 total). She immediately called her bank to report the fraudulent withdrawals. How much of this money will Patti lose because of the unauthorized withdrawals?

A. $0   **B.** $50   **C.** $500   **D.** $1000

The answer is C, $500. Because Patti waited more than two days after realizing the card was lost to report it to her financial institution, federal law states that she is liable for the first $500 in unauthorized uses. If she had notified the bank within two days, her loss would have been only $50. If Patti failed to notify her bank of the loss within 60 days, the law states that she would lose all of the money taken fraudulently. It's smart to immediately report a lost debit card!

LEARNING OBJECTIVES

After reading this chapter, you should be able to:

1 **List** and define the tools of monetary asset management and identify the types of financial services firms that provide those tools.

2 **Earn** interest and pay no or low fees on your checking accounts.

3 **Make** the best use of the benefits of savings accounts.

4 **Explain** the importance of placing excess funds in a money market account.

5 **Describe** electronic money management, including your legal protections.

6 **Discuss** your personal finances and money management more effectively with loved ones.

What Do You Recommend?

Mark Rosenberg and Trina Adams are to be married in two months. Both are employed full time and currently have their own apartments. Once married, they will move into Trina's apartment because it is larger. They plan to use Mark's rent money to begin saving for a down payment on a home to be purchased in four or five years. Mark has a checking account at a branch of a large regional commercial bank near his workplace where he deposits his paychecks. He also has three savings accounts—one at his bank and two small accounts at a savings and loan association near where he went to college. Mark pays about $30 per month in fees on his various accounts. In addition, he has a $10,000 certificate of deposit (CD) from an inheritance; this CD will mature in five months. Trina has her paycheck directly deposited into her share draft account at the credit union where she works. She has a savings account at the credit union as well as a money market account at a stock brokerage firm that was set up years ago when her father gave her 300 shares of stock. She also has $4300 in an individual retirement account invested through a mutual fund.

What would you recommend to Trina and Mark on the subject of managing checking and savings accounts regarding:

1. Where they can obtain the monetary asset management services that they need?

2. Their best use of checking accounts and savings accounts as they begin saving for a home?

3. The use of a money market account for their monetary asset management?

4. Their use of electronic banking in the future?

5. How they can best discuss the management of their money and finances?

FOR HELP with studying this chapter, visit the **Online Student Center:**

www.college.hmco.com/pic/garman9e

Good Money Habits in Managing Checking and Savings Accounts

Make the following your money habits when managing checking and savings accounts:

1. Use a free, interest-earning checking account for your day-to-day spending needs.

2. Use high-interest savings accounts for funds you will not need for six months to about five years in the future.

3. Use investments for needs that will not occur until five or more years in the future.

4. Maintain an emergency fund sufficient to cover three months of expenses.

5. Buy certificates of deposit when saved funds will not be needed until a specific future date.

6. Reconcile your account statements monthly.

monetary assets Cash and low-risk, near-cash items that can quickly be converted into cash.

Your financial success will depend heavily on how well you save money. Savings allows you to accumulate excess funds, or **monetary assets.** These assets were defined in Chapter 3 as cash and low-risk, near-cash items that can be readily converted to cash with little or no loss in value. If you are a typical college student, your monetary assets are the largest component of your net worth and are the major focus of the activities you consider "personal finance."

People use monetary assets in one of three ways. First, they spend them. They buy food, clothing, entertainment, and a long list of products and services. Spending often requires cash or the use of a check or a debit card to access funds in a checking account. (Using credit is covered in Chapters 6 and 7.) Checking accounts are appropriate places to keep money that you will spend within the next three to six months or so. The second way that people use monetary assets is to set aside funds to meet needs that will occur six months to five years in the future. You could keep these funds in a checking account, but savings accounts pay more interest. With savings accounts, the focus is on holding money safely until needed in the future. The third way that people use monetary assets is to make investments. Here the goal is to earn an even better return and actually earn money on your money. Investments are the best places to put money you will not need for 5, 10, or even 20 years in the future. The beauty of investments is that over long periods of time it is quite possible to earn three or four times more than the original amount deposited. Investments are examined in Chapters 13 through 16.

1   LEARNING OBJECTIVE

List and define the tools of monetary asset management and identify the types of financial services firms that provide those tools.

monetary asset (cash) management How you handle your monetary assets.

liquidity Ease with which an asset can be converted to cash.

What Is Monetary Asset Management?

Monetary asset (cash) management encompasses how you handle all of your monetary assets, including cash on hand, checking accounts, savings accounts and certificates of deposit, and money market accounts. The goal is to maximize interest earnings and to minimize fees while keeping funds safe and readily available for living expenses, emergencies, and saving and investment opportunities. Successful monetary asset management allows you to earn interest on your money while maintaining reasonable liquidity and safety. **Liquidity** refers to the speed and ease with which an asset can be converted to cash. Your funds are safe when they are free from financial risk.

The Three Tools of Monetary Asset Management

As illustrated in Figure 5.1, monetary asset management relies on three major tools:

1. Low-cost, interest-earning checking accounts from which to pay ongoing, current living expenses.

2. Interest-earning savings accounts in local financial institutions in which you deposit funds for upcoming expenditures or to accumulate funds for future investments.

3. Money market accounts in local financial institutions or other financial services

Checking account	Savings account	Money market account
• NOW checking (pays interest)	• Statement savings (+1/4%) • Certificate of deposit (+1% to +3%)	• Money market deposit account (+1/2%) • Super NOW (+3/4%) • Money market mutual fund (+1% to +5%) • Asset management account (+1% to +5%)

Figure 5.1

The Three Tools of Asset Management

(Percents are the amounts above NOW accounts.)

providers. These accounts pay higher interest rates than checking and savings accounts. They have limited check-writing privileges and, thus, are a cross between a checking and a savings account.

Who Provides Monetary Asset Management Services?

The **financial services industry** comprises companies that provide monetary asset management and other services. The firms in this industry provide checking, savings, and money market accounts. Quite often they also provide credit, insurance, investment, and financial planning services. These firms include depository institutions such as banks and credit unions, stock brokerage firms, mutual funds, financial services companies, and insurance companies. Table 5.1 matches these various types of firms with the financial products and services that they sell. As you can see, there is considerable overlap among the services they sell. For example, State Farm, which most people recognize as an insurance company, also owns a mutual fund and a bank.

financial services industry Companies that provide monetary asset management and other services.

Table 5.1   Today's Providers of Monetary Asset Management Services

Providers	What They Sell	Examples of Well-Known Company Names
Depository institutions (banks, mutual savings banks, savings and loan associations, and credit unions)	Checking, savings, lending, credit cards, investments, and trust advice	Bank One, Chase, Wells Fargo, Wachovia, Everbank (online)
Mutual funds	Money market mutual funds, tax-exempt funds, bond funds, and stock funds	Fidelity, T. Rowe Price, Vanguard
Stock brokerage firms	Securities investments (stocks and bonds), mutual funds, and real estate investment trusts	Merrill Lynch, Goldman/Sachs
Financial services companies	Checking, savings, lending, credit cards, securities investments, real estate, investments, insurance, accounting and legal advice, and financial planning	American Express, A. G. Edwards, Raymond James
Insurance companies	Property and liability, health and life insurance, credit services, financial planning services	Allstate, Aetna, State Farm

Did You Know?...

How to Reconcile Your Bank Accounts

It is a very good idea to maintain records of the activities occurring in your various banking accounts. You should record all checks written, debit card transactions, and deposits in your check register as they take place. It is also a good idea to go online every few days to confirm deposit and withdrawal (or checking) transactions.

You also should conduct an **account reconciliation** in which you compare your records with your bank's records, checking the accuracy of both sets of records and identifying any errors. The best time to do so is when you receive your monthly account statement from your bank. Account reconciliation is a three-step process:

1. Bring your own records up-to-date.
2. Bring the bank's records up-to-date.
3. Reconcile the results from Steps 1 and 2.

If the revised balance in your records and the revised balance from the bank statement differ, you will need to find where the error occurred. First, check the additions and subtractions in your records. Next, make sure that all previous entries in your records are properly reported on the account statement.

Looking for errors when Steps 1 and 2 yield differing results is a necessary but tedious task. Fortunately, it is less likely to be necessary today because of electronic banking. Many people go online frequently to check their balances and review their account activity for accuracy. In this way, they can catch errors early and are always very confident that their balances are exactly as shown in their own records. Here is a table you can use to guide your reconciling efforts.

STEP 1: Bring Your Own Records Up-to-Date	Amount	Comment
1. Enter balance from your check register.	$	
2. Add deposits not yet recorded.	$	
3. Subtract checks and other withdrawals not yet recorded.	$	
4. Subtract bank fees and charges included in the monthly statement and not yet recorded.	$	
5. Add interest earned.	$	
ADJUSTED CHECKBOOK REGISTER BALANCE	$	
STEP 2: Bring the Account Statement Up-to-Date		
1. Enter ending balance from bank statement.	$	
2. Add deposits made since bank statement closing date.	$	
3. Add outstanding checks written since bank statement closing date.	$	
ADJUSTED BANK STATEMENT BALANCE	$	

STEP 3: Compare adjusted checkbook register balance and adjusted bank statement balance. If the two balances do not match, identify where the error occurred.

account reconciliation Comparing your records with your bank's records, checking the accuracy of both sets of records, and identifying any errors.

How to Save

Americans have the lowest savings rates among the major countries of the world. When asked, they typically complain that there simply is no money left over at the end of the month. In a sense, they are correct, but they are thinking about savings in the wrong way. Wise financial planners take a different approach. They follow the adage "pay yourself first," which means to treat savings as the first expenditure after— or even before—getting paid. Build savings into your budget right from the beginning. In this way, you can effectively build funds to provide for large, irregular expenditures or unforeseen expenses; meet short-term goals; or save for retirement, a down payment on a home, or children's college education. Saving is not glamorous; slow and steady wins the race.

Your first savings goal is to accumulate enough money to cover living expenses (perhaps 70 percent of gross income) for three to six months. This money will serve as an **emergency fund** in case of job layoff, long illness, or other serious financial calamity. For a person with a $30,000 gross annual income, a three-month emergency fund would be $5250 ($30,000 ÷ 12 = $2500; $2500 × 0.70 = $1750 for each month). People who should consider keeping more funds available—perhaps income to cover six months to a year of living expenses—include those who depend heavily on commissions or bonuses or who own their own businesses.

Most people do not have a sufficient emergency fund. Instead, they rely on credit cards when an emergency or unforeseen need arises. This is an unwise way to manage finances. Other savings goals can be broken down into short-term goals and then monthly savings amounts calculated using the methods discussed in Chapter 3. If you have more than one or two goals, you can set up savings, or investment, accounts for each goal. In this way, you can keep track of your progress and keep money separately identified.

Savings Account Interest

The calculation of interest to be paid on deposits in financial institutions is primarily based on four variables:

1. Amount of money on deposit
2. Method of determining the balance
3. Interest rate applied
4. Frequency of compounding (such as annually, semiannually, quarterly, monthly, or daily)

The Truth in Savings Act requires depository institutions to disclose a uniform, standardized rate of interest so that depositors can easily compare various savings options. This rate, called the **annual percentage yield (APY),** is a percentage based on the total interest that would be received on a $100 deposit for a 365-day period given the institution's annual rate of simple interest and frequency of compounding. The more frequent the compounding, the greater the effective return for the saver. The institution must use the APY as its interest rate in advertising and in other disclosures to savers.

Wise money managers select the savings option that pays the highest APY and avoid institutions that assess excessive costs and penalties. Given the same APY, savers should choose an institution that compounds interest daily. Comparison shopping could easily earn you an extra $10 to $20 each year on a $1500 savings account balance. Smart savers also consider the fees and penalties outlined in Table 5.2 when deciding where to open a savings account.

An account with a grace period provides the depositor with a small financial benefit. A **grace period** is the period (in days) during which deposits or withdrawals can be made and still earn the same interest as other savings from a given day of the interest period. For example, if deposits are made by the tenth day of the month, interest might be earned from the first day of the month. For withdrawals, the grace period

Instant Message

Be a Regular Saver

Start saving regularly when you are young. Break long-term goals into short-term benchmarks. Then when sufficient amounts are accumulated, move the funds from savings into higher-yielding investments.

Instant Message

Use a Savings Calculator

A very easy-to-use savings calculator can be found at http://partners.financenter.com/kiplinger/calculate/us-eng/savings03.fcs. You can determine how much to save to reach your goal or find out what your savings will be worth at a future date.

annual percentage yield (APY) Return on total interest received on $100 deposit for 365-day period, given institution's simple annual interest rate and compounding frequency.

Instant Message

Focus on the APY

The best checking or savings account is the one with the highest APY. Once you have selected the account, make sure you manage it so that you avoid fees.

grace period Period (in days) for which deposits or withdrawals can be made without any penalty.

CHAPTER 6

Building and Maintaining Good Credit

! ? You Must Be Kidding, Right?

People with no prior credit history or one that shows poor repayment patterns in the past often wonder if they will ever be able to get credit. Simply put, why would any lender want to trust them? Which of the following is true today about the availability of credit for people in such situations?

A. No one will ever grant them credit.

B. If they wait a few years, their situation could change.

C. If they keep searching, they will find a lender that will treat them like everyone else.

D. Credit is relatively easy to obtain.

The answer is D. There are plenty of lenders that accept people with no or poor credit histories. The reason is the interest rate they will charge. Charging a high rate makes them willing to grant credit to high-risk applicants. Building and maintaining your good credit history will get you low interest rates!

LEARNING OBJECTIVES

After reading this chapter, you should be able to:

1 **Explain** reasons for and against using credit.

2 **Establish** your own debt limit.

3 **Achieve** a good credit reputation.

4 **Describe** common sources of consumer credit.

5 **Identify** signs of overindebtedness and describe options available for debt relief.

What Do You Recommend?

Carrie Savarin, age 25, is a nurse practitioner with the local health department. She earns $50,000 per year, with about $4000 of her income coming from overtime pay. Her employer provides a qualified tax-sheltered retirement plan to which Carrie contributes 4 percent of her salary and for which she receives an additional 4 percent matching contribution from her employer. (She could contribute up to 6 percent with an equal employer match.) Carrie has $19,000 in outstanding student loans on which she will pay $354 per month over the next five years, and her total credit card debt is $3000. Otherwise, she is debt free. Carrie would like to purchase a new or late-model used car to replace the car she has been driving since her senior year in high school. She has $2000 to use as a down payment.

What would you recommend to Carrie on the subject of building and maintaining good credit regarding.

1. Factors she should consider regarding her ability to take on additional debt?

2. The impact of her current debt on her ability to obtain a loan to buy a vehicle?

3. Where she might obtain financing for a vehicle loan?

4. The effect of taking on a loan on her overall financial planning?

FOR HELP with studying this chapter, visit the Online Student Center:

www.college.hmco.com/pic/garman9e

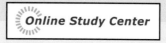

Good Money Habits in Building and Maintaining Good Credit

Make the following your money habits for building and maintaining good credit:

1. Protect your credit reputation just as you would guard your personal reputation.

2. Calculate your own debt limits before taking on any credit.

3. Obtain copies of your credit bureau reports regularly, and challenge all errors or omissions on them.

4. Never cosign a loan for anyone, including relatives.

5. Always repay your debts in a timely manner.

Your financial success hinges on your ability to make the sacrifices necessary to spend less than you earn. This means that you must use credit only when necessary, pay low interest rates, and pay off debts as quickly as possible. The term **credit** describes an arrangement in which goods, services, or money is received in exchange for a promise to repay at a future date. Most commonly, consumer credit takes the form of a **loan** that is repaid in equal payments over a set period of time or **credit cards,** which allow repeated use of credit as long as regular, monthly payments are maintained.

Most of us have conflicting feelings about the use of credit. On one hand, we may be attracted to the ease of using a credit card to pay for a vehicle or college expenses. On the other hand, we have all heard troubling stories about people who have over-used credit. There are good reasons for using credit despite its negative aspects. The key is to set reasonable debt limits for yourself. You also need to build a good credit reputation and know the best sources of credit. You need to be aware of your options for eliminating excessive debt if you ever get into credit difficulty.

credit A term used to describe an arrangement in which goods, services, or money is received in exchange for a promise to repay at a future date.

loan Consumer credit that is repaid in equal amounts over a set period of time.

credit cards Cards that allow repeated use of credit as long as the consumer makes regular monthly payments.

1 LEARNING OBJECTIVE

Explain reasons for and against using credit.

Reasons For and Against Using Credit

Credit represents a form of trust established between a lender and a borrower. If the lender believes that a prospective borrower has both the ability and the willingness to repay money, then credit will be extended. The borrower is expected to live up to that trust by repaying the lender. For the privilege of borrowing, a lender requires that a borrower pay interest and some other charges, such as processing fees.

One can distinguish between good and bad uses of credit. Among the good uses are mortgage loans to buy a home, loans to open a business, and student loans. These uses are seen as wise choices because the funds are invested in ways that have a long-term payoff. Bad uses of credit include using a credit card to support a lifestyle that you could not otherwise afford and taking out loans to buy overly expensive and otherwise unaffordable vehicles.

Good Uses of Credit

Credit can be used in very positive ways to enhance personal financial planning. Following are some of the reasons people use credit:

1. **For convenience.** Using credit cards simplifies the process of making many purchases. It provides a record of purchases, and it can be used as leverage if disputes later arise. Convenience use of credit is growing. For example, many of us now use credit cards at the grocery store and the gas station. Convenience use is justified *only* if the card balance is paid in full each month, however. After all, you do not want to be paying for today's restaurant meal for months or years in the future.

2. **For emergencies.** Consumers may use credit to pay for unexpected expenses such as emergency medical services or automobile repairs.

3. **To make reservations.** Most motels, hotels, and car rental agencies require some form of deposit to hold a reservation. A credit card number can serve as such a deposit, allowing guaranteed reservations to be made over the telephone. In many cases, the hotel will notify the credit card issuer to put a hold on your account for the anticipated total amount of the charge. This process is called **credit card blocking.**

credit card blocking Hotels or other service providers use a credit card number to secure reservations and charge the anticipated cost of services.

4. **To own expensive products sooner.** Buying "big ticket" items such as a computer or automobile on credit allows the consumer to enjoy immediate use of the product. Many expensive items would not be purchased (or would be bought only after several years of saving) without the opportunity to pay for them over time. The expected life of the product should be at least as long as the repayment period on the debt.

5. **To take advantage of free credit.** Merchants sometimes offer "free" credit for a period of time as an inducement to buy. Known as "same as cash" plans, these programs allow the buyer to pay later without incurring finance charges. The free credit lasts for a defined time period, but interest may be owed for the entire time period if the buyer pays even one day after the allotted free-credit period ends.

6. **To consolidate debts.** Consumers who have difficulty making credit repayments may resort to a **debt-consolidation loan,** through which the debtor exchanges several smaller debts with varying due dates and interest rates for a single large loan. Even when the debt-consolidation loan has a higher interest rate, the new payment can be smaller than the combined payments for the other debts because the term of the new loan is longer than the terms of the old ones.

> **debt-consolidation loan** A loan taken out to pay off several smaller debts.

7. **For protection against rip-offs and frauds.** Internet and telephone purchases made on a credit card can be contested with the credit card issuer under the guidelines of the Fair Credit Billing Act (discussed later).

8. **To obtain an education.** The high cost of education has forced many students to use student loans. This may be one of the better uses of credit, as the borrower is investing in himself or herself to raise the quality of life and/or income in the future.

The Downside of Credit

Despite its benefits, the use of credit has a downside. Negative aspects include interest costs, the potential for overspending, credit's negative effect on your financial flexibility, and concerns about privacy.

Use of Credit Reduces Financial Flexibility The greatest disadvantage of credit use comes from the loss of financial flexibility in personal money management. The money that you pay each month on your debts is money you could have spent elsewhere on other opportunities. Credit use also reduces your future buying power, as the money you pay out on a loan includes a finance charge as well as the principal. In fact, credit can be seen as a promise to "work for the creditor" in the future to pay off the debt.

It Is Tempting to Overspend A major disadvantage of credit is that its use often leads to overspending. Using a credit card to buy $425 worth of new clothes and paying $25 per month for 20 months (a total of $500: $425 + $75 interest charge) may seem less painful than paying cash for a planned purchase of only $300 worth of clothes. The problem is this: Once you begin carrying credit card debt, it may seem easier to buy more on credit, especially if you have more than three or four cards—as is typical for U.S. credit card holders.

Overindebtedness can be a real problem for credit users. Consumers with monthly nonmortgage debt repayments amounting to 16 percent of monthly take-home pay or more are considered to be seriously in debt. Misusing credit and not paying bills on time can give a consumer a poor credit reputation, damage employment prospects, increase the rates paid for insurance, and sometimes result in the loss of items purchased.

Interest Is Costly **Interest** represents the price of credit. It is the "rent" you pay while you use someone else's money. When stated in dollars, interest makes up part of the **finance charge,** which is the total dollar amount paid to use credit (including interest and any other required charges such as a loan application fee). The Truth in Lending Act requires lenders to state the finance charge both in dollars and as an

> **interest** In this context, interest is the "rent" you pay for using credit.

> **finance charge** Total dollar amount paid to use credit.

annual percentage rate (APR)
Expresses the cost of credit on a yearly basis as a percentage rate.

annual percentage rate (APR). The APR expresses the cost of credit on a yearly basis as a percentage rate. For example, a single-payment, one-year loan for $1000 with a finance charge of $140 has a 14 percent APR.

Knowing the APR simplifies making comparisons among credit arrangements. The lower the APR, the lower the true cost of the credit. The APR can be used to compare credit contracts with different time periods, finance charges, repayment schedules, and amounts borrowed. Many states have **usury laws** (sometimes called **small loan laws**) that establish the maximum loan amounts, interest rates, and credit-related fees for different types of loans from various sources. These maximum rates can vary from 18 percent to as much as 54 percent. The laws of the state in which the lending institution is located apply, rather than the laws of the state in which the borrower lives. These regulations apply to the annual fee, late payment fee, and other fees charged on a bank credit card.

identity theft When someone else uses your personal information to run up debt in your name or access your financial accounts.

card verification value The three- or four-digit code on the signature strip on the back of credit cards.

✔ CONCEPT CHECK 6.1

1. Which two good uses of credit seem most reasonable to you? Which do not?
2. Explain the two downsides of credit that would be most worrisome for you?
3. Distinguish between the APR and the finance charge on a debt.

Advice from a Pro

Guard Your Privacy

Identity theft is the most common form of consumer fraud in the United States. It occurs whenever someone else uses your personal information, such as a credit card number, to steal from merchants, from credit card companies, or from you. Armed with a very little personal information, a clever thief can borrow someone's credit identity and run up thousands of dollars in debt. To protect your privacy, follow these guidelines:

• Offer no personal information (such as your address, telephone number, or Social Security number) to merchants when using a credit card. If the merchant requires identification beyond the credit card (for example, a driver's license), do not allow such information to be written down or photocopied.

• Save all purchase and ATM receipts, and regularly check them against statements from creditors and sellers.

• Do not give out your credit card or checking account number on the telephone to anyone you do not know or did not telephone directly yourself.

• Never give your **card verification value** over the phone or online to a merchant unless you initiated the contact with the merchant. This is the three- or four-digit code in the signature strip on the back of a credit card.

• Review your credit bureau report at least once each year.

• Report lost or stolen credit cards and suspicious billing information without delay, especially if you make Internet purchases.

• If your credit card is lost or stolen, or if you ever suspect fraudulent use of an account, contact one of the national credit bureaus because any one of them can put a "fraud alert" on your file at all three companies.

• Tell all of your financial services companies (banks, lenders, insurance companies) that you want to "opt out" of any information-sharing programs they maintain with affiliated or external companies.

• Immediately change the marital status linked to your credit card account if you become married, separated, or divorced.

Brenda Cude
University of Georgia

You Should Set Your Own Debt Limit

2 **LEARNING OBJECTIVE**
Establish your own debt limit.

You, rather than a lender, should set your own **debt limit,** which is the overall maximum you believe you should owe based on your ability to meet the repayment obligations. Most people's debt limit is, and should be, lower than what lenders are willing to tender. Lenders are willing to take chances that some borrowers will not repay. By contrast, you should not take such a chance when making your own credit decisions.

debt limit Overall maximum you believe you should owe based on your ability to meet repayment obligations.

When considering a new loan, many people simply look at the monthly payment required. This view is shortsighted as it is easy to get a low monthly payment simply by lengthening the time period over which the loan will be repaid. You should assess your overall debt obligations. There are three ways to determine your debt limit:

1. Debt payments-to-disposable income method
2. Ratio of debt-to-equity method
3. Continuous-debt method

Debt Payments-to-Disposable Income Method

To use the **debt payments-to-disposable income method,** you first need to decide the percentage of your disposable personal income that can be spent for regular debt repayments, excluding the first mortgage loan on a home and credit card charges that are paid in full each month. **Disposable income** is the amount of your income remaining after taxes and withholding for such purposes as insurance and union dues. Table 6.1 shows some monthly debt-payment limits expressed as a percentage of disposable personal income. As the table indicates, with monthly payments representing 16 to 20 percent of monthly disposable personal income, a borrower is seriously over-indebted and fully extended; taking on additional debt would be unwise. This means that someone with an average income and an expensive car loan might not be able to afford to carry any credit card balances that carry over from month to month.

debt payments-to-disposable income method Percentage of disposable personal income available for regular debt repayments aside from set obligations.

disposable income Amount of income remaining after taxes and withholding for such purposes as insurance and union dues.

Once you decide the percentage that is appropriate for you, you can compare it with your **debt payments-to-disposable income ratio** as discussed in Chapter 3. In that chapter, we calculated a debt payments-to-disposable income ratio for the Hernandez family of 9.32 percent. As indicated by Table 6.1, they could take on new debt—but only cautiously.

Table 6.1 Debt-Payment Limits as a Percentage of Disposable Personal Income*

Percent	Current Debt Situation†	Borrower's Feelings	Take on Additional Debt?
0	No debt at all	No stress about personal finances	Taking on some consumer debt is fine
10 or less	Little debt	Borrower feels no stress from debt repayment obligations	More debt could be undertaken cautiously
11 to 15	Safe debt limit but fully extended financially	Borrower is moderately stressed about pressure from debt repayment obligations	Should not acquire more debt, and a debt consolidation loan from a credit union may be a good option
16 to 20	Seriously overindebted	Borrower starts to feel seriously stressed about debts and hopes no emergency arises	Absolutely should not take on more debt
21 to 25	Precariously overindebted	Borrower feels overwhelming stress and is desperate about debts	Contact a nonprofit credit counseling company
26 to 30	Excessively overindebted	Borrower feels hopeless and is painfully stressed about debts	Contact a bankruptcy attorney
311	Dangerously overindebted	Borrower knows his or her debts are so large that he or she is doomed to financial failure	Contact a bankruptcy attorney

*Excluding home mortgage loan repayments and convenience credit card purchases to be repaid in full when the bill arrives.
†People with a 16 percent or higher debt-payment limit as a percentage of personal income are "seriously overindebted." They may feel "seriously stressed" about their personal finances and begin to wonder if they are so overly indebted that they may never be able to get out of debt.

Table 6.2   Effects of Increasing Debt Payments on a Budget*

Gross income	$34,000	22%
Deductions for taxes, 401(k), insurance	$ 7,600	
Disposable personal income	$26,400	
Monthly Disposable income	$ 2,200	

	No Debt	10% Debt	15% Debt	20% Debt	25% Debt
Rent	$ 700	$ 700	$ 700	$ 700	$ 700
Savings and investments	250	**180**	**120**	**80**	**50**
Food	280	**250**	**240**	**220**	**210**
Utilities (telephone, electricity, heat)	130	130	130	**120**	120
Insurance (automobile, renter's, and life)	80	80	80	80	80
Transportation expenses	100	**90**	90	**80**	80
Charitable contributions	60	**50**	50	**40**	40
Entertainment	140	**120**	**110**	**100**	**80**
Clothing	50	**40**	**30**	**20**	20
Vacations and long weekends	60	**50**	**40**	40	**30**
Medical/dental expenses	60	**50**	50	50	50
Newspapers and magazines	40	**30**	30	30	**0**
Cable TV	50	50	**40**	40	**30**
Personal care	30	**20**	20	20	20
Gifts and holidays	40	**30**	30	30	30
Health club	60	60	60	60	60
Miscellaneous	70	**50**	50	50	50
Debt repayments	0	**220**	**330**	**440**	**550**
TOTAL	**$2,200**	**$2,200**	**$2,200**	**$2,200**	**$2,200**

*One person's decisions on where to cut back expenses to make increasing monthly debt payments.

Table 6.2 shows the effects on a budget of increasing debts. In the table, after deductions, disposable personal income amounts to $2200 per month. Current budgeted expenses (totaling the full $2200) are allocated in a sample distribution throughout the various categories. As you can see, increasing debt payments from $0 to $550 per month (for example, to buy a new automobile or home entertainment system on credit) has dramatic effects on this budget. A responsible financial manager must decide where to cut back to meet monthly credit repayments. As the debt load grows, each 5 percentage point increase makes it much more difficult to "find the money" and make the cutbacks. In this case, the borrower reduced expenditures on savings and investments immediately and then finally reduced the amount in this category to $50. Food was cut back, but only slightly. Utilities, automobile insurance, and rent are relatively fixed expenses; as a consequence, it is difficult to reduce these amounts without moving or buying a less expensive car. Entertainment expenses were steadily reduced, and newspapers and magazines were eliminated altogether.

Where would you make reductions? Spending a few minutes changing the figures in Table 6.2 will give you an idea of your priorities and the size of the debt limit that you might establish. Note that the debt payments-to-disposable income method focuses on the amount of monthly debt repayment—not the total debt. As a result, it also would be wise to consider the length of time that the severe financial situation caused by high debt payments might last. It could be years, many years.

Ratio of Debt-to-Equity Method

Another method for determining your debt limit involves calculating the ratio of your consumer debt to your assets. In Chapter 3, we performed such an analysis for the Hernandez family when we calculated their asset-to-debt ratio. The **debt-to-equity ratio** is similar except that it uses the **equity** in a person's assets (the amount by which the value of those assets exceeds debts), excluding the value of a primary residence and the first mortgage on that home. This ratio recognizes that mortgage debt does not get people into trouble. In fact, mortgage debt is backed up by excellent collateral—one's own home.

> **debt-to-equity ratio** Ratio of your consumer debt to your assets.

From Table 3.3 on page 69, we see that the Hernandez family has assets of $133,920 ($4420—monetary assets; $20,500—tangible assets less the value of their home; and $109,000—investment assets). Their debts (excluding their home mortgage) total $9365 ($120 + $1545 + $7700). With $9365 in debts and $133,920 in assets, the Hernandezes have equity of $124,555 ($133,920 − $9365), or a debt-to-equity ratio of 0.08 ($9365 ÷ $124,555).

The ratio of debt-to-equity method provides a quick idea of one's financial solvency. The larger the ratio, the riskier the likelihood of repayment. A ratio in excess of 0.33 is considered high. The Hernandezes are well under that limit, unlike the result found by calculating their debt payments-to-disposable income ratio. This contrast occurs primarily because of their real estate investment asset, on which they have no debt.

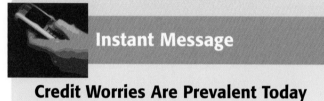

Instant Message

Credit Worries Are Prevalent Today

One in three U.S. households truly fears becoming overextended on credit, and more than one-half are concerned about making their monthly credit card payments.

Continuous-Debt Method

Another approach for determining your debt limit is the **continuous-debt method.** If you are unable to get completely out of debt every four years (except for a mortgage loan), you probably lean on debt too heavily. You could be developing a credit lifestyle in which you will never eliminate debt and will continuously pay out substantial amounts of income for finance charges—likely $1000 or more per year.

Dual-Earner Households Should Consider a Lower Debt Limit

Having two incomes in a household has its benefits. Two people, each of whom earns $32,000 per year, will gross $64,000, with a disposable personal income of around $48,000, or $4000 monthly. It may seem that the couple can afford a much higher level of debt than before the incomes were combined. While the guidelines given in Table 6.1 are realistic, they would allow a doubling of debt payments if the addition of a second earner doubled household earnings.

Many young couples adopt a lifestyle based on two incomes. Their spending grows in tandem with their rising incomes. After a while, they are spending and borrowing to the limit. This situation cannot go on forever, of course. Eventually they may begin to feel financially stressed and wonder, "How can we be so broke when we make so much money?" When a child comes along or a financial setback occurs, they may be in deep trouble. If one earner's income is reduced, perhaps because of a need to take care of family responsibilities, debts that had been manageable with two incomes quickly become overwhelming. Couples should avoid taking on excessive debt. Instead, they should set a reasonable limit and build savings accounts and make investments early in their lives together. That will truly protect their future financial security.

Did You Know?...

How to Manage Student Loan Debt

You should minimize your student loan debt because large debts make it more challenging to meet other financial goals such as buying a home and saving for retirement. Here are some tips for managing student loan debt:

1. **Choose the most advantageous repayment pattern allowed.** The standard repayment plan for student loan debt calls for equal monthly installments paid over ten years, but to pay the debt off faster, you can establish a graduated repayment plan whereby the payments are lower in the early years but then increase in later years.

2. **Pay electronically.** Make arrangements to have the monthly payment transferred electronically out of a checking account and you can receive a reduction in the interest rate.

3. **Make your repayments on time, every time.** In some programs, if you make the first 48 payments on time, the interest rate will be reduced by 2 percentage points. Failing to repay in a timely manner can have dire consequences, including forfeiture of federal and state income tax refunds, as well as Social Security and veterans' benefits.

4. **Consolidate your student loans.** Consolidating your education loans means that all your existing loans are paid off and one new loan is created. This strategy may allow for a much more convenient repayment schedule. The interest rate may be lower, the monthly payment is usually lower, and the amount of time for repayment may be longer under the new loan. Loans can be consolidated through a private bank or through one of three government programs: Collegiate Funding Services (www.cfsloans.com), Sallie Mae (www.salliemae.com), or Federal Direct Consolidation Loans (www.loanconsolidation.ed.gov).

Double incomes should not mean double debt.

✔ **CONCEPT CHECK 6.2**

1. Distinguish among the debt payments-to-disposable income, ratio of debt-to-equity, and continuous-debt methods for setting your debt limit.

2. What are the threshold levels for both the debt payments-to-disposable income and ratio of debt-to-equity methods that would indicate that a person is carrying too much debt?

3. Discuss how dual-earner households should consider their ability to carry additional debt.

Obtaining Credit and Building a Good Credit Reputation

3 LEARNING OBJECTIVE
Achieve a good credit reputation.

Credit is widely and readily available to many of us today. It is not unusual for a customer to walk into a retail store such as Target or Home Depot and be offered a credit card account that can be used immediately. However, if the applicant has not used credit previously (no credit) or if he or she has failed to honor credit agreements in the past (bad credit), an offer of credit is typically not extended. Your success in obtaining credit hinges on an understanding the credit approval process and having a good credit reputation.

The Credit Approval Process

To obtain credit, you must first complete a credit application. Based on the information in this application, the lender will investigate your credit history. The information is then evaluated (sometimes instantly via computer), and the lender decides whether to extend credit. When an application is approved, the rules of the account are contained in the credit agreement.

You Apply for Credit A **credit application** is a form or interview that requests information that sheds light on your ability and willingness to repay debts. This information helps lenders make informed decisions about whether they will be repaid by borrowers. Answering questions completely and honestly both on an application form and during an interview (if any) is important. If inconsistencies arise during the lender's subsequent investigation of the applicant's credit history, the lender could refuse the request for credit or charge a higher interest rate. At the time of application, always ask for a copy of the rules governing the account, including the APR and various repayment terms. However, these terms are not final and can change when the actual decision to lend is made. That is why you should read all credit contracts before signing.

Approximately 12 percent of all people who apply for credit are denied. Half of the unsuccessful applicants have no established **credit history** (a continuing record of a person's credit usage and repayment of debts) or their credit history contains negative information. A bad credit history is like having high blood pressure—you may not know you have a problem until something bad happens, such as when your loan application is rejected.

Did You Know?...

The Top 3 Financial Missteps with Credit

People slip up in building and maintaining good credit when they do the following:

1. Make late payments on credit cards

2. Pay more than 15 percent of disposable income toward nonmortgage debt payments

3. Fail to regularly check the accuracy of credit bureau files

credit application Form or interview that provides information about your ability and willingness to repay debts.

credit history Continuing record of a person's credit usage and repayment of debts.

The Lender Conducts a Credit Investigation

Upon receiving your completed credit application, the lender conducts a **credit investigation** and compares the findings with the information on your application. The goal of the investigation is to assign a **credit rating** to the applicant; this rating is the lender's evaluation of the applicant's creditworthiness. In assigning a credit rating, lenders will look at the applicant's prior credit usage; repayment patterns; and other important characteristics, such as income, length of employment, home ownership status, and credit history.

To conduct its investigation, the lender obtains a **credit report** from a **credit bureau** that keeps records of many borrowers' credit histories. Lenders pay a fee for each credit report requested. Credit bureaus compile information from merchants, utility companies, banks, court records, and creditors. Most of the more than 2000 local credit bureaus in the United States belong to national groups that collectively have access to the credit histories of more than 160 million adults.

Lenders use a **credit scoring** system (also known as **risk scoring**) in which a statistical measure is used to rate applicants on the basis of various factors deemed relevant to creditworthiness and the likelihood of repayment. All three of the major credit-reporting bureaus calculate and report credit scores to lenders. You also have the right to know your scores, although you usually must pay a fee to do so. The most well-known score is the FICO score developed by Fair, Isaac and Company.

The Lender Decides Whether to Accept the Application and Under What Terms

The approval or rejection of credit is based on the lender's judgment of the willingness and ability of the applicant to repay the debt. If the application is accepted, a contract is created that outlines the rules governing the account. For credit cards, this contract is called a **credit agreement.** For loans, the contract is called a **promissory note** (or simply, the **note**).

The actual lender always makes the decision about whether to grant credit. Credit scoring simply allows lenders to categorize credit users according to the perceived level of risk. Under the concept of **tiered pricing,** lenders may offer lower interest rates to applicants with the highest credit scores while charging steeper rates to more risky applicants. Even people with low credit scores usually can find some lender that will say yes, however. The interest rates will be higher for those borrowers. Of course,

credit report Information compiled by a credit bureau from merchants, utility companies, banks, court records, and creditors about your payment history.

credit bureau Firm that collects and keeps records of many borrowers' credit histories.

credit scoring (risk scoring) system Statistical measure used to rate applicants based on various factors deemed relevant to creditworthiness and the likelihood of repayment.

credit agreement Contract that stipulates repayment terms for credit cards.

promissory note (note) Contract that stipulates repayment terms for a loan.

unfair discrimination Making distinctions among individuals based on unfair criteria when granting credit.

Did You Know?...

Unfair Credit Discrimination Is Unlawful

The Equal Credit Opportunity Act (ECOA) prohibits certain types of **unfair discrimination** (making distinctions among individuals based on unfair criteria) when granting credit. Under this law, a lender must notify an applicant within 30 days about the lender's acceptance or rejection of a credit application. The ECOA also requires the creditor to provide the applicant with a written statement, if requested, detailing the reasons for refusing credit. Rejecting a credit application due to poor credit history is legal. Conversely, it is illegal to reject applicants on the basis of gender, race, age, national origin, religion, or receipt of Social Security income or public assistance. Credit applications cannot ask for information that could be used in a biased manner, such as marital status and childbearing plans. (Applicants may offer such information

voluntarily, however.) If discrimination is proved in court, the lender may be fined as much as $10,000.

A creditor cannot require an applicant to disclose income from alimony, separate maintenance payments, or child support payments. If the borrower wants this income to be counted during the lender's evaluation of the application, the creditor can consider whether that income stream is received consistently. Information about a spouse or former spouse may not be requested unless the spouse will use the account, it is a joint account, or repayment of debts will rely on the spouse's income or other financial support. The law requires that credit granted in both spouses' names be used to build a credit history for the parties as a couple as well as for each individual spouse.

Did You Know?...

How to Make Sense of FICO Credit Scores

Although the credit-scoring systems in use today go by a number of brand names, the most well known is the FICO score developed by Fair, Isaac and Company. (www.myfico.com). Because your credit file at each of the three major credit bureaus may differ, your credit score at each may differ as well. (See "Managing Your Credit Bureau File for Free" on page 170). Your FICO scores are vitally important because they dictate whether you will be granted credit and at what interest rates. Under the Fair and Accurate Credit Transactions Act of 2003, consumers must be told their credit scores upon request. A nominal fee (about $12) is charged for a credit score report.

FICO scores are produced via complex statistical models that correlate certain borrower characteristics with the likelihood of repayment. The exact methodologies employed in the models are closely held secrets, but the factors that are used in them are shared openly by Fair, Isaac and Company on the company's website:

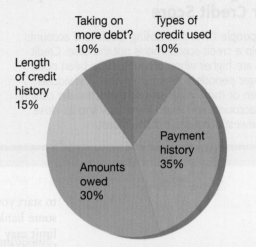

1. **Payment history.** Are you late with your payments? How late? How often? On how many of your accounts?

2. **Amounts owed.** What is the balance on each of your credit obligations? (Even if you pay in full each month, there might be a balance on a given date.) How do the amounts owed vary on various types of accounts, such as credit cards versus loans? How many accounts have balances? Are you "maxed out" or nearly so on your cards, regardless of the dollar amount of your balances? (Credit scores are negatively affected if you have a balance on any card in excess of 30 percent of the credit limit on that card.) On loans, how much of the original loan is still owed?

3. **Length of credit history.** How long have you had each account? How long has it been since you used the accounts?

4. **Taking on more debt.** How many new accounts do you have? How long has it been since you opened a new account? How many recent inquiries have been made by lenders to which you have made application? If you had a period of poor credit usage in the past, for how long have you been in good standing?

5. **Types of credit used.** Do you have a good mix of credit usage, with reliance on multiple types depending on the purpose of the credit (for example, not using a credit card to buy a boat)? How many accounts in total do you have?

The FICO website provides suggestions on how to improve your FICO scores. For example, if you are "maxed out" on two cards and have low balances on others, you might shift some of the large balances to other cards. If you have many dormant accounts, you should close them. The chart above indicates the importance of each of the five factors in the development of FICO scores.

---

some applicants represent such high risk that a lender will deny the application for credit. For this reason, you should always make sure that your credit bureau file is accurate before filling out a credit application.

Your Credit Reputation

The information about you that is contained in credit bureau files is one of the most important aspects of your financial life. It is used not only when lenders decide whether to approve your applications for credit but also when you apply for a job, insurance, and rental housing. Thus, it is important that you build a good credit reputation and confirm that the information in your file is as accurate and up-to-date as possible.

CHAPTER 7

Credit Cards and Consumer Loans

! ? You Must Be Kidding, Right?

College students who have a credit card in their own name (and most do) have an average debt of $2700 at graduation. If they maintain that level of debt for ten years (because their payments equal the charges they make plus interest), how much total interest will they pay?

A. $1200

B. $1800

C. $2700

D. $4860

The answer is D. A credit card with an 18 percent APR (typical for college students) translates to a 1.5 percent rate per month (18% ÷ 12). The $2700 debt multiplied by this rate equals $40.50 ($2700 × 0.015) per month in interest. And $40.50 multiplied by 120 months equals $4860. You must pay more than the amount you charge plus any interest owed for each month in order to reduce your credit card debt and avoid paying many thousands of dollars in interest over the years. Otherwise, you will be in debt forever!

LEARNING OBJECTIVES

After reading this chapter, you should be able to:

1 **Compare** the common types of consumer credit, including credit cards and installment loans.

2 **Describe** the types and features of credit card accounts.

3 **Manage** your credit card accounts to avoid fees and finance charges.

4 **Describe** the important features of consumer installment loans.

5 **Calculate** the interest and annual percentage rate on consumer loans.

What Do You Recommend?

Darrell Cochrane, a 31-year-old optician in Tampa, Florida, made $42,000 last year. Darrell avoided using credit and credit cards until he was 28 years old, when he missed three months of work due to a water-skiing accident. He made ends meet by obtaining two bank credit cards that, because of his lack of a credit history, carry 19.6 and 24 percent annual percentage rates (APRs). Darrell now has 11 credit card accounts open: five bank cards and six retail store cards. He uses them regularly, presenting whatever card a store will honor. He owes $13,000 on the 24 percent APR card and $4400 on the 19.6 percent APR card. His other three bank cards carry APRs of 11 percent, 12 percent, and 15 percent, and he owes $500 to $700 on each one. For the past year, Darrell has been making only the minimum payments on his bank cards. His retail cards all carry APRs in excess of 21 percent. Although he has managed to keep from running a balance on those cards during most months, occasionally these accounts have balances as well.

What would you recommend to Darrell on the subject of credit cards and consumer loans regarding:

1. His approach to using credit cards, including the number of cards he has?

2. Estimating the credit card interest charges he is paying each month?

3. How he might lower his interest expense each month?

4. Consolidating his credit card debts into one installment loan?

FOR HELP with studying this chapter, visit the Online Student Center:

college.hmco.com/pic/garman9e

Online Study Center

CHAPTER 8

Vehicle and Other Major Purchases

You Must Be Kidding, Right?

When Ryan Levelle graduated from college three years ago, he really wanted a fully equipped Pontiac G6. His monthly payment would be about $350 per month, about $70 more than he could afford. So that Ryan could meet his budget, the dealer suggested that he lease the vehicle and offered a 42-month lease option at $270 per month for 12,000 miles per year. The contract had a $0.30 per mile fee at the end of the lease for any excess mileage. Now, with six more months on his lease, Ryan is already 1500 miles over the 42,000 (3.5 × 12,000) total mileage limit in his contract. What is Ryan's best option at this point?

A. Turn back the vehicle now and pay the $450 (1500 × $0.30) for excess mileage.

B. Try to cut back on his driving to minimize his excess mileage fee, which could be more than $2500 if he keeps driving at the same rate as he has been.

C. Stop driving the car and pay $450 for excess mileage when he turns it back at the end of the lease.

D. Continue driving the vehicle and buy it at the end of the lease by paying the residual value agreed upon when he entered into the contract.

The answer is D. None of the other options is financially practical. Ryan learned a hard lesson. Leases require a lower monthly payment but have hidden costs that often are not known until the very end of the contract!

LEARNING OBJECTIVES

After reading this chapter, you should be able to:

1 **Explain** the three steps in the planned buying process that occur prior to interacting with sellers.

2 **Describe** the five aspects of major purchases that require comparison shopping.

3 **Negotiate** and decide effectively when making major purchases.

4 **Evaluate** your purchase decisions and, if necessary, effectively seek redress.

What Do You Recommend?

David and Lisa Cosgrove of Tacoma, Washington, are in their early 40s and have three children. They own three vehicles. Lisa drives an almost-new Toyota Camry; David uses a five-year-old Ford pickup; and Amber, the couple's 17-year-old daughter, drives a ten-year-old Dodge Neon. Recently, a fire in their garage destroyed both the Neon and the Camry. The Cosgroves received an insurance settlement of $21,900 on Lisa's car, although the loan payoff amount was $22,800. Amber's Neon was not insured for fire. The couple wants to obtain replacement cars that are similar to those destroyed.

What would you recommend to David and Lisa on automobiles and other major purchases regarding:

1. How to search for two vehicles to replace those destroyed?

2. Whether to replace Lisa's vehicle with a new or used vehicle?

3. Whether to lease or buy a vehicle?

4. How to decide between a rebate and a special low APR financing opportunity if they decide to purchase a new vehicle for Lisa?

5. How to negotiate with the sellers of the vehicles?

planned buying Thinking through all the details of a purchase from the initial desire to buy to your satisfaction after the purchase.

Planned buying entails thinking through all the details of a purchase from the initial desire to buy to your satisfaction after the purchase. You can use planned buying principles any time, but they are especially handy when you are buying a car or making other "big ticket" purchases. The seven distinct steps that lead you through the planned buying process are illustrated in Figure 8.1. Steps 1, 2, and 3 occur before you interact with sellers: determining your needs and wants, performing preshopping research, and fitting a purchase into your budget. Comparison shopping and other interactions with sellers comprise the fourth step in the buying process. Steps 5 and 6—negotiating and making the decision—follow. The seventh and final step—evaluation of the decision—is taken after making the purchase. After reading this chapter, you will understand enough about the planned buying process to save money when buying expensive goods while still meeting your needs and many of your wants.

Do Your Homework

1   LEARNING OBJECTIVE

Explain the three steps in the planned buying process that occur prior to interacting with sellers.

Let's look now at the first three steps, all of which should occur before you actually interact with sellers. They are, in a sense, the homework you do when preparing to buy.

What Do You Really Want?

need Item thought to be necessary.

want Item not necessary but desired.

A **need** is something thought to be a necessity; a **want** is unnecessary but desired. In truth, very few needs exist, yet in everyday language people talk often of "needing" certain things. In the planned buying process, it is best to avoid such thinking because once something is called a need, it may no longer be open to careful consideration. Instead, you should consider all purchase options to be wants. Of course, some wants are very important. The most important can be determined by prioritizing your wants. This approach allows for careful consideration of the benefits and costs of the options available. Costs should include opportunity costs as measured by some other goal or want that will become less attainable if a given want is satisfied. For example, buying a car with a retractable sunroof might mean that you cannot afford to purchase one with a remote start feature.

impulse buying Buying without fully considering priorities and alternatives.

generic products Goods that carry store brands or are sold under a general commodity name such as "whole-kernel corn" rather than a brand name, such as Del Monte.

Setting priorities becomes more difficult when a decision is complex such as when buying a car or home. Consider the case of Sharon Wilson, a respiratory therapist from St. Paul, Minnesota. Sharon has been late to work several times in the past few months because her 12-year-old car has been having mechanical problems. Sharon wants to avoid being late. But how? Should she buy a new car, a used car, lease a new car, repair her current car, or take the bus to work? After considering these options, Sharon decided to buy a new car. Now she must determine which features are of high or low priority. To do

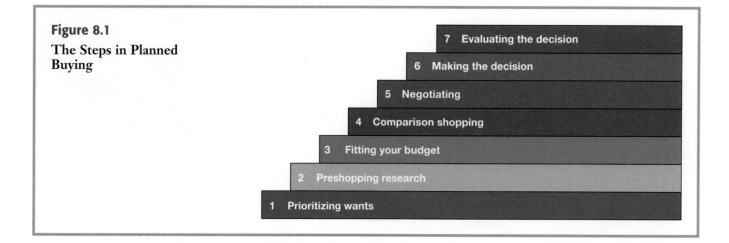

Figure 8.1

The Steps in Planned Buying

7 Evaluating the decision

6 Making the decision

5 Negotiating

4 Comparison shopping

3 Fitting your budget

2 Preshopping research

1 Prioritizing wants

Did You Know?...

How to Buy Smart

The ways that people waste money could fill the pages of a very long book. Fortunately, buying wisely can save you 10 or more percent during the course of a year. Smart buyers should practice the following habits:

Do Not Buy on Impulse

Buying without fully considering priorities and alternatives is called **impulse buying.** For example, let's say you're looking for a laptop computer and you decide to buy one on sale at a discount store. While at the store, you pick up two video games that you had not planned to buy. The extra $150 spent on the unplanned purchase ruins most of the benefits of your careful shopping for the computer itself.

Pay Cash

Paying cash whenever possible can save money in two ways. First, it helps control impulse buying, which is a temptation when you're paying with a credit card. Second, using credit adds to the cost of items you buy.

Buy at the Right Time

You can save $5 or $10 a week on food simply by stocking up on advertised specials. New cars are least expensive at the end of the month and the model year. Many items, such as sporting goods and clothing, are marked down near certain holidays and at the end of each season. But be certain that what you buy on sale is something you will really use.

Do Not Pay Extra for a "Name"

Buying generic and store-brand products represents a good way to save money. **Generic products** are sold under a general commodity name such as "whole-kernel corn" rather than a brand name such as Del Monte. Store-brand products, such as those sold by Sears (Kenmore), Kroger, or Safeway, are actually made by the brand-name manufacturers. Gasoline, vitamins, medicines, laundry and other soaps, and many grocery items are all products with minor quality differences.

Recognize the High Price of Convenience

Buying a few items daily at a convenience store rather than using a shopping list during a weekly visit to a supermarket can raise food bills by perhaps 30 percent. Shopping for furniture and appliances in one's local community may be convenient, but better prices on the same items may be found in larger, more competitive shopping areas or online.

AUTOMOBILE FEATURE	PRIORITY LEVEL		
	1	2	3
Adjustable steering column			✔
Side-impact airbags		✔	
Air conditioning		✔	
AM-FM radio	✔		
Antilock brakes		✔	
Automatic transmission	✔		
Keyless locking system	✔		
CD player			✔
Cruise control		✔	
4-Wheel (all-wheel) drive			✔
Power windows	✔		
Rear-window defroster	✔		
Sun roof / moon roof			✔
Theft-deterrent system			✔

Figure 8.2

Priority Worksheet (for Sharon Wilson)

preshopping research Gathering information before actually beginning to interact with sellers.

so, Sharon developed the worksheet shown in Figure 8.2. Such a worksheet makes it easier to formalize her wants and helps Sharon decide on the right car for her.

Become an Expert

Smart shoppers learn as much as they can about a product or service before buying. This process starts with **preshopping research**—gathering information before actually beginning to interact with sellers. Manufacturers, sellers, and service providers are all important sources of information about products and services during preshopping research. Two other sources are friends and consumer magazines. If you know someone who drives a car you're considering, ask that person's opinion of it. You can also research the car in *Consumer Reports*, a magazine that objectively tests and reports on numerous product categories. Monthly issues of *Consumer Reports* generally provide a two- to five-page narrative analyzing the products and summarizing the information in chart form. *Consumer Reports Buying Guide*, which is published every December, lists facts and figures for all kinds of products. And each year, the April issue of *Consumer Reports* is devoted entirely to the purchase of automobiles. All this and more can be seen at www.ConsumerReports.org.

When shopping for any product, it may help to review publications dedicated to the topic, such as *Popular Photography*, *PC World*, *Car and Driver*, and *Sound & Vision*. Keep in mind, however, that these trade magazines accept advertising for the products on which they report and thus are not likely to be as unbiased as *Consumer Reports*, which does not accept any advertising. Another unbiased source of information on wise buying (and many other personal finance topics) is the federal government's Consumer Information Center (www.pueblo.gsa.gov).

Good Money Habits in Vehicle and Other Major Purchases

Make the following your money habits in vehicle and other major purchases:

1. Think through all of your major purchases using the planned buying process.

2. When planning to buy vehicles, check repair ratings history in the April issue of *Consumer Reports* magazine.

3. Purchase late-model, high-quality used vehicles and check their ownership history at www.carfax.com and any recall history at www.nhtsa.gov.

4. Obtain price information from at least three sources and aggressively negotiate prices and financing terms for major purchases.

5. Never tell a seller what payment you can afford.

6. Promptly and firmly seek redress when dissatisfied with purchases or services.

What Price Should You Expect to Pay? Advertising is often a key source of information about prices. You can also obtain price information through catalogs, on the telephone, and over the Internet. This situation differs for big-ticket items. While the prices of furniture, appliances, and vehicles may be advertised, that price is rarely the lowest price you can expect to pay. This is because the seller has the authority to nego-

Time invested in preshopping research pays off in better purchase decisions.

tiate an even lower price, if necessary, to make a sale. Buyers should have a very good idea what price to expect to pay before going out to shop. Otherwise, they risk negotiating a price higher than necessary.

A key piece of price information for vehicles is the **manufacturer's suggested retail price (MSRP),** which is aptly named because it is simply the suggested initial asking price. On new automobiles, the MSRP—called the **sticker price**—appears on a window sticker in the vehicle. There is often a **dealer sticker price** as well, which includes additional charges tacked on by the dealer; many of these are nothing more than attempts to generate additional revenue. The sticker prices should in no way be seen as the price that needs to be paid for a new vehicle or other big-ticket item. Instead, it should be viewed as a starting point for negotiations. Smart buyers can research the average retail and wholesale prices on new and used vehicles by visiting the websites for Edmunds (www.edmunds.com), Kelley Blue Book (www.kbb.com), or the National Automobile Dealers Association (www.nadaguides.com).

What Is a Fair Interest Rate? Major purchases are often bought on credit. Interest rates for all types of loans, including vehicle loans, can be found at www.bankrate.com. Buyers should obtain multiple quotes from banks and credit unions. When shopping for a major purchase, ask your local bank or credit union for a **loan preapproval** before you visit sellers. This preshopping step will let you know how much you can borrow and at what interest rate.

A source of loans for new vehicles is sales financing arranged through the dealer or manufacturer. The interest rate on this credit is often low when manufacturers or dealers want to generate additional sales volume. The buyer must often choose between low-rate financing and a rebate (discussed later). See the Decision-Making Worksheet, "Choosing Between Low-Interest-Rate Dealer Financing and a Rebate," on page 212 for instructions on how to compare rebates, dealer/manufacturer financing, or other financing options.

Is a Rebate Available? Many sellers offer rebates to encourage people to buy. With a **rebate,** the seller refunds a portion of the purchase price of the product either as a direct payment or a credit against future purchases (often through a gift card). Vehicle manufacturers offer rebates of $1000 to $5000 to purchasers of new vehicles as a way to generate more sales volume or to move slow-selling models. In most cases, the buyer must choose between the rebate and a low APR loan offer also being offered by the manufacturer.

Many people choose to borrow the full price elsewhere and receive the rebate in cash. In effect, this option means that they are borrowing more money than the vehicle actually costs. Plus, the buyers also lose out on the opportunity for the low APR offer. The worksheet on page 212 provides a way to calculate whether a rebate or the low APR financing is the better option. If you do decide to take the rebate on a new vehicle, you should apply the money to the down payment on the vehicle or pay extra on the first monthly payment on the loan.

Rebates are common when purchasing products such as vehicles, cell phones, and computers. Why don't sellers simply lower the price of the item? First, rebate offers are temporary and thus do not affect the regular price of the item. Second, purchasers fail to redeem a high percentage (approaching 40 percent for some products) of rebates, which results in more profit for the seller.

Did You Know?...

Top 3 Financial Missteps in Big-Ticket Purchases

People slip up in purchasing vehicles and other big-ticket items when they do the following:

1. Rely upon the seller as their source of information for price, financing terms, and trade-in value

2. Tell a seller what they can afford to pay so the seller can avoid disclosing his or her lowest price

3. Don't complain when products fail to perform as expected

manufacturer's suggested retail price (MSRP)/sticker price Suggested initial asking price.

loan preapproval Oral commitment from a bank or credit union agreeing to furnish credit for a purchase; lets buyers know how much they can borrow and at what interest rate.

rebate A partial refund of a purchase price offered as an inducement to buy.

Decision-Making Worksheet

Choosing Between Low-Interest-Rate Dealer Financing and a Rebate

It is not uncommon to see ads for new vehicles offering low APRs for dealer-arranged loans. A cash rebate of $1000 to $3000 (or more) off the price of the car may be offered as an alternative to the low interest rate. If you intend to pay cash, then the cash rebate obviously represents the better deal. But which alternative is better when you can arrange your own financing?

To compare the two APRs accurately, you must add the opportunity cost of the forgone rebate to the finance charge of the dealer financing. The worksheet provides an example of this process. Suppose a dealer offers 2.9 percent financing for three years with a $907 finance charge; alternatively, you can receive a $3000 rebate if you arrange your own financing. The price of the car before the rebate is $22,000. Assume you can make a $2000 down payment and that you can get a 6.5 percent loan on your own. This worksheet can be found on the *Garman/Forgue* website, or you can find similar worksheets at www.bankrate.com (search for "calculators") or www.kiplingers.com/tools.

The lower of the values obtained in steps 3 and 4 is the better deal. In this instance, the financing that you arranged on your own is more attractive. In fact, any loan you arrange that carries an APR lower than 12 percent compares favorably with the dealer-arranged financing in this case.

Step		Example	Your Figures
1.	Determine the dollar amount of the rebate.	$3000	_____
2.	Add the rebate amount to the finance charge for the dealer financing (dollar cost of credit).	+ $ 907	_____
3.	Use the n-ratio APR formula from Chapter 7 [Equation (7.2) on page 201 and replicated here as Equation (8.1)] to calculate an adjusted APR for the dealer financing.		

$$APR = \frac{Y(95P + 9)F}{12P(P + 1)(4D + F)} \qquad (8.1)$$

where

APR = Annual percentage rate

Y = Number of payment periods in one year

F = Finance charge in dollars

D = Debt (amount borrowed)

P = Total number of scheduled payments

$$APR = \frac{(12)[(95 \times 36) + 9](\$3000 + \$907)}{(12 \times 36)(36 + 1)[(4 \times \$20,000) + (\$3000 + \$907)]}$$

12%

Step		Example	Your Figures
4.	Write in the APR that you arranged on your own.	6.5%	_____

What Is My Trade-in Worth? When buying vehicles, it is common, but not always advantageous, to trade in an old model when buying a new one. Vehicle buyers should know the true value of any vehicle they will trade in. Used-car trade-in values are available on the websites for Edmunds (edmunds.com), Kelley Blue Book (kbb.com), or the National Automobile Dealers Association (nadaguides.com). There you can find the likely trade-in value of the vehicle and the amount you could sell it for yourself. Armed with this information, you can more effectively negotiate a good trade-in allowance on your existing vehicle with a dealer.

Can I Afford It?

When considering a big-ticket item, everyone wonders, "Can I afford it?" An unaffordable cash purchase can wreck your budget for one or two months; the negative effects of an ill-advised credit purchase, however, may last for years.

One way to view the cost of a major expenditure is to consider the cost per use of the product. For example, Paul Lenz, an auto-worker from Dothan, Alabama, is considering buying a high-quality video camera. He has researched several models in the $700 to $750 price range. Paul figures that he would use the camera about 20 times per year and knows that the average video camera lasts about seven years, giving him 140 uses. Dividing this figure into the price of a $700 model yields a cost per use of $5 ($700 ÷ 140), excluding the cost of videotapes and maintenance. It might be possible for Paul to save money by renting or borrowing a camera when he needs one. Or he could buy a less expensive camera.

To see how this process works with a more expensive purchase, consider how Sharon Wilson (see page 215) might fit a new car into her budget. She estimates that the base sticker price of the car she wants will be about $16,000. This price includes her highest-priority wants. The lower-priority options will likely add a total of $2300 to the sticker price: side-impact airbags, $700; air conditioning, $700; antilock brakes, $600; and cruise control, $300. Buying a car with these features might cost Sharon $19,500 ($16,000 + $2300 for the options + $1200 for sales tax and title registration). She can use $2500 from her savings account as a down payment, receive $2000 for trading in her old car, and borrow the remaining $15,000. The actual price she will pay for the car will depend on her ability to negotiate the final price down from the sticker price. From her preshopping research, Sharon knows that the invoice price will be about 12 percent less than the sticker price, giving her some bargaining room. For example, Sharon might negotiate the price of the car down by 10 percent to $17,550 [$19,500 − ($19,500 × 0.10)].

The monthly payment that Sharon must fit into her budget will depend on five factors:

- Price she actually pays for the car
- Down payment she makes
- Time period for payback of the loan
- Amount she receives in trade for her old car
- Interest rate on the loan

For illustration, we will choose a down payment of $2500 and assume a 48-month time period (a common financing term). Sharon figures that she can get no more than $2000 for her old car. But what about the actual price and interest rate? Assuming that Sharon can reduce the price by 10 percent, she will need to borrow $13,050 ($17,550 − $2500 down − $2000 trade-in). If she obtains a loan with an 8 percent APR (based on her loan preapproval), Sharon estimates that her monthly payment would be about $318 (13.05 × 24.41, from Table 7.1 on page 199).

Table 8.1 shows Sharon's monthly budget. Her monthly take-home pay of $1765 is totally committed. To buy the automobile with options, she will need $318 per month and will have to change her budget drastically. For example, she could cut food expenditures ($30 per month); spend less on clothing ($50); cut entertainment, gifts, personal care, and miscellaneous items ($50, $10, $10, and $20, respectively); and put

Did You Know?...

About "Gap" Insurance

New cars and low-mileage used cars depreciate (go down in value) very quickly after purchase, often as much as 25 percent after leaving the dealer's lot. If you take out a vehicle loan with a low down payment, it is possible that the value of the vehicle will go down faster than the amount owed. As a result, you can owe more on the vehicle than it is worth. This situation is referred to as being **"upside down"** and can last for up to two years after the initial purchase.

Being upside down can be a big problem when a newer vehicle is totaled in an accident. In such cases, the insurance company will reimburse for the value of the vehicle, not the amount owed on the loan. Many car dealers sell **"gap" insurance** that pays off the remainder of the loan if the insurance payment is insufficient to do so. While gap insurance is attractive, it is very profitable for the dealer and not such a good deal for the buyer. You should consider the possibility of being upside down as a sign that you are not making a large enough down payment or that you are buying a vehicle that is too expensive for you.

"gap" insurance To insure against totaling a vehicle when one is upside down on it, dealers offer these programs that pay off the remainder of the loan if the insurance payment is insufficient to do so.

Instant Message

Be an Informed Shopper

Smart shoppers recognize that the seller is not an objective source of information. When making major purchases, you should go into the process with knowledge of what the item should cost, an appropriate interest rate if you will use credit, the availability of a rebate, and the value of any trade-in.

Advice from a Pro...

Tips for Buying Online

People use the Internet to shop for appliances, vehicles, furniture, and other big-ticket items. Here's how you can become a better online shopper:

1. Use only secure sites. A secure site will feature a key or lock symbol on its screens or have a URL starting with "https" ("s" for secure). Sites displaying the VeriSign symbol must meet certain security standards.

2. Only do business with sellers for which you have complete contact information, including a "snail mail" (postal) address and telephone number.

3. Review shipping policies and costs as well as return policies before placing your order.

4. Never use a debit card for online purchasing. When the debit card transaction is executed, your cash is immediately transferred from your account to the seller's account. It may be difficult to persuade a seller to give you a refund when you pay by debit card. Purchases made via credit cards give you more protection because you may be able to ask that a purchase be charged back (see Chapter 6).

5. Print and keep copies of all purchase documents, warranties, credit card authorizations, and shipping notices.

6. Use only one particular credit card for online purchases. This practice will serve you well if your account number is stolen. In such a case, you can notify the one credit card issuer of the theft and block the card's future use without affecting your other accounts.

7. Check the site's privacy policy. Sites that display the TRUSTe symbol or Better Business Bureau Online seal have agreed to meet certain privacy standards.

8. Opt out of any list sharing that the seller might conduct with other merchants.

9. Do not use your regular e-mail address. Set up a free address at Yahoo!, Hotmail, or other provider and use it solely for online transactions. This will reduce the spam coming into your everyday e-mail account.

Brenda J. Cude
University of Georgia

$50 less in savings (she was saving to buy a vehicle). In addition, her transportation-related expenses would change as follows: gasoline, −$20; maintenance and repairs, −$50; and insurance costs, +$20. (Always get an insurance quote before buying a vehicle.) In all, these efforts would raise only $270, still $48 short of the amount she needs for the car. Sharon's alternatives are to make more cutbacks in her budget, work overtime, or get a part-time job. She could also reduce her payments to about $264 per month by taking out a longer, 60-month loan (13.05 × $20.28, from Table 7.1 on page 199). She should be wary about having to operate on such a tight budget for five years, however. Sharon will pay much more in interest with a longer-term loan and she might want to consider a less expensive new car or a used car.

 ## CONCEPT CHECK 8.1

1. What is planned buying?

2. Distinguish between *needs* and *wants*, and explain why it may be better to act as if no needs exist.

3. Describe the types of information you need to be your own expert when making big-ticket purchases.

4. Summarize the process to determine whether you can afford a particular purchase.

Table 8.1 Fitting a Vehicle Payment into a Monthly Budget

	Prior Budget	Possible Cutbacks	New Budget
Food	$ 250	$ − 30	$ 220
Clothing/laundry	120	− 50	70
Vehicle maintenance and repairs	75	− 50	25
Auto insurance	60	20	80
Gasoline	90	− 20	70
Housing	450		450
Utilities	80		80
Telephone	50		50
Entertainment	150	− 50	100
Gifts	50	− 10	40
Church and charity	60		60
Personal care	60	− 10	50
Savings	200	− 50	150
Miscellaneous	70	− 20	50
TOTAL	**$1765**	**$ − 270**	**$1495**
Car payment			318
TOTAL WITH CAR PAYMENT	**$1765**	**$ − 270**	**$1813**

Use Comparison Shopping to Find the Best Buy

After completing the first three steps in planned buying, it is time to begin interacting with sellers. These interactions begin with comparison shopping. **Comparison shopping** is the process of comparing products or services to find the best buy. A **best buy** is a product or service that, in the buyer's opinion, represents acceptable quality at a fair or low price for that level of quality. Purchasing the product with the lowest price does not necessarily ensure a best buy; quality and features count, too. You can begin your comparison shopping online, but most likely you will need to visit different stores and talk to sellers directly.

Comparison shopping takes time and effort, but the payoff in both satisfaction and savings can be considerable. During the early steps in the comparison shopping process, shoppers should narrow their choices to specific makes and models and desired options. Then they should visit the appropriate sellers again. This time, shoppers will be much closer to the decision to buy and will be ready to discuss details, although they should not buy at this point. When comparison shopping, tell the salesperson exactly what interests you and ask about price and any dealer incentives and rebates that apply. You should inquire about financing options, leasing, warranties, and service contracts. Finally, test-drive the vehicle. The goal is to narrow the choice even further prior to negotiating for the very best deal, which is the next step in the buying process.

Compare Prices

Prices on big-ticket items such as autos, furniture, appliances, and electronic equipment are rarely the same from seller to seller and vary from week to week. Hundreds or even thousands of dollars can be saved by searching for the best prices. Experts recommend use of the "rule of three," which says to compare at least three alternatives before making any decision. When buying a car, compare the prices you find at dealers with the information from one of the websites devoted to vehicle prices listed on page 211.

Instant Message

Guard Your Privacy

Do not give out your Social Security number or allow the dealer to photocopy your driver's license before you go on a test drive. The dealer can then access your credit report and estimate how much you can afford to pay and your ability to obtain financing elsewhere.

Compare Financing Options

Sellers are not the only source of financing. Your bank or credit union loans money to make purchases. Also use websites such as bankrate.com or interest.com. Be on the lookout for "same as cash" offers on furniture, appliances, and electronics that allow you to delay interest or payment for, perhaps, 90 days to one year. If the product is paid off during this time period, you will not incur any finance charges. Be wary, however. Interest may be charged retroactively if a payment is late or if the purchase isn't fully paid off during the required time period.

Consider Leasing Instead of Buying

Leasing a new vehicle is an increasingly attractive option to people who are in the market for a car. About 20 percent of the new cars "sold" each year are actually leased. It is even possible to lease used cars. Is leasing a better deal than financing? You cannot answer this question until you understand some basics of leasing.

leasing Renting a product while ownership title remains with lease grantor.

When **leasing** a vehicle or any other product, you are, in effect, renting the product while the ownership title remains with the lease grantor. Regulation M issued by the Federal Reserve Board governs lease contracts. A requirement of this regulation is a mandatory disclosure of pertinent information about the lease that the consumer is considering. The disclosure form must summarize the offer of the lessor (leasing agency) to the lessee (consumer). The information in this form should be compared with the actual lease contract prior to signing to ensure that the lease signed is actually what was agreed upon verbally.

Did You Know?...

The Keys to a Safe Car

The following pointers may help you buy a safer vehicle:

- **Check government safety test results.** The federal government crash-tests motor vehicles to analyze their safety. For results on various makes and models, call the National Highway Traffic Safety Administration (NHTSA) "auto hotline" at (800) 424-9393 or visit www.safercar.gov.

- **Check on recalls.** When buying a used car, visit www.nhtsa.gov to see whether the vehicle has been recalled. If so, confirm that the repairs have been made to the car you're considering; if not, buy elsewhere. Dealers are required to fix for free vehicles recalled for safety reasons.

- **Consider a model with additional airbags.** All new cars have driver and passenger front-seat airbags. For added protection, consider new and used models that also provide side-impact airbags.

- **Look for antilock brakes.** Antilock brakes are believed to reduce the possibility of skidding during sudden stops. They are especially helpful in rain and inclement winter conditions.

- **Think about theft.** Some makes and models of vehicles are much more attractive to thieves than others. These vehicles also require higher auto insurance premiums. Visit www.nhtsa.gov and search "vehicle theft ratings."

Leasing Terminology   Five terms are important in leasing:

1. The **gross capitalized cost (gross cap cost)** includes the price of the vehicle plus what the leasor paid to finance the purchase plus any other items the lessee agree to pay for over the life of the lease, including insurance or a maintenance agreement.

2. **Capitalized cost reductions (cap cost reductions)** are monies paid on the lease at its inception, including any down payment, trade-in value, or rebate.

3. The **adjusted capitalized cost (adjusted cap cost)** is determined by subtracting the capitalized cost reductions from the gross capitalized cost.

4. The **residual value** is the projected value of a leased asset at the end of the lease time period.

5. The **money factor** (or **lease rate** or **lease factor**) measures the rent charge portion of your payment. Although the money factor is sometimes described by dealers as a figure for comparing leases, lease forms must carry the following disclosure about the money factor: "This percentage may not measure the overall cost of financing this lease."

Always negotiate the purchase price before discussing a lease. Leasing requires an initial outlay of cash to pay for the first month's lease payment and a security deposit. Payments are based on the capitalized cost of the asset minus any capitalized cost reductions and the residual value. This difference represents the cost of using the asset during the lease period; when divided by the number of months in the contract, it serves to establish the base for the monthly lease payment. (Some new vehicles are offered with single-payment leases in which the entire difference between the capitalized cost and residual value is paid up-front.) With monthly payment leases, the payments are lower than monthly loan payments for equivalent time periods because you are paying for only the reduction in the asset's value—not its entire cost. To compare the costs of leasing versus buying, use the Decision-Making Worksheet, "Comparing Automobile Financing and Leasing."

gross capitalized cost (gross cap cost) Includes vehicle price plus cost of any extra features such as insurance or maintenance agreements.

adjusted capitalized cost (adjusted cap cost) Subtracting the capitalized cost reductions from the gross capitalized cost.

residual value Projected value of leased asset at end of lease time period.

Open- and Closed-End Leases   A lease may be either open end or closed end. In an **open-end lease**, you must pay any difference between the projected residual value of the vehicle and its actual market value at the end of the lease period. When a vehicle depreciates more rapidly than expected, the holder of an open-end lease has to pay extra money when the lease expires. For example, a vehicle with an $11,000 residual value but a $10,250 market value would require an end-of-lease payment of $750 ($11,000 − $10,250). The Consumer Leasing Act limits this end-of-lease payment to a maximum of three times the average monthly payment.

Most vehicle leases are closed-end leases. In a **closed-end lease** (also called a **walkaway lease**), the holder pays no charge if the end-of-lease market value of the vehicle is lower than the originally projected residual value. However, closed-end leases may carry some type of end-of-lease charge if the vehicle has greater than normal wear or excess mileage. For example, a four-year closed-end lease might require a $0.30 per mile **excess mileage charge** in excess of 55,000 miles. If you actually drove the vehicle 60,000 miles during the four years, you would be charged an extra $1500 [$0.30 × 5000 (60,000 − 55,000)].

Additional Leasing Fees   Other charges are possible with a lease. An **acquisition fee** is either paid in cash or included in the gross capitalization cost. It pays for a credit report, application fee, and other paperwork. A **disposition fee** is assessed when you turn in the vehicle at the end of the lease and the lessor must prepare it for resale. An **early termination charge** may also be levied if you decide to end the lease prematurely. Be wary of a lease with an early termination charge, even if you do not

Instant Message

Buying Your Leased Vehicle

With either an open- or closed-end lease, you may purchase the vehicle at the end of the lease period. With an open-end lease, you would pay the actual cash value. With a closed-end lease, you would pay the residual value.

closed-end lease/walkaway lease Agreement in which the lessee pays no charge if the end-of-lease market value of the vehicle is lower than the originally projected residual value.

early termination charge Charge if lessee turns car in before the end of lease period.

Decision-Making Worksheet

Comparing Automobile Financing and Leasing

This worksheet can be used to compare leasing and borrowing to buy a vehicle. Remember that the cost of credit is the finance charge—the extra that you pay because you borrowed. Leases also carry costs, but they are hidden in the contract. Indeed, some may remain unknown until the end of the lease period. These lease costs, which are indicated by an asterisk (*), are negotiable and are defined in the text. Ask the dealer for the price of each item, as these fees must be disclosed by dealers. Then complete the worksheet and compare the dollar cost of leasing with the finance charge on a loan for the same time period.

To make the comparison accurately, you must know the underlying price of the car if you were purchasing it. Often you are not offered this value with a lease arrangement, so you should negotiate a price for the vehicle before mentioning your interest in leasing.

Shop for a lease through dealers and independent leasing companies because costs vary widely. This worksheet can be found on the *Garman/Forgue* website, or you can find similar worksheets at www.bankrate.com (search for "calculators") or www.kiplingers.com/tools.

Step		Example	Your Figures
1.	Monthly lease payment (36 payments of $275, for example)	$ 9,900	_____
2.	Plus acquisition fee* (if any)	300	_____
	Plus disposition charge* (if any)	300	_____
	Plus estimate of excess mileage charges* (if any)	0	_____
	Plus projected residual value of the vehicle	4,500	_____
3.	Amount for which you are responsible under the lease	15,000	_____
4.	Less the adjusted capitalized cost (gross capitalized cost* less the capitalized cost reductions*)	12,600	_____
5.	Dollar cost of leasing to be compared with a finance charge if you purchased the vehicle	2,400	_____

plan to end the lease early, because termination also occurs when a leased vehicle is traded in or is totally wrecked or stolen. Make sure you obtain a written disclosure of these charges well before you actually make your decision. The **early termination payoff** is the total amount you would need to repay if you end the lease agreement early; it includes both the early termination charge and the unpaid lease balance. In its early years, your lease may be financially upside down, which means that you owe more on the vehicle than it is worth.

Be Cautious About Leasing Getting a good deal on any vehicle can be very complicated—leasing is even more so. First, be cautious if you talk about buying all through the negotiation process only to be offered a lease at the last minute. Because the monthly charge will be lower, you may be tempted to sign a deal that actually costs considerably more. Second, make sure all oral agreements related to trade-in value, mileage charges, and rebates are included in the lease contract. Third, watch out for additional fees being assessed, especially near the very end of the negotiations or in the final written lease.

One option for people considering a lease is a balloon automobile loan. You can arrange this type of financing through your bank or credit union. With a **balloon automobile loan,** you actually buy the vehicle with the last monthly payment equal-

balloon automobile loan A loan that has a low monthly payment similar in amount to that required if the vehicle had been leased and with a large final payment similar in amount to the residual value under a lease.

ing the projected residual value of the vehicle at the end of the loan period. This arrangement effectively lowers all the other earlier monthly payments to make them more competitive with lease payments. When the final balloon payment is due, perhaps $1000 to $7000, the borrower generally has three options:

1. Sell the car and pay the balloon payment with the proceeds (with luck, the vehicle will sell for a high enough amount).

2. Pay the balloon payment and keep the vehicle.

3. Return the vehicle to the lender to cover the balloon payment.

Compare Warranties

Warranties are an important consideration in comparison shopping. Almost all products have **warranties**—assurances by sellers that goods are as promised and that certain steps will be taken to rectify problems—even if only in the form of implied warranties. The longer the warranty and the more it covers, the better the warranty.

Under an **implied warranty,** the product sold is warranted to be suitable for sale (a **warranty of merchantability**) and to work effectively (a **warranty of fitness**) whether or not a written warranty exists. Implied warranties are required by state law. To avoid them, the seller can state in writing that the product is sold **as is.** If you buy any product "as is," you have no legal recourse if it fails to perform, even if the salesperson made verbal "promises" to take care of any problems. Used cars are often sold "as is."

Written and oral warranties are called **express warranties.** Companies that offer written express warranties must do so under the provisions of the federal Magnuson-Moss Warranty Act if the product is sold for more than $15. This law provides that any written warranty offered must be classified as either a full warranty or a limited warranty. A **full warranty** includes three stringent requirements:

1. A product must be fixed at no cost to the buyer within a reasonable time after the owner has complained.

2. The owner will not have to undertake an unreasonable task to return the product for repair (such as ship back a refrigerator).

3. A defective product will be replaced with a new one or the buyer's money will be returned if the product cannot be fixed after a reasonable number of attempts.

A **limited warranty** includes less than a full warranty. For example, it may offer only free parts, not labor. Note that one part of a product could be covered by a full warranty (perhaps the engine on a lawnmower) and the rest of the unit by a limited warranty. Read all warranties carefully, and note that both full and limited warranties are valid for only a specified time period.

Extended Warranties Are Overpriced

An **extended warranty** (or **service contract**) is an agreement between the contract seller (the dealer, manufacturer, or an independent company) and the buyer of a product to provide repair or replacement for covered components of the product for some specified time period. Extended warranties are sometimes given names such as **maintenance agreement** or **buyer protection plan**. These contracts are purchased separately from the product itself (such as a vehicle, appliance, or electronics equipment). The cost is paid either in a lump sum or in monthly payments. Extended warranties are similar to insurance. For example, a 40-inch LC HDTV could have an extended warranty that promises to fix anything that goes wrong during the third and fourth years of ownership; the manufacturer's warranty covers the first two years. This contract might cost $120 for one year, or $10 per month.

Although buying an extended warranty might provide peace of mind, it is unwise financially because it makes little economic sense to insure against risks that can, if necessary, be paid for out of current income or savings. More than 80 percent of all

warranty Sellers' assurances that goods are as promised and that certain steps will be taken to rectify problems if they arise.

"as is" Way for seller to get around legal requirements for warranties; buyer takes all risk of nonperformance or other problems despite any salesperson's verbal assurances.

full warranty Warranty that meets three stringent promises: product must be fixed at no cost to buyer within reasonable time, owner will not have to undertake an unreasonable task to return product for repair, and defective product will be replaced with a new one or the buyer's money will be returned if product cannot be fixed.

limited warranty Any warranty that offers less than the three conditions for full warranty.

extended warranty/service contract/maintenance agreement/buyer protection plan Agreement between the seller and buyer of product to repair or replace covered product components for some specified time period; purchased separately from product itself.

tion fee on the car, which is projected to have a residual value of $8100 at the end of the lease. Use the Decision-Making Worksheet on page 218 to advise about Amanda whether she should buy or lease the car.

2. Kyle Parker of Fayetteville, Arkansas, has been shopping for a new car for several weeks. So far, he has negotiated a price of $27,000 on a model that carries a choice of a $2500 rebate or dealer financing at 2 percent APR. The dealer loan would require a $1000 down payment and a monthly payment of $564 for 48 months. Kyle has also arranged for a loan from his bank with a 7 percent APR. Use the Decision-Making Worksheet on page 212 to advise Kyle about whether he should use the dealer financing or take the rebate and use the financing from the bank.

Financial Planning Cases

Case 1
Purchase of a New Refrigerator

Tracy Sullivan, a financial consultant from Spokane, Washington, is remodeling her kitchen. Tracy, who lives alone, has decided to replace her refrigerator with a new model that offers more conveniences. She has narrowed her choices to two models. The first is a basic 20.2-cubic-foot model with a bottom freezer for $799. The second is a 25.4-cubic-foot model with side freezer for $999. Additional features for this model include icemaker, textured enamel surface, and ice and water dispenser. Tracy's credit union will loan her the necessary funds for one year at a 12 percent APR on the installment plan. Following is her budget, which includes $2140 in monthly take-home pay.

Food	$ 300
Entertainment	120
Clothing	60
Gifts	70
Charities	75
Car payment	330
Personal care	60
Automobile expenses	120
Savings	130
Housing	825
Miscellaneous	50
Total	**$2140**

(a) What preshopping research might Tracy do to select the best brand of refrigerator?

(b) Using the information in Table 7.1 on page 119 or the *Garman/Forgue* website, determine Tracy's monthly payment for the two models.

(c) Fit each of the two monthly payments into Tracy's budget.

(d) Advise Tracy to help her make her decision.

Case 2
A Dispute over New-Car Repairs

Christopher Hardison, a high school football coach from Oklahoma City, Oklahoma, purchased a new SUV for $28,000. He used the vehicle often; in fact, in less than nine months he had put 14,000 miles on it. A 24,000-mile, two-year warranty was still in effect for the power-train equipment, although Christopher had to pay the first $100 of each repair cost. After 16,500 miles and in month 11 of driving, the car experienced some severe problems with the transmission. Christopher took the vehicle to the dealer for repairs. A week later he picked the car up, but some transmission problems remained. When Christopher took the car back to the dealer, the dealer said that no further problems could be identified. Christopher was sure that the problem was still there, and he was amazed that the dealer would not correct it. The dealer told him he would take no other action.

(a) Was Christopher within his rights to take the car back for repairs? Explain why or why not.

(b) What logical steps might Christopher follow if he continues to be dissatisfied with the dealer's unwillingness or inability to repair the car?

(c) Should Christopher seek any help from the court system? If so, describe what he could do without spending money on attorney's fees.

Case 3
Victor and Maria Hernandez Buy a Third Car

The Hernandezes' older son, Hector, has reached the age at which it is time to consider purchasing a car for him. Victor and Maria have decided to give Maria's old car to Hector and buy a later-model used car for Maria.

(a) What sources can Victor and Maria use to access price and reliability information on various makes and models of used cars?

(b) What sources of used cars might be available to Victor and Maria, and what differences might exist among them?

(c) How might Victor and Maria check out the cars in which they are most interested?

(d) What strategies might Victor and Maria employ when they negotiate the price for the car they select?

Case 4
The Johnsons Decide to Buy a Car

The Johnsons have decided to move out of their apartment and into some form of owned housing. Although they have not decided what type of housing they will buy, they know that Belinda will no longer be able to ride the bus to work. Recognizing this fact, they are in the market for another car. They have decided not to buy a new car but think they have some room in their budget for a used car, given the raises each has received this year (see Table 3.8 on page 83). Harry and Belinda estimate that they could afford to spend about $3200 on an inexpensive used car by making a down payment of $600 and financing the remainder over 24 months at $120 per month.

(a) Make suggestions about how the $120 might be integrated into the Johnsons' budget (Table 3.8 on page 83) without changing the amount left over at the end of each month. Harry and Belinda want to retain that extra money to help defray some of the added expenses of home ownership.

(b) Which sources of used cars should they consider? Why?

(c) Assume that the Johnsons have narrowed their choices to two cars. Both have air conditioning, AM-FM radio, and automatic transmission. The first car is an eight-year-old Chevrolet Lumina with 102,000 miles; it is being sold for $3400 by a private individual. The hatchback-style car has a six-cylinder engine, and the seller has kept records of all repairs, tune-ups, and oil changes. The car will need new tires in about six months. The second car is a nine-year-old, two-door Ford Focus with 116,000 miles, being sold by a used-car dealership. It has a four-cylinder engine. Harry contacted the previous owner and found that the car was given in trade on a new car about three months ago. The previous owner cited no major mechanical problems but simply wanted a bigger car. The dealer is offering a written 30-day warranty on parts only. The asking price is $3200. Which car would you advise the Johnsons to buy? Why?

On the 'Net

Go to the Web pages indicated to complete these exercises. You can also go to the *Garman/Forgue* website at college.hmco.com/business/students for an expanded list of exercises. Under General Business, select the title of this text. Click on the Internet Exercises link for this chapter.

1. Visit the website for the Kelley Blue Book at http://www.kbb.com. For a used vehicle you currently own or one you would like to own, determine its "used car retail value," "trade-in value," and "private party value." Why do the three values differ?

2. Visit the website of *Consumer Reports* magazine at http://www.consumerreports.org and click on the "Cars" tab. You will be sent to a page containing tips on buying new and used cars. In what ways are the strategies similar and in what ways do they differ from the tips offered in this book for buying a used car?

3. Visit the website of the Federal Reserve Board at http://www.federalreserve.gov/consumers.htm where you will find a Web page titled "Keys to Vehicle Leasing" that expands upon the information in this book. Use this information to generate a list of pros and cons of leasing versus purchasing a vehicle. By clicking on "sample leasing form" on this Web page, you can view and print a copy of the required vehicle leasing disclosure form.

Visit the Garman/Forgue website ...

@college.hmco.com/business/students

Under General Business, select *Personal Finance 9e*. There, among other valuable resources, you will find a complete glossary, ACE questions, links to help you complete the chapter exercises, and links to other personal finance sites.

CHAPTER 9

Buying Your Home

You Must Be Kidding, Right?

Horst Brandt recently bought a new home and borrowed $140,000 at 6.75 percent interest for 30 years. His monthly payment for interest and principal will be $908. A friend suggested that Horst should have easily been able to find a loan at 6.5 percent with a monthly payment of $885. Horst dismissed his friend's comments, arguing that the difference in the monthly payments was no big deal. His friend replied, "Horst, it's not the monthly payment, it's the interest." How much more in interest will Horst pay over the life of the loan because he took a loan with the higher rate?

A. $350

B. $4200

C. $8460

D. $10,500

The answer is C. Horst will be making a higher payment for each and every month for 30 years. While the difference in the monthly payment seems small [$23 ($908 − $885) per month in this example], even a small difference in the interest rates on mortgage loans can add up to thousands of dollars in extra interest over the life of the loan. That is why searching for the lowest possible interest rate is so important when borrowing to buy a home!

LEARNING OBJECTIVES

After reading this chapter, you should be able to:

1 **Decide** whether renting or owning your home is better for you both financially and personally.

2 **Explain** the up-front and monthly costs of buying a home.

3 **Describe** the steps in the home-buying process.

4 **Distinguish among** the conventional and alternative ways of financing a home, and list the advantages and disadvantages of each.

5 **Identify** the important aspects of selling a home.

What Do You Recommend?

Libby Clark has worked for a major consumer electronics retailer since graduating from college. The company has operations across the country with regional headquarters in Atlanta, Denver, Minneapolis, and Boston. She has been based in the Atlanta area for the past three years and had begun thinking about buying a home there rather than renting her townhouse apartment. Then, last month, Libby was promoted to deputy regional director for the Denver region. The promotion represents a key step for becoming a regional director in four or five years. Regional directors may or may not be promoted from within their current region.

What do you recommend to Libby on the subject of buying a home regarding:

1. Buying or renting housing in the Denver area?

2. Steps she should take prior to actively looking at homes?

3. Finding a home and negotiating the purchase?

4. The closing process in home buying?

5. Selecting a type of mortgage to fit her needs?

6. Things to consider regarding the sale of her home should she ultimately be promoted to a position in another of the four regions?

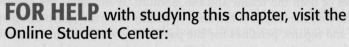

FOR HELP with studying this chapter, visit the **Online Student Center:**

www.college.hmco.com/pic/garman9e

Online Study Center

1. Visit the website for Bankrate.com (http://www .bankrate.com/brm/rate/mtg_home.asp), where you will find information on mortgage interest rates around the United States. View the information for the lenders in a large city near your home. How does the information compare with the interest rates on your own credit card account(s)? How do the rates in the city you selected compare with other rates found in the United States?

2. Visit the website for the United States Department of Housing and Urban Development, where you will find a calculator (http://www.hud.gov/buying/index .cfm#afford) that helps you determine the amount you can afford for the purchase of a home given your income and funds available for a down payment, closing costs, and other home-buying expenses. Enter the data requested for your current situation. What does the calculator tell you about your housing affordability? Change the entered data for some point in the future when you project a better financial situation for yourself. How do the results change?

3. Visit the website for the National Association of Realtors (realtor.com), where you can search for owned housing in various locales around the United States. Look for housing in your community of a type that would interest you and that is in your price range. Were you able to find housing that meets your criteria? Also search for similar housing in the San Diego, California (high-cost area), and Syracuse, New York (low-cost area), metropolitan areas. Compare these cost results with the housing found in your area.

Visit the Garman/Forgue website ...

@college.hmco.com/business/students

Under General Business, select *Personal Finance 9e*. There, among other valuable resources, you will find a complete glossary, ACE questions, links to help you complete the chapter exercises, and links to other personal finance sites.

PART 3

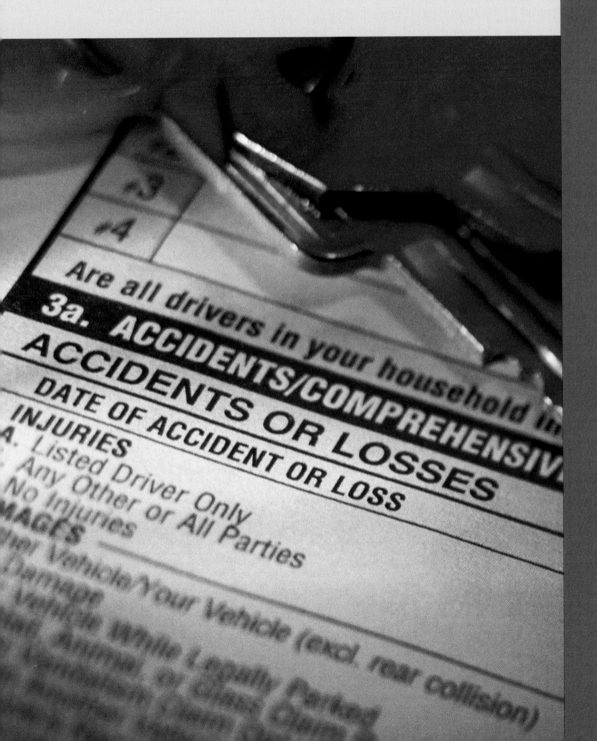

CHAPTER 10

Managing Property and Liability Risk

You Must Be Kidding, Right?

Tiffany Blake recently caused an automobile accident when she had a blowout on the freeway. Her car crossed the median and was struck by two other cars. The cost of repairs to Tiffany's car will be $13,200, which exceeds the car's $12,500 fair market value. The damage to the other two vehicles was $17,800 and $6400, respectively. Fortunately, no one was injured in the accident. On the advice of her insurance agent, Tiffany had purchased an auto insurance policy with a $500 collision deductible and liability limits of $25,000/$50,000/$15,000 when she purchased her car. What dollar amount of these losses will be covered by her policy?

A. $12,700   **B.** $27,000   **C.** $36,200   **D.** $37,400

The answer is B. Tiffany carried collision insurance, which covers her vehicle. The company will pay her $12,000, which is the fair market value of the vehicle less her $500 deductible. The company will take title to her vehicle, and she can use the $12,000 to find another car. The company will also pay $15,000 for the damage to the other vehicles. This is the limit for property damage liability under her policy. Tiffany will be personally responsible for the additional $9200 ($17,800 + $6,400 − $15,000) in damage to the other vehicles. Always buy high liability coverage limits!

LEARNING OBJECTIVES

After reading this chapter, you should be able to:

1 **Apply** the risk-management process to address the risks to your property and income.

2 **Explain** basic insurance terms and the relationship between risk and insurance.

3 **Design** a homeowner's or renter's insurance program to meet your needs.

4 **Design** an automobile insurance program to meet your needs.

5 **Describe** other types of property and liability insurance.

6 **Summarize** how to make an insurance claim.

What Do You Recommend?

George and Emily Cosgrove of Athens, Georgia, recently had a fire in their garage that destroyed two of their cars and did considerable damage to the garage and to the outside of their home. After receiving their reimbursements from their homeowner's and automobile insurance policies, the Cosgroves realized that they were severely underinsured. One vehicle was not insured for fire, and the insurance on their dwelling amounted to only 60 percent of its current replacement value.

What do you recommend to George and Emily about managing property and liability risk regarding:

1. The risk-management steps they should take to update their insurance coverages?

2. The relationship between severity and frequency of loss when deciding whether to buy insurance?

3. Adequately insuring their home?

4. The use of deductibles and policy limits to keep their automobile insurance premiums at a manageable level while still maintaining vital coverage?

FOR HELP with studying this chapter, visit the Online Student Center:

www.college.hmco.com/pic/garman9e

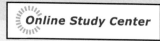

Up to this point, this book has focused on ways to manage your money and strategies for using financial resources to achieve your personal goals. But it is just as important to protect your resources and assets from the possibility of financial loss. Losses can result from accidents, acts of nature, illness or injury, and death. You can manage the risk of these losses through the effective use of insurance. Chapter 11 focuses on losses related to illness or injury, and Chapter 12 looks at losses related to death. This chapter focuses on losses that occur from accidents and acts of nature. Such losses stem from two possibilities. First, your property might be damaged. **Property insurance** protects you from financial losses resulting from the damage to or destruction of your property or possessions. Second, you might be held responsible, or liable, for losses suffered by others. **Liability insurance** protects you from financial losses suffered when you are held liable for the losses of others. The two major forms of property and liability insurance are insurance for your home and its contents and insurance for your ownership and use of vehicles.

property insurance Protection from financial losses resulting from the damage to or destruction of your property or possessions.

liability insurance Protection from financial losses suffered when you are held liable for others' losses.

risk Uncertainty about the outcome of a situation or event.

Risk and Risk Management

The Nature of Risk

1 LEARNING OBJECTIVE
Apply the risk-management process to address the risks to your property and income.

Risk is uncertainty about the outcome of a situation or event. It arises out of the possibility that the outcome will differ from what is expected. In the area of potential financial losses, risk consists of uncertainty about whether the financial loss will occur and how large it might be. There are two types of risk. **Speculative risk** exists in situations where there is potential for gain as well as for loss. Investments such as those made in the stock market involve speculative risk. **Pure risk** exists when there is no potential for gain, only the possibility of loss. Fires, automobile accidents, illness, and theft are examples of events involving pure risk. Insurance addresses pure risk.

Good Money Habits in Managing Property and Liability Risk

Make the following your money habits in managing property and liability insurance risk:

1. Always insure your home and vehicles.

2. Purchase insurance policies with very high liability limits to protect against the possibility of catastrophic losses.

3. Verify that your auto insurance policy covers rental car losses so you can wisely ignore sales pressure to purchase such overpriced coverage.

4. Always comparison shop for insurance locally as well as online.

5. Maintain a verifiable inventory of all your insured property so that you can collect what is coming to you in the event of a loss.

6. Once each year, reassess what types of and how much insurance coverage you need.

Many people think of "odds" or games of chance when they hear the word **risk**. In fact, risk and chance are different concepts. The difference between the two is subtle but very important. An event with a 95 percent chance of occurring is highly likely to occur. Thus, both uncertainty and risk are low. An event with a 0.000001 percent chance of occurring is highly likely *not* to occur. Thus, both uncertainty and risk are low. When an event has a moderate chance of occurring—5 percent, for example—the uncertainty and risk are relatively high because it is difficult to predict the one person in 20 who will experience the event. In such cases, insurance often represents a wise choice for reducing risk.

The Risk-Management Process

Risk management is the process of identifying and evaluating situations involving pure risk to determine and implement the appropriate means for its management. The goal is to minimize any risk or potential for risk through advance planning. Risk management entails making the most efficient arrangements before a loss occurs so as to minimize any after-loss effects on your financial status. It is an important part of overall personal financial management, as it preserves the benefits of your other financial planning efforts. Insurance is merely one of many possible ways of handling risk, and it is not always the best choice.

risk management Process of identifying and evaluating purely risky situations to determine and implement appropriate management.

Table 10.1   The Risk-Management Process

	Possessions	Activities	Accompanying Perils
Step 1 *Identify sources of risk.*	Vehicle House Jewelry	Driving Smoking Traveling	Accident Fire Theft
Step 2 *Estimate risk and potential losses.*	(a) Determine the likely frequency of losses associated with each exposure. (b) Determine the potential severity and magnitude of losses associated with each exposure.		
Step 3 *Choose how to handle risk.*	(a) Avoid risk. (b) Retain risk. (c) Control losses. (d) Transfer risk. (e) Reduce risk.		
Step 4 *Implement the risk-management plan.*	(a) Refrain from certain activities. (b) Take extra precautions. (c) Buy insurance.		
Step 5 *Evaluate and adjust the program.*			

The risk-management process involves five steps; Table 10.1 outlines these steps in the risk-management process.

Step 1: Identify Sources of Risk Sources of risk, called **exposures,** are the items you own and the activities in which you engage that expose you to potential financial loss. Owning and/or driving an automobile is a common exposure. In risk management, you take an inventory of what you own and what you do in order to identify your exposures to loss.

You face the possibility of loss in one of four ways:

1. First, you may suffer a loss to your property, such as can happen during a house fire.
2. Second, you could be held legally responsible for losses suffered by others such as if you cause an automobile accident.
3. Third, you may become ill or be injured and have costs associated with health care.
4. Fourth, you may suffer a loss of income as a result of illness, accident, or death.

You also need to identify the perils that you face. A **peril** is any event that can cause a financial loss. Fire, wind, theft, vehicle collision, illness, and death are all examples of perils.

peril Any event that can cause a financial loss.

Step 2: Estimate Risk and Potential Losses Once you identify your exposures to risk, you estimate both loss frequency and loss severity. **Loss frequency** refers to the likely number of times that a loss might occur over a period of time. **Loss severity** describes the potential magnitude of the loss(es).

Many people wonder whether they should buy insurance when loss frequency is low, for example if they are young and healthy or if they live in a safe neighborhood. This is not a good way to think about potential losses. If loss frequency is low, the insurance would simply cost less. Figure 10.1 illustrates the relationship between loss severity and loss frequency in risk management.

What is more important is loss severity. "How much might I lose?" is the question you should ask. When considering possible property losses, you simply make an estimate of the value of the property. Liability losses are more complicated because the severity of the loss depends on the circumstances of the person you harm. For example, if you caused an accident that permanently disabled a young heart surgeon with three small children, you would be liable for the surgeon's care, lost earnings over the surgeon's lifetime, and future care and education of the children. A loss of several million dollars is not out of the question in such a situation.

Step 3: Choose How to Handle Risk The risk of loss may be handled in five ways: risk avoidance, risk retention, loss control, risk transfer, and risk reduction. Each strategy may be appropriate for certain circumstances, and the mix that you choose will depend on the source of the risk, the size of the potential loss, your personal feelings about risk, and the financial resources you have available to pay for losses.

- **Risk avoidance.** The simplest way to handle risk is to avoid it. With this approach, you would refrain from owning items or engaging in activities that expose you to possible financial loss. For example, choosing not to own an airplane or not to skydive limits your exposure. Avoiding risk is not always practical, however.
- **Risk retention.** A second way to handle risk is to retain or accept it. The risk that the shrubbery around your house might die during a dry spell is such a retained risk. Conscious risk retention plays an important role in risk management. Risk retention due to ignorance or inaction is not effective risk management. For example, many people unwisely put off the purchase of life insurance because they consider it to be a morbid, unpleasant task.
- **Loss control.** Loss control, the third method of handling risk, is designed to reduce loss frequency and loss severity. For example, installing heavy-duty locks and doors will reduce the *frequency* of theft losses. Installing fire alarms and smoke detectors cannot prevent fires but will reduce the *severity* of losses from them. Insurance companies often require loss-control efforts or give discounts to policyholders who implement them.
- **Risk transfer.** A fourth way to handle risk is to transfer it. In a risk transfer, an insurance company agrees to reimburse you for a financial loss. For example, a professional football team's star run

Instant Message

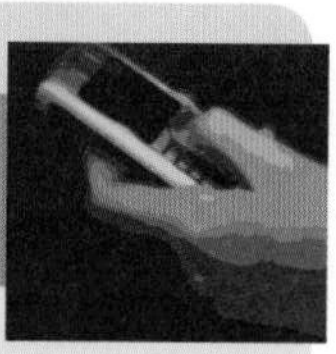

Driving Exposes You to Huge Potential Losses

The average driver will be involved in an accident approximately once every seven years, with the severity of these accidents ranging from a minor fender bender to catastrophic collisions bringing losses in the hundreds of thousands of dollars.

Did You Know?...

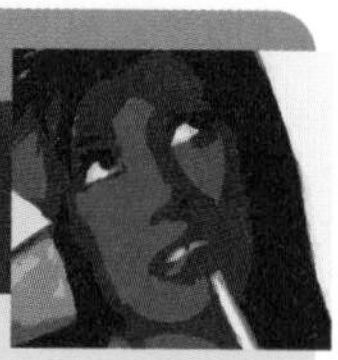

Top 3 Financial Missteps in Managing Property and Liability Risk

People slip up in managing property and liability risk when they do the following:

1. Buy only the legal minimum coverage on the liability insurance on their car
2. Fail to keep good records (e.g., lists, photos, receipts) that could serve to document insured property losses
3. Pay high premiums because they select low deductibles on property insurance for their home and car

Figure 10.1
The Relationship Between Severity and Frequency of Loss

	HIGH SEVERITY	LOW SEVERITY
LOW FREQUENCY	Purchase insurance to cover the potentially large losses. Their infrequency will make premiums affordable.	Consider retaining risk because the frequency and severity of loss are both low.
HIGH FREQUENCY	Purchase insurance. Loss control efforts can be useful in reducing the necessarily high premiums.	Retain risk but also budget for losses that are likely to be frequent.

ning back might take out an insurance policy on his legs. In this case, the uncertainty is simply transferred from the running back or his team to an insurance company. Insurance represents one method of transferring risk, although not all risk transfers can be classified as insurance because insurance goes beyond merely transferring risk to the actual reduction of risk.

- **Risk reduction.** The fifth way to handle risk is to reduce it to acceptable levels. Insurance is used by policyholders when they arrange for all or a portion of their risk to be covered by an insurance company, thereby reducing their personal level of risk.

risk reduction Includes mechanisms, such as insurance, that reduce the overall uncertainty about the magnitude of loss.

Step 4: Implement the Risk-Management Program The fourth step in risk management is to implement the risk-handling methods you have chosen. For most households, this means buying insurance to transfer and reduce risk. This involves selecting types of policies and coverage, dollar amounts of coverage, and sources of insurance protection.

People often wonder what types of insurance to buy and how many dollars of coverage to choose. You should use the maximum possible loss as a guide for the dollar amount of coverage to buy. This way of thinking makes use of the **large-loss principle:** Insure the losses that you cannot afford and assume the losses that you can reasonably afford. In other words, pay for small losses out of your own pocket and purchase as much insurance as necessary to cover large, catastrophic losses that will ruin you financially. The example earlier of an auto accident that injures a heart surgeon would bring you such ruin because you would be held responsible for those losses. Consequently, you would want high dollar amounts of liability coverage on your auto insurance.

large-loss principle A basic rule of risk management that encourages us to insure the losses that we cannot afford and assume the losses that we can reasonably afford.

Step 5: Evaluate and Adjust the Program The final step in risk management entails periodic review of your risk-management efforts. The risks people face in their lives change continually. Therefore, no risk-management plan should be put in place and then ignored for long periods of time. For certain exposures, such as ownership of an automobile, an annual review

Instant Message

Buy—Don't Be Sold—Insurance

Always remember that your goal is to "buy" the insurance you need at a fair price. Do not let yourself be "sold" more or less insurance coverage than you need at excessive prices. Visit www.insquote.com and www.quotesmith.com once you have decided what insurance you need.

Renters need home insurance, too.

is appropriate. For areas involving life insurance, a review should occur about once every three to five years or whenever family structure and employment situations change. The necessary adjustments should be implemented promptly to reflect changes over your life cycle. Many people stick with existing policies that no longer fit their needs (too little or too much coverage) simply because they buy once and ignore their insurance needs for years.

✔ *CONCEPT CHECK 10.1*

1. Distinguish between pure risk and speculative risk.
2. Explain the distinctions between risk and odds.
3. Describe the five steps of risk management.
4. Based on likelihood of loss and severity of loss, explain why one is more important when deciding whether to buy insurance.

Understanding How Insurance Works

2 LEARNING OBJECTIVE

Explain basic insurance terms and the relationship between risk and insurance.

insurance Mechanism for transferring and reducing pure risk through which a large number of individuals share in the financial losses suffered by members of the group as a whole.

premium Comparatively small, predictable fee with which individuals or companies can replace an uncertain—and possibly large—financial loss.

insurance policy Contract between the person buying insurance (the insured) and the insurance company (the insurer).

Insurance is a mechanism for transferring and reducing pure risk through which a large number of individuals share in the financial losses suffered by members of the group as a whole. Insurance protects each individual in the group by replacing an uncertain—and possibly large—financial loss with a certain but comparatively small fee. This fee, called the **premium,** has four components:

• The individual's share of the group's losses
• Insurance company reserves set aside to pay future losses
• A proportional share of the expenses of administering the insurance plan
• An allowance for profit (when the plan is administered by a profit-seeking company)

Insurance premiums are assessed on an annual or semiannual basis. You generally will be charged an extra amount if you choose to make the payments monthly.

The **insurance policy** is the contract between the person buying insurance (the **insured**) and the insurance company (the **insurer**). It contains language that describes the rights and responsibilities of both parties. Most people do not take the time to read and understand their insurance policies. As a result, insurance remains one of the least understood purchases people make. You can do a much better job of managing your risks if you understand the basic terms and concepts used in the field of insurance.

Instant Message

Can Your Insurance Company Honor Its Promises?

Insurance companies must have the financial strength to pay losses as promised. You can assess your company's financial strength at http://www.standardandpoors.com by clicking on "Ratings" and then "Insurance."

Hazards Make Losses More Likely to Occur

A **hazard** is any condition that increases the probability that a peril will occur. Driving under the influence of alcohol represents an especially dangerous hazard. Three types of hazards exist:

• A **physical hazard** is a particular characteristic of the insured person or property that increases the chance of loss. An example of a physical hazard is high blood pressure in a person covered by health insurance.
• A **morale hazard** exists when a person is indifferent to a peril. For example, a morale hazard exists if the insured party, knowing that theft insurance will pay for the loss, becomes careless about locking doors and windows.
• A **moral hazard** exists when an insured person wants a peril to occur so that he or she can collect on an insurance policy.

Insurance companies often limit or deny coverage if a loss occurs as a result of a morale or moral hazard.

Only Certain Losses Are Insurable

Certain minimum requirements must be met for a loss to be considered insurable—in particular, the loss must be fortuitous, financial, and personal. **Fortuitous losses** are unexpected in terms of both their timing and their magnitude. A loss caused by a lightning strike and fire to your home is fortuitous; a loss caused by a decline in the market value of your home is not because it is reasonable to expect home values to rise and fall over time. A **financial loss** is any decline in the value of income or assets in the present or future. Financial losses can be measured objectively in dollars and cents. When you become sick, you suffer as a result of the discomfort, inconvenience, lost wages, and medical bills. Insurance will cover only the lost wages and medical bills, however, because these losses—but not the others—can be objectively measured. Finally, **personal losses** can be directly suffered by specific individuals or organizations rather than society as whole.

The Principle of Indemnity Limits Insurance Payouts

The **principle of indemnity** states that insurance will pay *no more* than the actual financial loss suffered. For example, an automobile insurance policy will pay only the actual cash value of a stolen automobile. This principle prevents a person from gaining financially from a loss. Furthermore, it does not guarantee that insured losses will be totally reimbursed. Every policy includes **policy limits,** which specify the maximum dollar amounts that will be paid under the policy. These limits explain why there is no such thing as "full coverage" insurance—there is always the potential that a loss will exceed the limits on a policy. As a result, insurance purchasers must carefully select policy limits sufficient to cover their potential losses.

principle of indemnity Insurance will pay *no more* than the actual financial loss suffered.

policy limits Specify the maximum dollar amounts that will be paid under the policy.

Factors That Reduce the Cost of Insurance

Some specific features of insurance policies can lower your premiums without significantly reducing the protection offered. These features include deductibles, coinsurance, hazard reduction, and loss reduction.

Deductibles are requirements that you pay an initial portion of any loss. For example, automobile collision insurance often includes a $200 deductible. With such a policy, the first $200 of loss to the car must be paid by the insured. The insurer then pays the remainder of the loss, up to the limits of the policy. You usually have a choice of deductible amounts.

Coinsurance is a method by which the insured and the insurer share proportionately in the payment for a loss. For example, health insurance policies commonly require that the insured pay 20 percent of a loss and the insurer pay the remaining 80 percent. Substantial premium reductions can be realized through coinsurance, but you must be prepared to pay your share of losses. The following *deductible and coinsurance reimbursement formula* can be used to determine the amount of a loss that will be reimbursed when the policy includes a deductible and a coinsurance clause:

deductibles Requirements that the policyholder pays an initial portion of any loss.

coinsurance Method by which the insured and the insurer share proportionately in the payment for a loss.

$$R = (1 - CP)(L - D) \qquad (10.1)$$

where

R = Reimbursement
CP = Coinsurance percentage required of the insured
L = Loss
D = Deductible

As an example, assume you have a health insurance policy with a $100 deductible per hospital stay and a 20 percent coinsurance requirement. If the hospital bill is $1350, the reimbursement will be $1000, calculated as follows:

$$R = (1.00 - 0.20)(\$1350 - \$100)$$
$$= (0.80)(\$1250)$$
$$= \$1000$$

Hazard reduction is action taken by the insured to reduce the probability of a loss occurring. Insurance companies often offer reduced premiums to insureds who practice hazard reduction—for example, to nonsmokers.

Loss reduction is action taken by the insured to lessen the severity of loss if a peril occurs. Smoke alarms and fire extinguishers in the home are examples of loss reduction efforts. These items will not prevent fires, but their use may lead to less severe damage. Many property insurers offer reduced premiums to insureds who practice loss reduction.

The Essence of Insurance

Insurance consists of two basic elements: the reduction of risk and the sharing of losses. When you buy insurance, you exchange the uncertainty of a potentially large financial loss for the certainty of a fixed insurance premium, thereby reducing your

Did You Know?...

How to Read an Insurance Policy

Insurance policies do not invite casual reading. Consequently, many people fail to thoroughly examine their policies until a loss occurs, only to find that they had misunderstood the terms of the agreement. You can avoid such problems by systematically reading a policy before you purchase it, focusing on eight points:

1. **Perils covered.** Some policies list only the perils that are covered; others cover all perils except those listed. The definition of certain perils may differ from that used in everyday language.

2. **Property covered.** Like perils, the property covered under a policy may be listed individually, or only the excluded property may be listed. When the property is listed individually, any new acquisitions must be added to the policy.

3. **Types of losses covered.** Three types of property losses can occur: (a) the loss of the property itself, (b) extra expenses that may arise because the property is rendered unusable for a period of time, and (c) loss of income if the property was used in the insured's work.

4. **People covered.** Insurance policies may cover only certain individuals. This information usually appears on the first page of the policy but may be changed subsequently in later sections.

5. **Locations covered.** Where the loss occurs may have a bearing on whether it will be covered. It is especially important to know which locations are not covered.

6. **Time period of coverage.** Policies are generally written to cover specific time periods. Restrictions may exclude coverage during specific times of the day or certain days of the week or year.

7. **Loss control requirements.** Insurance policies often stipulate that certain loss control efforts must be maintained by the insured. For example, coverage for a vehicle may be denied if the owner knowingly allows it to be driven by an unlicensed person.

8. **Amount of coverage.** All insurance policies specify the maximum amount the insurer will pay for various types of losses.

The information on these eight points may be spread throughout a policy. In fact, coverage that appears to be provided in one location actually may be denied elsewhere. Carefully review the entire policy to determine the protection it provides. If necessary, telephone the salesperson or company to obtain clarification.

risk. Risk is reduced for the insurer as well through the **law of large numbers:** As the number of members in a group increases, predictions about the group's behavior become increasingly more accurate. This greater accuracy decreases uncertainty and, therefore, risk.

To illustrate, consider a city of 100,000 households in which the probability of a fire striking a household is 1 in 1000, or 0.1 percent. Thus, 100 home fires are likely to occur each year in this community. If we focus on groups of 100 households at a time, we cannot predict very accurately whether a fire will strike a house in a given group. Some groups might have two or three fires, while others might experience none. If we combine all the households into one group, however, we can more accurately predict that 100 fires will occur (100,000 × 0.001). Even if 103 fires occurred, our prediction would be in error by only a small percentage. Insurance companies, which may have millions of customers, can be even more accurate in their group predictions.

Individual insurance purchasers benefit regardless of whether they actually suffer a loss because of the reduction of risk. This is the essence of insurance. Reduced risk gives one the freedom to drive a car, own a home, and plan financially for the future with the knowledge that some unforeseen event will not result in financial disaster.

Who Sells Insurance

Sellers of insurance, called **insurance agents,** represent one or more insurance companies. They have the power to enter into, change, and cancel insurance policies on behalf of these companies. Two types of insurance agents exist: independent agents and exclusive agents.

law of large numbers As the number of members in a group increases, predictions about the group's behavior become increasingly accurate.

insurance agent Representative of an insurance company authorized to sell, modify, service, and terminate insurance contracts.

binder Temporary insurance contract replaced later by written policy.

underwriting Insurer's procedure for deciding which insurance applicants to accept.

Did You Know?...

How Companies Select Among Insurance Applicants

The purchase of insurance begins with an offer by the purchaser in the form of a written or oral policy application. The insurer typically issues a temporary insurance contract, called a **binder,** which is replaced at a later date with a written policy. The application then goes through a process of **underwriting**—that is, the insurer's procedure for deciding which insurance applicants to accept. To describe the process of underwriting, it is necessary to first understand how insurance rates are set.

An **insurance rate** is the price charged for each unit of insurance coverage. Rates represent the average cost of providing coverage to various **classes of insureds;** these classes consist of insureds who share similar characteristics. For example, automobile insurance policyholders may be classified by age, gender, marital status, and driving record, as well as by the make and model of vehicle that they drive.

When underwriters receive an application, they assign the applicant to the appropriate class. They then determine whether the rates established for that class are sufficient to provide coverage for that applicant. Underwriters divide insurance applicants into four groups:

- *Preferred* applicants have lower-than-average loss expectancies and may qualify for lower premiums.

- *Standard* applicants have average loss expectancies for their class and pay the standard rates.

- *Substandard* applicants have higher-than-average loss expectancies and may be charged higher premiums and have restrictions placed on the types or amounts of coverage they may purchase.

- *Unacceptable* applicants have loss expectancies that are much too high and are rejected.

It is common for insurance companies to use an applicant's credit report to provide information used in underwriting. (This is another reason for maintaining good credit and for making sure your credit bureau files are accurate!) You can save money by confirming with your agent that you have been placed in the proper class for premium-determination purposes. Verifying that you are in the proper class is also important because a claim may be denied if premiums were based on an inappropriate classification.

direct sellers Companies that market insurance policies through salaried employees, mail-order promotions, newspapers, the Internet, and even vending machines.

Independent insurance agents are independent business-people who act as third-party links between insurers and insureds. Such agents earn commissions from the companies they represent and will place each insurance customer with the company that they believe best meets that customer's particular needs.

Exclusive insurance agents represent only one insurance company for a specific type of insurance. They are employees of the insurance company they represent. Life insurance, for example, is often sold through exclusive insurance agents.

Not all companies use agents to market their policies. Companies referred to as **direct sellers** market their policies through salaried employees, mail-order promotions, newspapers, the Internet, and even vending machines. Any type of insurance can be sold directly. For risk managers who know what coverage they need, the lowest insurance premiums can be found with direct sellers.

Each type of seller presents both advantages and disadvantages. Independent agents may provide more personalized service and can select among several companies to meet a customer's needs. Exclusive agents can provide personalized service as well but are limited to the policies offered by the one company they represent; their sales commissions tend to be low.

✔ CONCEPT CHECK 10.2

1. Define *insurance*.
2. Distinguish among the three types of hazards.
3. Why is the principle of indemnity so important to insurance sellers?
4. Identify four key points to review when reading an insurance policy.
5. Summarize how to use deductibles, coinsurance, hazard reduction, and loss reduction to lower the cost of insurance.
6. Differentiate among independent agents, exclusive agents, and direct sellers.

Homeowner's Insurance

3   LEARNING OBJECTIVE
Design a homeowner's or renter's insurance program to meet your needs.

homeowner's insurance Combines liability and property insurance coverages that homeowners and renters typically need into single-package policies.

Whether you own or rent housing, you face the possibility of suffering property and liability losses. **Homeowner's insurance** combines the liability and property insurance coverages needed by homeowners and renters into a single-package policy. Four types of homeowner's insurance are available for people who own houses, another type for the owners of condominiums, and one other type for those who rent housing.

Coverages

The standard homeowner's insurance policy is divided into two sections.

Property Insurance Section I provides protection for various types of property damage losses, including the following: (1) damage to the dwelling, (2) damage to other structures on the property, (3) damage to personal property and dwelling contents, and (4) expenses arising out of a loss of use of the dwelling (for example, food and lodging). Additional coverages are usually provided for such items as debris removal, trees and shrubs, and fire department service charges.

An important variable related to Section I of a policy involves the number of loss-causing perils that are covered. **Named-perils policies** cover only those losses caused by perils that are specifically mentioned in the policy. **All-risk (or open-perils) policies** cover losses caused by all perils other than those specifically excluded by the policy. All-risk policies provide broader coverage because hundreds of perils can cause property losses, but only a few would be excluded.

Liability Insurance Section II deals with liability insurance. Whenever home-owners are negligent or otherwise fail to exercise due caution in protecting visitors, they may potentially suffer a liability loss. **Homeowner's general liability protection** applies when you are legally liable for the losses of another person. Homeowners often wish to take responsibility for the losses of another person regardless of the legal liability. Consider, for example, a guest's child who suffers burns from touching a hot barbecue grill. **Homeowner's no-fault medical payments protection** will pay for bodily injury losses suffered by visitors regardless of who was at fault. In the preceding example, such coverage would help pay for the medical treatment of the visitor's burns. **Homeowner's no-fault property damage protection** will pay for property losses suffered by visitors to your home. An example of such a loss might be damage to a friend's leather coat that was chewed by your dog.

Types of Homeowner's Insurance Policies

Six distinct types of homeowner's insurance policies exist: HO-1 through HO-4, HO-6, and HO-8. They are described in detail in Table 10.2 on page 280 and more generally in the sections that follow. The same terms and identifying numbers are generally used by most insurance companies.

Basic Form (HO-1) The **basic form (HO-1)** is a named-perils policy that covers 11 property-damage–causing perils and provides three areas of liability-related protection: personal liability, property damage liability, and medical payments. The most common perils that can cause property damage—fire and lightning, windstorm, theft, and smoke—are covered in the basic homeowner's policy. People who have finished basements (perhaps a TV room or spare bedroom) should purchase additional sewer backup coverage, as this possibility is not one of the 11 named perils.

Broad Form (HO-2) The **broad form (HO-2)** is a named-perils policy that covers 18 property-damage–causing perils and provides protection from the three liability-related exposures.

Special Form (HO-3) The **special form (HO-3)** provides open-perils protection (except for the commonly excluded perils of war, earthquake, and flood) for four types of property losses: losses to the dwelling, losses to other structures, landscaping losses, and losses generating additional living expenses. Contents and personal property are covered on a named-perils basis for 17 of the 18 common homeowner's perils (the exception is glass breakage). In terms of liability protection and in all other respects, the coverage under HO-3 is the same as under HO-2.

Renter's Contents Broad Form (HO-4) The **renter's contents broad form (HO-4)** is a named-perils policy that protects the insured from losses to the contents of a dwelling rather than the dwelling itself. It covers 17 perils and provides liability protection. HO-4 is ideal for renters because it provides protection from losses to dwelling contents and personal property and provides for additional living expenses if the dwelling is rendered uninhabitable by one of the covered perils. Although insurance is relatively inexpensive, only one-fourth of all renters carry HO-4 protection.

named-perils policies Cover only losses caused by perils that the policy specifically mentions.

all-risk (open-perils) policies Cover losses caused by all perils other than those that the policy specifically excludes.

homeowner's general liability protection Applies when you are legally liable for another person's losses, other than those that arise out of use of vehicles or your professional duties.

basic (homeowner's insurance) form (HO-1) Named-perils policy that covers 11 property-damage–causing perils and provides three areas of liability-related protection: personal liability, property damage liability, and medical payments.

special (homeowner's insurance) form (HO-3): Provides open-perils protection (except for the commonly excluded perils of war, earthquake, and flood) for four types of property losses.

renter's contents broad form (HO-4) Named-perils policy that protects the insured from losses to the contents of a rented dwelling rather than the dwelling itself.

Condominium Form (HO-6) The **condominium form (HO-6)** is a named-perils policy protecting condominium owners from the three principal losses they face: losses to contents and personal property, losses due to the additional living expenses that may arise if one of the covered perils occurs, and liability losses. (The building itself is insured by the management of the condominium.) Two additional coverages are included in the HO-6 policy as necessary to meet the specific needs of the condominium unit owner. The first is protection against losses to the structural alterations and additions that condominium owners sometimes make when they remodel their units. The second is supplemental coverage for the dwelling unit to protect the condominium owner if the building is not sufficiently insured.

Older Home Form (HO-8) The replacement value of an older home may be much higher than its market or actual cash value. The **older home form (HO-8)** is a named-perils policy that provides actual-cash-value protection on the dwelling. It does not provide that the dwelling be rebuilt to the same standards of style and quality, as those standards may be prohibitively expensive today. Instead, the policy provides that the dwelling be rebuilt to make it serviceable.

Buying Homeowner's Insurance

Three questions must be answered when buying a homeowner's policy. First, how much coverage will you need to replace the dwelling itself? Second, how much coverage will you need on the contents and personal property in general and for expensive items such as jewelry or antiques in particular? Third, how much coverage will you need for liability protection?

How Much Coverage Is Needed on Your Dwelling? Both property and liability losses can occur to owners or renters of housing. Your first step is to determine the dwelling's replacement value. You could either use the services of a professional liability appraiser or consult with your insurance agent to determine replacement value.

replacement-cost requirement Stipulates that a home *must* be insured for 80 percent of its replacement value (some companies require 100 percent) in order for any loss to be fully covered.

Homeowner's insurance policies usually contain a **replacement-cost requirement** that stipulates that a home *must* be insured for 80 percent of its replacement value (some companies require 100 percent). Thus, a home with a replacement value of $200,000 would need to be insured for $160,000 (or perhaps $200,000), and this amount would be the maximum that the insurance company would be obligated to pay for a total loss (after payment of the deductible by the policyholder). If you fail to meet your replacement-cost requirement, you will not be considered fully insured and must coinsure partial losses as well. The amount of reimbursement for partial losses will be calculated using the *replacement-cost-requirement formula:*

$$R = (L - D) \times [I \div (RV \times 0.80 \text{ or } 1.00)] \tag{10.2}$$

where

R = Reimbursement payable
L = Amount of loss
D = Deductible, if any
I = Amount of insurance actually carried
RV = Replacement value of the dwelling

Consider the example of Chris Shearer from East Lansing, Michigan, who owns a home with a replacement value of $200,000 with a $500 deductible. Chris had insured his home for $144,000, even though the policy required coverage of 80 percent of the replacement cost. Last month a fire in his home caused damage amounting to $80,500. Applying Equation (10.2), Chris's calculations are as follows:

$$R = (\$80,500 - \$500) \times [\$144,000 \div (\$200,000 \times 0.80)]$$
$$= \$80,000 \times (\$144,000 \div \$160,000)$$
$$= \$80,000 \times 0.90$$
$$= \$72,000$$

As this calculation shows, Chris will be reimbursed for only $72,000 of his loss. His failure to insure his house for 80 percent of its replacement cost, or $160,000 ($200,000 × 0.80), means he will be covered for only 90 percent ($144,000 ÷ $160,000) of its value, and he must pay 10 percent of any partial loss—in this case, $8000. Three out of four homes in the United States are underinsured by an average of 35 percent.

Meeting an 80 percent replacement-cost requirement enables you to avoid coinsurance on small losses but might still result in inadequate coverage on large losses that, though rare, exceed the policy limit. Thus, it is wise to insure your dwelling for 100 percent of its replacement cost. To do so, you can arrange to have your insurance company increase your coverage automatically each year to keep up with inflation in housing construction costs.

How Much Coverage Is Needed on Your Personal Property?

Making an inventory of, and placing a value on, all the contents of your home are time-consuming but important tasks. Table 10.3 shows the inventory and valuation for the contents of and personal property in a typical living room. You should conduct such an inventory for each room, the basement, garage, shed, and yard possessions. When totaled, these values will enable you to select proper policy coverage limits.

Most homeowner's policies will automatically cover contents and personal property for up to 50 percent of the coverage on the home. For example, if your home is insured for $240,000, you would have $120,000 in personal property insurance. If you need more coverage, simply notify your agent. Some types of personal property may be subject to specific item limits. For example, the typical homeowner's insurance policy provides maximum coverages of $200 for cash, $5000 for personal computers, and $1000 for jewelry. This is because most people do not have such items above these values. If your inventory reveals a higher valuation on such items, you can simply ask your company for extra coverage and pay the higher premium required.

Notice that Table 10.3 lists three estimates for the value of the contents of a room: the purchase price, the actual cash value, and the replacement cost. Historically, property insurance policies paid only the **actual cash value** of an item of personal property, which represents the purchase price of the property less depreciation. The *actual-cash-value (ACV) formula* is

$$ACV = P - [CA \times (P \div LE)] \qquad (10.3)$$

where

P = Purchase price of the property
CA = Current age of the property in years
LE = Life expectancy of the property in years

Consider the case of Marianna Kinard, a music teacher from Orangeburg, South Carolina, whose nine-year-old heating/air-conditioning unit was struck by lightning. The unit cost $2400 when new and had a total life expectancy of 12 years. Its actual cash value when it was struck by lightning was

$$ACV = \$2400 - [9 \times (\$2400 \div 12)]$$
$$= \$2400 - (9 \times \$200)$$
$$= \$600$$

Instant Message

Be Alert for Special Limits

Certain unusual and high-cost types of personal property carry special limits of liability as low as $200 or $1000. Such items include stamps, furs, jewelry, and guns. If you wish higher limits, simply notify your insurer.

actual cash value (of personal property) Represents the purchase price of the property less depreciation.

Table 10.2   Summary of Homeowner's Insurance Policies

	HO-1 (Basic Form)	HO-2 (Broad Form)	HO-3 (Special Form)
Perils covered (descriptions are given below)	Perils 1–11	Perils 1–18	All perils except those specifically excluded for buildings; perils 1–18 on personal property (does not include glass breakage)

Property coverage/limits

	HO-1 (Basic Form)	HO-2 (Broad Form)	HO-3 (Special Form)
House and any other attached buildings	Amount based on replacement cost, minimum $15,000	Amount based on replacement cost, minimum $15,000	Amount based on replacement cost, minimum $20,000
Detached buildings	10 percent of insurance on the home (minimum)	10 percent of insurance on the home (minimum)	10 percent of insurance on the home (minimum)
Trees, shrubs, plants, etc.	5 percent of insurance on the home, $500 maximum per item	5 percent of insurance on the home, $500 maximum per item	5 percent of insurance on the home, $500 maximum per item
Personal property	50 percent of insurance on the home (minimum)	50 percent of insurance on the home (minimum)	50 percent of insurance on the home (minimum)
Loss of use and/or additional living expense	10 percent of insurance on the home	20 percent of insurance on the home	20 percent of insurance on the home
Credit card, forgery, counterfeit money	$1000	$1000	$1000

Liability coverage/limits (for all policies)

Comprehensive personal liability	$100,000
No-fault medical payments	$1000
No-fault property damage	$500

Special limits of liability

For the following classes of personal property, special limits apply on a per-occurrence basis (e.g., per fire or theft): money, coins, bank notes, precious metals (gold, silver, etc.), $200; computers, $5000; securities, deeds, stocks, bonds, tickets, stamps, $1000; watercraft and trailers, including furnishings, equipment, and outboard motors, $1000; trailers other than for watercraft, $1000; jewelry, watches, furs, $1000; silverware, goldware, etc., $2500; guns, $2000.

List of perils covered

1. Fire, lightning
2. Windstorm, hail
3. Explosion
4. Riots
5. Damage by aircraft
6. Damage by vehicles owned or operated by people not covered by the homeowner's policy
7. Damage from smoke
8. Vandalism, malicious mischief
9. Theft
10. Glass breakage
11. Volcanic eruption
12. Falling objects (external sources)
13. Weight of ice, snow, sleet
14. Collapse of building or any part of building (specified perils only)
15. Leakage or overflow of water or steam from a plumbing, heating, or air-conditioning system
16. Bursting, cracking, burning, or bulging of a steam or hot water heating system, or of appliances for heating water
17. Freezing of plumbing, heating, and air-conditioning systems and home appliances
18. Injury to electrical appliances and devices (excluding tubes, transistors, and similar electronic components) from short circuits or other accidentally generated currents

Note: This table describes the standard policies. Specific items differ from company to company and from state to state. When you want a limit that exceeds the standard limit for your company, you usually can increase the limit by paying an additional premium.

HO-4 (Renter's Contents Broad Form) Perils 1–9,11–18	HO-6 For Condominium Owners) Perils 1–18	HO-8 (For Older Homes) Perils 1–11
10 percent of personal property insurance on additions and alterations to the apartment	$1000 on owner's additions and alterations to the unit	Amount based on actual cash value of the home
Not covered	Not covered (unless owned solely by the insured)	10 percent of insurance on the home (minimum)
10 percent of personal property insurance, $500 maximum per item	10 percent of personal property insurance, $500 maximum per item	5 percent of insurance on the home, $500 maximum per item
Chosen by the tenant to reflect the value of the items, minimum $6000	Chosen by the homeowner to reflect the value of the items, minimum $6000	50 percent of insurance on the home (minimum)
20 percent of personal property insurance	40 percent of personal property insurance	20 percent of insurance on the home
$1000	$1000	$1000

Table 10.3   Personal Property Checklist: Living Room

Item	Date Purchased	Purchase Price	Actual Cash Value	Replacement Cost
Furniture				
Sofa	8/03	$ 750	$ 375	$ 950
Chair	11/01	250	100	375
Lounger	12/04	575	300	695
Ottoman	12/04	100	50	120
Bookcase	4/06	275	225	300
End table (2)	7/07	300	250	300
Appliances				
TV	1/07	550	500	600
DVD	6/06	400	300	400
Wall clock	7/01	60	10	100
Furnishings				
Carpet	6/00	375	50	600
Painting	12/04	125	225	225
Floor lamp	4/02	150	50	225
Art (three items)	10/06	600	600	800
Table lamp	4/02	75	40	100
Table lamp	5/06	125	100	135
Throw pillows	7/03	45	20	60
TOTAL		$4755	$3195	$5985

(e) To whom and how much will David's medical protection pay?

(f) How much reimbursement will David receive for his car?

(g) How much will David be required to pay out of his own pocket?

David Smith's Accident: Who Pays What?

Coverage	David's Policy	Ashley's Policy
Liability (limits)		
Bodily injury		
Ashley		
Fran		
Cecilia		
Medical payments (limits)		
David		
Ashley		
Fran		
Cecilia		
Collision coverage (limits)		
David's car		
Ashley's car		
David's out-of-pocket expenses		
Fran's bodily injury		
Excess property damage losses		
Collision insurance deductible		
TOTAL		

Decision-Making Cases

Case 1
The Princes' Auto Insurance Is Not Renewed

Mark and Katrina Prince of Jacksonville, Florida, face a crisis. Their automobile insurance company has notified them that their current coverage expires in 30 days and will not be renewed. Both Mark and the Princes' younger son had minor, at-fault accidents during the past year. Their children are otherwise good drivers, as are both parents. The Princes are confused because they know families whose members have much worse driving records but still have insurance.

(a) Explain to Mark and Katrina why their policy might have been canceled.

(b) Use the box on page 283 to give Mark and Katrina some pointers on how to save money on their new policy.

Case 2
Abigail Contemplates a New Homeowner's Insurance Policy

Abigail Elizabeth Proctor of Bedford, Oregon, recently bought a home for $200,000. The previous owner had a $160,000 HO-1 policy on the property, and Abigail can simply pay the premiums to keep the same coverage in effect. Her insurance agent called her and cautioned that she would be better off to upgrade the policy to an HO-2 or HO-3 policy. Abigail has turned to you for advice. Use the information in Table 10.2 to advise her.

(a) What additional property protection would Abigail have if she purchased an HO-2 policy?

(b) What additional property protection would Abigail have if she purchased an HO-3 policy?

(c) What property protection would remain largely the same whether Abigail had an HO-1, HO-2, or HO-3 policy?

(d) Advise Abigail on what differences in liability protection, if any, exist among the three policies.

Case 3
A Student Buys Insurance for a Used Car

Makiko Iwanami, a student from Osaka, Japan, is in one of your classes. She is considering the purchase of a used car and has been told that she must buy automobile insurance to register the car and obtain license plates. Makiko has come to you for advice, and you have decided to focus on three aspects of automobile insurance.

(a) Explain how liability insurance works in the United States. Advise Makiko about which liability insurance limits she should select.

(b) Makiko is especially impressed that automobile insurance includes medical payments coverage because she has no health insurance. Explain why the medical payments coverage does not actually solve her health insurance problem, and describe the type of coverage it provides.

(c) Makiko plans to pay cash for the car and doesn't want to spend more than $3000. Outline the coverage provided by collision insurance and factors that might make such coverage optional for Makiko.

Case 4
An Argument About the Value of Insurance

You have been talking to some friends about insurance. One young married couple in the group believes that insurance is really a waste of money in most cases. They argue, "The odds of most bad events occurring are so low that you need not worry." Furthermore, they say, "Buying insurance is like pouring money down a hole; you rarely have anything to show for it in the end." Based on what you have learned from this chapter, how might you argue against this couple's point of view?

Case 5
The Hernandezes Consider Additional Liability Insurance

Victor and Maria's next-door neighbor, Jasmine Saunders, was recently sued over an automobile accident and was held liable for $437,000 in damages. Jasmine's automobile policy limits were 100/300/50. Because of the shortfall, she had to sell her house and move into an apartment. Victor and Maria are now concerned that a similar tragedy might potentially befall them. They have a homeowner's policy with $100,000 in comprehensive personal liability coverage, an automobile policy with 50/100/25 limits, and a small ($100,000) professional liability policy through Maria's employer.

(a) How might Victor and Maria more fully protect themselves through their homeowner's and automobile insurance policies?
(b) What additional benefits would they receive in buying an umbrella liability policy?

Case 6
The Johnsons Decide How to Manage Their Risks

The financial affairs of the Johnsons have become much more complicated since we began following them in Chapter 2. Both Harry ($275 per month) and Belinda ($300 per month) have been given raises at work. They have purchased a $125,000 condominium that has added about $400 per month to their housing expense. They have purchased a used car for $3200, adding about $120 per month to their expenses. As a result of these changes, Harry and Belinda realize that they now face greater risks in their financial affairs. They have decided to review their situation with an eye toward managing their risks more effectively. Use Table 10.1, their net

worth and income and expense statements at the end of Chapter 3, and other information in this chapter to answer the following questions:

(a) What are Harry and Belinda's major sources of risk from home and automobile ownership, and what is the potential magnitude of loss from each?
(b) Given the choices listed in step 3 of Table 10.1, how should the Johnsons handle the sources of risk listed in part a?

On the 'Net

Go to the Web pages indicated to complete these exercises. You can also go to the *Garman/Forgue* website at college.hmco.com/business/students for an expanded list of exercises. Under General Business, select the title of this text. Click on the Internet Exercises link for this chapter.

1. Visit the website for the Insurance Information Institute at http://www.iii.org/individuals/auto/a/stateautolaws/, where you will find a summary of the automobile insurance requirements in each state. Determine the minimum automobile insurance liability limits in your state. How do these minimums compare with those in other states? How well insured do you feel someone would be if they carried only these minimums?

2. Visit the website for the National Association of Insurance Commissioners, where you will find a map at http://www.naic.org/state_web_map.htm through which you can link to your state insurance regulator's website. If available in your state, obtain an insurance buyer's guide for automobile and homeowner's insurance that describes policy provisions and compares insurance rates. Use these rate comparisons to select two automobile insurance companies that would be appropriate for your needs. Write or telephone the companies to obtain specific premium quotations for the desired insurance protection. Do the same for single-family dwelling, condominium, or renter's insurance, depending on your circumstances.

3. Visit the website for the Insurance Institute for Highway Safety at http://www.iihs.org/ratings/default.aspx. For your own vehicle and one or two you would like to own, check how the vehicles stack up against the competition in terms of injury protection.

Visit the Garman/Forgue website ...

@college.hmco.com/business/students

Under General Business, select *Personal Finance 9e*. There, among other valuable resources, you will find a complete glossary, ACE questions, links to help you complete the chapter exercises, and links to other personal finance sites.

CHAPTER 11

Managing Health Expenses

You Must Be Kidding, Right?

Amber Parker is a 32-year-old married mother with two children, ages 3 and 4. She worked out of her home as a medical transcriptionist for a local hospital. Her employer offered a medical care plan that Amber had chosen from her menu of employment benefits. Last year Amber suffered severe head injuries in a bicycling accident. Amber's wounds have healed and she has regained her ability to speak but is not yet able to walk on her own or use her hands and arms very well. Amber is recuperating at home but requires a daily paid caregiver to assist with her personal needs. Her children now go to daycare, and it may be 5 years before she can work again. Which of the following aspects of her injury were covered by Amber's medical care plan?

A. Her hospital stay and surgery

B. Her at-home custodial care

C. The cost of daycare for her children

D. Her lost income

The answer is A. Having a medical care plan is a must, but your protection is incomplete until you have addressed the need for rehabilitation and custodial care and for the potential lost income from a period of disability!

LEARNING OBJECTIVES

After reading this chapter, you should be able to:

1 **Identify** ways that people can manage the financial burdens resulting from illness or injury.

2 **Distinguish** among the types of protection for direct medical expenses.

3 **Describe** the general benefits and limitations of medical care plans.

4 **Explain** how to protect yourself from the expenses for long-term care.

5 **Develop** a plan for protecting your income when you cannot work due to disability.

What Do You Recommend?

Danielle DiMartino is a 43-year-old single mother with two children, ages 10 and 14. Her 10-year-old daughter has a history of ear infections that require doctor's office visits four or five times per year. Danielle's 71-year-old mother lives with the family for financial reasons; she has hereditary high blood pressure and high cholesterol as well as diabetes. Danielle's mother has enrolled in Medicare Parts A and B.

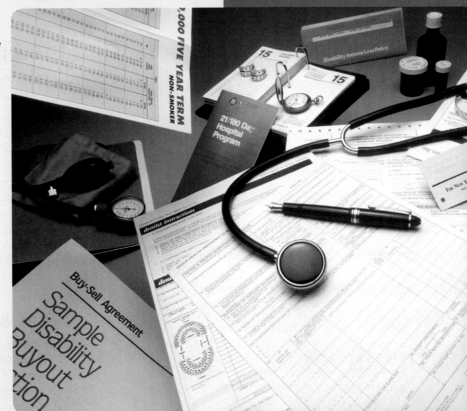

Danielle's employer sponsors a medical care plan to cover the company's workers, their spouses, and their dependents. Danielle has four options: (1) the basic HMO managed by a local university medical school/hospital with no additional cost for Danielle, but with additional cost of $122 per month to cover her children, (2) a health insurance plan with a PPO at that same medical center for an additional cost of $245 per month, (3) a traditional health insurance plan that provides access to virtually all medical care providers in her community for $455 per month, and (4) a high-deductible plan with a $5000 deductible at no additional cost. Danielle's employer offers no disability income or long-term care group plan. She does receive 10 sick days per year, which can accumulate to 60 days if not taken. Danielle has accumulated 30 days.

What would you recommend to Danielle DiMartino on the subject of managing health expenses regarding:

1. Choosing among the four alternatives available to her?

2. Danielle's concerns about providing for her mother's health care needs?

3. How Danielle can cover her long-term care and disability income risk?

FOR HELP with studying this chapter, visit the Online Student Center:

www.college.hmco.com/pic/garman9e

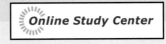

Few things in life are more important than your good health. When illness or injuries do strike, three possible issues may affect your finances. First, the direct cost of the required medical care, such as the cost of hospital stays, surgeries, and visits to the doctor's office, will have to be paid. Second, you will need to address the cost of your rehabilitation and custodial care. Nursing home care is an example of custodial care. Third, you will need to manage despite the loss of income that occurs when anyone who is employed cannot work due to illness or injury. This chapter looks at the ways you can address these three concerns.

group health plan Sold collectively to an entire group of people rather than to individuals, such as the group health care policies offered by employers.

Addressing the Financial Burdens of Illness or Injury

1 LEARNING OBJECTIVE
Identify ways that people can manage the financial burdens resulting from illness or injury.

On average, more than $7500 is spent on health care for each American each year. About 85 percent of Americans are covered by a medical care plan that will pay a portion of these costs. Those without a plan must pay even more.

You can obtain protection as an individual or as a member of a group. A **group health plan** is sold collectively to an entire group of people rather than to individuals. The medical care plan offered by many companies is an example of a group plan.

Each of the three types of losses resulting from illness or injury can be addressed in multiple ways. Of course, you can pay all of your own expenses. That is not always practical or smart. We provide a summary of your options here and in Table 11.1.

Instant Message

Group Health Plans Are Best

Participating in a group plan is desirable for three reasons: First, group health coverage costs less than an individual plan. Second, employers often pay all or the major portion of the cost. Third, people who have existing health problems are less likely to be rejected because of their condition.

1. Covering Your Direct Medical Care Costs

Direct medical care can be covered by an HMO, traditional health insurance, or a high-deductible health care plan (each is defined later). These three types of plans can cover as much as 90 to 100 percent of one's costs and comprise the plans typically offered by employers. Purchased individually, these plans can cost $400 or more per month for an individual and $700 or more for family coverage. Low-income individuals and families may qualify for **Medicaid,** a government health care program funded jointly by the federal and state governments. Finally, people age 65 or over can enroll in the **Medicare** program, which is the federal government's medical care program for the elderly.

2. Covering Your Rehabilitative and Custodial Care Costs

Instant Message

Three Ways to Obtain Medical Care Benefits

Medical benefits can come from three sources. First, your employer might provide them as an employee benefit. Second, you might qualify for a government program. Three, you can buy protection as an individual.

The elderly, people with chronic disease, and accident victims often have needs that go beyond direct medical care. At one extreme is the need for a stay in a nursing home and at the other might be a short period of time during which a patient receives rehabilitation. Medical care plans tend to cover only "medically necessary" care, not these rehabilitation and custodial needs. **Long-term care insurance** provides reimbursement for costs associated with intermediate-term and custodial care in a nursing facility or at home. Medicaid also provides protection here but only for low-income/low-wealth individuals. Those in the greatest need for assistance tend to be those in the middle-income range. They lack the financial resources to pay for nursing home care (perhaps $5000 per month) and have too high of an income to qualify for Medicaid.

3. Covering Your Lost Income

Anyone with a job can lose income when they become sick or are injured. Many employers offer sick days and other time off that can be used as necessary. Some employers may provide a disability income insurance plan that will replace a portion of income for a period of time. The employee may be required to pay all or a portion of the premium for such coverage. If your employer does not offer a plan, you can buy one on your own.

Workers who are eligible can collect **Social Security Disability Income Insurance** benefits if their disability is total (meaning they cannot work at any job) and will last one year (or until death if expected within one year). The amount of these benefits is based on the worker's average lifetime earnings and, thus, might be lower than necessary to fully support young workers. Finally, older workers who have built up considerable funds in a tax-sheltered retirement account may be able to utilize those funds to replace lost income when disabled.

Social Security Disability Income Insurance Under this government program, eligible workers can collect some income for up to one year if their disabilities are total, meaning that they cannot work at any job.

✓ CONCEPT CHECK 11.1

1. List three ways that group health plans are better than individually purchased plans.

2. Identify the five mechanisms available to help people pay for direct medical care costs.

3. Explain why someone might want to purchase long-term care insurance.

4. Explain how someone might replace the income lost due to illness or injury.

Did You Know?...

Top 3 Financial Missteps in Managing Health Expenses

1. Going unprotected for health care when changing jobs

2. Duplicating employer-provided health care protection with your spouse

3. Ignoring the need for protection of income during a period of disability

Sources of Protection from Direct Medical Care Costs

A **medical care plan** is a generic name for any program that pays or provides reimbursement for direct medical care expenditures. When a medical plan is available as an employee benefit, the employer typically pays the cost for the worker (and possibly other members of the worker's immediate family) for the lowest-cost plan the employer

2 LEARNING OBJECTIVE
Distinguish among the types of protection for direct medical expenses.

Good Money Habits in Managing Health Expenses

Make the following your money habits in managing health expenses:

1. Always maintain coverage for direct health care expenses.

2. When changing employers, consider continuing your medical care plan coverage using rights established through the COBRA law.

3. Working people should sign up for an employer-sponsored premium conversion plan and a flexible spending account for health care spending, when available, to save money on taxes.

4. If you are a frequent user of health care, reduce spending on deductibles and coinsurance by choosing an HMO or PPO.

5. Take advantage of employer-sponsored long-term disability income insurance or consider purchasing protection individually.

6. Regularly reevaluate your need for long-term care insurance against your resources for providing such care on your own.

Table 11.1   Types of Protection from Health-Related Expenses

	Type of Expense				
	Direct Medical Care			**Rehabilitative and Custodial Care**	**Lost Income**
Provider of Coverage?	Health maintenance organizations (HMOs) Medicare for those age 65 and over Medicaid for low-income/low-wealth individuals	Traditional health insurance Medicare for those age 65 and over Medicaid for low-income/low-wealth individuals	Consumer-driven health insurance plans	Long-term care insurance Medicaid for low-income/ low-wealth individuals	Disability income insurance Social Security for eligible workers and their families
Services Covered?	Provide hospital, surgi-cal, and medical ser-vices directly through their own hospital and physicians or under contract with such providers	Reimburses or pays for hospital, surgi-cal, medical, and other health care costs	Reimburse or pay for hospital, surgical, medical, and other health care costs that exceed a high deductible of $5000 or more	Reimburses for costs associ-ated with cus-todial care (not direct medical care)	Provides a monthly income to replace that lost when the insured is unable to work due to accident or injury
Payment Mode?	Charge a monthly fee on a prepaid basis	Charges monthly premiums for the insurance coverage	Charge monthly pre-miums for the insurance coverage	Charges monthly or annual premiums	Charges a monthly premium
Purchased By?	Individuals or by employers as an employee benefit	Individuals or by employers as an employee benefit	Individuals or by employers as an employee benefit	Individuals	Individuals or by employers as an employee benefit

offers. Employees can choose a higher-priced option or add family members to the coverage by paying an additional charge. New employees generally must make a choice among the available plans within the first few days of being hired.

Health Maintenance Organizations

health maintenance organizations (HMOs) Provide a broad range of health care services for a set monthly fee on a prepaid basis.

Health maintenance organizations (HMOs) provide a broad range of health care services for a set monthly fee on a prepaid basis. For the specific monthly fee, HMO members receive a wide array of health care services, including hospital, surgical, and preventive medical care. Some HMO plans require a small copayment of $5 to $20 for each office visit or prescription. A goal of HMOs is to catch problems early, thereby reducing the probability of subsequent high-cost medical treatment. HMO services are available to both groups and individuals.

The monthly fee charged by an HMO is based on the medical services that the average plan member would tend to use. HMOs do not put dollar limits on how much health care can be used. Instead, they list the types of medical care they will provide under the contract. HMOs are one of several types of **managed care plans.** Such

New employees must typically choose from among offered health care plans soon after being hired.

plans seek to control the conditions under which health care can be obtained. Examples of controls include preapproval of hospital admissions, restrictions on which hospital or doctor can be used, and mandates regarding the type of procedures that will be employed to treat a specific medical problem.

HMO subscribers are assigned a **primary-care physician** by the HMO or choose one from an approved list. The primary-care physician usually must order or approve referrals to specialized health care providers (for example, a cardiologist) within or outside the HMO. If the HMO itself does not provide a particular type of care, it refers the patient to a local hospital or clinic for those services. One HMO variation is the **individual practice organization (IPO),** a structure in which the HMO contracts with—rather than hires—groups of physicians. These physicians maintain their own offices in various locations around town and serve as the primary-care physicians and specialists for the HMO.

Traditional Health Insurance

Health insurance provides protection against financial losses resulting from illness and injury. It may cover hospital, surgical, and other medical expenditures. These coverages can be purchased separately, but most consumers and employers prefer **comprehensive health insurance** because it combines these protections into a single policy with policy limits of $1 million or more. Unlike with HMOs, where you are prepaying for health care in advance, health insurance is based on the concept of reimbursement for losses, with the patient choosing the type of care based on the advice of his or her physician. For this reason, health insurance plans are often referred to as **indemnity plans** because they compensate the insured for the cost of care received.

Health insurance plans often identify a **preferred provider organization (PPO).** A PPO is a group of medical care providers (doctors, hospitals, and other health care providers) who contract with a health insurance company to provide services at a discount. This discount is then passed along to the policyholders in the form of reductions or elimination of deductibles and coinsurance requirements if they choose the PPO providers for their medical care.

Consider the case of Dru Cameron, who works for a large marketing firm in Charlotte, North Carolina. Her firm's health insurance plan has contracted with a PPO representing a local university's teaching hospital and its affiliated physicians. Because Dru chose the university hospital for treatment of a broken ankle, she saved $150 on the $250 deductible and did not have to pay the usual 20 percent coinsurance share of office visit charges. She gave up the right to go to her family doctor, who is not a PPO member, although she could still see that physician for other health care needs in the future.

A **provider-sponsored network (PSN),** also called a **provider-sponsored association** is a group of cooperating physicians and hospitals who have banded together to offer a health insurance contract. Such networks operate primarily in rural areas, where access to HMOs may be limited. As a group, the members of the PSN coordinate and deliver health care services and manage the insurance plan financially. They contract with outside providers for medical services that are not available through members of the group.

Consumer-Driven Health Care

Consumer-driven health care is a term describing an approach to medical care that is different than that of typical HMOs and traditional health insurance. With these two latter approaches, consumers pay very little out of their own pocket for their medical care and, thus, have little incentive to minimize health care spending. The principle behind **consumer-driven health care** is that knowledgeable and informed patients/employees

Instant Message

Making Changes in Your Group Plan

When you work for an employer that offers a group health plan, you must wait until the next **open-enrollment period** to make changes in coverage or switch among alternative plans. Open-enrollment periods occur once each year and last for about one month. Open-enrollment period requirements are generally waived for such family changes as births, adoptions, divorce, and marriage.

Instant Message

The Difference Between Health Insurance and HMOs

Health insurance pays for or reimburses you for your care. HMOs actually provide your care.

health insurance Provides protection against financial losses resulting from illness and injury.

indemnity plan Health insurance based on reimbursement for losses with the type of care chosen by patients based upon their physicians' advice.

preferred provider organization (PPO) Group of medical care providers (doctors, hospitals, and other health care providers) who contract with a health insurance company to provide services at a discount.

consumer-driven health care Approach to medical care that assumes that knowledgeable and informed patients/employees will spend their own money more carefully than they would spend an employer's or health plan's funds.

How Much Must You Pay Out of Your Own Pocket?

Medical care plans contain provisions that specify the level of payments for covered expenses.

Deductibles **Deductibles** are clauses in medical care plans that require you to pay an initial portion of medical expenses annually before receiving reimbursement. A deductible of $200 per year, for example, would mean that the patient must pay the first $200 of the medical costs for the year. Family plans warrant special attention. Generally, they include a deductible for each family member (again, perhaps $200 per year) with a maximum family deductible (perhaps $500 per year). Once the deductible payments for individual family members reach the maximum family deductible ($500 in this example), further individual deductibles will be waived.

Copayments A **copayment,** which is a variation of a deductible, requires you to pay a specific dollar amount each time you have a specific covered expense item. A copayment is often required for visits to the doctor's office and prescription drugs. For example, you might have to pay $25 for each prescription, with the insurer paying the remainder. A copayment differs from a deductible in that it might require that you pay $35 for each office visit even after the deductible is met.

Coinsurance A **coinsurance clause** requires you to pay a proportion of any loss suffered. The typical share is 80/20, with the insurer paying the larger percentage. Usually, a coinsurance cap limits the annual out-of-pocket payments required of the patient when meeting the coinsurance. The following example illustrates how a deductible of $250 and an 80/20 coinsurance provision with a $1000 coinsurance cap work together to determine the coverage for an $8760 health care bill. Because the deductible is the responsibility of the insured party, the patient pays the first $250. The coinsurance ratio is applied to the remaining $8510 ($8760 − $250) until the portion paid by the patient reaches the coinsurance cap. Thus, $1000 is covered by the insured and $4000 by the insurer. The additional expenses of $3510 ($8510 − $1000 − $4000) are covered 100 percent by the insurance company up to the overall limits of coverage (perhaps $100,000). In this example, the insured party will pay $1250 ($250 deductible + $1000 coinsurance) and the insurer will pay $7510 ($4000 coinsurance + $3510 remaining charges).

deductibles Clauses in medical care plans that require you to pay an initial portion of medical expenses annually before receiving reimbursement.

copayment A variation of a deductible, requires you to pay a specific dollar amount each time you use your benefits for a specific covered expense item.

Policy Limits Policy limits specify the maximum dollar amounts that a health insurance plan will pay to reimburse a covered loss. To illustrate policy limits for a health insurance plan, we will consider the case of Karl Gruenfeld, an unmarried electrician from Las Vegas, New Mexico.

• **Item limits** specify the maximum reimbursement for a particular health care expense. Karl's policy contains a $75 maximum per X ray. Karl suffered a heart attack and had X-ray expenses of $840 (seven sets of X rays at $120 each). The policy will pay $525 (7 × $75) of this expense, and Karl must pay the remaining $315.

- **Episode limits** specify the maximum payment for health care expenses arising from a single episode of illness or injury, with each episode being considered separately. Karl's policy contains an episode limit of $25,000 for all covered expenses. After his heart attack, Karl was hospitalized for two weeks and incurred $31,223 in medical charges (including the covered portion of the X rays). His policy will pay $25,000 of these charges. One month later, Karl suffered burns in a cooking accident at his home and was hospitalized for two days, incurring hospital care costs of $4310. His policy will pay these expenses in full because the second hospitalization is considered a separate episode.

- Disputes may also center on whether a recurrence of an illness represents a separate episode. A **recurring clause** clarifies conditions under which a recurrence of an illness is considered a continuation of the first episode or a separate episode. If the recurrence is considered a separate episode, the deductible must be paid, but reimbursement will be available up to the full episode limit. If the recurrence is considered a continuation of the original episode, the second deductible will not apply, but the loss may exceed the episode limit.

- **Annual limits** specify the maximum payment for covered expenses occurring within one year. Consider Karl's heart attack and burn hospitalizations. If his policy had contained a $50,000 annual limit, Karl would have used $29,310 ($25,000 + $4310) of this amount and would have only $20,690 ($50,000 − $29,310) remaining for the year.

- A **lifetime** or **aggregate limit** places an overall maximum on the total amount of reimbursement available under a policy. If Karl's policy has an aggregate limit of $500,000, no more than $500,000 will be reimbursed for all medical expenses that Karl incurs during the life of the policy.

Coordination of Benefits A **coordination-of-benefits clause** prevents you from collecting insurance benefits that exceed the loss suffered. Such a clause designates the order in which plans will pay benefits if multiple plans apply to a loss. The primary plan is the first applied to any loss when more than one plan provides coverage. If it fails to reimburse 100 percent of the loss, then any secondary (or excess) plans will be applied in order until the loss is fully paid or until benefits are exhausted, whichever occurs first.

Instant Message

HMOs Do Not Have Dollar Limits

HMO plans generally do not have maximum policy limits specified in dollars. Instead, they limit the health care services they will provide for a specified diagnosis.

Instant Message

Know Your Limits

Aggregate dollar limits are always higher than time period limits, which are in turn higher than episode limits. A policy with high aggregate limits may seem attractive, but it may not be a good buy if the episode limits are too low. Analyze each limit separately to determine whether it provides sufficient protection.

lifetime/aggregate limit Places an overall maximum on the total amount of reimbursement available under a policy.

coordination-of-benefits clause Prevents you from collecting insurance benefits that exceed the loss suffered by noting the order in which plans will pay if you are covered by multiple plans.

✓ CONCEPT CHECK 11.3

1. What are preexisting conditions and how do they affect coverage under health plans?
2. Distinguish among a deductible, a copayment, and coinsurance.
3. Explain COBRA rights and portability rights that apply when you leave a job that has a group medical care plan.
4. Distinguish among item limits, episode limits, time period limits, and aggregate limits as used in medical care plans.
5. Distinguish among optionally renewable, guaranteed renewable, and noncancelable health care plans.
6. List three ways you can save on taxes when paying for health care or a health care plan.

CHAPTER 12

Life Insurance Planning

You Must Be Kidding, Right?

Michelle and Jason Bailey are in their mid-20s and expecting their first child next month. Each earns about $40,000 per year. Currently, they have $20,000 life insurance policies on each of their lives with the other named as the beneficiary. They bought these policies to pay for death-related expenses if tragedy struck. They are thinking about adding another $300,000 each to their protection to replace the income lost if one of them passed away. How much will Michelle and Jason each pay for this additional protection?

A. About $25 per month

B. About $50 per month

C. About $100 per month

D. About $200 per month

The answer is A. Term life insurance for people in their 20s costs about $1 per $1000 of coverage per year. Thus, Michelle and Jason could each buy this insurance for $300 each or about $25 per month. If they chose instead to buy cash-value life insurance, they would likely pay $200 or more each per month. Always buy inexpensive term life insurance to replace the lost income needed by your dependents if you were to pass away!

LEARNING OBJECTIVES

After reading this chapter, you should be able to:

1 **Understand** the reasons why you might need life insurance and calculate the appropriate amount of coverage.

2 **Distinguish** among types of life insurance.

3 **Explain** the major provisions of life insurance policies.

4 **Apply** a step-by-step strategy for implementing a life insurance plan.

What Do You Recommend?

Karen Bridgeman, age 28, and her husband Will, age 30, are planning to start a family in the next year. Both have small cash-value life insurance policies ($25,000 and $50,000, respectively) that their parents purchased when they were children. Karen is a real estate attorney and earns $90,000 per year. She plans to continue working after having a child. Karen's employer offers a 401(k) plan into which she contributes a maximum of 6 percent of her salary each year matched by her employer one-half of 1 percent for each 1 percent that Karen contributes. Her employer does not offer employer-paid life insurance. Will is a high-school teacher and track coach and makes $49,000 per year. His employer pays the full cost of his retirement pension plan. An optional supplemental retirement plan is available into which Will can contribute 5 percent of his salary, but he has not done so as yet. Will has an employer-provided life insurance policy equal to twice his annual salary. Will and Karen have no other life insurance on their lives.

What do you recommend to Karen and Will on the subject of life insurance planning regarding:

1. Their changing need for life insurance once they have a child?

2. What types of life insurance they should consider and whether they should purchase multiple policies?

3. Coordinating their retirement savings and other investments with their life insurance program?

4. Shopping for life insurance?

FOR HELP with studying this chapter, visit the Online Student Center:

www.college.hmco.com/pic/garman9e

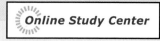

life insurance An insurance contract that promises to pay a dollar benefit to a beneficiary upon the death of the insured person.

Death is certain. Its timing is not. With this uncertainty comes financial risk. Two financial problems arise because you cannot know how long you will live. The first is the **risk of dying too soon.** This is the possibility that you might die before adequately providing for the financial well-being of loved ones, especially your spouse and children. **Life insurance** protects your loved ones against the possibility that you may die too soon. As you will see, term life insurance does this best. The second problem is the **risk of living too long.** This is the possibility that you will outlive your savings during retirement. Life insurance is not the best way to address the living-too-long problem. Instead, you should invest through tax-sheltered retirement savings plans.

Most Americans buy insufficient life insurance coverage. The need for life insurance is greatest in the child-rearing years. As children grow up, they need fewer years of financial support and a breadwinner's need for life insurance levels off and then declines. Eventually, growth in assets, primarily through a retirement plan, replaces the need for life insurance. Americans also tend to buy the wrong type of life insurance—cash-value life insurance—when term insurance costs 85 to 90 percent less. The best approach is to use the money saved by buying term insurance to invest in a tax-sheltered retirement plan. This approach is referred to as "buy term and invest the rest" and should be your mantra for life insurance planning.

How Much Life Insurance Do You Need?

1 LEARNING OBJECTIVE
Understand the reasons why you might need life insurance and calculate the appropriate amount of coverage.

The primary reason for buying life insurance is to allow the family members of the deceased to continue with their lives free from the financial burdens that death can bring. Income can be made available for the surviving spouse. Insurance proceeds can safeguard home ownership. College or other educational plans can remain intact. The bottom line? Your life insurance is for your loved ones, not for yourself.

Life insurance is the simplest form of insurance. It protects against only one peril—death. The policy pays out precisely the amount of insurance purchased. If the policy is for $100,000, then the policy will pay the **beneficiary** (the person named in the policy to receive the funds) an amount very close to $100,000. This payment will occur within a matter of a few days once a death certificate is presented to the insurance company. Beneficiaries may use the funds in any way they wish without paying income taxes on the proceeds. However, if the funds are put in the bank or invested in some way, the interest or investment returns will likely be subject to income taxation.

Good Money Habits in Life Insurance Planning

Make the following your money habits in life insurance planning:

1. Calculate your life insurance needs every three years or when major life events occur, such as the birth of a child.

2. Avoid being talked into buying types and amounts of life insurance that you do not need.

3. Shop for term life insurance on the Internet to obtain the lowest possible rates.

4. Employ the principle of "buy term life insurance and invest the rest" with guaranteed renewable or level-premium term life insurance.

5. Contribute the money saved by purchasing term rather than cash-value insurance into your retirement plan.

6. If you decide that you need a cash-value life insurance policy, get one with a guaranteed insurability option.

What Needs Must Be Met?

Financial losses that arise from dying too soon include expenditures for final expenses; the lost income of the deceased; and funds for a readjustment period, debt repayment, and education for children.

Final-Expense Needs **Final expenses** are one-time expenses occurring just prior to or after a death. Probably the largest of these expenses is for the funeral and burial of the deceased, which often cost more than $10,000. Travel expenses for family members to provide emotional support and to attend a funeral can be quite high as can food and lodging expenses for mourners. Severe and costly disruptions of family life can last as long as a month or more. These final expenses are one area of financial loss that is common to people of all ages. Nonetheless, they may not indicate a need for life insurance if existing assets are sufficient.

Income-Replacement Needs Once someone else becomes financially dependent on you, your lost income will be the major financial loss resulting from your premature death. Included in this lost income is the value of any essential employee benefits, such as health plan benefits for your dependents. Dual-earner families depend on both incomes to maintain the desired level of living and should protect both sources of income.

Readjustment-Period Needs Families often need a period of readjustment after the death of a loved one. This period may last for a few years and may have financial consequences that require substantial life insurance proceeds. For example, the death of a parent with young children may require the surviving spouse to forgo employment for a while. Similarly, a surviving employed spouse may need to take time off from a job to obtain further education.

Debt-Repayment Needs Many people expect life insurance proceeds to pay off installment loans, personal loans, and the outstanding balance on the home mortgage if a family income provider dies. Actually, a family that has provided adequately for the replacement of lost income probably will not need to make specific insurance provisions for the repayment of debts. It is sometimes helpful, however, to create a plan to pay off all debts other than the mortgage for no other reason than to simplify the financial lives of the survivors. Mortgage debt that was adequately being covered before death will continue to be covered if sufficient life insurance was purchased to replace lost income.

Instant Message

Husbands and Wives Need Their Own Life Insurance Plans

Husbands and wives should integrate their life insurance plans, but both need individual plans. This is true even if one partner makes the bulk of the family income. The cost of replacing the house-hold labor of a stay-at-home spouse should be included in life insurance planning.

Adequate life insurance can ensure that important financial goals, such as paying for a child's college education, are met should a parent die.

Social Security survivor's benefits Government program benefits paid to a surviving spouse and children.

College-Expense Needs Many families with small children already have a college savings plan in place. Adequate replacement of lost income should allow for continuation of the plan. Because most families will also use current income to handle expenses when the children are in college, the death of a family income provider may, therefore, impede the ability to meet this need. The solution: Earmark a dollar amount of life insurance proceeds for future college expenses.

Other Special Needs Many families have special needs that must be considered in the life insurance planning process. A family with a disabled child might have special needs if that child is likely to require medical or custodial care as an adult. Wealthier families might need extra life insurance to pay federal estate taxes and state inheritance taxes (covered in Chapter 18).

Government Benefits Can Reduce the Level of Need Widows, widowers, and their dependents may qualify for various government benefits—most notably **Social Security survivor's benefits,** which are paid to a surviving spouse and children. The level of benefits depends on income earned during the lifetime of the deceased that was subject to Social Security taxes. (Details on estimating Social Security benefits are provided in Appendix B and on the *Garman/Forgue* website.) If eligible, a family can receive as much as $25,000 per year, but these benefits generally cease when the youngest child reaches age 18.

Existing Insurance and Assets Reduce the Level of Need Employers often provide life insurance to their employees as an employee benefit. In addition, many people have existing life insurance that was purchased for them as children or that they purchased previously. These coverages can reduce the need for additional life insurance purchases.

As time passes, individuals and families usually acquire at least a minimal amount of savings and investments. The funds held in savings accounts, certificates of deposit, stocks, bonds, and mutual funds often are specifically earmarked for some special goal, such as retirement, travel, or college for children. In the event of a premature death, they could be used to pay final and readjustment expenses as well as to replace lost income, even though it might be wiser to retain these funds for their originally intended purpose. Pension funds and retirement plans of the deceased, such as 401(k) plans and IRAs (discussed in Chapter 17), may be viewed as resources. Younger families should be wary of using retirement money for living expenses after the death of an income provider, however, as this strategy may jeopardize the surviving spouse's retirement.

What Dollar Amount Do You Need?

Determining the magnitude of the possible losses resulting from a premature death can be complicated. Two methods are commonly used: a multiple-of-earnings approach and a needs-based approach. The needs-based approach is more accurate and reflects the changes in family status, income, assets, and age that will occur over your life cycle.

The Multiple-of-Earnings Approach: Easy But Flawed The **multiple-of-earnings approach** estimates the amount of life insurance needed by multiplying your income by some number, such as 5, 7, or 10. Thus, someone with an annual income of $40,000 would need $200,000 to $400,000 in life insurance.

Another multiple-of-earnings approach is to use the interest factors from Appendix Table A.4 for an expected investment rate of return and a given number of years of need. The logic here is that at death, the survivor could invest the funds received from the life insurance policy on the person who has died to provide a flow of income for the number of years desired. For example, a father who wishes to provide his family with income of $40,000 for 20 years at a real rate of return of 4 percent (after inflation and taxes) would need to have about $550,000 ($40,000 × 13.59) of life insurance protection on his life.

The shortcoming of the multiple-of-earnings approach can be seen in the wide range of dollar amounts that result. This approach addresses only one of the factors affecting life insurance needs—income-replacement—and does not take into consideration such factors as age, family situation, and other assets that could cover the lost income.

The Needs-Based Approach: A Better Method The **needs-based approach** to estimating life insurance needs considers all of the factors that might potentially affect the level of need. It improves upon the calculations of the multiple-of-earnings approach by including a more accurate assessment of income-replacement needs and incorporates factors that add to and reduce the level of need. The Decision-Making Worksheet, "The Needs-Based Approach to Life Insurance" (page 326), illustrates calculations made via the needs-based approach. You would be wise to calculate your current needs for life insurance and then to revisit those calculations every three years and when changes occur in your family situation or health status.

Calculating Life Insurance Needs for a Couple with Small Children

Consider the example of Zoel Raymond, a 35-year-old factory foreman from Holyoke, Massachusetts, who has a spouse (age 30) and three sons (ages 8, 7, and 3 years). Zoel earns $48,000 annually and desires to replace his income for 30 years, at which time his spouse would no longer need to support their children financially. The "Example" column of the Decision-Making Worksheet expands on the situation faced by Zoel.

1. **Final-expense needs.** Zoel estimates his final expenses for funeral, burial, and other expenses at $10,000.

2. **Income-replacement needs.** Zoel's income of $48,000 is multiplied by 0.75 and the interest factor of 17.292. This factor was used because Zoel decided that it would be best to replace his lost income for 30 years or until Mary, his wife, reached age 60 and passed through the Social Security blackout period. Zoel and Mary are moderate-risk investors and believe that she could earn a 4 percent after-tax, after-inflation rate of return on life insurance proceeds. Income-replacement needs based on these conditions amount to $622,512.

3. **Readjustment-period needs.** Mary is a columnist for a local newspaper, earning an annual income of $38,000. Allocating $19,000 for readjustment-period needs would allow her to take a six-month leave of absence from her job or meet other readjustment needs.

4. **Debt-repayment needs.** Zoel and Mary owe $10,000 on various credit cards and an auto loan. They also owe about

Top 3 Financial Missteps When Protecting Loved Ones Through Life Insurance

People slip up in personal finance when they do the following:

1. Let their life insurance agent convince them how much and what type of life insurance to buy

2. Buy their life insurance during their childbearing years through cash-value life insurance

3. Ignore their changing need for life insurance as their life progresses from young adulthood through retirement

needs-based approach A superior method of calculating the amount of insurance needed that considers all of the factors that might potentially affect the level of need.

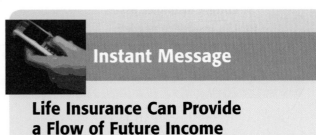

Instant Message

Life Insurance Can Provide a Flow of Future Income

Having the right amount of life insurance will allow your family to invest the proceeds received and then make withdrawals to replace the income you could have provided for them had you lived.

Decision-Making Worksheet

The Needs-Based Approach to Life Insurance

This worksheet provides a mechanism for estimating life insurance needs using the needs-based approach. The amounts needed for final expenses, income replacement, readjustment needs, debt repayment, college expenses, and other special needs are calculated and then reduced by funds available from government benefits and any current insurance or assets that could cover the need. This worksheet is also available on the *Garman/Forgue* website.

Factors Affecting Need	Example	Your Figures
1. Final-expense needs		
Includes funeral, burial, travel, and other items of expense just prior to and after death	$ 10,000	$_____
2. Income-replacement needs		
Multiply 75 percent of annual income* by the interest factor from Appendix Table A.4 that corresponds to the number of years that the income is to be replaced and the assumed after-tax, after-inflation rate of return. ($36,000 × 17.292 for 30 years at a 4% rate of return)	+ 622,512	+_____
3. Readjustment-period needs		
To cover employment interruptions and possible education expenses for surviving spouse and dependents	+ 19,000	+_____
4. Debt-repayment needs		
Provides repayment of short-term and installment debt, including credit cards and personal loans	+ 10,000	+_____
5. College-expense needs		
To provide a fund to help meet college expenses of dependents	+ 75,000	+_____
6. Other special needs	+ 0	+_____
7. Subtotal (combined effects of items 1–6)	+ $736,512	+_____
8. Government benefits		
Present value of Social Security survivor's benefits and other benefits		
Multiply monthly benefit estimate by 12 and use Table A.4 for the number of years that benefits will be received and the same interest rate that was used in item 1. ($2725 × 12 × 11.118 for 15 years of benefits and a 4% rate of return)	− 363,558	_____
9. Current insurance assets	− 98,000	_____
10. Life insurance needed	$274,954	$_____

*Seventy-five percent is used because about 25 percent of income is used for personal needs.

$128,000 on their home mortgage. Mary would like to pay off all debts except the mortgage debt if Zoel dies. The mortgage debt would be affordable if Zoel's income was adequately replaced.

5. **College-expense needs.** Zoel estimates that it would currently cost $25,000 for each of his sons to attend the local campus of a public university. If he dies, $25,000 of the life insurance proceeds could be invested for each son. If invested appropriately, the funds would grow at a rate sufficient to keep up with increasing costs of a college education.

6. **Other special needs.** Zoel and Mary do not have any unusual needs related to life insurance planning, so they entered zero for this factor.

7. **Subtotal.** The Raymonds total items 1 through 6 on the worksheet and determine that the family's financial needs arising out of Zoel's death would amount to $736,512. Although this sum seems large to them, they have access to two resources that can reduce this figure, as indicated in items 8 and 9.

8. **Government benefits.** Zoel estimates that his family would qualify for monthly Social Security survivor's benefits of $2725.* These benefits would be paid for 15 years, until his youngest son turns 18. The present value of this stream of benefits is $363,558 (from Appendix Table A.4), assuming a 4 percent return for 15 years.

9. **Current insurance and assets.** Zoel has a $50,000 life insurance policy purchased five years ago. His employer also pays for a group policy equal to his $48,000 gross annual income. Zoel's major assets include his home and his retirement plan. Because he does not want Mary to have to liquidate these assets if he dies, he includes only the $98,000 insurance coverage in item 9.

10. **Life insurance needed.** After subtracting worksheet items 8 and 9 from the subtotal, Zoel estimates that he needs an additional $274,954 in life insurance. This amount may seem like a large sum of insurance, but Zoel can meet this need through term life insurance for as little as $30 per month.

Because Mary earns an income that is about 80 percent of Zoel's, her life insurance needs may be about 20 percent lower. To determine the specific amount, the couple must complete a worksheet for her as well. Next, the Raymonds will need to decide what type of life insurance is best and from whom to buy the additional life insurance needed. These topics are covered later in this chapter.

Calculating Life Insurance Needs for a Young Professional
Irene Leech of Rancho Cucamonga, California, recently graduated with a degree in tourism management and has accepted a position paying $43,000 per year. Irene is single and lives with her sister. She owes $14,500 on a car loan and $21,800 in education loans. She has about $7000 in the bank. Among her employee benefits is an employer-paid term insurance policy equal to her annual salary.

Irene has been approached by a life insurance agent who used the multiple-of-earnings approach to suggest that she needs $215,000 in life insurance, or about five times her income. Does she? If you apply the needs-based approach to Irene's situation, you will see the following:

- Irene estimates her burial costs at $8000, which she entered for item 1. Because Irene has no dependents, she needs no insurance for income-replacement needs, readjustment-period needs, college-expense needs, or other special needs.
- Items 2, 3, 5, and 6 in the needs-based approach worksheet on page 326 are zero because Irene has no dependents.
- Irene's survivors will not qualify for any government benefits, so item 8 will also be zero.
- Irene would like to see her $14,500 automobile loan and $21,800 education loans repaid in the event of her death. She feels better knowing that her younger sister could inherit her car free and clear. She entered $36,300 for item 4.
- Irene has combined life insurance and assets of $50,000, so she entered that amount for item 8.

The resulting calculations show that Irene needs *no* additional life insurance ($8000 + $36,300 − $50,000 = −$5,700).

Instant Message

Social Security Survivor Benefits Have a Blackout Period

Once the youngest child reaches age 18, a surviving spouse enters the **Social Security blackout period** and is ineligible for Social Security survivor benefits. The blackout period ends when the surviving spouse reaches age 60. The surviving spouse may then collect survivor's benefits until age 62, and then may begin collecting Social Security retirement benefits based on his or her own or the deceased spouse's retirement account, whichever provides the higher payment.

*Your personal Social Security benefits can be estimated by requesting a Social Security Statement from the Social Security Administration (www.ssa.gov). Appendix B also provides estimates.

The agent suggested that Irene buy now while she is young and rates are low. This, too, is not a smart approach. The lesson here is that you should not buy life insurance simply to lock in low rates. That would be like buying car insurance before you own a car. Unless you have a personal or family-based medical history that might interfere with the purchase of life insurance when needed later, you, like Irene, can wait until family circumstances change to recalculate the need.

✔ CONCEPT CHECK 12.1

1. Distinguish between the dying-too-soon problem and the living-too-long problem and the best ways to address each.
2. List five types of needs that can be addressed through life insurance.
3. Explain why the multiple-of-earnings approach is less accurate than a needs-based approach to life insurance planning.
4. Identify two periods in a typical person's life cycle when the need for life insurance is low and one when it is high.

There Are But Two Basic Types of Life Insurance

2 LEARNING OBJECTIVE

Distinguish among types of life insurance.

term life insurance "Pure protection" against early death; pays benefits only if the insured dies within the time period (term) that the policy covers.

cash-value life insurance Pays benefits at death and includes a savings/investment element that can provide a reduced level of benefits to the policyholder prior to the death of the insured person.

face amount Dollar value of protection as listed in the policy and used to calculate the premium.

Many people are confused by the wide variety of life insurance plans available. But, in reality, there are only two types of life insurance: term life insurance and cash-value life insurance. **Term life insurance** is often described as "pure protection" because it pays benefits only if the insured person dies within the time period (term) covered by the policy. The policy must be renewed if coverage is desired for another time period. **Cash-value life insurance** pays benefits at death and includes a savings/investment element that can provide benefits to the policyholder prior to the death of the insured person. Thus, it includes a **cash value** representing the value of the investment element in the life insurance policy. Because of its investment aspect, many people automatically believe it is the better option. Cash-value life insurance costs much more than term insurance, however, and there are much better investment options.

Term Life Insurance

Term life insurance contracts are most often written for time periods (or terms) of 1, 5, 10, or even 20 years. If the insured survives the specified time period, the beneficiary receives no monetary benefits. Term insurance can be purchased in contracts with face amounts in multiples of $1000, usually with a minimum face amount of $50,000. The **face amount** is the dollar value of life insurance protection as listed in the policy and used to calculate the premium. Variations on term life insurance include decreasing term insurance, guaranteed renewable term insurance, convertible term insurance, and credit (term) life insurance.

Unless otherwise stipulated by the original contract, you must apply for a new contract and may be required to undergo a medical examination to renew the policy. The premium will increase with each renewal, reflecting your increasing age and greater likelihood of dying while the new policy remains in force. If you have a health problem, you may be denied a new policy or be asked to pay even higher premiums. For example, a $100,000 five-year renewable term policy for a man age 25 might have an annual premium of $100; at age 35, the policy might cost $135; and at age 45, it might cost $220. Term policies are much less expensive than cash-value policies at any given age because they do not include a savings/investment element.

Guaranteed Renewable Term Insurance Proving insurability at renewal may be difficult if you develop a health problem during the time period of a term policy. Term life insurance policies, however, are usually written as **guaranteed renewable term insurance.** The guarantee protects you against the possibility of becoming uninsurable. The number of renewals you can make without proving insurability may be limited, and a maximum age may be specified for these renewals (usually 65 or 70 years). Unless you are positive that you will not need a renewal, guaranteed renewable term insurance is recommended.

guaranteed renewable term insurance Protects you against the possibility of becoming uninsurable.

Level-Premium Term Insurance You can partially avoid term insurance premium increases as you grow older by buying **level-premium** (or **guaranteed level-premium) term insurance,** which is a term policy with a long time period (perhaps 5, 10, or 20 years). Under such a policy, the premiums remain constant throughout the entire life of the policy. Premiums charged in early years are higher than necessary to balance out the lower-than-necessary premiums in later years covered by the policy. Premiums on policies written for ten or more years usually remain constant for a five-year interval, then might increase to a new constant rate for another five- or ten-year interval. Such level-premium policies may include a **reenter provision,** requiring proof of good health at the beginning of each five-year interval. If health status changes, the insured must reenter the policy at a higher rate than originally anticipated. Be extremely wary of policies with such a provision, especially if you anticipate needing coverage beyond the initial level-premium interval.

level-premium term insurance Term policy with long term under which premiums remain constant. Also called guaranteed level-premium term insurance.

Decreasing Term Insurance With **decreasing term insurance,** the face amount of coverage declines annually, while the premiums remain constant. The owner chooses an initial face amount and a contract period, after which the face amount of the policy gradually declines (usually each year) to some minimum (such as $50,000) in the last year of the contract. For example, a woman age 35 might buy a 30-year $200,000 decreasing term policy that declines by $5000 each year. The major benefit of decreasing term policies is that they more closely fit changing insurance needs, which typically decline as a person ages.

Convertible Term Insurance **Convertible term insurance** offers the policyholder the option of exchanging a term policy for a cash-value policy without evidence of insurability. Usually, this conversion is available only in the early years of the term policy. Some policies provide for an automatic conversion from term to cash-value insurance after a specific number of years.

convertible term insurance Offers policyholders option of exchanging a term policy for a cash-value policy without evidence of insurability.

There are two ways to convert a term policy to a cash-value policy. First, you can simply request the conversion and begin paying the higher premiums required for the cash-value policy. The savings/investment element of the cash-value policy will begin accumulating as of the date of the conversion. Second, you can pay the company the cash value that would have built up had the policy originally been written on a cash-value basis. Although this lump sum may be a considerable amount, it does represent an asset for the policyholder. Furthermore, the new premiums will be based on your age at the time that you bought the original term policy, which may result in lower premiums.

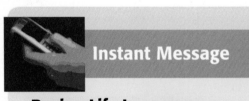

Instant Message

Buying Life Insurance Through a Group at Work

Unlike with health insurance, group life insurance rates are not lower than individual rates for people in good health. If you have a health condition, you can compare your group rates with what you must pay on your own.

Group Term Life Insurance **Group term life insurance** is issued to people as members of a group rather than as individuals. Most such policies are written for a large number of employees, with premiums being paid in full or in part by the employer. Group life insurance premiums are average rates based on the characteristics of the group as a whole. If you are insured under a group plan, you need not prove your insurability, and you can usually convert the policy to an individual basis without proof of insurability if you leave the group. Such convertibility represents a major benefit for people whose health status makes individual life insurance unaffordable or unattainable.

Credit Term Life Insurance **Credit term life insurance** will pay the remaining balance of a loan if the insured dies before repaying the debt. In essence, it is a decreasing term insurance policy with the creditor named as beneficiary. This product is usually grossly overpriced, and the only people who should consider its purchase are those who are uninsurable because of a serious health condition. Most people are insurable and can obtain term life coverage for a minimal cost, so they do not need credit term life insurance.

Some Forms of Cash-Value Life Insurance Pay a Fixed Return

Cash-value life insurance pays benefits upon the death of the insured and also incorporates a savings/investment element. This cash value belongs to the owner of the policy rather than to the beneficiary (although they can be the same person). While the insured is alive, the owner may obtain the cash value by borrowing from the insurance company or by surrendering and canceling the policy. Cash-value insurance is referred to as **permanent insurance** because it does not need to be renewed and because coverage is maintained for the entire life of the insured. The annual premiums for cash-value policies usually remain constant.

The premiums for cash-value policies are always higher than those for term policies providing the same amount of coverage. This difference arises because only a portion of the premium is used to provide the death benefit; the remainder is used to keep the premium level and to build the cash value. Figure 12.1 illustrates the premium differences between cash-value and term life insurance policies.

Cash-value life insurance actually represents a combination of decreasing term insurance and an investment account that adds up to the face amount of the policy. Figure 12.2 illustrates this concept. Initially, for example, you might have $100,000 of insurance and no savings. Several years later, you might have built up $2000 in savings within the policy. In the event of your death, your beneficiary would collect $100,000,

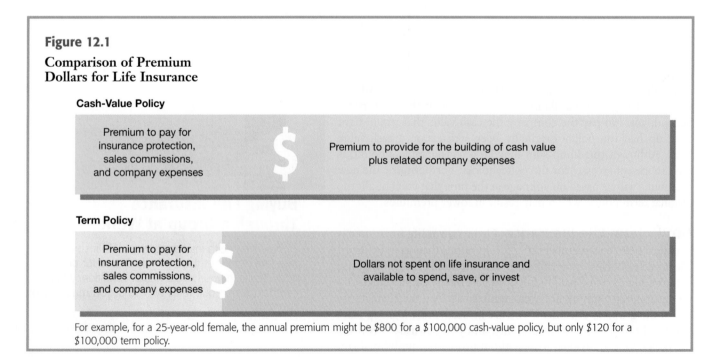

Figure 12.1

Comparison of Premium Dollars for Life Insurance

Cash-Value Policy

| Premium to pay for insurance protection, sales commissions, and company expenses | $ | Premium to provide for the building of cash value plus related company expenses |

Term Policy

| Premium to pay for insurance protection, sales commissions, and company expenses | $ | Dollars not spent on life insurance and available to spend, save, or invest |

For example, for a 25-year-old female, the annual premium might be $800 for a $100,000 cash-value policy, but only $120 for a $100,000 term policy.

of which $2000 would be your own money. If you lived long enough, the cash value could equal—and might surpass—the $100,000 figure. In effect, your beneficiary would then collect your "savings account" rather than an insurance payment.

Even though the cash value of a life insurance policy accumulates throughout your life, only the face amount of the policy will be paid upon your death. In many ways, cash values represent a kind of forced saving that allows funds to build up while you buy life insurance. Several types of cash-value life insurance are available that pay a fixed rate of investment return.

Whole Life Insurance
Whole, or **straight, life insurance** is a form of cash-value life insurance that provides lifetime life insurance protection and expects you to pay premiums for life. The policy remains in effect and does not need to be renewed as long as the premiums are paid on time.

Limited-Pay Whole Life Insurance
Limited-pay whole life insurance is whole life insurance that allows premium payments to cease before you reach the age of 100. Two common examples are *20-pay life policies*, which allow premium payments to cease after 20 years, and *paid-at-65 policies*, which require payment of premiums only until the insured turns 65. Although premiums need be paid only for the specified time period, the insurance protection lasts for your entire life. As you might expect, the annual premiums for limited-pay insurance policies are higher than those for whole life insurance policies because the insurance company has fewer years to collect premiums. Limited-pay policies are said to be **paid-up** when the owner can stop paying premiums. An extreme version of limited-pay life insurance is **single-premium life insurance,** in which the premium is paid once in the form of a lump sum.

Adjustable Life Insurance
The three cornerstones of cash-value life insurance are the premium, the face amount of the policy, and the rate of cash-value accumulation. **Adjustable life insurance** allows you to modify any one of these three components, with corresponding changes occurring in the other two. These changes may be made without providing new proof of insurability. For example, you might feel that inflation has increased your need for life insurance. Adjustable life insurance would allow you to increase the face amount. In return, your premiums could increase, the cash-value accumulation could slow, or some combination of the two could apply.

whole life insurance Form of cash-value life insurance that provides lifetime life insurance protection and expects the insured to pay premiums for life. Also called straight life insurance.

limited-pay whole life insurance Whole life insurance that allows premium payments to cease before the insured reaches the age of 100.

paid-up Point at which the owner of a whole life policy can stop paying premiums.

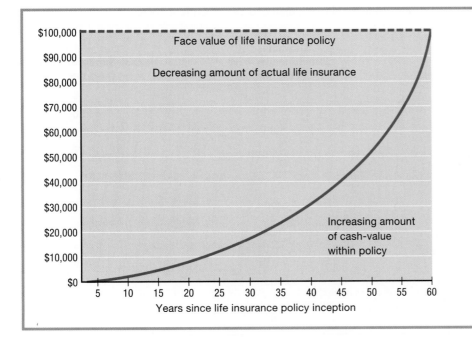

Figure 12.2

The Essence of Cash-Value Life Insurance

The $100,000 death benefit (face value) paid to the beneficiaries comprises a decreasing amount of life insurance and the policyholder's returned built-up cash values.

Modified Life Insurance **Modified life insurance** is whole life insurance for which the insurance company charges reduced premiums in the early years and higher premiums thereafter. The premiums are lower in early years because some of the protection during the early years is provided by term insurance. The period of reduced premiums can vary from one to five years. Modified life insurance is primarily designed for people whose life insurance needs are high (young parents, for example) but who cannot immediately afford the premiums required for a cash-value policy. Because it uses term insurance in the early years, modified life insurance accumulates cash value extremely slowly.

Endowment Life Insurance **Endowment life insurance** pays the face amount of the policy either upon the death of the insured or at some previously agreed-upon date, whichever occurs first. The date of payment, called the endowment date, is commonly some specified number of years after issuance of the policy (for example, 20 or 30 years) or some specified age (such as 65). New endowment policies are no longer being written, however, and this type of policy will be phased out as existing policies "endow" and are converted to cash.

Some Forms of Cash-Value Life Insurance Pay a Variable Return

The rate at which the cash value accumulates in a cash-value policy depends on the rate of return earned. Some forms of cash-value insurance have a guaranteed minimum rate of return, often 4 percent, but pay a higher current rate depending on the success of the investments made by the insurance company with your premiums. Table 12.1 illustrates these rates. An understanding of these policies requires an examination of the premium, the cost of the insurance protection portion, the rate of return on the invested funds, and the company's expense charges.

universal life insurance Provides the pure protection of term insurance and the cash-value buildup of whole life insurance, along with face amount variability, rate of cash-value accumulation, premiums, and rate of return.

Universal Life Insurance **Universal life insurance** provides both the pure protection of term insurance and the cash-value buildup of whole life insurance, along with variability in the face amount, rate of cash-value accumulation, premiums, and rate of return. Initially, the purchaser selects a face amount, and the company quotes an annual

Table 12.1   Cash-Value Buildup—Guaranteed Versus Current Rates

Policy Year	"Guaranteed" Cash-Surrender Value (4.0% rate)	"Current Rate" Cash-Surrender Value (7.6% rate)
1	$ 0	$ 0
2	0	236
3	585	886
4	1,280	1,577
5	1,993	2,377
6	2,723	3,187
7	3,470	4,212
8	4,234	5,258
9	5,016	6,302
10	5,816	7,419
15	10,089	14,748
20	14,738	25,812
25	19,888	39,419

Figures are illustrative for a $50,000 universal life policy; the annual premium is $684.

Advice from a Pro...

Don't Be Fooled by Vanishing-Premium or Return-of-Premium Policies

Life insurance agents often pitch **vanishing-premium life insurance,** which is designed to allow policyholders to cease making premium payments after just a few years. In these plans, cash-value accumulations are used to pay premiums that no longer must be paid. While attractive at first glance, these policies contain a significant hazard. If the growth in cash-value accumulations proves insufficient to pay the premium, the owner of the policy will be billed for the premium shortfall—possibly after many years of having not paid premiums. Always assume any life insurance charge that can be imposed will be imposed.

A similar type of plan is called a **return-of-premium policy.** Here the policy promises to return all the premi-

ums paid if the insured person maintains the policy and lives past a certain number of years—usually 30. These policies cost more so that the extra funds can be invested to provide for the return of premiums. Insurance companies promote these policies as a way to avoid "wasting" your money. In reality, what they are trying to do is entice you to keep the policy in effect for a long time even if you do not need the coverage anymore. Instead buy term insurance and decide for yourself when it is best to drop a policy.

Hyungsoo Kim
University of Kentucky, Lexington, Kentucky

premium. The annual premium goes into the cash-value fund, from which the company deducts the cost of providing the insurance protection and charges for company expenses. As time goes by, the owner of the policy may reduce or increase the premium, with corresponding changes occurring in the insurance protection or amount added to cash value. If premiums drop below the amount necessary to cover the insurance protection and expenses, funds are removed from the cash-value account to cover the shortfall.

Essentially, universal life insurance combines annual term insurance with an investment program. Universal life policies are usually available in initial face amounts of $100,000 or more. The rate of return is tied to some interest rate prevailing in the financial markets or is dictated by the insurance company. The rate of return often exceeds those available under fixed-rate cash-value policies.

Variable Life Insurance

Variable life insurance allows you to choose the investments made with your cash-value accumulations and to share in any gains or losses. The face amount of your policy and the policy's cash value may rise or fall based on changes in the rates of return on the invested funds. The face amount of the policy usually will not drop below the originally agreed-upon amount, however. Instead, the cash value will fluctuate. If you are unfamiliar with markets for corporate stocks and bonds and mutual funds, however, you should probably avoid variable life insurance. Many variable life insurance policies contain provisions calling for the payment of fees and sales charges before the policyholder can share in any investment returns. Variable life insurance policies should be read and analyzed very carefully before purchase.

Variable-Universal Life Insurance

Variable-universal life insurance is a form of universal life insurance that gives the policyholder some choice in the investments made with the cash value accumulated by the policy. It is sometimes called **flexible-premium variable life insurance.** The most popular form of cash-value life insurance, it most closely embodies the philosophy of "buy term and invest the difference." Because you select the investment vehicles (a combination of stocks, bonds, or money market mutual funds), you can potentially realize a higher rate of return than is possible under other cash-value policy types. With this flexibility comes the risk of a lower rate of return, of course. As a result, variable-universal life policies usually provide no minimum guaranteed rate of return. Table 12.2 summarizes the features of term life insurance, cash-value insurance with a fixed return, and cash-value insurance with a variable return.

variable-universal life insurance
Form of universal life insurance that gives the policyholder some choice in the investments made with the cash value accumulated by the policy. Also called flexible-premium variable life insurance.

Table 12.2   Comparisons of Three Popular Life Insurance Policies

Feature	Term Insurance	Cash-Value Life Insurance	
		Whole Life Insurance	**Variable Life Insurance**
Cash-value accumulation	None	Fixed rate of accumulation	Variable accumulation as premium and interest rates vary
Rate of return paid on cash accumulations	Not applicable	Fixed	Variable with interest rates in the economy or as specified by company
Face amount	Fixed or declining during term of the policy; changeable at renewal	Fixed	Variable
Premiums	Low with increases at renewal	High and fixed	High but variable within limits
Cost of the death benefit portion	Low, with interest at renewal	Unknown	Known but can vary and may hide some expense charges
Company expense charges	Low but unknown; hidden in premium	Unknown; hidden in premium	Known; may be high

Variable-universal life insurance also carries higher commissions and is more likely to require annual fees than other forms of life insurance. A 2 percent annual fee would change a policy with an annual return of 7 percent on its investments to one with a net 5 percent return. You should also compare the policy's investment component with alternative investments. (Investments are covered in Chapters 13 to 16.)

✔ CONCEPT CHECK 12.2

1. List three similarities and three differences between term life insurance and cash-value life insurance.
2. Explain why the premiums for term insurance are so much lower than those of cash-value life insurance.
3. Describe the benefit of buying guaranteed renewable term insurance.
4. Explain why the amount of "insurance" declines over time under a cash-value life insurance policy.
5. Distinguish between cash-value life insurance with a fixed return and with a variable return.

---

owner/policyholder Retains all rights and privileges granted by the policy, including the right to amend the policy and the right to designate who receives the proceeds.

insured Individual whose life is insured

3   LEARNING OBJECTIVE

Explain the major provisions of life insurance policies.

Understanding Your Life Insurance Policy

A **life insurance policy** is the written contract between the insurer and the policyholder. It contains all of the information relevant to the agreement. Several parties will be named in the life insurance contract (policy). The **owner,** or **policyholder,** retains all rights and privileges granted by the policy, including the right to amend the policy and the right to designate who receives the proceeds. The **insured** is the person whose life is insured. In addition to the beneficiary, the owner will name a **contingent beneficiary** who will become the beneficiary if the original beneficiary dies before the insured. Although the owner and the insured are often the same person, it is possible for four different people to play all these roles.

Policy Terms and Provisions Unique to Life Insurance

Life insurance policies define the terminology used in the policy and outline the basic provisions of such insurance. This information serves to clarify the meaning of the policy and the protection afforded the insurer and the policyholder.

The Application The **life insurance application** is the policyholder's offer to purchase a policy. It provides information and becomes part of the life insurance policy (the contract). Any errors or omissions in the application may allow the insurance company to deny a request for payment of the death benefit.

Lives Covered Most life insurance policies cover the life of a single person—the insured. It is also possible to cover two or more people with one policy, however. **First-to-die policies** cover more than one person but pay only when the first insured dies. These policies are less costly than separate policies written on each person, but the survivor then has no coverage after the first person dies. An alternative is the **survivorship joint life policy,** which pays when the last person covered dies.

first-to-die policies Cover more than one person but pay only when the first insured dies.

survivorship joint life policy Pays when the last person covered dies.

The Incontestability Clause Life insurance policies generally include an **incontestability clause** that places a time limit—usually two years after issuance of

incontestability clause Places a time limit on the right of the insurance company to deny a claim.

Did You Know?...

How Insurance Policies Are Organized

All insurance policies include five basic components, each of which provides specific information. These five elements, in order of their usual location in the policy, are as follows: declarations, insuring agreements, exclusions, conditions, and endorsements.

- **Declarations** provide the basic descriptive information about the insured person or property, the premium to be paid, the time period of the coverage, and the policy limits. Also included may be promises by the insured to take steps to control the losses associated with a specific peril. For example, a life insurance purchaser may promise not to smoke in exchange for paying a discounted premium. The information in the declarations is used to help determine the premium and for identification purposes.

- **Insuring agreements** are the broadly defined coverages provided under the policy. The insurer makes these promises in return for the premium paid by the insured. For example, in life insurance, the insurer promises to pay the death benefit amount to the beneficiary in the event of the insured's death. In automobile insurance, the insuring agreements will often include definitions of a motor vehicle or insured premises to clarify the promises made.

- **Exclusions** narrow the focus and eliminate specific coverages broadly stated in the insuring agreements.

The insurer makes no promise to pay for these exceptions and special circumstances. For example, suicide is commonly excluded during the first two years of a life insurance policy. A common automobile insurance exclusion denies coverage under a family policy if the car is used primarily for business purposes. People who do not understand the exclusions in their policies may believe they are covered for a loss when, in fact, they are not.

- **Conditions** impose obligations on both the insured and the insurer by establishing the ground rules of the agreement. For example, they might include procedures for making a claim after a loss, rules for cancellation of the policy by either party, and procedures for changing the terms of the policy. The insured who fails to adhere to the procedures or obligations described in the conditions may be denied coverage when a loss occurs.

- **Endorsements** (or **riders,** as they are sometimes called in life insurance) are amendments and additions to the basic insurance policy that can both expand and limit coverage to accommodate specific needs. When the terms of an endorsement or rider differ from the terms of the basic policy, the endorsement will be considered valid. Endorsements may be requested at any time during the life of the policy to expand coverage, raise the policy limits, and make other changes.

Step-by-Step Strategies for Buying Life Insurance

4 LEARNING OBJECTIVE

Apply a step-by-step strategy for implementing a life insurance plan.

In a recent year, more than $140 billion of new life insurance was purchased in the United States. Did each individual really need to be covered by life insurance? Was the policy purchased the right one, and was it purchased from a reputable company and agent? Did the buyer pay the right price?

First Ask Whether or Not, and For How Much, Your Life Should Be Insured

Anyone whose death will result in financial losses to others should be covered by life insurance unless other resources are sufficient to cover the losses. At a minimum, there will be final expenses such as for funeral and burial. Beyond that, the need depends on the person's family situation. Parents with minor children almost always need life insurance.

People who generally do not need life insurance include children and people with no dependents who have no desire to leave an estate. People who are sometimes unnecessarily insured include retirees who may have already built up assets sufficient to provide for income for survivors and to cover final expenses. The only way to really know how much additional life insurance you need is through the needs-based calculations covered earlier in this chapter. You should do this yourself and not rely on an insurance agent who has a vested interest in selling you some life insurance.

Did You Know?...

About Life Insurance After Divorce

If you receive income from a former spouse through either alimony or child support, life insurance on that person is advisable. If a policy that was purchased while a couple was married remains in effect, it is wise to keep it. To be certain that the correct beneficiary is named, have that requirement stated in a court order and/or made part of the divorce decree. The custodial parent should then be named as owner of the policy, thereby preventing the noncustodial parent from making any changes in the policy. Noncustodial parents will also need life insurance on their former spouses because they will probably receive custody of the children if the former spouse dies and may need additional income to support them.

Then Properly Integrate Your Life Insurance into Your Overall Financial Planning

Advertising and sales promotion literature for cash-value life insurance often pushes the idea that this type of insurance is a good investment and is appropriate as a retirement savings vehicle. Most independent personal finance experts would disagree strongly. Instead, they typically advise people to take a broader perspective and think of life insurance as just one facet of their plans. Specifically, you should always think in terms of the two longevity risks: the risk of dying too soon and the risk of living too long. Term life insurance most effectively solves the dying-too-soon problem. Investing through tax-sheltered retirement plans most effectively solves the living-too-long problem.

Your need for life insurance will change significantly over the course of your life. So should your life insurance plan. You should reassess your plan every two or three years and any time your family or employment situation changes. Keep these facts in mind:

- During childhood and while single, your need for life insurance is either nonexistent or very small because few, if any, other people rely on you for financial support.
- With marriage comes the increased responsibility for another person, although life insurance needs probably remain low because spouses usually have the potential to support themselves if the other partner were to die.
- The arrival of children, however, triggers a sharp increase in life insurance needs. Children often require as many as 25 years of parental support, during which time they usually have little ability to provide for themselves.
- As children grow older, the number of years of their remaining dependency declines, reducing the need for life insurance.

Did You Know? ...

The Tax Consequences of Protecting Loved Ones Through Life Insurance

Some people consider cash-value life insurance to be a tax-advantaged way to invest for retirement. Life insurance does have some tax-sheltering aspects because the cash value built up in the policy is not subject to income taxes. For a number of other reasons, however, cash-value life insurance does not compare favorably with qualified retirement plans available through your employer or with IRAs (discussed in Chapter 17)

1. The rate of return on cash-value life insurance has historically lagged well behind what can be achieved by a diversified portfolio of stock and bond mutual funds. Mutual funds can be purchased through various tax-sheltered retirement accounts (discussed in Chapters 1, 4, and 17).

2. The commissions and expense charges on cash-value life insurance are much higher than those associated with most no-load mutual funds. This is especially true for index mutual funds. (See Chapter 15.)

3. The premiums paid on life insurance policies cannot be used to reduce taxable income; however, contributions to individual retirement accounts and 401(k) plans do offer this significant advantage.

You should be contributing the maximum amount possible into available tax-sheltered retirement plans before you consider the purchase of cash-value life insurance as a retirement savings vehicle.

- Parents with grown children see a reduced need for life insurance because their retirement investment program will have grown large enough to cover the losses that death might bring.
- Retirement and widowhood reduce the need for life insurance or may even eliminate it altogether.

Figure 12.3 depicts a life insurance and investment plan recommended over an individual's life cycle. This plan is built on two cornerstones: (1) the purchase of term insurance for the bulk of life insurance needs (because term insurance is more flexible than cash-value insurance and provides more protection for each premium dollar) and (2) a systematic, regular investment program. The first type of life insurance to buy is a permanent cash-value policy with a guaranteed insurability option. A $20,000 to $50,000

As a family ages, life insurance needs typically decrease.

Advice from a Pro...

Buy Term and Invest the Rest

The principle behind the strategy "buy term and invest the rest" is simple: If you invest the money difference between the cost of premiums for a term life insurance policy and the cost of premiums for a far more expensive cash-value policy, you will *always* come out ahead financially. To see why, consider the buildup of protection shown in the accompanying table for Seth Cameron, a 30-year-old who is considering life insurance policies. Seth could pay an $870 annual premium to buy a $100,000 whole life policy. Alternatively, he could spend $130 for the first-year premium of a $100,000 five-year renewable term policy and invest the $740 difference ($870 − $130) in a mutual fund account and earn a 5 percent after-tax rate of return.

If Seth dies tomorrow, the policy's beneficiary would receive both the $100,000 in insurance proceeds and the $740 in savings. After five years (age 35), Seth's annual $740 in savings would have grown to $4293; if he dies at that time, the total death benefit would be $104,293. If Seth dies years into the future, the estate is even further ahead because of the growing principal in the account. By age 60, Seth's mutual fund investment would have grown to $58,052. If the fund earned higher than 5 percent annually, the amount would be much greater.

By the time Seth reached age 60, the term insurance premiums would exceed the premiums for the cash-value policy. However, his need for life insurance would presumably be eliminated or greatly reduced at that point. If Seth's children were self-supporting by then, he could probably drop the term insurance policy altogether. Nevertheless, his mutual fund account would remain to provide a financial nest egg of $58,052 or more to his heirs.

With the "buy term and invest the rest" strategy, Seth would have been insured more than 30 years at total premium cost of just $7450. By contrast, the cash-value policy would have required total premiums of $26,100 ($870 × 30) and the policy's cash value at year 30 would be about $44,000.

For "buy term and invest the rest" to work, however, the difference between the term and cash-value policy premiums must, in fact, be invested on a regular basis. Many people say that they will invest this money but then fail to follow through on that promise. You can succeed with a little discipline. The easiest way to ensure that your money is actually invested is to set up an **automatic investment program (AIP)** in which a mutual fund is authorized to withdraw money from your checking account, perhaps monthly, to buy mutual fund shares. When you agree to invest the "difference" automatically, the strategy will work well for you. (See Chapters 13 and 15.)

Jordan Goodman
Moneyanswers.com

Estate Buildup if a Term Life Insurance Buyer Invests the Difference

Age	Premium for Five-Year Renewable Term	Difference (Not Spent on Whole Life)	Total Investment and Earnings* at 5%	Total Estate
30	$ 130	$ 740	$ 740	$100,740
35	150	720	4,293	104,293
40	180	690	9,657	109,657
45	210	660	16,328	116,328
50	240	630	24,668	124,668
55	580	290	35,139	135,139
60			58,052	58,052

*This illustration makes the following assumptions: The whole life policy premium for the same $100,000 in coverage is fixed at $870 every year; the buyer pays the five-year renewable term premium at the beginning of each year; and the difference is invested. Those amounts stay in the investments account all year, as does the previous year's ending balance. Investments earn a compounded 5 percent after-tax annual rate of return. Upon the insured's death, the beneficiary would receive the $100,000 face amount of the term life insurance policy plus the amount built up in the investments account earning 5 percent.

policy is sufficient to cover final expenses, the only permanent need that is present throughout life. The remainder of your life insurance should consist of multiple term insurance policies that you start buying when you begin to have dependents. These should be five- or ten-year, level-premium, guaranteed renewable policies in increments of $100,000 or more. The policies should be layered so that you can drop policies as your need declines. By the time you reach retirement, you will have dropped all your term policies and the cash-value policy can remain to pay final expenses or be cashed in to provide a little retirement income. Of course, this scenario requires that you implement an investment program to save for retirement. Chapters 13 through 17 cover investments in sufficient detail to provide you with the necessary tools to construct this program.

Where and How to Buy Your Life Insurance

The most important feature of any life insurance company is its ability to pay its obligations. The company you choose must have the stability and financial strength to survive for the many years your policy will remain in force. Ratings of the financial strengths of insurance companies are available from A.M. Best Company (www .ambest.com) and Standard & Poor's (www.standardandpoors.com).

You Can Easily Buy Life Insurance Online
Smart personal financial managers take a do-it-yourself approach to life insurance. They regularly calculate their needs and decide what types of insurance to buy and cancel in what increments. This allows them to use a **premium quote service** that offers computer-generated comparisons among 20 to 80 different companies. Premium quote services can be found at www .quotesmith.com, www.quotescout.com, and www.accuquote.com. These websites also offer online life insurance needs calculators and a wealth of information on life insurance from an unbiased perspective. In addition, all the major life insurance companies have an online purchase system. Term insurance is easiest to buy this way, but even cash-value insurance can be purchased online.

premium quote service Offers computer-generated comparisons among 20 to 80 different companies.

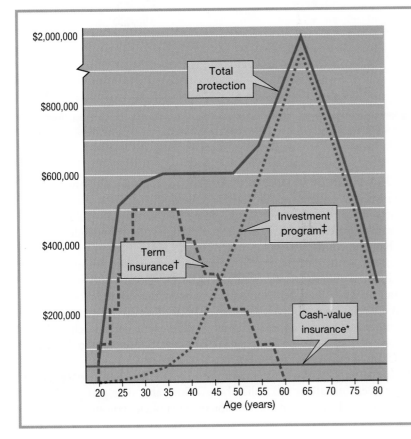

Figure 12.3

Life Insurance and Investment Planning over the Life Cycle

*With a guaranteed insurability option and paid-up at 65.

†Term insurance policies.

††Includes vested employer-sponsored retirement [e.g., 401(k)] plans. (See Chapter 17.)

Did You Know?...

How to Layer Your Term Insurance Policies for $60 per Month

Trying to meet one's life insurance needs with just one or two life insurance policies is not the best way to obtain protection over the life cycle. Life insurance needs fluctuate over one's lifetime, and you will need flexibility. Your life insurance needs are low (burial, debt repayment) until the moment when your first child is born or adopted. Then the need can easily spike up to $200,000 or $500,000 (or more). This need will remain high until the youngest child is approximately ten years old and then will decrease until your retirement age. You can meet the bulk of this need by **layering term insurance policies** so that coverage grows and then can be decreased as your needs change.

An example is provided in the chart below. It assumes that the person is age 25 when a first child is born and age 30 when a last child is born. In this example, the parents buy several level-premium term policies near the birth of the first child, with the policies having differing time periods. They buy another policy when their last child is born and another as the first child gets close to college age. As the children go out on their own, some of the earliest policies expire, thereby reducing the overall amount of insurance as the parents' needs decline.

One benefit of layering is affordability. Based on premium rates for healthy nonsmokers, the cost for the plan illustrated here would never be more than approximately $60 per month.

Age	Buy	Policies in Force at Each Age	Total Coverage at Each Age
25	Policy 1, $100,000, 30 years	#1, #2, #3	$450,000
	Policy 2, $150,000, 25 years		
	Policy 3, $200,000, 20 years		
30	Policy 4, $150,000, 25 years	#1, #2, #3, #4	600,000
35		#1, #2, #3, #4	600,000
40	Policy 5, $50,000, 20 years	#1, #2, #3, #4, #5	650,000
45		#1, #2, #4, #5	450,000
50		#1, #4, #5	300,000
55		#5	50,000
60			0

layering term insurance policies Purchasing level-premium term policies so that coverage grows when you need it most and then can be decreased as your needs change.

insurance agent Representative of an insurance company authorized to sell, modify, service, and terminate insurance contracts.

Or You Can Use a Local Insurance Agent An **insurance agent** is a representative of an insurance company authorized to sell, modify, service, and terminate insurance contracts. In the United States, life insurance is typically sold through exclusive agents who represent only one company, although some independent agents represent more than one company.

The life insurance agent must be qualified to design a program tailored to your specific needs and should understand the dynamics of family relationships, which influence all life insurance needs. The agent should have earned a professional designation, such as chartered life underwriter (CLU). To earn the CLU, an agent must have three years of experience and pass a ten-course program in life insurance counseling. Some agents also may have earned the certified financial planner (CFP) or chartered financial consultant (ChFC) designation (see page 344).

Your agent should be willing to take the time to provide personal service and to answer all of your questions about the policy both before and after you purchase it. Always ask an agent about the first-year commission on any policies you are considering.

In addition, you should check your agent's reputation with your state's insurance and securities investment regulatory agencies.

Compare Costs Among Policies The price people pay for life insurance depends on their age, health, and lifestyle. Age is important, of course, because the probability of dying increases with age. A person who has a health problem such as heart disease or diabetes may pay considerably higher rates for life insurance or may not be able to obtain coverage at any price. People with hazardous occupations (police officers) or dangerous hobbies (skydivers) are often required to pay higher life insurance premiums as well. Life insurance companies typically offer their lowest prices to "preferred" applicants whose health status and lifestyle (for example, nonsmokers) suggest longevity. "Standard" and "impaired" applicants would pay more. Because companies differ in how they assign these labels to applicants, you should shop around for the best treatment.

Instant Message

State Insurance Departments Are a Good Consumer Resource

You can find information about life insurance companies through your state's insurance regulatory agency (www.naic.org/state_web_map.htm).

Popular magazines such as *Kiplinger's Personal Finance Magazine*, *Consumer Reports*, and *Money* regularly publish articles that give average or typical premiums for different types of policies. In addition, your state department of insurance may publish life insurance buyer's guides containing price guidelines that may prove useful in selecting companies with the lowest prices. These independent life insurance agents or groups of agents concentrate on marketing term life insurance at the lowest possible rates.

Term life insurance premiums are usually quoted in dollars per $1000 of coverage. Generally, the higher the face amount of the policy, the lower the rate per $1000. For example, a company might sell term life insurance for $1 per $1000 per year when purchased in face amounts of $100,000 or more and for $1.25 per $1000 per year for policies of less than $100,000. Policies with face amounts of $1 million can cost less than $0.50 per $1000 per year for people younger than age 35.

It is easy to pay too much for term life insurance, especially if you do not comparison shop. The rates shown in Table 12.4 represent good values for term insurance. Note that smokers pay much higher premiums than nonsmokers because as a group smokers die ten years earlier than nonsmokers. Men pay more than women because they typically die three years earlier. Table 12.5 lists annual premiums that are near the average required for various types of insurance policies.

Did You Know?...

About Life Insurance Sales Commissions

Sales commissions are paid to the selling insurance agent every year that a life insurance policy remains in force. Very low sales commissions tend to be charged on term insurance policies—perhaps 10 percent or less of the premium if the policy is purchased directly rather than through an agent. Sales commissions typically represent as much as 90 percent of the first-year premium paid for a cash-value life insurance policy. Over the next several years, commissions drop considerably (perhaps to 50, 40, 30, 20, and 10 percent) so that more of the premium builds cash value.

You can buy all types of life insurance policies with low commissions by mail, on the Internet, and through fee-only financial planners and fee-for-service insurance agents. Even policies sold with a low commission rate may have a **surrender charge**, which is a fee assessed if the policyholder withdraws some or all of the cash value accumulated. This charge is often highest in the early years of the policy but may be reduced or eliminated in later years. The policy illustrated in Table 12.1 has a surrender charge, for example. Ask about commissions and surrender charges whenever you shop for life insurance. Be wary of policies that have both high commissions and surrender charges.

4 **Apply a step-by-step strategy for implementing a life insurance plan.**

Life insurance should be purchased to address the dying-too-soon problem. Your investments should manage the living-too-long problem. Addressing these two problems appropriately requires a small amount of cash-value life insurance, high amounts of term insurance while you are raising children, and a sound investment program to prepare for your retirement years. You should not purchase life insurance until you have determined the actual dollar amount and type of policy you need and compared premiums using various life insurance cost indices.

Let's Talk About It

1. What were your feelings about the need for life insurance before you read this chapter? What are they now?

2. Are you covered by life insurance? If so, how much? Do you feel that you are over- or underinsured?

3. Why do you think people persist in buying cash-value life insurance when, in most cases, they would be better off buying term insurance and investing the money saved into a tax-sheltered retirement account?

4. In many married-couple families, one of the spouses is the primary breadwinner and the other focuses more on homemaking duties. In your view, how does such an arrangement affect the approach that should be taken for each spouse in terms of life insurance?

5. Many young people today choose to cohabitate rather than marry (at least for some time period). Should this affect their thinking about life insurance?

Do the Numbers

1. Andrew Blake of Tuscaloosa, Alabama, is single and has been working as an admissions counselor at a university for three years. Andrew owns a home valued at $156,000 on which he owes $135,000. He has a two-year-old vehicle valued at $12,500 on which he owes $8000. He has about $3800 remaining on his student loans. His retirement account has grown to $7800, and he owns some stock valued at $4400. He has no life insurance and is considering buying some. How much should he buy?

2. Kyle and Laura Parker have been married for three years. They recently bought a home costing $212,000 using a $190,000 mortgage. They have no other debts. Kyle earns $42,000 per year and Laura $41,000. Each has a retirement plan valued at approximately $10,000. They recently received a mail offer from their mortgage lender for a mortgage life insurance policy of $190,000. Their only life insurance currently is a $20,000 cash-value survivorship joint life policy. They each would like to provide the other with support for five years if one of them should die. Assuming $10,000

in final expenses, calculate the amount of life insurance they need using the needs-based approach. Assume a 4% interest rate.

3. Lauren Crow of Davis, California, has a $100,000 participating cash-value policy written on her life. The policy has accumulated $4700 in cash value; Lauren has borrowed $3000 of this value. The policy also has accumulated unpaid dividends of $1666. Yesterday Lauren paid her premium of $1200 for the coming year. What is the current death benefit from this policy?

Financial Planning Cases

Case 1
Life Insurance for a Newly Married Couple

Just-married couples sometimes overindulge in the type and amount of life insurance that they buy. John and Nicole Greenwood of Gunnison, Colorado, took a different approach. Both were working and had a small amount of life insurance provided through their respective employee benefit programs: John, $40,000, and Nicole, $50,000. During their discussion of life insurance needs and related costs, they decided that if Nicole completed her master's degree in industrial psychology, she would have better employment opportunities. Consequently, they decided to use money they had available for additional life insurance to pay for Nicole's education. They both feel, however, that they do not want to have inadequate life insurance.

(a) In what way does Nicole's return to school alter the Greenwoods' life insurance needs?

(b) Would you agree that the amount of life insurance provided by the Greenwoods' respective employers is adequate while Nicole is in school? Explain your response.

(c) Summarize how the Greenwoods' life insurance needs might change over their life cycle.

Case 2
Fraternity Members Contemplate Permanent Life Insurance

Zachary Chen is a college student from Santa Ana, California. Soon to graduate, Zachary was approached recently by a life insurance agent, who set up a group meeting for several members of his fraternity. During the meeting, the agent presented six life insurance plans and was very persuasive about the benefits of a universal life insurance plan that his company calls Affordable Life II. Under the plan, the prospective graduate can buy $100,000 of permanent life insurance for a very low premium during the first five years and then pay a higher premium later when income presumably will have increased. Zachary was confused after the meeting, as were his friends. Armed with your knowledge from this personal finance book, you have been asked to respond to some of their questions.

(a) Do you think universal life insurance is a good deal for these people? Why or why not?

(b) How can the individual fraternity members decide how much life insurance they need?

(c) Life insurance cannot be as confusing as the agent made it seem. What clearer explanation would you give to the fraternity members?

(d) What type of life insurance, if any, would you advise for the fraternity brothers?

(e) How would they know if a life insurance policy is offered at a fair price?

Case 3
A Married Couple with Children Address Their Life Insurance Needs

Joseph and Samantha Hensley of Savannah, Georgia, are a married couple in their mid-30s. They have two children, ages five and three, and Samantha is pregnant with their third child. Samantha is a book indexer who earned $15,000 after taxes last year. Because she performs much of her work at home, it is unlikely that she will need to curtail her work after the baby is born. Joseph is a family therapist; he earned $48,000 last year after taxes. Because both are self-employed, Samantha and Joseph do not have access to group life insurance. They are each covered by $50,000 universal life policies they purchased three years ago. In addition, Joseph is covered by a $50,000, five-year guaranteed renewable term policy, which will expire next year. The Hensleys are currently reassessing their life insurance program. As a preliminary step in their analysis, they have determined that Samantha's account with Social Security would yield the family about $1094 per month, or an annual benefit of $13,128, if she were to die. For Joseph, the figure would be $2072 per month, or an annual benefit of $24,864. Both agree that they would like to support each of their children to age 22, but to date they have been unable to start a college savings fund. The couple estimates that it would cost $80,000 to put each child through a regional university in their state as measured in today's dollars. They expect that burial expenses for each spouse would total about $10,000, and they would like to have a lump sum of life insurance clearly marked for paying off their $155,000 home mortgage. They also feel that each spouse would want to take a six-month leave from work if the other were to die.

(a) Calculate the amount of life insurance that Samantha needs based on the information given. Use the Decision-Making Worksheet on page 326 or the *Garman/Forgue* website. Assume a 3 percent rate of return after taxes and inflation and an income need for 22 years because the unborn child will need financial support for that many years.

(b) Calculate the amount of life insurance that Joseph needs based on the information given. Use the Decision-Making Worksheet on page 326 or the *Garman/Forgue* website. Assume a 3 percent rate of return after taxes and inflation and an income need for 22 years because the unborn child will need financial support for that many years.

(c) If Samantha and Joseph purchased term insurance to cover their additional needs, how much more would each need to spend on life insurance?

Case 4
Victor and Maria Hernandez Contemplate Switching Life Insurance Policies

Victor and Maria Hernandez have a total of $200,000 in life insurance. Victor has a $50,000 cash-value policy purchased more than 20 years ago when the couple was first married (now with a $16,000 cash value) and a $100,000 group term policy through his employer. Maria has a $50,000 group term insurance policy through her employer. The couple has been approached by a life insurance agent who thinks that they need to change their policy mix because, he says, they are inadequately insured. Specifically, the agent has suggested that Victor cash in his cash-value policy and buy a new variable-universal life insurance policy.

(a) If Victor cashes in his policy, what options would he have when receiving the cash value?

(b) Determine what the $16,000 in cash value in Victor's life insurance policy would be worth in 20 years if that sum were invested somewhere else and earned an 8 percent annual return. (Hint: Use the *Garman/Forgue* website.)

(c) Would cashing in the policy be a wise decision? Why or why not?

(d) As the Hernandezes' children are now grown and out on their own, and both Victor and Maria are employed full time, give general reasons why Victor may need more or less insurance.

(e) Explain why it would be a bad idea for Victor to buy a variable-universal life insurance policy.

Case 5
The Johnsons Change Their Life Insurance Coverage

Harry and Belinda Johnson spend $9 per month on life insurance in the form of a premium on a $10,000, paid-at-65 cash-value policy on Harry. Belinda has a group term insurance policy from her employer with a face amount of $59,400 (1.5 times her annual salary). By choosing a group life insurance plan from his menu of employee benefits, Harry now has $30,900 (his annual salary) of group term life insurance. Harry and Belinda have decided that, because they have no children, they could reduce their life insurance needs by protecting one another's income for only four years, assuming the survivor would be able to fend for himself or herself after that time. They also realize that their savings fund is so low that it would have no bearing on their life insurance needs. Harry and Belinda are basing their calculations on a projected 4 percent rate of return after taxes and inflation. They also estimate the following expenses: $8000 for final expenses, $4000 for readjustment expenses, and $5000 for repayment of short-term debts.

(a) Should the $3000 interest earnings from Harry's trust fund be included in his annual income for the purposes of calculating the likely dollar loss if he were to die? (See the discussions about the Johnsons at the end of Chapter 3.) Explain your response.

(b) Based on your response to the previous question, how much more life insurance does Harry need? Use the Decision-Making Worksheet on page 326 to arrive at your answer.

(c) Repeat the calculations to arrive at the additional life insurance needed on Belinda's life.

(d) How might the Johnsons most economically meet any additional life insurance needs you have determined they may have?

(e) In addition to their life insurance planning, how might the Johnsons begin to prepare for their retirement years?

On the 'Net

Go to the Web pages indicated to complete these exercises. You can also go to the *Garman/Forgue* website at college.hmco.com/business/students for an expanded list of exercises. Under General Business, select the title of this text. Click on the Internet Exercises link for this chapter.

1. Visit the website for QuoteSmith at www.quotesmith.com to obtain a quote for the annual premium on a $200,000 guaranteed renewable, ten-year term policy for you. Then call a life insurance agent in your community to obtain a quote on the same term insurance coverage. How do the term rates quoted by your local agent compare with the rates found over the Internet? Also, ask for the quote on a $100,000 universal life policy with guaranteed insurability and waiver-of-premium options. Ask the agent to explain why the quotes for the two types of policies differ. Analyze his or her response based on what you learned in this chapter.

2. Visit the website for A.M. Best Company at www.ambest.com/ratings and check the ratings for the insurance company recommended by the agent in Exercise 1 as well as the company with the lowest cost for term insurance that you found on the Web. What do the ratings tell you about the relative strengths of those companies?

3. Visit the www.life-line.org website. Click on "Life Insurance" then "How much do I need" and then "Insurance needs calculator." Calculate your current need for life insurance. Then recalculate your need for five years from now given your estimates of your income and family situation.

Visit the Garman/Forgue website...

@college.hmco.com/business/students

Under General Business, select *Personal Finance 9e.* There, among other valuable resources, you will find a complete glossary, ACE questions, links to help you complete the chapter exercises, and links to other personal finance sites.

PART 4

CHAPTER 13

Investment Fundamentals

You Must Be Kidding, Right?

Twins Laura and Lauren Jackson have worked for the same employer for many years. They have always differed in their investment philosophies toward saving for retirement. Laura invested $5000 for 10 years starting at age 25 and never added any more money to the account. Lauren invested $5000 per year for 20 years starting at age 35 and never contributed more to her account. Assuming that they both earn an 8 percent annual return, how much more money will Laura have accumulated for retirement than Lauren by the time they reach age 65?

    A. $144,000   **B.** $235,000   **C.** $494,000   **D.** $729,000

The answer is B, $235,000. Laura's account balance at age 65 is projected at $729,000 and Lauren's is $494,000. Even though Laura saved for only 10 years compared with Lauren's 20 years of saving, Laura's long-term investment approach had her starting to save for retirement early in her working career. Thus, she accumulated 48 percent more money than her sister ($235,000 ÷ $494,000). Starting early on long-term investment goals is a money-winning idea!

LEARNING OBJECTIVES

After reading this chapter, you should be able to:

1   **Explain** how to get started as an investor.

2   **Discover** your own investment philosophy.

3   **Identify** the kinds of investments that match your interests.

4   **Describe** the major factors that affect the rate of return on investments.

5   **Decide** which of the five long-term investment strategies you will utilize.

6   **Create** your own investment plan.

What Do You Recommend?

Jennifer and Julia are sisters, both in their 20s. Jennifer drives a leased BMW convertible, and she makes about $42,000, including tips, as a part-time bartender at two different restaurants. Although she has no employee benefits, she enjoys having flexible work hours so that she can go to the beach and the local nightspots. Currently, Jennifer has $10,000 in credit card debt. She has $1500 in a bank savings account, and two years ago she opened an individual retirement account (IRA) with a $1000 investment in a mutual fund. Her sister Julia drives a paid-for Geo, pays her credit card purchases in full each month, and sacrifices some of her salary by putting $100 per month into her employer's company stock through her 401(k) retirement account. Over the past seven years, the stock price, which was once about $40, has risen to almost $70, and Julia's 401(k) plan is now worth about $16,000. Julia also has invested about $14,000 in aggressive-growth mutual funds, and she plans to use that money for a down payment on a home purchase. She earns $58,000 as a manager of a restaurant, plus she receives an annual bonus ranging from $2000 to $4000 every January that she uses for a spring vacation in Mexico. Julia's employer provides many employee benefits.

What do you recommend to Jennifer and Julia on the subject of investment fundamentals regarding:

1. Getting more money to save and invest?

2. Prerequisites to investing for Jennifer?

3. Portfolio diversification for Julia?

4. Dollar-cost averaging for Jennifer?

5. Investment alternatives for Julia?

FOR HELP with studying this chapter, visit the Online Student Center:

www.college.hmco.com/pic/garman9e

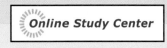
Online Study Center

At many points in this book, we have encouraged you to set aside funds for the future, especially by accumulating funds through regular savings. This approach is a wise course of action, but building real wealth requires an additional consideration—earning a good rate of return on your money. The difference in the return is a major distinction between mere savings and investing. Many successful investors ultimately become able to live off the earnings on their accumulated wealth, sometimes without spending the wealth itself.

To help secure a desirable future lifestyle, you cannot spend every dollar that you earn today. Instead, you must sacrifice by setting aside some of your current income and investing it. To be financially successful, it is wise to start investing early in life, invest regularly, and stay invested. Why? Because, for every five years you delay investing, you will have to double your monthly investment amount to achieve the same goals. Remember: You—and no one else—are responsible for your own financial success.

This chapter begins by examining how to get started in investments. It then helps you identify your personal investment philosophy. The next section gives an overview of investment possibilities—whether you as an investor want to lend or own and whether you prefer to be a short- or long-term investor. We also examine the major factors that affect an investment's rate of return, such as market risk, inflation, time horizon, and taxes. Rather than trying to time the market, the wise investor uses the investment strategies of buy and hold, portfolio diversification, asset allocation, modern portfolio theory, and dollar-cost averaging. The chapter closes with step-by-step details on how to create your own investment plan.

Starting Your Investment Program

1　LEARNING OBJECTIVE
Explain how to get started as an investor.

Starting an investment program requires understanding how investing differs from savings, getting ready to invest, and deciding why you want to invest. Then after you find the money to invest, you can contemplate the types of returns you might anticipate from your investments.

Investing Is More Than Saving

investing Putting saved money to work so that it makes you even more money.

Savings is the accumulation of excess funds by intentionally spending less than you earn. Investing is more. **Investing** is taking some of the money you are saving and putting it to work so that it makes you even more money. Your goals and the time it will take to reach those goals dictate the investment strategies you follow and the investment alternatives you choose.

securities Assets suitable for investment, including stocks, bonds, and mutual funds.

The most common ways that people invest are by putting money into assets called **securities,** such as stocks, bonds, and mutual funds (often through their employer-sponsored retirement accounts), and by buying real estate. **Stocks** are shares of ownership in a corporation, and bonds represent loans to companies and governments. All of your investment assets make up your **portfolio,** the collection of investments assembled to meet your investment goals.

stocks Shares of ownership in a corporation.

portfolio Collection of investments assembled to meet your investment goals.

Are You Ready to Invest?

Here are signs you are ready to begin an investment program:
- **You balance your budget.** If you find yourself constantly running short of cash toward the end of the month or if you make only minimum payments on your credit card balances, you need to institute budget controls so you can live within your means.
- **You are able to save regularly.** A good financial manager forgoes some spending to save regularly to build an emergency fund, acquire goods and services, and

achieve other goals. You can't invest unless you have some savings with which to begin.

- **You use credit wisely.** Pay off any high-interest debt. Pay credit card bills in full each month. Have a maximum credit limit sufficient to meet personal financial emergencies.
- **You carry adequate insurance.** Liability insurance protects your assets and lifestyle in the event you are sued. Health insurance is a must. Term life insurance protects the lifestyle of dependents.

Decide Why You Want to Invest

When you have reasons to invest, such as to buy a home or plan for a financially satisfying retirement, you will be more likely to consider "investments" as a high-priority category in your budget. Your investments can increase your income and help maximize your enjoyment of life. People invest for four reasons:

- To achieve financial goals, such as a taking vacation, purchasing a new car, making a down payment on a home, financing a child's education, or starting a business
- To gain wealth and a feeling of financial security
- To increase current income
- To meet retirement income needs

Where Can You Get the Money to Invest?

You must save money to have it for investing, and here are some suggestions:

- **Pay yourself first.** "Pay yourself" every time you receive income by earmarking in your budget money for saving.
- **Save—don't spend—extra funds.** When unexpected money arrives, save part or all of it. Examples of extra money are a year-end employer bonus, a commission check, a salary raise, a gift of money, an inheritance, and an income tax refund. Also, when you have a surplus in a monthly budget category, save it.
- **Participate in your employer's retirement plan.** When your employer offers to match your contribution to a 401(k) retirement plan, it's free money.

Good Money Habits in Investing Fundamentals

Make the following your money habits in investing fundamentals:

1. Sacrifice some of your income by investing for your future needs and lifestyle.
2. Start early in life to invest in a diversified portfolio of assets consistent with your investment philosophy.
3. When investing for the long term, willingly accept more risk.
4. Invest regularly through your employer's retirement plan using an asset allocation strategy.
5. Invest no more than 10 percent of your portfolio in your company stock, or any single company stock, for that matter.
6. Follow the buy-and-hold long-term approach to investing.
7. Invest in stocks, mutual funds, bonds, and real estate, not life insurance or annuities.

If you want to *save $1,000* this year, ask yourself these questions…before you buy!

1. Did I plan to buy this?
2. If I have to pay cash, do I still want it?
3. What will happen if I don't buy this?
4. Do I need this… or just want it?

- **Make saving automatic.** Have funds automatically transferred from your bank to a savings account as well as from your paycheck to your retirement plan.
- **Make installment payments to yourself.** If you make installment repayments on a debt or lease, continue to make the "payments" to your savings account after the debt has been repaid.
- **Break a habit.** Put aside the money you would have spent on a former habit, such as buying lottery tickets.
- **Get a part-time job.** Save the after-tax money earned from an extra job.
- **Scrimp for one month.** To succeed, cut back and question every possible expense. Knowing that this level of frugality will end after 30 days will help motivate you.

What Investment Returns Are Possible?

Figure 13.1 shows the long-term rates of return on some popular investments. When people invest their money, they take a **financial risk** (also called **business risk**)—namely, the possibility that the investment will fail to pay them any return to the investor. Later in the chapter, investing poses a number of other kinds of risk. At the extremes, a company could have a very good year earning a considerable profit, or it could go bankrupt, causing investors to lose all of their money.

Investors hope that their investments will earn them a positive **total return**, which is the income an investment generates from current income and capital gains. **Current income** is money received while you own an investment. It is usually received on a regular basis as interest, rent, or dividends. As we have noted elsewhere in the text, **interest** is the charge for borrowing money. Investors in bonds earn interest. **Rent** is payment received in return for allowing someone to use your real estate property, such as land or a building. A **dividend** is a portion of a company's earnings that the firm pays out to its shareholders. For example, Nina Hernandez from Oneonta, New York, purchased 100 shares of H&M stock at $45 per share ($4500) last year. The company paid dividends of $3 per share during the year, so Nina received $300 in cash dividends as current income.

A **capital gain** occurs only when you actually sell the investment; it results from an increase in the value of the initial investment. It is calculated by subtracting the total amount paid for the investment (including purchase transaction costs) from the higher price at which it is sold (minus any sales transaction costs). For example, if the price of H&M company stock rose to $52 during the year, Nina could sell it for a capital gain. If Nina paid a transaction cost of $1 per share at both purchase and time of sale, her capital gain would be $500 [($5200 − $100) − ($4500 + $100)].

Capital losses can occur as well. For most investments, a trade-off arises between capital gains and current income. Investments with potential for high capital gains often pay little current income, and investments that pay substantial current income generally have little or no potential for capital gains. Long-term investors are usually willing to forgo current income in favor of possibly earning substantial future capital gains.

The **rate of return, or yield,** is the total return on an investment expressed as a percentage of its price. It is usually stated on an annualized basis. For example, if Nina sells the H&M stock for $52 per share after one year, she will have a total return of $800 ($300 in dividends plus $500 in capital gains). Her yield would be 17.78 percent ($800 ÷ $4500).

---

financial risk Possibility that an investment will fail to pay a return to the investor.

total return Income an investment generates from current income and capital gains.

current income Money received while you own an investment; usually received regularly as interest, rent, or dividends.

interest Charge for borrowing money; bond investors earn interest.

capital gain Increase in the value of an initial investment (less costs) realized upon the sale of the investment.

Instant Message

Creating Wealth

For most people it is difficult to accumulate wealth by saving out of earnings. Most wealth comes from capital gains. To create wealth use your savings to invest in stocks, bonds, or real estate and/or start a business.

capital loss Decrease in paper value of an initial investment; only realized if sold.

rate of return/yield Total return on an investment expressed as a percentage of its price.

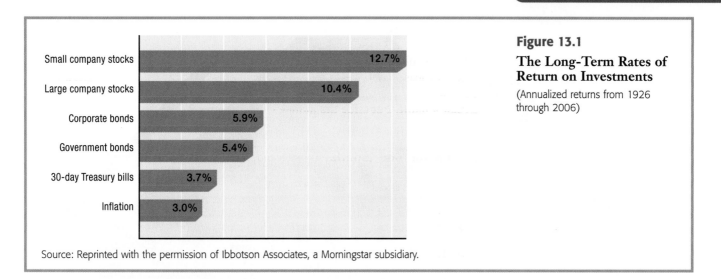

Figure 13.1

The Long-Term Rates of Return on Investments

(Annualized returns from 1926 through 2006)

Source: Reprinted with the permission of Ibbotson Associates, a Morningstar subsidiary.

✓ CONCEPT CHECK 13.1

1. What should you do before you are ready to invest?
2. Identify three ways that you personally could find some money to invest in the next five years.
3. What are the two parts of an investor's total return?

Discover Your Investment Philosophy

Achieving financial success requires that you understand your investment philosophy and adhere to it when investing. Thus, you also need to know about investment risk and what to do about it.

2 LEARNING OBJECTIVE
Discover your own investment philosophy.

How to Handle Investment Risk

Pure risk, which exists when there is no potential for gain, only the possibility of loss, was discussed in Chapter 10. Investments, in contrast, are subject to **speculative risk,** which exists in situations that offer potential for gain as well as for loss. **Investment risk** represents the uncertainty that the yield on an investment will deviate from what is expected. For most investments, the greater the risk, the higher the potential return. This potential for gain is what motivates people to accept increasingly greater levels of risk, as illustrated in Figure 13.2. Nevertheless, many people remain seriously averse to risk.

Investors need the promise of a high return to warrant placing their money at risk in an investment. If you want a completely safe investment, you can invest in U.S. Treasury securities (discussed in Chapter 14), which are backed by the full faith and credit of the U.S. government. With this sort of investment, you loan your money to the federal government and it is later returned with interest. One form of Treasury securities is the short-term Treasury bill, or **T-bill,** which is a government IOU of one year of less. Because T-bills are risk-free investments, they pay too low a return for most people.

If you invest only in T-bills, you will miss out on the significantly higher returns that other investments, such as stocks and stock mutual funds, can provide. When making investments, people demand a **risk premium** for their willingness to make

speculative risk Involves the potential for either gain or loss; equity investments might do either.

investment risk The possibility that the yield on an investment will deviate from its expected return.

risk premium Amount that risk-averse investors require for taking on a riskier investment rather than a risk-free investment like U.S. government securities. The riskier the investment, the greater the premium demanded.

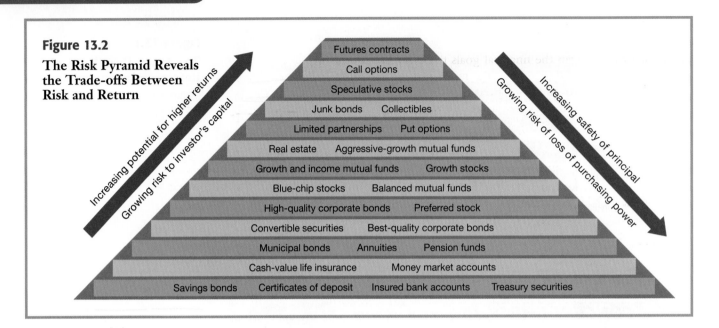

Figure 13.2

The Risk Pyramid Reveals the Trade-offs Between Risk and Return

Increasing potential for higher returns

Growing risk to investor's capital

Increasing safety of principal

Growing risk of loss of purchasing power

Futures contracts

Call options

Speculative stocks

Junk bonds   Collectibles

Limited partnerships   Put options

Real estate   Aggressive-growth mutual funds

Growth and income mutual funds   Growth stocks

Blue-chip stocks   Balanced mutual funds

High-quality corporate bonds   Preferred stock

Convertible securities   Best-quality corporate bonds

Municipal bonds   Annuities   Pension funds

Cash-value life insurance   Money market accounts

Savings bonds   Certificates of deposit   Insured bank accounts   Treasury securities

---

Instant Message

Accept More Risk

Most investors are too risk averse. You can accept more risk when investing for long-term goals.

---

investments for which there is no guarantee of future success. This risk premium constitutes the difference between a riskier investment's return and the totally safe return on the T-bill. Industry experts figure the risk premium for most investors is 3 percent or higher, although it varies depending upon the investment alternative. A top-quality corporate bond pays about 2 percentage points more than T-bills, so if the latter rate is 4.5 percent, the potential return to the bond investor should be about 6.5 percent. Because stocks historically earn at least 5 percentage points more than T-bills, the anticipated return to the stock investor should be 9.5 percent (0.045 + 0.05) or more. Higher-risk investments carry higher risk premiums. A variety of investment alternatives are available to fit each investor's requirements.

Ultraconservative Investors Are Really Just Savers

The securities markets offer many ways to save that present no risk of losing your principal and still earn respectable—albeit limited—returns. These financial vehicles include federally insured savings accounts, certificates of deposit, and EE bonds. Ultraconservative investors, especially those who cannot sleep at night if they think their money is at risk, do not consider putting money into investments, choosing instead to stick with the 100 percent safe options backed by the U.S. federal government. Over the course of a year, an ultraconservative investor who places $1000 in one of these options will not lose a penny and will likely gain $20 to $30. In actuality, ultraconservative investors are not really investors. They are savers. As a result, they do not get ahead financially over the long term because taxes and inflation offset most, if not all, of their interest earnings.

What Is Your Investment Philosophy?

Investors have to take risks that are appropriate to reach their financial goals. The task is to find the right balance and make choices accordingly. You must weigh the risks of an investment with the likelihood of not reaching your goal. Your **risk tolerance** is your ability to weather changes in the values of your investments. To be successful in investing, your tolerance for risk must be factored into your investment philosophy.

risk tolerance An investor's ability and willingness to weather changes in security prices, that is, to weather market risk.

An **investment philosophy** is one's general approach to tolerance for risk in investments, whether it is conservative, moderate, or aggressive, given the financial goals to be achieved. The more risk you take, within reason, the more you can expect to earn and accumulate over the long term. Smart investors follow their investment philosophy without wavering; they do not change course unless their basic objectives change.

Are You a Conservative Investor?

If you have a **conservative investment philosophy,** you accept very little risk and are generally rewarded with relatively low rates of return for seeking the twin goals of a moderate amount of current income and preservation of capital. **Preservation of capital** means that you do not want to lose any of the money you have invested. In short, you could be characterized as risk averse.

Conservative investors focus on protecting themselves. They do so by carefully avoiding losses and trying to stay with investments that demonstrate gains, often for long time periods (perhaps for five or ten years). Tactically, they rarely sell their investments. Investors who are approaching retirement or who are planning to withdraw money from their investments in the near future often adhere to a conservative investment philosophy.

Conservative investors typically consider investing in obligations issued by the government. Examples include Treasury bills, notes, and bonds (insured as to timely payment of principal and interest by the U.S. government), municipal bonds, high-quality (blue-chip) corporate bonds and stocks, balanced mutual funds (which own both stocks and bonds), certificates of deposit, and annuities. A **bond** is essentially a loan that the investor makes to a government or a corporation. Thus, a bond is a debt of the issuer. Over the course of a year, a conservative investor with $1000 could possibly lose $20 and is likely to gain $50 to $60.

Are You a Moderate Investor?

People with a **moderate investment philosophy** seek capital gains through slow and steady growth in the value of their investments along with some current income. They invite only a fair amount of risk of capital loss. Most have no immediate need for the funds but instead focus on laying the investment foundation for later years or building on such a base. Moderate investors are fairly com-

Instant Message

Take a Risk-Tolerance Quiz

Take a risk-tolerance quiz at the following websites:
Bankrate.com: www.bankrate.com/brm/news/investing/20011127a.asp
MSN: www.moneycentral.msn.com/investor/calcs/n_riskq/main.asp
AOL: http://money.aol.com/investing (and "Take the Quiz")

investment philosophy Investor's general tolerance for risk in investments, whether it is conservative, moderate, or aggressive, given the investor's financial goals.

bond A debt instrument issued by an organization that promises repayment at a specific time and the right to receive regular interest payments during the life of the bond; from investor's standpoint, a loan that the investor makes to a government or a corporation.

moderate investment philosophy Investors with this philosophy accept some risk as they seek capital gains through slow and steady growth in investment value along with current income.

Did You Know?...

Americans Are Lousy at Investing Their Money

Over the past decade, the most popular type of investor in America—the average person who puts money into stock mutual funds—earned 6.2 percent a year, according to the consulting firm Dalbar. That is about half of what the S&P 500 stock market average delivered during that time. Over the past 20 years, the figures are worse, investors producing gains of 3.7 percent compared with stock market averages of 13.2 percent annually.

Why? American investors are inept. They make emotional errors when they fail to stay within the bounds of their personal investment philosophy. Greed leads to bad decisions, such as chasing the latest investment fad. Impatience leads to jumping in and out of investments. Investors who buy what they do not understand often wind up with a mishmash of investments. They buy high and sell low. This unhappy result arises when people forget to match their financial decisions with their disposition toward risk.

fortable during rising and falling market conditions. They remain secure in the knowledge that they are investing for the long term. Their tactics might include spreading investment funds among several choices and trading some assets perhaps once a year.

People seeking moderate returns consider investing in dividend-paying common stocks, growth and income mutual funds, high-quality corporate bonds, government bonds, and real estate. Over the course of a year, a moderate investor with $1000 could possibly lose $150 and is likely to gain $80 to $100.

Are You an Aggressive Investor? If you choose to strive for a very high return by accepting a high level of risk, you have an **aggressive investment philosophy.** As such, you could be characterized as a risk seeker. Aggressive investors primarily seek capital gains. Many such investors take a short-term approach, remaining confident that they can profit substantially during major upswings in market prices.

People seeking exceptionally high returns consider investing in common stocks of new or fast-growing companies, high-yielding junk bonds, and aggressive-growth mutual funds. Such investors may put their money into limited real estate partnerships, undeveloped land, precious metals, gems, commodity futures, stock-index futures, and collectibles. Devotees of this investment philosophy sometimes do not spread their funds among many alternatives. Also, they may adopt short-term tactics to increase capital gains. For example, aggressive investors might place most of their investment funds in a single stock in the hope that it will rise 10 percent over 90 days, giving an annual yield of more than 40 percent. Those shares could then be sold and the money invested elsewhere.

Investment tactics for aggressive investors are discussed in Chapter 16. Aggressive investors must be emotionally and financially able to weather substantial short-term losses—such as a downward swing in a stock's price of 30 or 40 percent even though they might expect that an upswing in price will occur in the future. Over the course of a year, an aggressive investor with $1000 could possibly lose $300 and could gain $150 or even more.

Should You Take an Active or Passive Investing Approach?

Another aspect of your personal investment philosophy is your level of involvement in investing. That is, do you want to be an active or passive investor?

Active Investing An **active investor** carefully studies the economy, market trends, and investment alternatives; regularly monitors these factors; and makes decisions to buy and sell, perhaps three or four or more times a year, with or without the advice of a professional. In addition, because the prices of many investments vary with certain news events, world happenings, and economic and political variables, active investors stay alert. Knowing what is going on in the larger world helps active investors understand when to buy or to sell investments quickly so as to reap profits or reduce losses.

Passive Investing A **passive investor** does not actively engage in trading of securities or spend large amounts of time monitoring his or her investments. Such an individual may make regular investments in securities, such as mutual funds (described in Chapter 15), and his or her assets are rarely sold for short-term profits. Instead, passive investors simply aim to match the returns of the entire market. They ignore "hot" tips and the investment of the day touted in the financial press. They keep their emotions in check, and they earn higher returns than active investors over the long term. Most long-term investors utilize a passive approach.

Once you have clarified your investment philosophy and how involved you want to be as an investor, you will be able to make future investing decisions with confi-

aggressive investment philosophy Investors with this philosophy primarily seek capital gains, often with a short time horizon.

active investor An investor who wishes to manage her own account by carefully studying the economy, market trends, and investment alternatives; regularly monitoring these factors; and buying and selling three to four times a year, with or without the advice of a professional.

passive investor An investor who does not actively engage in trading securities or monitoring his or her investments; seeks to match the market return via mutual funds or other managed investments in the longer term.

An active investor keeps a close watch on the economy and financial markets.

dence and conviction. You will be able to show patience by following your long-term views rather than make emotional and wrong decisions—in other words, mistakes—about your money. The investments you choose and the returns earned are likely to match your investment philosophy.

✓ CONCEPT CHECK 13.2

1. Summarize your investment philosophy and general approach to tolerance for risk.

2. Indicate whether you view yourself as an active or passive investor, and explain why.

Identify the Kinds of Investments You Want to Make

The investments you choose should match your interests. Before investing, think about lending versus owning, short term versus long term, and how to select investments that are likely to provide your desired potential total return.

3 LEARNING OBJECTIVE

Identify the kinds of investments that match your interests.

Do You Want to Lend or Own?

You can invest money in two ways, by lending or by owning. When you lend your money, you receive some form of IOU and the promise of repayment plus interest. The interest is a form of current income while you hold the investment. Lending investments rarely result in capital gains.

You can lend by depositing money in banks, credit unions, and savings and loan associations (via savings accounts and certificates of deposit) or by lending money to governments (via Treasury notes and bonds as well as state and local bonds), businesses (corporate bonds), mortgage-backed bonds (such as Ginnie Maes), and life insurance companies (annuities). Such lending investments, or **debts**, generally offer both a fixed maturity and a fixed income. With a **fixed maturity**, the borrower agrees to repay the principal to the investor on a specific date. With a **fixed income**, the borrower agrees to pay the investor a specific rate of return for use of the principal. Such investments allow lenders to be fairly confident that they will receive a certain amount of interest income for a specified period of time and that the borrowed funds will eventually be returned. Thus, the return is somewhat assured. No matter how much profit the borrower makes with your funds, the investing lender receives only the fixed return promised at the time of the initial investment.

Alternatively, you may invest money through ownership of an asset. Ownership investments are often called **equities.** You can buy common or preferred corporate stock (to obtain part ownership in a corporation) in publicly owned companies, purchase shares in a mutual fund company (which invests your funds in corporate stocks and bonds), put money into your own business, purchase real estate, buy commodity futures (pork bellies or oranges), or buy investment-quality collectibles (such as rare antiques or stamps). Ownership investments have the potential for providing current income; however, the emphasis is usually upon achieving substantial capital gains.

debts Lending investments that typically offer both a fixed maturity and a fixed income.

fixed maturity Specific date on which borrower agrees to repay the principal to the investor.

fixed income Specific rate of return that borrower agrees to pay the investor for use of the principal (initial investment).

equities Ownership equities such as common or preferred stocks, equity mutual funds, real estate, and so on that focus on capital gains more than on income.

Instant Message

Financial Planning on the Web

To obtain an overall assessment of your financial progress in life and advice on how to achieve your goals, you may want a financial plan. Prices vary from $250 to $500 or more. Check out Fidelity.com, Schwab.com, TrowePrice.com, and Vanguard.com. Answers to specific questions for $50 to $100 may be obtained on the Web and over the telephone from companies such as Myfinancialadvice.com.

Making Short-, Intermediate-, and Long-Term Investments

If you are investing for a short-term time horizon of less than a year or an intermediate-term of perhaps up to five years, you want to be confident that you preserve the value of what you have. After all, you don't want to lose money in an investment when you need to use that money for a near-term goal, such as college tuition, or be forced to sell an investment because you need cash in a hurry. People with a short or intermediate time horizon require investments that offer some predictability and stability. As a result, these investors are usually more interested in current income than capital gains. If you are investing to achieve long-term goals, by contrast, you want your money to grow, and, therefore, you are likely to keep your money in the same investments for 10 or 15 years. Long-term investors usually invite more risk by seeking capital gains as well as current income. Table 13.1 provides an overview of investment alternatives.

Choose Investments for Their Components of Total Return

When investing, you want to select a portfolio of investments that will provide the necessary potential total return through current income and capital gains in the proportions that you desire. One stock might provide an anticipated cash dividend of

Table 13.1 Overview of Investment Alternatives

This chapter provides background information to help you to initially assess which types of investments might best suit your needs. The next three chapters examine details of investment alternatives. After reading those chapters, you will have learned enough about investments to make informed decisions.

- **Stocks.** Shares of ownership in the assets and earnings of a business corporation. Examples: Blue-chip stocks (like Dow Chemical, Exxon Mobil, and General Electric), well-known growth stocks (like Microsoft and McDonald's), lesser-known growth stocks (like American Greeting and Panera Bread), and income stocks (like water and electricity companies).
- **Bonds.** Interest-bearing negotiable certificates of long-term debt issued by a corporation, a municipality (such as a city or state), or the federal government. Examples: U.S. savings bonds, Series EE bonds, corporate bonds, high-yield corporate bonds, municipal bonds, and zero-coupon bonds.
- **Mutual funds.** An investment company that combines the funds of investors who have purchased shares of ownership in it and then invests that money in a diversified portfolio of stocks and bonds issued by other corporations or governments. Examples: Fidelity Growth Fund, Calvert Social Investment, and Vanguard Growth Index.
- **Real estate.** Property consisting of land; all structures permanently attached to that land; and accompanying rights and privileges, such as crop and mineral rights. Examples: residential housing units, commercial properties, residential lots, raw land.
- **High-risk investments.** Alternatives that have the potential for significant fluctuations in return over short time periods, perhaps only days or weeks. Examples: collectibles (baseball cards, posters, sports jerseys, comic books, stamps, rare coins, antiques), precious metals and stones, and options and futures contracts.

1.5 percent and an expected annual price appreciation of 10 percent, for a total anticipated return of 11.5 percent. Another choice offering the same projected total return might be a stock with expected annual cash dividends of 3.5 percent and capital gains of 8 percent.

✓ CONCEPT CHECK 13.3

1. Summarize your personal views on lending or owning investments.
2. Which type of investment return—current income or capital gains—seems more attractive to you? Why?

Risks and Other Factors Affect the Investor's Return

Because of the uncertainty that surrounds investments, people often follow a conservative course in an effort to keep their risk low. Being too conservative when investing means that they also risk not reaching their financial goals. To be a successful investor, you must understand the major factors that affect the rate of return on investments. Being informed, you can then take the appropriate risks when making investment decisions.

4 LEARNING OBJECTIVE
Describe the major factors that affect the rate of return on investments.

Random and Market Risk

Random risk (also called **unsystematic risk**) is the risk associated with owning only one investment of a particular type (such as stock in one company) that, by chance, may do very poorly in the future because of uncontrollable or random factors, such as labor unrest, lawsuits, and product recalls. If you invest in only one stock, its value might rise or fall. If you invest in two or three stocks, the odds are lessened that all of their prices will fall. Such **diversification**—the process of reducing risk by spreading investment money among several investment opportunities—provides one effective method of managing random risk. It results in a potential rate of return on all of the investments that is lower than the potential return on a single alternative, but the

random/unsystematic risk Risk associated with owning only one investment of a particular type (such as stock in one company) that, by chance, may do very poorly in the future due to uncontrollable or random factors that do not affect the rest of the market.

return is more predictable and the risk of loss is lower. Diversification averages out the high and low returns.

Research suggests that you can cut random risk in half by diversifying into as few as five stocks or bonds; you can eliminate random risk by holding 15 or more stocks or bonds. Rational investors diversify so as to reduce random risk.

Diversification among stocks or bonds cannot eliminate all risks. Some risk would exist even if you owned all of the stocks in a market because stock (and bond) prices in general move up and down over time. This movement results in **market risk** (also known as **systematic** or **undiversifiable risk**). In this case, the value of an investment may drop due to influences and events that affect all similar investments. Examples include a change in economic, social, political, or general market conditions; fluctuations in investor preferences; or other broad market-moving factors, such as a recession or a terrorist attack.

Market risk is the risk that remains after an investor's portfolio has been fully diversified within a particular market, such as stocks. Over the years, market risk has averaged about 8 percent. As a consequence of this risk, the return on any single securities investment (such as a stock), through no fault of its own, might vary up and down about 8 percent annually. The total risk in an investment consists of the sum of the random risk and the market risk.

market risk/systematic risk/ undiversifiable risk Risk that the value of an investment may drop due to influences and events that affect all similar investments.

Other Types of Investment Risks

A number of other investment risks affect investor returns:

- **Business failure risk. Business failure risk,** also called **financial risk,** is the possibility that the investment will fail, perhaps go bankrupt, and result in a massive or total loss of one's invested funds. Investigate thoroughly before investing. See Chapters 14, 15, and 16.

- **Inflation risk.** Inflation risk may be the most important concern for the long-term investor. **Inflation risk,** also called **purchasing power risk,** is the danger that your money will not grow as fast as inflation and therefore not be worth as much in the future as it is today. Over the long term, inflation in the United States has averaged 3.1 percent annually. Thus, the cumulative effects of inflation diminish your investment return. Historically, common stocks and real estate have reduced inflation risk, as values tend to rise with inflation over several years. However, houses, real estate, and other ownership investments are also subject to **deflation risk.** This is the chance that the value of an investment will decline when overall prices decline.

- **Time risk.** The role of time affects all investments. The sooner your invested money is supposed to be returned to you—the **time horizon** of an investment—the less the likelihood that something could go wrong. The more time your money is invested, the more it is at risk. For taking longer-term risks, investors expect and normally receive higher returns.

- **Business-cycle risk.** As we discussed in Chapter 1, economic growth usually does not occur in a smooth and steady manner. Instead, periods of expansion lasting three or four years are often followed by contractions in the economy, called recessions, that may last about a year. The profits of most industries follow the business cycle. Some businesses do not experience business-cycle risk because they continue to earn profits during economic downturns. Examples are gasoline retailers, supermarkets, and utility companies.

- **Market-volatility risk.** All investments are subject to occasional sharp changes in price as a result of events affecting a particular company or the overall market for similar investments. For example, the value of a single stock, such as that of

Instant Message

Time Reduces the Risk of Owning Stock

Since 1927 the worst 20-year performance for stocks was a gain of 3 percent. The worst over 10 years was only −1 percent; over 1 year it was −43 percent. The chance of making money during any one year in the stock market over the past 80 years is 66 percent. Over 5 years, the probability increases to 81 percent; over 10 years it rises to 89 percent.

a technology company like Microsoft, might change 10 or even 30 percent in a single day. Also, all technology stocks could decline 2 or perhaps 5 percent if two or three competitors announce poor earnings. In an average year, the price of a typical stock fluctuates up and down by about 50 percent; thus, the price of a stock selling for $30 per share in January might range from $15 to $45 before the end of the following December.

- **Liquidity risk. Liquidity** is the speed and ease with which an asset can be converted to cash. You can convert your savings into cash instantly. You can sell your stocks and bonds in one day, although it may take four days to have the proceeds available in cash. Real estate is *illiquid* because it may take weeks, months, or years to sell.
- **Reinvestment risk.** Reinvestment risk is the risk that the return on a future investment will not be the same as the return earned by the original investment.
- **Marketability risk.** When you have to sell a certain asset quickly, it may not sell at or near the market price. This possibility is referred to as **marketability risk.** Selling real estate in a hurry, for example, may require the seller to substantially reduce the price in order to sell to a willing buyer.

Transaction Costs Reduce Returns

Buying and selling investments may result in a number of transaction costs. Examples include "fix-up costs" when preparing a home for sale, appraisals for collectibles, and storage costs for precious metals. **Commissions** are usually the largest transaction cost in investments. These are fees or percentages of the units or selling price paid to salespeople, agents, and companies for their services—that is, to buy or sell an investment. The commission charged to buy an investment (one commission) and then later sell it (a second commission) is partially based on the value of the transaction. Typical ranges for commissions are as follows: stocks, 1.5 to 2.5 percent (although trades can be made on the Internet for less than $20); bonds, 0 to 2.0 percent; mutual funds, 0 to 8.5 percent; real estate, 4.5 to 7.5 percent; options and futures contracts, 4.0 to 6.0 percent; limited partnerships, 10.0 to 15.0 percent; and collectibles, 15.0 to 30.0 percent. You can increase your investment returns by holding down transaction costs.

commissions Fees or percentages of the selling price paid to salespeople, agents, and companies for their services in buying or selling an investment.

Commissions

Leverage May Increase Returns

Another factor that can affect return on investment is **leverage**. In the leveraging process, borrowed funds are used to make an investment with the goal of earning a rate of return in excess of the after-tax costs of borrowing. Investing in real estate for its rental income provides an illustration of leverage, as shown in Table 13.2 Assume

leverage Using borrowed funds to invest with the goal of earning a rate of return in excess of the after-tax costs of borrowing.

Table 13.2 Leverage Illustration: Buying Real Estate

	Pay Cash	Use Credit
Purchase price of office building	$300,000	$300,000
Amount borrowed	0	− 270,000
Amount invested	300,000	30,000
Rental income ($2500 per month)	30,000	30,000
Minus tax-deductible interest (6.5%, 30-year loan on $270,000)	− 0	− 17,450
Net earnings before taxes	30,000	12,550
Minus income tax liability (25% bracket)	− 7,500	− 3,137
Rental earnings after taxes	$22,500	$9,413
	÷ 300,000	÷ 30,000
Percentage return on amount invested	7.5%	31.38%

Did You Know?...

The Tax Consequences in Investment Fundamentals

There are some favorable aspects to income taxes to think about when making investments.

1. **After-tax return.** When comparing similar investments, your objective is to earn the best after-tax return. This return is the net amount earned on an investment after payment of income taxes. [See Equation (4.1) on page 122.]

2. **Income versus capital gain.** Current investment income, such as dividends and interest, is taxed at one's marginal tax bracket, likely 25 percent. Capital gains are taxed at special lower rates, likely at 5 or 15 percent.

3. **Tax-deferred investments.** The income and capital gains from investments within employer-sponsored retirement accounts are not subject to income taxes until the funds are withdrawn.

4. **Tax-exempt income.** Income earned from municipal bonds is exempt from income taxes.

5. **Tax-exempt investments.** The income and capital gains from investments within Roth IRA accounts are never subject to income taxes.

that a person can buy a small office building either by making a $30,000 down payment and borrowing $270,000 or by paying $300,000 cash. If the rental income is $30,000 annually ($2500 per month) and the person pays income taxes at a 25 percent rate, a higher return can be obtained using credit to buy the building because the yield would be 31.38 percent versus a 7.5 percent yield when paying cash.

Leverage can prove particularly beneficial when substantial capital gains occur, as this strategy sharply boosts the return on the investment. Assume that at the end of one year, the value of the building described in the previous example has appreciated 7 percent and you could sell it for $321,000 (excluding commission costs). If you had purchased the property for $300,000 cash and then sold it for $321,000, the capital gain on the sale would be 7 percent (the $21,000 return divided by the $300,000 originally invested). If you had bought it using credit, the capital gain would be 70 percent (the $21,000 return divided by the $30,000 originally invested, ignoring transaction costs, taxes, and inflation).

Leverage has a potential negative side as well. In the preceding example, if you used credit to purchase the property, you would need a minimum rental income of $20,479 (using Table 9.4 on page 252, 6½ percent interest on a 30-year loan) just to make the mortgage loan payments. A few months of vacancy or expensive repairs to the building could result in a losing situation. Furthermore, any decline in value would be magnified when you use leverage. You can become financially overextended by using leverage for investments, a factor that you should not ignore.

✓ CONCEPT CHECK 13.4

1. Distinguish between random risk and market risk.
2. Summarize three other risks that may affect investment returns.
3. Explain how transactions costs, leverage, and income taxes increase or decrease investment returns.

Establishing Your Long-Term Investment Strategy

Investing is not rocket science! Anyone reading this book and following its recommendations for making long-term investments can become a successful investor. To succeed, you must establish your own long-term investment strategies. Fortunately, this is easy because there are only five strategies to follow, and they all "hang together." And once learned, as the Nike slogan goes, you "Just do it!" And don't forget to start investing as early in life as possible, as illustrated in Figure 13.3 and Table 13.3.

Long-term investors seek growth in the value of their investments that exceeds the rate of inflation. In other words, they want their investments to provide a positive **real rate of return.** This is the return after subtracting the effects of both inflation and income taxes. A long-term investor generally wants to hold an investment as long as it provides a return commensurate with its risk, often for 10 or 15 years or more.

In addition to understanding the overall economic picture (see Chapter 1), long-term investors understand how the **securities markets** (places where stocks and bonds

5 LEARNING OBJECTIVE

Decide which of the five long-term investment strategies you will utilize.

real rate of return Return on an investment after subtracting the effects of inflation and income taxes.

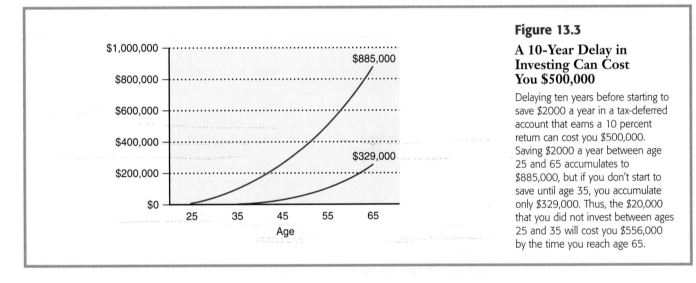

Figure 13.3

A 10-Year Delay in Investing Can Cost You $500,000

Delaying ten years before starting to save $2000 a year in a tax-deferred account that earns a 10 percent return can cost you $500,000. Saving $2000 a year between age 25 and 65 accumulates to $885,000, but if you don't start to save until age 35, you accumulate only $329,000. Thus, the $20,000 that you did not invest between ages 25 and 35 will cost you $556,000 by the time you reach age 65.

Table 13.3 The Wisdom of Starting to Invest Early in Life

Age	Early Investor*		Late Investor†	
	Cumulative Investment	**Account Value**	**Cumulative Investment**	**Account Value**
30	$ 2,000	$ 2,180	$ 0	$ 0
35	10,000	13,047	0	0
40	20,000	33,121	2,000	2,180
45	0	50,960	10,000	13,047
50	0	78,408	20,000	33,121
55	0	120,641	30,000	64,007
60	0	185,621	40,000	111,529
65	0	285,601	50,000	184,648

Conclusion: $20,000 gets the early investor $285,601; $50,000 gets the late investor only $184,648.

*The early investor invested $2000 at the beginning of every year from ages 30 to 39 (ten years of cumulative investing totaling $20,000), and the funds compounded at 9 percent annually.
†The late investor invested $2000 at the beginning of every year from ages 40 to 64 (25 years of cumulative investing totaling $50,000), and the funds compounded at 9 percent annually.

Did You Know?...

Calculate the Real Rate of Return (After Taxes and Inflation) on Investments

1. Identify the <u>rate of return before income taxes.</u> Perhaps you think that a stock will offer a return of 10 percent in one year, including current income and capital gains.

2. Subtract the effects of your marginal tax rate on the rate of return to <u>obtain the after-tax return.</u> If you are in the 25 percent federal income tax bracket, the calculation is $(1 - 0.25) \times 0.10 = 0.075 = 7.5$ percent.

3. Subtract the effects of inflation from the after-tax return to <u>obtain the real rate of return</u> on the investment after taxes and inflation. If you estimate an annual inflation of 4 percent, the calculation gives 3.5 percent (7.5 percent − 4.0 percent). Thus, your before-tax rate of return of 10 percent provides a real rate of return of 3.5 percent after taxes and inflation.

are traded) are performing as a whole. That is, are the markets moving up, moving down, or remaining stagnant? A securities market in which prices have declined in value by 20 percent or more from previous highs, often over the course of several weeks or months, is called a bear market. Since 1926, several bear markets have occurred, with the most recent bear market lasting from 2000 to 2002. In contrast, a bull market results when securities prices have risen 20 percent or more over time. Historically, the more than 20 bull markets have seen an average gain of 110 percent. The bull market of the 1990s saw stock prices increase more than 300 percent!

A **bull** in the market is a person who expects securities prices to go up; a **bear** expects the general market to decline. The origin of these terms is unknown, but some suggest that they refer to the ways that the animals attack: Bears thrust their claws downward, and bulls move their horns upward. Bear markets last, on average, about 9 months; bull markets average 29 months in length.

Long-Term Investors Understand Market Timing

Long-term investors must be able to withstand some market volatility, the likelihood of large price swings in their chosen securities. Although they do not like to be described as such, some long-term investors are **market timers.** Market timing entails shifting your money into cash or bonds when you think stocks and stock mutual funds are overpriced and then later reinvesting your money in stocks and stock mutual funds when you think they have gotten cheap. Market timers pull out of stocks or bonds in anticipation of a market decline or hold back from investing until the market "settles down." In this scenario, investors try to "time" their investments, hoping to capture most of the upside of rising stock prices while avoiding most of the downside.

To succeed in timing the market, you need to know just the right time to buy and just the right time to sell. Research shows that most of the market's gains are realized in a few trading days that occur every now and then. If market timers are out of the market on those days, they lose. In times of rising markets, it is very easy for market timers to sell too early and as a result miss out on much larger profits as the bull market continues to push up prices even more. Those who sell after a sudden drop in investment value, a "down market," actually lock in their losses.

bear market Market in which securities prices have declined in value by 20 percent or more from previous highs, often over the course of several weeks or months.

bull market Market in which securities prices have risen 20 percent or more over time.

market timers Long-term investors who pull out of stocks or bonds in anticipation of a market decline or hold back from investing until the market "settles down"—that is, when they expect prices to climb.

Instant Message

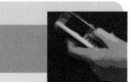

Out of the Market? You Missed a 45% Gain

If you had been out of stocks during the market's ten best days in the past decade, according to Charles Schwab, you would have missed out on 45 percent of the gains.

Very few market timers succeed in simultaneously lowering their risk and raising their returns. In fact, research shows that most of these investors earn returns far worse than the averages, in part because they pay lots of transaction fees. The reality is that market timing increases market risk. Short-term buying and selling is more like gambling than investing. What contributes the most to successful investing is not timing, but time.

Strategy 1: Buy and Hold Anticipates Long-Term Economic Growth

The secret to investment success is benign neglect. Long-term investors need to relax with the confidence and knowledge that investing regularly and not trading frequently will create a substantial portfolio over time. Long-term investors do not follow or react emotionally to the day-to-day changes that occur in the market. Ignore them is the best advice. Because most people are sensitive to short-term losses, daily monitoring could motivate one to make shortsighted buying and selling decisions. Selling high-quality assets in a bear market is a poor strategy because bear markets are so short in duration. It is tough to do, but it is smart to buy more shares when prices are lower during normal market downturns because rising prices in a bull market always follow a bear market. Investors who remain invested in the stock market are rewarded with the opportunity to earn the historic average return of the equities markets, which is 11.4 percent annually.

Most long-term investors use the **buy-and-hold** (also called **buy-to-hold**) approach to investing. That is, they buy a widely diversified mix of stocks and/or mutual funds, reinvest the dividends by buying more stocks and mutual funds, and hold on to those investments almost indefinitely. With this approach, the investor expects that the values of the assets will increase over the long run in tandem with the growth of the U.S. and world economies. The investments may pay some current income as well. The investor's emphasis is on holding the assets through both good and bad economic times with the confidence that their values will go up over the long term. This is a wise strategy.

Buy and hold does not mean buy and ignore. Investors are unwise to blindly hold on to an investment for years. Instead, review all holdings at least once a year to make

buy and hold/buy to hold Investment strategy in which investors buy a widely diversified mix of stocks and/or mutual funds, reinvest the dividends by buying more stocks and mutual funds, and hold on to those investments almost indefinitely.

Short-term buying and selling is more like gambling than investing.

sure that each remains a good investment. Questions to ask: "Is the valuation too high?" "Has the fundamental outlook of the company changed?" "Does this asset still fit my investment plan?" "Would I buy it today?" If necessary, sell the asset.

Strategy 2: Dollar-Cost Averaging Buys at "Below-Average" Costs

dollar-cost averaging/cost averaging Systematic program of investing equal sums of money at regular intervals regardless of the price of the investment.

Dollar-cost averaging (or **cost averaging**) is a systematic program of investing equal sums of money at regular intervals regardless of the price of the investment. In this approach, the same fixed dollar amount is invested in the same stock or mutual fund at regular intervals over a long time. Since investments generally rise more than they fall, the "averaging" means that you purchase more shares when the price is down and fewer shares when the price is high. Most of the shares are, therefore, purchased at **below-average costs.**

below-average costs "Averaging" means that you purchase more shares when the price is down and fewer shares when the price is high, so most of your shares are purchased at below-average cost.

This strategy avoids the risks and responsibilities of investment timing because the stock purchases are made regularly (usually every month) regardless of the price. It also ignores all outside events and short-term gyrations of the market, providing the investor with a disciplined buying strategy. A well-diversified stock mutual fund would be an excellent choice for dollar-cost averaging.

Table 13.4 shows the results of dollar-cost averaging for a stock under varying market conditions. (Commissions are excluded.) As an example, assume that you invest $300 into a stock every three months. Notice that dollar-cost averaging is successful in all three scenarios illustrated.

Dollar-Cost Averaging in a Fluctuating Market To illustrate the effects of dollar-cost averaging, assume that you first invested funds during the "fluctuating market" shown in Table 13.4. Because the initial price is $15 per share, you receive 20 shares for your investment of $300. Then the market drops—an extreme but easy-to-follow example—and the price falls to $10 per share. When you buy $300 worth of the stock now, you receive 30 shares. Three months later, the market price rebounds to $15 and you invest another $300, receiving 20 shares. The price then drops and rises again.

average share price Calculated by dividing the share price total by the number of investment periods.

You now own 120 shares, thanks to your total investment of $1500. The **average share price** is calculated by averaging the amounts paid for the investment: Simply divide the share price total by the number of investment periods. In this example, the

Table 13.4 Dollar-Cost Averaging for a Stock or Mutual Fund Investment

Fluctuating Market			Declining Market			Rising Market		
Regular Investment	Share Price	Shares Acquired	Regular Investment	Share Price	Shares Acquired	Regular Investment	Share Price	Shares Acquired
$300	$15	20	$300	$15	20	$300	$6	50
300	10	30	300	10	30	300	10	30
300	15	20	300	10	30	300	12	25
300	10	30	300	6	50	300	15	20
300	15	20	300	5	60	300	20	15
Totals $1,500	$65	120	$1,500	$46	190	$1,500	$63	140
Average share price: $13.00 ($65 ÷ 5)*			Average share price: $9.20 ($46 ÷ 5)*			Average share price: $12.60 ($63 ÷ 5)*		
Average share cost: $12.50 ($1500 ÷ 120)†			Average share cost: $7.89 ($1500 ÷ 190)†			Average share cost: $10.71 ($1500 ÷ 140)†		

*Sum of share price total ÷ number of investment periods.
†Total amount invested ÷ total shares purchased.

Advice from a Pro...

Buy Shares of Stock Directly Using a Dividend-Reinvestment Plan

More than 1000 well-known companies allow investors to purchase shares of stock directly from them without the assistance of a stockbroker and then to continue to invest on a regular basis without paying brokerage commissions. Such a program is known as a **dividend-reinvestment plan (DRIP).** You simply sign up with the company, agreeing to buy a certain number of shares and to reinvest cash dividends into more shares of stock for little or no transaction fees. Investors' accounts are credited with fractional shares, too.

Wal-Mart is illustrative. It requires a minimum investment of $250, and continuing investments of $50 thereafter. The enrollment fee is $20 plus $0.10 per share. Most companies will buy back shares for a transaction fee of only $10. Companies offering DRIPs include Ameritech, ExxonMobil, Home Depot, Tenneco, Wal-Mart, McDonalds, and Sears. For a list of companies offering direct purchases, see the Securities Transfer Association at www.netstockdirect.com or the Direct Stock Purchase Plan Clearinghouse at www.dripinvestor.com/clearinghouse/home.asp.

Buying shares regularly through a DRIP is a great example of dollar-cost averaging. It allows you to take advantage of fluctuating stock prices by purchasing on a regular basis at below-average costs.

Linda Gorham
Berklee College of Music, Boston, Massachusetts

---

average share price is $13 ($65 ÷ 5). The **average share cost,** a more meaningful figure, is the actual cost basis of the investment used for income tax purposes. It is calculated by dividing the total amount invested by the total shares purchased. In this example, it is $12.50 ($1500 ÷ 120). Based on the recent price of $15 per share, each of your 120 shares is worth on average $2.50 ($15 − $12.50) more than you paid for it. Thus, your gain is $300 (120 × $2.50; or $15 × 120 = $1800, $1800 − $1500 = $300).

average share cost Actual cost basis of the investment used for income tax purposes, calculated by dividing the total amount invested by the total shares purchased.

Dollar-Cost Averaging in a Declining Market

Markets may also decline over a time period. The "declining market" columns in Table 13.4 (representing a prolonged bear market of 15 months) show purchases of 190 shares for increasingly lower prices that eventually reach $5 per share at the bottom of the business cycle. In a declining market, if you keep investing using dollar-cost averaging, you will purchase a large volume of shares. If you sell when the market is down substantially, you will not profit. In this example, you have purchased 190 shares at an average cost of $7.89, and they now have a depressed price of $5. Selling at this point would result in a substantial loss of $550 [$1500 − (190 × $5)]. Dollar-cost averaging requires that you continue to invest if the longer-term prospects suggest an eventual increase in price.

Dollar-Cost Averaging in a Rising Market

During the "rising market" in Table 13.4, you continue to invest but buy fewer shares. The $1500 investment during the bull market bought only 140 shares for an average cost of $10.71. In this rising market, you profit because your 140 shares have a recent market price of $20 per share, for a total value of $2800 (140 × $20).

Almost anyone can profit in a rising market. If you use dollar-cost averaging over the long term, you will continue to buy in rising, falling, and fluctuating markets. The overall result will be that you buy more shares when the cost is down, thereby lowering the average share cost to below-average prices. The totals in Table 13.4, for example, reveal an overall investment of $4500 ($1500 + $1500 + $1500) used to purchase 450 shares (120 + 190 + 140) for an average cost of $10 per share ($4500 ÷ 450). With the recent market price at $20, you will realize a long-term gain of $4500 ($20 current market price × 450 shares = $9000; $9000 − $4500 invested = $4500 gain). Note that the dollar-cost averaging method would remain valid if the time interval for investing were monthly, quarterly, or even semiannually; benefits are derived from the regularity of investing.

Dollar-Cost Averaging Offers Two Advantages First, it reduces the average cost of shares of stock purchased over a relatively long period. Profits occur when prices for an investment fluctuate and eventually go up. Although this approach does not eliminate the possibility of loss, it does limit losses during times of declining prices. Profits accelerate during rising prices. Second, dollar-cost averaging dictates investor discipline. This strategy of investing is not particularly glamorous, but it is the only approach that is almost guaranteed to make a profit for the investor. It takes neither brilliance nor luck, just discipline. People who invest through individual retirement accounts (IRAs), employee stock ownership programs, and 401(k) retirement plans (discussed in Chapter 17) enjoy the benefits of dollar-cost averaging when they invest regularly.

Strategy 3: Portfolio Diversification Reduces Portfolio Volatility

Owning too much of any one investment creates too great a financial risk. Experts advise that you never keep more than 10 percent of your assets in one investment, including your employer's stock. Many workers who did not diversify properly have seen their retirement funds disappear or be drastically reduced in value when their employers' stocks plunged in price.

Diversification is the single most important rule in investing. **Portfolio diversification** is the practice of selecting a collection of different asset classes of investments (such as stocks, bonds, mutual funds, real estate, and cash) that are chosen not only for their potential returns but also for their dissimilar risk-return characteristics.

The goal of portfolio diversification is to create a collection of investments that will provide an acceptable level of return and an acceptable exposure to risk. This outcome can be achieved because asset classes typically react differently to economic and marketplace changes. The major benefit of having a diversified portfolio is that when one asset class performs poorly, there is a good chance that another will perform well, and vice versa.

For example, you might buy a number of mutual funds, perhaps including a balanced fund, an asset-allocation fund, a life-cycle fund, and an aggressive-growth fund. Similarly, you could invest in three or four stocks within an industry group, instead of just one, and then invest in several industry groups, plus invest in a bond mutual fund and a certificate of deposit.

Diversification reduces portfolio volatility while averaging out an investor's return. (See Figure 13.4.) Diversification lowers the odds that you will lose money investing and increases the odds that you will make money.

Strategy 4: Asset Allocation Keeps You in the Right Investment Categories at the Right Time

Research shows that more than 90 percent of returns earned by long-term investors result from having one's assets allocated in a diversified portfolio. Most of the return comes not from specific investments but rather is derived from owning the right asset categories at the right time.

Asset allocation, a form of diversification, is deciding on the proportions of your investment portfolio that will be devoted to various categories of assets. Asset allocation helps preserve capital by selecting assets so as to protect the entire portfolio from negative events while remaining in a position to gain from positive events. This strategy helps control your exposure to risk.

portfolio diversification Practice of selecting a collection of different asset classes of investments (such as stocks, bonds, mutual funds, real estate, and cash) that are chosen not only for their potential returns but also for their dissimilar risk-return characteristics.

asset allocation Form of diversification in which investor decides on proportions of an investment portfolio that will be devoted to various categories of assets.

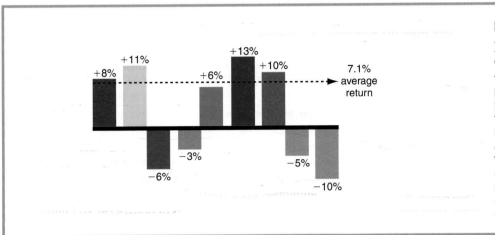

Figure 13.4

Diversification Averages Out an Investor's Return

The chart at the left represents a hypothetical mix of winning and losing investments after one year. The investment on the far left, for instance, increased in value 8 percent; another declined 10 percent. While some investments lost value, over the year those losses were offset with the gains of others, and the overall portfolio earned a 7.1 percent average return.

To achieve an appropriate mix of growth, income, and stability in your portfolio, you need a combination of three investments: (1) stocks and/or stock mutual funds *(equities)*, (2) bonds *(debt)*, and (3) *cash* (or cash equivalents like Treasury securities). Asset allocation requires that you keep your equities, debt, and cash at a fixed ratio for long time periods, occasionally rebalancing the allocations, perhaps quarterly or annually, so as to continue to meet your investment objectives.

Your allocation proportions and investment choices need to reflect your age, income, family responsibilities, financial resources, risk tolerance, goals, retirement plans, and investment time horizon. You need not change the proportions of your asset allocation until your broad investment goals change—possibly not for another five or ten years. When your investment objectives change, perhaps because of marriage, birth of a child, child graduating from college, loss of employment, divorce, or death of a spouse, you will need to change your asset allocation as well.

Figure 13.5 illustrates model portfolios that reflect varying degrees of risk tolerance and time horizons. A young, risk-tolerant, long-term investor with an aggressive investment philosophy might have a portfolio that is 100 percent in equities because equities offer the highest return over the long term and

Instant Message

Asset Allocation Rules of Thumb

Consider these two rules of thumb to guide the stock and bond allocation of your portfolio:

1. The percent to invest in equities is 110 minus your age, multiplied by 1.25. For example, if you are 40 years old, calculate as follows: $110 - 40 = 70$; $70 \times 1.25 = 87.5$. Therefore, a 40-year old investor is advised to maintain a portfolio where 87.5 percent of the assets are in equities and 12.5 percent in bonds (or cash equivalents).

2. The percent to invest in equities is found by subtracting your age from 120. Put the resulting number in the form of the percentage of your portfolio to invest in stocks. Put the remainder in bonds. So if you are age 30, put 90 percent $(120 - 30)$ in stocks and 10 percent in bonds. Every year, subtract your age from 120 again and rebalance your portfolio as needed.

Did You Know?...

Employers Offer Automatic Portfolio Rebalancing

Employees who participate in their employer-sponsored retirement plan may have access to services to automatically rebalance their retirement assets. Instead of being a do-it-yourself investor, a worker can sign up for the services of a **limited managed account**. Once you have decided on your preferred asset allocation and signed a contract with a vender approved by your employer, the company sells and buys your mutual fund assets on your behalf to adjust your portfolio back to your specific standards. Your professional money manager does this on a quarterly basis for an annual fee of as little as $150.

Asset Allocation Using the Sharpe Ratio

When creating your asset allocation proportions, you want the most risk-efficient portfolio for a collection of securities given a certain level of risk tolerance. The Sharpe Ratio helps you find the best proportions of securities to use in a portfolio that also contains cash. Input your proportions of stocks, bonds, and cash at www.moneychimp.com/articles/risk/portfolio.htm.

nothing in cash (money market funds). Younger investors also have ample time to ride out market fluctuations and make up any major losses. A moderate approach with a time horizon of six to ten years might have an equities-bond-cash portfolio of 60/30/10 percent.

You must reset your asset allocation at least once a year. Here is why. Assume you have a moderate investment philosophy and started out with a 50/40/10 bond-equities-cash portfolio, and a year later stock values increased and bond prices decreased. The result: Your portfolio is now 49 percent toward stocks and 42 in bonds. It is too risky. As shown in Figure 13.6, this means selling some of your equities and using the proceeds to buy more bonds, thus rebalancing it according to your previously determined asset allocations. When rebalancing, you will be selling high and buying low—the goal of all investors.

Figure 13.5

Model Portfolios and Time Horizons

0–5 Years	6–10 Years	11+ Years	Risk Tolerance/ Investment Philosophy
10% Cash 30% Bonds 60% Equities	20% Bonds 80% Equities	100% Equities	High Risk/Aggressive
20% Cash 40% Bonds 40% Equities	10% Cash 30% Bonds 60% Equities	20% Bonds 80% Equities	Moderate Risk/Moderate
35% Cash 40% Bonds 25% Equities	20% Cash 40% Bonds 40% Equities	10% Cash 30% Bonds 60% Equities	Low Risk/Conservative

---

Figure 13.6

Rebalancing Assets in Your Portfolio

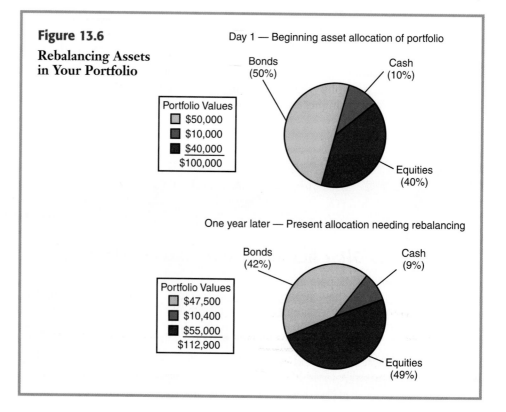

Day 1 — Beginning asset allocation of portfolio

Bonds (50%)   Cash (10%)

Portfolio Values
- $50,000
- $10,000
- $40,000
- $100,000

Equities (40%)

One year later — Present allocation needing rebalancing

Bonds (42%)   Cash (9%)

Portfolio Values
- $47,500
- $10,400
- $55,000
- $112,900

Equities (49%)

Strategy 5: Modern Portfolio Theory Evolves from Asset Allocation

A sophisticated application of asset allocation can be accomplished using **modern portfolio theory (MPT).** Here, the goal is to identify the investor's acceptable level of risk tolerance and then find an optimal portfolio of assets that will have the highest expected returns for that level of risk. A popular form of MPT is **Monte Carlo analysis.** This technique performs a large number of trial runs of a particular portfolio mix of investments, called simulations. It calculates hundreds or even thousands of possible investment combinations to determine the probability that a particular selection of investments will reach an investor's goal, such as a specific retirement income at a certain point in the future. See the green and yellow portions in Figure 13.7.

Many software programs can be used to assist investors in creating an efficient portfolio. Products are available from Financial Engines, Morningstar, and Vanguard; access and use

Did You Know?...

Top 3 Financial Missteps in Investing

People slip up in investing fundamentals when they do the following:

1. Invest only money that is left over at the end of the month

2. Follow a conservative investment philosophy for long-term goals

3. Fail to regularly rebalance the assets in their portfolio

How we create your Forecast

Overview

How much you'll have in the future depends on how your investments perform over time. To give you our best estimate, we explore thousands of possible economic scenarios using a technique known as "Monte Carlo" simulation. The animation below is a visual representation of this process.

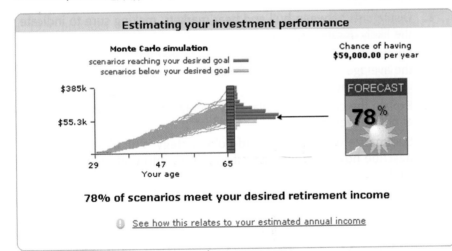

Figure 13.7

Monte Carlo Analysis from Financial Engines

(The analysis and recommendations pictured are hypothetical and are provided for illustrative purposes only. This illustration should not be relied on for investment advice.)

Source: Copyright © Financial Engines. Used used with permission.

Each economic scenario we explore makes different, realistic assumptions about inflation, interest rates, and returns on asset classes (stocks, bonds, and so forth) for each year of possible growth.

To make sense out of the thousands of estimated portfolio values, we carefully sort and count them. Then we show you three very important numbers. Your median estimate is the most likely of the three, but you should be prepared for the downside just in case:

- **Upside:** if your investments perform well, you may end up with a portfolio in the best 5% of the scenarios.
- **Median:** if your investments perform average, you may end up with a portfolio near the middle of the scenarios.
- **Downside:** if your investments perform poorly, you may end up with a portfolio in the worst 5% of the scenarios.

CHAPTER 14

Investing in Stocks and Bonds

! ? You Must Be Kidding, Right?

Brothers Ricky and Marvin Morton differ in investment philosophies—Marvin is conservative and Ricky holds a moderate investing outlook. Their father left each of them $100,000 when he died ten years ago, and Ricky invested in common stocks while Marvin invested in corporate bonds. After ten years, how much more money is Ricky likely to have in his account than Marvin?

A. $97,000   **B.** $163,000   **C.** $260,000   **D.** $357,000

The answer is A, $97,000. In U.S. securities markets, one could typically expect to obtain a long-term average annual return of 10 percent on common stocks compared with 5 percent on corporate bonds. Thus, a common stock portfolio that returned 10 percent annually would accumulate to $260,000 in ten years while a bond portfolio earning 5 percent annually over the same time period would grow to $163,000. Dividing $97,000 ($260,000 − $163,000) by $163,000 reveals that Ricky's willingness to accept more risk by investing in common stocks may provide him with a balance bigger than his brother's by a whopping 60 percent!

LEARNING OBJECTIVES

After reading this chapter, you should be able to:

1 **Explain** how stocks and bonds are used as investments.

2 **Classify** common stocks according to their major characteristics.

3 **Describe** fundamental and numerical ways to evaluate stock values.

4 **Determine** whether an investment's potential rate of return is sufficient.

5 **Use** the Internet to evaluate common stocks in which to invest.

6 **Summarize** how stocks are bought and sold.

7 **Describe** how to invest in bonds.

What Do You Recommend?

Caitlin Diaz, age 42, is a senior Web designer for a communications company in Lansing, Michigan. She earns $92,000 annually. From her salary, Caitlin contributes $200 per month to her 401(k) retirement account, through which she invests in the company's stock. Caitlin is divorced and has custody of her three children, 10-year-old twins and a 12-year-old. Her ex-husband pays $1500 per month in child support. Caitlin and her former spouse contribute $3000 each annually to a college fund for their children. Over the past 15 years, Caitlin has built a $300,000 stock portfolio after starting by investing the proceeds of a $50,000 life insurance policy following the death of her first husband. Currently, her portfolio is allocated 40 percent into preferred stocks (paying 4.5 percent), 30 percent into cyclical, blue-chip common stocks (P/E ratio of 18), 10 percent into Treasury bonds (paying 5.2 percent), 10 percent into municipal bonds (paying 3.7 percent), and 10 percent into AAA corporate bonds (paying 5.6 percent). Today's comparable corporate bonds pay 5 percent. Caitlin's total return in recent years has been about 6 percent annually. Her investment goals are to have sufficient cash to pay for her children's education and to retire in about 18 years.

What do you recommend to Caitlin on the subject of stocks and bonds regarding:

1. Investing for retirement in 18 years?

2. Owning blue-chip common stocks and preferred stocks rather than other common stocks given Caitlin's investment time horizon?

3. The wisdom of owning municipal bonds rather than corporate bonds?

4. The likely selling price of her corporate bonds, if sold today? 417

5. Investments that might be appropriate to fund her children's education?

FOR HELP with studying this chapter, visit the Online Student Center:

www.college.hmco.com/pic/garman9e

stocks have included Quality Systems, Longs Drug Stores, and Urban Outfitters. Their betas are usually 1.5 or more.

Value Stocks

A **value stock** is one that tends to trade at a low price relative to its company fundamentals (dividends, earnings, sales, and so on) and thus is considered undervalued by a value investor. A **value investor** believes that the market isn't always efficient and that it is possible to find companies trading for less than they are worth. Value stocks often operate within industries that benefit from a growing economy. Stocks that have a relatively high dividend yield, low price/sales ratio, and/or low P/E ratio are classified as value stocks. The low valuations that value stocks enjoy are often a result of some type of bad news (poor earnings report, bad press, legal issues, and so on). Although their stock prices may have changed, some past examples of value stocks have included General Motors, General Electric, DuPont, Merck, Citigroup, and AT&T.

Speculative Stocks

The term **speculative stock** describes the stock of a company that has a potential for substantial earnings at some time in the future. These stocks are considered speculative because those earnings may never be realized. A speculative stock may have a spotty earnings record or is so new that no earnings pattern has emerged. Investors in these companies accept some risk because they expect the companies to be highly profitable in the future. They hope that the company will make a new discovery, invent a new product, or generate valuable information that later may push up the price of the stock, creating substantial capital gains.

Examples of speculative companies include computer graphics firms, Internet applications firms, small oil exploration businesses, genetic engineering firms, and some pharmaceutical manufacturers. For these firms, the P/E ratio fluctuates widely in tandem with the company's fortunes, and beta values exceeding 2.0 are common. For every speculative company that succeeds, many others do poorly or fail altogether.

Tech Stocks

Tech stocks are those in the technology sector. Technology firms are dominant in the stock market and include firms that offer technology-based products and services, biotechnology, Internet services, network services, wireless communications, and more. Some are large blue-chip firms, such as Microsoft and Cisco Systems, while most are speculative ventures, such as Human Genome Sciences and Cognus Corporation.

Blue-Chip Stocks

The term **blue-chip stock** suggests a company that has been around for a long time, has a well-regarded reputation, dominates its industry (often with annual revenues of $1 billion or more), and is known for being a solid, relatively safe investment. Typically, blue-chip companies have a history of both good earnings and consistent cash dividends, and they grow at approximately the same rate as the overall economy. The term comes from poker, in which the highest chip denomination is colored blue.

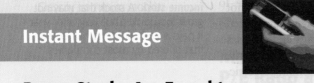

Did You Know?...

Most Stocks Are Cyclical and Some Are Countercyclical

The term **cyclical stock** describes the stock of a company whose profits are greatly influenced by changes in the economic business cycle. Such companies operate in consumer-dependent industries, such as automobiles, housing, airlines, retailing, and heavy machinery. The market prices of cyclical stocks mirror the general state of the economy and reflect the various phases of the business cycle. During times of prosperity and economic expansion, corporate earnings rise, profits grow, and stock prices climb; during a recession, these measures decline sharply. The stock of many firms characterized as blue-chip, income, growth, value, or speculative stocks can be described as cyclical stocks. Cyclical stocks have a beta of about 1.0.

A stock with a beta that is less than 1.0 or even a negative beta is called a **countercyclical** (or **defensive**) **stock** because it exhibits price changes contrary to movements in the business cycle. These stocks perform well even in an environment characterized by weak economic activity and sliding interest rates. Cigarette smokers, for example, do not quit during a recession, and people usually continue to go to movies, consume soft drinks, purchase cat and dog food, buy electric utility service, and go grocery shopping. The prices of countercyclical stocks remain steady during an economic recession.

Blue-chip stock shares are widely held by individual investors, mutual funds, and pension plans. The earnings of blue-chip companies (whose stocks are usually considered income stocks or well-known growth stocks) are expected to increase at a consistent but unspectacular rate because these highly stable firms are the leaders in their industries. Examples of such stocks are Wal-Mart, Coca-Cola, Berkshire Hathaway, and Exxon Mobil. Investing in such companies is considered much less risky than investing in other types of firms.

Large-Cap, Small-Cap, and Midcap Stocks

A company's size classification in the stock market is based on its **market capitalization.** This is the total value of a company's common stock shares determined at its current market price. **Large-cap stocks** are those of firms that have issued $3 billion to $4 billion (or more) of stocks. Most are considered blue-chip companies, too. Examples include Texaco, Microsoft, Time Warner, and General Foods. Stocks of midsize and smaller firms often outperform large-cap stocks.

Midcap stocks are the stocks of those remaining companies that are quite substantial in terms of capitalization—perhaps $750 million to $3 billion in size—but not among the very largest firms. Examples include Wendy's and Starbucks. A **small-cap stock** is stock of a company that has a capitalization of less than $750 million. **Microcaps** are firms with less than $100 million in capitalization, and perhaps as little as $10 million. When the smaller firms achieve substantial increases in sales and earnings, their stock prices typically jump quite sharply.

✓ CONCEPT CHECK 14.2

1. Distinguish between income stocks and growth stocks.
2. Explain how a value stock might or might not differ from a blue-chip stock or a tech stock.
3. Explain how a stock with a beta of 1.0 differs from ones with a beta of 1.2 and 2.5.

How to Evaluate Stock Values

3 LEARNING OBJECTIVE
Describe fundamental and numerical ways to evaluate stock values.

How do you know whether buying a particular stock is a good idea? Or when you should sell shares that you hold? To get answers, first use fundamental research analysis. Second, understand that evaluating stocks is largely about earnings. Third, use numerical measures to evaluate stock values. And fourth, use beta values to compare a stock to similar investments.

Use Fundamental Analysis to Evaluate Stocks

fundamental analysis School of thought in market analysis that assumes each stock has an intrinsic (or true) value based on its expected stream of future earnings.

The premise underlying **fundamental analysis** is that each stock has an intrinsic (or true) value based on its expected stream of future earnings. Most professional stock analysts and investors take this approach to investing as they research economic, corporate, and industry financials. Fundamental analysis suggests that you can identify some stocks that will outperform others. The fundamental approach presumes that a stock's basic value is largely determined by current and future earnings trends, expected levels of interest rates, industry outlook, and management's expertise. The aim is to seek out sound stocks—perhaps even unfashionable ones—that are priced below what they ought to be.

technical analysis Method of evaluating securities that uses statistics generated by market activity, such as past prices and volume, over time to determine when to buy or sell a stock.

An opposing and minority view on valuing common stocks is advocated by proponents of **technical analysis,** often newsletter authors. This method of evaluating securities analyzes statistics generated by market activity, such as past prices and volume. Technical analysts do not attempt to measure a security's intrinsic value but instead use charts, graphs, mathematics, and software programs to identify and predict future price movements. Technical analysis has proved to be of little value, although some novice investors may find technical analysts' logic appealing.

There are numerous websites that offer fundamental and technical analysis of stocks. The Motley Fool does so with a sense of humor.

Corporate Earnings Are Most Important

Corporate earnings are the profits a company makes during a specific time period. If a company cannot generate earnings now or in the future, stock market analysts and investors are not going to be impressed. As people reach this conclusion, there quickly will be more sellers than buyers of the company's common stock, and that will depress the stock's market price. Here are some numerical indicators of earnings.

corporate earnings The profits a company makes during a specific time period indicate to many analysts whether to buy or sell a stock.

Earnings per Share A company's **earnings per share (EPS)** is annual profit divided by the number of outstanding shares. It indicates the income that a company has available, on a per-share basis, to pay dividends and reinvest as retained earnings. The EPS is a measure of the firm's profitability on a common-stock-per-share basis, and it is helpful because investors can use it to compare financial conditions of many companies. The EPS is reported in the business section of many newspapers.

In our example, assume that, next year after payment of $9000 in dividends to preferred stockholders, Running Paws had a net profit of $32,000. With 20,000 shares of stock, the company's EPS would be $1.60 ($32,000 ÷ 20,000).

earnings per share (EPS) A firm's profit divided by the number of outstanding shares; analysts follow EPS because it indicates the income that a company has available to pay dividends and reinvest as retained earnings—used to compare stocks across the board.

Price/Sales Ratio The **price/sales ratio (P/S ratio)** indicates the number of dollars it takes to buy a dollar's worth of a company's annual revenues. The P/S is obtained by dividing a company's total market capitalization by its sales for the past four quarters. For example, if Running Paws Cat Food Company's common stock currently sells for $25 per share and 20,000 shares of the company's stock are outstanding, its total capitalization is $500,000. If company revenues (sales of cat food) were $750,000 over the past year, the stock's P/S would be 0.67 ($500,000 ÷ $750,000). Stock analysts suggest investors avoid companies with a P/S greater than 1.5 and favor those having a P/S of less than 0.75. Many investors ignore the P/S, but it works better than the highly acclaimed P/E ratio in predicting which companies provide the best return, as explained in James P. O'Shaughnessy's *What Works on Wall Street.*

price/sales ratio (P/S ratio) Tells the number of dollars it takes to buy a dollar's worth of a company's annual revenues; calculated by dividing company's total market capitalization by its sales for the past four quarters.

Numerical Measures to Evaluate Stock Prices

Several other numerical measures are used to evaluate stock performance. These numbers are readily available to investors on the Internet. Here are some numerical indicators that will help you assess future stock prices.

Cash Dividends Stocks usually pay dividends. Cash dividends are distributions made in cash to holders of stock. They are the current income that you receive while you own shares in the company. The firm's board of directors usually declares a dividend on a quarterly basis (four times per corporate year), typically at the end of March, June, September, and December. Dividends are ordinarily paid out of current earnings, but, in the event of unprofitable times (low earnings or none), the money might come from cash reserves held by the company. Occasionally, a company will borrow to pay the dividend so as to maintain its reputation of consistently paying dividends. Later profits can be used to repay any funds borrowed for this purpose.

Dividends per Share The **dividends per share** measure translates the total cash dividends paid out by a company to common stockholders into a per-share figure. For example, Running Paws might elect to declare a total cash dividend of $8000 for the year to common stockholders. In that case, cash dividends per share would amount to $0.40 ($8000 ÷ 20,000 shares).

dividends per share Translates the total cash dividends paid out by a company to common stockholders into a per-share figure.

Dividend Payout Ratio The **dividend payout ratio** is the dividends per share divided by earnings per share. It helps you judge the likelihood of future dividends. For example, imagine that Running Paws Cat Food Company earned $32,000 (after paying preferred stockholders), paid out a cash dividend of $8000 to company stockholders, and retained the remaining $24,000 to facilitate growth of the company. In

dividend payout ratio Dividends per share divided by earnings per share; helps judge likelihood of future dividends.

this case, the dividend payout ratio equals 0.25 ($8000 ÷ $32,000). For that year, Running Paws paid a dividend equal to 25 percent of earnings. Newer companies usually retain most, if not all, of their profits to facilitate growth. An investor interested in growth would, therefore, seek a company with a low payout ratio. The lower the payout ratio, the greater the likelihood that the company will grow, resulting in capital gains for investors.

dividend yield Cash dividend to an investor expressed as a percentage of the current market price of a security.

Dividend Yield The **dividend yield** is the cash dividend paid to an investor expressed as a percentage of the current market price of a security. For example, the $0.40 cash dividend of Running Paws divided by the current $25 market price for its stock reveals a dividend yield of 1.6 percent ($0.40 ÷ $25). Growth and speculative companies typically pay little or no cash dividends, so they have limited dividend yields. Such companies are attractive to investors who are interested in capital gains.

book value/shareholder's equity Net worth of a company, determined by subtracting total liabilities from assets.

Book Value Book value (also known as **shareholder's equity**) is the net worth of a company, which is determined by subtracting the company's total liabilities from its assets. It theoretically indicates a company's worth if its assets were sold, its debts were paid off, and the net proceeds were distributed to the investors who own the outstanding shares of common stock.

book value per share Reflects the book value of a company divided by the number of shares of common stock outstanding.

Book Value per Share The **book value per share** reflects the book value of a company divided by the number of shares of common stock outstanding. Running Paws has a net worth of $230,000, which, when divided by 20,000 shares, gives a book value per share of $11.50.

Often little relationship exists between the book value of a company and its earnings or the market price of its stock. A stock's price usually exceeds its book value per share. The reason is that stockholders bid up the stock price because they anticipate earnings and dividends in the future and expect the market price to rise even more. When the book value per share exceeds the price per share, the stock may truly be underpriced.

price-to-book ratio (P/B ratio) Current stock price divided by the per-share net value of a firm's plant, equipment, and other assets (book value); helps investors identify stocks that are value rich. Also called market-to-book ratio.

Price-to-Book Ratio The **price-to-book ratio (P/B ratio)**, also called the **market-to-book ratio**, identifies firms that are asset rich, such as many banks, brokerage firms, and insurance companies. The P/B ratio is the current stock price divided by the per-share net value of the company's plant, equipment, and other assets (book value). It tells you the premium that you are paying for the net assets of the company.

Did You Know...

About Employee Stock Options

Many employers give stock options to attract and retain employees. An **employee stock option (ESO)** is a gift, like a bonus, from an employer to an employee that allows employees to benefit from the appreciation of their employer's stock without putting any money down. The company gives the employee the right and opportunity to "exercise" the option by buying the stock sometime in the future at an "exercise" or "striking" price established when the option was given. If the company prospers, when the employee eventually decides to exercise the options, the current share price may be much higher than the exercise price, thus allowing the employee to buy the shares at a considerable discount.

In the Running Paws example, the book value per share of $11.50 would be divided into the recent price at which the stock was sold ($25 in this case); thus, the P/B ratio for Running Paws is 2.17. The current P/B ratio for most stocks lies between 2.1 and 1.0. The lower the ratio, the less highly a company's assets have been valued, indicating that the stock may be currently underpriced. If the ratio is less than 1, the assets may be utilized ineffectively. In such cases, an underperforming and undervalued company may become a target of a corporate takeover.

✔ CONCEPT CHECK 14.3

1. What is the focus of fundamental analysis?
2. Distinguish between earnings per share and the price/earnings ratio.
3. Summarize the differences among dividend payout ratio, dividends per share, and dividend yield.

Calculating a Stock's Potential Rate of Return

There is but a single reason to make an investment: to obtain a positive return. One indicator of return is an investment's **alpha statistic,** which quantifies the difference between an investment's expected return and its actual recent performance (outperforming or underperforming) given its risk. A stock or mutual fund with a positive alpha means the company did better than expected for its level of risk; a negative alpha indicates poor performance. Alphas for individual stocks, mutual funds, and other investments are available online through brokerage firms and advisory services. Alphas are an important statistic, but they are based on past performance and, thus, provide only a guide for future performance.

While you cannot know the exact performance of any investment in advance, you certainly will want to pay no more than the "right price" for the investment given its potential rate of return. Calculating returns on a potential investment involves five steps. Armed with these data, you will be better positioned to make informed decisions:

1. Use beta to estimate the level of risk of the investment.
2. Estimate the market risk.
3. Calculate the required rate of return.
4. Calculate the potential rate of return on the investment.
5. Compare the required rate of return with the potential rate of return on the investment.

Use Beta to Estimate the Risk of the Investment

Beta is a useful piece of information when you want to estimate the rate of return you require on an investment in a stock, bond, or mutual fund before putting your money at risk. Betas for individual stocks, mutual funds, and other investments are available online from brokerage firms, advisory services, and investment magazines.

The following example illustrates how to use beta to estimate the amount of risk in an investment portfolio. Assume you are willing to accept more risk than the general investor and that you buy a stock with a beta of 1.5. If the average price of all stocks rises by 20 percent over time, the price of the stock you chose might rise by 30 percent,

4 LEARNING OBJECTIVE
Determine whether an investment's potential rate of return is sufficient.

alpha statistic Quantifies the difference between an investment's expected return and its actual recent performance (outperforming or underperforming) given its risk; positive values indicate better-than-market performance.

which is the beta of 1.5 multiplied by the increase in the market (1.5 × 20%). If the average price of all stocks drops in value by 10 percent, the price of the stock you chose might drop by 15 percent (1.5 × 10%).

Estimate the Market Risk

To estimate the required rate of return on an investment, you need to quantify the market risk. **Market risk,** also known as **systematic risk,** which we discussed in Chapter 13, is the risk associated with the effects of the overall economy on securities markets. It often causes the market price of a particular stock or bond to change, even though nothing has changed in the fundamental values underlying that security. Historical records indicate that 8 percent represents a realistic estimate of market risk for U.S. stocks.

Calculate Your Required Rate of Return

The return on short-term U.S. Treasury bills has historically exceeded the rate of inflation by a slight degree. Thus, when T-bills pay 5 percent interest, the inflation rate might hover around 4 percent. This circumstance provides almost no gain for the investor. For this reason, investors often use the yield on Treasury bills as a base number that provides a zero **real rate of return**—that is, a zero return on investment after inflation and income taxes.

To calculate your required rate of return on an investment, multiply the beta value of an investment by the estimated market risk and then add the risk-free T-bill rate, as shown in Equation (14.1). For current T-bill rates, see

http://www.treasurydirect.gov/indiv/products/prod_tbills_glance.htm, and

http://www.treasurydirect.gov/RI/OFBills. Use Equation (14.1) to determine an *estimate of the required rate of return on an investment.*

$$\text{Estimate of the required rate of return on an investment} = \text{T-bill rate} + (\text{beta} \times \text{market risk}) \qquad (14.1)$$

For example, assume you are considering investing in Running Paws Cat Food Company, which has a beta of 1.5. If you assume a market risk of 8 percent and the current T-bill rate is 2.0 percent, the total rate of return you will require on this investment is 14.0 percent [2.0 + (1.5 × 8.0)]. Investors need the promise of a return higher than 14 percent to put their money at risk in this investment.

Calculate the Stock's Potential Rate of Return

potential rate of return Determined by adding anticipated income (from dividends, interest, rents, or other sources) to future value of investment and then subtracting investment's original cost.

The **potential return** for any investment over a period of years can be determined by adding anticipated income (from dividends, interest, rents, or other sources) to the future value of the investment and then subtracting the investment's original cost. The investor using fundamental analysis can obtain the figures needed to construct the expected stream of future earnings for a company from a variety of sources. For example, you can use estimates for earnings and dividends gathered from large investment data firms such as Value Line or Standard & Poor's, an individual stock analyst's projections, or figures from the company itself, or you can create your own numbers.

Add Up Projected Income and Price Appreciation Table 14.1 illustrates how to sum up the projected income and price appreciation. You can convert these figures into a **potential rate of return** by calculating the approximate compound yield, as shown in Equation (14.2). This figure can then be compared with returns on other investments.

Table 14.1 One Investor's Projections of the Earnings and Dividends for Running Paws Cat Food Company

End of Year	Earnings	Dividend Income
1	$2.76	$0.76
2	3.17	0.87
3	3.65	1.00
4	4.20	1.15
5	4.83	1.33
Total dividends		$5.11
Average annual dividend ($5.11 ÷ 5)		$1.02

Example: Running Paws Cat Food Company Based on a recommendation from his stockbroker, Martin Crane, a Seattle resident, is considering Running Paws Cat Food Company as a potential investment. Martin figures that the company's stock might provide a better return than inflation and income taxes for about five years. He has determined the following information about this stock investment: It is currently priced at $30 per share, its most recent 12-month earnings amounted to $2.40 per share, and the cash dividend for the same period was $0.66 per share.

Martin began the task of projecting the future value of one share of the stock by using the earnings per share information. He first calculated the P/E ratio to be 12.5 ($30 ÷ $2.40). Next, as illustrated in Table 14.1, Martin applied a 15 percent rate of growth estimate (the same rate that occurred in previous years, according to Running Paws' annual report) for the earnings per share for each year ($2.40 × 1.15 = $2.76; $2.76 × 1.15 = $3.17; and so forth). Using a P/E ratio of 12.5 (the same as the current ratio), Martin estimated the market price at the end of the fifth year to be $60.38 (12.5 × $4.83). This calculation gives a projected net appreciation in stock price over five years of $30.38 ($60.38 minus the current price of $30).

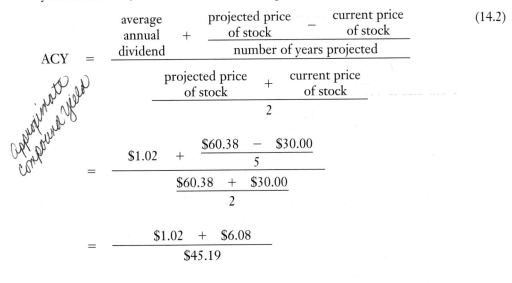

To project the future income of the investment in Running Paws—the anticipated cash dividends—Table 14.1 shows that Martin estimated a 15 percent growth rate in the cash dividend ($0.66 × 1.15 = $0.76; $0.76 × 1.15 = $0.87; and so forth). Adding the projected cash dividends over five years gives a total of $5.11. Martin obtained the potential return for one share of Running Paws over five years by adding anticipated dividend income ($5.11) to the future value of the investment ($60.38) less its original cost ($30.00), for a result of $35.49 ($5.11 + $30.38). Thus, Martin has projected that $30 invested in one share of Running Paws will earn a potential total return of $35.49 in five years.

The question now becomes, what is the percentage yield for this dollar return? The **approximate compound yield (ACY)** provides a measure of the annualized compound growth of any long-term investment. You can determine this value by using Equation (14.2). The calculation requires use of an *annual average* dividend rather than the specific projected dividends. In this example, the annual average dividend of $1.02 is computed by dividing the $5.11 in dividend income by five years. Substituting the data from Table 14.1 into Equation (14.2) and using the average annual dividend figure results in an approximate compound yield of 15.7 percent on the potential investment in one share of Running Paws stock for five years. (This formula can be found on the *Garman/Forgue* website.)

Compare the Required Rate of Return with the Potential Rate of Return on the Investment

Now the moment of decision making is at hand. You compare the estimated required rate of return on an investment (given its risk) with the investment's potential projected rate of return. In our example involving Running Paws Cat Food Company, the risk suggested a required rate of return of 14.0 percent. The investment's potential rate of return was projected to be 15.7 percent, which suggests that Running Paws is a good buy for Martin at the current selling price of $30—that is, the stock is underpriced. Once armed with projected rate of return information for an investment, you can compare it with other investments.

CONCEPT CHECK 14.4

1. Explain why individuals considering investing in stocks begin by thinking about the return on U.S. Treasury bills.

2. Calculate what might happen in the future to your stock with a beta of 2.0 if all stocks rise by 20 percent next year.

3. Summarize the steps in calculating the potential rate of return on a stock investment.

How to Use the Internet to Evaluate and Select Stocks

5 **LEARNING OBJECTIVE**
Use the Internet to evaluate common stocks in which to invest.

An overwhelming amount of information is available on stock investments. With more than 8000 U.S. public companies to choose from and another 50,000 stocks in other countries, stock selection takes time. Hundreds of investment resources exist, including television and radio shows, books, websites, blogs, and newsletters. What approach should you take? Use the Internet because everything you need is online. The Internet is a source of up-to-the minute, high-quality information on investments.

Begin by Setting Criteria for Your Stock Investments

The process of setting criteria for a stock investment starts with a review of your investment plan, as discussed in Chapter 13 and illustrated in Figure 13.8 on page 378. To make informed selections of the specific stock investments that match your investment goals, philosophy, and time horizon, begin by making decisions on criteria for your stock investments:

• What classifications of stocks are best suited for your goals?
• What market capitalization meets your desires?

- What specific numeric measures do you require on beta, sales, profitability, P/E ratio, dividends, payout ratio, and market price?
- What projected EPS growth do you require?
- Do you want to invest in an industry leader?

Basic Investment Information

Comprehensive investment websites provide updated news headlines; market overviews; market statistics; industry statistics; industry trends; corporate stock symbols; current stock market prices; specific company profiles, history, financials, prices, and outlook for the future; tips on how to build a portfolio; and stock-screening tools with search capabilities. Following are some popular websites for investing:
- The Motley Fool (www.fool.com)
- *Kiplinger's Personal Finance* (www.kiplinger.com/personalfinance/)
- CNNMoney.com (www.money.cnn.com/pf/index.html)
- Yahoo! Finance (www.finance.yahoo.com/marketupdate?u)
- BusinessWeek.com (www.businessweek.com/investor/)
- SmartMoney.com (http://www.smartmoney.com/)
- AOL Money Basics (http://money.aol.com/basics/index)

Stock Screening

You can research stocks, bonds, and mutual funds by using **stock-screening tools** available on the Internet. Screening enables you to quickly sift through vast databases of hundreds of companies to find those that best suit your investment objectives. For example, you can use the Kiplinger screening tool to filter thousands of stocks using 27 search criteria, and you can use Kiplinger's or another company's tools to identify dividend-paying stocks, small companies, and growth companies. You simply set the standard for screening, such as high P/E ratios, and the program sorts out the investment choices, including five-year EPS growth projections by professional stock analysts. You may be surprised to find how easy it is to screen stocks. The following websites offer stock-screening tools:
- Yahoo! Finance (screen.yahoo.com/stocks.html)
- Morningstar (http://screen.morningstar.com/stockselector.html?hsection=tool centerstsel)

stock-screening tools Enable you to quickly sift through vast databases of hundreds of companies to find those that best suit your investment objectives.

Did You Know?...

How to Use Online Stock Calculators

You can perform almost any kind of mathematical calculation necessary in investing by using one of the online investment websites. For example, by using AOL Money Basics (http://money.aol.com/calculators/stocks), you can get answers to these questions:

- Which is better: income or growth stock?
- What is my current yield from dividends?
- How much do commissions and fees affect my stock's rate of return?

- What stock price will achieve my target rate of return?
- What is the return on my stock if I sell now?
- Should I wait a year to sell my stock?
- Should I sell my stock now and invest the money elsewhere?

- MSN Money (http://moneycentral.msn.com/investor/finder/customstocksdl.asp)
- MarketWatch (www.marketwatch.com/)
- BusinessWeek.com (www.businessweek.com/investor/)

Security Analysts' Research Reports

Stock analysts working for independent stock advisory firms or stock brokerages write research reports on companies and industries, as illustrated in Figure 14.1 with a report from Standard & Poor's. Reports based on fundamental analysis are quite informative. The quality of advice is uneven, ranging from brilliant to pedestrian as analysts have a tendency to run with the herd and make similar recommendations. They often recommend buying certain stocks and rarely suggest selling. The prudent investor interprets "hold" recommendations as a signal to sell.

Corporate News

Public companies must regularly report their financial status to the government and the public. Corporate filings required by the Securities and Exchange Commission are available on the Internet from the Electronic Data Gathering and Retrieval (EDGAR) project (www.edgar-online.com). Top online sources for stock, bond, and mutual fund information include Morningstar (morningstar.com) and Bloomberg (bloomberg .com). Each public company has its own website that offers insights from management about the future of the firm, and it is easy to request a company's annual report.

annual report Legally required yearly report about financial performance, activities, and prospects sent to major stockholders and made available to the general public.

Annual Reports Companies issue an annual report once a year (hence the name), both in hard-copy format and online. Today's **annual report** is mostly a numbers-free publication that looks like a slick marketing magazine. While annual reports do contain some summarized financial information, they serve more as promotional corporate brochures.

10-K report A firm's financial statements and activity details for any publicly traded company appear in this mandatory report sent to the SEC annually.

10-K Reports The financial statements and details on a public company are contained in its **10-K report,** which every company registered with the SEC is required to file once each year to ensure public availability of accurate current information about the firm. It summarizes the firm's financial activities for the year. A 10-K report

Though annual reports contain some important information, many are mainly marketing tools for the corporation

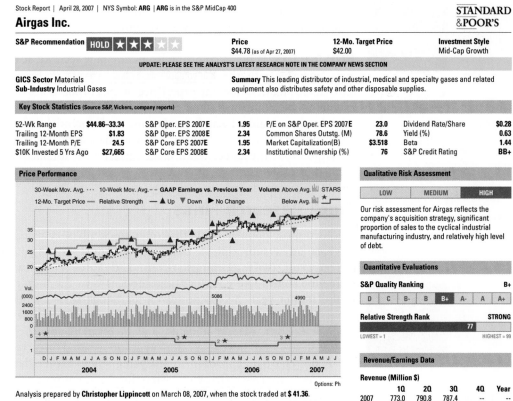

Stock Report | April 28, 2007 | NYS Symbol: **ARG** | **ARG** is in the S&P MidCap 400

STANDARD &POOR'S

Airgas Inc.

S&P Recommendation HOLD ★★★☆☆

Price	**12-Mo. Target Price**	**Investment Style**
$44.78 (as of Apr 27, 2007)	$42.00	Mid-Cap Growth

UPDATE: PLEASE SEE THE ANALYST'S LATEST RESEARCH NOTE IN THE COMPANY NEWS SECTION

GICS Sector Materials
Sub-Industry Industrial Gases

Summary This leading distributor of industrial, medical and specialty gases and related equipment also distributes safety and other disposable supplies.

Key Stock Statistics (Source S&P, Vickers, company reports)

52-Wk Range	$44.86–33.34	S&P Oper. EPS 2007E	1.95	P/E on S&P Oper. EPS 2007E	23.0	Dividend Rate/Share	$0.28
Trailing 12-Month EPS	$1.83	S&P Oper. EPS 2008E	2.34	Common Shares Outstg. (M)	78.6	Yield (%)	0.63
Trailing 12-Month P/E	24.5	S&P Core EPS 2007E	1.95	Market Capitalization(B)	$3.518	Beta	1.44
$10K Invested 5 Yrs Ago	$27,665	S&P Core EPS 2008E	2.34	Institutional Ownership (%)	76	S&P Credit Rating	BB+

Price Performance

30-Week Mov. Avg. · · · · 10-Week Mov. Avg. - - - GAAP Earnings vs. Previous Year Volume Above Avg. STARS
12-Mo. Target Price — Relative Strength ▲ Up ▼ Down ► No Change Below Avg. ★

Options: Ph

Analysis prepared by **Christopher Lippincott** on March 08, 2007, when the stock traded at **$ 41.36**.

Highlights

➤ We expect revenues to increase 11% in FY 07 (Mar.) and 8% in FY 08, driven primarily by a 10% forecasted increase in distribution revenues in FY 07 and 7% in FY 08. We believe the industrial manufacturing, energy and non-residential construction end markets will continue to support core revenue growth through FY 07. We anticipate additional revenue growth will come from the medical and safety products platforms, higher prices and acquisitions.

➤ We believe operating margins should expand in FY 07 and FY 08 as price increases, driven by high capacity utilization, and operating leverage offset rising commodity supply and transportation costs. Additionally, we expect lower SG&A expenses as a percentage of sales to help improve operating margins.

➤ We forecast that operating EPS will be $1.95 in FY 07 and $2.34 in FY 08.

Investment Rationale/Risk

➤ In our view, the company should see internal sales expansion that exceeds GDP growth from several target markets. We expect ARG to continue to gain market share as it consolidates a highly fragmented packaged gas industry via an ongoing acquisition strategy. While we believe ARG should continue to post strong earnings growth and generate free cash flow, in our view the shares are fully valued.

➤ Risks to our recommendation and target price include warmer than normal winter weather, lower than expected price increases and sudden increases in commodity and transportation costs.

➤ Our 12-month target price of $42 represents a combination of two valuation metrics. Our discounted cash flow model, which assumes a 4% growth rate in perpetuity and an 11% discount rate, indicates an intrinsic value of $41. In terms of relative valuation, we assume a P/E multiple of 19.5X for 2007, a slight premium to peers, which suggests a value of $43. By blending these methodologies, we arrive at our target price.

Qualitative Risk Assessment

LOW	MEDIUM	HIGH

Our risk assessment for Airgas reflects the company's acquisition strategy, significant proportion of sales to the cyclical industrial manufacturing industry, and relatively high level of debt.

Quantitative Evaluations

S&P Quality Ranking B+

D	C	B-	B	B+	A-	A	A+

Relative Strength Rank STRONG

77

LOWEST = 1   HIGHEST = 99

Revenue/Earnings Data

Revenue (Million $)

	1Q	2Q	3Q	4Q	Year
2007	773.0	790.8	787.4	--	--
2006	690.7	714.4	702.4	746.9	2,830
2005	544.0	599.8	611.5	656.1	2,411
2004	461.1	460.5	451.9	522.1	1,895
2003	457.7	451.1	435.3	442.9	1,787
2002	415.7	412.0	392.4	416.0	1,636

Earnings Per Share ($)

2007	0.48	0.49	0.40	E0.52	E1.95
2006	0.38	0.38	0.41	0.45	1.62
2005	0.29	0.30	0.30	0.31	1.20
2004	0.25	0.26	0.28	0.29	1.07
2003	0.20	0.27	0.23	0.25	0.94
2002	0.19	0.21	0.17	0.12	0.69

Fiscal year ended Mar. 31. Next earnings report expected: Early May. EPS Estimates based on S&P Operating Earnings; historical GAAP earnings are as reported.

Dividend Data (Dates: mm/dd Payment Date: mm/dd/yy)

Amount ($)	Date Decl.	Ex-Div. Date	Stk. of Record	Payment Date
0.070	05/23	06/13	06/15	06/30/06
0.070	08/09	09/13	09/15	09/29/06
0.070	11/22	12/13	12/15	12/29/06
0.070	01/16	03/13	03/15	03/30/07

Dividends have been paid since 2003. Source: Company reports.

Please read the Required Disclosures and Analyst Certification on the last page of this report.
Redistribution or reproduction is prohibited without written permission. Copyright ©2007 The McGraw-Hill Companies, Inc.

The McGraw·Hill Companies

Figure 14.1

Stock Analyst's Report

Reprinted by permission of Standard & Poor's, a division of the McGraw-Hill Companies, Copyright © 2007.

includes information on sales, earnings, profit, and legal problems, and it forecasts the company's future. You can obtain 10-K reports from the SEC online (www.sec.gov).

Prospectus   When a company issues any new security, it files a **prospectus** with the Securities and Exchange Commission. This disclosure describes the experience of the corporation's management, the company's financial status, any anticipated legal matters that could affect the company, and potential risks of investing in the firm. The language is legalistic and full of technical jargon, but the interested investor may find it useful to sift through the details.

Stock Research Firms

The two most popular firms that offer stock advisory research services on a subscription basis to individual investors are Morningstar (www.morningstar.com) and Value Line (www.valueline.com). The cost for these services is in the hundreds of dollars per year. A Google search for "stock advisory newsletters" will reveal several dozen firms that offer guidance on stock selections, market updates, and investment advice. You may wish to avoid those that offer suggestions based on a "technical" or "chartist" approach to analyzing stocks rather than a mainstream approach that emphasizes fundamental research.

Economic Data

Investors need to stay aware of trends in the general economy. You need to know the stage of the business cycle (recession or prosperity) and the current interest and inflation rates, and you need to understand how economic conditions are likely to change over the next 12 to 18 months. (This topic was examined in Chapter 1.) Economic information is available through almost all media:

- Search engines: Yahoo!, Google, and Momma
- Big newspapers: *USA Today, Los Angeles Times, The Wall Street Journal*
- Business news: *BusinessWeek, Fortune, Forbes, Financial World*
- Personal finance: *Money* magazine and *Kiplinger's Personal Finance Magazine*
- Investment sources: *The Wall Street Journal, Barron's, Investor's Business Daily, MarketWatch*
- News magazines: *U.S. News & World Report, Time*

Stock Market Data

Reports on securities market indexes are provided around the clock in almost every media. "The Dow went up 30 points today." "The S&P 500 rose 68 points." When it is reported that "the Dow rose 110 points today in heavy trading," realize that these "points" are changes in the index, not actual dollar changes in the value of the stocks. A **securities market index** is an indicator of market performance. It measures the average value of a number of securities chosen as a sample to reflect the behavior of a more general market. Indexes aim to provide a comprehensive, unbiased, and stable barometer of a broad market. Investors use the indexes to determine trends to help in their decision making. Popular indexes include the following:

Dow Jones Industrial Average The Dow Jones Industrial Average (DJIA) is the most widely reported of all indexes. The DJIA follows prices of only 30 actively traded blue-chip stocks, including well-known companies such as American Express, AT&T, Caterpillar, Citigroup, Coca-Cola, Wal-Mart, and Walt Disney. The average is calculated by adding the closing prices of the 30 stocks and dividing by a number adjusted for splits, spinoffs, and dividends.

Standard & Poor's 500 Index The popular Standard & Poor's (S&P) 500 Index reports price movements of 500 stocks of large, established, publicly traded firms. It includes stocks of 400 industrial firms, 40 financial institutions, 40 public utilities, and 20 transportation companies. Companies with the highest market values influence the index the greatest.

NASDAQ Composite Index The NASDAQ Composite Index takes into account virtually all U.S. stocks (about 3000) traded in the over-the-counter market in the automated quotations system operated by the National Association of Securities Dealers. It provides a measure of companies not as popular or as large as those traded on the NYSE, including price behavior of many smaller, more speculative companies, although some big companies (such as Cisco Systems, Intel, and Microsoft) are listed as well.

Russell 3000 Index The Russell 3000 Index measures the performance of the 3000 largest U.S. companies based on total market capitalization.

Wilshire 5000 Index The Wilshire 5000 Index represents the total market value of practically all the 6000-plus U.S.-headquartered stocks that trade on major exchanges.

Foreign Stock Exchanges Stock exchanges are located in major cities throughout the world, including London, Sydney, Tokyo, Toronto, and Kuala Lumpur. U.S. investors often check the stock exchanges throughout the night to gain a hint of what might happen that day in the U.S. stock market.

Securities Exchanges (Stock Markets)

As we first noted in Chapter 13, a **securities exchange** (also called a **stock market**) is a market where agents of buyers and sellers can find each other easily by providing an orderly, open plan to trade securities. Each exchange has its own rules, is subject to government regulation, and provides constant supervision and self-regulation. The transactions are performed in an organized physical location, such as the New York Stock Exchange (also known as the "Big Board") and the American Stock Exchange, both in New York City. NYSE Euronet is the first trans-Atlantic stock exchange, and it is the world's biggest. For the convenience of traders, regional stock exchanges are located in Boston, Chicago, Philadelphia, and San Francisco. They all are called **organized exchanges.**

The electronic marketplace for securities transactions is called the **over-the-counter (OTC) marketplace.** In the OTC market, buyers and sellers negotiate transaction prices through a sophisticated telecommunications network connecting brokerage firms. The National Association of Securities Dealers (NASD) operates the network. Its **NASDAQ** automated quotations system provides prices on securities offered by more than 3200 domestic and foreign companies.

securities exchange/stock market Market where agents of buyers and sellers can find each other easily by providing an orderly, open plan to trade securities.

organized exchanges Actual physical location for a market, at which some securities prices are set by open outcry. Organized exchanges are quickly merging with electronic markets.

over-the-counter (OTC) marketplace Electronic marketplace for securities transactions.

NASDAQ National Association of Securities Dealers Automated Quotations system, which provides instantaneous information on securities offered by more than 3200 domestic and foreign companies.

Figure 14.2

How Stocks Are Quoted

1	2	3	4	5	6	7	8	9	10
YTD	52 WEEKS				YLD		VOL		NET
%CHG	HI	LO	STOCK (SYM)	DIV	%	PE	100S	LAST	CNG
+17.2	45.29	28.70	Walgreen	WAG	.14	.4	44	27540	39.45	+0.59
+ 3.7	20.56	14.00	WallaceCS	WCS	.66	3.4	17	714	19.70	+0.06
+ 0.1	34.50	23.00	WaddReed A	WDR	.35	1.1	25	2228	32.24	+0.04
+ 8.6	63.08	41.50	WalMart	WMT	.28	.4	42	104572	62.52	+0.82

+18.7	17.50	8.55▲	WacknhutCorr	WHC	...	18	448	16.45 − 0.40
+ 0.1	34.50	23	WaddlReed A	WDR	.35	1.1	25	2228	32.24 + 0.04
+17.2	45.29	28.70	Walgreen	WAG	.14	.4	44	27540	39.45 + 0.59
+ 3.7	20.56	14	WallaceCS	WCS	.66	3.4	17	714	19.70 + 0.06
+ 8.6	63.08	41.50	WalMart	WMT	.28	.4	42	104572	62.52 + 0.82
+ 9.6	14.65	7.60	WalterInd	WLT	.12	1.0	12	1625	12.40 − 0.10
+ 3.1	42.99	26.52	WashMut	WM s	1.00f	3.0	11	45891	33.71 − 0.45
			WashMut	PIES	4.00	5.4	...	14	74.10 − 0.40
			WashPost B	WPO	5.60	.9	25	51	596.90 − 0.60
			WashREIT	WRE	1.33	4.9	20	590	26.99 − 0.11
			WasteMgt	WMI	.01	...	34	15675	27.46 − 0.52
			WtrPikTch	PIK	...	11	51	9.48 + 0.38
			WatersCp	WAT	...	26	17787	32.76 + 1.31
			Watsco	WSO	.12f	.7	19	3016	17.05 + 1.46
			WatsnPharm	WPI	...	28	10379	30.22 + 0.06
			WatsonWyatt A	WW	...	18	3106	26.45 + 0.95
			WattsInd A	WTS	.24	1.5	16	3198	16.20 + 0.45
			WausaMosin	WMO	.34	2.9	62	1503	11.87	...
			Weatherford	WFT	...	26	16527	46.09 − 0.40
			WeiderNutrtn A	WNI	.15	8.6	dd	251	1.75 + 0.01
			WeightWatchers	WTW n	...	1128	35.82 + 0.62
			WeingtnRlty	WRI	3.33f	6.5	18	943	50.87 − 0.04
			WeisMkts	WMK	1.08	3.8	18	121	28.09 − 0.01
			Wellman	WLM	.36	2.3	61	1194	15.90 − 0.11
+ 3.2	131.25	81.65▲	WelptHlth	WLP	...	19	4837	120.59 + 3.09
+12.8	51.71	38.25	WellsFargo	WFC	1.04	2.1	25	45366	49.05 + 0.16
+ 1.0	25.75	24.75	WellsFargo QUIPS	WPF n	...	410	25.38 − 0.27
+ 9.6	32.78	20	Wendys	WEN	.24	.8	19	5596	31.97 − 0.44
+ 6.9	63.25	45.10	Wendys TECONS		2.50	4.0	...	15	62.25 − 0.55
+44.0	9.50	3.95	Wescolnt	WCC		17	240	7.13 + 0.37

Looking Up a Stock Price

The only thing that affects the price of a stock is supply and demand. When more people want to buy, the price goes up. When more people want to sell, the price goes down. If you know the company's stock symbol (search Google for "stock symbols"), the current price of any stock may be obtained by inputting the company symbol into Google or any of the other popular investment websites, such as Yahoo! Finance, MSN Money, and MarketWatch.

The millions of daily buying and selling transactions involving stocks, bonds, and mutual funds are summarized in the *Wall Street Journal*, the most widely read financial newspaper in the United States. Many daily newspapers publish abbreviated information, and security prices are quoted and traded to two decimal points. Stock quotations that might appear in the *Wall Street Journal* for Wal-Mart, a retailer, are illustrated in Figure 14.2.

Column 1: YTD % Change. The numbers in this column report the "year to date (YTD) as a percentage" change in the price (+8.6%) of Wal-Mart stock since January 1 of the current calendar year.

Columns 2 and 3: 52 Weeks, High and Low. This column shows that Wal-Mart stock traded at a high price of $63.08 and a low price of $41.50 during the previous 52 weeks, not including the previous trading day.

Column 4: Stock and Sym. This column gives the name of the stock (Wal-Mart in this example) and its abbreviated trading symbol (WMT).

Column 5: Div. The dividend amount is based on the last quarterly declaration by the company. For example, Wal-Mart last paid a quarterly dividend that, when converted to an annual basis, amounts to an estimated $0.28 annual dividend.

Column 6: Yld %. The figure in this column represents the yield as a percentage of dividend income, calculated by dividing the current price of the stock into the recent estimated dividend. The yield of the Wal-Mart stock is 0.4 percent.

Column 7: PE. This figure provides the price/earnings ratio based on the current price. The earnings figure used to calculate the price is not published in the newspaper but is the latest available. When Wal-Mart's "last" or closing price of $62.52 is divided by earnings, it gives a P/E ratio of 42.

Column 8: Vol 100s. This figure indicates the total volume of trading activity for the stock measured in hundreds of shares. Thus, 10,457,200 shares of Wal-Mart were traded on that day.

Column 9: Last. The price of the last trade of the day before the market closed for Wal-Mart was $62.52.

Column 10: Net Cng. The net change, +$0.82, represents the difference between the closing price (last) on this day and the closing price of the previous trading day. Today's Wal-Mart closing (last) price of $62.52 was up $0.82 from the previous closing price, which must have been $61.70.

Using Portfolio Tracking to Monitor Your Investments

Keeping track of investments requires record keeping, particularly for income tax purposes. These tasks can be performed easily using a computer software program. **Portfolio tracking** automatically updates the value of your portfolio after you enter the symbols of the stocks you own and the number of shares held. Online portfolio tracking services also alert you to events that may affect your stocks. Tracking helps you stay on top of your holdings so you know which stocks are performing well, which are underperforming, and which might need to be sold. See MSN Money (http://moneycentral.msn.com), E*Trade (https://us.etrade.com/e/t/home), Morningstar (www.morningstar.com), and InvestorGuide.com.

portfolio tracking Automatically updates the value of your portfolio after you enter the symbols of the stocks you own and the number of shares held.

✓ CONCEPT CHECK 14.5

1. Give three examples of the types of website resources available to investors on the Internet.
2. List five places where you can obtain investment information on a specific stock.
3. Distinguish between the Dow Jones Industrial Average and the S&P 500.
4. Where can you go to look up stock symbols and prices?

Buying and Selling Stocks

Securities transactions require the use of a licensed broker serving as a middleman between the seller and the buyer and collecting a fee on each purchase or sale of securities. A **stockbroker** (also known as an **account executive**) is licensed to buy and sell securities on behalf of the brokerage firm's clients. You can buy or sell securities through an online or human stockbroker who works for a brokerage firm that has access to the securities markets. Brokerage firms often provide investors with investment advice. As a matter of convenience and to facilitate resale, investors prefer to leave securities certificates in the name of their brokerage firm rather than take physical possession themselves. Securities certificates kept in the brokerage firm's name instead of the name of the individual investor are known as the **security's street name.**

Brokers have a duty to assess each client's suitability for particular investments. Regulations also require that they disclose when they are selling securities owned by the firm for which they work. Figure 14.3 shows the flow of securities transactions.

6 LEARNING OBJECTIVE
Summarize how stocks are bought and sold.

stockbroker/account executive Professional who is licensed to buy and sell securities on behalf of the brokerage firm's clients.

security's street name Securities certificates kept in the brokerage firm's name instead of the name of the individual investor.

Discount, Online, and Full-Service Brokers

To trade securities, you will need a brokerage firm to act as your agent. You can open an account at a full-service general brokerage firm or a discount brokerage firm. Each charges a commission for any trading it conducts on your behalf. You should make clear to the brokerage firm, in writing, your investment objectives and your desired level of risk. You can open an account rather easily at any brokerage firm. A **cash account**

cash account A brokerage account that requires an initial deposit (perhaps as little as $100) and specifies that full settlement is due to the brokerage firm within three business days after a buy or sell order has been given.

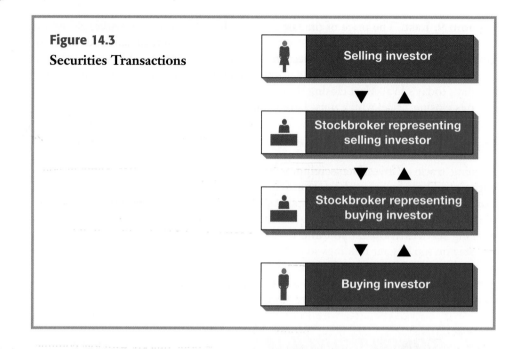

Figure 14.3
Securities Transactions

Selling investor

Stockbroker representing selling investor

Stockbroker representing buying investor

Buying investor

Did You Know?...

How Over-the-Counter Securities Transactions Are Executed

In an OTC sale, a stockbroker at a brokerage firm representing a buyer communicates with another brokerage firm that has the desired securities. The second brokerage firm is more accurately known as a **broker/dealer** because, in addition to offering the usual brokerage services, it can "make a market" for one or more securities. That is, broker/dealers both buy and sell securities. Market making occurs when a broker/dealer attempts to provide a continuous market by maintaining an inventory of specific securities to sell to other brokerage firms and stands ready to buy reasonable quantities of the same securities at market prices. To avoid potential conflicts of interest with a client, when a stockbroker sells securities in which the brokerage firm has made a market, the buying investor must be informed of that fact.

Did You Know?...

Initial Public Offerings of Securities

Companies that need capital to begin or expand their operations sell new issues of stocks, bonds, or both to the investing public. New issues of stock are referred to as **initial public offerings (IPOs). Investment banking firms** serve as intermediaries between companies issuing new stocks and bonds and the investing public. Buyers and sellers negotiate prices on the IPO shares over one or more days and buy the shares, thus raising the funds for the corporation. After that, shares of the stock will be bought and sold every day on a stock exchange. A company's later capital needs may be financed by reinvesting corporate profits or by selling additional new stock issues or bonds.

requires an initial deposit (perhaps as little as $100) and specifies that full settlement is due to the brokerage firm within three business days after a buy or sell order has been given. After each transaction, your account is debited or credited and written confirmation is immediately forwarded to you. All brokers offer such services.

Discount Brokers Many investors use **discount brokers** because they charge commissions to execute trades that are often 30 to 80 percent less than the fees charged by full-service brokers. These brokers feature low commissions because they have lower overhead and may offer fewer customer services. That is, they focus on a single function: efficiently executing orders to buy and sell securities. Some discount brokerage firms do not conduct research or provide investment advice. Transactions can be completed online as well as via a toll-free telephone number; investors can also obtain price quotes, check the status of their accounts, and transfer funds online or by phone. Discounters include Ameritrade, Scottrade, E*Trade, ShareBuilder, and BUYandHOLD.

Online brokers (also called **Internet** or **electronic brokers**) have reduced the cost of executing a trade to perhaps $20 or even $10 because their primary business is online trading. Online **day trading** occurs when an investor buys and sells stocks quickly throughout the day with the hope that the price will move enough to cover transaction costs and earn some profits. Day traders do not own stocks overnight. Transactions are executed online because they can be done quickly with low commissions. Day trading is a risky practice. One of billionaire Warren Buffett's commandments for getting ahead in personal finance states, "You will lose money if you trade stocks actively."

discount brokers Charge commissions to execute trades that are often 30 to 80 percent less than the fees charged by full-service brokers, but also offer fewer services.

online brokers Such brokers, also called Internet or electronic brokers, have reduced the cost of executing a trade to perhaps $20 or even $10 because their primary business is online trading.

day trading Occurs when an investor buys and sells stocks quickly throughout a day with the hope that prices will move enough to cover transaction costs and earn some profits.

Did You Know?...

Regulations Protect Against Investment Fraud

Public trust is vital to the success of the securities industry; without it, consumers will not invest. Regulation of securities markets aims to provide investors with accurate and reliable information about securities, maintain ethical standards, and prevent fraud against investors. This regulation occurs at four levels:

1. The **Securities and Exchange Commission (SEC)**, a federal government agency, focuses on ensuring disclosure of information about securities to the investing public and on approving the rules and regulations employed by the organized securities exchanges. The SEC requires registration of listed securities with appropriate and updated information. It also prohibits manipulative practices, such as using insider information for illegal personal gain or causing the price of a security to rise or fall for false reasons. All states require registration of securities sold within their states, and they, too, regulate the securities industry.

2. The Financial Industry Regulatory Authority (FINRA) and other self-regulatory organizations enforce standards of conduct for their members and their member organizations. They dictate rules for listing and for trading securities.

3. Individual brokerage firms have established standards of conduct for brokers that govern how they deal with investors.

4. The U.S. Congress decides when investors need more federal laws. Congress created a limited insurance program to protect the investing public. Although investment losses are not covered, the Security Investors Protection Corporation (SIPC) protects investors when an SEC-registered brokerage firm goes bankrupt. Each of an investor's accounts at a brokerage firm is protected against financial loss as a result of unreturned securities and cash up to a total of $500,000, but no more than $100,000 in cash.

general (full-service) brokerage firms Offer a full range of services to customers, including investment advice and research.

Advice from a Pro...

Check Your Stockbroker's Background

You can check the background of a stockbroker or a brokerage firm via the Financial Industry Regulatory Authority (www.finra.org and click on FINRA BrokerCheck). Some investors neglect to investigate a stockbroker or firm and lose money as a result. The broker may abscond with the investor's funds; at other times, the investor receives poor advice. Don't let it happen to you!

Allen Martin
California State University–Northridge

round lots Standard units of trading of 100 shares of stock and $1000 or $5000 par value for bonds.

odd lot An amount of a security that is less than the normal unit of trading for that particular security; for stocks, any transaction less than 100 shares is usually considered to be an odd lot.

floor broker Brokerage firm's contact person at an exchange.

specialist Person on floor of an exchange who handles trades of a particular stock in an effort to maintain a fair and orderly market.

Full-Service General Brokerage Firms A traditional **general brokerage firm** offers a full range of services to customers, including investment information and advice; research reports on companies, industries, general economic trends, and world events; an investment newsletter; recommendations to buy, sell, or hold stocks; execution of securities transactions by humans and online; and margin loans. Investors receive monthly statements summarizing all of the transactions in their account and commissions, dividends, and interest. Commissions and fees are higher than those of discount and online brokers; however, investors can discuss their investments with a qualified professional.

Broker Commissions and Fees

Brokerage firms receive a commission on each securities transaction to cover the direct expenses of executing the transaction and other overhead expenses. They have established fee schedules that they use when dealing with any except the largest investors. The fees reflect a commission rate that declines as the total value of the transaction increases. For example, in lieu of a minimum commission charge of $25, a brokerage firm might charge 2.8 percent on a transaction amounting to less than $800, 1.8 percent on transactions between $800 and $2500, 1.6 percent on amounts between $2500 and $5000, and 1.2 percent on amounts exceeding $5000.

Transaction costs are based on sales of **round lots,** which are standard units of trading of 100 shares of stock and $1000 or $5000 par value for bonds. An **odd lot** is an amount of a security that is less than the normal unit of trading for that particular security; for stocks, any transaction less than 100 shares is usually considered to be an odd lot. When brokerage firms buy or sell shares in odd lots, they may charge a fee of 12.5 cents (called an **eighth**) per share on the odd-lot portion of the transaction, which is called the **differential.**

The payment of commissions can quickly reduce the return on any investment. A purchase commission of 2 percent added to a sales commission of another 2 percent, for example, means that the investor has to earn a 4 percent yield just to pay the transaction costs. Brokerage commissions typically range from $25 to 3 percent of the value of the transaction. The easiest way to hold down investing costs is to find a brokerage firm that charges low commissions.

How to Order Stock Transactions

Hundreds of millions of shares of securities are traded daily on the stock markets in the United States. Every trade brings together a buyer and a seller to complete the transaction at a given price.

The Process of Trading Stocks Assume you instruct brokerage firm A to purchase a certain number of shares at a specific price. The firm relays the buy order to its representative, who coordinates trading. Because the brokerage firm has a seat on the exchange, the buy order is then given to the brokerage firm's contact person at the exchange—a **floor broker.** This broker contacts a **specialist,** a person on the floor of the exchange who handles trades of that particular stock in an effort to maintain a fair and orderly market. The buy order is then filled, either by taking shares from the specialist's own inventory or by matching it with another investor's sell order.

Matched or Negotiated Stock Price

Securities prices are either matched or negotiated.

Matched Price On the organized stock exchanges, a match must occur between the buyer's price and the seller's price for a sale to take place. Therefore, a specialist could hold a specific order for a few minutes, a few hours, or even a week before making a match. With actively traded issues, a transaction is completed in just a few minutes. A slower-selling security can be traded more quickly if an investor is willing to accept the current market price (as discussed later).

Negotiated Price. In the over-the-counter market, the final transaction price is negotiated because two prices are involved. The **bid price** is the highest price anyone has declared that he or she wants to pay for a security. Thus, it represents the amount a brokerage firm is willing to pay for a particular security. The **ask price** is the lowest price anyone will accept at that time for a particular security. Thus, it represents the amount for which another brokerage firm is willing to sell a particular security. The **spread** represents the difference between the bid price at which a broker/dealer will buy shares and the higher ask price at which the broker/dealer will sell shares. The spread can be as little as 5 cents per share, but it can range from 10 to 20 cents for OTC stocks. In addition to paying the ask price, investors typically pay a nominal sales commission to their stockbroker for executing the transaction.

    If a buyer does not want to pay the asking price, he or she instructs the stockbroker to offer a lower bid price, which may or may not be accepted. If it is refused, the buyer might cancel the first order and raise the bid slightly in a second order in the hope that the owner will sell the shares at that price. Otherwise, the buyer may have to pay the full ask price to complete the deal. OTC trades usually occur at prices somewhere between the bid and ask figures.

Types of Stock Orders

Basically, there are only two types of orders—buy and sell. The stockbroker will buy or sell securities according to prescribed instructions in a process called **executing an order.** Those instructions can place constraints on the prices at which those orders are carried out. Following are examples of instructions that may accompany stock orders:

Market Order. A **market order** instructs the stockbroker to execute an order at the prevailing market price—that is, the current selling price of the stock. A stockbroker can generally conduct the desired transaction within a few minutes. The floor broker tries to match the instructions from many investors with the narrow range of prices available from the specialist. Traders on the floor of the stock market typically shout and signal back and forth as part of this effort to match buyers and sellers. Most trades are market orders.

Limit Order. A **limit order** instructs the stockbroker to buy or sell a stock at a specific price. It may include instructions to buy at the best possible price but not above a specified limit, or to sell at the best possible price but not below a specified limit. A limit order provides some protection against buying a security at a price higher than desired or selling at a price deemed too low. The stockbroker transmits the limit order to the specialist. The order is executed if and when the specified price (or better) is reached and all other previously received orders on the specialist's book have been considered.

    A disadvantage for buyers who place a limit order is that they might miss an excellent opportunity. For example, assume you place a limit order with your stockbroker to buy 100 shares of Running Paws common stock at $60.50 or lower. You have read in the newspaper that the stock has recently been selling at $61 and $61.25, and you hope to save $0.50 to $1.00 on each share. On that same day, the company announces publicly that it plans to expand into the dog food area for the first time. Investor confidence in the new sales effort pushes the price up to $70. If you had given your stockbroker a market order instead, you would have purchased 100 shares of Running Paws at perhaps

bid price Declared highest price anyone wants to pay for a security.

ask price Declared lowest price that anyone is willing to accept to sell a security.

spread Represents difference between bid price at which a broker/dealer will buy shares and higher ask price at which the broker/dealer will sell shares.

market order Instructs the stockbroker to execute an order at the prevailing market price—that is, the current selling price of the stock.

limit order Instructs the stockbroker to buy or sell a stock at a specific price.

$61.50, which would have given you an immediate profit of $850 ($70 − $61.50 = $8.50; $8.50 × 100 shares = $850) on an initial investment of $6150 ($61.50 × 100).

A disadvantage for sellers placing a limit order is that it could result in no sale if the price drops because of negative news. Assume that you bought stock at $50 that is currently selling at $58 and that you have placed a limit order to sell at a price of no less than $60 so as to take your profit. The price could creep up to $59 and then fall back to $48, however. In this event, you did not sell the securities because the limit order was priced too high, and they are now worth less than what you originally paid for them. A limit order is best used when you expect great fluctuations in the price of a stock and when you buy or sell infrequently traded securities on the over-the-counter market. Limit orders account for about one-third of all trades.

Stop Order (Stop-Loss Order). A **stop order** instructs a stockbroker to sell your shares of stock at the market price if a stock declines to or goes below a specified price. It is often called a **stop-loss order** because the investor uses it to protect against a sharp drop in price and thus to stop a loss. The specialist executes the order as soon as the stop-order price is reached and a buyer is matched at the next market price.

As an example of how to stop a loss, assume you bought 100 shares of Running Paws stock at $70. You are nervous about the company's entry into the competitive dog food business, however, and you fear that it might lose money. As a consequence, you place a stop order to sell your shares if the price drops to $56, thereby limiting your potential loss to 20 percent ($70 − $56 = $14; $14 ÷ $70 = 0.20). Some months later, you read in the financial section of your newspaper that even after six months Running Paws still has less than 1 percent of the dog food market. You call your stockbroker, who informs you that the price of Running Paws stock dropped drastically in response to the article, which was published in the previous day's *Wall Street Journal*. The broker reports that all of your shares were sold at $55, that the current price is $49, and that the sales transaction notice is already in the mail to your home. The stop order cut your losses to slightly more than 20 percent ($70 − $55 = $15; $15 ÷ $70 = 21.4 percent) and saved an additional loss of $6 ($55 − $49) per share. Thus, the stop order limited your loss to $1500 [(100 × $70 = $7000) − (100 × $55 = $5500)] instead of $2100 [(100 × $70 = $7000) − (100 × $49 = $4900)].

You can use a stop order to protect your profits, too. Assume you bought 100 shares of Alpo Dog Food Company at $60 per share, which now has a current selling price of $75. Your paper profit is $1500 ($75 − $60 = $15; $15 × 100 shares = $1500), less commissions. To protect part of that profit, you place a stop order with your stockbroker to sell at $65 if the price drops that low. If your stock is sold, you will have a real profit of $500 ($65 − $60 = $5; $5 × 100 shares = $500). If Alpo Dog Food stock climbs in price instead, perhaps in response to the bad news about Running Paws, the stop order would have cost you nothing. If the price does climb, you might replace the stop order with one having a higher price to lock in an even greater amount of profit.

Time Limits. Investors have several ways to place time limits on their orders to buy or sell stocks. A **fill-or-kill order** instructs the stockbroker to buy or sell the stock at the market price immediately or else cancel the order. A **day order** is valid only for the remainder of the trading day during which it was given to the brokerage firm. Unless otherwise indicated, any order received by a stockbroker is assumed to be a day order. A **week order** remains valid until the close of trading on Friday of the current week. A **month order** is effective until the close of trading on the last business day of the current month. An **open order**, also called a **good-til-canceled (GTC) order**, remains valid until executed by the stockbroker or canceled by the investor. If you give an order longer than a week in duration, you should carefully monitor events and then alter the order if the situation changes substantially.

stop order Instructs a stockbroker to sell your shares of stock at the market price if a stock declines to or goes below a specified price.

Did You Know?...

The Tax Consequences of Investing in Stocks and Bonds

The government encourages investing through tax policies that favor investors.

- Money invested in qualified tax-sheltered retirement plans accumulates tax free, thereby avoiding current income taxes on interest, dividends, and capital gains for many years. As a result, balances can build up more quickly than funds in traditional investment accounts. Income taxes must be paid on such money when it is eventually withdrawn.

- Taxes are low on dividend income. Funds put into regular investment accounts represent "after-tax money" (you earn an income, you pay taxes on that income, and then you invest some of the remaining money). Taxes are due on any interest, dividends, and capital gains in the year in which the income is received. Interest is taxable at the investor's marginal tax rate. Dividend income is taxed at a maximum rate of 15 percent for most people; a 5 percent rate applies to lower-income taxpayers.

- Capital gains taxes are low. No tax liability is incurred for any capital gains until the stock, bond, mutual fund, real estate, or other investment is sold. When you sell an investment, such as a stock, the gain or loss is calculated by analyzing what you paid for the investment plus broker commissions and loads minus the selling price minus commissions or redemption fees. Short-term gains (for investments held for one year or less) are taxed at the same rates as ordinary income. Long-term gains (for investments held at least a year and a day) are taxed at special rates: The federal rate is 15 percent, but taxpayers in the 10 to 15 percent tax brackets pay a long-term capital gains tax of 5 percent. The long-term capital gain rate for collectibles such as stamps and coins is 28 percent.

- Capital losses can be used to offset capital gains or even your regular income. See Chapter 4.

Margin Buying and Selling Short Are Risky Trading Techniques

For investors interested in taking on additional risk, there are two advanced trading techniques, and both involve using credit: buying stocks on margin and selling short. Buying stocks on margin involves using a line of credit from a stockbroker, thereby enabling the investor to effectively control many more shares with a small amount of cash. Investors who sell shares of stock short are actually selling shares they do not own.

Margin Trading Is Buying Stocks on Credit   Some investors open a margin account with a brokerage firm in addition to their cash account so they can buy securities using credit. Opening a **margin account** requires making a substantial deposit of cash or securities ($2000 or more) and permits the purchase of other securities using credit granted by the brokerage firm. Using a margin account to purchase securities, or **margin buying,** allows the investor to apply leverage that magnifies returns. In essence, the investor borrows money from the brokerage firm to buy more stocks and bonds than would be possible with his or her available cash. Both brokerage firms and the Federal Reserve Board regulate the use of credit to buy securities.

The **margin rate** is the percentage of the value (or equity) in an investment that is not borrowed. In recent years, it has ranged from 25 to 40 percent. Thus, if the margin rate is 40 percent, you can buy securities by putting up only 40 percent of the total price and borrowing the remainder from the brokerage firm. The securities purchased, as well as other securities in the margin account, are used as collateral. Margin lending is financed at competitive interest rates.

margin account Account at a brokerage firm that requires a substantial deposit of cash or securities and permits the purchase of other securities using credit granted by the brokerage firm.

margin buying Using a margin account to buy securities; allows the investor to apply leverage that magnifies returns—or losses.

margin rate Set by the Fed, percentage of the value (or equity) in an investment that is not borrowed—recently 25 to 40 percent.

Buying on Margin Can Increase Returns. Buying on margin is commonly used to increase the individual's return on investment. For example, assume that Greenfield Computer Company common stock is selling for $80 per share. You want to buy 100 shares, requiring a total expenditure of $8000. Using your margin account, you will make a cash payment of $3200 (0.40 × $8000), with the brokerage firm lending you the difference of $4800 ($8000 − $3200). For the sake of simplicity, we will omit commissions from this example and assume that the brokerage firm lends the funds at 10 percent interest. Thus, your equity (market value minus amount borrowed) in the investment is $3200. If, as illustrated in Table 14.2, the price of Greenfield stock increases from $80 to $92 at the end of a year, you can sell your investment for proceeds of $9200, minus the amount invested ($3200), the amount borrowed ($4800), and the cost of borrowing ($4800 × 0.10 = $480), for a return of $720. Because you invested equity of only $3200 to obtain a profit of $720, you have earned a return of 22.5 percent ($720 ÷ $3200). If you had put up the entire $8000 and not bought on margin, your return on investment would have been only 15 percent ($9200 − $8000 = $1200; $1200 ÷ $8000 = 0.15). In this way, you can use credit to increase the rate of return on your own investment. Those with an aggressive investment philosophy might buy on margin because it gives them the opportunity to obtain a higher rate of return.

Table 14.2 How Buying on Margin Affects Investment Returns

	Cash Transaction	Margin Transaction
Price of stock rises (from $80 to $92 per share)		
Buy 100 shares at $80 (amount invested)	−$8,000	−$3,200
Sell 100 shares at $92 (proceeds)	9,200	9,200
Net proceeds	$1,200	$6,000
Minus amount borrowed	—	−4,800
Net	$1,200	$1,200
Minus cost of borrowing	—	−480
Return	$1,200	$720
Yield (return ÷ amount invested)	+15.0% ✓	+22.5% ✓
Price of stock declines (from $80 to $70 per share)		
Buy 100 shares at $80 (amount invested)	−$8,000	−$3,200
Sell 100 shares at $70 (proceeds)	7,000	7,000
Net proceeds	−$1,000	$3,800
Minus amount borrowed	—	−4,800
Net	−$1,000	−$1,000
Minus cost of borrowing	—	−480
Return	−$1,000	−$1,480
Yield (return ÷ amount invested)	−12.5%	−46.25% ✓
Price of stock declines (from $80 to $60 per share)		
Buy 100 shares at $80 (amount invested)	−$8,000	−$3,200
Sell 100 shares at $60 (proceeds)	6,000	6,000
Net proceeds	−$2,000	$2,800
Minus amount borrowed	—	−4,800
Net	−$2,000	−$2,000
Minus cost of borrowing	—	−480
Return	−$2,000	−$2,480
Yield (return ÷ amount invested)	−25.0%	−77.5% ✓

Buying on Margin Can Increase Losses. If the price of a security bought on margin declines, however, leverage can work against you, as Table 14.2 also illustrates. For example, if the price of the Greenfield stock bought at $80 dropped to $70 after a year, you would lose $10 per share on the 100 shares, for a total loss of $1000. Your proceeds from selling the stock would be only $7000. If you bought the stock on 40 percent margin, these proceeds are offset by the cost of the investment ($3200), the margin loan from the broker ($4800), and interest on the loan ($480), for a total deduction of $8480 and a net loss of $1480 ($7000 − $8480). Thus, a loss of $1480 on an investment of $3200 is a negative return of 46.25 percent (−$1480 ÷ $3200). The same $10 loss per share (from a price of $80 to $70 per share) would have been a negative loss of only 12.5 percent if the stocks were not bought on margin ($7000 − $8000 = −$1000; −$1000 ÷ $8000 = −0.125). Similarly, the example cited in Table 14.2 shows the magnitude of the loss due to a $20 decline in value as a negative return of 77.5 percent, compared with a loss of only 25 percent if the investor had not bought on margin.

Did You Know?...

How to Determine a Margin Call Stock Price

To determine the price at which a margin call for a stock will occur, use the formula given in Equation (14.3). This formula also appears on the *Garman/Forgue* website.

$$\text{Margin call stock price} = \frac{\text{amount owed broker} \div (1 - \text{margin call requirement})}{\text{number of shares bought}} \quad (14.3)$$

$$\$64 = \frac{\$4800 \div (1 - 0.25)}{100}$$

Substituting the figures from the Running Paws text example, the investor will receive a margin call if the stock price dropped below $64, as equity at this point is 25 percent.

A Margin Call Makes Matters Even Worse. When the price of a stock declines to the point where the investor's equity is less than the required percentage, the brokerage firm will make a telephone call to the investor. A representative of the firm will tell the investor to immediately either put up more collateral (money or other stocks) or face having the investment liquidated. This procedure is known as a **margin call.** If the investor fails to put up the additional cash or securities to maintain a required level of equity in the margin account, the broker will sell the securities at the market price, resulting in a sharp financial loss to the investor. The investor is required to repay the broker for any losses. The margin call concept protects the broker that has loaned money on securities.

For example, in Table 14.2, the 100 shares of Greenfield priced at $80 were originally valued at $8000, consisting of investor's equity of $3200, or 40 percent ($3200 ÷ $8000), and $4800 borrowed from the brokerage firm. Assume that the stock price drops to $60 per share, resulting in a current market value of $6000 for the investment. Because the investor still owes $4800, his or her equity has dropped to $1200 ($6000 − $4800), which is now only 20 percent of the value of the securities ($1200 ÷ $6000), rather than the required 40 percent. The broker, operating with a 25 percent margin requirement, will immediately make a margin call and demand that funds or collateral be added to the account to bring the equity up to a minimum of 25 percent. In this example, to maintain a 25 percent margin, an additional $300 ($6000 × 0.25 = $1500; $1500 − $1200 = $300) would be required.

margin call If a stock price declines to the point that the investor's equity is less than the required percentage, a representative of the brokerage firm makes a phone call and tells the investor to either put up more money or securities or face having the position bought on margin liquidated.

Selling Short Is Selling Stocks Borrowed from Your Broker
Buying a security with the hope that it will go up in value—the goal of most investors—is called **buying long.** You might suspect, however, that the price of a security will drop. You can earn profits when the price of a security declines by **selling short.** In this trading technique, investors sell securities they do not own (borrowing them from a broker) and later buy the same number of shares of the security at a lower price (returning them to the broker). Thus, the investor earns a profit on the transaction. Brokerage firms require an investor to maintain a margin account when selling short

buying long Buying a security (especially on margin) with the hope that the stock price will rise.

selling short Investors selling securities they do not own (borrowing them from a broker) and later buying the same number of shares of the security at a lower price (returning them to the broker).

covering a position When an investor using a margin account buys back securities sold short or sells securities bought long.

because it provides some assurance that the investor can repay the firm for the borrowed stock, if necessary. As a result, some or all of an investor's funds deposited in a margin account are effectively tied up during a short sale. Many brokers hold the proceeds of a short sale, without paying interest, until the customer **covers the position** by buying it back for delivery to the broker.

An Example of Short Selling. As an example, suppose you believe that the price of Greenfield stock will drop substantially over the next several months. You have heard that some top managers of the company may resign and that competitors are expected to introduce newer products. Accordingly, you instruct your broker to sell 100 shares of Greenfield at $80 per share ($80 × 100 = $8000). In this illustration, assume that you have a 40 percent margin requirement, which means you have committed $3200 (0.40 × $8000). The shares are actually borrowed by the broker from another investor or another broker. Several months later, Greenfield announces lower profits because of strong competition, and the share price drops to $70. Now you instruct your broker to buy 100 shares at the new price and use the purchased shares to repay the borrowed shares. You gain a profit of $1000 ($8000 − $7000), ignoring commissions, providing a return of 31.3 percent ($1000 ÷ $3200).

Using Margin to Sell Short. A very small price drop can provide big profits for the short-term investor who sells short *and* uses margin-buying techniques. As an example, imagine that you sell 100 shares of a $10 stock with a 40 percent margin requirement. The committed funds amount to $400 (0.40 × $1000). Even if the price of the stock declines by only $1, you still earn a significant profit: 100 shares sold at $10 equals $1000, minus 100 shares bought at $9 equals $900, for a profit of $100 and a return of 25 percent ($100 ÷ $400). The price could decline in just a day or two. This possibility of a fast, high return explains the allure of such investments.

Almost unlimited losses can occur with the use of margin to sell short if the price rises rather than falls. If the $10 stock soars to $22, for example, the loss will exceed the original investment: 100 shares sold at $10 equals $1000, minus 100 shares bought at $22 equals $2200, for a loss of $1200 and a negative return of 550 percent ($2200 ÷ $400). When the price of a security rises, short sellers are subject to margin calls.

Only a small proportion of investors sell stocks short because this approach is so risky. Selling short and buying on margin are techniques to be used only by sophisticated investors. Rydex Investments and ProFunds sell short index mutual funds, allowing market timers to profit during bear markets.

Did You Know?...

Top 3 Financial Missteps of Investing in Stocks and Bonds

People slip up in investing in stocks and bonds when they do the following:

1. Seek to invest in just one stock that promises to make them a lot of money
2. Neglect to carefully research investment choices
3. Hold onto a lousy investment too long instead of cutting losses by selling it

✔ CONCEPT CHECK 14.6

1. Summarize the differences among discount, online, and full-service brokers.
2. Distinguish between round lot and odd lot broker's commissions.
3. Summarize the differences among types of stock orders: market, limit, and stop order.
4. Explain what buying on margin is and how it can go wrong for an investor.
5. Explain what selling short is and how it can go wrong for an investor.

Investing in Bonds

Investment-grade bonds offer investors a reasonable certainty of regularly receiving the periodic income (interest) and retrieving the amount originally invested (principal). Bonds are usually issued at a **par value** (also known as **face value**) of $1000. An investor typically earns a low to moderate return on bond investments, an appropriate yield when compared with the higher total returns earned on riskier stocks and stock mutual funds. Fewer than 800 of the 23,000 largest U.S. companies that issue bonds meet the highest investment-grade rating standards. Owning some bonds (or bond mutual funds) along with stocks and cash diversifies an investment portfolio. The Bond Market Association (http://www.investinginbonds.com/) sponsors a bond website.

Speculative-grade bonds pay a high interest rate. These are often called **junk bonds,** and they are long-term, high-risk, high-interest-rate corporate (or municipal) IOUs issued by companies (or municipalities) with poor or no credit ratings. The interest rates paid investors on junk bonds are 3.5 to 8 percent higher than those of Treasury bonds. Also called **high-yield bonds,** they carry investment ratings that are below traditional investment grade and carry a higher default risk. The **default rate** on high-quality bonds is less than 1 percent. The default rate on junk bonds over time has ranged from a low of 2 percent to a whopping 31 percent. For more information, see Bond Pickers (www.bondpickers.com) or www.defaultrisk.com or search Google using "high-yield bond offerings."

Individual investors often avoid buying individual junk bonds because of the substantial financial risk involved with owning too few investments. Instead, they reduce risk by diversifying their investments through a "high-yield income" bond mutual fund (see Chapter 15) that has junk bonds in its portfolio.

Corporate, U.S. Government, and Municipal Bonds

Three types of bonds are available: corporate bonds, U.S. government securities, and municipal government bonds.

Corporate Bonds **Corporate bonds** are interest-bearing certificates of long-term debt issued by a corporation. They represent a needed source of funds for corporations. The dollar value of newly issued bonds is three times the dollar value of newly issued stocks. Because of tax regulations, corporations often finance major projects by issuing long-term bonds instead of selling stocks. One reason they do so is that payments of dividends to common and preferred stockholders are not tax deductible for corporations, unlike interest paid to bondholders. State laws require corporations to make bond interest payments on time. Therefore, companies in financial difficulty are required to pay bondholders before paying any short-term creditors.

Compared with other bonds, corporate bonds pay the highest interest rates. The default risk varies with the issuer. To help you in appraising the risks and potential rewards of bond investments, independent advisory services, such as Moody's Investors Service and Standard & Poor's, grade bonds for credit risk. These firms publish unbiased ratings of the financial conditions of corporations and municipalities that issue bonds. A **bond rating** represents the opinion of an outsider on the quality—or creditworthiness—of the issuing organization. It reflects the likelihood that the issuing organization will be able to repay its debt. Ratings for each bond issue are continually reevaluated, and they often change after the original security has been sold to the public. Investors have access to measures of the **default risk** (or **credit risk**), which is the uncertainty associated with not receiving the promised periodic interest payments and the principal amount when it becomes due at maturity. Bond rating directories are available in large libraries and online.

Table 14.3 shows the bond ratings used by Moody's and Standard & Poor's. The higher the rating, the greater the probable safety of the bond and the lower the default risk. The lower the rating of the bond, the higher the stated interest rate or the effec-

7 LEARNING OBJECTIVE
Describe how to invest in bonds.

investment-grade bonds Offer investors a reasonable certainty of regularly receiving periodic income (interest) and retrieving the amount originally invested (principal).

par value/face value Some multiple of $1000 that is printed on a bond when issued and repaid at maturity.

speculative-grade bonds Long-term, high-risk, high-interest-rate corporate (or municipal) IOUs issued by companies (or municipalities) with poor or no credit ratings. Also called junk bonds or high-yield bonds.

default rate Percentage of bonds that do not repay principal at maturity and sometimes cease interest payments in the interim.

corporate bonds Interest-bearing certificates of long-term debt issued by a corporation.

bond rating An impartial outsider's opinion of the quality—or creditworthiness—of the issuing organization.

default risk/credit risk Uncertainty associated with not receiving the promised periodic interest payments and the principal amount when it becomes due at maturity.

Table 14.3 Summary of Bond Ratings

| Ratings | | Interpretation of Ratings |
Moody's	Standard & Poor's	
Aaa Aa A	AAA AA A	High investment quality suggests ability to repay principal and interest on time. Aaa and AAA bonds are generally referred to as "gilt-edged" because issuers have demonstrated profitability over the years and have paid their bondholders their interest without interruption; thus, they carry the smallest risk.
Baa Ba	BBB BB B	Medium-quality investments that adequately provide security to principal and interest. They are neither highly protected nor poorly secured; thus, they may have some speculative characteristics.
B Caa Ca	CCC CC C	Lack characteristics of a desirable investment and investors have decreasing assurance of repayment as the rating declines. Elements of danger may be present regarding repayment of principal and interest.
C	DDD DD D	In default with little prospect of regaining any investment standing.

Note: Bonds rated Baa and higher by Moody's and BBB and higher by S&P are investment-grade quality; Ba, BB, and lower-rated bonds are junk bonds.

tive interest rate. When bonds are reduced in price from their face amount, more risk is involved. Higher ratings denote confidence that the issuer will not default and, if necessary, that the bond can readily be sold before its maturity date. Investment-grade corporate bonds may provide returns as much as 1.5 percentage points higher than the returns available on comparable U.S. Treasury securities.

U.S. Government Bills, Notes, and Bonds U.S. Treasury securities are the world's safest investment because the government has never defaulted on its debt. U.S. Treasury securities are backed by the "full faith, credit, and taxing power of the U.S. government," and this all but guarantees the timely payment of principal and interest.

U.S. government securities are classified into two groups: (1) Treasury bills, notes, and bonds and (2) federal agency issue notes, bonds, and certificates. Treasury bills, notes, and bonds are collectively known as **Treasury securities,** or **Treasuries.** The federal government uses these debt instruments to finance the public national debt. Treasury securities have excellent liquidity and are simple to acquire and sell. Previously issued marketable Treasury securities are bought and sold in securities markets through brokers. New issues can be purchased online using the Treasury Direct Plan (www.savingsbonds.gov).

The interest rates on federal government securities are lower than those on corporate bonds because they are virtually risk free. The possibility of default is near zero. Individuals with a conservative investment philosophy are often attracted to the certainty offered by U.S. government securities. Investors can purchase Treasury securities through their bank or broker or directly from the Treasury. Investors often buy Treasury issues to protect a portion of their assets and to diversify their portfolios. Although interest income is subject to federal income taxes, interest earned on Treasury securities is exempt from state and local income taxes.

Treasury Bills, Notes, and Bonds **Treasury bills,** or **T-bills,** are short-term U.S. government securities issued with maturities of a year or less. They are sold at a discount from their face value (par). The difference between the original purchase price and what the Treasury pays you at maturity, the gain or "par," is interest. This interest is exempt from state and local income taxes but is reported as interest income on your federal tax return in the year the Treasury bill matures. Stated as an interest rate, the return on such investments is called a **discount yield.** For example, if you buy a $10,000 26-week Treasury bill for $9750 and hold it until maturity, your interest will be $250. An investor can hold a bill until maturity or sell it before it is due.

Treasury securities Known as Treasuries, securities issued by the U.S. government, including bills, notes, and bonds.

Treasury bills Known as T-bills, U.S. government securities with maturities of one year or less.

discount yield Difference between the original purchase price of a T-bill and what the Treasury pays you at maturity—the gain, or "par," is interest.

When a bill matures, the proceeds can be reinvested into another bill or redeemed and the principal will be deposited into the investor's checking or savings account.

A **Treasury note** or **bond** is a fixed-principal, fixed-interest-rate government security issued for an intermediate term or long term. Notes are issued for two, three, five, or ten years and bonds have a maturity of more than ten years. Notes and bonds exist only as electronic entries in accounts. The interest rate is higher than the rates for T-bills because the lending period is longer. Owners of Treasury notes and bonds receive interest payments every six months, which is reported as interest income on their federal tax return in the year received. When the security matures, the investor is repaid the principal. Investors can hold a note or bond until maturity or sell it.

I bonds are nonmarketable savings bonds backed by the U.S. government that pay an earnings rate that is a combination of two rates: a fixed interest rate that is set when the investor buys the bond and a semiannual variable interest rate tied to inflation that protects the investor's purchasing power. They are sold at face value, such as $50 for a $50 bond. Interest stops accruing 30 years after issue, and I bonds pay off only when redeemed. If you redeem an I bond within the first five years, you will forfeit the three most recent months' interest; after five years, you will not be penalized. The maximum purchase allowed in one calendar year is $30,000. All earnings on savings bonds are exempt from both state and local income taxes, while federal taxes can be deferred until the bonds are either redeemed or reach final maturity. I bonds cashed in to pay education expenses are tax exempt.

TIPS, also known as **Treasury Inflation-Protected Securities,** are marketable Treasury bonds whose principal increases with inflation and decreases with deflation. These inflation-indexed $1000 bonds are the only investment that guarantees that the investor's return will outpace inflation. TIPS bonds are sold in terms from 5 to 30 years, and interest is paid to TIPS owners every six months until they mature. The interest rate is set when the security is purchased, and the rate never changes. The principal is adjusted every six months according to the rise and fall of the consumer price index (CPI); if inflation occurs and the CPI rises, the principal increases. The government sends the interest payment on the new principal to the investor's account.

The fixed interest rate on TIPS is applied to the inflation-adjusted principal; so if inflation occurs throughout the life of a TIPS security, every interest payment will be greater than the one before it. The amount of each interest payment is determined by multiplying the inflation-adjusted principal by one-half the interest rate. The inflation-adjusted amount added to the principal on a TIPS bond every six months is taxable, even though the investor does not receive the money until the bond matures. Thus, TIPS bonds pay "phantom taxable interest income," like **zero-coupon bonds** (described on page 422), so the investor pays federal income taxes on the interest earned each year. The investor uses other funds to pay the taxes on that income.

When TIPS mature, the federal government pays the inflation-adjusted principal (or the original principal if it is greater). Investors can hold a TIPS bond until it matures or sell it before it matures. The interest on TIPS bonds can be excluded from federal income tax when the bond owner pays tuition and fees for higher education in the year the bonds are redeemed.

U.S. government savings bonds are nonmarketable, interest-bearing bonds. **Series EE savings bonds** are issued at a sharp discount from face value and pay no annual interest, and they may be redeemed at full value upon maturity. For example, a $100 savings bond might be purchased for half of its face amount, $50. The interest, compounded semiannually, accumulates within the bond itself, and the return to the investor comes from redeeming the bond at its stated face value at the maturity date. Interest on Series EE bonds is exempt from state and local taxes. There is no federal income tax liability on the interest at redemption if the proceeds are used to fund the

Instant Message

Reinvestment Risk

As we noted in Chapter 13, **reinvestment risk** is the risk that the return on a future investment will not be the same as the return earned by the original investment. This term is often heard in the context of bonds during periods of falling interest rates when the coupon payments are reinvested at less than the yield to maturity at the time of purchase.

Treasury note/Treasury bond Fixed-principal, fixed-interest-rate government security issued for an intermediate term or long term. Notes mature in ten years or less; bonds mature in more than ten years.

I bonds Nonmarketable savings bonds backed by the U.S. government that pay an earnings rate that combines two rates: a fixed interest rate set when the investor buys the bond and a semiannual variable interest rate tied to inflation that protects the investor's purchasing power.

Treasury Inflation-Protected Securities (TIPS) Marketable Treasury bonds whose value increases with inflation. These inflation-indexed $1000 bonds are the only investment that guarantees that the investor's return will outpace inflation.

zero-coupon bonds (zeros or deep discount bonds) Municipal, corporate, and Treasury bonds that are issued at a sharp discount from face value and pay no annual interest but are redeemed at full face value upon maturity.

U.S. government savings bonds Non-marketable, interest-bearing bonds issued by the U.S. Treasury.

Series EE savings bonds Nonmarketable, interest-bearing bonds issued by the federal government that are issued at a sharp discount from face value and pay no annual interest, and they may be redeemed at full value upon maturity.

child's college education. (**Series HH savings bonds** [no longer sold] were issued at par and acquired only by exchanging Series EE bonds. Interest on Series HH bonds is exempt from state and local taxes.)

Federal Agency Debt Issues More than 100 different bonds, notes, and certificates of debt are issued by various federal agencies that are government sponsored but stockholder owned. Examples of these agencies include Government National Mortgage Association (Ginnie Mae), Federal National Mortgage Association (Fannie Mae), and Student Loan Marketing Association (Sallie Mae). Ginnie Mae and Fannie Mae buy mortgage loans from lenders, thereby supplying them with more cash to make loans. Each security represents interest in a pool of mortgages that are sold to institutions and investors in units of $25,000 (they can also be purchased in smaller units through a mutual fund). When homeowners make their monthly mortgage payments to Ginnie Mae, part of the principal and interest is passed to investors.

The assets and resources of the issuing agency back these agency issues. Although the federal government does not guarantee the debt issued by such agencies, investors nevertheless believe it would step in if an agency faced default. Agency issues are not as widely publicized as Treasury securities, yet they often pay a yield that is three-quarters of a percentage point higher than the yield for comparable-term Treasury securities because of their somewhat higher degree of risk.

Municipal Government Bonds As we discussed in Chapter 4, **municipal government bonds** (also called **munis**) are long-term debts issued by local governments (cities, states, and various districts and political subdivisions) and their agencies. Their proceeds are used to finance public improvement projects, such as roads, bridges, and parks, or to pay ongoing expenses. Moody's Bond Record rates some 20,000 munis, and twice as many unrated securities exist. Bonds range in quality from AAA-rated state highway bonds to unrated securities issued by local governmental parking authorities.

The investor's interest income on municipal bonds is not subject to federal income taxes. This is because the U.S. Constitution requires that municipal bond interest be exempt from federal income tax. Because the interest income is tax free, municipal bonds are also known as **tax-free bonds** or **tax-exempt bonds.** Interest income on munis also is exempt from state and local income taxes when the investor lives in the state that issued the bond.

Municipal bonds offer a lower stated return than other bonds. However, if your marginal tax rate is higher than 25 percent, it generally makes economic sense to invest in municipal bonds because the after-tax return on a muni might be higher than that of a corporate bond. To compare the after-tax returns of investments, see page 122.

Capital gains on the sale of munis are taxable. Such gains may be realized when bonds are bought at a discount and then sold at a higher price or redeemed for full value at maturity. Bonds bought at a premium also may appreciate to produce a gain.

Unique Characteristics of Bond Investing

Bonds have certain characteristics that distinguish them from other investment alternatives.

Coupon Rate The bond's **coupon rate** (also known as the **coupon, coupon yield,** or **stated interest rate**) is the interest rate printed on the certificate when the bond is issued. It reflects the total annual fixed rate of interest that will be paid. For example, Leslie Geradine Sherman, a retired teacher from Laramie, Wyoming, bought a 20-year, $1000 Running Paws Cat Food Company bond last week with a

municipal government bonds (munis) Long-term debts (bonds) issued by local governments (cities, states, and various districts and political subdivisions) and their agencies. Interest from munis, also known as tax-free bonds or tax-exempt bonds, is exempt from federal income tax.

coupon rate/coupon/coupon yield/ stated interest rate Interest rate printed on the certificate when the bond is issued.

coupon rate of 7 percent that promises to pay her $70 in interest annually (bonds pay interest in two semiannual installments—$35 in this instance). A disadvantage of bonds is that the investment does not provide the automatic benefit of compounding of interest; therefore, investors have no choice but to find other places to invest interest payments.

Serial or Sinking Fund

The coupon rate of a bond remains the same until the maturity date, when the face amount is due and the debt is required to be paid off (or **retired**). Corporate bonds often mature in 20 to 30 years. Occasionally, bonds are retired serially; that is, each bond is numbered consecutively and matures according to a prenumbered schedule at stated intervals. These investments are known as **serial bonds.** Many bonds include a **sinking fund** through which money is set aside with a trustee each year for repayment of the principal portion of the debt. The details about each bond issue are contained in its **indenture.** This written, legal agreement between a group of bondholders (representing each bondholder) and the debtor describes the terms of the debt by setting forth the maturity date, interest rate, and other factors.

Secured or Unsecured

Bonds are issued as either secured or unsecured. A corporation issuing a **secured bond** pledges specific assets as collateral in the indenture or has the principal and interest guaranteed by another corporation or a government agency. In the event of default, the trustee could take legal action to seize and sell such assets. In the event of bankruptcy, the claims of secured creditors are paid first.

An **unsecured bond** (or **debenture**) does not name collateral as security for the debt and is backed only by the good faith and reputation of the issuing agency. Although secured bonds might appear safer than unsecured bonds, this assumption may not be true. The strong financial reputations of many large corporations enable them to offer unsecured bonds that are safer than the secured bonds of many other companies. All federal government bonds are unsecured and are backed by the U.S. government.

Registered and Issued

By law, all bonds issued now are **registered bonds.** This provides for the recording of the bondholder's name so that checks or electronic funds transfers for payment of interest and principal can be safely forwarded when due. The Internal Revenue Service is notified of the payments as well. A registered bond can be transferred only when the registered owner endorses the transaction.

Book Entry

All bonds today are issued in **book-entry form,** which means that certificates are not issued. Instead, an account is set up in the name of the issuing organization or the brokerage firm that sold the bond, and interest is paid into this account when due. In the past, all corporations issued **bearer bonds** (also called **coupon bonds** because owners redeemed the coupons for interest). Some of these older bonds are still traded today.

Callable

An issuer might desire to exercise a **call option** when interest rates drop substantially. For example, assume a company issues bonds paying a $90 annual dividend (9 percent coupon rate). When interest rates drop perhaps to 7 percent, the 9 percent bonds may represent too high a cost for borrowing to the corporation. If the bonds have a **callable** feature, according to dates and terms detailed in the indenture, the issuer can redeem the bonds before the maturity date. In such a case, the issuer repurchases the bond at par value or by paying a premium, often one year's worth of interest. Approximately 80 percent of long-term bonds are classified as callable.

---

serial bonds Bonds that are retired serially; that is, each bond is numbered consecutively and matures according to a prenumbered schedule at stated intervals.

sinking fund Bond feature through which money is set aside with a trustee each year for repayment of the principal portion of the debt at maturity.

indenture Written, legal agreement between bondholders and debtor that describes terms of the debt by setting forth the maturity date, interest rate, and other details.

secured bond Pledges specific assets as collateral in indenture or has the principal and interest guaranteed by another corporation or government agency.

unsecured bond/debenture Does not name collateral as security for debt; backed only by the good faith and reputation of the issuing agency.

registered bond Bondholder's name is recorded so that checks or electronic funds transfers for payment of interest and principal can be safely forwarded when due.

book-entry form Bond certificates aren't issued; rather, account is set up in name of the issuing organization or the brokerage firm that sold the bond, and interest is paid into this account when due.

call option Stipulation in an indenture that allows issuer to repurchase the bond at par value or by paying a premium, often one year's worth of interest. Bonds are thus callable.

Advice from a Pro...

Zero-Coupon Bonds Pay Phantom Interest

Zero-coupon bonds (also called **zeros** or **deep discount bonds**) are municipal, corporate, and Treasury bonds that pay no annual interest. They are sold to investors at sharp discounts from their face value and may be redeemed at full value upon maturity. For example, a 7 percent, $1000 zero-coupon bond to be redeemed in the year 2025 might sell today for $258. Zeros pay no current income to investors, so investors do not have to be concerned about where to reinvest interest payments. The semiannual interest accumulates within the bond itself, and the return to the investor comes from redeeming the bond at its stated face value at the maturity date. In this manner, zeros operate much like Series EE savings bonds and T-bills. The maturity date for a zero could range from a few months to as long as 30 years.

Parents often invest in zero-coupon bonds to help pay for their children's college education, and they wisely establish ownership of the zeros in the child's name. The phantom income "paid" to the child is generally so small that little, if any, income taxes are due.

Treasury zeros, unlike other zeros, are not callable. People planning for retirement buy zeros because they know exactly how much will be received at maturity. Even though the investor receives no interest money until maturity, the investor still pays income taxes every year on the interest that accumulates within the bond. Investors can avoid income taxes altogether by buying zeros in a qualified tax-sheltered retirement plan account.

Elizabeth Dolan
University of New Hampshire

Evaluating Bond Prices and Returns

Factors that affect bond prices and returns to the investor include interest rates, premiums and discounts, current yield, and yield to maturity.

Interest Rate Risk Results in Variable Value A bond's price, or its value on any given day, is affected by a host of factors. These include its type, coupon rate, availability in the marketplace, demand for the bond, prices for similar bonds, the underlying credit quality of the issuer, and the number of years before it matures. Most important, the price also varies because of fluctuations in current **market interest rates** in the general economy. The state of the economy and the supply and demand for credit affect market interest rates. These are the current long- and short-term interest rates paid on various types of corporate and government debts that carry similar levels of risk.

Long-term rates are largely set by bond investors' buying and selling decisions, primarily based on their expectations of future inflation. Short-term interest rates are manipulated by the Federal Reserve Board, which is popularly known as the Fed. When the economy slows, the Fed often lowers the interest rates on short-term Treasury issues in an attempt to stimulate economic activity by making borrowing cheaper. When inflation rises, the Fed often raises interest rates.

As we noted in Chapter 13, **interest rate risk** is the risk that interest rates will increase and bond prices will fall, thereby lowering the prices on older bond issues. This decline in value ensures that an older bond and a newly issued bond will offer potential investors approximately the same yield. Bonds generally have a **fixed yield** (the interest income payment remains the same) but a **variable value.** For example, assume that you buy a 20-year, $1000 bond with a stated annual interest rate of 8 percent, or an annual return of $80 ($1000 × 0.08). If interest rates in the general economy jump to 10 percent after one year, no one will want to buy your bond for $1000 because it pays only $80 per year. If you want to sell it at that time, the price of

market interest rates Current long- and short-term interest rates paid on various types of corporate and government debts that carry similar levels of risk.

interest rate risk Risk that interest rates will rise and bond prices will fall, thereby lowering the prices on older bond issues.

fixed yield Interest income payment remains the same regardless of bond's price.

variable value Because interest rates change, bonds may trade at a premium (more than face value) or at a discount (less than par) so that the yield equals the current yield for bonds with similar maturities and risk levels.

the bond will have to be lowered, perhaps to $800 [Equation (14.4), the *bond-selling price formula*, shows the calculation involved].

$$\text{Bond selling price} = \frac{\text{annual interest income in dollars}}{\text{current market interest rate}} \qquad (14.4)$$

Conversely, if interest rates on newly issued bonds slip to 6 percent after one year, the price of your bond will increase sharply (perhaps to $1333). This occurs because investors will be willing to pay a **premium** (a sum of money paid in addition to a regular price) to own your bond paying 8 percent when other rates are only 6 percent. Remember that bond yields and prices move in opposite directions—as one goes up, the other goes down.

Bond prices are most volatile in the following circumstances: (1) when bonds are sold at less than face value when first issued, (2) when the stated rate is low, and (3) when the bond maturity time is long. The investor who holds a bond to maturity might ignore such information, but the person considering selling before maturity might be shocked to see price swings of 20 percent or more, as illustrated on page 424. A person with a moderate or aggressive investment philosophy might regard such rapid price changes as opportunities.

premium A sum of money paid in addition to a regular price.

Premiums and Discounts When a bond is first issued, it is sold in one of three ways: (1) at its face value (the value of the bond stated on the certificate and the amount the investor will receive when the bond matures), (2) at a discount below its face value, or (3) at a premium above its face value. After a bond is issued, its market price changes in order to provide a competitive effective rate of return for anyone interested in purchasing it from the original bondholder.

As an example, assume that Running Paws Cat Food Company decided to issue 20-year bonds at 8.8 percent. While the bonds were being printed and prepared for sale, the market interest rate on comparable bonds rose to 9 percent. In this instance, Running Paws will sell the bonds at a slight discount to provide a competitive return. Discounts and premiums on bonds reflect changing interest rates in the economy and the number of years to maturity.

Current Yield The **current yield** equals the bond's fixed annual interest payment divided by its bond price. It is a measure of the current annual income (the total of both semiannual interest payments in dollars) expressed as a percentage when divided by the bond's current market price. When you buy a bond at par, its current yield equals its coupon yield. For example, a bond with a 5.5 percent coupon yield purchased at par for $1000 has a current yield of 5.5 percent. As bond prices fluctuate because of interest rate changes and other factors, the current yield also changes. For example, if Leslie paid $940 for a $1000 bond paying $55 per year, the bond's current yield is 5.85 percent, as shown by the *current yield formula*, Equation (14.5).

current yield Equals the bond's fixed annual interest payment divided by its bond price.

$$\begin{aligned} \text{Current yield} &= \frac{\text{current annual income}}{\text{current market price}} \qquad (14.5) \\[6pt] &= \frac{\$55}{\$940} \\[6pt] &= 5.85\% \end{aligned}$$

A bond's current yield is based on the purchase price, not on the prices at which it later trades. The current yields for many bonds based on that day's market prices are available online and are published in the financial section of many newspapers.

The total return on a bond investment consists of the same components as the return on any investment: current income and capital gains. In Leslie's case, she will receive $1000 at the maturity date (20 years from now), even though she paid only $940 for the bond; therefore, her anticipated total return (or effective yield) will be

Did You Know?…

How Far Bond Prices Will Move When Interest Rates Change

On any given day, the major determinant of bond prices is the prevailing level of interest rates in the economy. Figure 14.4 illustrates the price changes for bonds when interest rates rise or fall. Rising interest rates reduce bond prices and falling rates increase bond prices. The longer the time until maturity of a bond, the more sensitive the price to interest rate changes. Thus, prices for long-term bonds fluctuate much more dramatically than those for short-term securities.

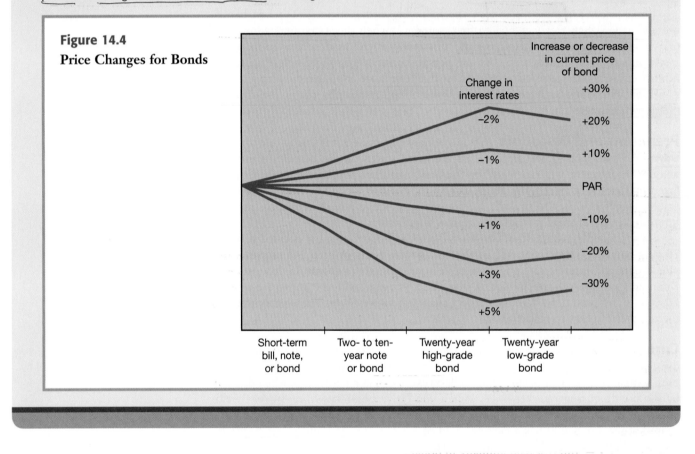

Figure 14.4

Price Changes for Bonds

higher than the 5.85 percent current yield. How much higher is accurately revealed by the yield to maturity (discussed next).

yield to maturity (YTM) Total annual effective rate of return earned by a bondholder on a bond if the security is held to maturity—takes into consideration both the price at which the bond sold and the coupon interest rate to arrive at effective rate of return.

Yield to Maturity

Yield to maturity (YTM) is the total annual effective rate of return earned by a bondholder on a bond if the security is held to maturity. The YTM is the internal rate of return on cash flows of a fixed-income security. The YTM reflects both the current income and any difference if the bond was purchased at a price other than its face value spread over the life of the bond. The market price of a bond equals the present value of its future interest payments and the present value of its face value when the bond matures. Three generalizations can be made about the yield to maturity:

1. If a bond is purchased for exactly its face value, the YTM is the same as the coupon rate printed on the certificate.

Did You Know?...

How to Estimate the Selling Price of a Bond After Interest Rates Have Changed

Bond prices are influenced partially by supply and demand but mostly by the cost of money. If you paid $1000 for a 20-year, 7 percent bond and then were forced to sell it after interest rates on comparable bonds had increased to 9 percent, you would lose more than $200. You can estimate the selling price of an existing bond (assuming it is more than a few years from maturity) after interest rates change by using the bond-selling price formula given in Equation (14.4) on page 423.

Using Equation (14.4), the selling price equals $777.78 ($70 ÷ 0.09) for the preceding example. If you bought the bond for $1000, you will lose $222.22 if you sell it for $777.78. If interest rates drop to 5.5 percent instead of increasing, however, you could sell your 7 percent bond at a profit of $272.72 ($70 ÷ 0.055 = $1272.72; $1272 − $1000 = $272.72). If you keep the bond until maturity, the issuer is obligated to retire it for $1000. An online financial calculator or brokerage firm can perform exact calculations of selling prices.

2. If a bond is purchased at a premium, the YTM will be lower than the coupon rate.

3. If a bond is purchased at a discount, the YTM will be higher than the coupon rate.

For example, because Leslie bought her 20-year bond with a coupon rate of 5.5 percent at a discount for $940, her yield to maturity must be greater than the coupon rate because she will receive $60 more than she paid for the bond when she receives the $1000 at maturity. Exactly how much greater can be determined by calculating an approximate yield to maturity when contemplating a bond purchase because bonds that seem comparable may have different YTMs. The *yield to maturity (YTM) formula,* Equation (14.6), which is duplicated on the *Garman/Forgue* website, factors in the approximate appreciation when a bond is bought at a discount or at a premium:

$$\text{YTM} = \frac{I + [(FV - CV)/N]}{(FV + CV)/2} \tag{14.6}$$

where

I = Interest paid annually in dollars
FV = Face value
CV = Current value (price)
N = Number of years until maturity

If Leslie paid $940 for a 20-year bond with a 5.5 percent coupon rate, the YTM is calculated as follows:

$$\text{YTM} = \frac{\$55 + [(\$1000 - \$940)/20]}{(\$1000 + \$940)/2}$$

$$= \frac{\$58}{\$970}$$

$$= 5.98\%$$

If you plan to buy and hold a bond until its maturity, you should compare YTMs instead of current yields when considering a purchase because YTMs fairly represent all factors. The current yield on a bond is not an effective measure of the total annual return to the investor; in fact, the fewer years until maturity, the worse an indicator it becomes. As just calculated, Leslie's 20-year bond with a coupon rate of 5.5 percent and a current yield of 5.85 percent has a YTM of 5.98 percent. If the same bond had been purchased with only 10 years until maturity, the YTM would be 6.29 percent; with 5 years until maturity, the YTM would be 6.90 percent; and with 2 years until maturity, the YTM would be 8.76 percent. Exact YTMs are online and listed in detailed bond tables available at large libraries and at brokers' offices.

Six Decisions for Bond Investors Individuals interested in investing in bonds can review resources on the website of The Bond Market Association (http://www.investinginbonds.com/). It offers a free, searchable database of the latest corporate, government, municipal, and mortgage-backed bond issues and prices. Bond investors must make six decisions:

1. **Decide on credit quality.** Consider Treasury/agency, investment-grade corporate and municipal, and below investment-grade corporate and municipal.

2. **Decide on maturity.** Consider the time schedule of your financial needs: short, medium or long term. Bonds with a short maturity have the lowest current yield but excellent price stability. Medium maturity bonds pay close to the higher rates earned on long-term bonds and enjoy much greater price stability.

3. **Determine the after-tax return.** Assuming equivalent risk, choose the bond that provides the better after-tax return because tax-exempt securities may offer a higher after-tax return than taxable alternatives. To compare the after-tax return of investments, see page 122.

4. **Select the highest yield to maturity.** Given similar bond securities with comparable risk, maturity, and tax equivalency, investors are wise to choose the one that offers the highest yield to maturity, as calculated by Equation (14.6).

5. **Consider selling.** When interest rates have dropped, consider selling because you can profit when rate decreases push up the value of your bond. Consider selling also if the bond rating has seriously slipped because it could mean greater risk and possible default.

6. **Think about investing in bond mutual funds.** Consider whether it is smarter to invest in bond mutual funds rather than individual bonds. This topic is examined in Chapter 15.

✓ CONCEPT CHECK 14.7

1. Distinguish between investment- and speculative-grade bonds.
2. Give some reasons why individuals often invest in corporate bonds rather than Treasuries.
3. Summarize the differences among Treasury bonds, I bonds, and TIPS bonds.
4. Explain what interest rate risk is and tell what calculation individuals considering bond investments avoid that problem when buying an existing bond.

What Do You Recommend Now?

Now that you have read the chapter on stocks and bonds, what do you recommend to Caitlin Diaz in the case at the beginning of the chapter regarding:

1. Investing for retirement in 18 years?

2. Owning blue-chip common stocks and preferred stocks rather than other common stocks given Caitlin's investment time horizon?

3. The wisdom of owning municipal bonds rather than corporate bonds?

4. The likely selling price of her corporate bonds, if sold today?

5. Investments that might be appropriate to fund her children's education?

Big Picture Summary of Learning Objectives

1 Explain how stocks and bonds are used as investments.

Individual investors provide the money corporations use to create sales and earn profits. The investor shares in those profits.

2 Classify common stocks according to their major characteristics.

Common stocks may be broadly classified as either income or growth stocks. Other terms used to describe stocks are *blue chip*, *value*, *speculative*, and *tech*. Market capitalization is used to classify large-cap, midcap, and small-cap stocks.

3 Describe fundamental and numerical ways to evaluate stock values.

The investor studies certain fundamental factors, such as the company's sales, assets, earnings, products or services, markets, and management, to determine a company's basic value. To do so, investors examine several revealing ratios such as price/earnings, price/sales, and dividend payout, as well as revealing numbers such as book value per share. Individuals also estimate the value of a company by using beta to compare its history and expected future profitability with those of competing stocks.

4 Determine whether an investment's potential rate of return is sufficient.

Estimating and calculating returns on a potential investment involve using beta to estimate the level of risk of the investment, estimating the market risk, calculating the required rate of return, calculating the potential rate of return on the investment, and comparing the required rate of return with the potential rate of return on the investment.

5 Use the Internet to evaluate common stocks in which to invest.

Individuals begin evaluating stocks by setting criteria for a stock investment. This may involve using stock-screening software; obtaining security analysts' research reports, annual reports, 10-K reports, and prospectuses; acquiring economic and stock market data; and using portfolio-tracking services.

6 Summarize how stocks are bought and sold.

Securities transactions require the use of a licensed broker serving as a middleman between the seller and the buyer. You can buy or sell securities through an online or human stockbroker who works for a brokerage firm that has access to the securities markets. Many individuals use discount and online brokers rather than full-service brokers. Types of stock orders include market, limit, and stop orders. Buying on margin and selling short are risky trading techniques.

7 Describe how to invest in bonds.

Investment-grade bonds offer a reasonable certainty of regularly receiving the periodic income (interest) and retrieving the amount originally invested (principal). Junk bonds are available, too. Corporate bonds usually pay higher returns than government bonds. Interest-rate risk results in variable value in bond investments.

Let's Talk About It

1. Make a list of three products and services that you buy on a weekly or monthly basis and the companies that sell them. Offer your initial views on whether each company would be a good place to invest money.

2. The text introduced a variety of ways to measure stock performance. Name two of those measures that you might use in your own decision making. Offer reasons for selecting those measures.

3. You have just heard that Microsoft's stock price dropped $5. If you had the money, would you buy 100 shares? Give three reasons why or why not.

4. Review the three basic classifications of common stock and the other descriptive terms. Based on your personal comfort level for risk, which type of stock would be of interest to you? Give three reasons why.

5. If you had an investment portfolio of stocks worth $20,000, identify three sources for information that you would likely use to keep abreast of current information affecting your investments.

6. Do you think anyone really calculates the potential rate of return on a particular investment? Should they? If so, offer a reason why.

7. Buying on margin and selling short both involve using credit. Would you invest this way? Give two reasons why or why not.

8. Do bonds interest you as an investment? Why or why not?

Do the Numbers

1. A stock sells at $15 per share.

   (a) What is the EPS for the company if it has a P/E ratio of 20?

   (b) If the company's dividend yield is 5 percent, what is its dividend per share?

   (c) What is the book value of the company if the price-to-book ratio is 1.5 and it has 100,000 shares of stock outstanding?

2. What is the market price of a $1000, 20-year, 8.8 percent bond if comparable market interest rates drop to 7.0 percent?

3. What is the market price of a $1000, 20-year, 8.8 percent bond if comparable market interest rates rise to 9.6 percent?

4. For a municipal bond paying 5.4 percent for a taxpayer in the 25 percent tax bracket, what is the equivalent taxable yield? (Hint: See the footnote on page 122.)

5. For a municipal bond paying 5.7 percent for a taxpayer in the 33 percent tax bracket, what is the equivalent taxable yield? (Hint: See the footnote on page 122.)

6. A corporate bond maturing in 20 years with a coupon rate of 8.9 percent was purchased for $980.

   (a) What is its current yield?

   (b) What will be its selling price if comparable market interest rates drop 2 percent in two years?

   (c) Calculate the bond's YTM using Equation (14.6) or the *Garman/Forgue* website.

7. A corporate bond maturing in 18 years with a coupon rate of 8.2 percent was purchased for $1100.

   (a) What is its current yield?

   (b) Calculate the bond's YTM using Equation (14.6) or the *Garman/Forgue* website.

   (c) What will the bond's selling price be if comparable market interest rates rise 1.5 percent in two years?

8. Michael Margolis is a single parent and a motivational training consultant from Rancho Cucamonga, California. He is wondering about potential returns on investments given certain amounts of risk. Michael invested a total of $6000 in three stocks ($2000 in each) with different betas: stock A with a beta of 0.8, stock B with a beta of 1.7, and stock C with a beta of 2.5.

   (a) If the stock market rises 12 percent over the next year, what will be the likely value of each investment?

   (b) If the stock market declines 8 percent over the next year, what will be the likely value of each investment?

9. Xiao and Shiao Jing-jian, newlyweds from New Castle, Delaware, have decided to begin investing for the future. Xiao is a 7-Eleven store manager, and Shiao is a high-school math teacher. The couple intends to take $3000 out of their savings for investment purposes and then continue to invest an additional $200 to $400 per month. Both have a moderate investment philosophy and seek some cash dividends as well as price appreciation.

   (a) Calculate the five-year return on the investment choices in the table on page 429. Put your calculations in tabular form like that shown in Table 14.1. (Hint: At the end of the first year, the EPS for Running Paws will be $2.40 with a dividend of $0.66, and the EPS for Eagle Packaging will be $2.76 with a projected dividend of $0.86.)

   (b) Using the appropriate P/E ratios, what are the estimated market prices of the Running Paws and Eagle Packaging stocks after five years?

   (c) Show your calculations in determining the projected price appreciations for the two stocks over the five years.

(d) Add the projected price appreciation of each stock to its projected cash dividends, and show the total five-year percentage returns for the two stocks.

(e) Determine the average annual dividend for each stock, and use these figures in calculating the approximate compound yields for each.

(f) Assume that the beta is 2.5 for Running Paws and 2.8 for Eagle Packaging. If the market went up 20 percent during the year, what would be the likely stock prices for Running Paws and Eagle Packaging?

(g) Assume that inflation is approximately 4 percent and the return on high-quality, long-term corporate bonds is 8 percent. Given the Jing-jians' investment philosophy, explain why you would recommend (1) Running Paws, (2) Eagle Packaging, or (3) a high-quality, long-term corporate bond as a growth investment. Support your answer by calculating the potential rate of return using the information on page 399 or by using the *Garman/Forgue* website. The Jing-jians are in the 25 percent marginal tax bracket.

	Running Paws	Eagle Packaging
Currrent price	$30.00	$48.00
Current earnings per share (EPS)	$2.00	$2.30
Current quarterly cash dividend	$0.15	$0.18
Current P/E ratio	15	21
Projected earnings annual growth rate	20%	20%
Projected cash dividend growth rate	10%	10%

Financial Planning Cases

Case 1
Two Brothers' Attitudes Toward Investments

Kyle Broffoski, a guidance counselor in Gainesville, Florida, has purchased several corporate and government bonds over the years, and his total bond investment now exceeds $40,000. He prefers a variable-value investment with some inflation protection. His brother Ike, a highly paid physician, has more than $150,000 invested in various blue-chip income stocks in a variety of industries.

(a) Justify Kyle's attitude toward bond investments.

(b) Justify Ike's attitude toward stock investments.

(c) Explain why both brothers might be happy investing some of their money in TIPS bonds.

Case 2
A College Student Ponders Investing in the Stock Market

Richard Ford of Savannah, Georgia, has $5000 that he wants to invest in the stock market. Richard is in college on a scholarship and does not plan to use the $5000 or any dividend income for another five years, when he plans to buy a new automobile. He is currently considering a stock selling for $25 per share with an EPS of $1.25. Last year, the company earned $900,000, of which $250,000 was paid out in dividends.

(a) What classification of common stock would you recommend to Richard? Why?

(b) Calculate the P/E ratio and the dividend payout ratio for this stock. Given this information and your recommendation, would this stock be an appropriate purchase for Richard? Why or why not?

(c) Identify the components of the total return Richard might expect, and estimate how much he might expect annually from each component.

Case 3
An Aggressive Investor Seeks Rewards in the Bond Market

Karry Varcoe works as a drug manufacturer's representative based in Newton, Iowa. She has an aggressive investment philosophy and believes that interest rates will drop over the next year or two because of an expected economic slowdown. Karry, who is in the 25 percent marginal tax rate, wants to profit in the bond market by buying and selling during the next several months. She has asked your advice on how to invest her $15,000.

(a) If Karry buys corporate or municipal bonds, what rating should her selections have? Why?

(b) Karry has a choice between two $1000 bonds: a corporate bond with a coupon rate of 8.4 percent and a municipal bond with a coupon rate of 5.8 percent. Which bond provides the better after-tax return? [Hint: See Equation (4.1) on page 122.]

(c) If Karry buys 15 30-year, $1000 corporate bonds with an 8.4 percent coupon rate for $960 each, what is her current yield? [Hint: Use Equation (14.5).]

(d) If market interest rates for comparable corporate bonds drop 2 percent over the next 12 months (from 8.4 percent to 6.4 percent), what will be the approximate selling price of Karry corporate bonds in (c)? [Hint: Use Equation (14.4).]

(e) Assuming market interest rates drop 2 percent in 12 months, how much is Karry's capital gain on the $15,000 investment if she sells? How much was her current return for the two semiannual interest payments? How much was her total return, both in dollars and as an annual yield? (Ignore transaction costs.)

(f) If Karry is wrong in her projections and interest rates go up 1 percent over the year, what would be the probable selling price of her corporate bonds? [Hint: Use Equation (14.4).] Explain why you would advise her to sell or not to sell.

Case 4
Victor and Maria Hernandez Wonder About Investing

Victor and Maria are considering making investments in stocks and bonds. They plan to invest between $8000 and $9000 every year for the next 13 years.

(a) Why should Victor and Maria consider buying common stock as an investment?

(b) If Victor and Maria bought a stock with a market price of $50 and a beta value of 1.8, what would be the likely price of an $8000 investment after one year if the general market for stocks rose 20 percent?

(c) What would the same investment be worth if the general market for stocks dropped 20 percent?

(d) Assume that Victor and Maria bought $8000 in 13-year bonds with a coupon rate of 8 percent and that interest rates dropped to 7 percent after one year. What is the approximate current selling price of their bonds if they were to sell? [Hint: Use Equation (14.4) or visit the *Garman/Forgue* website.]

(e) If inflation averages 3 percent for the next 13 years, and the issuer redeems their $8000 bond, how much buying power will the Hernandez family have with their $8000?

Case 5
The Johnsons Want Greater Yields on Investments

Harry and Belinda Johnson have saved $6000 toward a down payment on a luxury automobile they hope to purchase in the next three to five years. Because they are not receiving a very high rate of return on their money market account, they are seeking greater yields with bond investments. Examine the following table, which identifies eight investment alternatives, and then respond to the questions that follow. The coupon rates vary because the issue dates range widely, and market prices are above par because older bonds paid higher interest than today's issues.

(a) What is the current yield of each investment alternative? Use Equation (14.5) or visit the *Garman/Forgue* website. (Write your responses in the proper column in the table.)

(b) What is the yield to maturity for each investment alternative? (Write your responses in the proper column in the table.) You may calculate the YTMs by using Equation (14.6) or by visiting the *Garman/Forgue* website.

(c) Knowing that the Johnsons follow a moderate investment philosophy, which one of the six corporate bonds would you recommend? Why?

(d) Given that the Johnsons are in the 25 percent federal marginal tax rate, what is the equivalent taxable yield for the municipal bond choice? Should they invest in your recommendation in part (c) or in the municipal bond? Why? You may calculate the equivalent taxable yield using the footnote on page 122.

(e) Which three of the eight alternatives would you recommend as a group so that the Johnsons would have some diversification protection for their $6000? Why do you suggest that combination?

(f) Assume that the Johnsons bought all three of your recommendations in part (e). If market interest rates drop by 2 percent in two years because of a severe economic slowdown (for example, from 5.1 percent to 3.1 percent), what are your recommendations for buying or selling each alternative? Why? Support your answer by calculating the selling price for each bond using Equation (14.4) or by visiting the *Garman/Forgue* website.

Name of Issue	Bond Denomination	Coupon Rate Percent	Years Until Maturity	Moody's Rating	Market Price	Current Yield	YTM
Corporate ABC	$1000	7.0	4	Aa	$1400		
Corporate DEF	1000	7.5	20	Aa	1550		
Corporate GHI	1000	5.9	12	Baa	1250		
Corporate JKL	1000	7.8	5	Aaa	1500		
Corporate MNO	1000	6.1	15	B	1260		
Corporate PQR	1000	5.8	11	B	1200		
Treasury note	1000	7.9	3	—	1600		
Municipal bond	1000	4.1	20	Aa	1200		

On the 'Net

Go to the Web pages indicated to complete these exercises. You can also go to the *Garman/Forgue* website at college.hmco.com/business/students for an expanded list of exercises. Under General Business, select the title of this text. Click on the Internet Exercises link for this chapter.

1. Visit the website for the U.S. Treasury Department at http://www.treasurydirect.gov/ and enter its Institutional section, where you will find the results of recent auctions for Treasury notes and bonds. What do the results of the auctions over the past year tell you about market expectations for movement of interest rates in the future? (Hint: Compare auction rates for bonds and notes with similar maturity periods.)

2. Visit the website for Kiplinger.com. at http://www .kiplinger.com where you can find stock quotes for most publicly traded companies. Type in the symbols for the following companies: Coca-Cola (KO), Google (GOOG), Microsoft (MSFT), and Disney (DIS). Evaluate these four firms on the basis of earnings per share, dividend yield, and price/earnings ratio. What do these data suggest to you about the relative attractiveness of these companies for investors?

3. Visit the website for Yahoo! Finance, where you can find a stock-screener utility at http://screen.yahoo .com/stocks.html. Search among the S&P 500 stocks for companies with a $50 minimum share price. How many companies meet this criterion? Select again using a P/E ratio from 0 to 20. How many companies meet this new criterion? Why is this list longer? Do you recognize any of the companies on either list?

Visit the Garman/Forgue website ...

@college.hmco.com/business/students
Under General Business, select *Personal Finance 9e.* There, among other valuable resources, you will find a complete glossary, ACE questions, links to help you complete the chapter exercises, and links to other personal finance sites.

CHAPTER 15

Investing Through Mutual Funds

You Must Be Kidding, Right?

Twins Amanda and Daniel invest in mutual funds. Amanda majored in finance. For more than 20 years she invested in managed funds, counting on intelligent professional financial advisers to select the winning companies more often than not. Daniel majored in English; he invested in unmanaged index funds that achieve the same return as a particular market index by buying and holding all or a representative selection of securities in the index. After 20 years of investing, what is the likelihood that Amanda's investment portfolio balance will be better than Daniel's?

A. 10%   **B.** 20%   **C.** 30%   **D.** 40%

The answer is B or A but never C or D. Managed mutual funds generally do not earn returns for investors that exceed the overall market indexes. The fact is, the average mutual fund manager earns a lower return at least 80 percent of the time. In most years, only 10 percent beat the market averages. Finding a mutual fund investment manager who can consistently beat the market is very challenging!

LEARNING OBJECTIVES

After reading this chapter, you should be able to:

1 **Describe** the features, services, and advantages of investing in mutual funds.

2 **Differentiate** mutual funds by investment objectives, types, and characteristics.

3 **Summarize** the fees and charges involved in buying and selling mutual funds.

4 **Establish** strategies to evaluate and select mutual funds that meet your investment goals.

What Do You Recommend?

David and Sarah Gent, a couple in their early 30s, have a 2-year-old child, and they enjoy living in a moderately priced downtown apartment. David, a librarian section manager, earns $44,000 annually. Sarah earns $59,000 as a merchandise buyer for a specialty store. They are big savers: Together they have been putting $1000 to $2000 per month into certificates of deposit, and the couple now has a portfolio balance worth $120,000 paying about 4 percent annually. The Gents are conservative investors and want to retire in about 20 years.

What would you recommend to David and Sarah on the subject of investing through mutual funds regarding:

1. Redeeming their certificates of deposit and investing their retirement money in mutual funds?

2. Investing in growth and income mutual funds instead of income funds?

3. Buying no-load rather than load funds?

4. Buying life-cycle mutual funds instead of balanced mutual funds?

5. Buying mutual funds through their employers' 401(k) retirement accounts?

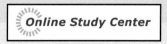

Most investors prefer to avoid stocks and bonds because of the high financial risk associated with owning too few investments. The average investor usually cannot accumulate a portfolio diversified enough to minimize the risk linked to the failure of a single holding. Investors often also lack the ability and time required to research individual securities and manage such a portfolio. To avoid these problems, many people invest *in* the stock and bond markets *through* mutual funds, which typically buy hundreds of different stocks and bonds. Mutual funds make it easy and convenient for investors to open an account and continue investing. Half of all households invest through mutual funds. The investor in mutual funds, using common sense and a little knowledge of the world of investments, can obtain very good returns.

Why Invest in Mutual Funds?

1 LEARNING OBJECTIVE
Describe the features, services, and advantages of investing in mutual funds.

mutual fund Investment company that pools funds by selling shares to investors and makes diversified investments to achieve financial goals of income or growth, or both.

A **mutual fund** is an investment company that pools funds obtained by selling shares to investors and makes investments to achieve the financial goal of income or growth, or both. Mutual funds invest in a diversified portfolio of stocks, bonds, short-term money market instruments, and other securities or assets.

The fund might own common stock and bonds in such companies as General Motors, IBM, Sears, or Running Paws Cat Food Company (our example from Chapter 14). The combined holdings are known as a **portfolio,** as we noted in Chapter 13 and as shown graphically in Figure 15.1. The mutual fund company owns the investments it makes and the mutual fund investors own the mutual fund company. Unlike corporate shareholders, holders of mutual funds have no say in running the company, although they have equity interest in the pool of assets and a residual claim on the profits.

Net Asset Value

net asset value (NAV) Per-share value of a mutual fund.

One measure of the investor's claim on assets is the net asset value. The **net asset value (NAV)** is the price one pays (excluding any transaction costs) to buy a share of a mutual fund; it is the per-share value of the mutual fund. It is calculated by summing the values of all the securities in the fund's portfolio, subtracting liabilities, and then dividing by the total number of shares outstanding.

Figure 15.1
How a Mutual Fund Works

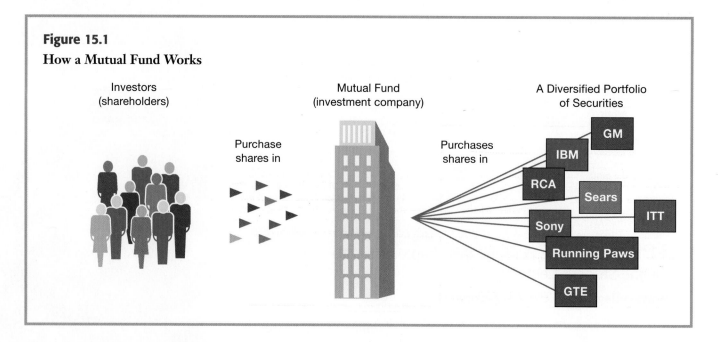

$$\text{Net asset value} = \frac{\text{market value of assets} - \text{market value of liabilities}}{\text{number of shares}} \qquad (15.1)$$

For example, a mutual fund has 10 million shares outstanding, a portfolio worth $100 million, and its liabilities are $5 million. The net asset value of a single share is

$$\text{Net asset value} = \frac{\$100,000,000 - \$5,000,000}{10,000,000} = \frac{\$95,000,000}{10,000,000} = \$9.50 \text{ per share}$$

The NAV rises or falls to reflect changes in the market value of the investments held by the mutual fund company. This value is calculated daily after the major U.S. stock exchanges close, and a new NAV is posted in the financial media. If the assets held in a mutual fund increase in value, the NAV will rise. For example, if a mutual fund owns IBM and General Electric common stocks and the prices of those stocks increase, the increased value of the underlying securities is reflected in the NAV of fund shares. The increase in NAV due to rising portfolio values is price appreciation. When investors sell shares at a net asset value higher than that paid when they purchased the shares (after transaction costs), they will have a capital gain.

Dividend Income and Capital Gains

A **mutual fund dividend** is income paid to investors out of profits that the mutual fund has earned from its investments. The dividend represents both ordinary income dividend distributions and capital gains distributions. **Ordinary income dividend distributions** occur when the fund pays out dividend income and interest (monthly, quarterly, or annually) it has received from securities it owns. **Capital gains distributions** represent the net gains (capital gains minus capital losses) that a fund realizes when it sells securities that were held in the fund's portfolio. Mutual funds distribute capital gains once a year, even though the gains occur throughout the year whenever securities are sold at a profit. When a fund pays out these distributions, the NAV drops by the amount paid. Figure 15.2 illustrates theses sources of mutual fund returns.

Good Money Habits in Mutual Funds

Make the following your money habits when investing through mutual funds:

1. Match your investment philosophy and financial goals to a mutual fund's objectives.
2. Invest only in no-load mutual funds that have low expenses and have no or a low 12b-1 fee.
3. Get the right mix of asset classes in your long-term fund investments and learn to love consistency.
4. Sign up for automatic reinvestment of your mutual fund dividends.
5. Invest regularly through your employer's retirement plan.
6. Rebalance your portfolio at least once a year.

mutual fund dividend Income paid to investors out of profits earned by the mutual fund from its investments.

Sources of Investor Returns from Owning a Share in a Mutual Fund		
Current Income (returns received while you own a share)		Capital Gains (returns received when you sell your share)
Ordinary Dividend Income Distributions	Capital Gains Distributions	
The mutual fund receives dividends from the stocks and interest from the bonds it holds in its portfolio. These are passed on to you every three months (quarterly).	The mutual fund occasionally sells stocks and bonds in its portfolio. When it receives more from the sale than it paid for the securities, it achieves a capital gain. The gains are passed along to you each year (annually).	When you sell your share in the mutual fund, you receive the NAV of the share at its current market price. If that price is higher than the price you paid at purchase, you have a capital gain due to the increase in NAV. Your capital gain will be reduced by transaction costs.

Figure 15.2

Sources of Investor Returns from Owning Mutual Fund Shares

Advantages of Investing Through Mutual Funds

open-end mutual funds Issue redeemable shares that investors purchase directly from the fund (or through a broker for the fund).

The type of mutual fund that is the focus in this chapter is an **open-end mutual fund.** Accounting for more than 90 percent of all funds, open-end mutual funds issue redeemable shares that investors purchase directly from the fund (or through a broker for the fund) instead of purchasing from investors on a stock market. They are always ready to sell new shares of ownership and to buy back previously sold shares at the fund's current NAV. Open-end mutual funds, numbering more than 8100, outnumber companies listed on the New York Stock Exchange (approximately 2800). Mutual funds offer a number of advantages to investors.

Diversification Mutual funds are broadly diversified in financial markets. They might own several hundred different securities, and all are represented in a single mutual fund share. The individual with $500 or $5000 to invest could never obtain such diversification. A diversified portfolio reduces the risk if a company or sector fails. **Random risk,** or **nonsystematic risk,** as we discussed in Chapter 13, is reduced. Recall that random risk arises when one owns only one investment of a particular type (such as stock in one company) that, by chance, may do very poorly in the future due to uncontrollable or random factors. Many investors find it easier to achieve diversification through ownership of mutual funds that own stocks and bonds rather than picking and then owning individual stocks and bonds.

Affordability Individuals can invest in mutual funds with relatively low dollar amounts for initial purchases, such as $250 or $1000. Subsequent purchases can be as little as $50.

Professional Management Many investors lack the knowledge, time, and commitment to worry about which of their stocks and bonds to buy and sell. Mutual fund investors like the fact that professional investment advisers registered with the Securities and Exchange Commission manage their investment portfolio. The fund management company may control many millions or billions of dollars of assets. The **fund investment advisers** have access to the best research, and they select, buy, sell, and monitor the performance of the securities purchased; they oversee the portfolio. Investment advisers use the most current information, analytical tools, and investment techniques available. Fund investment advisers (money managers, securities analysts, and traders) share the same investment objective as the individual investor: to make money by increasing the net asset value of the mutual fund.

fund investment advisers Have access to the best research; they select, buy, sell, and monitor the performance of the securities purchased; thus, they oversee the portfolio.

Liquidity Mutual funds have good **liquidity,** a term we discussed in Chapters 5 and 13. You can very easily convert mutual fund shares into cash without loss of value because the investor sells (**redeems**) the shares back to the investment company. To do so, individuals simply pick up the telephone or go online. The price the investor gets depends upon the value of the portfolio and the resulting NAV.

redeems When an investor sells shares.

Low Transaction Costs Because mutual funds trade in large quantities of shares, they pay far less in brokerage commissions than individual investors. Lower transaction costs result in higher returns for investors. Individuals purchase mutual fund shares from the fund itself (or through a broker for the fund) instead of from other investors on a secondary market, such as the New York Stock Exchange or NASDAQ stock market. Shares bought and sold are at the NAV plus any fees and charges that the fund imposes, and these are often low. While some funds charge significant fees on purchases and redemptions, individuals need not invest in them.

Uncomplicated Investment Choices Selecting a mutual fund is easier than selecting specific stocks or bonds. Mutual funds state their investment objectives, allowing investors to select funds that almost perfectly match their own objectives.

Did You Know?...

Mutual Fund Disadvantages

There are some disadvantages for mutual fund investors:

1. **Performance is often lower than the market.** Despite having intelligent professionals make investment decisions for mutual funds, they often do not deliver annual returns higher than the stock market averages, such as the S&P 500. It is hard for a mutual fund to beat the market averages (an index has no transaction costs) when the fund has to pay administrative and brokerage expenses, particularly over many years.

2. **Diversification may not really exist.** Mutual funds that specialize in particular segments of investments, such as biotechnology, Southeast Asia, or precious metals, are not diversified across asset classifications.

They may have a diversified investment portfolio of 50 precious metals companies within that sector, but **market risk** exists because stock prices move up and down over time due to influences and events that affect all similar investments.

3. **Costs can be high.** While individual investors can choose among thousands of mutual funds for the net asset value, some funds charge substantial commissions and fees on purchases and sales. These can run from 2 to 8.5 percent. Mutual fund investors pay annual management fees regardless of how the fund performs, and some funds have "hidden fees." And although these are not out-of-pocket expenses, they reduce the NAV.

Identifying mutual funds that meet certain investment criteria can be done easily using mutual fund screening software. This topic is examined later in this chapter.

Unique Mutual Fund Services

Mutual funds offer a number of valuable services that are unique to this type of investment and that are helpful and appealing to investors.

Convenience Mutual funds are extremely convenient for investors. Funds make it easy to open an account and invest in and sell shares. Fund prices are widely quoted. Services include toll-free telephone numbers, detailed records of transactions, and various checking and savings alternatives. Funds handle all the paperwork and record keeping, including accounting for fractional shares, so it is simple for investors to calculate taxable gains and losses when shares are sold.

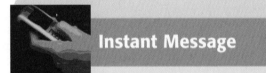

Instant Message

Reasons Why People Invest in Mutual Funds

Individuals invest in mutual funds to (1) obtain diversification in their investment portfolio, (2) employ the services of investment professionals, (3) earn an attractive rate of return that matches their investment philosophy and meets their investment goals, and (4) enjoy the conveniences of mutual fund investing.

Ease of Buying and Selling Shares Opening an account with a mutual fund company is just as simple as opening a checking account. After sending the fund your initial investment, you can easily buy more shares. Any number of shares can be sold at any time, or you can simply ask that a specific dollar amount be taken out by selling the appropriate number of shares. Each share is redeemed at the closing price—that is, the NAV—at the end of the trading day. Shares can be bought and sold by communicating with the company via telephone, wire, fax, mail, or online.

Check Writing and Electronic Transfers Mutual funds often offer interest-earning money market mutual funds in which investors can accumulate cash, accept dividends, or hold their money while making decisions about investing. They can write checks from money market funds. A money market fund invests exclusively in cash and cash equivalents. Investors can electronically transfer funds to and from mutual funds and banks.

Distribution of or Automatic Reinvestment of Income and Capital Gains

Unlike most other investments, mutual funds allow investors to choose to receive interest, dividends, and capital gains payments or have them automatically reinvested to purchase additional fund shares (often without paying any commissions). This is **automatic reinvestment,** and it produces the same effects as the compounding of interest because the investor earns money on past earnings. Fractional shares are acquired as needed. Automatic reinvestment is one of the most appealing aspects of mutual funds for investors. Most shareholders reinvest their mutual fund income as this keeps all their capital fully invested because it is wise to do so, as illustrated in Figure 15.3.

Telephone and Internet Exchange Privileges

An **exchange privilege** (also called a **switching, conversion,** or **transfer privilege**) permits mutual fund shareholders to easily swap shares on a dollar-for-dollar basis for shares in another mutual fund within a mutual fund family. Telephone and online transfers from one fund to another, such as moving money from a domestic stock fund to a Taiwan international fund, can be accomplished at no cost or for only a small charge, typically $5 or $10 per transaction, called an **exchange fee. A mutual fund family,** and there are more than 400 (see http://biz.yahoo.com/p/fam/a-b.html), is an investment management company that offers a number of different funds to the investing public, each with its own investment objectives.

Beneficiary Designation

When opening a mutual fund account, the investor is given the opportunity to complete a form to designate a beneficiary in case of the investor's death. A **beneficiary designation** enables the shareholder to name one or more beneficiaries so that the proceeds go to them without going through probate. The delays and expenses of probate are discussed in Chapter 18.

Automatic Investment

Funds often allow investors to make periodic monthly or quarterly payments using money automatically transferred from their bank

---

automatic reinvestment When investors choose to automatically reinvest any interest, dividends, and capital gains payments to purchase additional fund shares.

exchange privilege Permits mutual fund shareholders to easily swap shares on a dollar-for-dollar basis for shares in another mutual fund within a mutual fund family. Also called switching, conversion, or transfer privilege.

exchange fees Small amount charged to move money among funds within a mutual fund family.

mutual fund family Investment management company that offers a number of different funds to the investing public, each with its own investment objectives or philosophies of investing.

beneficiary designation Allows fund holder to name one or more beneficiaries so that the proceeds bypass probate proceedings if the original shareholder dies.

Figure 15.3

The Wisdom of Automatic Dividend Reinvestment

Reinvesting income greatly compounds share ownership. Figure 15.3 illustrates the positive results obtained by reinvesting dividends. The initial $10,000 investment in Vanguard's S&P 500 Index Fund grew to $110,897 over 20 years, instead of $66,931, because of the reinvestment of dividends. According to Standard & Poor's Dave Guarino, "Automatic reinvestment of dividends is one of the most overlooked ways of accumulating wealth. In addition to the benefits of compounding, it also provides a mechanism to dollar-cost average investments."

Source: Data copyright © 2007 Standard & Poor's, a dvision of the McGraw-Hill Companies, Inc. Reprinted with permission.

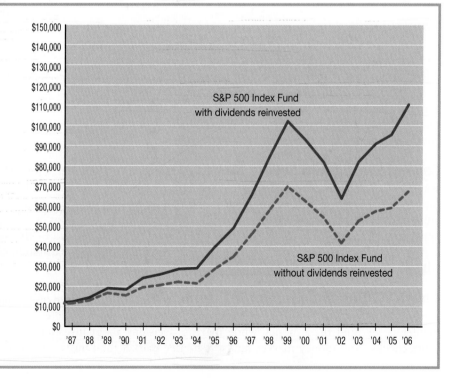

accounts or paychecks to the mutual fund company. You can invest as little as $25 monthly or quarterly. You can change your investment selections without penalty by contacting the fund. This is an example of dollar-cost averaging. By regularly investing in mutual funds, you can build a substantial portfolio of assets over time.

Effortless Establishment of Retirement Plans Mutual funds are perhaps the best option available to people saving for retirement through 401(k) plans and IRAs (topics examined in Chapter 17). An employee can direct his employer to transfer a specified dollar amount from every paycheck to a mutual fund to buy shares for a 401(k) plan; individuals can buy shares for their IRA accounts, too.

Multiple Income Withdrawal Options Mutual funds offer **withdrawal options** (also called **systematic withdrawal plans**) to shareholders who want to receive income on a regular basis from their mutual fund investments. Once enrolled in a withdrawal plan, the minimum withdrawal amount is $50. The fund forwards the amounts to you (or to anyone you designate) at regular intervals (monthly or quarterly). You can make regular withdrawals by (1) taking a set dollar amount each month, (2) cashing in a set number of shares each month, (3) taking the current income as cash, or (4) taking a portion of the asset growth.

withdrawal options/systematic withdrawal plans Arrangements with a mutual fund company for shareholders who want to receive income on a regular basis from their mutual fund investments.

Did You Know?...

Other Investment Companies

The Investment Company Act of 1940 distinguishes among investment companies. Open-end mutual funds are by far the most widely owned investment companies. Four other types exist:

1. **Closed-end mutual fund. Closed-end mutual funds** issue a limited and fixed number of shares at inception and do not buy them back. These companies operate with a fixed amount of capital. Closed-end shares are bought and sold on a stock exchange or in the over-the-counter market. After the original issue is sold, the price of a share depends primarily on the supply and demand in the market rather than the performance of the investment company assets. Closed-end shares are actively traded like common stocks and bonds, primarily on the New York Stock Exchange.

2. **Real estate investment trusts.** A special kind of closed-end investment company is a **real estate investment trust (REIT).** REITs invest in a portfolio of assets as defined in the trust agreement, such as properties, like office buildings and shopping centers (called an equity REIT), or mortgages (a mortgage REIT). Hybrid REITs invest in both. REITs have no predetermined life span. REIT shares are traded on stock exchanges, although many are illiquid investments.

3. **Unit investment trusts.** A **unit investment trust (UIT)** is a closed-end investment company that makes a one-time public offering of only a specific, fixed number of units. A UIT buys and holds an unmanaged fixed portfolio of fixed-maturity securities, such as municipal bonds, for a period of time. This could be a few months or perhaps 50 years. Each unit represents a proportionate ownership interest in the specific portfolio of perhaps 10 to 50 securities. Sold by brokers for perhaps $250 to $1000 a unit, there is no trading of these securities, although brokers may repurchase and resell them.

4. **Exchange-traded fund.** An **exchange-traded fund (ETF)** is a basket of passively managed securities structured like an index fund (described elsewhere in this chapter) as it owns all or a representative set of securities that duplicate the performance of a market segment or index. There are ETFs for the S&P 500, called Spiders; the Dow Jones Industrial Average, called Diamonds; and Qubes based on the NASDAQ 100. ETF prices are set by market forces since they are listed on securities markets [primarily on the American Stock Exchange (AMEX)] and traded throughout the day by brokers. One in four investors have ETFs in their portfolios, likely because of the extremely low costs. *Enhanced* ETFs are available that track an index but overweigh companies with the greatest potential; that's a "managed ETF."

Fund Objectives, Types, and Characteristics

2   LEARNING OBJECTIVE
Differentiate mutual funds by investment objectives, types, and characteristics.

managed funds Each fund's professional managers constantly evaluate and choose securities to buy or sell, using a specific investment approach.

Most mutual funds are **managed funds,** meaning that professional managers are constantly evaluating and choosing securities using a specific investment approach. On a daily basis, active managers select the stocks and bonds in which to invest and sell them when they deem appropriate. The managers earn a fee for their services, and ultimately their choices are responsible for the performance of the fund. Often, however, investing in a managed mutual fund is not the best choice for investors. Index funds are unmanaged, and they are often the best choice for investors; they are discussed later in the chapter.

Before investing in any specific mutual fund, decide whether the fund's investment objectives are a good fit for you. The Securities and Exchange Commission requires funds to disclose their investment objective. Mutual funds may be classified in one of three categories: income, growth, and growth and income. Each type has different features, risks, and reward characteristics. The name of a fund gives a clue to its objectives.

Income Objective

A mutual fund with an income objective invests in securities that pay regular income in dividends or interest. One key to earning a good return is to buy a fund that has low expenses.

Money Market Funds Mutual fund companies and brokerage firms offer **money market funds.** They invest in highly liquid, relatively safe securities with very short maturities (always less than one year), such as certificates of deposit, government securities, and commercial paper (i.e., short-term obligations issued by corporations). You can write checks or use an ATM card to access a money market fund account. Issuers keep the NAV (the price of each share of the fund) at $1.

As we discussed in Chapter 5, money market funds (and there are more than 1000 of them) pay a higher rate of return than accounts offered through banks and credit unions. While money market funds are not insured by a federal agency, they are considered extremely safe. **Tax-exempt money market funds** limit their investments to tax-exempt municipal securities with maturities of less than 90 days. The earnings are tax free to investors. **Government securities money market funds** appeal to investors' concerns about safety by investing solely in Treasury bills and other short-term securities backed by the U.S. government.

tax-exempt money market funds Funds that limit their investments to tax-exempt municipal securities with maturities of 90 days or less.

government securities money market funds Appeal to investor concerns about safety by investing solely in U.S. Treasury bills and other short-term securities backed by the U.S. government.

Bond Funds Bond funds (also called **fixed-income funds**) aim to earn current income higher than a money market fund without incurring undue risk by investing in a portfolio of bonds and other investments, such as preferred stocks and common stocks that pay high dividends. They do not ignore capital gains, however. Bond fund prices fluctuate with changing interest rates. Bond funds are categorized by what they own and the maturities of their portfolio holdings.

- **Short-term corporate bond funds** invest in securities maturing in 1 to 5 years.
- **Short-term U.S. government bond funds** invest in Treasury issues maturing in 1 to 5 years.
- **Intermediate corporate bond funds** invest in investment-grade corporate securities with 5- to 10-year maturities.
- **Intermediate government bond funds** invest in Treasuries with 5- to 10-year maturities.
- **Long-term corporate bond funds** specialize in investment-grade securities maturing in 10 to 30 years.
- **Long-term U.S. government bond funds** invest in Treasury and zero-coupon bonds with maturities of 10 years or longer.
- **Mortgage-backed funds** invest in mortgage-backed securities issued by agencies of the U.S. government, such as Ginnie Mae (GNMA).
- **Junk bond funds** invest in high-yield, high-risk corporate bonds.
- **Municipal bond (tax-exempt) funds** invest in municipal bonds that provide tax-free income. Both investment-grade and high-yield municipal bond funds exist.
- **Single-state municipal bond funds** invest in debt issues of only one state.
- **World bond funds** invest in debt securities offered by foreign corporations and governments.

Instant Message

Invest in Bond Funds Rather Than Bonds

There are three advantages for people investing in bond funds rather than bonds: (1) Bond funds are more liquid because shares can be readily sold; (2) bond funds provide cost-effective diversification because shares are inexpensive (perhaps $10, $20, or $40 a share) compared with buying a single bond for $1000, $5000, or $10,000; (3) bond funds (but not bonds) automatically reinvest interest and other income.

Growth Objective

A mutual fund that has a growth objective seeks capital appreciation. It invests in the common stock of companies that have above average growth potential, firms that may not pay a regular dividend but have the potential for large capital gains. Growth funds carry a fair amount of risk exposure, and this is reflected in substantial price volatility. **Aggressive growth funds** (also known as **maximum capital gains funds**) seek the greatest long-term capital appreciation. Also known as **capital appreciation funds,** they make investments in speculative stocks with volatile price swings. They may employ high-risk investment techniques, such as borrowing money for leverage, short selling, hedging, and options. Lots of buying and selling occurs to enhance returns.

aggressive growth funds Make investments in speculative stocks with volatile price swings, seeking the greatest long-term capital appreciation possible. Also known as maximum capital gains funds and capital appreciation funds.

Did You Know?...

Stable-Value Funds Available in Employer-Sponsored Retirement Plans

Stable-value funds are primarily available through employer-sponsored retirement plans. This is a different breed of fund. Stable-value funds get their name in part because they buy an insurance policy designed to allow the fund to redeem shares at a stable price regardless of overall market prices. This gives investors some assurance that the fund will be able to maintain the net asset value of the portfolio. Stable-value funds invest in high-quality, intermediate-term investments, including **guaranteed investment contracts (GICs)** offered by insurance companies. A GIC guarantees the owner a fixed or floating interest rate for a predetermined period of time, and the return of principal is guaranteed.

growth funds Seek long-term capital appreciation by investing in common stocks of companies with higher-than-average revenue and earnings growth, often the larger and well-established firms.

growth and income funds Invest in companies that have a high likelihood of both dividend income and price appreciation; less risk-oriented than aggressive growth funds or growth funds.

value funds Specialize in stocks that are fundamentally sound whose prices appear to be low (low P/E ratios) based on the logic that such stocks are currently out of favor and undervalued by the market.

Growth funds seek long-term capital appreciation by investing in the common stocks of companies with higher-than-average revenue and earnings growth, often the larger and well-established firms. Such companies (like Wal-Mart, Microsoft, and Coca-Cola) tend to reinvest most of their earnings to facilitate future growth.

Growth and income funds invest in companies that have a high likelihood of both dividend income and price appreciation.

Value funds specialize in stocks that are fundamentally sound and whose prices appear to be low (low P/E ratios), based on the logic that such stocks are currently out of favor and undervalued by the market.

Midcap funds invest in the stocks of midsize companies with a market capitalization of less than $1 billion that are expected to grow rapidly.

Small-cap funds (or **small company growth funds**) invest in lesser-known companies with a market capitalization of less than $500 million that offer strong potential for growth.

Microcap funds invest in high-risk companies with a market capitalization of less than $300 million.

Sector funds concentrate their investment holdings in one or more industries that make up a targeted part of the economy that is expected to grow, perhaps very rapidly, such as energy, biotechnology, health care, and financial services.

Regional funds invest in securities listed on stock exchanges in a specific region of the world, such as the Pacific Rim, Australia, or Europe.

Precious metals and gold funds invest in securities associated with gold, silver, and other precious metals.

Global funds invest in growth stocks of companies listed on foreign exchanges as well as in the United States, usually multinational firms.

International funds invest only in foreign stocks throughout the world.

Emerging market funds seek out stocks in countries whose economies are small but growing. Fund prices are volatile because these countries tend to be less stable politically.

Advice from a Pro...

Invest Only "Fun Money" Aggressively

People with a moderate or conservative investment philosophy may have the occasional urge to invest aggressively in a speculative mutual fund or other security. Once the investor has his or her financial plan in place, taking on more risk is acceptable—but *only* within the limits of the individual's "fun money." **Fun money** is a sum of investment money that you can afford to lose without doing serious damage to your total portfolio.

Resolve to trade with a specific sum, such as $5000, or perhaps no more than 2 or 3 percent of your portfolio. Decide mentally that if and when the money is gone, it has been spent on an activity that you enjoyed trying, but accept that the money lost is lost forever. In particular, avoid the temptation to "throw good money after bad" in trying to recover your losses. Speculative investing is not much different from gambling but, if armed with information, you might avoid losing 100 percent of your fun money. The biggest danger of fun-money investing is that you might be successful. Success can give you the confidence—albeit perhaps false confidence—that you are a great investor. While you might be the next Warren Buffet, such success is likely to tempt you to aggressively invest even more of the assets in your total portfolio. That approach can result in disaster.

Investing in aggressive growth mutual funds for some might be a lot of fun, particularly when the amount of money at stake is small. Over time, you will be best served by pursuing a disciplined investing plan with a focus on diversification. As financial columnist Jane Bryant Quinn observes, "The money you really need for life is better off in broadly diversified mutual funds, where a mistake is not forever."

Robert O. Weagley
University of Missouri–Columbia

Did You Know?...

Quant Funds

Charles Schwab, Janus, and other investment companies offer **quant funds (quantitative funds)** to investors. Computers make the buy and sell decisions based strictly on constant crunching of hundreds or thousands of numbers according to the criteria they are programmed to monitor. Why? Only people, not computers, have bad days in making investment decisions.

Vanguard quant funds look for the best growth prospects and lowest valuations. Schwab likes rapid earnings. Janus prefers stock movement volatility.

Growth and Income Objective

A mutual fund that has a combined growth and income objective seeks a balanced return made up of current income and capital gains. Such funds heavily invest in common stocks. They seek a return not as low as offered by funds with an income objective but not as high as that offered by funds with a growth objective. They invite less risk than growth funds.

Growth and income funds invest in companies expected to show average or better growth and pay steady or rising dividends.

Equity-income funds invest in well-known companies with a long history of paying high dividends as they emphasize income and capital preservation.

Socially conscious funds invest in companies that meet some predefined standard of moral and ethical behavior. Criteria could be progressive employee relations, strong records of community involvement, an excellent record on environmental issues, respect for human rights, and safe products (as well as no "sinful" products such as tobacco, guns, alcohol, gambling). See www.socialinvest.org for examples.

Balanced funds (or **hybrid funds**) keep a set mix of stocks and bonds, often 60 percent stocks and 40 percent bonds, in order to earn a well-balanced return of income and long-term capital gains. **Blend funds** invest in a combination of stocks and money market securities, but no fixed-income securities, such as bonds.

Asset allocation funds invest in a mix of assets (usually stocks, bonds, and cash equivalents and sometimes international assets, gold, and real estate), and they buy and sell regularly to reduce risk while trying to outperform the market. The asset mix may be based on risk tolerance (aggressive, moderate, and conservative).

Life-cycle funds are asset allocation funds that offer investors premixed portfolios of stocks, bonds, and cash that investors of a certain age and risk tolerance might prefer. These are targeted to people in their 30s, 40s, 50s, 60s, and 70s. They are also known as **target retirement funds.** Life-cycle funds shift assets from aggressive to moderate to conservative securities as the retirement target approaches. They seek to first grow and then preserve the portfolio assets. This is a no-hassle, "buy-and-forget" way to invest.

Mutual fund funds earn a return by investing in other mutual funds. This provides extensive diversification, but expenses and fees are higher than average.

socially conscious funds Invest in companies that meet some predefined standard of moral and ethical behavior.

balanced funds Keep a set mix of stocks and bonds, often 60 percent stocks and 40 percent bonds, in order to earn a well-balanced return of income and long-term capital gains.

Instant Message

Index Funds Are Unmanaged

An **index fund** is a mutual fund whose investment objective is to achieve the same return as a particular market index by buying and holding all or a representative selection of securities in it. An S&P 500 index fund would effectively mirror the companies in the index, which are primarily large-cap U.S. stocks. A Russell 2000 Index Fund invests in the 2000 small-cap stocks in the index. Index funds offer a guarantee that the investor will get the same return that the market obtains.

Index funds are called **unmanaged funds** because their managers do not evaluate or select individual securities. Being unmanaged, annual management fees are extremely low, perhaps only 0.20 to 0.30 percent. Both index funds and ETFs follow market benchmarks, and ETF management fees often are lower. The returns achieved by actively managed stock funds typically trail the stock market averages by about 1.5 percentage points per year.

Burton Malkiel, professor of economics at Princeton University, says that very few individual investors or fund managers will do better than the indexes. "It's like looking for a needle in a haystack." He recommends that investors buy the haystack.

Fees and Charges of Mutual Fund Investing

3 LEARNING OBJECTIVE
Summarize the fees and charges involved in buying and selling mutual funds.

Individuals who invest through mutual funds pay transaction costs that often are less than those associated with buying individual stocks, bonds, and cash equivalent securities. Mutual fund investors do pay certain fees and charges for the benefits of diversification, professional management, liquidity, check writing, and record keeping. Funds also pay their operating expenses out of fund assets, and this means that investors indirectly pay these costs.

Shareholder fees are charged directly to investors for specific transactions, such as purchases, redemptions, or exchanges. **Annual fund operating expenses** are the normal operating costs of the business that are deducted from fund assets before earnings are distributed to shareholders. The fees and charges associated with investing in mutual funds are many, and they can be confusing; some can be avoided.

Did You Know?...

Top 3 Financial Missteps in Mutual Fund Investing

People slip up in mutual fund investing when they do the following:

1. Buy funds with high fees and expenses
2. Withdraw dividends rather than reinvesting
3. Chase performance by investing in "hot" funds

Load and No-Load Funds

All mutual funds are classified as either load or no-load funds. This refers to whether or not they assess a sales charge, or load, when shares are purchased. Table 15.1 shows the basic fund classes.

Load Funds Always Charge Transaction Fees Funds that levy a sales charge for purchases are called **load funds.** Load funds are generally *sold* by stock brokerage firms, banks, and financial planners rather than marketed directly to investors by a mutual fund company. The load is the commission used to compensate brokers.

This commission, also called a **front-end load,** typically amounts to 3 to 8.5 percent of the amount invested; this reduces the amount available to purchase fund shares. For example, assume that you and a salesperson have discussed the investment potential of the Conglomerate Cat and Dog Food Mutual Fund and you decide to invest $10,000. Because this load fund charges a commission of 8.5 percent (the maximum permitted by the Securities and Exchange Commission), the salesperson receives $850 ($10,000 × 0.085). As a result, only $9150 of your money is actually available to purchase shares. Such a commission is much higher than stock transaction costs, which are usually 0.25 percent to 2 percent of the security's purchase price.

The sales charge may be shown either as the stated commission or as a percentage of the amount invested. The **stated commission** (8.5 percent in our example) is always somewhat misleading. In contrast, the **percentage of the amount invested** is a more accurate figure because it is based on the actual money invested and working. A stated commission of 8.5 percent actually amounts to 9.3 percent of the amount invested: $10,000 − $9150 = $850; $850 ÷ $9150 = 9.3%. If you

shareholder fees Charged directly to investors for specific transactions, such as purchases, redemptions, or exchanges.

annual fund operating expenses Normal operating costs of the business that are deducted from fund assets before shareholders receive earnings.

load funds Mutual funds that always charge a "load" or sales charge upon purchase; the load is the commission used to compensate brokers.

front-end load A sales charge paid when an individual buys an investment, reducing the amount available to purchase fund shares.

Table 15.1 Load Fund Share Classes

A single mutual fund company may offer more than one class of shares to investors: Class A, B, or C. Realize that Classes A, B, and C all are the same fund. Each class invests in the same investment portfolio of securities and has the same investment objectives but has different shareholder distribution arrangements and services, resulting in dissimilar fees and expenses and therefore performance results. To determine which class of shares suits your needs, use the Mutual Fund Expense Analyzer of NASD (National Association of Securities Dealers) (http://apps.nasd.com/investor_Information/ea/nasd/mfetf.aspx) and the U.S. Securities and Exchange Commission's Mutual Fund Cost Calculator (http://www.sec.gov/investor/tools/mfcc/mfcc-intsec.htm). Investors in no-load funds can avoid most of these charges, although some no-load funds do assess 12b-1 fees and back-end loads.

Share Class	Characteristics	Who Should Invest?
A	Front-end load (usually modest); small 12b-1 fee; low annual expenses	Long-term investors
B	No front-end load; substantial back-end loads up to ten years; maximum 12b-1 fees; substantial annual expenses; might convert to Class A shares with a lower 12b-1 fee after a set period of time	Should be avoided as too expensive
C	Low front-end load; small back-end load; modest 12b-1 fee; highest annual expenses	Short-term investors; better than Class B shares

want to invest a full $10,000 in this load fund, you will need to pay out $10,930 [$10,930 − ($10,930 × 8.5%) = $10,000]. Investments of $10,000 or more often receive a discount on the load (see the "Breakpoints on Load Funds" box).

So-called **low-load funds** may carry a sales charge of perhaps 1 to 3 percent. These funds may also be sold by brokers and are sold via mail and sometimes through mutual fund retailers located in shopping centers. About half of all mutual funds levy a load.

No-Load Funds

A **no-load mutual fund** sells shares at the net asset value without the addition of sales charges. These mutual fund companies let people purchase shares directly from the mutual fund company without the services of a broker, banker, or financial planner. Interested investors simply seek out advertisements for these funds in financial newspapers, magazines, and the Internet and make contact through toll-free telephone numbers, online, or mail. The SEC does allow funds to be called "no-load" even though they assess a "service fee" of 0.25 percent or less when shares are purchased.

Some No-Load Funds Assess 12b-1 Fees

A **12b-1 fee** (named for the SEC rule that permits the charge) is an annual charge deducted by the fund company from a fund's assets to compensate underwriters and brokers for fund sales as well as to pay for advertising, marketing, distribution, and promotional costs. A 12b-1 fee is also known as a **distribution fee.** For load funds, these charges also pay for **trailing commissions,** which is compensation paid to salespeople for months or years in the future.

Instant Message

No-Load Mutual Fund Investors Avoid Bad Brokers

No-load mutual fund investors do not have to deal with persuasive salespeople, potentially bad financial advice, and outrageous sales commissions.

Instant Message

Breakpoints on Load Funds

The investment levels required to obtain a reduced sales load are referred to as **breakpoints,** and these start at $10,000. Funds are not required to offer breakpoints in the fund's sales load, but if they exist they must be disclosed. You have to ask how a fund establishes breakpoint discounts. NASD's Mutual Fund Breakpoint search tool (http://tools1.nasd.com/nbst/) can help you determine whether you are entitled to breakpoint discounts.

Although the funds do not call 12b-1 fees "loads" because they are not charged up front, they have the same effect as loads—that is, they reduce the investor's return.

These **hidden fees** decrease a shareholder's earning power each year without being described as a sales commission. A 12b-1 fee is actually a "perpetual sales load" because it is assessed on the initial investment as well as on reinvested dividends, every year, forever. The SEC caps 12b-1 fees at 0.75 percent, although it permits a 0.25 percent "service fee," which brings the total cap to 1 percent. Some funds stop assessing 12b-1 fees after four to eight years.

Some No-Load Funds Assess Deferred Load and Redemption Fees

Approximately 60 percent of no-load mutual funds (and many load funds) assess additional fees for transactions, such as deferred load and redemption charges. A **deferred load**, also known as a **back-end load**, is a sales commission that is imposed only when shares are sold. Deferred loads are often on a sliding scale. The fee may decline 1 percentage point for each year the investor owns the fund. For example, a fund might charge a 6 percent fee if an investor redeems the shares within one year of purchase, and then the fee declines on an annual basis, until it reaches zero after six years.

A **redemption charge** (or **exit fee**) is similar to a deferred load, although often it is much lower; it is used to reduce excessive trading of fund shares. The fee is usually 1 percent of the value of the shares redeemed. It disappears after the investment has been held for six months or a year. Long-term investors should not shy away from funds with redemption fees that disappear after a year.

Disclosure of Fees in Standardized Expense Table

The SEC requires that a mutual fund's prospectus include a **standardized expense table** within its first three pages that describes and illustrates in an identical manner the effects of all of its fees and other expenses. (See Table 15.2.) This description must estimate the hypothetical total costs that a mutual fund investor would pay on a $1000 investment that earns 5 percent annually and is withdrawn after ten years. All figures must be adjusted to reflect the effects of loads and fees. Also look for the fund's **expense ratio,** the expense per dollar of assets under management. Some mutual funds are much more efficient than others, and the expense ratio could range from 0.2 percent to more than 4 percent. Expense ratios average 1.45 percent for diversified stock funds and 0.40 percent for index funds.

What's Best: Load or No Load? Low Fee or High Fee?

The sales commissions charged by load funds indisputably reduce total returns as illustrated in Table 15.3. When investment results are adjusted to account for the effects of sales charges, no-load mutual funds have an initial advantage because the investor has more money at work. In general, the shorter the time period you own the shares, the greater the negative impact of loads on the total return for the mutual fund investor. Up-front load charges are costly to the investor in the short run (less than five years), whereas annual 12b-1 charges are very costly over the long run.

If you pay 1 percent per year in 12b-1 fees for a mutual fund in which you invest for ten years, you will be giving up nearly 10 percent of your investment amount in trailing commissions. Yikes! You would be well advised to invest in a load fund rather than pay 12b-1 assessments if you plan to own the fund for more than five years.

Independent research has found that over five-year periods, lower-cost funds always deliver returns better than those offered by higher-cost funds. Even a small difference in fees can seriously affect long-term returns. For example, a

---

deferred load/back-end load A sales commission that is imposed only when shares are sold; often charges are on a sliding scale, with the fee dropping 1 percentage point per year that the investor stays in the fund.

redemption charge/exit fee Similar to a deferred load but often much lower; used to reduce excessive trading of fund shares.

standardized expense table SEC-required information that describes and illustrates mutual fund charges in an identical manner so that investors can accurately compare the effects of all of a fund's fees and other expenses relative to other funds.

expense ratio Expense per dollar of assets under management.

Table 15.2 Mutual Fund Fee Table Required by Federal Law

This illustrative mutual fund fee table is hypothetical, and the estimated expenses are based on the U.S. Securities and Exchange Commission's Mutual Fund Cost Calculator (www.sec.gov/investor/tools/mfcc/get-started.htm).

Shareholder Fees		Annual Fund Operating Expenses	
A Maximum Sales Charge (Load) Imposed on Purchases (as a percentage of offering price)	4.5%	G Management Fee	0.52%
		H Distribution (12b-1) Fee	0.25%
		I Other Expenses	0.20%
B Maximum Deferred Sales Charge (Load)	None		
		J Total Annual Fund Operating Expenses (Expense Ratio)	0.97%
C Maximum Sales Charge (Load) on Reinvested Dividends	None	**K Example** This example is intended to help an investor compare the cost of investing in different funds. The example assumes a $10,000 investment in the fund for one, three, five, and ten years and then a redemption of all fund shares at the end of those periods. The example also assumes that an investment returns 5 percent each year and that the fund's operating expenses remain the same. Although actual costs may be higher or lower, based on these assumptions an investor's estimated expenses would be:	
D Redemption Fee	None	1 year	$547
E Exchange Fee	None	3 years	$754
F Annual Account Maintenance Fee	None	5 years	$977
		10 years	$1,617

Source: *Guide to Understanding Mutual Funds,* copyright © by the Investment Company Institute (www.ici.org). Reprinted with permission.

Table 15.3 Effect of Loads and Fees on Mutual Fund Returns (Estimated figures based on a $10,000 investment and assuming a 10 percent gain each year.)

Years	No-Load*	3% Front-end Load	8.5% Front-end Load	5.5% Front-end Load with 0.25% 12b-1	5% Back-end Load with 1% 12b-1†
>1	$10,890	$10,560	$ 9,960	$10,260	$10,280
3	12,900	12,500	11,800	12,150	12,230
5	15,320	14,860	14,020	14,380	14,460
7	18,170	17,620	16,620	18,000	16,930
10	23,470	22,770	21,480	21,200	20,200

*1 percent annual management fee.
†A declining redemption fee of 5 percent the first year that goes to zero after the fifth year.

Did You Know?...

The Total Long-Term Returns for Stock Mutual Funds Are Roughly the Same

Data from the Investment Company Institute reveal that the type of stock mutual fund in which you invest over the long term makes very little difference. Over 10 or 20 years, the average annual returns for different types of diversified stock funds (growth, domestic equity, growth and income, equity income, and balanced)

converge around 11 percent (11.2 percent, according to Ibbotson Associates). The only secret to obtaining such a good return is to remain patient and keep investing. Returns over one, three, and five years vary widely, but over the long term, the returns of major categories of diversified stock mutual funds are roughly the same.

Instant Message

Keep Your Mutual Fund Costs Low

John C. Bogle, who started the no-load mutual fund powerhouse Vanguard, says in *The Little Book of Commonsense Investing* that the costs of the average managed mutual fund is 2.5 percent, while the classic index fund's cost is 0.2 percent. Over time compounding costs greatly reduce compounding returns.

$50,000 portfolio earning an 8 percent annual return would grow to $176,182 in 20 years with a 1.5 percent management fee. By comparison, over the same time span it would grow to $193,484 with a 1.0 percent fee and to $212,393 with a 0.5 percent fee. Over 30 years, the returns with these fee rates would be $330,718, $380,613, and $437,748, respectively. The negative effects of high fees on long-term returns are enormous.

The investor would be wise to invest in no-load fee mutual funds that have low management fees. "If you pick your own funds, sales charges [and loads] are a total waste of money," observes Fred W. Frailey, editor of *Kiplinger's Personal Finance Magazine*.

✔ CONCEPT CHECK 15.3

1. Give three examples of fees and charges associated with load funds.
2. Which is better for most investors, load or no-load fund?
3. Summarize the effects of loads on investment returns.

Selecting Funds in Which to Invest

4 LEARNING OBJECTIVE
Establish strategies to evaluate and select mutual funds that meet your investment goals.

Selecting mutual funds in which to invest is usually a do-it-yourself effort. A tremendous amount of objective information is available to help potential investors evaluate and select funds. To explain the process of selecting funds, let's follow Jessica Shipp's decision making. She is in sales and earns $51,000 annually; she lives in Sacramento, California. Figure 15.4 illustrates the process of selecting mutual fund investments, and Table 15.4 contains performance data for a number of large-cap mutual funds from *Consumer Reports* magazine.

Review Your Investment Philosophy and Investment Goals

Jessica began by reviewing her investment philosophy and financial goals. These topics were examined in Chapter 13. Jessica has a moderate investment philosophy, and

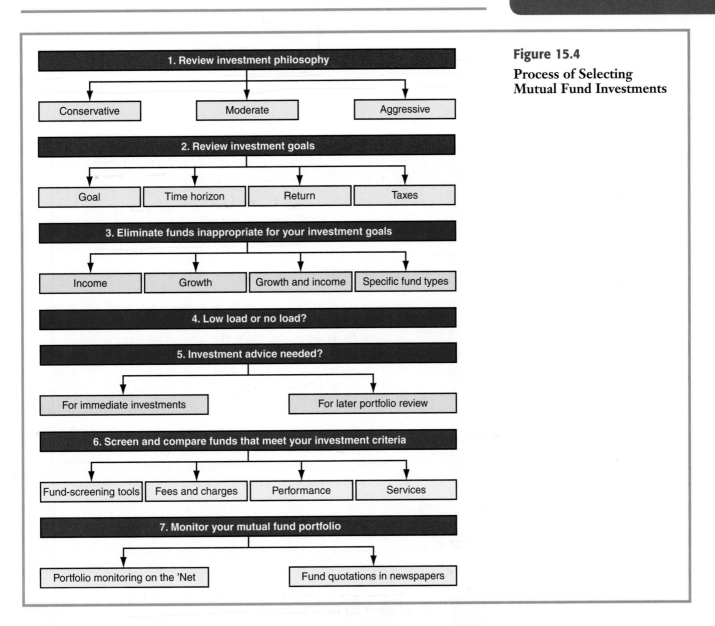

Figure 15.4

Process of Selecting Mutual Fund Investments

Capital Strategies Community Investment Fund is a mutual fund that provides returns through socially oriented investment vehicles. The fund fosters economic development in America's underserved communities, including victims of Hurricane Katrina.

Table 15.4 Mutual Fund Performance

Ratings
large-cap funds

Key no.	Fund name & ticker	Fund type	Load	Consistency score	Annualized returns 10-yr.	5-yr.	Best/worst 12 months	Expense ratio	Tax-cost ratio	Manager tenure (years)	Fund stewardship grade	Minimum initial investment
1	Gabelli Equity Income AAA GABEX	Value		89	11.2	11.3	39.1 / -14.4	1.46	1.79	15	C	1,000
2	TCW Dividend Focused N TGIGX	Value		86	11.4	11.0	46.2 / -18.6	1.25	2.14	5	C	2,000
3	Manning & Napier Pro-Blend Maxm Term A EXHAX	Blend		85	11.5	10.2	41.5 / -22.7	1.20	2.10	11	NA	2,000
4	American Century Value Inv TWVLX	Value		84	10.8	10.3	40.7 / -19.8	.99	2.92	13	B	2,500
5	Parnassus Equity Income PRBLX	Blend		84	10.5	7.8	33.6 / -7.7	.99	1.91	5	C	2,000
6	Weitz Value WVALX	Value		84	14.1	8.4	58.8 / -20.3	1.12	1.61	20	A	5,000
7	ING Corporate Leaders Trust B LEXCX	Value		84	9.2	11.9	32.2 / -18.5	.50	1.56	6	NA	1,000
8	American Funds Fundamental Invs A ANCFX	Blend	•	84	10.2	9.2	42.5 / -24.0	.60	1.47	22	A	250
9	T. Rowe Price Equity Income PRFDX	Value		83	9.9	9.3	36.4 / -21.9	.71	1.82	13	A	2,500
10	Weitz Partners Value WPVLX	Value		83	14.1	7.9	61.1 / -20.8	1.14	1.36	23	A	5,000
11	Mairs & Power Growth MPGFX	Blend		83	12.1	9.8	39.7 / -16.1	.70	.90	7	B	2,500
12	Vanguard Windsor II VWNFX	Value		83	9.8	10.1	47.0 / -23.5	.34	1.57	21	B	10,000
13	Homestead Value HOVLX	Value		82	9.6	11.3	38.7 / -21.8	.76	.99	16	NA	500
14	American Funds Amcap A AMCPX	Growth	•	82	10.1	5.1	49.5 / -19.1	.65	1.52	21	B	250
15	Van Kampen Growth & Income A ACGIX	Value	•	82	10.3	8.0	39.4 / -22.6	.80	1.87	16	C	0
16	American Beacon Lg Cap Value Plan AAGPX	Value		82	9.4	12.0	47.9 / -24.1	.86	1.87	19	NA	2,500
17	T. Rowe Price Personal Strat Growth TRSGX	Blend		81	9.2	9.9	37.4 / -16.8	.92	1.01	8	B	2,500
18	American Century Equity Income Inv TWEIX	Value		81	12.3	10.6	37.8 / -12.1	.98	3.03	12	B	2,500
19	BlackRock Equity Dividend A MDDVX	Value	•	81	9.8	10.3	38.8 / -18.9	1.07	1.88	5	NA	1,000
	VANGUARD 500 INDEX VFINX			NA	8.0	6.0	47.8 / -26.7	.18	.51	NA	B	3,000

Consistency score scale: 0 — P F G VG E — 100

Note: The above examples were chosen to meet the requirements of the end-of-chapter questions on pages 444–445.
Source: © 2007 by Consumers Union of U.S., Inc. Yonkers, NY 10703-1057, a nonprofit organization. Reprinted with permission from the February 2007 issue of CONSUMER REPORTS® for educational purposes only. No commercial use or reproduction permitted. www.ConsumerReports.org.

she has a written investment plan (Figure 13.8 on page 378). The investment goal she is interested in investing in for now is retirement, and her investment time horizon is the next 30 years or more. She anticipates an annual return of at least 7 to 8 percent. She does not care about income taxes because these investments will be made within Jessica's tax-deferred 401(k) retirement plan at work.

Jessica does not have any lump sums available in a savings or money market account to use for investing. To help fund her retirement plans, she decided to have $200 a month withheld from her paycheck to invest in a mutual fund with a growth investment objective. Jessica's employer's 401(k) plan offers about 20 funds as well as company stock.

Eliminate Funds Inappropriate for Your Investment Goals

Jessica began by reviewing all fund classifications (pages 440 and 443) and balancing the risks and returns of various funds as illustrated in Figure 15.5. She wants to eliminate mutual funds inappropriate for her retirement investment goal.

Instant Message

Morningstar Ratings

Many investors review Morningstar mutual fund ratings for guidance in selecting funds in which to invest. Five stars indicate the best and one star indicates the worst. (See www.Morningstar.com or www.cnnmoney.com.) The star ratings are backward-looking, quantitative measures of past returns that are adjusted for risk, costs, and sales charges. Other fund analysts (*Kiplinger's Personal Finance Magazine*, *Money* magazine, *Consumer Reports*, and other investment publications) offer forward-looking, subjective recommendations of funds that they think have the best chance at success.

Did You Know?...

How to Learn About Mutual Funds

Information on mutual fund investing is vast, and current information about mutual funds is available from numerous sources.

Websites Focusing on Mutual Funds

- Yahoo! Finance (http://finance.yahoo.com/funds)
- The Motley Fool (http://www.fool.com/mutualfunds/mutualfunds.htm?source=LN)
- *Kiplinger's Personal Finance* (http://www.kiplinger.com/personalfinance/investing/funds/index.html)
- CNNMoney.com (http://money.cnn.com/pf/funds/index.html)
- BusinessWeek Online (http://www.businessweek.com/investor/funds.html)
- SmartMoney.com (http://www.smartmoney.com/funds/?nav=dropTab)
- AOL Money & Finance (http://money.aol.com/investing/funds?icid=investing:mutualfunds)

Personal Finance Magazines

Kiplinger's Personal Finance Magazine, *Money*, *BusinessWeek*, *Consumer Reports*, *Forbes*, *Fortune*, and *Worth*. Comprehensive examinations of the performance of numerous mutual funds are featured every year in the late August issue of *Forbes*, the October issue of *Money*, a late February issue of *BusinessWeek*, and the September issue of *Kiplinger's Personal Finance Magazine*.

Financial Press

The Wall Street Journal, *Barron's*, *Investor's Business Daily*, and the business sections of newspapers such as *The New York Times* and *USA Today*.

Online News and Quote Services

CompuServe, Dow Jones News/Retrieval—Private Investor Edition, Farcast, Personal Journal, Quotecom, and Reuters Money Network.

Mutual Fund Investment Publications and Websites

Morningstar Mutual Funds, *Morningstar No-Load Funds*, *Mutual Funds Update*, *Investment Companies Yearbook*, *IBC/Donoghue's Mutual Funds Almanac*, Standard & Poor's, *Lipper Mutual Fund Profiles*, Moody's, and *The Value Line Mutual Fund Survey*. Dozens of newsletters that specialize in mutual funds are available, too. Morningstar (www.morningstar.com) and the Investment Company Institute (www.ici.org) provide information on thousands of funds. Some charge fees, and others are free.

Figure 15.5

Balancing Risk and Returns on Mutual Funds

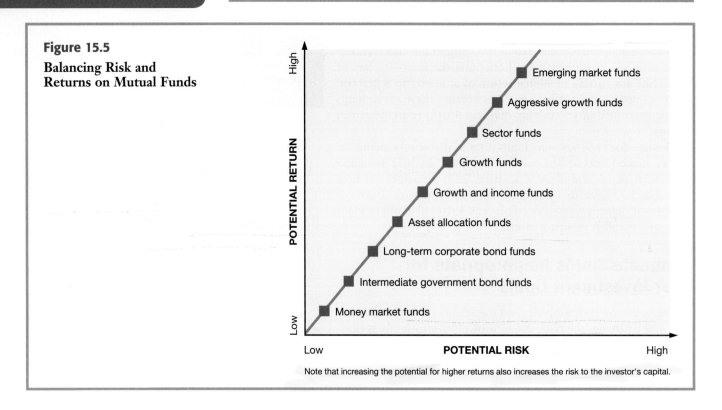

Note that increasing the potential for higher returns also increases the risk to the investor's capital.

Jessica recognizes that increasing the potential for higher returns also increases the risk to the investor's capital. Therefore, she eliminated the following types of funds: aggressive income funds, sector funds, aggressive growth funds, and international equity funds, as well as stock in the company where she works. She also realizes that investing too conservatively invites the risk of failure to achieve her goal of a financially successful retirement. Therefore, Jessica eliminated money market funds, bond funds, and balanced funds.

Load or No-Load Funds?

The sales commissions charged by load funds indisputably reduce total returns. Jessica reasoned that since no-load mutual funds have an initial advantage—the investor has more money at work—she preferred no-load funds. Because her $200 a month was going into investment for retirement, she also thought that 12b-1 fees would be very costly over the long term. For the same reason, she wanted to avoid high management fees. She did not care about back-end loads and exit fees, as these largely disappear over time. Jessica decided to invest in one or more no-load mutual funds with no or low 12b-1 fees and very low management fees.

Investment Advice Needed?

Because Jessica is going to invest in no-load funds, she figured she did not need the services of a broker or financial adviser. Instead, she plans to use the tremendous resources that are available via the Vanguard website—information, education, and professional advice. Jessica's employer offers investing and retirement planning seminars and workshops provided by Vanguard, T. Rowe Price, and other companies. Significant others are welcome to attend. Employer-sponsored financial advice may cover an employee's entire financial situation, including debt reduction, college planning, spousal assets, real estate, and other investments. Once Jessica's retirement assets build up to a substantial amount, perhaps $20,000 or more, she might be wise to seek additional professional investment advice.

Did You Know?...

About Mutual Fund Volatility

Volatility characterizes a mutual fund's (or any security's) tendency to rise or fall in price over a period of time. A measure of volatility is the **standard deviation,** which gauges the degree to which a security's historical return rises above or falls below its long-term average return—and therefore may be likely to do so again in the future. A standard deviation is a probability indicator, not an economic forecast. The bigger an investment's standard deviation, the more volatile its price may be in the future. High volatility suggests greater long-term rewards but a greater-than-normal risk of short-term losses during economic downturns. Other common measures of risk are beta, the Sharpe Ratio, and R-squared.

Kiplinger's Personal Finance Magazine provides a volatility ranking for mutual funds. Its system measures the volatility of a fund's results on a scale ranging from 1 (least volatile) to 10 (most volatile), indicating how much the fund's NAV could decline in a falling market or increase in a rising market relative to other mutual funds. Morningstar publishes a "downside risk" score for each fund based on how its record compares with the average for its peers. *U.S. News & World Report* uses OPI (overall performance index) as a measure of an investment's returns and volatility compared with similar funds. Conservative investors can use standard deviations to avoid the most volatile stock funds, while aggressive investors might seek them out.

Screen and Compare Funds That Meet Your Investment Criteria

When comparing the track records of mutual funds, there are a number of criteria to consider. These may include expenses; net asset value; minimum initial purchase; size of fund; ratings; past performance (perhaps one, three, five, and ten years); best and worst performance in up and down markets (volatility); fund manager tenure; and services. Jessica is interested in value, growth and blend funds, low management fees, and no or low 12b-1 fees.

Jessica started searching for mutual fund investments at Vanguard (https://flagship.vanguard.com/VGApp/hnw/FundsMFSIntro?FROM=VAN), considered among the best mutual fund selection websites. A **fund screener** or **fund-screening tool** permits an individual to screen all of the mutual funds in the market. Other mutual fund screening tools are available at the following websites:

- Yahoo! Finance (http://finance.yahoo.com/funds)
- Kiplinger.com (www.Kiplinger.com/investing/funds/)
- CNNMoney.com (http://money.cnn.com/pf/funds/)
- Fidelity (http://personal.fidelity.com/products/funds/?refhp=pr&ut=B10)

Jessica focused on large-cap funds, including those shown in Table 15.4. She researched funds using the Vanguard fund screener. She obtained online a profile prospectus from Vanguard on each of the funds she liked. A **profile prospectus** (or **fund profile**) describes the mutual fund, its investment objectives, and how it tries to achieve its objectives. Written in lay language, it offers a two- to four-page summary presentation of information contained in an SEC-required legal prospectus that answers 11 key investor questions, including risks, fees, and details about the fund's ten-year performance record.

After reading fund details, looking at the numbers, and comparing performance, Jessica decided to split her monthly $200 investment between Vanguard Windsor II (VWNFX) and T. Rowe Price Equity Income (PRFDX), partly because of their low fees. (The minimum initial investment fee is waived for investments via her employer's retirement plan.) Jessica almost decided to invest solely in the Vanguard 500 Index

fund screener/fund-screening tool Permits investors to screen all of the mutual funds in the market to gauge performance.

profile prospectus/fund profile Describes the mutual fund, its investment objectives, and how it tries to achieve its objectives in lay terms rather than the legal language used in a regular prospectus.

Did You Know?...

The Tax Consequences of Mutual Fund Investing

Ordinary income dividend distributions, capital gains distributions, and realized gains from the sale of mutual funds are generally subject to taxation.

- In regular investment accounts:
  - When you buy and hold mutual fund shares, you owe income taxes on any ordinary income dividends and on the fund's capital gains in the year you receive or reinvest them.
  - When you sell shares, you owe taxes on the capital gains earned on the difference between what you paid for the shares and the selling price (less transaction costs).
  - When purchasing a mutual fund in December, determine whether the fund has already

made its end-of-year capital gains distribution. If you buy the fund before the **record date** (the date established by an issuer to determine who is eligible to receive a dividend or distribution), you will receive the income but you also will owe capital gains taxes for the whole year. Buying after the record date avoids that situation because you will not receive the distribution.

- Interest from a tax-exempt municipal bond fund is exempt from federal income taxes.
- In retirement accounts [such as a 401(k) or traditional IRA account], taxes are deferred until withdrawn.

fund, but she thinks the fund managers will beat the average market returns. Jessica might be right, or she might be wrong.

The next step is for Jessica to contact the human resources department at her employer and sign the documents to withhold $200 a month from her paycheck and invest $100 into each of the two funds. Jessica also knows that for every dollar invested she gets an immediate 50 percent return because her employer's policy is to match 401(k) contributions 50 cents on the dollar for the first 6 percent of earnings. Jessica's 401(k) balance in 12 months, therefore, will show $2400 in contributions and $1200 in employer matching contributions (that's an immediate 50 percent return on her $2400!), plus whatever gain occurs (hopefully not a loss) in NAV. Jessica's 401(k) balance next year is likely to be more than $3600. Chapter 17 examines retirement planning.

The Internet offers a broad variety of investment advice.

Monitor Your Mutual Fund Portfolio

Tracking your portfolio is imperative because investors do not want to keep an underperforming mutual fund in their portfolio for very long, assuming other similar funds are doing better. Detailed records are also useful when preparing income tax returns. If Jessica wants to invest outside of her 401(k) plan in the same or other no-load funds, she can purchase funds directly from mutual fund investment companies, such as family fund companies like Fidelity, T. Rowe Price, or any other mutual fund, like Gabelli, Neuberger, or Calvert.

Use Portfolio Monitoring on the 'Net Monitoring a mutual fund portfolio is easy using any of the top-rated mutual fund websites cited earlier. For example, see Yahoo!'s portfolio manager capabilities at http://finance.yahoo.com/funds/monitoring_funds.

Check Fund Quotations in Newspapers You can check closing prices online any time on any of the financial websites cited earlier or read quotes in newspapers. See Figure 15.6 for an illustration. Newspapers' quotations for no-load mutual funds list the name of the fund followed by columns for its net asset value, net change from the previous day, and year-to-date percentage return. For example, within the group listing for Fidelity Investments mutual funds, the Balanced Fund (abbreviated as Balanc) has a net asset value (NAV) of $15.14, a change in the net asset value (NET CHG) of −$0.20 from the closing price of the previous trading day, and a year-to-date percentage return (YTD %RET) of 1.1 percent. In mutual funds, the NAV is also known as the **mutual fund bid price.** Shareholders receive this amount per share when they redeem their shares—that is, the company is willing to pay this amount to buy the shares back. Also, the NAV is the amount per share an investor will pay to purchase a fund, assuming it is a no-load fund. A no-load fund is indicated as such by the alphabetic letter n at the end of the fund's name.

mutual fund bid price Same as NAV (net asset value).

The **mutual fund ask price** (or **offer price**) is the price at which a mutual fund's share can be purchased by investors. It equals the current NAV per share plus sales charges, if any. If you wanted to buy or sell shares of Fidelity Balanced Fund, a no-load (note the superscript *n* in Figure 15.6) mutual fund, the price would be $15.14 per share. The funds listed without "n" are load funds. The SEC requires that appropriate footnotes appear in newspaper listings of mutual funds to indicate other expenses and charges.

mutual fund ask price Price at which an investor can purchase a mutual fund's shares; current NAV per share plus sales charges.

Fidelity Invest

A Mgr	15.83	−0.24	− 4.3	GovtInc	9.82	+0.02	+ 2.5
AggrGr r	22.68	−0.76	− 37.1	GroCo	55.13	−1.97	− 22.6
AggrInt	11.60	−0.15	− 12.8	GroInc	38.56	−0.69	− 7.9
AMgrAggr	11.73	−0.35	− 10.0	GroIncII	9.33	−0.18	− 8.7
AMgrGr	14.83	−0.29	− 6.8	HighInc r	8.81	−0.01	− 2.5
AMgrIn	11.38x	−0.11	− 0.4	Indepndnc	16.46	−0.60	− 25.0
Balanc	15.14	−0.20	+ 1.1	IntBd	10.16	+0.02	+ 4.4
BluCh	44.52	−1.34	− 13.6	IntGov	9.66	+0.02	+ 3.6
Canad r	19.30	−0.21	− 8.2	IntGr	19.31	−0.26	− 15.0
CapAp	21.53	−0.57	− 3.1	IntlBnd	7.83	+0.04	− 4.2
ChinaReg	13.61	−0.08	− 7.4	InvGB	7.20	+0.01	+ 3.7
CoInc r	7.35	−0.04	− 1.3	Japan r	11.86	−0.21	− 13.7
		−5.55	− 7.6	JpnSmCo r	7.64	−0.09	− 4.3
		−0.45	− 11.2	LargeCap	15.56	−0.41	− 12.3
		−0.28	− 5.2	LatinAm r	12.62	−0.13	− 3.4
		−0.29	− 0.5	LevCoSt	10.56	−0.15	+ 4.9
		−0.35	− 12.1	LowP r	26.61	−0.29	+ 15.1
		−0.29	− 5.2	MagIn	107.84	−2.46	− 8.9
		−0.39	− 11.2	MidCap	23.86	−0.49	− 8.1
		−0.68	− 3.9	MtgSec	10.78	+0.02	+ 3.5
		−0.15	− 11.7	NewMkt r	11.38	−0.04	+ 4.9
		−0.09	− 4.5	NewMill	27.27	−1.25	− 19.2
		−0.86	− 2.8	Nordic	19.60	−0.12	− 25.0
		−0.47	− 4.9	OTC	32.41	−1.42	− 21.0
		−0.21	− 18.8	Ovrse	29.16	−0.57	− 15.2
		−0.13	− 15.0	PcBas r	15.37	−0.27	− 11.1
		−4.03	− 8.2	Puritn	18.38	−0.19	− 0.9
		−0.33	− 1.2	RealE	19.49	−0.05	+ 8.3
		−1.02	− 7.6	STBF	8.74	+0.02	+ 4.4
		−0.06	− 10.3	SmallCap r	13.54	−0.20	+ 0.2
		−0.40	− 8.4	SmCapSlc	15.06	−0.25	− 7.2
GNMA	10.79	+0.01	+ 3.7	SE Asia r	10.68	−0.10	− 6.6
GloBal	15.90	−0.16	− 8.8	StratInc	9.13	+0.01	+ 3.2

NAME	NAV	NET CHG	YTD %RET
Fidelity Invest			
Balanc^{n}	15.14	− 0.20	+ 1.1
Contra	43.67	− 0.45	− 11.2
MidCap^{n}	23.86	− 0.49	− 8.1
MagIn	107.84	− 2.46	− 8.9

Figure 15.6
How Mutual Funds Are Quoted

> ✓ **CONCEPT CHECK 15.4**
>
> **1.** Tell why it is important to review your investment philosophy and goals when selecting mutual fund investments.
> **2.** Explain how you would eliminate funds inappropriate for your investment goals, given your situation and assuming you were working full time.

What Do You Recommend Now?

Now that you have read the chapter on mutual funds, what do you recommend to David and Sarah Gent in the case at the beginning of the chapter regarding:

1. Redeeming their certificates of deposit and investing their retirement money in mutual funds?

2. Investing in growth and income mutual funds instead of income funds?

3. Buying no-load rather than load funds?

4. Buying life-cycle mutual funds instead of balanced mutual funds?

5. Buying mutual funds through their employers' 401(k) retirement accounts?

Big Picture Summary of Learning Objectives

1 Describe the features, services, and advantages of investing in mutual funds.

A mutual fund is an investment company that pools funds obtained by selling shares to investors and makes investments to achieve the financial goal of income or growth, or both. The net asset value (NAV) is the per-share value of the fund. Advantages of mutual funds include diversification, affordability, and professional management. Unique services include ease of buying and selling, check writing, and effortless establishment of retirement plans.

2 Differentiate mutual funds by investment objectives, types, and characteristics.

A mutual fund with an income objective invests in securities that pay regular income in dividends or inter-est. A fund that has a growth objective seeks capital appreciation. A fund that has a combined growth and income objective seeks a balanced return made up of current income and capital gains. The name of a fund, such as aggressive growth fund, gives a clue to its objectives. Index funds and ETFs are popular because they earn the same return as a particular market index.

3 Summarize the fees and charges involved in buying and selling mutual funds.

Individuals who invest through mutual funds pay shareholder fees for specific transactions, such as purchases, redemptions, or exchanges. They also pay annual fund operating expenses that are deducted from fund assets before earnings are distributed to shareholders. Investors may be faced with load and no-load funds, 12b-1 fees, and deferred load and redemption fees.

4 **Establish strategies to evaluate and select mutual funds that meet your investment goals.**

The process of selecting mutual funds in which to invest is usually a do-it-yourself effort. The steps are (1) review investment philosophy, (2) review investment goals, (3) eliminate funds inappropriate for your investment goals, (4) choose low- or no-load funds, (5) decide whether investment advice is needed, (6) screen and compare funds that meet your investment criteria, and (7) monitor your mutual fund portfolio.

Let's Talk About It

1. Review the objectives of mutual funds and the characteristics of various funds. Based on your investment philosophy and risk tolerance, which one type of fund would be of most interest to you if you are saving to buy a home several years from now? Give reasons why.

2. Assume you graduated from college a few years ago, had a good job paying $55,000 annually, and wanted to invest $300 per month in mutual funds for retirement. Which combination of two or more mutual funds would you think appropriate? Give reasons for each of your selections.

3. Assume that your uncle gave you $50,000 to invest solely in mutual funds. Based on your point in the life cycle and your investment philosophy, identify your investment goals and explain how would you spread your money into different funds.

4. Identify the types of mutual funds that would be good choices to meet the following investment objectives: emergency fund, house down payment, college fund for 2-year-old child, and retirement fund for a 25-year-old. Give two reasons why each of your recommendations would be appropriate.

5. Which is a better choice for you, load or no-load mutual funds? Give some reasons.

Do the Numbers

1. Last January George Jetson, from Tarpon Springs, Florida, invested $1000 by buying 100 shares of the Can't Lose Mutual Fund, an aggressive growth no-load mutual fund. George reinvested his dividends all year. So far, the NAV for George's investment has risen from $10 per share to $13.25.

   (a) What is the percentage increase in the value of George's mutual fund?

   (b) If George redeemed his mutual fund investment for $13.25 per share, how much profit would he realize?

   (c) Assuming George pays income taxes at the 25 percent rate, how much income tax will he have to pay if he sells his shares?

   (d) Assuming George pays income taxes at the 25 percent rate, how much income tax will he have to pay if he chooses not to sell his shares but to remain invested?

2. Two years ago, Stephanie, from Pocatello, Idaho, invested $1000 by buying 125 shares ($8 per share NAV) in the Can't Lose Mutual Fund, an aggressive growth no-load mutual fund. Last year she made two additional investments of $500 each (50 shares at $10 and 40 shares at $12.50). Stephanie reinvested all of her dividends. So far, the NAV for her investment has risen from $8 per share to $13.25. Late in the year, she sold 60 shares at $13.25.

   (a) What were the proceeds from Stephanie's sale of the 60 shares?

   (b) To use the Internal Revenue Service's average-cost basis method of determining the average price paid for one share, begin by calculating the average price paid for the shares. In this instance, the $2000 is divided by 215 shares (125 shares + 50 shares + 40 shares). What was the average price paid by Stephanie?

   (c) To finally determine the average-cost basis of shares sold, you multiply the average price per share times the number of shares sold—in this case, 60. What is the total cost basis for Stephanie's 60 shares?

   (d) Assuming that Stephanie has to pay income taxes on the difference between the sales price for the 60 shares and their cost, how much is this difference?

   (e) If Stephanie's mutual fund transactions were conducted within an IRS-qualified tax-sheltered retirement account, what would her income tax liability be if she were paying income taxes at the 25 percent rate?

Financial Planning Cases

Case 1
Matching Mutual Fund Investments to Economic Projections

Glenn Sandler, a realtor for the past ten years in Kankakee, Illinois, is married and has two children. He is interested in investing in mutual funds. Glenn wants to put half of his $20,000 of accumulated savings into a stock mutual fund and then continue to invest $200 monthly for the foreseeable future, perhaps using the money for retirement starting in about 25 years. Glenn has limited his choices to the mutual funds listed in Table 15.4.

(a) Glenn wants to invest the full $10,000 now and diversify his holdings into two mutual funds. Which two funds listed in Table 15.4 do you recommend as investments for his $10,000? Why?

(b) Glenn also wants to invest $200 per month into one mutual fund over the next 25 years. Which of the funds listed in Table 15.4 would you recommend? Why?

Case 2
Selection of a Mutual Fund as Part of a Retirement Plan

Etta Mae Westbrook, a single mother of a six-year-old child, works in a marketing firm in Mishawaka, Indiana, and is willing to invest $2000 to $3000 per year in a mutual fund. She wants the investment income to supplement her retirement pension starting in approximately 20 years and she has a moderate investment philosophy. Advise Etta Mae by responding to the following questions:

(a) Should Etta Mae invest in a mutual fund with a growth objective or one with a growth and income objective? Why?

(b) Etta Mae wants to invest in a mutual fund that focuses on common stocks. Which two stock funds in Table 15.4 would you recommend that she avoid? Why?

(c) Explain your reasons for suggesting Etta Mae invest in a load fund or a no-load fund.

Case 3
Victor and Maria Invest for Retirement

Victor and Maria Hernandez plan to retire in less than 15 years. Their current investment portfolio is distributed as follows: 40 percent in growth mutual funds, 40 percent in corporate bonds and bond mutual funds, and 20 percent in cash equivalents. They have decided to increase the amount of risk in their portfolio by taking 10 percent from their cash equivalent investments and investing in some mutual funds with strong growth possibilities.

(a) Of the mutual funds listed in Table 15.4, which two would you recommend to meet the Hernandezes' goals? Why?

(b) If those two investments perform over the next decade as well as they did in the past five years,

would you recommend that the Hernandezes remain invested in those two funds during their retirement years? Why or why not?

Case 4
The Johnsons Decide to Invest Through Mutual Funds

After learning about mutual funds, the Johnsons are confident that they are a great way to invest, especially because of the diversification and professional management that funds offer. The couple has a financial nest egg of $9500 to invest through mutual funds. They also want to invest another $300 per month on a regular basis.

Although not yet completely firm, Harry and Belinda's goals at this point are as follows:
- They want to continue to build for retirement income.
- They will need about $10,000 in six to eight years to use as supplemental income if Belinda has a baby and does not work for six months.
- They might buy a superexpensive luxury automobile requiring a $10,000 down payment if they decide not to have a child.

Knowing that the Johnsons have a moderate investment philosophy, that they live on a reasonable budget, and that they have a well-established cash-management plan, advise them on their mutual fund investments by responding to the following questions:

(a) After looking at Table 15.4, which two types of funds would you recommend to meet the Johnsons' goals? Why?

(b) How would you divide the $9500 between the two types of funds? Why?

(c) How much of the $300 monthly investment amount would you allocate to each type of fund? Why?

(d) Some comparable mutual fund performance data on stock funds are shown in Table 15.4. Using only that information and assuming that you are recommending some funds for the Johnsons' retirement needs, which three funds would you recommend? Why?

(e) Assume that all three funds have above-average performance over the next ten years. A bear market then occurs, causing the NAVs to drop 25 percent from the previous year. Would you recommend that the Johnsons sell their accumulated shares in the funds? Why or why not?

(f) Determine the value of their $9500 investment in ten years, assuming that the three funds' NAVs increase 13 percent annually for the next ten years. (Use the *Garman/Forgue* website.)

On the 'Net

Go to the Web pages indicated to complete these exercises. You can also go to the *Garman/Forgue* website at college .hmco.com/business/students for an expanded list of exercises. Under General Business, select the title of this text. Click on the Internet Exercises link for this chapter.

1. Visit the website for Vanguard Investments and visit its education section at https://flagship.vanguard.com/ VGApp/hnw/planningeducation/education. Compare the information provided in the "Mutual fund basics" section with the information in this text chapter. Develop a list of ten key points that every beginning investor in mutual funds should know. Also list four advantages that investing in stock mutual funds provides as opposed to direct purchase of stock.

2. Visit the website for CNNMoney. On its "Mutual Fund" page at http://money.cnn.com/pf/funds/index .html, access its "Fund winners and fund losers" section to review the best- and worst-performing funds over the past three months, past one year, and past five years. What differences do you detect in the lists? What might this information tell you about the approach that might be taken by investors with longer time horizons?

3. Visit the website for the Financial Industry Regulatory Authority (FINRA) at www.investopedia.com/terms /f/finra.asp, where you will find an "expense analyzer" for comparing the expenses of mutual funds. Compare the expenses for three of the funds identified as examples in this chapter.

Visit the Garman/Forgue website

@college.hmco.com/business/students

Under General Business, select *Personal Finance 9e*. There, among other valuable resources, you will find a complete glossary, ACE questions, links to help you complete the chapter exercises, and links to other personal finance sites.

CHAPTER 16

Real Estate and High-Risk Investments

You Must Be Kidding, Right?

Friends Richard Belisle and Nicholas Stevenson both have aggressive investment philosophies. Richard invests primarily in residential real estate, and Nicholas invests in commodities futures contracts. As longtime investors, they consider themselves experts, but occasionally each has experienced financial losses. What are the odds that the typical investor will make money investing in commodities futures contracts?

A. 50%

B. 30%

C. 20%

D. 10%

The answer is D. Ninety percent of individual investors in futures contracts lose money. Funds used for these investments should be only those that one can afford to lose!

LEARNING OBJECTIVES

After reading this chapter, you should be able to:

1 **Demonstrate** how you can make money investing in real estate.

2 **Calculate** the right price to pay for real estate and how to finance your purchase.

3 **Assess** the disadvantages of investing in real estate.

4 **Summarize** the risks and challenges of investing in collectibles, precious metals, and gems.

5 **Explain** why options and futures are high-risk investments.

What Do You Recommend?

Jamie Day, a 37-year-old marketing manager for a large corporation in Long Beach, California, earns $110,000 per year. She saves about $1800 each month beyond her contributions to her employer's 401(k) retirement plan. To date, Jamie has been investing her 401(k) plan money primarily in aggressive stock mutual funds and the remainder in her employer's company stock. She has found excellent success investing in the mutual funds within the plan, and her investments have grown at a healthy pace through the years. Her total 401(k) holdings are worth $260,000.

Ever since her grandfather gave her some stocks as a child, Jamie has loved investing—and she has enjoyed a good track record with her efforts. Jamie is an active trader, often trading every three or four weeks, primarily in the oil, technology, and prescription drug industries. Every year she has some losses as well as gains. Her private portfolio is currently worth $160,000. Jamie has never bought or sold options or futures contracts, but her stockbroker suggested that she consider them. Jamie also has a friend who owns several residential rental properties who has asked her to consider investing as her partner in her next real estate venture.

What would you recommend to Jamie on the subject of real estate and high-risk investments regarding:

1. Investing in real estate?

2. Putting some of her money in a high-risk investment, like collectibles?

3. Investing in options and futures contracts?

FOR HELP with studying this chapter, visit the Online Student Center:

www.college.hmco.com/pic/garman9e

461

A home tends to accomplish more than just putting a roof over your head. It is also an investment because housing values increase over the long term. But real estate investing is not the same as buying a home in which to live. Investing in real estate can provide you extra income now and give a boost to your future retirement plans. But to do so you have to do a lot of things right. Real estate is not rocket science, but investors must know a lot about taxes, financing, insurance, community economics, and dealing with difficult tenants. Real estate investments are complex, and they are much riskier than investing in mutual funds and stocks.

You also might consider owning tangible assets such as collectibles, precious metals, and gems for their investment potential. Or you may be attracted to options and futures contracts investments. All these are referred to as **high-risk (or speculative) investments** because they have the potential for significant fluctuations in return, sometimes over short time periods. They are suitable only for investors with a moderate-to-aggressive investment philosophy.

high-risk/speculative investments
Present potential for significant fluctuations in return, sometimes over short time periods.

Making Money Investing in Real Estate

1   **LEARNING OBJECTIVE**
Demonstrate how you can make money investing in real estate.

real estate Property consisting of land, all structures permanently attached to that land, and accompanying rights and privileges, such as crops and mineral rights.

"Anyone can get rich investing in real estate." This may be true, but it may not be the whole truth. It sounds too easy when successful real estate investors tell their stories: "My rental properties freed me from having a full-time job." "I have more income now than when I was in the rat race working." "I fixed up and sold three homes and now I own seven." "I can pay off all my mortgages in 13 years and never lift a finger again."

Real estate is property consisting of land, all structures permanently attached to that land, and accompanying rights and privileges, such as crops and mineral rights. A real estate investment is termed **direct ownership** when an investor holds actual legal title to the property. For example, you can invest directly as an individual or jointly with other investors to buy properties designed for residential living, such as houses, duplexes, apartments, mobile homes, and condominiums. You also could invest in commercial properties designed for business uses, such as office buildings, medical centers, gasoline stations, and motels. You might buy raw land or residential lots, although they are extremely risky.

Good Money Habits in Real Estate and High-Risk Investments

Make the following your money habits when investing in real estate and high-risk investments:

1. Consider the disadvantages before investing in real estate.

2. Invest only in real estate properties that have a positive cash flow.

3. Finance real estate investments with conventional mortgages, not mortgages with adjustable interest terms.

4. Use the discounted cash-flow method to help determine the right price to pay.

5. If you put money into high-risk assets, limit your investment to no more than 10 percent of your portfolio.

Current Income and Capital Gains

Following are two key questions for real estate investors:
- Can you make current income while you own?
- Can you profit with capital gains when you sell the property?

The most important consideration for real estate investors is whether the rental income will be sufficient to make a profit. If you invest in a property and you are paying out more than the rental income coming in, you face three risks: (1) whether you can afford to continue paying out that money every month, (2) whether the price on the property will increase, and (3) whether the property actually will sell for more than what you paid for it.

To measure the current income in a real estate market, investors can begin by using the **price-to-rent ratio.** This numerical relationship might range from 11 to 26 depending upon local market conditions—meaning how high housing prices are. The larger the number, the less likely the investor can make money. In San Diego, California, a condominium renting for $1500 a month might sell for the sky-high price of $390,000 for a ratio of 21.7 ($12 \times \$1500 = \$18,000$; $\$390,000 \div \$18,000 = 21.7$), while a similar one in Dallas, Texas, might cost only $165,000 for a ratio of 9.17

$(12 \times \$1500 = \$18,000; \$165,000 \div \$18,000 = 9.17)$. Buying property with a high ratio will provide a profit only with a future increase in the value of the property.

Investors also calculate the rental yield on properties. This is a computation of how much income the investor might pocket from rent each year before mortgage payments as a percentage of the purchase price. Most properties yield about 4 percent of income annually, although the rental yield may be as little as 1 or 2 percent and as high as 8 or 9 percent. Less expensive properties often offer higher yields. The formula assumes half of rental income goes for expenses (other than debt repayment).

rental yield A computation of how much income the investor might pocket from rent each year (before mortgage payments) as a percentage of the purchase price; divide the annual rent by 2 and then divide by the purchase price.

$$\text{Rental yield} = \frac{(\text{rent} \div 2)}{\text{purchase price}} \qquad (16.1)$$

	Example A	Example B
Purchase price	$500,000	$150,000
Annual rent	36,000	26,000
Yield	3.6%	8.67%

Current Income Results from Positive Cash Flow

In real estate investing, current income takes the form of positive cash flow. For an income-producing real estate investment, you pay operating expenses out of rental income. If the property has a mortgage (a common occurrence), payments toward the mortgage principal and interest also must be made out of rental income. Operating expenses such as vacancies, taxes, mortgage payments, and repairs may eat up half of rental income.

The amount of rental income you have left after paying all operating expenses is called **cash flow.** The amount of cash flow—obtained by subtracting any cash outlays from the cash income—depends on the amount of rent received, the amount of expenses paid, and the amount necessary to repay the mortgage debt. Investors usually prefer a positive cash flow to a negative cash flow because any shortages represent out-of-pocket expenses for the investor.

cash flow Amount of rental income you have left after paying all operating expenses.

Many real estate investments will not generate a positive cash flow, even though they may offer the likelihood of high potential returns through price appreciation. Investors might manage a negative cash flow for a few years while waiting for capital gains to later materialize when selling the property.

Price Appreciation Leads to Capital Gains

The capital gain earned in a real estate investment comes from **price appreciation.** It is the amount above ownership costs for which an investment is sold. In real estate, ownership costs include the original purchase price as well as expenditures for any capital improvements made to a property prior to sale. **Capital improvements** are costs incurred in making changes in real property, beyond maintenance and repairs, that add to its value. Paneling a living room, adding a new roof, and putting up a fence represent capital improvements. **Repairs** are expenses (usually tax deductible against an investor's cash-flow income) necessary to maintain the value of the property. Repainting, mending roof leaks, and fixing plumbing are examples of repairs.

capital improvements Costs incurred in making value-enhancing changes (beyond maintenance and repair) in real property.

repairs Usually tax-deductible expenses necessary to maintain property value.

As an example, assume that Andrew Webb, an unmarried schoolteacher from Fayetteville, Arkansas, bought a small rental house as an investment five years ago for $120,000 in cash that he received as an inheritance. He fixed some roof leaks (repairs) for $1000 and then added a new shed and some kitchen cabinets (capital improvements) at a cost of $10,000 before selling the property this year for $160,000. As a

Did You Know?...

What to Do Before Investing in Real Estate

1. Set up a limited liability corporation to own your real estate investments as it protects your personal assets in case someone injured on your rental property sues you.

2. Hire an accountant experienced in real estate investing.

3. Line up financing options before searching for properties.

4. Hire an inspector to inspect the physical condition of the property.

5. Hire a licensed contractor for plumbing, electrical, and expensive repair jobs rather than doing them yourself.

6. Consider hiring a management company to tend to your property; the cost is 5 to 10 percent of rental income.

7. Set aside $5000 as a contingency fund for unanticipated property problems.

8. Consider investing in properties only in locales where there are thriving businesses located near good schools, supermarkets, and public transportation.

result, Andrew happily realized a capital gain of $30,000 ($160,000 minus the $120,000 purchase price minus $10,000 in capital improvements).

Residential real estate values can generally be expected to increase 3 percent annually, about the rate of inflation, or a little above. In some markets, prices might jump 10 percent or more in one year and perhaps continue rising for two or three more years. Prices can decline, too, as even in hot regional real estate markets prices in individual neighborhoods may decline. Prices can drop 10 or 20 percent in one year. In markets in which real estate is hard to sell (too many properties on the market and too few buyers), perhaps because of job losses in a slow regional economy, residential housing prices might decline 2 or 3 percent annually for a long time.

If you cannot forecast the future of what you invest in, such as price appreciation on a property in a local housing market, you are speculating. Using a mortgage loan invites more risk. While price appreciation is where the big profits are in real estate investing, you can reduce risk by investing in property for which the expected rental income exceeds projected mortgage payments, property taxes, and maintenance costs.

Leverage Can Increase an Investor's Return

As we noted in Chapter 13, **leverage** involves using borrowed funds to make an investment with the goal of earning a rate of return in excess of the after-tax costs of borrowing. Lenders allow investors to borrow from 75 to 95 percent of the price of a property.

Suppose that Andrew, instead of paying cash for the house, had made a down payment of $25,000 and borrowed the remainder. What effect would this borrowing have on his return? In the first instance, Andrew paid $120,000 cash for the property and earned a 25 percent return on his investment ($30,000 ÷ $120,000) over the five-year period, or roughly 5 percent per year. In the second situation, using leverage, he would have an apparent return of 120 percent ($30,000 ÷ $25,000), or roughly 24 percent per year. The true return would be lower because of mortgage payments, interest expenses, property taxes, and repairs but would still be a double-digit return.

The **loan-to-value ratio** measures the amount of leverage in a real estate investment project. It is calculated by dividing the amount of debt by the value of the total

loan-to-value ratio Measures the amount of leverage in a real estate investment project by dividing the total amount of debt by the market price of the investment.

original investment. For example, because his down payment was $25,000 on the $120,000 property, Andrew had a loan-to-value ratio of 79 percent ($95,000 ÷ $120,000), or 79 percent leverage.

Beneficial Tax Treatments

The U.S. Congress, through provisions in the Internal Revenue Code, encourages real estate investments by giving investors five special tax treatments. The first three may increase the real estate investor's income while the last two may enhance capital gains.

1. Depreciation Is Tax Deductible Investors in real estate become successful by understanding the "numbers" of real estate investing. For example, assume that Jisue Han, a lawyer from Huntsville, Alabama, invested $200,000 in a residential building ($170,000) and land ($30,000). She rents the property to a tenant for $24,000 per year. You might think that Jisue has to pay income taxes on the entire $24,000 in rental income. Wrong. IRS regulations allow taxpayers to deduct depreciation from rental income. **Depreciation** represents the decline in value of an asset over time due to normal wear and tear and obsolescence. A proportionate amount of a capital asset representing depreciation may be deducted against income each year over the asset's estimated life. Land cannot be depreciated.

Jisue can deduct an equal part of the building's cost over the estimated life of the property. IRS guidelines provide that residential properties may be depreciated over 27.5 years while nonresidential properties are allowed 39 years. Jisue calculates (from Table 16.1) the amount she can annually deduct from income to be $6182 ($170,000 ÷ 27.5). Table 16.1 shows the effects of depreciation on her income taxes, assuming Jisue pays income taxes at a combined federal and state rate of 36 percent. In this example, the depreciation deduction lowers taxable income on the property from $24,000 to $17,818 ($24,000 − $6182) and increases the return on the investment to 8.79 percent.

2. Interest Is Tax Deductible Real estate investors incur many business expenses in attempting to earn a profit: interest on a mortgage, real estate taxes, insurance, utilities, capital improvements, and repairs. The largest of these costs often is the interest expense, as properties are often purchased with a mortgage loan. Table 16.2 illustrates the effect of interest expenses on income taxes. Assume Jisue borrowed $175,000 to purchase her $200,000 property. After deducting annual depreciation of $6182 and interest expenses of $13,050, her taxable income is reduced to $4768. Because her income tax liability is only $1716, Jisue's after-tax return of $9234 yields 36.94 percent on her leveraged investment.

Did You Know?...

Top 3 Financial Missteps in Real Estate and High-Risk Investment Investing

People slip up in real estate and high-risk investment when they do the following:

1. Failing to factor in income lost due to vacancies and collection costs for tenants who do not pay

2. Not setting enough money aside for maintenance, repairs, unanticipated capital improvements, and rising real estate taxes

3. Assuming that real estate prices will go up and interest rates will not increase

depreciation Decline in value of an asset over time due to normal wear and tear and obsolescence.

Table 16.1 Effect of Depreciation on Income Taxes and Return

			Without Depreciation	With Depreciation
Total amount invested	$200,000	Gross rental income	$24,000	$24,000
Cost of land	− 30,000	Less annual depreciation expense	0	6,182
Cost of rental building	$170,000	Taxable income	24,000	17,818
Depreciation for 27.5 years	$ 6,182	Income taxes (36 percent combined federal and state tax rate)	8,640	6,414
		After-tax return	$15,360	$17,586
		After-tax yield (divide return by $200,000)	7.68%	8.79%

Table 16.2 Additional Effect of Interest Paid on Income Taxes on Return

Gross rental income	$24,000
Less annual depreciation deduction	− 6,182
Subtotal	$17,818
Less interest expense for the year (7.5 percent mortgage loan)	− 13,050
Taxable income	$ 4,768
Cash flow after paying interest ($24,000 − $13,050)	10,950
Less income tax liability (0.36 × $4,768)	− 1,716
After-tax return ($10,950 − $1,716)	$ 9,234
After-tax yield [$9,234 ÷ ($200,000 − $175,000)]	36.94%

Tax laws permit investors to deduct interest expenses (with the amount of the deduction allowed depending on the investor's marginal tax bracket). The interest deduction gives Jisue a cash flow after paying mortgage interest of $10,950 ($24,000 − $13,050). In essence, the $13,050 in interest is paid with $4698 ($13,050 × 36 percent combined federal and state income tax rate) of the money that was not sent to the federal and state governments and $8352 ($13,050 − $4698) of Jisue's money.

3. Rental Income Tax Regulations on Vacation Homes

If you rent out your vacation property for 14 or fewer days during the year, you can pocket the income tax-free, regardless of how much you charge. The IRS does not want to hear about this gain. The home is considered a personal residence, so you can deduct mortgage interest and property taxes just as you would for your principal residence.

Renting a vacation home for more than 14 days turns the endeavor into a business, and you must report all rental income. You also can deduct rental expenses up to the level of rental income you report. When your adjusted gross income (AGI) is less than $100,000, a maximum of $25,000 of rental-related losses may be deducted each year to offset income from *any* source, including your salary. The $25,000 limit is gradually phased out as your AGI moves between $100,000 and $150,000. This ability to shelter income from taxes represents a terrific benefit for people who invest in real estate on a small scale.

4. Capital Gains Are Taxed at Reduced Rates

Capital gains on real estate are realized through price appreciation. For most taxpayers, long-term capital gains are taxed at a rate of 15 percent, and taxpayers in the 10 to 15 percent tax brackets pay a long-term capital gains tax of 5 percent. (See Chapter 4.)

5. Tax-Free Exchanges

Another special tax treatment results when a real estate investor trades equity in one property for equity in a similar property. If none of the people involved in the trade receives any other form of property or money, the transaction is considered a **tax-free exchange.** If one person receives some money or other property, only that person has to report the extra proceeds as a taxable gain. For example, assume you bought a residential rental property five years ago for $220,000 and today it is worth much more money. You trade it with your friend by giving $10,000 in cash for your friend's $280,000 single-family rental home. Your friend needs to report only the $10,000 as income this year. In contrast, you do not need to report your long-term gain, $50,000 ($280,000 − $10,000 − $220,000), until you actually sell the new property.

tax-free exchange Arises when a real estate investor trades equity in one property for equity in a similar property and no other forms of property or money change hands.

Did You Know?...

About Real Estate Seminars

Infomercials and Internet ads tout the money to be make after attending seminars with names such as the Enlightened Millionaire Institute, The Real Estate Goddess, Carlton Sheets, and Ron LeGrand. Inspirational! Spiritual! Motivating! Practical! The seminars offer advice on marketing and deal making and sell participants books, tapes, additional seminars, and personal mentoring for thousands of dollars more.

Beginner real estate entrepreneurs are encouraged to pursue "no money down" and "little money down" schemes to make a quick fortune buying and selling real estate. The basic idea is to buy "distressed properties" at no more than 70 percent of their value from motivated sellers (such as after a death, divorce, foreclosure notice, or bankruptcy) by persuading them to do what may not be in their best interest.

Those sitting in weekend-long real estate seminars at a hotel meeting room with 400 people or a convention center with thousands of other novices (read that as "suckers") listening to get-rich gurus can cost each attendee big bucks, $599 to $5000. Real estate investing is very competitive, as investors may own one in four homes in a community.

If real estate seminars lead to novices making great profits, why aren't all local real estate agents rich? And retired in Hawaii? Seminar promoters are the ones who are making money off these schemes. For a critique of the real estate seminar industry, see John T. Reed's views (http://www.johntreed.com/Reedgururating.html) and the Australian Securities and Exchange Commission (http://www.asic.gov.au/fido/fido.nsf/byheadline/ Investment+seminars+homepage?openDocument).

CONCEPT CHECK 16.1

1. What are the two key questions for real estate investors?

2. Distinguish between the price-to-rent ratio and the rental yield as measures of current income.

3. Give an example of how leverage can increase an investor's yield in real estate.

4. Explain how two beneficial tax treatments are helpful to real estate investors.

> **discounted cash-flow method** Effective way to estimate the value or asking price of a real estate investment based on after-tax cash flow and the return on the invested dollars discounted over time to reflect a discounted yield.

Pricing and Financing Real Estate Investments

Sure ways to go wrong in a real estate investment are to pay too much for the property and finance it incorrectly.

2 LEARNING OBJECTIVE
Calculate the right price to pay for real estate and how to finance your purchase.

Pay the Right Price

The **discounted cash-flow method** is an effective way to estimate the value or asking price of a real estate investment. It emphasizes after-tax cash flow and the return on the invested dollars discounted over time to reflect a discounted yield. Software programs are available to calculate the discounted cash flows. You also can use Appendix Table A.2, as illustrated in Table 16.3.

Prices typically decline as the inventory of houses for sale goes up.

Table 16.3　Discounted Cash-Flow to Estimate Price

	After-Tax Cash Flow	Present Value of $1 at 10 Percent*	Present Value of After-Tax Cash Flow
1 year	$ 4,000	0.909	$ 3,636
2 years	4,200	0.826	3,469
3 years	4,400	0.751	3,304
4 years	4,600	0.683	3,142
5 years	4,800	0.621	2,981
Sell property	$265,000	0.621	164,565
Present value of property			$181,097

*From Appendix Table A.2.

Instant Message

Find Information on Home Prices

To find prices on homes where you live, check out www.realtor.org and http://www.huduser.org/.

To see how this method works, assume that you require an after-tax rate of return of 10 percent on a condominium advertised for sale at $200,000. You estimate that rents can be increased each year for five years. After all expenses are paid, you expect to have after-tax cash flows of $4000, $4200, $4400, $4600, and $4800 for the five years. Assuming some price appreciation, you anticipate selling the property for $265,000 after all expenses are incurred. How much should you pay now to buy the property?

Table 16.3 explains how to answer this question. Multiply the estimated after-tax cash flows and the expected proceeds of $265,000 to be realized on the sale of the property by the present value of a dollar at 10 percent (the required rate of return). Add the present values together to obtain the total present value of the property—in this case, $181,097. The asking price of $200,000 is too high for you to earn an after-tax return of 10 percent. Your choices are to negotiate the price down, accept a return of less than 10 percent, hope that the sale price of the property will be higher than

$265,000 five years from now, or consider another investment. The discounted cash-flow method provides an effective way to estimate real estate values because it takes into account the selling price of the property, the effect of income taxes, and the time value of money.

Financing a Real Estate Investment

Borrowing to finance a real estate investment is more expensive than borrowing to buy one's own home, often 0.5 to 1.5 percent percentage points above the rate for customary homebuyers. There is more risk because the investor does not live in the property. The minimum down payment for investors is often 20 or 25 percent. Most investors finance real estate investments with conventional fixed-rate, fixed-term mortgage loans.

To make a smaller down payment and get a lower mortgage rate, some real estate investors buy a home, live in it for a year, and then rent it out as an investment. Another way to finance a real estate investment is through **seller financing** (or **owner financing**). This occurs when a seller is willing to self-finance a loan by accepting a promissory note from the buyer who makes monthly mortgage payments. No lending agency is involved. Investing buyers pay higher interest rates for seller financing. The seller may accept little or no down payment in exchange for an even higher interest rate, perhaps 1½ to 2½ percent above conventional mortgage rates. Owner-financed deals can be transacted very quickly.

A popular way to start in real estate investing is to purchase **sweat equity property.** With this approach, you seek a property that needs repairs but has good underlying value. You buy this fixer-upper at a favorable price and "sweat" by spending many hours cleaning, painting, and repairing it to rent or sell at a profit.

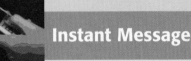

Instant Message

Own Real Estate Indirectly

In an indirect investment in real estate, a trustee, not the investor, holds actual legal title to the property. Examples are real estate syndicates, limited partnerships, and **real estate investment trusts (REITs),** which we discussed in Chapter 15. REITs typically specialize in a segment of the real estate market, such as shopping centers, apartment buildings, or medical offices. Investors can obtain information on these alternatives from brokerage firms.

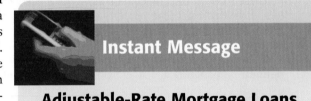

Instant Message

Adjustable-Rate Mortgage Loans Are Risky

It is risky to buy real estate by financing it with an adjustable-rate mortgage loan (see Chapter 9). When rates begin to rise—and they eventually will—the higher rates mean the investor is forced to write bigger and bigger monthly checks to the lender.

✓ CONCEPT CHECK 16.2

1. Summarize how the discounted cash-flow method helps determine the right price to pay for a real estate investment.

2. List three ways to finance a real estate investment, and tell why a conventional mortgage might be safer than another financing method.

seller financing/owner financing
When seller self-finances a buyer's loan by accepting a promissory note from buyer, who makes monthly mortgage payments at a slightly higher rate.

Disadvantages of Real Estate Investing

Real estate investing can be very profitable. But it does have some significant disadvantages.

- **Business risk.** It is quite possible to lose money in real estate investments. A local recession can depress prices. Zoning changes can slash housing values. Some property values simply decline, and so do rents. Rents will not keep up with costs in communities in which industries and jobs are moving elsewhere or in deteriorating neighborhoods.
- **Complexity.** Real estate investments require much more investigation than do most other investments. Numerous assumptions about financial details in the future also must be made.

3 LEARNING OBJECTIVE
Assess the disadvantages of investing in real estate.

Did You Know?...

Timesharing Is Not an Investment

Timesharing is the joint ownership or lease of vacation property through which the principals occupy the property individually for set periods of time. Timesharing is not an investment, although it is promoted as a way to simultaneously invest and obtain vacation housing. For $5000 to $20,000, buyers can purchase one or more weeks' use of luxury vacation housing furnished right down to the salt-and-pepper shakers. Timeshare owners pay an annual maintenance fee of perhaps $100 to $300 for each week of ownership.

With **deeded timesharing,** the buyer obtains a legal title or deed to limited time periods of use of real estate. Purchasers become secured creditors who are guaranteed continued use of the property throughout any bankruptcy proceedings. They also really own their week (or two) of the property.

Most timeshares are sold without a deed. **Non-deeded timesharing** is a legal right-to-use purchase of a limited, preplanned timesharing period of use of a property. It is a long-term lease, license, or club membership permitting use of a hotel suite, condominium, or other accommodation, and the right to use expires in 20 to 25 years. It does not grant legal real estate ownership interest to the purchaser. If the true owner of the property—the developer—goes bankrupt, problems abound. Creditors can lock out the timeshare purchasers (technically they are tenants) from the premises.

It is very hard to sell a timeshare. A survey from the Resort Property Owners Association says that the average timeshare unit languishes on the market for 4.4 years before being sold. At any point in time, 60 percent of all timeshares are up for sale. Timeshare sellers rarely receive more than 50 percent of their original investment in the sale. If you are interested in such property for vacation purposes, buy a deeded timeshare. Timeshare commissions are 25 percent of the price.

- **Large initial investment.** Direct investment in real estate generally requires many thousands of dollars, often with an initial outlay of $15,000, $30,000, or $50,000.
- **Lack of diversification.** So much capital is required in real estate investing that spreading risk is almost impossible.
- **Dealing with tenants.** Someone has to screen rental applicants for their credit histories, criminal records, work references, and experience with previous landlords. State laws may make it impossible to evict a deadbeat tenant for several months. Picking the wrong tenants can quickly turn a real estate property into a financial loss.
- **Time-consuming management demands.** Managing a real estate investment requires time for conducting regular inspections of the property, dealing with insurance companies, making repairs, and collecting overdue rents.
- **Low current income.** Expenses may reduce the cash-flow return to less than 2 percent or even generate a net loss in a given year.
- **Unpredictable costs.** Estimating costs is problematic. Investors cannot control increasing real estate tax assessments or when a central air-conditioning unit might break down.
- **Interest rate risk.** As we noted in Chapter 13, when interest rates rise, fewer people can afford to buy homes, and this puts downward pressure on prices and rents.
- **Legal fees.** The services of a real estate attorney will be needed to help handle the real estate purchase, sale, building inspections, zoning issues, tenant problems, insurance disputes, and any liability issues.
- **Illiquidity.** Real estate is expensive, and the market for investment property is much smaller than the securities market. As a result, it is common to experience trouble in selling. It may take months or even a year or more to find a buyer, arrange the financing, and close the sale of a real estate investment.

- **High transfer costs.** Substantial transfer costs, often representing 6 to 7 percent of the property's sale price, plus money for fix-up costs, may be incurred when real estate is bought or sold.

✓ CONCEPT CHECK 16.3

1. Summarize why illiquidity, transfer costs, and unpredictable costs are disadvantages in real estate investing.

2. Do you think you could successfully deal with tenants and the time-consuming management demands required in real estate investing? Why or why not?

Investing in Collectibles, Precious Metals, and Gems

Investors usually think of assets as something they would like to own for the long term. When investing in collectibles, precious metals, and gems, the investor owns illiquid real assets, not intangible items represented by pieces of paper. While an asset may be bought for its long-term investment potential, a profit might be earned in the short term. A speculator buys in the hope that someone else will pay more for an asset in the not-too-distant future. Speculators often buy or sell in expectation of profiting from market fluctuations. If you put money into these illiquid assets, limit such speculative investing to no more than 10 percent of your portfolio.

4 LEARNING OBJECTIVE
Summarize the risks and challenges of investing in collectibles, precious metals, and gems.

Collectibles

Collectibles are cultural artifacts that have value because of their beauty, age, scarcity, or popularity. They include baseball cards, posters, sports memorabilia, guns, photographs, paintings, ceramics, comic books, watches, lunchboxes, matchbooks, glassware, spoons, stamps, rare coins, art, rugs, cars, and antiques. The collectible markets are fueled by nostalgia, limited availability, and "what is hot to own today."

collectibles Cultural artifacts that have value because of their beauty, age, scarcity, or popularity, such as antiques, stamps, rare coins, art, baseball cards, and so on.

Making a Profit on Collectibles Is Not Easy
A key to success in collectibles is to invest in quality—the higher the better. Although buying collectibles can be fun and easy, turning a profit may not. The only return on collectibles occurs through price appreciation, and you must sell to realize a profit. That could be hard for you to do if the collectibles give you pleasure.

Items that are almost certain to lose value include those that are mass-produced and marketed as collectibles or limited editions. Another risk is the wholesale-to-retail price spread. Prices on collectibles vary greatly from item to item and year to year. Markets are fickle. If the investor needs to convert the asset to cash, a sale may take days, weeks, or months, and the seller may be forced to accept a lower price. The collectibles industry is rife with forgeries, scams, and frauds, particularly in sports memorabilia.

Buying and Selling Collectibles on the 'Net
You can buy collectibles on the Internet, using eBay for example, purchasing in minutes what you might never have found after searching for years in magazines, junk shops, flea markets, and auctions. Buying collectibles on the Internet is efficient and convenient, and it is easy to compare products and prices. It's hard to inspect them before purchase, however. Search Google for "collectibles." This is a very risky way to invest!

Did You Know?...

The Tax Consequences of an Income-Producing Real Estate Investment

When you are considering a real estate investment, you use the investment amount (purchase price or down payment) to begin the process of estimating the likely rate of return. This calculation may then be compared with other investment alternatives. Because some of the many assumptions in real estate calculations could be incorrect, caution is warranted in real estate analyses.

The following table shows five-year estimates for a hypothetical residential property in Bozeman, Montana, with a purchase price of $200,000. The building will be purchased with a $150,000 mortgage loan, so the buyer has to make a $50,000 down payment plus pay $8000 in closing costs. The gross rental income of $18,000 annually is projected to rise at an annual rate of 5 percent, vacancies and unpaid rent at 10 percent, real

estate taxes at 7 percent, insurance at 8 percent, and maintenance at 10 percent. Virtually the entire payment for the 30-year, $150,000, 8 percent, fixed-rate mortgage loan is assumed to be interest during these early years. For income tax purposes, the land is valued at $20,000, and the building is depreciated over 27.5 years. The amount of annual straight-line depreciation is calculated to be $6546 ($200,000 − $20,000 = $180,000; $180,000 ÷ 27.5 = $6546).

Note (in line D) how challenging it is to earn current income from rental properties. During the first year, the total cash-flow loss is projected to be $2808. However, because the income tax laws permit depreciation (line E, $6546) to be recorded as a real estate investment expense,

Estimates for a Successful Real Estate Investment

	Year				
	1	2	3	4	5
A. Gross rental income	$ 18,000	$18,900	$ 19,845	$ 20,837	$ 21,879
Less vacancies and unpaid rent	1,800	1,890	1,985	2,084	2,188
B. Projected gross income	$ 16,200	$17,010	$ 17,860	$ 18,753	$ 19,691
C. Less operating expenses					
Principal and Interest (P + I)	$ 13,208	$13,208	$ 13,208	$ 13,208	$ 13,208
Real estate taxes (T)	2,600	2,782	2,977	3,185	3,408
Insurance (I)	800	864	933	1,008	1,089
Maintenance	2,400	2,640	2,904	3,194	3,513
Total operating expenses	$ 19,008	$ 19,494	$ 20,022	$ 20,595	$ 21,218
D. Total cash flow (negative)	$(2,808)	$(2,484)	$(2,162)	$(1,842)	$(1,527)
E. Less depreciation expense	6,546	6,546	6,546	6,546	6,546
F. Taxable income (or loss) (D − E)	$(9,354)	$(9,030)	$(8,708)	$(8,388)	$(8,073)
G. Annual tax savings (30 percent marginal rate)	2,806	2,709	2,612	2,516	2,422
H. Net cash-flow gain (or loss) after taxes (G − D)	$ (2)	$ 225	$ 450	$ 674	$ 895

even though it is not an out-of-pocket cost, the total taxable loss (line F) is projected to be $9354. This loss can be deducted on the investor's income tax returns. Because the investor pays a 30 percent combined federal and state income tax rate, the loss results in a first-year annual tax savings of $2806. Therefore, instead of sending the $2806 to the government in taxes, the investor can use that amount to help pay the operating expenses of the investment. Consequently, the net cash-flow income (line D) of $2808 is reduced by tax savings (line G) of $2806 to result in a net cash-flow gain after taxes of $2 ($2808 − $2806).

Assume that the property appreciates in value at an annual rate of 6 percent and will be worth $267,645 (line K) in five years ($200,000 × 1.06 × 1.06 × 1.06 × 1.06 × 1.06). If it is sold at this price, a 6 percent real estate sales commission of $16,059 ($267,645 × 0.06) would reduce the net proceeds to $251,586 ($267,645 − $16,059).

Now we can calculate the **crude annual rate of return** on the property, as shown in the second table. A crude rate of return is a rough measure of the yield on amounts invested that assumes that equal portions of the gain are earned each year. The total return in this example was substantial. The investor made out-of-pocket cash investments of $50,000 for the down payment and $8000 in closing costs, and we subtract the accumulated net cash flow (line N) of $2242 (adding all the numbers across line H because the investor already has received that money) for a total investment (line O) of $55,758. The investor has a capital gain (line M) of $76,316. After dividing to determine the before-tax total return (line R) to obtain 137 percent, the crude annual rate of return (line S) is 27.4 percent annually over the five years (137 percent ÷ 5 years).

Crude Rate of Return on a Successful Real Estate Investment

I.	**Taxable cost**	
	Purchase price	$200,000
	($50,000 down payment; $150,000 loan)	
	Closing costs	8,000
	Subtotal	208,000
J.	Less accumulated depreciation	32,730
	Taxable cost (adjusted basis)	$175,270

	Proceeds (after paying off mortgage)	
K.	Sale price	$ 267,645
	Less sales commission	16,059
	Net proceeds	$251,586
L.	Less taxable cost (J)	175,270
M	Taxable proceeds (capital gain)	$ 76,316

	Amount invested	
	Down payment	$ 50,000
	Closing costs	8,000
N.	Less accumulated net cash-flow gains	(2,242)
O.	Total invested	$ 55,758

	Crude annual rate of return	
P.	Total invested	$ 55,758
Q.	Taxable proceeds (capital gain from M)	$ 76,316
R.	Before-tax total return ($ 76,316 ÷ $55,758)	137%
S.	Crude before-tax annual rate of return (137 percent ÷ 5 years)	27.4%

Selling collectibles at a profit is not a sure thing.

Gold and Other Metals

There is an allure to owning gold. It is beautiful to look at, hold, and own. Gold is a uniquely private, personal, and portable way to hold some genuine wealth. People around the world occasionally invest some of their assets in gold to preserve capital, reasoning that if their national economies crash they will be able to trade gold even if their country's paper currency is devalued. The prices of gold tend to increase in times of economic and political turmoil, war, and high inflation because investors fear a future that may be worse than today, perhaps a lot worse. Some other metals have a similar appeal to investors.

gold bullion A refined and stamped weight of precious metal.

Gold Bullion Gold bullion is often thought of as the large gold "bricks" that weigh about 28 pounds that people imagine are stored in Fort Knox. Each is worth more than $100,000. The term simply means a refined and stamped weight of precious metal. Gold bullion is traditionally purchased and traded in 1- and 10-ounce gold bars. Gold is expensive to own. There are fees for refining, fabricating, and shipping bullion. A sales charge of 5 to 8 percent is common. There are storage costs. When gold is sold, the bank or dealer buying it from an investor may insist on reassaying its quality, yet another cost for the investor. The investor may also need to purchase insurance against fire and theft.

Gold Bullion Coins Some costs of investing in gold can be avoided by those wanting to take physical possession of gold bullion itself by owning modern

CHAPTER 16: Real Estate and High-Risk Investments

475

gold bullion coins, each containing 1 troy ounce (31.15 grams) of pure gold issued by the various world mints. The most popular coins are the South African Krugerrand, Canadian Maple Leaf, and U.S. American Eagle. Other gold bullion coins are available, including the Great Britain Sovereign, Australian Kangaroo Nugget, and Chinese Panda. Minimum orders are 10 coins, and commissions are 2 to 4 percent when buying and selling. These gold bullion coins have total liquidity worldwide.

Gold Stocks and Mutual Funds People usually do not invest in gold because it does not pay interest or dividends. Also, gold has been in a bear market for most of the past 25 years, government central banks have tons of stored bullion that they could sell (which would depress prices), and almost no one recommends gold as an investment.

Promoters (and that is the correct term because traders only make money when something sells) always tell investors that they are crazy not to participate in the "ongoing gold boom." They are confident that economic conditions today are similar to the 1970s when gold prices moved from $38 to more than $800. Investors deeply worried about the future, instead of owning gold, often find it more convenient to put some of their assets in the cash of the world's two safest currencies, the U.S. dollar and the euro.

Investors wanting to capitalize on world crises and rising gold prices may invest in the stocks of gold mining companies and in mutual funds that own gold companies. You may have heard of the Homestake Gold Mine, one of the early enterprises associated with the Gold Rush of 1876 in the northern Black Hills of what was then Dakota Territory. There are a handful of gold mining companies in the United States and dozens around the world. When there is turmoil in the world and people are fearful about the future, the prices of gold stocks rise, including gold mutual funds and gold exchange-traded funds (ETFs). Search Google for information, and you will find many scams.

Silver, Platinum, Palladium, Rhodium Some less popular metals also appeal to some investors. Silver, platinum, palladium, and rhodium are metals used industrially and occasionally in jewelry. The values of these metals rise and fall with changes in demand. An investor might reason that since palladium is used in auto production that when China's demand for vehicles increases substantially the price of the metal will soar.

gold bullion coins Various world mints issue these coins, which contain 1 troy ounce (31.15 grams) of pure gold.

Did You Know?...

Scams Abound in Collectibles, Precious Metals, and Gems

The average investor can't tell a diamond from cubic zirconium or a Monet from a Manet. The values of collectibles, gold, other precious metals, and precious gems rely in part upon the authority of "experts" who purport to determine their worth, and such blind trust invites risk for potential investors. When an asset does not generate a readily quantifiable return (such as rent, interest, or dividends), its value is determined by supply and demand—and rumors. Scams and frauds abound with these investments, as promoters and telemarketers tell tales about skyrocketing prices and high profit potentials to encourage their purchase. Collectibles, precious metals, and gems are not wise choices for the casual investor.

Precious Stones and Gems

Precious stones and gems, such as diamonds, sapphires, rubies, and emeralds, are also examples of high-risk investments. Investors purchase investment-grade gems as "loose gems" rather than as pieces of jewelry. Wholesale firms, not jewelers, sell the best-quality precious gems. The gem certification process may be touted as a science, but it is educated guesswork. Obtaining two assessments of a stone's quality, particularly on stones of less than 1 carat, is likely to result in a variation of at least 10 percent.

Novice investors often buy at retail and then wind up trying to sell at retail. This approach is the opposite of smart investing—that is, buying low and selling high. Sales commissions on precious stones are high, and reselling is very difficult. Losing 15 to 50 percent of one's investment upon selling is common.

✔ **CONCEPT CHECK 16.4**

1. Identify one collectible that might be an interesting investment, and explain why it might be difficult to make a profit.

2. Explain why some investors buy gold and other precious metals, and tell why that type of investment might be appealing or unappealing to you.

3. Identify some risks of investing in precious stones and gems.

Investing in Options and Futures Contracts

5 LEARNING OBJECTIVE
Explain why options and futures are high-risk investments.

Derivative securities are available for commodities, equities, bonds, interest rates, exchange rates, and indexes (such as a stock market idex, consumer price index, and weather conditions). A **derivative** (or **derivative security**) is an instrument used by people to trade or manage more easily the asset upon which these instruments are based. Investors choose derivatives to either reduce risk by hedging agains losses or take on additional risk by speculating. The investor's returns are derived solely from changes in the underlying asset's price behavior. Two of the most common derivative instruments are options and futures contracts.

derivative/derivative security A financial instrument that people trade in order to more easily manage the underlying asset upon which these instruments are based that can be used to reduce risk or take on additional risk.

Options Allow You to Buy or Sell an Asset at a Predetermined Price

An **option** is a contract to buy or sell an asset at some point in the future at a specified price. The most common type of option is a **stock option.*** This security gives the holder (purchaser) the right, but not the obligation, to buy or sell a specific number of shares (normally 100) of a certain stock at a specified price (the **striking price**) before a specified date (the **expiration date,** typically three, six, or nine months).

option Contract to buy or sell a financial asset at a specified point in the future at a specified price.

stock option Security that gives the holder the right to buy or sell a specific number of shares (normally 100) of a certain stock at a specified (striking) price before a specified expiration date.

Options Are Created by an Option Writer An **option writer** signs an option contract through a brokerage firm and promises either to buy or to sell a specified asset for a fixed striking price. In return, the option writer receives an **option premium** (the price of the option itself) for standing ready to buy or sell the asset at the wishes of the option purchaser. Once written and sold, an option may change

option writer Agrees to sell an option contract that promises either to buy or to sell a specified asset for a fixed striking price.

*Recall from Chapter 14 that some employers give stock options as a way to attract and retain employees. If the price of the underlying stock increases sufficiently, the employee can profit by exercising the option to buy the shares at the predetermined price and then quickly selling the shares at the higher current price.

hands many times before its expiration. The **option holder** is the person who actually owns the option contract. The original option writer always remains responsible for buying or selling the asset if requested by the holder of the option contract.

Two types of option contracts exist: calls and puts. A **call option** gives the option holder (buyer) the right, but not the obligation, to *buy* the optioned asset from the option writer at the striking price. A **put option** gives the option holder (buyer) the right, but not the obligation, to *sell* the optioned asset to the option writer at the striking price. "How to Make Sense of Option Contracts" explains the relationships between option writers and option holders for both puts and calls.

Most option contracts expire without being exercised by the option holder, and the option writer is the only person to earn a profit. The profit results from the option premium charged when the option was originally sold. Buying and selling options are techniques used by both conservative and aggressive investors.

Conservative Writers Profit by Selling Covered Calls
Selling calls can be a fairly safe way to generate income by conservative option writers who own the underlying asset (the stock). When they sell a call, it is described as a **covered option** because the writer owns the underlying stock. (If the writer does not own the asset, it is a **naked option,** a speculative position.) When used effectively by conservative option writers, calls can potentially pick up an extra return of perhaps 1 to 2 percent every three months and minimize risk at the same time. In effect, this conservative investor protects himself financially by hedging his investment against loss due to price fluctuation.

You can profit by selling a call on stock already owned, giving the buyer the right to purchase your shares at any time during a relatively short period at a fixed strike price. Here is an example.

Assume you have 1000 shares of ABC stock originally bought for $56 (total investment of $56,000) and you write a call to sell the shares at a strike price of $60.

option holder Person who buys and then owns an option contract.

call option Gives option holder the right to buy the optioned asset from the option writer at the striking price at any time before the expiration date.

put option Gives option holder the right to sell the optioned asset to the option writer at the striking price at any time before the option expires.

covered option Option for a security that the writer owns and thus the writer can settle any call options contract with relatively little risk.

naked option Speculative option that the writer does not own thus exposing the writer to unlimited risk (if selling a call) or substantial risk (if selling a put).

Did You Know?…

How to Make Sense of Option Contracts

An option is a contract that gives its holder the right, but not the obligation, to buy or sell an asset at a specified price. The two principal players in the options game are the option writer and the option holder. Their relationships are summarized below.

Option holder has the right to buy or sell.	Calls		Option writer has possible obligation to sell or buy.
	Call option Has option to buy stock at a specific price	**Call obligation** Is obligated to sell stock at a specific price	
	Put option Has option to sell stock at a specific price	**Put obligation** Is obligated to purchase stock at a specific price	
	Puts		

The option price is $2, so you gain an instant premium of $2000 (omitting commissions). Three scenarios are possible:

1. If the stock price does not change in three months, the call expires. As the covered call writer, you profit from the $2000 premium.

2. If the stock price rises to $65, the holder exercises the call and buys the stock at $60. Your profit is $6000 ($4000 from appreciation in the stock price from $56 to $60, plus the $2000 premium). You missed out on potentially greater profits, however, because you sold the stocks at the striking price of $60. Without the option, you could have sold the stock at $65 per share.

3. If the stock price drops to $50, the buyer of the call will not exercise it because the market price is less than the striking price. You keep the $2000 premium, which cuts your loss from $6000 to $4000 ($56 − $50 = $6; $6 × 1000 = $6000).

Conservative Investors Reduce Risks by Purchasing Covered Puts

Buying puts is a way to immunize a conservative investor's portfolio against severe price declines because they set up a "collar" to safeguard profits. Puts allow the holder of the contract to sell an asset at a specific striking price for a certain time period, commonly three months. For example, if you own 1000 shares of ABC stock originally purchased at $56 per share (total investment of $56,000), you hope that the market price of the stock will go up. If it goes down instead, you may suffer a loss. To reduce this risk, you could buy a put for 1000 shares at a striking price close to the purchase price of the stock—for example, $52. The total price of the option contract might be $2000 ($2 per share). Three scenarios are possible:

1. If the stock price does not change in three months, the put expires, and you are out only the $2000.

2. If the stock price rises to $65, you allow the put to expire because it is greater than the striking price, and again you are out only the $2000. Alternatively, you could sell your shares at $65 and realize a profit of $7000 ($65 × 1000 = $65,000; $65,000 − $56,000 − $2000 = $7000).

3. If the stock price drops to $50, you would exercise the put and sell your stock at the striking price of $52, thereby hedging your loss from $6000 ($56 − $50 = $6; $6 × 1000 = $6000) to $4000 ($56 − $52 = $4; $4 × 1000 = $4000).

Speculative Investors Try to Profit with Options

Aggressive investors in the options market attempt to profit in two ways. First, because a market typically exists for each security for a period of three months, the investor can hope for an increase in the value of the option. For example, if the price of a stock is rising, the holder of a call option might sell it to another investor for a higher price than that originally paid. Second, the investor can exercise the option at the striking price, take ownership of the underlying securities, and sell them at a profit.

Investors take a particularly speculative position when they do not own the underlying asset, as when they sell naked calls or sell naked puts. Option traders can suffer considerable losses. For example, the writer of a put may incur a loss when the market price of an optioned asset drops below the striking price. The writer would be forced to buy the asset from the option holder at a price higher than the market price. Writing naked options is high-risk investing.

Instant Message

Options Industry Websites

Websites for learning about the options industry include www.optionscentral.com, www.tradeking.com, www.cboe.com, and www.optionsxpress.com.

Instant Message

LEAPS

A **LEAP** is a Long-term Equity AnticiPation Security. It is an option with a much longer term than traditional stock or index options. Like options, a stock-related LEAP may be a call or a put, meaning that the owner has the right to purchase or sell shares of the stock at a given price on or before some set, future date. Unlike options, the given date may be up to two and a half years away.

Speculative Investors Buy Calls to Create Tremendous Leverage

The lure of a call is that the option holder can control a relatively large asset with a small amount of capital for a specified period of time. If the market price of the asset rises to exceed the striking price plus the premium, the holder could make a substantial profit. For example, Jeremy Dietrich, a technology expert from Aurora, Colorado, bought a stock option call on Xerox in March, when the stock was selling for $55 per share. The striking price is $60, the expiration date is the third Friday in March, and the price (premium) of the call is $2 per share. The option contract cost is $200 ($2 × 100 shares under his control). Jeremy hopes that the per-share price for Xerox will rise. He prefers not to buy the stock outright because 100 shares of Xerox would cost him a great deal more—$5500 ($55 × 100).

For Jeremy to break even on the call option deal, the price of Xerox shares must rise to $62 before the call expires, as shown in Equation (16.3). If Jeremy exercises the call option, he can buy the stock at $60 from the option writer and sell it on the market for the current market price of $62 (ignoring commissions). In this instance, he earns $2 per share ($62 − $60), which offsets the $2 per share purchase price of the option. If the price of Xerox stock rises to $65, Jeremy would make a $3 profit per share, for a total profit of $300. Based on his $200 investment, this gain amounts to a 150 percent return ($300 ÷ $200) earned over a short period. If the Xerox stock price fails to reach $60 by late March, Jeremy's $200 in calls will expire with no value at all, and he will lose the amount he paid (invested) for the options.

Advice from a Pro...

How to Calculate Breakeven Prices for Option Contracts

Investors need to know the **breakeven price** for option contracts. At this price, the cost of a contract is negated by a profit (or the cost is reduced by hedging a loss). The breakeven prices for two types of option contracts—puts and calls—are calculated using Equations (16.2) and (16.3), respectively. (Both formulas appear on the *Garman/Forgue* website.) If the striking price on a put option contract was $52 and the option contract cost $2000 and provided for the control of 1000 shares of stock, then the breakeven price of a share of the stock would be $50, as the calculation shows. If the striking price on a call was $60 and the option contract cost $200 and provided for the control of 100 shares of stock, then the breakeven price of a share of the stock would be $62.

$$\text{Breakeven price on puts} = \text{striking price} - \frac{\text{contrast cost}}{\text{number of shares under control}} \qquad (16.2)$$

$$= \$52 - \frac{\$2000}{1000}$$

$$= \$50$$

$$\text{Breakeven price on calls} = \text{striking price} + \frac{\text{contrast cost}}{\text{number of shares under control}} \qquad (16.3)$$

$$= \$60 + \frac{\$200}{100}$$

$$= \$62$$

When calculating the breakeven prices for both puts and calls, it is critical to include all transaction costs in the contract cost. These costs include the option premium and perhaps sizable commissions paid to brokers. Commissions will be paid on the option contract itself, and subsequent commissions may be paid related to execution or sale of the option contract. In the preceding put example, a price below $50 triggers the sale of 1000 shares that will come at an additional, and perhaps unanticipated, commission cost. This possibility leads to some sage advice: When planning, always consider the full and subsequent costs of the deal.

Jonathan Fox
The Ohio State University

Did You Know?...

About Hedge Funds

A **hedge fund** is a global company, beyond the regulations of the U.S. Securities and Exchange Commission, that uses unconventional investment strategies. Hedge funds trade options and commodities, sell short, use leverage, risk arbitrage, buy and sell currencies, and invest in undervalued securities (poorly performing companies, those in bankruptcy, companies that may be merged). Hedge funds can profit in times of market volatility as well as in a falling market. The investors are partners. Fees charged by the hedge fund manager are 2 to 5 percent of assets under management and 20 to 40 percent of the profits of the fund.

Most hedge funds are global companies. Outside the reach of the SEC, none of the 8000 hedge funds can be offered or advertised to the general investing public in the United States. They are limited to "accredited investors and purchasers" who have incomes over $200,000 and a net worth over $1 million and who own more than $5 million in investments. Some hedge funds have had catastrophic losses and have gone bankrupt.

Selling Options You would want to sell a put or a call when the option's market price has risen sufficiently due to changes in the market price of the underlying asset to ensure a profit. Alternatively, you might sell an option to prevent further losses if its market price is dropping.

Commodities Futures Contracts

futures contract Type of exchange-traded standardized forward contract that specifies the size of the contract, quality of product to be delivered, and delivery date.

A **futures contract** is similar to an option in that it is a type of forward contract that is standardized (usually in terms of size of contract, quality of product to be delivered, and delivery date) and traded on an organized exchange. The difference is that futures contracts require the holder to buy the asset on the date specified. If the holder does not want to buy the asset, he or she must sell the contract to some other investor or to someone who wants to actually use the asset.

Futures contracts usually focus on agricultural, commercial, and mining products. Organized commodities markets include the New York Coffee and Sugar Exchange; New York Cocoa Exchange; CME Group (pigs, pork bellies, eggs, potatoes, and cattle); Chicago Board of Trade (corn, wheat, soybeans, soybean oil, oats, silver, and plywood); International Monetary Market (foreign currencies and U.S. Treasury bills); New York Commodity Exchange (gold and silver); and New York Mercantile Exchange (platinum).

Economic Need Creates Futures Markets A farmer planting a 10,000-bushel soybean crop in Eureka, Illinois, might want to sell part of it now to ensure the receipt of a certain price when the crop is actually harvested. Similarly, a food-processing company might want to purchase soybeans now to protect itself against sharp price increases in the future. Similarly, an orange juice manufacturer might want to lock in a supply of oranges at a definite price now rather than run the risk that a winter freeze might push up prices. These economic needs create futures markets.

Speculators May Trade in Futures Markets The speculative investor who buys or sells a commodity contract is hoping that the market price of the commodity will rise (or fall) before the contract matures, usually 3 to 18 months after it is

Did You Know?...

Sure Ways to Lose Money in Investing

If you don't know a lot about the specific investments you are considering, you are sure to lose money. You may lose a lot. If you are a long-term investor, never consider these risky investments.

- Margin trading
- Short selling

- Options (puts and calls)
- Commodity futures (pork bellies, oranges)
- Limited real estate partnerships
- Gold, precious metals and gems
- Infomercial investment schemes

written. Futures offer the potential for extremely high profits because all futures contracts by definition are highly leveraged. Depending on the commodity, the volatility of the market, and the brokerage house requirements, an investor can put up as little as 5 to 15 percent of the total value of the contract. Some contracts require a deposit of only $300. Commissions average about $20 for each purchase and sale.

To illustrate the use of leverage in buying futures contracts, assume that Danielle Anthony, a scuba-diving instructor from Largo, Florida, purchases a wheat contract for 5000 bushels at $3.80 per bushel in July. The contract value is $19,000 ($3.80 × 5000), but Danielle puts up only $2500. Each $0.01 increase in the price of wheat represents a total of $50 profit to her ($0.01 × 5000). If the price rises $0.50 to reach $4.30 by late July, Danielle is "in the money" and will make $2500 ($0.50 × 5000 bushels) and double her investment by directing the futures exchange to close out her position. The theory is that she could buy the wheat for $3.80 per bushel (as stipulated in the contract) rather than the market price of $4.30 in late July. As an investor, Danielle does not actually want the wheat; she wants her profit by selling her contract. Another investor, perhaps a bread company, is likely to purchase that futures contract to obtain wheat at a below-market price.

The potential for loss exists, too. If the price drops $0.50 to reach $3.30, Danielle would lose $2500. If the price declines, the broker will make a margin call and ask Danielle to provide more money to back up the contract. If Danielle does not have these additional funds, the broker can legally sell her contract and "close out" the position, which results in a true cash loss for Danielle. Because of the risks involved, brokerage houses require their futures customers to have a minimum net worth of $50,000 to $75,000, exclusive of home and life insurance.

In each commodity transaction, a winner and a loser will emerge. A buyer of a futures contract benefits if the price of the commodity increases, but the seller suffers. When prices decline, the reverse is true. An estimated 90 percent of investors in the futures market lose money; 5 percent (mostly the professionals) make good profits from the losers; and the remaining 5 percent break even.

Futures Are a Zero-Sum Game Investors need to be aware that they are dealing in very sophisticated markets when they trade in options or futures. Trading in futures is a **zero-sum game** in which the wealth of all investors remains the same; the trading simply redistributes the wealth among those traders. Each profit must be offset by an equivalent loss; therefore, the average rate of return for all investors in futures is zero. The return actually becomes negative if transaction costs are included. In the world of options and futures, losers outnumber winners.

zero-sum game Situation in which the wealth of all investors remains the same; the trading simply redistributes the wealth among those traders. Each profit must be offset by an equivalent loss; therefore, the average rate of return for all investors in futures is zero.

✓ CONCEPT CHECK 16.5

1. Distinguish between a call and a put for the options investor.
2. Summarize two ways a person with a conservative investment philosophy can profit in options.
3. Explain how a speculative options investor can lose a lot of money.
4. Offer reasons why futures contracts are not appropriate for the average investor.

What Do You Recommend Now?

Now that you have read the chapter on real estate and high-risk investments, what do you recommend to Jamie regarding:

1. Investing in real estate?
2. Putting some of her money in a high-risk investment, like collectibles?
3. Investing in options and futures contracts?

Big Picture Summary of Learning Objectives

1 Demonstrate how you can make money investing in real estate.

The key questions for real estate investors are: "Can you make current income while you own the property?" and "Can you profit with capital gains when you sell the property?" To help find answers, investors calculate the price-to-rent ratio and rental yield. Leverage enhances real estate returns, and the IRS offers investors five beneficial tax treatments, including depreciation and tax-deductible interest.

2 Calculate the right price to pay for real estate and how to finance your purchase.

The discounted cash-flow method is an effective way to estimate the value or asking price of a real estate investment. It takes into account the selling price of the property, the effect of income taxes, and the time value of money. There are many ways to finance a real estate investment, although a conventional mortgage loan is the most popular.

3 Assess the disadvantages of investing in real estate.

There are many disadvantages in real estate investing: large initial investment, lack of diversification, dealing with tenants, low current income, unpredictable costs, illiquidity, and high transfer costs.

4 Summarize the risks and challenges of investing in collectibles, precious metals, and gems.

When investing in collectibles, precious metals, and gems, the investor owns illiquid real assets, not intangible items represented by pieces of paper. The investor's only return comes from price appreciation, as they do not pay interest or dividends. While prices are set by supply and demand, promoters hype these high-risk investments. Changing investor tastes and rumors also influence prices.

5 Explain why options and futures are high-risk investments.

Derivatives, such as options and futures, are instruments used by market participants to trade or manage more easily the asset upon which these instruments are based. While all types of investors can profit in options, only "speculators" with an aggressive investment philosophy should consider trading in futures. Most investors in derivatives lose money, and losses can accumulate quickly.

Let's Talk About It

1. Assume you have $30,000 in cash. Give reasons why you might want to invest that money in a real estate

investment. Offer two reasons why others might not be willing to invest in real estate.

2. The text describes several disadvantages of real estate investments. Identify two that might stop you from investing in real estate. Identify ways to circumvent those two obstacles.

3. Explain why timeshares should never be considered an investment. What are some reasons why people buy timeshares?

4. What percentage of your portfolio do you think should be invested in high-risk investments? Explain.

5. Both options and futures are high-risk investments. Identify one that seems like an unwise idea, and explain why it is unappealing.

Do the Numbers

1. Justin Nicholas, an electrician from Great Bend, Kansas, is interested in the numbers of real estate investments. He has reviewed the figures in Table 16.2 and is impressed with the potential 36.9 percent return after taxes. Justin is in the 25 percent marginal tax bracket. Answer the following questions to help guide his investment decisions:

   (a) Substitute Justin's 25 percent marginal tax bracket in Table 16.2, and calculate the taxable income and return after taxes.

   (b) Why does real estate appear to be a favorable investment for Justin?

   (c) What one factor might be changed in Table 16.2 to increase Justin's return?

   (d) Calculate the after-tax return for Justin, assuming that he bought the property and financed it with a 7 percent, $170,000 mortgage with annual interest costs of $11,175.

2. Elizabeth Bennett, a caterer from New Orleans, Louisiana, is considering buying a vacation condominium apartment for $265,000 in Park City, Utah. Elizabeth hopes to rent the condo to others to keep her costs down. Answer the following questions to help Elizabeth with her decisions:

   (a) Elizabeth's $210,000, 30-year mortgage loan costs $16,766 annually (from Table 9.4 on page 252). She figures that $1020 of her $1397 monthly mortgage payment will go for interest. On top of that are monthly expenses for property taxes ($140), homeowner's insurance ($80), and homeowner's association fee ($100). These amounts total $1717 a month. Which of these costs will be tax deductible?

   (b) If Elizabeth is in the 30 percent combined federal and state marginal tax bracket, how much less in taxes will she pay if she buys this condo?

   (c) Given that she should would like to personally use the condo for vacations totaling 10 to 12 days per year, how many days will Elizabeth have to rent it

out before she would become eligible to deduct rental losses from her taxes?

   (d) Because Park City is primarily a winter ski resort, few condo renters can be found in the off season; therefore, Elizabeth is concerned about qualifying to deduct rental losses. Assuming she could rent the condo for $400 per day, summarize the IRS-approved rental alternative she could use to generate some tax-free income. Calculate the maximum amount of money Elizabeth could obtain using that plan.

   (e) Figure Elizabeth's annual net out-of-pocket cost to buy the condominium and rent it out minimally for tax-free income. List the costs and total on an annualized basis. Next, deduct the savings on income taxes as well as the presumed rental for the number of IRS-allowed days.

   (f) Using the figure derived in part (e), what would Elizabeth's out-of-pocket cost per day be to use the condo herself if she stayed there ten days each year? Fifteen days each year?

Financial Planning Cases

Case 1
Real Estate or Stocks?

Junhee Chang, a senior research analyst in Austin, Texas, has bought and sold high-technology stocks profitably for years. Lately some of her stock investments have done poorly, including one company that went bankrupt. Emily, a longtime friend at work, has suggested that the two of them invest in real estate together because property values in some neighborhoods have been rising. Emily has looked at three small office buildings and some residential duplexes as possible investments.

   (a) Contrast the wisdom of investing in commercial office buildings versus the attraction of investing in residential properties.

   (b) List three of the advantages associated with real estate investments.

   (c) List three things that can go wrong for real estate investors.

Case 2
From Real Estate to Options and Futures

Brandon Williams and Jason Richardson, longtime partners in Berkeley, California, have bought and sold real estate properties for ten years. They have profited on every transaction and now have a portfolio of real estate worth about $4.7 million, on which they owe only $2.9 million. Jason has read about investing in options and futures contracts, and last week he talked with a stockbroker about the possibilities.

   (a) Offer some reasons why Jason might gain by investing $100,000 or $200,000 in options and futures contracts.

   (b) List some of the risks of options trading for Brandon and Jason.

   (c) From an investor's point of view, contrast trading in futures contracts with buying highly leveraged real estate.

Case 3
Victor and Maria Consider Hedging an Investment with Puts

Victor and Maria Hernandez invested in 200 shares of Pharmacia Corporation common stock at $93 per share. They purchased the stock because the company is testing a new drug that may represent a significant medical breakthrough. The stock's value has already risen $8 in three months, in anticipation of the U.S. Food and Drug Administration's approval of the new drug. Many observers believe that the price of the stock could reach $120 if the drug is successful. If it does not prove to be the breakthrough anticipated, the price of the stock could drop back to the $85 range, or even lower. The Hernandezes are optimistic but feel that they should hedge their position a bit. As a result, they have decided to purchase two nine-month Pharmacia 100-share puts for $3 per share at a striking price of $93 per share. Ignore commissions when answering the following questions.

   (a) What price would the Pharmacia stock need to reach for the Hernandezes to break even on their investment?

   (b) How much would the Hernandezes gain if they sold the stock for $102 six months from now?

   (c) How much would the return be as a percentage on an annualized basis?

   (d) If the price of the stock dropped to $85 in six months, how much would the Hernandezes lose?

Case 4
The Johnsons Consider a Real Estate Investment

Harry and Belinda Johnson are considering purchasing a residential income property as an investment. The Johnsons want to achieve an after-tax total return of 10 percent. They are considering a property with an asking price of $190,000 that should produce $27,000 in gross rental income and $15,000 in net operating income.

   (a) Calculate the present value of after-tax cash flow for the property, assuming that the after-tax cash-flow numbers are $8000 for the first year, $8400 for the second year, $8800 for the third year, $9200 for the fourth year, and $9600 for the fifth year, and that the selling price of the property will be $220,000 in five years. Prepare your information in a format similar to Table 16.3, using Appendix Table A.2 or the *Garman/Forgue* website to discount the future after-tax cash flows to their present values.

   (b) Give the Johnsons your advice on whether they should invest in the property at its current price of $190,000.

On the 'Net

Go to the Web pages indicated to complete these exercises. You can also go to the *Garman/Forgue* website at college.hmco.com/business/students for an expanded list of exercises. Under General Business, select the title of this text. Click on the Internet Exercises link for this chapter.

1. Visit the website for the Chicago Board of Trade (www.cbot.com). In its Education section, use the tutorials and glossary to answer the following questions:

   (a) What is a futures contract?

   (b) What is the difference between a stock market and a futures exchange?

   (c) Browse the site further to learn about the commodities that are traded on the CBOT.

2. Visit the website for Investopedia.com. Search "reducing risk with options" at www.investopedia.com. There you will see an article on how option investing can serve to reduce risk. When might investors want to use options in their investment portfolios?

Visit the Garman/Forgue website...

@college.hmco.com/business/students

Under General Business, select *Personal Finance 9e*. There, among other valuable resources, you will find a complete glossary, ACE questions, links to help you complete the chapter exercises, and links to other personal finance sites.

PART 5

CHAPTER 17

Retirement Planning

You Must Be Kidding, Right?

Lindsey Jones is 27 years old, and she recently took a new job. Lindsey had accumulated $6000 in her previous employer's 401(k) retirement plan, and she withdrew it to pay for her wedding. How much less money will Lindsey have at retirement at age 67 if she could have earned 9 percent on the $6000?

A. $6000   **B.** $24,000   **C.** $48,000   **D.** $188,000

The answer is D. Spending retirement money for discretionary purposes, instead of keeping it in a tax-deferred account where it can compound for many years, is unwise. The lesson is to keep your retirement money where it belongs!

LEARNING OBJECTIVES

After reading this chapter, you should be able to:

1 **Recognize** that you are solely responsible for funding your retirement and must sacrifice some current spending and invest for your future lifestyle.

2 **Estimate** your Social Security retirement income benefit.

3 **Calculate** your estimated retirement savings needs in today's dollars.

4 **Understand** why you should save for retirement within tax-sheltered retirement accounts.

5 **Distinguish** among the types of employer-sponsored retirement plans.

6 **Explain** the various types of personally established tax-sheltered retirement accounts.

7 **Recognize** that professional investment advice for retirement assets is available, including Monte Carlo simulations.

8 **Describe** techniques for living in retirement without running out of money.

What Do You Recommend?

Maryanne Johnson, age 32, worked for a previous employer for eight years. When she left that job, Maryanne left her retirement money (now worth $90,000) in that employer's defined-contribution plan. After getting divorced and remarried four years ago, she has been working as an assistant food services manager for a large convention center in Indianapolis, Indiana, earning $80,000 per year. Maryanne contributes $267 each month (4 percent of her salary) to her account in her employer's 401(k) retirement plan. Her current employer provides a 100 percent match for the first 4 percent of Maryanne's salary contributions. Today, Maryanne's 401(k) account balance is $21,000. Her investments are equally divided among three mutual funds: a growth fund, a value fund, and an S&P index fund.

Maryanne's husband, Bob, is permanently disabled, and most of his medical expenses are paid for through Maryanne's health benefits at work. Bob receives $1000 per month in disability insurance benefits, and he earns about $5000 per year as a freelance cartoonist. Maryanne is hoping that she and Bob can retire when she is age 55.

What do you recommend to Maryanne and Bob on the subject of retirement and estate planning regarding:

1. The major steps in the process to determine the amount of Maryanne and Bob's retirement savings goal?

2. How Bob's net income could be invested in a personal tax-sheltered retirement account?

3. The kinds of investment accounts into which they might put additional money over the next 23 years if they determined they needed $1 million to meet their retirement savings goal?

4. The investment strategies that Maryanne and Bob might follow for accumulating their retirement funds?

FOR HELP with studying this chapter, visit the Online Student Center:

www.college.hmco.com/pic/garman9e

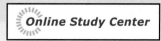

Online Study Center

Today's Americans are healthier, are better educated, will live longer, and have higher expectations than their counterparts from earlier generations. Your view may include retiring to a comfortable and happy life with little stress and lots of leisure. Enjoying financial security during your retirement years is not a matter of luck, as it takes planning and action. You must invest money you save during your working years, and do so wisely. Then when you no longer want to work or are unable, all your money can work for you.

To invest for your future lifestyle in retirement, you simply sacrifice some current spending. By starting early and contributing regularly, you can turn small monthly investments into hundreds, then thousands, and eventually millions of dollars over the years. You can have a lot of fun investing, but realize that building assets for retirement is serious business. While compiling this seemingly enormous sum may seem like an impossible proposition today, you can, and you need to do it.

retirement The time in life when the major sources of income change from earned income (such as salary or wages) to employer-based retirement benefits, private savings and investments, income from Social Security, and perhaps part-time employment.

1 LEARNING OBJECTIVE

Recognize that you are solely responsible for funding your retirement and must sacrifice some current spending and invest for your future lifestyle.

Retirement Planning Is Your Responsibility

Retirement is the time in life when the major sources of income change from earned income (such as salary or wages) to employer-based retirement benefits, private savings and investments, income from Social Security, and perhaps part-time employment. (See Figure 17.1.) Planning for retirement has changed dramatically in recent years. Yesterday's employer-provided pensions were commonly a reward for 30-plus years of working for one employer, but they are no longer widely available. Instead, most employers today offer "voluntary" retirement plans to which employees may or may not choose to contribute.

As a result, both the responsibility of investing funds for retirement and the risk of making poor investments with these funds has been shifted from the employer to the employee. You cannot count on your boss in retirement. You must accept the fact that you—and only you—are solely responsible for meeting your retirement needs.

On the day when your regular full-time paycheck stops, you are retired. If you have not saved enough money to enjoy the lifestyle you prefer, you will have to lower your level of living, continue working part time, or do both. Many of today's retirees continue to work part time because they need to supplement their retirement income, enjoy working, and want an employer's subsidized health care benefits. Others continue working simply because they must do so to survive. You may choose to save and invest for your retirement, or you can work forever.

Financial planners say that people need 80 to 100 percent of their pre-retirement gross income (along with Social Security) to meet their expenses in retirement and maintain their lifestyle. This amount includes what you have to pay in income taxes. Achieving this goal will be a big challenge, but it is one you can meet successfully. As the American Savings Education Council says, "You have the power to choose today how you will spend your retirement tomorrow."

To prepare for a financially successful retirement, you must build a sufficient amount of savings and investments to sup-

Good Money Habits in Retirement Planning

Make the following your money habits in retirement planning:

1. Save early and often by beginning early in life to invest in mutual funds through tax-sheltered retirement accounts and continuing to invest every year.

2. Take enough risk to increase the likelihood that you will have enough money in retirement.

3. Save within an employer-sponsored retirement plan at least the amount required to obtain the full matching contribution from your employer.

4. Diversify your investments and limit company stock to no more than 10 percent of your portfolio.

5. Contribute to Roth IRA and traditional IRA accounts to supplement your employer-sponsored plans.

6. Keep your hands off your retirement money. Do not borrow it. Do not withdraw it. When changing employers, roll over the funds into the new employer's plan or a rollover IRA.

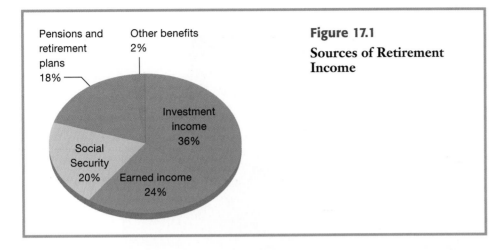

Figure 17.1

Sources of Retirement Income

plement other sources of income in retirement, such as monthly checks from the **Social Security Administration (SSA).** To succeed in this endeavor, during your 30 or 40 years in the workforce you must select among the various retirement plans and accounts that are available to you and adequately fund them through regular and consistent savings. You must make sound investment decisions regarding your retirement assets. You are advised to start early to save and invest for retirement and to continue this effort throughout your working years. You can then let the magical powers of compounding fully fund your needs and wants during the latter third of your life.

Instant Message

Cost of Delaying Saving for Retirement

Making steady contributions of $3000 every year to a tax-sheltered retirement account earning 8 percent annually for 30 years will accumulate to $340,000. Delaying 10 years before beginning to save accumulates only $137,000.

✔ CONCEPT CHECK 17.1

1. Summarize why retirement planning has changed in recent years and has now become each individual's responsibility.

2. List some financial planning actions that individuals must do during their working life to prepare for retirement.

3. Comment on the cost of delaying saving for retirement.

Understanding Your Social Security Retirement Income Benefits

The Social Security program has become the most successful and popular domestic government program in U.S. history. Funding for Social Security benefits comes from a compulsory payroll tax split equally between employee and employer. Social Security taxes withheld from wages are called **FICA taxes** (named for the Federal Insurance Contributions Act). The amounts withheld are put into the Social Security trust fund accounts from which benefits are paid to current program recipients.

Federal Insurance Contributions Act (FICA) Act that authorizes Social Security and Medicare tax withdrawals from employee paychecks; amounts withheld go into Social Security trust fund accounts, which pay benefits to current retirees.

2 LEARNING OBJECTIVE
Estimate your Social Security retirement income benefit.

Understanding your Social Security benefits is a key component of retirement planning.

Did You Know?...

About Women and Retirement Planning

Women are less likely to get retirement benefits from their employers (30 percent of women receive such benefits as compared with 50 percent of men). This occurs, in part, because women are more likely to work for employers who do not offer a retirement plan. Because of their lower average incomes, women also receive less income than men from Social Security (about $800 per month compared with $975). Women live longer than men, so women may need to save more money for retirement than men do.

maximum taxable yearly earnings (MTYE) The maximum amount to which the FICA tax is applied.

Your Contributions to Social Security and Medicare

Wage earners pay both FICA and Medicare taxes to the SSA. The FICA tax is paid on wage income up to the **maximum taxable yearly earnings (MTYE),** which comprises the maximum amount to which the FICA tax is applied. The MTYE figure—$97,500 for last year—is adjusted annually for inflation.* The FICA tax rate has been 12.4 percent, consisting of 6.2 percent paid by employees and 6.2 percent paid by employers. Self-employed workers pay a FICA tax rate of 12.4 percent, twice that of wage earners, because they are their own employers. Thus, a self-employed person earning $97,500 per year would pay $12,090 ($97,500 × 0.062 × 2) in FICA taxes on that income.

Wage earners and their employers also pay a 1.45 percent Medicare tax on all earnings. The MTYE limit does not apply to the Medicare tax. Thus, the typical worker sends 7.65 (6.2 + 1.45) percent of his or her earnings to the SSA. For example, a person earning $35,000 pays a combined FICA and Medicare tax of $2678 ($35,000 × 0.0765) and a person earning $110,000 pays $6045 ($97,500 × 0.062) plus $1595 ($110,000 × 0.0145), or a total of $7640.

How You Become Qualified for Social Security Benefits

You must be insured under the Social Security program before retirement, survivors, or disability insurance benefits can be paid to you or your family. The Social Security program covers nine out of every ten U.S. employees. Some federal, state, and local government employees are exempt because their employers have instituted other plans.

*All tax-related information in this chapter applies to the year 2007.

To qualify for benefits, a worker accumulates credits for employment in any work subject to the FICA taxes, including part-time and temporary employment. The periods of employment in which you earn credits need not be consecutive. Military service also provides credits. You earn **Social Security credits** for a certain amount of work covered under Social Security during a calendar year. For example, workers receive one credit if they earned $1000 during any one of the four 90-day periods during the year and the annual maximum of four credits if they earned $4000 (4 × $1000). The dollar figure required for each credit earned is raised annually to keep pace with inflation.

The number of credits you have earned determines your eligibility for retirement benefits and for disability or survivors benefits if you become disabled or die. Table 17.1 shows the length-of-work requirements to receive Social Security benefits. The SSA recognizes four statuses of eligibility:

Fully Insured **Fully insured** status requires 40 credits and provides the worker and his or her family with benefits under the retirement, survivors, and disability programs. Once obtained, this status cannot be lost even if the person never works again. Although it is required to receive retirement benefits, "fully insured" status does not imply that the worker will receive the maximum benefits allowable.

Currently Insured To achieve **currently insured status,** six credits must be earned in the most recent three years. This status provides for some survivors or disability benefits but no retirement benefits. To remain eligible for these benefits, a worker must continue to earn at least six credits every three years or meet a minimum number of covered years of work established by the SSA.

Transitionally Insured **Transitionally insured** status applies only to retired workers who reach the age of 72 without accumulating 40 credits (ten years). These people are eligible for limited retirement benefits.

Not Insured Workers younger than age 72 who have fewer than six credits of work experience are **not insured.**

How to Estimate Your Social Security Retirement Benefits

The actual dollar amount of Social Security benefits is based on the average of the highest 35 years of earnings during the working years. Your actual earnings are first adjusted, or **indexed,** to account for changes in average wages since the year the earnings were received. The SSA then calculates your average monthly indexed earnings during the 35 years in which you earned the most. The agency applies a formula to these earnings to arrive at your **basic retirement benefit** (or **primary insurance amount).** This is the amount you would receive at your **full-benefit retirement age**—67 for those born in 1960 or later.

You can compute your own retirement benefit estimate using a program that you can download to your computer from http://www.ssa.gov/OACT/anypia/. You will have three choices concerning when you want to begin receiving Social Security retirement benefits.

1. Begin Receiving Benefits at Your Full-Benefit Age
Once you have reached your full-benefit retirement age, you are eligible to receive your basic monthly retirement benefit. You can begin collecting these benefits even if you con-

Social Security credits Accumulated quarterly credits to qualify for Social Security benefits obtained by paying FICA taxes.

Instant Message

The Future of Social Security

The taxes collected from workers currently exceed the benefits paid to retirees. By 2030 the ability of the Social Security trust fund to meet Americans' retirement needs will exceed the taxes being collected. While many young people doubt that Social Security will provide them benefits, Congress will continue the nation's most popular government program. Simple fixes favored by people of both parties and all age groups are to increase the wage cap, increase the payroll tax, and change the benefit formula.

fully insured Social Security status Requires 40 credits and provides workers and their families with benefits under the retirement, survivors, and disability programs; once status is earned, it cannot be taken away even if the eligible worker never works again.

currently insured status Requires workers to earn six credits in the most recent three years; provides for some survivors or disability benefits but no retirement benefits.

indexed A procedure used by the Social Security Administration to adjust the earnings during one's working years to reflect increases in average wages for all workers over time; used in the process of calculating SSA benefits.

basic retirement benefit/primary insurance amount Amount of Social Security benefits a worker would receive at his or her full-benefit retirement age, which is 67 for those born after 1960.

Table 17.1   Length-of-Work Requirements for Social Security Benefits

Types of Benefits	Payable to	Minimum Years of Work Under Social Security
Retirement	You, your spouse, child, dependent spouse 62 or older	10 years (fully insured status).
Survivors*		
Full	Widow(er) 60 or older, disabled widow(er) 50-59, widow(er) if caring for child 18 years or younger, dependent children, dependent widow(er) 62 or older, disabled dependent widow(er) 50–61, dependent parent at 62	10 years (fully insured status).
Current	Widow(er) caring for child 18 years or younger, dependent children	1½ years of last 3 years before death (currently insured status).
Disability	You and your dependents	If younger than age 24, you need 1½ years of work in the 3 years prior to disablement; if between ages 24 and 31, you need to work half the time between when you turned 21 and your date of disablement; if age 31 or older, you must have 5 years of credit during the 10 years prior to disablement.
Medicare		
Hospitalization (Part A: automatic benefits)	Anyone 65 or older plus some others, such as the disabled	Anyone qualified for the Social Security retirement program is qualified for Medicare Part A at age 65; others may qualify by paying a monthly premium for Part A.
Medical expense (Part B: voluntary benefits)	Anyone eligible for Part A and anyone else 65 or older (payment of monthly premiums required)	No prior work under Social Security is required.

*A lump-sum death benefit no greater than $255 is also granted to dependents of those either fully or currently insured.
Source: U.S. Department of Health and Human Services.

tinue working full or part time. Your level of employment income will not affect your level of benefits, though it may affect the income taxes that you pay on your Social Security benefits (as discussed later in this chapter).

2. Begin Receiving Reduced Benefits at a Younger Age You can choose to start receiving retirement benefits as early as age 62, regardless of your full-benefit retirement age. If you do so, however, your basic retirement benefit will be permanently reduced. The check will be permanently reduced 30 percent for people born after 1960. If you choose to take the earliest Social Security retirement benefits, you will be ahead financially if you do not survive to about age 80. Sixty percent of retirees elect to take their Social Security benefits early.

People considering early Social Security retirement benefits need to be aware that their checks will be reduced if they have earned income above the annual limit ($12,000 this year). Those who earn more than the annual limit have their Social Security benefits reduced $1 for every $2 in earnings. A person entitled to $750 per month ($9000 per year) in early retirement benefits who has an earned income of more than $30,000 should not apply for early Social Security benefits because he or she makes too much money to be eligible for any benefit.

3. Begin Receiving Larger Benefits at a Later Age You can delay taking benefits beyond your full-benefit retirement age. In such a case, your benefit would

Advice from a Pro...

How to Collect Retirement Benefits and Social Security from a Divorced Spouse

Federal law allows courts to split retirement money between husbands and wives at their divorce. To receive a share of a private-sector defined-benefit or defined-contribution retirement plan, a former spouse needs her (or his) attorney to prepare a **qualified domestic-relations order (QDRO).** Upon approval by the court, a QDRO establishes the rights of an alternate payee to receive all or a portion of a participant's retirement plan benefits upon divorce or as soon as the participant leaves a job or reaches retirement age. In the case of public-sector pensions, a **domestic-relations order** (or court order acceptable for processing) must be filed instead of a QDRO.

Rules on receiving benefits from other pension plans vary depending on the laws of the state in which the divorce occurred, the specific rules in the plan, and the competence of your legal representation. Be sure to ask your lawyer to explain your rights under various scenarios, including the death or disability of your ex-spouse or your own remarriage. Annuities and individual retirement accounts also may be divided as part of a divorce agreement.

To qualify for Social Security retirement benefits based on your former spouse's earnings, your marriage must have lasted at least ten years, you must be unmarried and have been divorced for at least two years, and both you and your ex-spouse must be at least 62 years old. Your benefits will not be affected if the ex-spouse remarries. You will lose the right to benefits based on your former spouse's earnings if you remarry, unless your second marriage also ended in divorce. Your benefit amount consists of 50 percent of a living divorced spouse's benefit or 100 percent of a deceased ex-spouse's benefit. Social Security is the only plan that provides automatic benefits to a divorced spouse.

Sue Alexander Greninger
University of Texas at Austin

be permanently increased by as much as 8 percent per year. You can continue to work even after you begin taking these delayed benefits. Again, your level of employment income will not affect your level of benefits, but it may affect the income taxes that you pay on your Social Security benefits.

Check the Accuracy of Your Social Security Statement

The **Social Security Statement** is a document that the SSA periodically sends to all workers. It includes a record of your earnings history, a record of how much you and your various employers paid in Social Security taxes, and an estimate of the benefits that you and your family might be eligible for now and in the future. You can also request a Social Security Statement at any time at www.ssa.gov/statement/ or by telephone at (800) 772-1213. When reviewing this statement, make sure that the SSA's records are up-to-date and accurate. Workers have three years to correct any errors.

✓ CONCEPT CHECK 17.2

1. Summarize how workers become qualified for Social Security benefits.
2. Distinguish between the benefits provided under Social Security for a worker who is fully insured and a worker who is currently insured.
3. Explain what happens if you choose to retire earlier than your full retirement age, which is probably 67.

How to Calculate Your Estimated Retirement Needs in Today's Dollars

3 LEARNING OBJECTIVE

Calculate your estimated retirement savings needs in today's dollars.

retirement savings goal/retirement nest egg Total amount of accumulated savings and investments needed to support desired retirement lifestyle.

To plan for a financially successful retirement, you first need to set a goal. Otherwise, as one of the most quoted figures in sports, Yogi Berra, says, "If you don't know where you are going, you will end up somewhere else." Your **retirement savings goal,** or **retirement nest egg,** is the total amount of accumulated savings and investments needed to support your desired retirement lifestyle.*

Setting a personally meaningful retirement goal will help motivate you to take the necessary saving and investing actions. If you begin to save and invest for retirement early in life, the compounding effect on money over time will make it fairly easy for you to reach your retirement savings goal.

Projecting Your Annual Retirement Expenses and Income

Projecting your annual retirement expenses in current dollars and being knowledgeable about the sources of income that might support these expenditures lead logically to a key question that may be asked in several ways: "How much money must be set aside to provide that support?" or "What is my retirement savings goal?" or "How large a retirement nest egg do I need?" You can use the Decision-Making Worksheet, "Estimating Your Retirement Savings Goal in Today's Dollars," to calculate this amount. In the following example, you will see how to use this worksheet to arrive at the amount that you would need to save each year to realize your desired, financially comfortable retirement lifestyle. Couples can use the same worksheet, but each person should prepare a worksheet. You do not have to remain clueless about how much money you will need when you retire. Simply do the math.

An Illustration of Retirement Needs

Consider the case of Erik McKartmann, aged 35 and single, the manager of a weight-loss business in South Park, Colorado. Erik currently earns $50,000 per year. He has been contributing $160 per month ($1920 annually) into his account established through his employer's 401(k) plan. Erik plans to retire at age 62.

1. Erik has chosen not to develop a retirement budget at this time. Instead, he multiplied his current salary by 70 percent to arrive at an annual income (in current dollars) needed in retirement of $35,000 ($50,000 × 0.70). This amount was entered on line 1 of the worksheet. If Erik wants to increase the amount of dollars to support a higher retirement lifestyle, he can simply increase the percentage in the calculation.

2. Erik checked the SSA website to estimate his benefits. At age 62, he could expect a monthly benefit of $1100 (in current dollars). Multiplying by 12 gave an expected annual Social Security benefit of $13,200 (in current dollars), which Erik entered on line 2 of the worksheet.

3. Line 3 of the worksheet, which calls for Erik's expected pension benefit, is appropriate for defined-benefit plans. After discussing his expected employer pension with the benefits counselor at work, Erik found that his anticipated benefit under the plan would amount to approximately $5800 annually, assuming that he remained with the company until his retirement, so he entered that figure on line 3.

*If you want to spend only five minutes to get a basic idea of the savings you will need when you retire, see the American Savings Education Council's *Ballpark Estimate* (www.choosetosave.org/ballpark/) for a one-page worksheet.

Decision-Making Worksheet

Estimating Your Retirement Savings Goal in Today's Dollars

This worksheet will help you calculate the amount you need to set aside each year in today's dollars so that you will have adequate funds for your retirement. The example here assumes that a single person is now 35 years old, will retire at age 62, has a current income of $50,000, currently saves and invests about $2000 per year, contributes zero to an employer-sponsored retirement plan, anticipates needing a retirement income of $35,000 per year assuming a spending lifestyle at 70 percent of current income ($50,000 × 0.70), and will live an additional 20 years beyond retirement. Investment returns are assumed to be 3 percent after inflation—a fair estimate for a typical portfolio. The financial needs would differ if the growth rate of the investments was less than 3 percent. This approach simplifies the calculations and puts the numbers to estimate retirement needs into today's dollars. The amount saved must be higher if substantial inflation occurs.

		Example	Your Numbers
1.	Annual income needed at retirement in today's dollars (Use carefully estimated numbers or a certain percentage, such as 70% or 80%.)	$ 35,000	_____
2.	Estimated Social Security retirement benefit in today's dollars	$ 13,200	_____
3.	Estimated employer pension benefit in today's dollars (Ask your retirement bene-fit adviser to make an estimate of your future pension, assuming that you remain in the same job at the same salary, or make your own conservative estimate.)	$ 5,800	_____
4.	Total estimated retirement income from Social Security and employer pension in today's dollars (line 2 + line 3)	$ 19,000	_____
5.	Additional income needed at retirement in today's dollars (line 1 − line 4)	$ 16,000	_____
6.	Amount you must have at retirement in today's dollars to receive additional annual income in retirement (line 5) for 20 years (from Appendix Table A.4, assuming a 3% return over 20 years, or 14.8775 × $16,000)	$238,040	_____
7.	Amount already available as savings and investments in today's dollars (add lines 7A through 7D, and record the total on line 7E)		
	A Employer savings plans, such as a 401(k), SEP-IRA, or profit-sharing plan	0	
	B IRAs and Keoghs	$ 24,000	
	C Other investments, such as mutual funds, stocks, bonds, real estate, and other assets available for retirement	$ 13,000	
	D If you wish to include a portion of the equity in your home as savings, enter its present value minus the cost of another home in retirement	0	
	E Total retirement savings (add lines A through D)	$ 37,000	_____
8.	Future value of current savings/investments at time of retirement (using Appendix Table A.1 and a growth rate of 3% over 27 years, the factor is 2.2213; thus, 2.2213 × $37,000)	$ 82,188	_____
9.	Additional retirement savings and investments needed at time of retirement (line 6 − line 8)	$155,852	_____
10.	Annual savings needed (to reach amount in line 9) before retirement (using Appendix Table A.3 and a growth rate of 3% over 27 years, the factor is 40.7096; thus, $155,852 ÷ 40.7096)	$ 3,828	_____
11.	Current annual contribution to savings and investment plans	$ 2,000	_____
12.	Additional amount of annual savings that you need to set aside in today's dollars to achieve retirement goal (in line 1) (line 10 − line 11)	$ 1,828	_____

4. Erik adds lines 2 and 3 to determine his total estimated retirement income from Social Security and his employer pension. The amount on line 4 would be $19,000 ($13,200 + $5800).

5. Subtracting line 4 from line 1 reveals that Erik would need an additional income of $16,000 ($35,000 − $19,000) in today's dollars from savings and investments to meet his annual retirement income needs.

6. At this point, Erik has considered only his annual needs and benefits. Because he plans to retire at age 62, Erik will need income for 20 years based on his life expectancy. (Of course, Erik could live well into his 80s, which would mean that he would need the inflation-adjusted equivalent of his annual retirement expenditures for more than 20 years.) Using Appendix Table A.4 and assuming a return that is 3 percent above the inflation rate, Erik finds the multiplier 14.8775 where 3 percent and 20 years intersect. He then calculates that he needs an additional amount of $238,040 (14.8775 × $16,000) at retirement. That's a big number! And it is in current dollars. The number does not dissuade Erik from saving because he knows he has time and the magic of compounding on his side.

7. Erik's current savings and investments can be used to offset the $238,040 he will need for retirement. Erik has zero savings in his employer's 401(k) account; however, he does have some money invested in an IRA ($24,000), plus some other investments ($13,000). These amounts are totaled ($37,000) and recorded on line 7E.

8. If left untouched, the $37,000 that Erik has built up will continue to earn interest and dividends until he retires. Because he has 27 more years until retirement, Erik can use Appendix Table A.1 and, assuming a growth rate of 3 percent over 27 years, find the factor 2.2213 and multiply it by the total amount in line 7. Erik's $37,000 should have a future value of $82,188 at his retirement, so he puts this amount on line 8.

9. Subtracting line 8 from line 6 reveals that Erik's retirement nest egg will need an additional $155,852 at the time of retirement.

10. Using Appendix Table A.3 and a growth rate of 3 percent over 27 years, Erik finds a factor of 40.7096. When divided into $155,852, it reveals that he needs savings and investments of $3828 per year until retirement.

11. Erik records his current savings and investments of $2000 per year on line 11.

Planning an active retirement can include working part time at something you love.

Advice from a Pro...

Buy Your Retirement on the Layaway Plan

The large retirement savings goal dollar amount scares some people. To allay such concerns, the following novel approach to thinking about retirement saving has been suggested. You can look at your retirement as something you "buy." The "retail price" is the retirement nest egg goal itself. From that amount, you can subtract "discounts" for anticipated income from Social Security, employer-sponsored retirement accounts, personal retirement accounts, and any other funds you expect to have

accumulated. Then you identify the difference—the shortfall indicated on line 9 of the Decision-Making Worksheet—and buy it on a "layaway plan." The additional amounts you periodically save and invest are, therefore, the "layaway payments" with which you "buy" your retirement. This is smart thinking!

Dennis R. Ackley
Ackey & Associates, Kansas City, Missouri

12. Erik subtracts line 11 from line 10 to determine the additional amount of annual savings that he should set aside in today's dollars to achieve his retirement goal. His shortfall totals $1828 per year. By saving an extra $153 each month ($1828 ÷ 12), he can reach his retirement goal established in step 1.

Suggestions to Fund Erik's Retirement Goal

Erik needs to continue what he is doing—saving and investing—plus save a little more so he can enjoy his lifestyle when his full-time career ends. Erik should discuss with his benefits counselor how much he can save and invest via the company's new 401(k) program.

Erik needs to save more for retirement by contributing an additional $1828 per year into his account within his employer's 401(k) plan—that is, about 3.7 percent of his salary. To create an extra margin of safety, and if the rules of his employer's retirement plan permit it, he could save even more of his salary. His employer might also make a matching contribution (discussed later) of some of Erik's 401(k) contributions.

The additional $1828 in current dollars assumes that the growth of his investments will be 3 percent higher than the inflation rate, a reasonable assumption. If his income goes up sharply, Erik should increase his savings because he will have a much larger amount of income to replace at retirement. Redoing the calculations every few years will help keep Erik informed and on track for a financially successful retirement.

Instant Message

Save 10% of Your Pay

Saving and investing 10% of your pay can provide a lump sum of $1,540,000 at age 65, while saving only 6% will provide only $924,000. Calculations are based on a 25-year old with a salary of $40,000 who receives 3 percent annual pay increases and the invested sums earn an 8 percent annual return.

✔ CONCEPT CHECK 17.3

1. List the steps in the process of estimating your retirement savings goal in today's dollars.
2. In the text example, what can Erik do to save more for his retirement?
3. Give your impression of the idea of buying retirement on the "layaway plan."

Why Invest in Tax-Sheltered Retirement Accounts?

4 **LEARNING OBJECTIVE**
Understand why you should save for retirement within tax-sheltered retirement accounts.

after-tax money Funds put into regular investment accounts; subject to income taxes.

tax-sheltered retirement accounts Retirement account for which all earnings from the invested funds are not subject to income taxes.

pretax money Investing with pretax money to a tax-sheltered retirement account comes out of your earnings before income taxes are calculated, thus gaining an immediate elimination of part of your income tax liability for the current year.

tax-deferred income Income earned on funds in tax-sheltered retirement accounts for which the individual does not have to pay income taxes on the earnings (interest, dividends, and capital gains) reinvested within the retirement account.

The funds you put into regular investment accounts represent **after-tax money.** Assume, for example, that a person in the 25 percent tax bracket earns an extra $1000 and is considering investing those funds. She will pay $250 in income taxes on the extra income, which leaves only $750 in after-tax money available to invest. Furthermore, all earnings from the invested funds are also subject to income taxes each year as they are accrued. Matters are much different when you invest in **tax-sheltered retirement accounts.**

Your Contributions May Be Tax Deductible

Contributions may be "deductible" from your taxable income in the year the contributions are made. In this situation, you pay zero taxes on the contributed amount of income in the current year. This means that you are investing with **pretax money,** and the salary amount you defer, or contribute, to a tax-sheltered retirement account comes out of your earnings before income taxes are calculated. Thus, you gain an immediate elimination of part of your income tax liability for the current year. The advantage of using tax-deductible contributions is illustrated in Table 17.2. The maximum contribution varies (discussed later) depending upon the type of tax-sheltered account you are using.

Your Earnings Are Tax Deferred

Income earned on funds in tax-sheltered retirement accounts accumulates **tax deferred.** In other words, the individual does not have to pay income taxes on the earnings (interest, dividends, and capital gains) reinvested within the retirement account. A **withdrawal** is a removal of assets from an account.

You Can Accumulate More Money

You will have much more money when it is time to retire if you use tax-sheltered accounts for your investing instead of personal taxable accounts. The following examples assume that a person who pays combined federal and state income taxes at a 25 percent rate invests $3000 per year for 20 years in a diversified portfolio of stocks,

Table 17.2 The Smart "Net-Pay" Numbers of 401(k) Participation

Samantha Smarty participates in her employer's 401(k) retirement plan, and contributes $3600 of her $60,000 income. Her contributions are tax deductible, so this reduces her federal income taxes by $1900 ($9600 − $7700), and it takes another $500 off her state income tax liability ($3100 − $2600). Samantha's net take-home pay is reduced by only $800 ($47,300 − $46,500). What a good financial deal!

	Not Participating in 401(k) Plan	Participating in 401(k) Plan
Income	$60,000	$60,000
Contribution to plan	- 0 -	3,600
Taxable income	60,000	56,400
Federal income tax	9,600	7,700
State income tax	3,100	2,600
Tax-home pay	$47,300	$46,100

bonds, and mutual funds that earns 8 percent annually. Calculations are from Appendix Table A.3.

Example 1—$110,357: Make Annual After-Tax Investments That Are Not Tax Sheltered

The sum of $3000 in after-tax money is invested in a personal taxable account every year for 20 years. Because the 8 percent return is subject to annual income taxes, the return rate is effectively reduced to 6 percent [8 percent $\times$ (1 − 0.25)]. A $3000 annual investment for 20 years that earns 6 percent annually will grow to $110,357. The person has invested $60,000.

Example 2—$137,286: Make Annual After-Tax Investments That Are Tax Sheltered

The sum of $3000 in after-tax money is invested in a tax-sheltered account every year for 20 years. Because no income taxes are assessed on the interest, dividends, and capital gains while they accumulate, the return rate is 8 percent. A $3000 annual investment for 20 years that earns 8 percent annually will grow to $137,286. The person has invested $60,000.

Example 3—$137,286: Make Annual Pretax Investments That Are Tax Sheltered

The $3000 in pretax money is invested in a tax-sheltered account every year for 20 years. Pretax contributions to retirement accounts reduce the current year's income tax liability, so the investor saves $750 ($3000 $\times$ 0.25) in income taxes. Instead of the $750 going to the government, those dollars are used to reduce the amount the person had to invest. A $3000 annual investment for 20 years that earns 8 percent annually will grow to $137,286. Of the $60,000 invested, the person put in only $45,000 because $15,000 was money that would have otherwise gone to the IRS.

Example 4—$171,608: Make Annual Investments That Tax-Shelter Growth Plus Invest the Money That Would Have Gone to the IRS in Taxes

The $3000 in pretax money is invested in a tax-sheltered account every year for 20 years. Pretax contributions to qualified accounts reduce the current year's income tax liability, so the investor saves $750 ($3000 $\times$ 0.25) in income taxes. This time, however, the investor uses that $750 to help fund a larger contribution—$3750 instead of $3000. A $3750 annual investment for 20 years ($75,000 invested, although only $60,000 was the investor's money and $15,000 was money that would have otherwise gone to the IRS) that earns 8 percent annually will grow to $171,608.

You Have Ownership and Portability

Portability means that upon termination of employment, an employee can keep his or her savings in a tax-sheltered account by transferring the retirement funds from the employer's account to another account without penalty. Assets held in tax-sheltered retirement accounts are always owned by the person who opened the account (once the person is vested, as discussed later).

Your Withdrawals Might Be Tax Free

Taxes may or may not be due in the future when withdrawals occur. IRS regulations permit tax-free withdrawals from only one type of retirement account, the Roth IRA, which is discussed later. **Tax free** means that withdrawals are never taxed.

portability Upon termination of employment, employees with portable benefits can keep their savings in tax-sheltered accounts, transferring retirement funds from employer's account directly to another account without penalty.

Instant Message

Beneficiary Designation Form

When you open a retirement account, you must sign a **beneficiary designation form.** This document contractually determines who will inherit the funds in that retirement account in case you die before the funds are distributed. This designation generally overrides any provisions in a will, and it keeps those assets out of one's estate, as discussed in Chapter 18.

✓ **CONCEPT CHECK 17.4**

1. Distinguish between after-tax money put into investments and pretax money.
2. Give your impression of the logic of the "net pay" numbers of participating in a 401(k) plan.
3. Explain what is meant by tax-sheltered investment growth on money contributed to qualified retirement accounts.

Employer-Sponsored Retirement Plans

5 LEARNING OBJECTIVE

Distinguish among the types of employer-sponsored retirement plans.

Employers usually offer retirement plans to their employees because the promise of a secure retirement represents an effective way to recruit and retain valuable workers. An **employer-sponsored retirement** plan is an IRS-approved plan offered by an employer. These are called **qualified** plans. Approximately one-third of all workers at small firms voluntarily participate in an employer-sponsored retirement plan, compared with four-fifths of workers in medium-size to large firms. Participating in such a plan can serve as the cornerstone of your retirement planning. If you do not have access to an employer plan, you should make alternative preparations for retirement (discussed later in this chapter).

Employee Retirement Income Security Act (ERISA) Regulates employer-sponsored plans by calling for proper plan reporting and disclosure to participants in defined-contribution, defined-benefit, and cash-balance plans.

The **Employee Retirement Income Security Act (ERISA)** does not require companies to offer retirement plans, but it does regulate those plans that are provided. ERISA calls for proper plan reporting and disclosure to participants. Three types of employer-sponsored retirement plans are available: defined-contribution, defined-benefit, and cash-balance.

Defined-Contribution Retirement Plan— Today's Standard

defined-contribution plan A retirement plan designed to provide a lump-sum at retirement; it is distinguished by its "contributions"— the total amount of money put into each participating employee's individual account. (Also called *salary reduction plan*.)

A **defined-contribution retirement plan** is designed to provide a lump sum at retirement. It is distinguished by its "contributions"—that is, the total amount of money put into each participating employee's individual account. The eventual retirement benefit in such an employer-sponsored plan consists solely of assets (including investment earnings) that have accumulated in the various individual accounts. In a **noncontributory plan,** money to fund the retirement plan is contributed only by the employer. In a **contributory plan,** money to fund the plan is provided by both the employer and the participant or solely by the employee. Most plans are contributory.

noncontributory plan An employer-sponsored defined-contribution retirement plan in which only the employer makes contributions.

When you elect to participate and contribute to such a retirement plan, you take a portion of your salary and postpone receiving it. That money goes into your account. Because it goes there before you receive it, those funds are not subject to income taxes. Defined-contribution retirement plans are also known as **salary-reduction plans** because the contributed income is not included in an employee's salary. The tax-free contributions are designated as such on the employee's W-2 form. Financial expert Steve Lansing says a defined-contribution plan can be viewed as an interest-free loan from the government, via the income taxes saved, to help finance one's retirement.

contributory plan The most common type of employee-sponsored defined-contribution retirement plan; accepts employee as well as employer contributions.

Each employee's contributions are deposited with a **trustee** (usually a financial institution, bank, or trust company that has fiduciary responsibility for holding certain assets), which invests the money in various securities, including mutual funds, and sometimes the stock of the employer. Each employee's funds are managed in a separate account.

automatic enrollment plan Plan in which the employer withholds up to 6 percent of an employee's salary and places it into a defined-contribution retirement plan.

Employers who offer a defined-contribution account may choose to establish an **automatic enrollment plan** for employees. Employees are registered and the employer withholds up to 3 percent of the employee's salary and puts that amount into each worker's account in an automatically diversified portfolio. Over time, the employer may choose to automatically increase the withholding to 6 percent, or the company maximum. Employees have the right to opt out of this kind of "automatic" plan, although taking such action defeats a valuable way to save for retirement.

Defined-contribution retirement plans are also called **self-directed** because the employee controls the assets in his or her account. The individual selects how to invest, how much risk to take, how much to invest, and how often contributions are made to the account.

Over time, the balance amassed in such an account consists of the contributions plus any investment income and gains, minus expenses and losses. The contributions devoted to the account are specified (defined). The future amount in the account at retirement will not be known until the individual decides to begin making withdrawals. This uncertainty occurs because the sum available to the retiree depends on the success of the investments made.

self-directed In defined-contribution plans, employees control the assets in their account—how often to make contributions to the account, how much to contribute, how much risk to take, and how to invest.

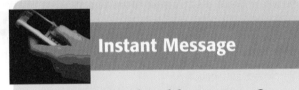

Instant Message

How Much Should You Save?

Only about half of twentysomethings say they have a retirement plan, such as an IRA or 401(k). People who start saving and investing for retirement during their 20s should aim to reserve 12 to 15 percent of their pretax income every year, *including* employer contributions, for this purpose. Those who have delayed planning for retirement until their late 30s or 40s should begin investing 20 to 25 percent annually in an effort to catch up, and they also may have to be more aggressive in their investment choices.

Names of Defined-Contribution Plans

Several types of employer-sponsored defined-contribution plans exist. The most common are the 401(k), 403(b), and 457 plans (named after sections of the IRS tax code) and the SIMPLE IRA. Each plan is restricted to a specific group of workers. You may contribute to these plans only if your employer offers them.

The **401(k) plan** is the best-known defined-contribution plan. It is designed for employees of private corporations. Eligible employees of nonprofit organizations (colleges, hospitals, religious organizations, and some other not-for-profit institutions) may contribute to a **403(b) plan** that has the same contribution limits. Employees of state and local governments and non-church controlled tax-exempt organizations may contribute to **457 plans.** Only employees (not employers) make contributions into the plan. When the employing organization has 100 or fewer employees, it may set up a **Savings Incentive Match Plan for Employees IRA (SIMPLE IRA).** Regulations vary somewhat for each type of plan.

401(k) plan Defined-contribution plan designed for employees of private corporations.

403(b) plan Defined-contribution plan designed for eligible employees of not-for-profit institutions, such as colleges, hospitals, and religious organizations.

Matching Contributions

Many employers offer a full or partial **matching contribution** (up to a certain limit) to the employee's account in proportion to each dollar of contributions made by the participant. The match might be $1.00 per $1.00 up to the first 3 percent of pay. More common is $0.50 per $1.00 up to the first 6 percent of pay. Because your employer makes a contribution to your account every time you do, in effect you obtain an "instant return" on your retirement savings. Saving $4000 a year with a $0.50 employer match immediately puts $2000 more into your retirement account. This concept is illustrated in Table 17.3.

matching contribution Employer benefit that offers a full or partial matching contribution to a participating employee's account in proportion to each dollar of contributions made by the participant.

Limits on Contributions

There are limits on the maximum amount of income that an employee may contribute to an employer-sponsored plan. The maximum contribution limit to 401(k), 403(b), and 457 plans is $15,500; the maximum is $10,500 for SIMPLE IRA plans. These figures rise yearly with inflation.

Catch-up Provision

A **catch-up provision** permits workers age 50 or older to contribute an additional $5000 to most employer-sponsored plans. Millions of people who are getting a late start on saving—including women who have gone back to work after raising children—can put more money away for retirement.

catch-up provision Permits workers age 50 or older to contribute an additional $5000 to most employer-sponsored plans ($1000 limit on IRA accounts).

Vesting Gives You Rights to Your Benefits

Employers may require a waiting period of one year before allowing new employees to participate in the com-

Table 17.3   How Much You Give Up Without Matching Contributions

You might consider working only for employers who offer matching contributions to your retirement account. For example, the matching 100 percent employer contributions shown below increase the retirement account balance after 30 years from $317,193 to $475,789 with a 2 percent match and to $634,386 with a 4 percent match. By increasing the employee's contribution from 4 percent ($70,000 × 0.04 = $2800) to 6 percent ($70,000 × 0.06 = $4200) to obtain the full 100 percent employer match on the first 6 percent of salary, the sum rises to almost $1 million after 30 years earning an 8 percent annual return. You should make contributions to your account at least up to the amount where you obtain the largest matching contribution from your employer. After all, the matching contributions are "free money."

Salary $70,000	Employee contribution	100% match of 2% of salary	100% match of 4% of salary	100% match of 6% of salary
Employee contribution	$ 2,800	$ 2,800	$ 2,800	$ 4,200
Employer contributions	$ 0	$ 1,400	$ 2,800	$ 4,200
Total annual contributions	$ 2,800	$ 4,200	$ 5,600	$ 8,400
Account balance after 30 years earning 8%	$317,193	$ 475,789	$634,386	$951,579

pany's retirement plan. To be eligible for any retirement benefits, an employee must first participate in the employer-sponsored retirement plan.

vesting Ensures that a retirement plan participant has the right to take full possession of all employer contributions and earnings if employee is dismissed, resigns, or retires.

Vesting ensures that a retirement plan participant has the right to take full possession of all employer contributions and earnings if the employee is dismissed, resigns, or retires. If an employee has not worked long enough for the employer to be vested before leaving his or her job, the employer's contributions are forfeited back to the employer's plan. The employee has no rights to any of those funds. Once vested, the worker has a legal right to the entire amount of money in his or her account in a defined-contribution plan. No matter when you leave an employer, you always have a vested right to the money that you personally contributed to that retirement account. Some employers permit immediate vesting, whereby the employees owns the money just as soon as the employer deposits funds into their retirement accounts.

Employees, by law, must be vested no later than specified by one of the following options:

cliff vesting Schedule under which employee is fully vested within three years of employment.

- **Cliff vesting.** The employee is fully vested within three years of employment.
- **Graduated vesting.** Employees must be at least 20 percent vested after two years of service and gain an additional 20 percent of vesting for each subsequent year until, at the end of year six, the account is fully vested.

graduated vesting Schedule under which employees must be at least 20 percent vested after two years of service and gain an additional 20 percent of vesting for each subsequent year until, at the end of year six, the account is fully vested.

Retirement Plan Contribution Tax Credit for Low-Income and Moderate-Income Savers

Singles with adjusted gross incomes of less than $25,000 and joint filers earning less than $50,000 can claim a nonrefundable **retirement plan contribution credit** (also known as a **saver's tax credit**). This credit ranges from 10 to 50 percent of every dollar they contribute to an IRA or employer-sponsored retirement plan up to $2000.

retirement plan contribution credit/ saver's tax credit Program to encourage low-income individuals to save for retirement, this tax credit ranges from 10 to 50 percent of every dollar they contribute to an IRA or employer-sponsored retirement plan up to $2000.

Defined-Benefit Retirement Plan— Yesterday's Standard

defined-benefit retirement plan Employer-sponsored retirement plan that pays lifetime monthly annuity payments to retirees based on a predetermined formula.

The second type of employer-sponsored retirement plan, a **defined-benefit retirement plan,** pays lifetime monthly annuity payments to retirees based on a predetermined formula, usually in the form of annuity payments to retirees. It is commonly called a "pension" or a "final-average plan." A **pension** is a sum of money paid regularly as a retirement benefit. Pensions are paid to retirees, and sometimes their survivors, by the Social Security Administration, various government agencies, and some employers.

Benefits in defined-benefit plans are based on the years of service at the employer, average pay in the last few working years, and a percentage. For example, an employee

Did You Know?...

How to Avoid Rollover Penalties When Changing Employers or Retiring

When changing employers or retiring, you may have four choices:

1. **Leave it.** You may be able to leave the money invested in your account at your former employer until you wish to begin taking withdrawals.

2. **Transfer it.** You may be able to transfer the money to a retirement account at a new employer.

3. **Transfer it.** You can transfer the money to an IRA.

4. **Take it.** You can take the money in cash and pay income taxes and penalties.

Options 2, 3, and 4 result in a **lump-sum distribution** because all the funds are removed from a retirement account at one time. Such a transfer must be executed correctly according to the IRS's "rollover regulations" or the taxpayer will be subject to a substantial tax bill, a **rollover penalty,** and perhaps a need to borrow money to pay the IRS. A **rollover** is the action of moving assets from one tax-sheltered account to another tax-sheltered account or to an IRA within 60 days of a distribution. This procedure preserves the benefits of having funds in a tax-sheltered account.

The IRS's **20 percent withholding rule,** the rollover penalty, applies if the participant takes direct possession of the funds (choice 4 in the previous list). This rule requires that an employer collect a 20 percent tax from any lump-sum distribution that is paid directly to a former employee. This amount is forwarded to the IRS to prepay some of the income taxes that will be owed on the withdrawn funds. To avoid the 20 percent withholding rule, a **trustee-to-trustee rollover** must occur. In this procedure (choices 2 and 3 in the list), the funds go directly from the previous employer's trustee to the trustee of the new account, with no payment to the employee occurring.

For example, a $300,000 lump-sum distribution made directly to an employee would result in that person receiving $240,000 and the employer withholding $60,000 for the IRS. Government regulations further require that the employee put the entire $300,000 into an account at another employer or a **rollover IRA** (an IRA opened to accept rollover funds) within 60 days— even though only $240,000 was actually received by the employee. The investor must supply the difference ($60,000 in this instance) on his or her own. Substantial penalties are assessed for noncompliance. The 20 percent amount that was withheld may be retrieved the following tax year by filing an income tax return to claim a refund. The IRS wants taxpayers to transfer retirement funds in such a way that the previously untaxed money remains accountable and, eventually, taxable.

---

might have a defined annual retirement benefit of 2 percent multiplied by the number of years of service and multiplied by the average annual income during the last five years of employment. In this example, a worker with 20 years' service and an average income of $48,000 over the last five years of work would have an annual benefit of $19,200 (20 × 0.02 × $48,000), or $1600 per month. In another example, an employee with 30 years of service might qualify for 60 percent of the average income over the last five years of work. With a $48,000 average salary over those five years, this worker might receive $28,800 annually, or $2400 per month.

Since the employer contributes all the money, it assumes all the investment risks associated with creating sufficient funds to pay future benefits. Defined-benefit plans were the "standard" a generation ago, but today they are offered by less than one-fourth of employers, primarily because the other retirement plan alternatives are less costly.

Some employers offer both defined-benefit and defined-contribution plans to their employees. Vesting requirements and participant rights are the same for all retirement plans.

Normal or Early Retirement? The earlier you retire, the smaller your monthly retirement pension from a defined-benefit plan will be because you will likely receive income for more years as a retired person. To illustrate, assume you are eligible for a full retirement pension of $24,000 per year at age 65. Your benefit may be

disability benefits Substantially reduced benefits paid to employees who become disabled prior to retirement.

joint and survivor benefit/survivor's benefit Annuity whose payments continue to a surviving spouse after the participant's death; often equals at least 50 percent of participant's benefit.

reduced 5 percent per year if you retire at age 58 or reduced 3 percent per year if you retire at age 62. Smaller monthly pension payments are paid to the early retiree in a defined-benefit plan so that he or she will receive, in theory, the same present value amount of benefits as the person who retires later.

The financial advantage of taking early retirement depends in part on the person's life expectancy and the rate at which benefits are reduced. People who expect to live for a shorter period than the average expectancy may achieve a better financial position by retiring early. Most employees are allowed to work for as long as they choose, but companies generally do not increase benefits for employees who postpone retirement beyond age 65.

Disability and Survivors Benefits Survivors and disability benefits also represent concerns for workers who have spouses or children or are financially responsible for caring for others. A person's full retirement pension forms the basis for any benefits paid to survivors and, when part of a retirement plan, for disability benefits as well. **Disability benefits** can be paid to employees who become disabled prior to retirement. People receiving either survivors or disability benefits are entitled to an amount that is substantially less than the full retirement amount. For example, if you were entitled to a retirement benefit of $2000 per month, your disability benefit might be only $1100 per month.

If a survivor is entitled to benefits, that pension amount must be paid over two people's lives instead of a single person's life; consequently, the monthly payment is different. Using the benefit described in the preceding example, if your surviving spouse is five years older than you, he or she might be entitled to $1300 per month. In contrast, if your spouse is five years younger, he or she might be entitled to only $900 per month.

A qualified **joint and survivor benefit** (or **survivor's benefit**) is an annuity whose payments continue to the surviving spouse after the participant's death, often equal to at least 50 percent of the participant's benefit. This requirement can be waived if desired, but only after marriage—not in a prenuptial agreement. Federal law dictates that a spouse or ex-spouse who qualifies for benefits under the plan of a spouse or former spouse must agree in writing to a waiver of the spousal benefit. This **spousal consent requirement** protects the interests of surviving spouses. If the spouse does waive his or her survivors benefits, the worker's retirement benefit will increase. Upon the worker's death, the spouse will not receive any survivors benefits when a waiver has been signed. Unless a spouse has his or her own retirement benefits, it is usually wise to keep the spousal benefit.

Cash-Balance Plan— The Newest Retirement Deal

A number of employers have established or amended their existing retirement plans to create a third type of employer-sponsored retirement plan, a hybrid of the defined-contribution and defined-benefit plans. A **cash-balance plan** is a defined-benefit plan that gives each participant an interest-earning account credited with a percentage of pay on a monthly basis. It is distinguished by the "balance of money" in an employee's account at any point in time. The employer contributes 100 percent of the funds and the employees contribute nothing. The employer contributes a straight percentage of perhaps 5 percent of the employee's salary every payday to his or her specific cash-balance account. Interest on cash-balance accounts is credited at a rate (perhaps 5 percent) guaranteed by the employer, and the employer assumes all the investment risk. As a result, the amount in the account grows at a regular rate. Employees can look ahead 5 or 25 years and calculate how much money will be in their account.

Vesting requirements for cash-balance plans are the same as those for other employer-sponsored retirement plans. At separation from employment or retirement, the vested employee has the right to all money in the account.

Many large employers are shifting to cash-balance retirement plans in part because they are often much less costly to administer. Cash-balance plans are controversial because when substituted for a defined-benefit plan, they typically give older workers smaller benefits. Recognizing this concern, many cash-balance plans now provide a higher contribution, sometimes as large as 10 percent, for those employees age 55 and older. Younger workers who are more inclined to move from job to job may appreciate a benefit that can move with them, rather than one that offers a substantial payout only after decades of job loyalty.

Additional Employer-Sponsored Plans

Some employers offer supplemental savings plans to employees.

ESOP An **employee stock-ownership plan (ESOP)** is a benefit plan through which the employer makes tax-deductible gifts of company stock into a trust, which are then allocated into accounts for individual employees. When employees leave the company, they get their shares of stock and can sell them. In effect, the retirement fund consists of stock in the company. If the company prospers over time, the employees will own some valuable stock; if the company does poorly or goes bankrupt, the stock may be worthless. (Note that an ESOP is not an employee stock option, examined in Chapter 14, page 396, as an ESO is a gift, like a bonus, from an employer to an employee that allows employees to benefit from the appreciation of their employer's stock without putting any money down.)

To be properly diversified, experts recommend that employees have no more than 10 percent of their retirement assets invested in their employer's company stock. The **2006 Pension Protection Act** provides that companies cannot require that you buy company stock to qualify for a match. If your contributions continue to be matched with stock, you are able to trade out of those shares after three years. If you already own company shares, you can sell a third at a time, over three years.

Profit-Sharing Plan A **profit-sharing plan** is an employer-sponsored plan that shares some of the profits with employees in the form of end-of-year cash or common stock contributions to employees' 401(k) accounts. The level of contributions made to the plan may reflect each person's performance as well as the level of profits achieved by the employer. Contributions might be fixed (perhaps at 10 percent of profits) or be discretionary. They can vary from year to year. Some companies offer a voluntary profit-sharing plan through which employees can regularly purchase shares of stock in the company at discounted prices.

employee stock-ownership plan (ESOP) Benefit plan in which employers make tax-deductible gifts of company stock into trusts, which are then allocated into employee accounts.

profit-sharing plan Employer-sponsored plan that allocates some of the employer profits to employees in the form of end-of-year cash or common stock contributions to employees' 401(k) accounts.

1. Summarize the main differences between defined-contribution and defined-benefit pension plans.
2. Explain why defined-contribution retirement plans are called self-directed.
3. Offer your impressions of working for an employer that offers a sizable matching contribution compared with one that does not.
4. Distinguish between an employee stock ownership plan (ESOP) and a profit-sharing plan.

You Can Also Contribute to Personal Retirement Accounts

6 LEARNING OBJECTIVE

Explain the various types of personally established tax-sheltered retirement accounts.

IRS regulations allow you to take advantage of other personally established, self-directed tax-sheltered retirement accounts. These are especially important if your employer offers no retirement plan. But even if you do have a plan at work, you can benefit from personally established plans.

Individual Retirement Accounts

individual retirement account (IRA)
Personal retirement account to which a person can make annual contributions that provide tax-deferred growth and then decide how to invest the funds within the IRA.

An **individual retirement account (IRA)** is a personal retirement account to which a person can make annual contributions. These accounts are created and funded at the discretion of the individual who sets them up. An IRA is much like any other account opened at a bank, credit union, brokerage firm, or mutual fund company. An IRA is not an investment but rather an account in which to hold investments, such as stocks and mutual funds. You can invest IRA money almost any way you desire, including collectibles like art, gems, stamps, antiques, rugs, metals, guns, and certain coins and metals. You may change investments whenever you please.

You should consider investing in an IRA to augment your retirement savings. IRAs are similar to 401(k) plans in that you do not pay taxes each year on capital gains, dividends, and other distributions from securities held within the account. The maximum contribution you may make to an IRA is $5000. An additional catch-up contribution of $1000 to an IRA may be made by people age 50 and older. You may not borrow from an IRA.

To fund the account, you may make a new contribution or transfer a lump-sum distribution received from another employer plan or another IRA account to your IRA account. Taxpayers can even opt on their tax return to allocate part or all of their refund for direct deposit into an IRA account.

traditional (regular) IRA Account that offers tax-deferred growth; the initial contribution may be tax deductible for the year that the IRA was funded.

Traditional IRAs A **traditional** (or **regular**) **IRA** offers tax-deferred growth. Your contributions may be tax deductible, which means that you can use all or part of your contributions to reduce your taxable income. Qualifying depends on how much your earnings are (restrictions exist to prevent some high-income earners from getting the deduction) and whether you and your spouse are eligible to participate in an employer-sponsored retirement plan. To see whether you qualify for a tax-deductible IRA, use the following guidelines:

1. If you have no retirement plan at work, you can invest in a traditional IRA and deduct the entire amount from your taxes.

2. If you are married and you are not an active participant in an employer retirement plan but your spouse is an active participant, you may deduct all of your contribution to a traditional IRA.

Did You Know?...

Tax-Sheltered Retirement Accounts Offer Flexibility

Both employer-sponsored and individual tax-sheltered retirement accounts offer flexibility on where you can invest. Options may include trust accounts at financial institutions, such as a bank, credit union, savings and loan association, or mutual fund. Individuals often invest in mutual funds and stocks, particularly index funds. You can change investments whenever desired. You may choose to contribute once to a tax-sheltered retirement account and then never do so again, or you can contribute regularly for many years.

3. If you have a retirement plan at work, you may fully or partially deduct your IRA contribution only if your adjusted gross income qualifies. Also, if either spouse participates in an employer-sponsored retirement plan, the allowable contribution depends on the couple's income. The amount begins to be reduced for single taxpayers earning about $80,000 and $160,000 for joint returns.

4. If you have a nonworking spouse, that person may contribute to a spousal IRA. Each partner may invest up to the limit and deduct the full amount if the combined compensation of both spouses is at least equal to the contributed amount.

Distributions from traditional IRAs may be fully or partially taxable. If the account is funded solely by tax-deductible contributions, any distributions are fully taxable when received. If you also made nondeductible contributions, logically some amount should not be taxed at withdrawal as it has already been taxed earlier. You should maintain adequate records of all IRA contributions—even for 40 years or more—to avoid paying too much in taxes. That means saving all annual reports of account activities. The IRS requires that withdrawals from traditional IRAs begin no later than age 70½.

Roth IRAs A **Roth IRA** is a nondeductible, after-tax IRA that offers significant tax and retirement planning advantages for taxpayers earning less than approximately $110,000. Contributions of up to $5000 annually to Roth IRAs are not tax deductible and funds in the account grow tax free. Once you remove money from a Roth IRA, it is a withdrawal (not a loan), and you cannot put it back. Tax-free and penalty-free withdrawals of earnings may be made after a five-year waiting period if you are older than age 59½ or you are disabled. Tax-free withdrawals may be made for qualifying first-time home-buyer expenses or to pay for educational expenses. There is no mandatory withdrawal schedule for Roth IRAs, and money in the account can pass to an heir free of estate taxes. A traditional IRA may be converted to a Roth IRA.*

*A Roth 401(k) plan exists, although it is offered by few employers.

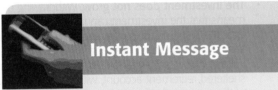

Instant Message

Roth IRA or Regular IRA?

Mutual fund websites provide worksheets to help you decide (in five minutes) whether a traditional IRA or a Roth IRA is best for you. See www.troweprice.com, www.kiplinger.com, or www.fidelity.com. These calculations will be based on your current age, current marginal tax rate, expected annual yield, years to retirement, years in retirement, and marginal income tax rate during the distribution years.

Instant Message

Extra Money to Invest for Retirement

The best place to invest for retirement is in a 401(k) plan. Once you have earned the full company match, put extra money into a Roth IRA.

spousal IRA Account set up for spouse who does not work for wages; offers tax-deferred growth and tax deductibility.

Roth IRA IRA funded with after-tax money (and thus it is not tax deductible) that grows on a tax-deferred basis; withdrawals are not subject to taxation.

Did You Know?...

If You Choose "Low-Cost" Over "High-Cost" Funds

Investing for retirement in low-cost or ultra-low-cost funds, such as an index fund or exchange-traded fund, is the single most effective strategy to fatten your retirement nest egg. The following calculations are based on research from T. Rowe Price and *Money*. Assume you are 30 years old, earn $40,000, and invest 6 percent of your salary with a $0.50 match on $1.00. Your salary increases 3 percent annually and your investments earn 8 percent a year. Low mutual fund expenses dramatically increase your retirement nest egg.

Cost of mutual fund expenses	Retirement Nest Egg at Age 65
High expenses (1.5%)	$664,000
Moderate expenses (1.0%)	$732,000
Low expenses (0.5%)	$819,000
Ultra-low expenses (0.25%)	$852,000

Did You Know?...

Top 3 Financial Missteps in Retirement Planning

People slip up in retirement planning when they do the following:

1. Never starting (or starting late) to begin to save for retirement
2. Putting away too little money
3. Using high-expense mutual funds for your 401(k) or IRA accounts

Annual fees should be no more than one-third of 1 percent of your assets. Financial firms, such as Fidelity and Vanguard, offer similar services on a private basis, although the annual fee might be as high as 1 percent.

Monte Carlo Simulations to Help Guide Retirement Investment Decisions

Employer-based financial advice must follow the requirements of the Pension Protection Act, including keeping employees informed about any possible conflicts of interest. The advice must be based on computer simulations of projected investment performance. Monte Carlo simulations are an evolution of the long-term investment strategy of asset allocation, as discussed in Chapter 13 (see pages 375-376).

Monte Carlo simulations, named for the famous casino site, can be used to model the performance of hundreds or even thousands of individual mutual funds and stocks through fluctuating securities markets. The simulations allow you to estimate the probability of reaching your financial goals. This sophisticated application of asset allocation identifies the investor's acceptable level of risk tolerance and then finds an optimal portfolio of assets that will have the highest expected returns for that level of risk.

The mathematical simulations are based on long-term historical risk and return characteristics for various mixes of stock, bond, and short-term investment asset classes. Each simulation estimates how much you need to save if your investments performed better or worse than expected, and it gives the odds that your assets will last throughout the retirement time period after you choose a given set of investments and establish a withdrawal amount. Note that these calculations are probabilities, not certainties.

By using Monte Carlo simulations, investors can get a more realistic view of how much their current investments may yield in retirement. Investors may learn that they are playing it too safe by investing too conservatively, and this may prevent them from reaching their goals. By evaluating the trade-offs among various combinations of retirement plan contribution levels, diverse investment mixes, overall portfolio risk,

Did You Know?...

How to Invest 401(k) or IRA Money

Recall from Chapter 13 that most of the returns earned by long-term investors come not from owning a few specific investments but rather from owning a diverse portfolio of investments that you hold on to for many years. This can be accomplished through asset allocation, with your portfolio containing certain proportions of equities (stocks), debt (bonds), and cash (money market) equivalents or mutual funds that invest in those types of alternatives. Retirement plans should be invested this way as well.

When you sign up for your 401(k) plan at work, your employer will have established a number of investment vehicles from which you must choose. These are usually arranged through one or two mutual fund companies. You will likely have a stock fund, a growth stock fund, an index fund, a bond fund, and a money market fund at a minimum. In addition, you will likely be able to invest in your own company's stock and in an annuity. What should you choose for your contributions?

You should allocate no more than 10 percent to your company's stock because of the need to diversify. Similarly, you should not have more than 10 percent going into a money market fund because its returns are too low to build the financial nest egg you will need. Annuities, if desired, may be purchased with your money when you retire, so you should wait until then to make

that decision. So that leaves various stock and bond funds.

A young, risk-tolerant, long-term 401(k) investor with an aggressive investment philosophy might have a portfolio with 100 percent in a growth stock fund. A more moderate approach might have a stock fund/bond fund/money market fund portfolio allocated 60/30/10 percent, respectively. As a young investor, you do not need to be conservative with your retirement money because you will have the time to ride out the ups and downs of the stock market. You can keep the same proportions of your asset allocation until your broad investment goals change—possibly not for another 25 or 30 years as you approach retirement.

IRA money should be invested in a similar fashion. You can invest in individual stocks (even your own company's) but should hold your investments in any one stock to below 10 percent to achieve diversification. You will need to make your own arrangements with a mutual fund company for the remainder of your portfolio. This is very easy to do because all the major mutual fund companies and stock brokerage firms have IRA account options. But watch your expenses in these funds. Expense ratios should not exceed 1 percent.

projected retirement age, and retirement income goals, Monte Carlo simulations let you understand how certain changes in these factors will affect the chance that you will have enough money in retirement. Some investors may have to learn to be comfortable with increased risk while others may have to save more or work longer. See Figure 17.2 for illustrative Monte Carlo calculations.

Monte Carlo simulations can be performed with any of the top-rated retirement planning computer software programs: Financial Engines (www.financialengines .com), Morningstar (www.morningstar.com) Vanguard (www.vanguard.com), Fidelity (www.fidelity.com), Quicken (www.Intuit.com), PricewaterhouseCoopers (www .PricewaterhouseCoopers.com), and T. Rowe Price (www.troweprice.com). Many employers provide free access to these software programs as part of the educational efforts associated with a 401(k) plan. These services include retirement forecasts, portfolio monitoring, newsletters, and information on finances and investing. To try out interactive Monte Carlo simulations, see www.moneychimp.com/articles/risk/riskintro.htm.

When you take the appropriate retirement planning action steps, including a moderate amount of risk when investing, you will be able to relax with the confidence that you are making wise decisions about your investment assets and the knowledge that your money will grow and will be there to fund your lifestyle during the last third of your life.

Did You Know?...

Tax Consequences in Retirement Planning

Tax-deferred retirement plans, like 401(k) plans and traditional IRAs, provide these benefits:

- Your contributions are tax deductible and are not subject to federal, state, and local income taxes.

- No income taxes are due on any earnings on the assets until withdrawn.

- Withdrawals are subject to income taxes at your marginal tax rate, which in retirement may be lower than your tax rate today.

- Other retirement income, such as from Social Security, pensions, employment, interest, dividends, and capital gains, is subject to income taxes.

- When you die, any beneficiary may choose to roll your 401(k) assets into his or her IRA tax free.

---

per month ($21,796 ÷ 12 months) before taxes, for 20 years before the fund was depleted. But what if they live for 30 more years? The factor for 30 years is 13.7648, and the answer is $18,162, or $1513 per month. Table 17.4 indicates how long retirement money will last given certain withdrawal rates.

A slightly higher rate of withdrawal can significantly decrease your years of retirement income. For example, a portfolio of $1 million with a 4 percent annual withdrawal rate could provide 20-plus more years of retirement income than the same portfolio with a 5 percent annual withdrawal rate. People planning for retirement should be cautious and withdraw at a rate, perhaps 3½ to 4 percent, that is not likely to deplete their funds too rapidly. Then they can be more confident that their money will last the desired number of years.

Buy an Annuity and Receive Monthly Checks

Rather than continuing to manage their own investments during retirement and make planned withdrawals over the years, some people take a portion of their retirement nest egg (such as one-third or one-half) to buy an annuity. An **annuity** is a contract made with an insurance company that provides for a series of payments to be received at stated intervals (usually monthly) for a fixed or variable time period. For retirees who buy an annuity, this means that an insurance company will manage a lump sum of their retirement nest egg and promise to send monthly distribution payments according to an agreed-upon schedule, usually for the life of the person covered by the annuity (the **annuitant**).

This is best accomplished by purchasing an **immediate annuity** with a single payment during retirement. The income payments will then begin at the end of the first month after purchase. People who buy an immediate annuity typically do so with a lump sum of money rolled over from an individual retirement account, from an employer's defined-contribution retirement account, from the cash-value or death benefit of a life insurance policy, or from other savings and investments.

Annuities offer several options for drawing down the funds used to purchase the annuity. In the following examples of hypothetical income payments, assume that a 70-year-old retiree has purchased an annuity for $100,000. A **straight annuity** might provide a lifetime income of perhaps $790 monthly for the rest of the life of the annuitant only. An **installment-certain annuity** might provide a payment of $680 monthly for the rest of the life of the annuitant with a guarantee that if the person dies before receiving a specific number of payments his or her beneficiary will receive a

annuity Contract made with an insurance company that provides for a series of payments to be received at stated intervals (usually monthly) for a fixed or variable time period.

annuitant Person covered by an annuity who is to receive the benefits.

immediate annuity Annuity, often funded by a lump sum from the death benefit of a life insurance policy or lump sum from a defined-contribution plan, that begins payments one month after purchase.

straight annuity Provides lifetime payments for the life of the annuitant only.

certain number of payments for a particular time period (such as ten years in this example). A **joint-and-survivor annuity** might provide $640 monthly for as long as one of the two people-usually a husband and wife-is alive.

The purchase of an annuity can involve a variety of high sales commissions and fees, and, as such, they can substantially reduce the amount of income paid out. The trade-off is between the guaranteed payouts from an annuity that often carry high costs and the high risks of managing one's retirement investments. Those considering buying an annuity perhaps might begin with the low-fee, AAA-rated industry leader TIAA-CREF.

Another type of annuity is a **deferred annuity.** Here the person pays premiums during his or her life and income payments start at some future date, such as at retirement. A common type of deferred annuity sold by insurance salespeople is called a **variable annuity.** This is an annuity whose value rises and falls like mutual funds, and it pays a limited death benefit via an insurance contract. Variable annuities are sold very aggressively because sellers earn commissions of 5 percent or more, and they charge annual fees that often average 3 percent or more. An investor will have to wait 15 to 20 years before an annuity becomes as efficient an investment as a mutual fund. Variable annuities are not a practical investment for 99 percent of investors.

People should absolutely, positively not consider investing in an annuity until *all* other tax-sheltered vehicles to save and invest for retirement have been maximized. This means that people saving for retirement first contribute the legally permitted maximum amounts to 401(k), traditional IRA, and Roth IRA accounts, perhaps totaling $20,000 each year. The tax-sheltered benefits of these retirement accounts are far better than those offered by a salesperson promoting a deferred annuity. Annuities are replete with numerous restrictions, administrative charges, commissions, purchase fees, withdrawal charges, and penalties. If you need life insurance, buy term life insurance, not an annuity (see Chapter 12); if you need to save for retirement, invest in mutual funds through tax-sheltered retirement accounts.

Consider Working Part Time

For a variety of reasons, including reducing the worry of outliving one's retirement income, instead of retiring completely, some people choose to work part time for a while during their early retirement years. They either continue working for their last employer or go to work part time for a new employer. Reasons include wanting the extra income, enjoying being with coworkers, and obtaining employer-provided health care benefits. Predictions are that many retirees will work part time if for no other reason than to continue to feel active and be a contributing member of society.

joint-and-survivor annuity Provides monthly payments for as long as one of the two people—usually a husband and wife—is alive.

Instant Message

Employers Offer Annuities

There is no need to select an annuity as an investment option within an IRA or inside your employer's 401(k) plan as you save for retirement. Moving some of your money into an annuity is a decision that can wait until you reach retirement age.

Instant Message

What Retirement Money to Spend First

When deciding which money to draw down during retirement, take funds from your taxable account first, and let the tax-sheltered accounts continue to grow.

1. Taxable assets (mutual funds, stocks, bonds, CDs in regular accounts)
2. Tax-deferred assets [IRA, rollover IRA, employer savings plan, and 401(k)]
3. Tax-free assets (Roth IRAs)

deferred annuity Annuity plan in which annuitants pay premiums during their working lives, then take income payments at some future date, such as retirement.

variable annuity Annuity whose value rises and falls like mutual funds and pays a limited death benefit via an insurance contract. Not as efficient as a mutual fund; costs are high for little return.

✓ CONCEPT CHECK 17.8

1. Use Appendix Table A.4 to determine how much money per month could be withdrawn from a $500,000 nest egg over 20 years, assuming it will earn a 6-percent annual return in the future.

2. Offer some positive and negative observations on the wisdom of buying an annuity with all or some of your retirement nest egg money when you retire.

What Do You Recommend Now?

Now that you have read the chapter on retirement planning, what do you recommend to Maryanne and Bob Johnson in the case at the beginning of the chapter regarding:

1. The major steps in the process to determine the amount of Maryanne and Bob's retirement savings goal?

2. How Bob's net income could be invested in a personal tax-sheltered retirement account?

3. The kinds of investment accounts into which they might put additional money over the next 23 years if they determined they needed $1 million to meet their retirement savings goal?

4. The investment strategies that Maryanne and Bob might follow for accumulating their retirement funds?

Big Picture Summary of Learning Objectives

1 Recognize that you are solely responsible for funding your retirement and must sacrifice some current spending and invest for your future lifestyle.

The responsibility of investing for retirement and the risk of making poor investments have been shifted from the employer to the employee. You are solely responsible for meeting your retirement needs, which may include health care costs.

2 Estimate your Social Security retirement income benefit.

The Social Security program is funded through FICA taxes on employees and employers, and the amounts withheld are put into trust fund accounts from which benefits are paid to current program recipients. Congress is expected to take action to maintain the solvency of the Social Security program. You must be fully insured under the Social Security program before retirement benefits can be paid.

3 Calculate your estimated retirement savings needs in today's dollars.

Your retirement nest egg is the total amount of accumulated savings and investments needed to support your desired retirement. This is calculated by projecting your annual retirement expenses and income and determining the amount of annual savings you need to set aside in today's dollars to achieve your retirement goal.

4 Understand why you should save for retirement within tax-sheltered retirement accounts.

Saving in tax-sheltered retirement accounts has tax advantages. Your contributions may be tax deductible and earnings may be tax deferred; thus, you can accumulate more money for retirement.

5 Distinguish among the types of employer-sponsored retirement plans.

The three major types of employer-sponsored retirement plans are defined-contribution, defined-benefit, and cash-balance. Some employers make matching contributions to their employees' accounts. To receive benefits, an employee must be vested in an employer-sponsored retirement plan.

6 Explain the various types of personally established tax-sheltered retirement accounts.

IRS regulations allow you to take advantage of personally established tax-sheltered retirement plans, including the traditional individual retirement account, or IRA, for which contributions are tax deductible and withdrawals are taxed. After-tax contributions may be made to Roth IRAs in which earnings accumulate tax free and withdrawals are not taxed.

7 Recognize that professional investment advice for retirement assets is available, including Monte Carlo simulations.

Employers often provide financial advice for retirement assets, and the advice must be based in part on Monte Carlo simulations. These calculations allow you to estimate the probability of reaching your financial goals.

8 Describe techniques for living in retirement without running out of money.

Your choices at retirement are to carefully manage your retirement account withdrawals, consider purchasing an annuity with a portion of your retirement funds, and/or work part time during your early retirement years. There are tables and techniques to calculate how long your money will last.

Let's Talk About It

1. Do you know anyone who has estimated his or her retirement savings goal in today's dollars? Offer two reasons why many people do not perform those calculations. Offer two reasons why it would be smart for people to determine a financial target.

2. If you go to work for an employer that does not sponsor a retirement plan, which kind of personal retirement account would you establish? A traditional IRA or a Roth IRA? Give two reasons to support your response. How much money do you think could accumulate in the account before retirement?

3. What kinds of people do you think are likely to not plan ahead and save for retirement in a tax-sheltered account? What might be done to help those people prepare for retirement?

4. Of all the mistakes that people make when planning for retirement, which one might be likely to negatively affect your retirement planning? Give two reasons why.

5. If you had $10,000 in your employer's 401(k) plan retirement account, explain how you would invest these funds. Tell why.

Do the Numbers

1. Timothy Clum, of Charlotte, North Carolina, is considering the tax consequences of investing $2000 at the end of each year for 20 years, assuming that the investment earns 6 percent annually.

   (a) How much will the account total if the growth in the investment remains sheltered from taxes?

   (b) How much will the account total if the investments are not sheltered from taxes? (Hint: Use Appendix Table A.3 or the *Garman/Forgue* website.)

2. Over the years, Kyle and Erica Paget, of Joplin, Missouri, have accumulated $200,000 and $220,000, respectively, in their employer-sponsored retirement plans. If the amounts in their two accounts earn a 6 percent rate of return over Kyle and Erica's anticipated 20 years of retirement, how large an amount could be withdrawn from the two accounts each month? Use the *Garman/Forgue* website or Appendix Table A.4 to make your calculations.

3. Kyle Paget from Question 2 is an aggressive investor and lucky. Assume that his $200,000 retirement nest egg will earn 8 percent while his wife Erica's invest-

ments earn 6 percent. How large an amount could be withdrawn from the two funds each month over the next 20 years? Use the *Garman/Forgue* website or Appendix Table A.4 to make your calculations.

4. Christine and Nathan Riley desire an annual retirement income of $40,000. They expect to live for 30 years past retirement. Assuming that the couple could earn a 3 percent after-tax and after-inflation rate of return on their investments, what amount of accumulated savings and investments would they need? Use Appendix Table A.4 or the *Garman/Forgue* website to solve for the answer.

5. Alicia and Juan Selenas, of Fargo, North Dakota, hope to sell their large home for $280,000 and retire to a smaller residence valued at $150,000. After they sell the property, they plan to invest the $130,000 in equity ($280,000 − $150,000, omitting selling expenses) and earn a 4 percent after-tax return. Approximately how much annual income will be earned? Use Appendix Table A.4 or the *Garman/Forgue* website to solve for the answer.

6. Kathryn Ake, of Plymouth, New Hampshire, plans to invest $3000 in a mutual fund for the next 25 years to accumulate savings for retirement. Her twin sister, Kristin, plans to invest the same amount for the same length of time in the same mutual fund. Instead of investing with after-tax money, Kristin will invest through an employer-sponsored retirement plan. If both mutual fund accounts provide a 9 percent rate of return, how much more will Kristin have in her retirement account after 25 years? How much will Kristin have if she also invests the amount saved in income taxes? Assume both women pay income taxes at a 25 percent rate. Use Appendix Table A.3 or the *Garman/Forgue* website to solve for the answer.

7. Jenna Cowley is currently putting $9500 per year into her tax-sheltered employer-sponsored retirement plan at work. Jenna's employer will match $0.50 for each $1 that each employee contributes to his or her retirement account on amounts up to 6 percent of the employee's salary—$4200 in Jenna's case, as her annual salary is $70,000. How much will Jenna accumulate after 18 years if her annual $9500 investments plus the employer's $2100 contributions grow at a 2 percent rate of return after taxes and inflation? (Jenna assumes that her increases in salary will equal the value of inflation and income taxes, so her real income will not change.) Use Appendix Table A.3 or the *Garman/Forgue* website to solve for the answer.

8. Benjamin Chan, of New Brunswick, New Jersey, wants to invest $4000 annually for his retirement 30 years from now. He has a conservative investment philosophy and expects to earn a return of 3 percent in a tax-sheltered account. If he took a more aggressive investment approach and earned a return of 5 percent, how much more would Benjamin accumulate? Use Appendix Table A.3 or the *Garman/Forgue* website to solve for the answer.

Financial Planning Cases

Case 1
Estimating Early and Normal Retirement Benefits

Patrick Dietrick of Las Cruces, New Mexico, age 35, is single and does not expect to marry. He is busily making plans for his retirement from employment in state government. He is anxious to maintain his current lifestyle without "scrimping" but still wants to actively save more for his retirement to take advantage of compounding. Currently, Patrick earns $40,000 per year, with an adjusted gross income of $39,000 and an after-tax income of $29,000. He anticipates receiving $10,000 from Social Security annually and $13,000 per year in a defined-benefit pension upon his retirement at age 65. If he retires at age 55, his pension benefits will be lowered to approximately $9000. To date, Patrick has about $10,000 in investments.

(a) Using the Decision-Making Worksheet on page 495, calculate the additional amount of annual savings that Patrick needs to set aside to reach his goal of retiring at age 55 with 70 percent of his current income.

(b) What amount of savings for retirement would Patrick need if he decided to work to age 65? What amount is needed if he waits until the full retirement age of 67? Use the same worksheet to solve for the answer.

(c) Would you recommend that Patrick invest in a traditional IRA or a Roth IRA? Why or why not?

Case 2
Calculation of Annual Savings Needed to Meet a Retirement Goal

Jessica Amberlin, age 40, single, and from Sacramento, California, is trying to estimate the amount she needs to save annually to meet her retirement needs. Jessica currently earns $30,000 per year. She expects to need 80 percent of her current salary to live on at retirement. Jessica anticipates that she will receive $800 per month in Social Security benefits. Using the Decision-Making Worksheet on page 495, answer the following questions.

(a) What annual income would Jessica need for retirement?

(b) What would her annual expected Social Security benefit be?

(c) Jessica expects to receive $500 per month from her defined-benefit pension at work. What is her annual benefit?

(d) How much annual retirement income will she need from savings?

(e) How much will Jessica need to save by retirement in today's dollars if she plans to retire at age 65?

(f) Jessica currently has $5000 in a traditional IRA. Assuming a growth rate of 8 percent, what will be the value of her IRA when she retires?

(g) How much will she still need to save?

(h) What is the amount she needs to save each year to reach this goal?

Case 3
Deciding How to Invest Retirement Money

Emily Borden, from Georgetown, Delaware, recently graduated from college and started her first full-time job with a midsize company. Emily's employer offers a 401(k) defined-contribution, tax-sheltered retirement account in which she and her employer can place funds. She must select one or more options from among these seven investment choices: (1) her company's stock, (2) a low-risk bond mutual fund, (3) a growth stock fund, (4) an aggressive growth stock fund, (5) a stock index fund, (6) a money market fund, or (7) an annuity. Into which option(s) would you suggest she invest, and indicate what percentage of the overall 100 percent of deposited funds she should put into that option. Explain the reasons for your choices.

Case 4
Victor and Maria's Retirement Plans

Victor, now age 61, and Maria, age 59, are retiring at the end of the year. Since his retail management employer changed from a defined-benefit retirement plan to a defined-contribution plan ten years ago, Victor has been contributing the maximum amount of his salary to several different mutual funds offered through the plan, although his employer never matched any of his contributions. Victor's tax-sheltered account, which now has a balance of $144,000, has been growing at a rate of 9 percent through the years. Under the previous defined-benefit plan, Victor is entitled to a single-life pension of $360 per month or a joint and survivor option paying $240 per month. The value of Victor's investment of $20,000 in Pharmacia stock eight years ago has now grown to $56,000.

Maria's earlier career as a dental hygienist provided no retirement program, although she did save $10,000 through her credit union, which was later used to purchase zero-coupon bonds now worth $28,000. Maria's second career as a pharmaceutical representative for Pharmacia allowed her to contribute about $27,000 to her retirement account over the past nine years. Pharmacia matched a portion of her contributions, and that account is now worth $112,000; its growth rate has ranged from 6 to 10 percent annually. When Maria's mother died last year, Maria inherited her home, which is rented for $900 per month; the house has a market value of $170,000. The Hernandezes' personal residence is worth $180,000. They pay combined federal and state income taxes at a 30 percent rate.

(a) Sum up the present values of the Hernandezes' assets, excluding their personal residence, and identify which assets derive from tax-sheltered accounts.

(b) Assume that the Hernandezes sold their stocks, bonds, and rental property, realizing a gain of $238,000 after income taxes and commissions. If that sum earned a 7 percent rate of return over the Hernandezes' anticipated 20 years of retirement, how large an amount could be withdrawn each month? How large an amount could be withdrawn each month if they needed the money over 30 years? How large an amount could be withdrawn each month if the proceeds earned 6 percent for 20 years? For 30 years?

(c) Victor's $144,000 and Maria's $112,000 in retirement funds have been sheltered from income taxes for many years. Explain the advantages the couple realized by leaving the money in the tax-sheltered accounts. Offer them a rationale to keep the money in the accounts as long as possible before making withdrawals.

Case 5
The Johnsons Consider Retirement Planning

Harry Johnson's father, William, was recently forced into early retirement at age 63 because of poor health. In addition to the psychological drawbacks of the unanticipated retirement, William's financial situation is poor because he had not planned adequately for retirement. His situation has inspired Harry and Belinda to take a look at their own retirement planning. Together they now make about $66,000 per year and would like to have a similar level of living when they retire. Harry and Belinda are both 28 years old, and although their retirement is a long way off, they know that the sooner they start a retirement account, the larger their retirement nest egg will be.

(a) Belinda believes that the couple could maintain their current level of living if their retirement income represented 75 percent of their current annual income after adjusting for inflation. Assuming a 4 percent inflation rate, what would Harry and Belinda's annual income need to be when they retire at age 68? (Hint: Use Appendix Table A.1 or visit the *Garman/Forgue* website.)

(b) Both Harry and Belinda are covered by defined-contribution retirement plans at work. Harry's employer contributes $1000 per year, and Belinda's employer contributes $2000 per year. Assuming a 7 percent rate of return, what would their retirement nest egg total 40 years from now? (Hint:

Use Appendix Table A.3 or visit the *Garman/Forgue* website.)

(c) For how many years would the retirement nest egg provide the amount of income indicated in Question 1? Assume a 4 percent return after taxes and inflation. (Hint: Use Appendix Table A.4 or visit the *Garman/Forgue* website.)

(d) One of Harry's dreams is to retire at age 55. What would the answers to Questions a, b, and c be if he and Belinda were to retire at that age?

(e) How would early retirement at age 55 affect the couple's Social Security benefits?

(f) What would you advise Harry and Belinda to do to meet their income needs for retirement?

On the 'Net

Go to the Web pages indicated to complete these exercises. You can also go to the *Garman/Forgue* website at college .hmco.com/business/students for an expanded list of exercises. Under General Business, select the title of this text. Click on the Internet Exercises link for this chapter.

1. Visit the website for the Social Security Administration. There you will find a quick benefits calculator at http://www.ssa.gov/planners/calculators.htm that can be used to estimate your Social Security benefit in today's dollars. Use an income figure that approximates what you expect to earn in the first full year after graduating from college. When the calculator provides your answer, click on "break-even age" to see when you would be better off if you had waited until age 67 to begin taking benefits rather than age 62.

2. Visit the website for the U.S. Department of Labor. There you will find an article on 401(k) fees and the effects they can have on retirement savings at http://www.dol.gov/ebsa/publications/undrstndgrtrmnt .html. Develop a list of six questions that employees with a 401(k) plan might ask their employers about the fees charged under their plans.

3. Visit the website of the American Association of Retired Persons (AARP), where you will find AARP's views on how to fix the Social Security system at http://www.aarp.org/bulletin/socialsec/ss_ideas.html. How would the suggestions affect your retirement planning? Which of the suggestions would you support? Which would you oppose?

Visit the Garman/Forgue website...

@college.hmco.com/business/students

Under General Business, select *Personal Finance 9e*. There, among other valuable resources, you will find a complete glossary, ACE questions, links to help you complete the chapter exercises, and links to other personal finance sites.

CHAPTER 18

Estate Planning

! ? You Must Be Kidding, Right?

Michael and Jessica have two children. In addition, Michael has a child from his previous marriage to Ashley. Unfortunately, one day a big bus hit and killed Michael. The assets in his IRA and 401(k) accounts amount to $700,000. Who is likely to get the $700,000 now that Michael has died?

A. First wife, Ashley

B. Second wife, Jessica

C. Children of first or second wife

D. Michael's mother

The answer is D, Michael's mother. Why? If Michael was like many unmarried guys starting a career who designate their mothers as the beneficiary, his mom will get all the money if he neglected to change the beneficiary and designate either of his wives or his children on his retirement accounts. And his first wife, Ashley, would get all the money if, when Michael married Jessica, he failed to fill out the form to change the beneficiary designation to his second wife. As you can see, estate planning, like designating beneficiaries, is not just for old people!

LEARNING OBJECTIVES

After reading this chapter, you should be able to:

1 **Identify** the ways that your estate can be transferred through contracts and a will.

2 **Determine** how trusts can be used to transfer assets and reduce estate taxes.

3 **Summarize** the benefits of preparing advance directive documents.

4 **List** the questions and documents needed to simplify the settlement and transfer of your estate.

5 **Explain** the potential impact of estate and inheritance taxes.

What Do You Recommend?

Orlando Molina, age 34, the ballet master at a professional ballet company, recently remarried after being single for several years. He shares custody of his son with his first wife. Orlando married into a ready-made family: Giselle, his new wife, who was divorced from her husband two years ago, has two children, Jamie and Jon. Like many married couples, Orlando and Giselle, who is a modern dance choreographer, have a variety of financial assets. These include bank accounts, money market accounts, mutual fund accounts, 401(k) plans, Roth IRAs, and whole life insurance policies. They also plan to buy a larger home in the near future. Soon after they returned from their honeymoon, Orlando's father, who is only 56 years of age, had a serious stroke. Despite undergoing physical therapy, he is now in a nursing home and likely will reside there for the remainder of his life. The financial and emotional impacts of the elder Mr. Molina's illness have forced Orlando and Giselle to talk about some delicate financial circumstances in their own family.

What do you recommend to Orlando and Giselle on the subject of estate planning regarding:

1. Beneficiary designations for their financial assets?

2. Joint ownership of their home, vehicles, and other property?

3. Making a will?

4. Establishing guardianship for the children?

5. Using advance directive documents to avoid a situation like that confronting Orlando's father?

6. Establishing trusts for their children?

FOR HELP with studying this chapter, visit the
Online Student Center:

www.college.hmco.com/pic/garman9e

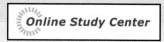

You will work hard over the course of your life to build an **estate.** Everyone has an estate. Your estate consist of your worldly possessions and financial wealth less any debts you owe. As this book amply illustrates, you can and should develop and execute plans for spending, for saving, for investing, for pre-retirement asset accumulation, for protection of those assets, and for the spend-down years of retirement. Now is the time to think about your final financial planning task, the plan to transfer your estate to others. College-educated people now in their 20s may have an estate worth $2 million or more at retirement. They will want to avoid having these assets become depleted because of an extended end-of-life hospital stay, mental incapacitation, or a catastrophic health problem. They also will want to have their estate transferred to the desired people and organizations at death.

This book's closing chapter offers guidance in making these transfers through proper estate planning. **Estate planning** comprises the definite arrangements you make during your lifetime that are consistent with your wishes for the administration, disposition, and transfer of your wealth and worldly possessions to your dependents and others when you die. Estate planning takes into consideration the needs of your survivors, making sure the greatest amount of the estate passes to the intended beneficiaries. It involves both financial and legal considerations, and a common goal is to minimize both taxes and legal costs. Protecting and transferring your estate can be an emotional process, and it is both smart and practical to take the fundamental steps while you are young and then update them as your life progresses.

estate planning Definite arrangements made during your lifetime that are consistent with your wishes for the administration, disposition, and transfer of your wealth and worldly possessions to your dependents and others when you die.

probate court Special court specifically charged to conduct the distribution of assets of people who have died.

probate Court-supervised process that allows creditors to present claims against an estate and ensures the transfer of a decedent's assets to the rightful beneficiaries according to a properly executed and valid will or, when no will exists, to the people, agencies, or organizations required by state law.

1 LEARNING OBJECTIVE

Identify the ways that your estate can be transferred through contracts and a will.

How Your Estate Is Transferred

The deceased person cannot "walk away" from his or her debts when death occurs. Before any money is distributed to heirs, state law requires that all of the deceased's creditors be notified of the death, usually by posting a notice in a local newspaper. In this manner, creditors can collect what they are owed from the estate. Surviving relatives have no personal obligation to repay the decedent's creditors for debts that exceed the assets of the estate.

Good Money Habits in Estate Planning

Make the following your money habits in estate planning:

1. Every three years or whenever your family situation changes, review the beneficiary and ownership designations in your life insurance policies, retirement plans, bank accounts, and other assets to make certain they will transfer the property according to your wishes.

2. Always have both an up-to-date will and a letter of last instructions and revise them as major life events occur.

3. Prepare and regularly update advance directive documents so others can make the right decisions for you if you become incapacitated.

4. Once a year, discuss with your spouse or significant other your family's financial and estate plans.

5. Be positive that certain family members or friends know where you keep financial records, advance directives, your will, and an estate planning checklist.

Probate

When planning for the disposal of your estate, realize that your surviving family members do not conduct the distribution of your assets after death. The distributions are either set up by you before your death or conducted by a **probate court**—a special court that is specifically charged to conduct the distribution of assets of people who have died. **Probate** is a court-supervised process that allows creditors to present claims against an estate and ensures the transfer of a decedent's assets to the rightful beneficiaries according to a properly executed and valid will or, when no will exists, to the people, agencies, or organizations required by state law.

Probate and Nonprobate Property

Figure 18.1 illustrates the different ways that your property can be distributed after your death. **Nonprobate property,** which does not go through probate, includes assets transferred to survivors by contract (such as naming a beneficiary for your retirement plan or with bank accounts owned with another person through joint tenancy with right of survivorship). Trusts (discussed in the next section) can also be used to transfer assets outside of probate.

The remaining probate property goes through the court-supervised probate process of publicly administering the disposition of an estate. A decedent's **probate property** consists of what

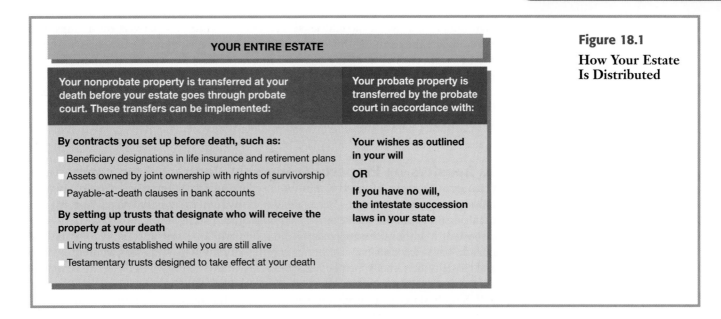

Figure 18.1
How Your Estate Is Distributed

the decedent owned individually and totally in his or her name, as well as the value of assets jointly owned through tenancy in common. In the latter case, the heirs will receive the deceased's share, but not the co-owner's share. In some states, the decedent's half of community property owned with a spouse is included in a person's estate. Avoiding probate may save some costs (the probate process can charge a fee based on the net worth of the deceased) and time and maintain privacy (the probate process is public). Also, the probate process can take between 4 and 18 months.

The proceeds of life insurance if payable to the estate of the deceased—exactly the wrong thing to do—(instead of being payable directly to beneficiaries) are included in one's estate as well. While the beneficiary does not have to pay income taxes on the life insurance proceeds, the amount is included in a person's estate for federal estate tax purposes if the deceased, while alive, retained any ownership interest, such as the right to change beneficiaries or to borrow against any cash value of the policy. Assigning ownership of the policy to someone else, such as the beneficiary, prior to death solves this problem.

Transfer Your Estate by Contracts

Described next are three ways to transfer by contract most or all of one's estate. (Trusts are a special form of contract that is discussed later in this chapter.) Transferring your estate by contract is an easy do-it-yourself project. You just have to take a few minutes of time to fill out the appropriate forms.

1. Transfers by Beneficiary Contract Designation
The forms one fills out to open investment accounts or title certain assets often require a named beneficiary. Examples are IRAs, 401(k) plans, Keogh plans, bank and credit union accounts, stock brokerage accounts, mutual funds, and life and disability income insurance policies. A **beneficiary** is a person or organization designated to receive a benefit. A **beneficiary designation** is a legal form signed by the owner of an asset providing that the property goes to a certain person or organization in the event of the owner's death. The form also contains a place to designate a **contingent** (or **secondary**) **beneficiary** in case the first-named beneficiary has died. If no one has been named as beneficiary for a particular asset or if that person and a named contingent beneficiary have died, the property will go to one's estate and to probate court for distribution.

Retirement plan administrators are required by the Employee Retirement Income Security Act (ERISA) to pay benefits in the plan to the beneficiaries identified in the

beneficiary designation Legal form signed by the owner of an asset providing that the property goes to a certain person or organization in the event of the owner's death.

contingent beneficiary The beneficiary in case the first-named beneficiary has died; also called the secondary beneficiary.

plan documents. Some people leave retirement savings to parents or siblings and never update the forms. If the employee dies without changing the beneficiary, an ex-spouse might inherit all of the plan assets, even if state law views his children as the rightful heirs.

Keeping your beneficiary designations current is extremely important, particularly if you become a parent or get divorced or remarried. Divorce does not terminate an ex-spouse's status as the named beneficiary of a retirement plan or a life insurance policy.

2. Transfers by Property Ownership Contract Designation **Joint tenancy with right of survivorship** (also called **joint tenancy;** see page 146) is the most common form of joint ownership, especially for husbands and wives. In this case, each person owns the whole of the asset, such as a bank account or home, and can dispose of it without the approval of the other owners. Assets owned in this way can include bank accounts, stocks, bonds, real estate, mutual funds, government bonds, and virtually any other type of asset. Upon the death of one owner, the surviving owners receive the property by operation of law rather than through the provisions of a will. Simply stated, the surviving owners owned the entire asset before the death and own all of it after death.

3. Transfers by Payable-at-Death Contract Designation It is often impractical, undesirable, or inappropriate to own certain types of property using joint tenancy. For example, two elderly unmarried siblings might want each other to have access to funds in individual savings accounts earmarked to pay for their funerals but not have those accounts be available to the other sibling during life. They could, of course, designate each other as heirs in their wills. However, the funds would then remain tied up until the probate process is complete. To solve this dilemma, each could name the other to receive the funds upon their death using a **payable-at-death designation** for the account. To access the funds, the surviving sibling would simply need to present the death certificate to the bank and show proper identification, and access to the account would be granted.

Transfer the Rest of Your Estate by Will

A will is one of the primary—and smartest—ways to transfer your assets upon your death. You need a will unless all of your property is nonprobate property or will be

---

joint tenancy with right of survivorship/joint tenancy Most common form of joint ownership, especially for husbands and wives, in which each person owns the whole of the asset, such as a bank account or home, and can dispose of it without the approval of the other owner(s).

payable-at-death designation Status granted to individuals who are not joint tenants and who might need to access accounts without going through probate—the deceased signs the designation before death and the designee simply presents a death certificate to access the accounts.

Did You Know?...

How to Transfer Retirement Assets

As a condition of opening a retirement account, such as an IRA or 401(k), you are required to complete the form identifying your named beneficiary(ies) and contingent beneficiary(ies), the latter in case a primary beneficiary dies before you do. You may designate as a beneficiary a spouse, child, or anyone else. Upon your death, a recipient (or his or her heirs) can choose to take the money directly or have the funds transferred into an existing or new IRA account. An IRA's tax shelter can last as long as

its beneficiaries do. Transferring assets to a young child may keep the tax collector away for many years. Be certain to change your beneficiary when major life events occur, such as divorce, remarriage, or the birth of a child. Otherwise, the originally named beneficiaries (e.g., ex-spouse, ex-spouse's sister) *will* get the funds no matter what! Company pensions operate in a similar manner, although typically the only beneficiary eligible to receive money is a surviving spouse.

Did You Know?...

Last Will and Testament of Harry Johnson

1 Introduction
Being of sound mind and memory, I Harry Johnson, do hereby publish this as my Last Will and Testament. I am married to Belinda Johnson, and my mother is Melinda Johnson.

2 Payment of Debts and Expenses
I hereby direct my Executor to pay my medical expenses, funeral expenses, debts, and the costs of settling my estate.

3 Distribution of Assets
I give my wife one-half of my possessions and all my personal effects. I give my mother one-quarter of my possessions. I give to Common Cause, a nonprofit organization, one-quarter of my possessions. If my wife, Belinda Johnson, predisposes me, I give her share to my mother, Melinda Johnson.

4 Simultaneous Death of Beneficiary
If any beneficiary of this Will, including any beneficiary of any trust established by this Will, other than my wife, shall die within 60 days of my death or prior to the distribution of my estate, I hereby declare that I shall be deemed to have survived such person.

5 Appointment of Executor and Guardian
I appoint my father-in-law, Martin Anderson, to be the Executor of this will and my estate, and provide if this executor is unable or unwilling to serve then I appoint the Trust Department of the Bank of America as alternate Executor. My Executor shall be authorized to carry out all provisions of this Will and pay my just debts, obligations, and funeral expenses.

6 Power of the Executor
The executor of this will has the power to receive payments, buy or sell assets, and pay debts and taxes owed on behalf of my estate.

7 Payment of Taxes
I direct my executor to pay all taxes imposed by governments.

8 Execution
In witness therefore, I hereby set my hand to this last Will and Testament, which consists of one page, this 31st day of January 2008.

9 Witness Clause
The above-named person signed in our presence and in our opinion is mentally competent.

Witness 1	Address	Date
Witness 2	Address	Date

transferred by contract. A will is not estate planning. It is written after all the other aspects of estate planning are completed.

Transfers with a Will Go to Your Desired Heirs
A **will** is a written document in which a person, the **testator,** tells how his or her remaining assets should be given away after death. If you die without a will, the probate court will follow state law to determine how your assets will be distributed.

A simple will that is prepared by an attorney can cost $125 to $400. Minor changes in a will may be made with a **codicil** instead of revoking the existing will and writing a completely new one, as you would when making major changes. People usually know exactly what they want to do with their property, so they can use software and online programs to prepare an uncomplicated will. Examples include BuildaWill .com, Kiplinger's WILLPower, LegalZoom, and Quicken WillMaker.*

If you die with a valid will, the probate court will transfer or distribute your property according to your wishes. A person who inherits or is entitled by law or by the terms of a will to inherit some asset is called an **heir.** A will that is properly drafted,

*Visit www.courttv.com/people/wills to see some wills of famous people.

will Written document in which a person tells how his or her remaining assets should be given away after death; without a will, the property will be distributed according to state probate law.

testator Writer of a will and owner of the estate.

codicil Legal instrument with which one can make minor changes to a will.

heir Person who inherits or is entitled by law or by the terms of a will to inherit some asset.

Preparing a will ensures appropriate distribution of your assets upon your death.

executor/personal representative Person responsible for carrying out the provisions of a will and managing the assets until the estate is passed on to heirs.

guardian Person responsible for caring for and raising any child under the age of 18 and for managing the child's estate.

letter of last instructions Nonlegal instrument that may contain suggestions and recommendations regarding funeral and burial instructions, organ donation wishes, material to be included in the obituary, contact information for relatives and friends, and other information useful to the survivors, such as the location of important documents.

signed, and witnessed is unlikely to be successfully challenged by someone who is dissatisfied with the intended distribution of assets. If you have a complicated estate, you should seek the assistance of an attorney who specializes in estate planning.

Your will should name an **executor** (or **personal representative**). This person ought to be good with paperwork because he or she is responsible for carrying out the provisions of a will and managing the assets until the estate is passed on to heirs. The executor identifies assets, collects any money due, pays off debts, liquidates assets, files final income tax and estate tax returns, and with the court's permission distributes the balance of any remaining money and property to the beneficiaries. Some people select a friend or relative to perform the executor's duties, whereas others name an accountant or attorney to play this role. The executor's fee for carrying out these complicated tasks ranges from 1 to 5 percent of the estate.

If you have minor children, you should appoint a legal **guardian** for each child in your will. This person is responsible for caring for and raising any child under the age of 18 and for managing the child's estate. The guardian should be someone who shares your values and views on child rearing. Financial columnist Michelle Singletary suggests that you might avoid as potential guardians those who are too old, too ill, or too tired from raising their own children, and those who don't really know the children. Consider naming an alternate candidate in case your first choice cannot take on this responsibility. If you have not taken steps to name a legal guardian, the court will appoint one.

Many people prepare a nonlegal **letter of last instructions** along with their will that may contain suggestions and recommendations regarding funeral and burial instructions, organ donation wishes, material to be included in the obituary, contact information for relatives and friends, and other information useful to the survivors, such as the location of important documents. A letter of last instructions may specify that certain pieces of jewelry or art are to go to specific people. If the will contains different instructions on these matters, the will prevails. Family members and others are not legally bound by details in a letter of last instructions.

Your original will and letter of last instructions should be kept in a safe place, such as a safe-deposit box or at an attorney's office. Copies may be given to certain family members or friends.

Without a Will, Your Property May Not Go to the Correct Heirs When a person dies without a valid will, the deceased is assumed to have died **intestate.** In such a case, the probate court will divide all property according to a set formula and transfer assets to the legal heirs. If no surviving relatives exist (a rare situation), the estate will go to the state by **right of escheat.** Your friends and charities will get nothing. If you die without leaving a valid will, the intestate succession laws in the state in which you lived prior to death then determine how your property will be divided. This legal determination may force your heirs to share money in ways you did not intend, and those provisions may exclude distribution of your assets to nonmarital partners, step-children, friends, and charities. The probate court will also ensure that the debts, income taxes, and expenses of the deceased are paid. Dying intestate can cost much more in taxes and cause legal, bureaucratic, and emotional struggles for survivors.

When one dies without a will, the manner in which the assets are divided varies enormously from state to state. For example, one state might make the following distributions of a $120,000 estate: If a person with no surviving kin except a spouse dies without a will, the spouse receives the entire estate of $120,000. If the deceased had children with that spouse, the spouse takes $60,000 and the balance is divided equally between the spouse and their children. If the couple was not married, the children would get 100 percent. If the deceased also had children from another marriage, one-half of the estate goes to the spouse and the balance is divided among all his children. If a spouse and a parent survive the decedent, the spouse receives $60,000 and one-half of the balance, with the remainder passing to the parent.

As you can see, state laws contain a number of complex provisions that govern what constitutes a legal heir and how much (if any) of an estate an heir may be entitled to receive. What may appear least fair in the intestate distributions just described is that, if the decedent has no children, his or her spouse may be required to share the assets with a distant relative. More than half of all adults and two-thirds of all parents with dependent children do not have wills.

intestate When a person dies without a legal will.

right of escheat Law by which an estate transfers to the state if no surviving relatives exist.

Instant Message

Do-It-Yourself Estate Planning

Routine legal estate planning matters can be handled without a lawyer. Nolo (www.nolo.com) is a publisher of self-help, lawyer-prepared legal books on such topics as writing a will or living trust and other ways to minimize estate taxes.

✔ CONCEPT CHECK 18.1

1. What is probate, and why do people try to avoid probate court?
2. Distinguish between probate and nonprobate property.
3. Give three examples of how people transfer some estates by contract.
4. Give an example of what could happen to one's estate when one dies without a will.

Use of Trusts to Transfer Assets and Reduce Estate Taxes

Properly drawn trusts can save you and your family time, trouble, and money. These laudable objectives can be achieved only with the assistance of an experienced attorney who specializes in carefully drafting, planning, and executing strategies and techniques in estate planning.

2 LEARNING OBJECTIVE
Determine how trusts can be used to transfer assets and reduce estate taxes.

trust Legal arrangement between you as the creator of the trust and the trustee, the person designated to faithfully and wisely manage any assets in the trust to your benefit and to the benefit of your heirs.

grantor/settler/donor/trustor Creator of a trust.

trustee Person charged with carrying out the trust for the benefit of the grantor(s) and heirs.

By creating one or more trusts, portions of an estate can be transferred in a contractual manner to others in a way that avoids probate and may reduce or eliminate the federal estate tax. A **trust** is a legal arrangement between you as the **grantor** or creator of the trust and the **trustee,** the person designated to control and manage any assets in the trust. The agreement requires the trustee to faithfully and wisely manage and administer the assets to the benefit of the grantor and others. Trusts can be established to take effect during the grantor's life as well as upon his or her death.

People who should consider setting up a trust include those who have complex estates, hold relatively few liquid assets, desire privacy for their heirs, fear a battle over the provisions of a will, or live in a state with high probate costs or cumbersome probate procedures. Trusts may be created to safeguard the inheritances of survivors, reduce estate taxes, fund a child's education, provide the down payment on someone's home, provide financial assistance for minor children, manage property for young children or disabled elders, and provide income for future generations.

Some of the terms associated with trusts are as follows:

- **Grantor:** The person who makes a grant of assets to establish a trust. Also called the **settler, donor,** or **trustor.**
- **Trustee:** The person or corporation to whom the property is entrusted to manage for the use and benefit of the beneficiary or beneficiaries.
- **Corpus:** The assets put into a trust. Also called the *trust estate* or *fund.*
- **Beneficiary:** The person for whose benefit a trust is created. Also called the **donee.**
- **Remainder beneficiaries:** The parties named in the trust who are to receive the corpus upon termination of the trust agreement.

living trust A trust that takes effect while the grantor is still alive.

testamentary trust A trust that takes effect only upon the grantor's death.

Living Trusts

Trusts fall into two broad categories: (1) **living trusts** and (2) **testamentary trusts** that go into effect upon death.

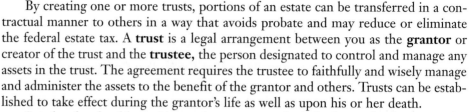

 Did You Know?...

Spouses Have Legal Rights to Each Other's Estates

The **partnership theory of marriage rights** presumes that wedded couples intend to share their fortunes equally. Thus, property acquired during the marriage and titled in the name of only one partner (other than property acquired by gift or inheritance) becomes the property of both spouses. A decedent who disinherits a surviving spouse or who leaves that person with less than a fair share of the estate is judged to have reneged on the partnership. A surviving spouse disinherited in this manner has some claim in probate court to a portion of the decedent's estate if he or she chooses to elect that option. All states give a surviving spouse the right to claim one-fourth to one-half of the other spouse's estate, no matter what a will provides. The remaining portion may pass to other heirs.

Furthermore, in states with **community property laws,*** the law assumes that the surviving spouse owns half of everything that both partners earned during the marriage,

no matter how much was actually contributed by either partner and even if only one spouse held legal title to the property. States with community property laws provide the same spousal rights for marriages that end in divorce.

Community property consists of property acquired during marriage, except for separable property. **Separable property** is a property wholly owned by one spouse. That is, separable property belonged to one spouse before marriage or was received by that person as a gift or an inheritance during the marriage.

You may not disinherit a spouse unless that person's right to inheritance was voluntarily given up in a signed agreement—and even that type of document might be challenged in court. States often limit the right to contest a will by providing that survivors have six months to challenge it and claim a legal share. Domestic partners usually have no legal claim on the estate of their deceased partners.

*Arizona, California, Idaho, Louisiana, Nevada, New Mexico, Puerto Rico, Texas, Washington, and Wisconsin.

Revocable Living Trusts.

A **revocable living trust** is used to protect and manage a person's assets. The person creating the trust maintains the right to change its terms or cancel the trust at any time, for any reason, during his or her lifetime. Thus, the grantor retains control over the assets for as long as he or she lives. Revocable living trusts often establish the grantor as the trustee. A revocable living trust can provide for the orderly management and distribution of assets if the grantor becomes incapacitated or incompetent. A new trustee can easily be named. A revocable living trust operates much like a will and can prove difficult to contest. Its assets stay in the estate of the grantor.

Irrevocable Living Trusts

An **irrevocable living trust** is an arrangement in which the grantor relinquishes ownership and control of property. Usually this involves a gift of the property to the trust. It cannot be changed or undone by the grantor during his or her lifetime. The grantor gives up three key rights under an irrevocable living trust: (1) control of the property, (2) change of the beneficiaries, and (3) change of the trustees. Because irrevocable trusts are generally considered separate tax entities, the trust pays any income taxes due. The assets in the trust bypass probate; however, transfers to a trust made within three years of death may be brought back into the decedent's estate for tax purposes.

Testamentary Trusts

The second broad category of trusts used in connection with estate planning comprises **testamentary trusts.** A testamentary trust becomes effective upon the death of the grantor according to the terms of the grantor's will or a revocable living trust. Such trusts can be designed to provide money or asset management after the grantor's death, to provide income for a surviving spouse and children, and to give assets to grandchildren or great-grandchildren while providing income from the assets to the surviving spouse and children, among other things.

revocable living trust Grantor maintains the right to change the trust's terms or cancel it at any time, for any reason, during his or her lifetime.

irrevocable living trust Arrangement in which the grantor permanently gives up ownership and the right to control of the property, to change the beneficiaries, and to change the trustees.

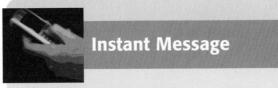

Instant Message

Special Needs Trust

Some states have passed laws that allow parents to set aside money in a trust specifically for the benefit of a disabled child or adult while letting him or her retain all public benefits, like Medicaid or welfare. This kind of trust is called a **special needs trust.** It provides lifelong access to supplemental and emergency funds to cover expenses that public assistance does not. The trustee makes all the decisions to pay for access to ensure suitable health, safety, and welfare. Without special arrangements, income from a trust will count against a special needs child who is receiving public aid.

Did You Know?...

Use of a Charitable Remainder Trust to Boost Current Income

Effective use of an **irrevocable charitable remainder trust (CRT)** is popular for people who want to leave a portion of their estate to charity because it can boost one's income during the grantor's lifetime. You set up the trust and irrevocably give it assets. The trust then pays you income from the assets in the trust for a set period, usually for life, and possibly your spouse's life as well. The charity eventually receives the corpus of the CRT when you (and your spouse, if so arranged) die. For example, Amy Louisanta, a widow from Hyattsville, Maryland, increased the after-tax income on her $60,000 investment portfolio from $1000 to $4800 per year by earmarking the assets for the National Wildlife Federation. According to her attorney, Matthew Paul, the CRT that Amy created quickly sold the assets without incurring any capital gains taxes and then reinvested the proceeds.

A CRT works well for people who show wealth on paper because of appreciated assets. The projected future value of the gift can be discounted to a present value. This amount can then be written off as a charitable contribution on Amy's current income tax return, saving her even more money. It is wise to give to a CRT because the donor can avoid capital gains taxes while still realizing the full benefit of the asset's current value.

✓ CONCEPT CHECK 18.2

1. List some reasons why people establish trusts.
2. Distinguish between a grantor and a trustee.
3. Summarize the difference between living and testamentary trusts.
4. Explain what is so important about the difference between revocable and irrevocable trusts.

Prepare Advance Directive Documents in Case You Become Incapacitated

3   LEARNING OBJECTIVE

Summarize the benefits of preparing advance directive documents.

You can retain your dignity and save your loved ones the burden of making some very challenging decisions by writing down what you want to happen if you become incapacitated. Many illnesses, such as Alzheimer's disease, strokes, and cancer, can result in a period of mental incompetence and physical disability before death. Give copies of these documents to members of your family and other responsible people in your life, and your wishes in these matters may be controlled as you desire.

Instant Message

Estate Planning for Unmarried Couples

While state laws are evolving on the rights of unmarried couples, a loved one can be protected and have some legal power. To do so, name each other in these estate planning documents: titling of assets, beneficiaries, durable power of attorney, health care durable power of attorney, living will, will, and, if appropriate, guardianship of children.

Instant Message

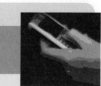

Estate Planning on the Web

- American Bar Association (http://www.abanet.org/rppt/public/home.html)
- Nolo (http://www.nolo.com/resource.cfm/catID/FD1795A9-8049-422C-9087838F86A2BC2B/309/)
- Cornell Law School (http://www.law.cornell.edu/wex/index.php/Estate_Planning)
- National Association of Estate Planners & Councils (http://www.naepc.org/)

Powers of Attorney

People over age 50 or 60 often create a **durable power of attorney** well in advance of the onset of any medical problems. This is a document in which you appoint someone, called an attorney-in-fact, to handle your legal or business matters and sign his or her name to documents. It stays in effect as long as you live, unless you explicitly revoke it. This document should detail the specific aspects of your affairs that it covers and should even mention specific institutions (banks or brokerage firms, for example) and account numbers. A durable power of attorney gives the designated person virtually absolute power to manage your financial affairs, so choose a trusted individual who knows your wishes.

A **limited** (or **special**) **power of attorney** is narrower in scope and could be restricted to one specified act or a certain time period, such as signing your name at the closing of the sale of a home or managing your investment accounts. A **springing power of attorney** "jumps" into effect when a specified event occurs, usually mental incapacitation or disability. This is often used to allow a spouse or family member to manage the grantor's affairs in case illness or injury makes him or her unable to act, while allowing him or her to retain power before the incapacity occurs.

Advance Medical Directives

An **advance medical directive** is a medical guideline that pertains to treatment preferences, including the designation of a surrogate decision maker in the event that a patient becomes unable to make medical decisions on his or her own behalf as a result of coma, dementia, brain death, or other serious medical condition. A **living will** specifies what types of medical treatment are desired. It commonly states that "If I suffer an incurable, irreversible illness,

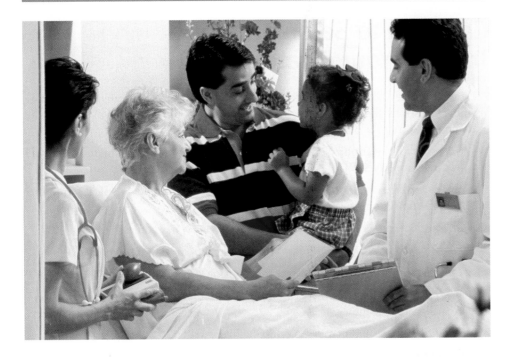

Medical directives and health care proxies can help family members make appropriate decisions when a loved one is incapacitated.

disease, or condition and my attending physician determines that my condition is terminal, I direct that life-sustaining measures that would serve only to prolong my dying be withheld or discontinued."

This document may relieve family members of making a painful decision to allow a person's life to end. To be effective and to avoid varying interpretations, a living will must speak to specific circumstances. For example, a living will could dictate a "do not resuscitate order" designed to prohibit health care providers from attempting cardiopulmonary resuscitation (CPR) in case of cardiac or respiratory arrest. Federal law requires hospitals to inform patients of their rights to make such decisions about medical care. Living wills need to conform precisely to the statutes in the state in which the person lives.

A **health care proxy** is a legal document in which individuals designate another person to make health care decisions if they are rendered incapable of making their wishes known. The person designated in the health care proxy has, in essence, the same rights to request or refuse treatment that the individual would have if capable of making and communicating decisions.

Instant Message

Steps in Estate Planning

1. Inventory everything you own and owe.
2. Record reasonable estimates of each item's current value.
3. Prepare advance directives.
4. Create a comprehensive estate planning checklist describing all essential assets, documents, and financial information and where they are located.
5. Sit down with your spouse or significant other and discuss your wishes about who should get what and under what circumstances.
6. Decide which estate planning tools are the most appropriate choices for your situation.

✓ CONCEPT CHECK 18.3

1. What does a durable power of attorney accomplish, and who should consider having one?
2. Distinguish between a limited power of attorney and a springing power of attorney.
3. Summarize the difference between a living will and a health care proxy.

health care proxy Legal document that appoints another person to make health care decisions if the writer of the proxy is rendered incapable of making his or her wishes known.

Checklist to Settle and Transfer Your Estate

4 LEARNING OBJECTIVE

List the questions and documents needed to simplify the settlement and transfer of your estate.

Creating a master checklist to your financial world by providing answers to estate planning questions and detailing the locations of related documents will simplify the settlement and transfer of your estate.

1. *Current will.* Location? Contact information for attorney? For financial adviser? For insurance agent?

2. *Powers of attorney.* Durable power of attorney? Advance medical directive? Medical power of attorney?

3. *Letter of last instructions.* Document locations? Who has copies?

4. *Funeral and burial arrangements.* Written instructions? Who has copies?

5. *Trusts.* Location? Attorney contact information?

6. *Official documents.* Birth? Prenuptial agreements? Marriage? Divorce? Guardianship? Military?

7. *Social Security numbers.* Yours? Spouse? Children?

8. *Computer passwords.* Passwords for computer?

9. *Safe-deposit box.* Location? Key? Written record of contents?

10. *Employer.* Employee benefits? Contact information for supervisors and human resources department?

11. *Life insurance.* Policies? Employer group policy? Beneficiaries? Contingent beneficiaries? Agent(s)? Details on collecting benefits?

12. *Pension.* Potential benefits? Veterans benefits?

13. *Retirement accounts.* IRA? 401(k)? Keogh? Annuities? Employer pension plans? Passwords?

14. *Social Security and Veterans Administration.* Current or potential benefits? Discharge papers? Records?

15. *Health insurance.* Coverage details? Employer policy?

16. *Disability income and long-term care insurance.* Policies?

17. *Financial statements.* Balance sheet, including artwork and family heirlooms? Cash-flow statement? Value of estate?

18. *Budget.* Details? Old records?

19. *Liabilities.* Credit cards? Vehicle loans/leases? Personal loans? Mortgages? Passwords?

20. *Cash management.* Bank information? Checking? Savings? Money market? Passwords? Certificates of deposit?

21. *Housing.* Deeds? Titles? Rental properties? Title insurance? Timeshares? Homeowner's policies?

22. *Automobiles/recreational vehicles.* Titles? Insurance policies?

23. *Investment assets.* Brokerage accounts? Mutual fund statements? Stocks? Bonds? Other assets? Written investment objectives? Passwords?

24. *Business interests.* Agreements? Ownership interest in a family-owned business? Legal counsel?

25. *Tax returns.* Last year's return? Previous returns? Current year's information? Gift and estate tax?

CONCEPT CHECK 18.4

1. List five estate planning documents that should be easily found by your survivors.

2. List five different types of assets about which your survivors will need detailed information in order to claim them after your death.

Estate and Inheritance Taxes

The **federal estate tax** is assessed against the estate of a deceased person before property (real estate, stocks and bonds, business interests, and so on) is transferred to heirs or assigned according to terms of a will or state intestacy laws. It is a tax on the deceased's estate, not on the beneficiary who is to receive the property.

The first $2.0 million of a taxable estate is exempt from the federal estate tax. Referred to as the **exclusion amount,** it is the value of assets that may be transferred to heirs without incurring an estate tax. The **marital deduction** allows an estate to pass on an unlimited amount of assets to a surviving spouse free of estate taxes. When the surviving spouse who inherited assets dies, the estate would be subject to any federal estate taxes in effect at that time.

You are not likely to be subject to federal estate taxes because out of about 2.4 million deaths each year, only 18,000 estates must pay estate taxes; that is less than 1 percent. Most estate taxes are paid by the extremely wealthy. Because of exemptions, trusts, gifts, and other estate planning actions, the average tax bite on an estate of $1 to $2 million is 4.7 percent and it is 10.5 percent on estates of $2 to $3.5 million. Current law has the federal estate tax being repealed and going to zero in 2010. The law expires in 2011, meaning that the older estate tax rates, which are higher, will become law again that year unless Congress changes it. Seventeen states and the District of Columbia have a state estate tax, and since most are coupled with the federal estate tax, the state tax is zero when the federal tax is zero.

Eight states* impose an **inheritance tax** assessed by the decedent's state of residence on *beneficiaries* who receive inherited property. This tax is based on how much the beneficiaries get and their right to receive it. In those states, transfers to spouses, children, and other close relatives may be either exempt or subject to a lower state inheritance tax rate. The beneficiaries are responsible for paying inheritance taxes, although typically the estate pays the taxes before distributing any remaining assets to the heirs.

5 LEARNING OBJECTIVE
Explain the potential impact of estate and inheritance taxes.

Did You Know?...

Top 3 Financial Missteps in Estate Planning

People slip up in estate planning when they do the following:

1. Not having a will

2. Not having signed advance directive documents

3. Forgetting to update forms you have signed that contractually award assets, like life insurance and retirement and checking accounts, to ex-spouses, parents, siblings, and others because those instructions override your will.

federal estate tax Assessed against a deceased person's estate before property (real estate, stocks and bonds, business interests, and so on) is transferred to heirs or assigned according to terms of a will or state intestacy laws.

exclusion amount The value of assets that may be transferred to heirs without incurring an estate tax— currently $2 million.

marital deduction Allows an estate to pass on an unlimited amount of assets to a surviving spouse free of estate taxes.

CONCEPT CHECK 18.5

1. What is the exclusion amount on the federal estate tax?

2. Tell how the marital deduction works in estate planning.

3. Comment on the likely impact of estate taxes and inheritance taxes at the state level on most people.

*Connecticut, Indiana, Iowa, Kentucky, Maryland, Nebraska, New Jersey, and Pennsylvania.

Advice from a Pro...

Ten Things Every Spouse Must Know

The following checklist contains items spouses should know about financial, estate, tax, and investment planning. After all, it is never what we know that will get us in trouble, but rather what we don't know.

1. Understand your current financial situation—assets and liabilities, net worth, and family income and expenses.

2. Have a plan for all emergencies. Know exactly what financial resources would be needed if your spouse were to become disabled or unemployed. Make certain your auto, homeowner's, and medical insurance coverage are adequate for your situation. Have sufficient cash on hand to pay your deductibles.

3. Carry sufficient life insurance on yourself and your spouse. Determine whether sufficient resources are available to raise your family and provide for your children's education if you or your spouse were to die. Know what benefits your spouse's employer offers and what benefits have been selected. Know who is the beneficiary at your spouse's death and if both you and your spouse were to die. Consider naming a trust as beneficiary instead of naming minor-age children as beneficiaries.

4. Verify that your estate documents (wills, trusts, guardianships, durable powers of attorney, and so on) reflect your current wishes for your family.

5. Understand your income taxes and pursue aggressive, but legal, strategies for reducing your tax liabilities. Don't sign a return you don't understand.

6. Create a written investment plan and follow it. Understand the rate of return that you must realize on your investments to achieve your goal. Monitor your results quarterly.

7. Know how to invest—when to buy and sell—so that you can consistently obtain a rate of return that will allow your family to achieve and maintain financial independence. Do not expect someone else to care more about your money than you do.

8. Have a plan for funding your children's education, home ownership, and your retirement. Complete sample FAFSA forms when your child enters high school so you will understand what the government believes your family should be able to contribute for your child's college education.

9. Thoroughly understand your employer- and government-provided benefits. If they are not sufficient to achieve your goals, make a career change. There is no sense in riding a dead horse.

10. Communicate with your children and other members of your family to teach them about financial, estate, tax, and investment planning. Remember, the most expensive form of education is to learn through your own bad experiences.

Lorraine R. Decker
Decker & Associates Inc., www.DeckerUSA.com

Source: Decker, Lorraine R., CLU, ChFC, MSFS, President, Decker & Associates Inc., "Ten Things Every Spouse Must Know About Finance, Estate Tax, and Investment Planning." Copyright © 2008 by Decker & Associates Inc. Reprinted with permission.

What Do You Recommend Now?

Now that you have read the chapter on estate planning, what do you recommend to Orlando and Giselle Molina in the case at the beginning of the chapter regarding:

1. Beneficiary designations for their financial assets?

2. Joint ownership of their home, vehicles, and other property?

3. Making a will?

4. Establishing guardianship for the children?

5. Using advance directive documents to avoid a situation like that confronting Orlando's father?

6. Establishing trusts for their children?

Big Picture Summary of Learning Objectives

1 Identify the ways that your estate can be transferred through contracts and a will.

After inventorying everything you own and owe, you may find that you can readily transfer most or all of your estate with a will and via contracts. Nonprobate property, which does not go through the court process of probate, includes assets transferred to survivors by contract (such as naming a beneficiary for your retirement plan or with bank accounts owned with another person through joint tenancy with right of survivorship).

2 Determine how trusts can be used to transfer assets and reduce estate taxes.

By creating one or more trusts, portions of an estate can be transferred in a contractual manner to others in a way that avoids probate and may reduce or eliminate the federal estate tax. A trust is a legal arrangement between you as the grantor or creator of the trust and the trustee, the person designated to control and manage any assets in the trust. Revocable and irrevocable trusts are used in estate planning as well as testamentary trusts.

3 Summarize the benefits of preparing advance directive documents.

Making advance directives can save your loved ones the burden of making some challenging decisions in case you become incapacitated. These documents include durable power of attorney, limited power of attorney, living will, and health care directive.

4 List the questions and documents needed to simplify the settlement and transfer of your estate.

Creating a master list of "*CliffsNotes*" to your financial world by providing answers to estate planning questions and listing the locations of related documents will simplify the settlement and transfer of your estate.

5 Explain the potential impact of estate and inheritance taxes.

The federal estate tax affects less than 1 percent of estates, and a surviving spouse may use the marital deduction to completely avoid the tax during his or her lifetime. Some states have state estate and inheritance taxes.

Let's Talk About It

1. Do college students really need a will at this point in their lives? Why or why not? What probably would happen to the typical college student's assets if he or she died without a will?

2. What are some criteria that you would use to select the executor for your estate or the guardian for your children if you and your spouse or significant other died at the same time?

3. If you were thinking about signing a living will, what are some provisions that you might put into the document?

4. Identify topics that you would cover in your letter of last instructions.

5. Do you think it is appropriate for parents and grandparents to put conditions in a trust set up for their

children or grandchildren that relate to the behavior of those assets?

Do the Numbers

1. Christopher Marcos, of Compton, California, died recently without a valid will. His probate estate for federal estate tax purposes was $3.2 million. Christopher's wife, Amanda, and three children were his only survivors. Answer the following questions, assuming that Christopher's state of residence followed the typical guidelines of division (one-half for the spouse with the children equally splitting the remainder):

   (a) What will be the proportional division of assets for the wife and children?

   (b) What dollar amount will be inherited by Amanda?

   (c) If Amanda now dies without a will, what will be the proportional division of assets, assuming that she has no other children?

   (d) If Amanda has personal assets (beyond her inheritance from Christopher) that have a fair market value of $400,000, when she dies, how much will her estate total?

   (e) Assuming Amanda's estate paid $15,000 for her funeral expenses, $14,000 for probate costs, and $180,000 to pay off the remaining debts and mortgages, what was Amanda's taxable estate?

2. Laura Kim of Southington, Connecticut, lives with her elderly grandmother, Haejeong. Her grandmother owns two profitable auto parts stores that are worth millions. Because current law has the federal estate tax going to zero in 2010, the pair is wondering how these taxes might affect Haejeong's estate. Laura hopes that her grandmother, who is in excellent health, lives at least another 20 years. If she doesn't, the federal estate tax will apply in all years except 2010. If Haejeong's probate estate is valued at $3.5 million, calculate the following:

   (a) The amount of the federal estate tax if she dies in 2008 (exclusion is $2 million; 45 percent tax rate)

   (b) The amount of the federal estate tax if she dies in 2010 (zero taxes)

Financial Planning Cases

Case 1
A Couple Considers the Ramifications of Dying Intestate

Melissa Merryweather of Savannah, Georgia, is a 34-year-old police detective earning $58,000 per year. She and her husband, Joshua, have two children in elementary school. They own a modestly furnished home and two late-model cars. Melissa also owns a snowmobile. Both spouses have

401(k) retirement accounts through their employers, and their employers also provide them with $50,000 group term life policies. Melissa also has a $50,000 term life policy of her own. The couple has about $5000 in their joint checking account. Neither has a will.

   (a) List four negative things that could happen if either Melissa or Joshua were to die without a will.

   (b) What would be the most important negative consequence of not having a will if both Melissa and Joshua were to die together in an accident?

   (c) Which assets could be jointly owned so that they will automatically transfer to the other spouse if either Melissa or Joshua dies?

   (d) What qualities should Melissa and Joshua look for when naming the executors of their wills?

   (e) Once they have completed and signed their wills, where should the Merryweathers keep the original documents and any copies?

Case 2
A Lottery Winner Practices Estate Planning

Your good friend and next-door neighbor, Brandon, has just announced that he has the sole winning ticket in the $7 million lottery drawing of last week. Brandon is 60 years old and divorced. He has two adult children (Nicole and Heather) and four grandchildren. Recognizing that you are not an attorney, and knowing that your friend needs personal finance advice, offer some estate planning suggestions regarding the following points:

   (a) Assume that Brandon's taxable estate now amounts to $7,200,000 and after the $2,000,000 exclusion, his remaining estate could be taxed at 20 percent. If he died tomorrow, how much would he owe? Give him that figure while offering him a single piece of advice.

   (b) Name two types of trusts that Brandon might consider to reduce his eventual estate taxes and summarize what those trusts might help him accomplish.

   (c) Offer some suggestions on how Brandon might use life insurance to avoid estate taxes.

   (d) Offer Branson some suggestions for things he might want to put into his letter of last instructions.

Case 3
Victor and Maria Update Their Estate Plans

Since retiring earlier this year, Victor and Maria have found that their assets amount to approximately $800,000, made up of the following: Victor's half-interest in their home

($90,000), his tax-sheltered pension plan ($144,000), his stock ($56,000), his personal property ($50,000), Maria's half-interest in their home ($90,000), the inherited home from her mother ($120,000), her tax-sheltered pension plan ($112,000), the present value (obtained from Victor's employer) of the survivors benefits under her husband's defined-benefit pension plan ($60,000), personal property ($50,000), and her zero-coupon bonds ($28,000).

(a) Offer the Hernandezes advice about how each might establish a durable power of attorney.

(b) Should both Victor and Maria have living wills and medical powers of attorney? Why or why not?

(c) Victor purchased his $100,000 term life insurance policy through his employer, and he has been paying on his privately purchased $50,000 whole life insurance policy for many years (which now has a cash value of $30,000). Maria is listed as the beneficiary on both policies. Assuming that Victor owns both policies, what advice can you offer regarding ownership of the two policies?

(d) After adding up the value of the estate, what is the likelihood of having to pay federal estate taxes if Victor dies?

(e) Offer Victor and Maria some suggestions on how to ease the transfer of assets to their adult children and grandchildren while avoiding estate taxes.

Case 4
Belinda Johnson Helps Her Uncle Plan His Estate

Belinda Johnson has been approached by her uncle, Ryan Lawrence, who seeks advice about planning his estate. She has been handling some of Ryan's investments, and he trusts her judgment on financial matters. Ryan has a net worth of $2,340,000. At age 54, he is concerned about preparing his finances so that as much as possible of his estate will go to his heirs according to his wishes. Ryan has no will but has written down some of his ideas. He has no wife or children but wants to be able to provide for his mother, four nephews, Belinda, and a disabled sister.

(a) What is the first action Ryan should take in planning his estate?

(b) Why might an irrevocable living trust be a good idea for Ryan in providing for his mother and sister?

(c) What other types of trusts might Ryan use in his estate planning?

On the 'Net

Go to the Web pages indicated to complete these exercises. You can also go to the *Garman/Forgue* website at college.hmco.com/business/students for an expanded list of exercises. Under General Business, select the title of this text. Click on the Internet Exercises link for this chapter.

1. Visit the website for Legacy Writer at www.legacywriter.com. Click on "Living Wills," where you can begin the process of developing a living will and other advance directives. Finishing the process will require payment of a fee, but for this exercise simply answer the questions asked. After doing so, is an advance directive something you would consider? Why or why not?

2. Upon death, a person's will can become a public document through the probate process. Visit the Court TV website at http://www.courttv.com/archive/legaldocs/newsmakers/wills/, where the wills of some famous people have been posted. Select a person whose will interests you. Identify one of the estate planning techniques outlined in this chapter that were used by that person.

3. Visit the website for the Internal Revenue Service at http://www.irs.gov/formspubs/article/0,,id=112782,00.html, where you can find information on the federal gift and estate tax. Is this a tax you ever expect to pay? What are your views on this tax as an appropriate way to provide revenue to support government operations?

Visit the Garman/Forgue website...

@college.hmco.com/business/students

Under General Business, select *Personal Finance 9e*. There, among other valuable resources, you will find a complete glossary, ACE questions, links to help you complete the chapter exercises, and links to other personal finance sites.

APPENDIXES

Present and Future Value Tables

Many problems in personal finance involve decisions about money values at varying points in time. These values can be directly and fairly compared only when they are adjusted to a common point in time. Chapter 1 introduced the basic time value concepts. This appendix offers more details about the time value of money. In addition, it provides tables listing the future and present value of $1 with which to make calculations.

Four assumptions must be made to eliminate unnecessary complications:

1. Each planning period is one year long.

2. Only annual interest rates are considered.

3. Interest rates are the same during each of the annual periods.

4. Interest is compounded and continues earning a return in subsequent periods.

Tables of present and future values can be constructed to make these adjustments. **Future values** are derived from the principles of compounding the dollar values ahead in time. **Present values** are derived by discounting (which is the inverse of compounding) the dollar values and transferring them to an earlier point in time.

It is usually unnecessary to precisely identify whether the interest is paid/received at the *beginning* of a period or at the end of a period, or to know whether interest compounds daily or quarterly instead of annually. (These calculations require even more tables.) The following present and future value tables assume that money is accumulated, received, paid, compounded, or whatever at the *end* of a period. The tables can be used to compute the mathematics of personal finance with high certainty and to confirm (or reject as inaccurate) what people tell you about financial matters.

The most significant task is to find the correct table. Accordingly, each table is clearly described here, and illustrations of its use appear on the facing page where possible. In addition, the appropriate mathematical equation is shown and can be easily solved using a calculator.

Illustrations Using Table A.1: Future Value of a Single Amount ($1)

To use Table A.1 on page A-5, locate the future value factor for the time period and the interest rate.

1. You invest $500 at a 15 percent rate of return for 12 years. How much will you have at the end of that 12-year period?

   The future value factor is 5.350; hence, the solution is $500 × 5.350, or $2675.

2. Property values in your neighborhood are increasing at a rate of 5 percent per year. If your home is presently worth $90,000, what will its worth be in 7 years?

   The future value factor is 1.407; hence, the solution is $90,000 × 1.407, or $126,630.

3. You need to amass $40,000 in the next 10 years to make a balloon payment on your home mortgage. You have $17,000 available to invest. What annual interest rate must be earned to realize the $40,000?

   $40,000 ÷ $17,000 = 2.353. Read down the periods (n) column to 10 years and across to 2.367 (close enough), which is found under the 9 percent column. Hence, the $17,000 invested at 9 percent for 10 years will grow to a future value of slightly more than $40,000.

4. An apartment building is currently valued at $160,000, and it has been appreciating at 8 percent per year. If this rate continues, in how many years will it be worth $300,000?

   $300,000 ÷ $160,000 = 1.875. Read down the 8 percent column until you reach 1.851 (close enough to 1.875). This number corresponds to a period of 8 years. Hence, the $160,000 property appreciating at 8 percent annually will grow to a future value of $300,000 in slightly more than 8 years.

5. You have the choice of receiving a down payment from someone who wants to purchase your rental property as $15,000 today or as a personal note for $25,000 payable in 6 years. If you could expect to earn 8 percent on such funds, which is the better choice?

   The future value factor is 1.587; hence, the future value of $15,000 at 8 percent is $15,000 × 1.587, or $23,805. Thus, it would be better to take the note for $25,000.

6. How much will an automobile now priced at $20,000 cost in 4 years, assuming an annual inflation rate of 5 percent?

   Read down the 5 percent column and across the row for 4 years to locate the future value factor of 1.216. Hence, the solution is $20,000 × 1.216, or $24,320.

7. How large a lump-sum investment do you need now to have $20,000 available in 5 years, assuming a 10 percent annual rate of return?

   The $20,000 future value is divided by 1.611 (10 percent at 5 years), resulting in a current lump-sum investment of $12,415.

8. You have $5000 now and need $10,000 in 9 years. What rate of return is needed to reach that goal?

   Divide the future value of $10,000 by the present value of the lump sum of $5000 to obtain a future value factor of 2.0. In the row for 9 years, locate the future value factor of 1.999 (very close to 2.0). Read up the column to find that an 8 percent return on investment is needed.

9. How many years will it take your lump-sum investment of $10,000 to grow to $16,000, given an annual rate of return of 7 percent?

Divide the future value of $16,000 by the present value of the $10,000 lump sum to compute a future value factor of 1.6; look down the 7 percent column to find 1.606 (close enough). Read across the row to find that an investment period of 7 years is needed.

An alternative approach is to use a calculator to determine the future value, *FV,* of a sum of money invested today, assuming that the amount remains in the investment for a specified number of time periods (usually years) and that it earns a certain rate of return each period. The equation is

$$FV = PV\,(1.0 + i)^n \tag{A.1}$$

where

$$FV = \textit{Future Value}$$
$$PV = \textit{Present Value} \text{ of the investment}$$
$$i = \textit{Interest} \text{ rate per period}$$
$$n = \textit{Number} \text{ of periods the PV is invested}$$

Table A.1 Future Value of a Single Amount ($1 at the End of n Periods)
(Used to Compute the Compounded Future Value of a Known Lump Sum)

n	1%	2%	3%	4%	5%	6%	7%	8%	9%	10%	11%	12%	13%	14%	15%	16%	17%	18%	19%	20%
1	1.0100	1.0200	1.0300	1.0400	1.0500	1.0600	1.0700	1.0800	1.0900	1.1000	1.1100	1.1200	1.1300	1.1400	1.1500	1.1600	1.1700	1.1800	1.1900	1.2000
2	1.0201	1.0404	1.0609	1.0816	1.1025	1.1236	1.1449	1.1664	1.1881	1.2100	1.2321	1.2544	1.2769	1.2996	1.3225	1.3456	1.3689	1.3924	1.4161	1.4400
3	1.0303	1.0612	1.0927	1.1249	1.1576	1.1910	1.2250	1.2597	1.2950	1.3310	1.3676	1.4049	1.4429	1.4815	1.5209	1.5609	1.6016	1.6430	1.6852	1.7280
4	1.0406	1.0824	1.1255	1.1699	1.2155	1.2625	1.3108	1.3605	1.4116	1.4641	1.5181	1.5735	1.6305	1.6890	1.7490	1.8106	1.8739	1.9388	2.0053	2.0736
5	1.0510	1.1041	1.1593	1.2167	1.2763	1.3382	1.4026	1.4693	1.5386	1.6105	1.6851	1.7623	1.8424	1.9254	2.0114	2.1003	2.1924	2.2878	2.3864	2.4883
6	1.0615	1.1262	1.1941	1.2653	1.3401	1.4185	1.5007	1.5869	1.6771	1.7716	1.8704	1.9738	2.0820	2.1950	2.3131	2.4364	2.5652	2.6996	2.8398	2.9860
7	1.0721	1.1487	1.2299	1.3159	1.4071	1.5036	1.6058	1.7138	1.8280	1.9487	2.0762	2.2107	2.3526	2.5023	2.6600	2.8262	3.0012	3.1855	3.3793	3.5832
8	1.0829	1.1717	1.2668	1.3686	1.4775	1.5938	1.7182	1.8509	1.9926	2.1436	2.3045	2.4760	2.6584	2.8526	3.0590	3.2784	3.5115	3.7589	4.0214	4.2998
9	1.0937	1.1951	1.3048	1.4233	1.5513	1.6895	1.8385	1.9990	2.1719	2.3579	2.5580	2.7731	3.0040	3.2519	3.5179	3.8030	4.1084	4.4355	4.7854	5.1598
10	1.1046	1.2190	1.3439	1.4802	1.6289	1.7908	1.9672	2.1589	2.3674	2.5937	2.8394	3.1058	3.3946	3.7072	4.0456	4.4114	4.8068	5.2338	5.6947	6.1917
11	1.1157	1.2434	1.3842	1.5395	1.7103	1.8983	2.1049	2.3316	2.5804	2.8531	3.1518	3.4785	3.8359	4.2262	4.6524	5.1173	5.6240	6.1759	6.7767	7.4301
12	1.1268	1.2682	1.4258	1.6010	1.7959	2.0122	2.2522	2.5182	2.8127	3.1384	3.4985	3.8960	4.3345	4.8179	5.3503	5.9360	6.5801	7.2876	8.0642	8.9161
13	1.1381	1.2936	1.4685	1.6651	1.8856	2.1329	2.4098	2.7196	3.0658	3.4523	3.8833	4.3635	4.8980	5.4924	6.1528	6.8858	7.6987	8.5994	9.5964	10.6993
14	1.1495	1.3195	1.5126	1.7317	1.9799	2.2609	2.5785	2.9372	3.3417	3.7975	4.3104	4.8871	5.5348	6.2613	7.0757	7.9875	9.0075	10.1472	11.4198	12.8392
15	1.1610	1.3459	1.5580	1.8009	2.0789	2.3966	2.7590	3.1722	3.6425	4.1772	4.7846	5.4736	6.2543	7.1379	8.1371	9.2655	10.5387	11.9737	13.5895	15.4070
16	1.1726	1.3728	1.6047	1.8730	2.1829	2.5404	2.9522	3.4259	3.9703	4.5950	5.3109	6.1304	7.0673	8.1372	9.3576	10.7480	12.3303	14.1290	16.1715	18.4884
17	1.1843	1.4002	1.6528	1.9479	2.2920	2.6928	3.1588	3.7000	4.3276	5.0545	5.8951	6.8660	7.9861	9.2765	10.7613	12.4677	14.4265	16.6722	19.2441	22.1861
18	1.1961	1.4282	1.7024	2.0258	2.4066	2.8543	3.3799	3.9960	4.7171	5.5599	6.5436	7.6900	9.0243	10.5752	12.3755	14.4625	16.8790	19.6733	22.9005	26.6233
19	1.2081	1.4568	1.7535	2.1068	2.5270	3.0256	3.6165	4.3157	5.1417	6.1159	7.2633	8.6128	10.1974	12.0557	14.2318	16.7765	19.7484	23.2144	27.2516	31.9480
20	1.2202	1.4859	1.8061	2.1911	2.6533	3.2071	3.8697	4.6610	5.6044	6.7275	8.0623	9.6463	11.5231	13.7435	16.3665	19.4608	23.1056	27.3930	32.4294	38.3376
21	1.2324	1.5157	1.8603	2.2788	2.7860	3.3996	4.1406	5.0338	6.1088	7.4002	8.9492	10.8038	13.0211	15.6676	18.8215	22.5745	27.0336	32.3238	38.5910	46.0051
22	1.2447	1.5460	1.9161	2.3699	2.9253	3.6035	4.4304	5.4365	6.6586	8.1403	9.9336	12.1003	14.7138	17.8610	21.6447	26.1864	31.6293	38.1421	45.9233	55.2061
23	1.2572	1.5769	1.9736	2.4647	3.0715	3.8197	4.7405	5.8715	7.2579	8.9543	11.0263	13.5523	16.6266	20.3616	24.8915	30.3762	37.0062	45.0076	54.6487	66.2474
24	1.2697	1.6084	2.0328	2.5633	3.2251	4.0489	5.0724	6.3412	7.9111	9.8497	12.2392	15.1786	18.7881	23.2122	28.6252	35.2364	43.2973	53.1090	65.0320	79.4968
25	1.2824	1.6406	2.0938	2.6658	3.3864	4.2919	5.4274	6.8485	8.6231	10.8347	13.5855	17.0001	21.2305	26.4619	32.9190	40.8742	50.6578	62.6686	77.3881	95.3962
26	1.2953	1.6734	2.1566	2.7725	3.5557	4.5494	5.8074	7.3964	9.3992	11.9182	15.0799	19.0401	23.9905	30.1666	37.8568	47.4141	59.2697	73.9490	92.0918	114.4755
27	1.3082	1.7069	2.2213	2.8834	3.7335	4.8223	6.2139	7.9881	10.2451	13.1100	16.7386	21.3249	27.1093	34.3899	43.5353	55.0004	69.3455	87.2598	109.5893	137.3706
28	1.3213	1.7410	2.2879	2.9987	3.9201	5.1117	6.6488	8.6271	11.1671	14.4210	18.5799	23.8839	30.6335	39.2045	50.0656	63.8004	81.1342	102.9666	130.4112	164.8447
29	1.3345	1.7758	2.3566	3.1187	4.1161	5.4184	7.1143	9.3173	12.1722	15.8631	20.6237	26.7499	34.6158	44.6931	57.5755	74.0085	94.9271	121.5005	155.1893	197.8136
30	1.3478	1.8114	2.4273	3.2434	4.3219	5.7435	7.6123	10.0627	13.2677	17.4494	22.8923	29.9599	39.1159	50.9502	66.2118	85.8499	111.0647	143.3706	184.6753	237.3763
40	1.4889	2.2080	3.2620	4.8010	7.0400	10.2857	14.9745	21.7245	31.4094	45.2593	65.0009	93.0510	132.7816	188.8835	267.8635	378.7212	533.8687	750.3783	1051.668	1469.772
50	1.6446	2.6916	4.3839	7.1067	11.4674	18.4202	29.4570	46.9016	74.3575	117.3909	184.5648	289.0022	450.7359	700.2330	1083.657	1670.704	2566.215	3927.357	5988.914	9100.438

Illustrations Using Table A.2: Present Value of a Single Amount ($1)

To use this table, locate the present value factor for the time period and the interest rate.

1. You want to begin a college fund for your newborn child; you hope to accumulate $30,000 by 18 years from now. If a current investment opportunity yields 7 percent, how much must you invest in a lump sum to realize the $30,000 when needed?

The present value factor is 0.296; hence, the solution is $30,000 × 0.296, or $8880.

2. You hope to retire in 25 years and want to deposit a single lump sum that will grow to $250,000 at that time. If you can now invest at 8 percent, how much must you invest to realize the $250,000 when needed?

The present value factor is 0.146; hence, the solution is $250,000 × 0.146, or $36,500. The present value of $250,000 received 25 years from now is $36,500 if the interest rate is 8 percent.

3. You have the choice of receiving a down payment from someone who wants to purchase your rental property as $15,000 today or as a personal note for $25,000 payable in 6 years. If you could expect to earn 8 percent on such funds, which is the better choice?

The present value factor is 0.630; hence, the solution is $25,000 × 0.630, or $15,750. Thus, the present value of $25,000 received in 6 years is greater than $15,000 received now, and the personal note is the better choice.

4. You own a $1000 bond paying 8 percent annually until its maturity in 5 years. You need to sell the bond now, even though the market rate of interest on similar bonds has increased to 10 percent. What discounted market price for the bond will allow the new buyer to earn a yield of 10 percent?

First, compute the present value of the future interest payments of $80 per year for 5 years at 10 percent (using Table A.4): $80 × 3.791, or $303.28. Second, compute the present value of the future principal repayment of $1000 after 5 years at 10 percent: $1000 × 0.621, or $621.00. Hence, the market price is the sum of the two present values ($303.28 + $621.00), or $924.28.

An alternative approach is to use a calculator to determine the present value, *PV,* of a single payment received some time in the future. The equation, which is a rearrangement of the future value Equation (A.1), is

$$PV = \frac{FV}{(1.0 + i)^n} \qquad (A.2)$$

where

$$PV = \textit{Present Value of the investment}$$
$$FV = \textit{Future Value}$$
$$i = \textit{Interest rate per period}$$
$$n = \textit{Number of periods the PV is invested}$$

Table A.2 Present Value of a Single Amount ($1)
(Used to Compute the Discounted Present Value of Some Known Future Single Lump Sum)

n	1%	2%	3%	4%	5%	6%	7%	8%	9%	10%	11%	12%	13%	14%	15%	16%	17%	18%	19%	20%
1	0.9901	0.9804	0.9709	0.9615	0.9524	0.9434	0.9346	0.9259	0.9174	0.9091	0.9009	0.8929	0.8850	0.8772	0.8696	0.8621	0.8547	0.8475	0.8403	0.8333
2	0.9803	0.9612	0.9426	0.9246	0.9070	0.8900	0.8734	0.8573	0.8417	0.8264	0.8116	0.7972	0.7831	0.7695	0.7561	0.7432	0.7305	0.7182	0.7062	0.6944
3	0.9706	0.9423	0.9151	0.8890	0.8638	0.8396	0.8163	0.7938	0.7722	0.7513	0.7312	0.7118	0.6931	0.6750	0.6575	0.6407	0.6244	0.6086	0.5934	0.5787
4	0.9610	0.9238	0.8885	0.8548	0.8227	0.7921	0.7629	0.7350	0.7084	0.6830	0.6587	0.6355	0.6133	0.5921	0.5718	0.5523	0.5337	0.5158	0.4987	0.4823
5	0.9515	0.9057	0.8626	0.8219	0.7835	0.7473	0.7130	0.6806	0.6499	0.6209	0.5935	0.5674	0.5428	0.5194	0.4972	0.4761	0.4561	0.4371	0.4190	0.4019
6	0.9420	0.8880	0.8375	0.7903	0.7462	0.7050	0.6663	0.6302	0.5963	0.5645	0.5346	0.5066	0.4803	0.4556	0.4323	0.4104	0.3898	0.3704	0.3521	0.3349
7	0.9327	0.8706	0.8131	0.7599	0.7107	0.6651	0.6227	0.5835	0.5470	0.5132	0.4817	0.4523	0.4251	0.3996	0.3759	0.3538	0.3332	0.3139	0.2959	0.2791
8	0.9235	0.8535	0.7894	0.7307	0.6768	0.6274	0.5820	0.5403	0.5019	0.4665	0.4339	0.4039	0.3762	0.3506	0.3269	0.3050	0.2848	0.2660	0.2487	0.2326
9	0.9143	0.8368	0.7664	0.7026	0.6446	0.5919	0.5439	0.5002	0.4604	0.4241	0.3909	0.3606	0.3329	0.3075	0.2843	0.2630	0.2434	0.2255	0.2090	0.1938
10	0.9053	0.8203	0.7441	0.6756	0.6139	0.5584	0.5083	0.4632	0.4224	0.3855	0.3522	0.3220	0.2946	0.2697	0.2472	0.2267	0.2080	0.1911	0.1756	0.1615
11	0.8963	0.8043	0.7224	0.6496	0.5847	0.5268	0.4751	0.4289	0.3875	0.3505	0.3173	0.2875	0.2607	0.2366	0.2149	0.1954	0.1778	0.1619	0.1476	0.1346
12	0.8874	0.7885	0.7014	0.6246	0.5568	0.4970	0.4440	0.3971	0.3555	0.3186	0.2858	0.2567	0.2307	0.2076	0.1869	0.1685	0.1520	0.1372	0.1240	0.1122
13	0.8787	0.7730	0.6810	0.6006	0.5303	0.4688	0.4150	0.3677	0.3262	0.2897	0.2575	0.2292	0.2042	0.1821	0.1625	0.1452	0.1299	0.1163	0.1042	0.0935
14	0.8700	0.7579	0.6611	0.5775	0.5051	0.4423	0.3878	0.3405	0.2992	0.2633	0.2320	0.2046	0.1807	0.1597	0.1413	0.1252	0.1110	0.0985	0.0876	0.0779
15	0.8613	0.7430	0.6419	0.5553	0.4810	0.4173	0.3624	0.3152	0.2745	0.2394	0.2090	0.1827	0.1599	0.1401	0.1229	0.1079	0.0949	0.0835	0.0736	0.0649
16	0.8528	0.7284	0.6232	0.5339	0.4581	0.3936	0.3387	0.2919	0.2519	0.2176	0.1883	0.1631	0.1415	0.1229	0.1069	0.0930	0.0811	0.0708	0.0618	0.0541
17	0.8444	0.7142	0.6050	0.5134	0.4363	0.3714	0.3166	0.2703	0.2311	0.1978	0.1696	0.1456	0.1252	0.1078	0.0929	0.0802	0.0693	0.0600	0.0520	0.0451
18	0.8360	0.7002	0.5874	0.4936	0.4155	0.3503	0.2959	0.2502	0.2120	0.1799	0.1528	0.1300	0.1108	0.0946	0.0808	0.0691	0.0592	0.0508	0.0437	0.0376
19	0.8277	0.6864	0.5703	0.4746	0.3957	0.3305	0.2765	0.2317	0.1945	0.1635	0.1377	0.1161	0.0981	0.0829	0.0703	0.0596	0.0506	0.0431	0.0367	0.0313
20	0.8195	0.6730	0.5537	0.4564	0.3769	0.3118	0.2584	0.2145	0.1784	0.1486	0.1240	0.1037	0.0868	0.0728	0.0611	0.0514	0.0433	0.0365	0.0308	0.0261
21	0.8114	0.6598	0.5375	0.4388	0.3589	0.2942	0.2415	0.1987	0.1637	0.1351	0.1117	0.0926	0.0768	0.0638	0.0531	0.0443	0.0370	0.0309	0.0259	0.0217
22	0.8034	0.6468	0.5219	0.4220	0.3418	0.2775	0.2257	0.1839	0.1502	0.1228	0.1007	0.0826	0.0680	0.0560	0.0462	0.0382	0.0316	0.0262	0.0218	0.0181
23	0.7954	0.6342	0.5067	0.4057	0.3256	0.2618	0.2109	0.1703	0.1378	0.1117	0.0907	0.0738	0.0601	0.0491	0.0402	0.0329	0.0270	0.0222	0.0183	0.0151
24	0.7876	0.6217	0.4919	0.3901	0.3101	0.2470	0.1971	0.1577	0.1264	0.1015	0.0817	0.0659	0.0532	0.0431	0.0349	0.0284	0.0231	0.0188	0.0154	0.0126
25	0.7798	0.6095	0.4776	0.3751	0.2953	0.2330	0.1842	0.1460	0.1160	0.0923	0.0736	0.0588	0.0471	0.0378	0.0304	0.0245	0.0197	0.0160	0.0129	0.0105
26	0.7720	0.5976	0.4637	0.3607	0.2812	0.2198	0.1722	0.1352	0.1064	0.0839	0.0663	0.0525	0.0417	0.0331	0.0264	0.0211	0.0169	0.0135	0.0109	0.0087
27	0.7644	0.5859	0.4502	0.3468	0.2678	0.2074	0.1609	0.1252	0.0976	0.0763	0.0597	0.0469	0.0369	0.0291	0.0230	0.0182	0.0144	0.0115	0.0091	0.0073
28	0.7568	0.5744	0.4371	0.3335	0.2551	0.1956	0.1504	0.1159	0.0895	0.0693	0.0538	0.0419	0.0326	0.0255	0.0200	0.0157	0.0123	0.0097	0.0077	0.0061
29	0.7493	0.5631	0.4243	0.3207	0.2429	0.1846	0.1406	0.1073	0.0822	0.0630	0.0485	0.0374	0.0289	0.0224	0.0174	0.0135	0.0105	0.0082	0.0064	0.0051
30	0.7419	0.5521	0.4120	0.3083	0.2314	0.1741	0.1314	0.0994	0.0754	0.0573	0.0437	0.0334	0.0256	0.0196	0.0151	0.0116	0.0090	0.0070	0.0054	0.0042
40	0.6717	0.4529	0.3066	0.2083	0.1420	0.0972	0.0668	0.0460	0.0318	0.0221	0.0154	0.0107	0.0075	0.0053	0.0037	0.0026	0.0019	0.0013	0.0010	0.0007
50	0.6080	0.3715	0.2281	0.1407	0.0872	0.0543	0.0339	0.0213	0.0134	0.0085	0.0054	0.0035	0.0022	0.0014	0.0009	0.0006	0.0004	0.0003	0.0002	0.0001

Illustrations Using Table A.3: Future Value of a Series of Equal Amounts (an Annuity of $1 per Period)

To use this table, locate the future value factor for the time period and the interest rate.

1. You plan to retire after 16 years. To provide for that retirement, you initiate a savings program of $7000 per year in an investment yielding 8 percent. What will the value of the retirement fund be at the beginning of the seventeenth year?

   Your last payment into the fund will occur at the end of the sixteenth year, so scan down the periods (*n*) column for period 16, and then move across until you reach the column for 8 percent. The future value factor is 30.32. Hence, the solution is $7000 × 30.32, or $212,240.

2. What will be the value of an investment if you put $2000 into a retirement plan yielding 7 percent annually for 25 years?

   The future value factor is 63.250. Hence, the solution is $2000 × 63.250, or $126,500.

3. You are trying to decide between putting $3000 or $4000 annually for the next 20 years into an investment yielding 7 percent for retirement purposes. What is the difference in the value of investing the extra $1000 for 20 years?

   The future value factor is 41.0. Hence, the solution is $1000 × 41.0, or $41,000.

4. You will receive an annuity payment of $1200 at the end of each year for 6 years. What will be the total value of this stream of income invested at 7 percent by the time you receive the last payment?

   The appropriate future value factor for 6 years at 7 percent is 7.153. Hence, the solution is $1200 × 7.153, or $8584.

5. How many years of investing $1200 annually at 9 percent will it take to reach a goal of $11,000?

   Divide the future value of $11,000 by the lump sum of $1200 to find a future value factor of 9.17. Look down the 9 percent column to find 9.200 (close enough). Read across the row to find that an investment period of 7 years is needed.

6. If you plan to invest $1200 annually for 9 years, what rate of return is needed to reach a goal of $15,000?

   Divide the future value goal of $15,000 by $1200 to derive the future value factor 12.5. Look across the row for 9 years to locate the future value factor of 12.49 (close enough). Read up the column to find that you need an 8 percent return.

   An alternative approach is to use a calculator to determine the total future value, *FV*, of a stream of equal payments (an annuity). The equation is

$$FV = \frac{[(1.0 + i)^n - 1.0] \times A}{i} \qquad \text{(A.3)}$$

where

$$FV = \textit{Future Value of the investment}$$
$$i = \textit{Interest rate per period}$$
$$n = \textit{Number of periods the PV is invested}$$
$$A = \textit{Amount of the annuity}$$

Table A.3 Future Value of a Series of Equal Amounts (an Annuity of $1 Paid at the End of Each Period)
(Used to Compute the Compounded Future Value of a Stream of Income Payments)

n	1%	2%	3%	4%	5%	6%	7%	8%	9%	10%	11%	12%	13%	14%	15%	16%	17%	18%	19%	20%
1	1.0000	1.0000	1.0000	1.0000	1.0000	1.0000	1.0000	1.0000	1.0000	1.0000	1.0000	1.0000	1.0000	1.0000	1.0000	1.0000	1.0000	1.0000	1.0000	1.0000
2	2.0100	2.0200	2.0300	2.0400	2.0500	2.0600	2.0700	2.0800	2.0900	2.1000	2.1100	2.1200	2.1300	2.1400	2.1500	2.1600	2.1700	2.1800	2.1900	2.2000
3	3.0301	3.0604	3.0909	3.1216	3.1525	3.1836	3.2149	3.2464	3.2781	3.3100	3.3421	3.3744	3.4069	3.4396	3.4725	3.5056	3.5389	3.5724	3.6061	3.6400
4	4.0604	4.1216	4.1836	4.2465	4.3101	4.3746	4.4399	4.5061	4.5731	4.6410	4.7097	4.7793	4.8498	4.9211	4.9934	5.0665	5.1405	5.2154	5.2913	5.3680
5	5.1010	5.2040	5.3091	5.4163	5.5256	5.6371	5.7507	5.8666	5.9847	6.1051	6.2278	6.3528	6.4803	6.6101	6.7424	6.8771	7.0144	7.1542	7.2966	7.4416
6	6.1520	6.3081	6.4684	6.6330	6.8019	6.9753	7.1533	7.3359	7.5233	7.7156	7.9129	8.1152	8.3227	8.5355	8.7537	8.9775	9.2068	9.4420	9.6830	9.9299
7	7.2135	7.4343	7.6625	7.8983	8.1420	8.3938	8.6540	8.9228	9.2004	9.4872	9.7833	10.0890	10.4047	10.7305	11.0668	11.4139	11.7720	12.1415	12.5227	12.9159
8	8.2857	8.5830	8.8923	9.2142	9.5491	9.8975	10.2598	10.6366	11.0285	11.4359	11.8594	12.2997	12.7573	13.2328	13.7268	14.2401	14.7733	15.3270	15.9020	16.4991
9	9.3685	9.7546	10.1591	10.5828	11.0266	11.4913	11.9780	12.4876	13.0210	13.5795	14.1640	14.7757	15.4157	16.0853	16.7858	17.5185	18.2847	19.0859	19.9234	20.7989
10	10.4622	10.9497	11.4639	12.0061	12.5779	13.1808	13.8164	14.4866	15.1929	15.9374	16.7220	17.5487	18.4197	19.3373	20.3037	21.3215	22.3931	23.5213	24.7089	25.9587
11	11.5668	12.1687	12.8078	13.4864	14.2068	14.9716	15.7836	16.6455	17.5603	18.5312	19.5614	20.6546	21.8143	23.0445	24.3493	25.7329	27.1999	28.7551	30.4035	32.1504
12	12.6825	13.4121	14.1920	15.0258	15.9171	16.8699	17.8885	18.9771	20.1407	21.3843	22.7132	24.1331	25.6502	27.2707	29.0017	30.8502	32.8239	34.9311	37.1802	39.5805
13	13.8093	14.6803	15.6178	16.6268	17.7130	18.8821	20.1406	21.4953	22.9534	24.5227	26.2116	28.0291	29.9847	32.0887	34.3519	36.7862	39.4040	42.2187	45.2445	48.4966
14	14.9474	15.9739	17.0863	18.2919	19.5986	21.0151	22.5505	24.2149	26.0192	27.9750	30.0949	32.3926	34.8827	37.5811	40.5047	43.6720	47.1027	50.8180	54.8409	59.1959
15	16.0969	17.2934	18.5989	20.0236	21.5786	23.2760	25.1290	27.1521	29.3609	31.7725	34.4054	37.2797	40.4175	43.8424	47.5804	51.6595	56.1101	60.9653	66.2607	72.0351
16	17.2579	18.6393	20.1569	21.8245	23.6575	25.6725	27.8881	30.3243	33.0034	35.9497	39.1899	42.7533	46.6717	50.9804	55.7175	60.9250	66.6488	72.9390	79.8502	87.4421
17	18.4304	20.0121	21.7616	23.6975	25.8404	28.2129	30.8402	33.7502	36.9737	40.5447	44.5008	48.8837	53.7391	59.1176	65.0751	71.6730	78.9791	87.0680	96.0217	105.9306
18	19.6147	21.4123	23.4144	25.6454	28.1324	30.9057	33.9990	37.4502	41.3013	45.5992	50.3959	55.7497	61.7251	68.3941	75.8364	84.1407	93.4056	103.7403	115.2659	128.1167
19	20.8109	22.8406	25.1169	27.6712	30.5390	33.7600	37.3790	41.4463	46.0185	51.1591	56.9395	63.4397	70.7494	78.9692	88.2118	98.6032	110.2846	123.4135	138.1664	154.7400
20	22.0190	24.2974	26.8704	29.7781	33.0660	36.7856	40.9955	45.7620	51.1601	57.2750	64.2028	72.0524	80.9468	91.0249	102.4436	115.3797	130.0329	146.6280	165.4180	186.6880
21	23.2392	25.7833	28.6765	31.9692	35.7193	39.9927	44.8652	50.4229	56.7645	64.0025	72.2651	81.6987	92.4699	104.7684	118.8101	134.8405	153.1385	174.0210	197.8474	225.0256
22	24.4716	27.2990	30.5368	34.2480	38.5052	43.3923	49.0057	55.4568	62.8733	71.4027	81.2143	92.5026	105.4910	120.4360	137.6316	157.4150	180.1721	206.3448	236.4384	271.0307
23	25.7163	28.8450	32.4529	36.6179	41.4305	46.9958	53.4361	60.8933	69.5319	79.5430	91.1479	104.6029	120.2048	138.2970	159.2764	183.6014	211.8013	244.4868	282.3618	326.2368
24	26.9735	30.4219	34.4265	39.0826	44.5020	50.8156	58.1767	66.7648	76.7898	88.4973	102.1741	118.1552	136.8315	158.6586	184.1678	213.9776	248.8075	289.4945	337.0105	392.4842
25	28.2432	32.0303	36.4593	41.6459	47.7271	54.8645	63.2490	73.1059	84.7009	98.3471	114.4133	133.3339	155.6196	181.8708	212.7930	249.2140	292.1048	342.6035	402.0424	471.9811
26	29.5256	33.6709	38.5530	44.3117	51.1135	59.1564	68.6765	79.9544	93.3240	109.1818	127.9988	150.3339	176.8501	208.3327	245.7120	290.0883	342.7626	405.2721	479.4305	567.3773
27	30.8209	35.3443	40.7096	47.0842	54.6691	63.7058	74.4838	87.3508	102.7231	121.0999	143.0786	169.3740	200.8406	238.4993	283.5688	337.5024	402.0323	479.2211	571.5223	681.8527
28	32.1291	37.0512	42.9309	49.9676	58.4026	68.5281	80.6977	95.3388	112.9682	134.2099	159.8173	190.6989	227.9499	272.8892	327.1041	392.5027	471.3778	566.4808	681.1116	819.2233
29	33.4504	38.7922	45.2188	52.9663	62.3227	73.6398	87.3465	103.9659	124.1354	148.6309	178.3972	214.5827	258.5834	312.0937	377.1697	456.3032	552.5120	669.4474	811.5228	984.0679
30	34.7849	40.5681	47.5754	56.0849	66.4389	79.0582	94.4608	113.2832	136.3075	164.4940	199.0209	241.3327	293.1992	356.7868	434.7451	530.3117	647.4390	790.9479	966.7121	1181.882
40	48.8864	60.4020	75.4013	95.0255	120.7998	154.7620	199.6351	259.0565	337.8824	442.5925	581.8260	767.0914	1013.704	1342.025	1779.090	2360.757	3134.522	4163.212	5529.829	7343.856
50	64.4632	84.5794	112.7969	152.6671	209.3480	290.3359	406.5289	573.7701	815.0834	1163.908	1668.771	2400.018	3459.507	4994.522	7217.714	10435.65	15089.50	21813.09	31515.33	45497.17

Illustrations Using Table A.4: Present Value of Series of Equal Amounts (an Annuity of $1 per Period)

To use this table, locate the present value factor for the time period and the interest rate.

1. You are entering into a contract that will provide you with an income of $1000 at the end of the year for the next 10 years. If the annual interest rate is 7 percent, what is the present value of that stream of payments?

   The present value factor is 7.024; hence, the solution is $1000 × 7.024, or $7024.

2. You expect to have $250,000 available in a retirement plan when you retire. If the amount invested yields 8 percent and you hope to live an additional 20 years, how much can you withdraw each year so that the fund will just be liquidated after 20 years?

   The present value factor for 20 years at 8 percent is 9.818. Hence, the solution is $250,000 ÷ 9.818, or $25,463.

3. You have received an inheritance of $60,000 that you invested so that it earns 9 percent. If you withdraw $8000 annually to supplement your income, in how many years will the fund run out?

   Solving for n, $60,000 ÷ $8000 = 7.5. Scan down the 9 percent column until you find a present value factor close to 7.5, which is 7.487. The row indicates 13 years; thus, the fund will be depleted in approximately 13 years with $8000 annual withdrawals.

4. A seller offers to finance the sale of a building to you as an investment. The mortgage loan of $280,000 will be for 20 years and requires an annual mortgage payment of $24,000. Should you finance the purchase through the seller or borrow the funds from a financial institution at a current rate of 10 percent?

   $280,000 ÷ $24,000 = 11.667. Scan down the periods (n) column to 20 years and then read across to locate the figure closest to 11.667, which is 11.470. The column indicates 6 percent; thus, seller financing offers a lower interest rate.

5. You have the opportunity to purchase an office building for $750,000 with an expected life of 20 years. Looking over the financial details, you see that the before-tax net rental income is $90,000. If you want a return of at least 15 percent, how much should you pay for the building?

   The present value factor for 20 years at 15 percent is 6.259, and $90,000 × 6.259 = $563,310. Thus, the price is too high for you to earn a return of 15 percent.

An alternative approach is to use a calculator to determine the present value, PV, of a stream of payments. The equation is

$$PV = \frac{[1.0 - 1.0 \ / (1.0 + i)^n] \times A}{i} \qquad \text{(A.4)}$$

where

$$PV = \textit{Present Value} \text{ of the investment}$$
$$i = \textit{Interest} \text{ rate per period}$$
$$n = \textit{Number} \text{ of periods the } PV \text{ is invested}$$
$$A = \textit{Amount} \text{ of the annuity}$$

Table A.4 Present Value of a Series of Equal Amounts (an Annuity of $1 Received at the End of Each Period)
(Used to Compute the Discounted Present Value of a Stream of Income Payments)

n	1%	2%	3%	4%	5%	6%	7%	8%	9%	10%	11%	12%	13%	14%	15%	16%	17%	18%	19%	20%
1	0.9901	0.9804	0.9709	0.9615	0.9524	0.9434	0.9346	0.9259	0.9174	0.9091	0.9009	0.8929	0.8850	0.8772	0.8696	0.8621	0.8547	0.8475	0.8403	0.8333
2	1.9704	1.9416	1.9135	1.8861	1.8594	1.8334	1.8080	1.7833	1.7591	1.7355	1.7125	1.6901	1.6681	1.6467	1.6257	1.6052	1.5852	1.5656	1.5465	1.5278
3	2.9410	2.8839	2.8286	2.7751	2.7232	2.6730	2.6243	2.5771	2.5313	2.4869	2.4437	2.4018	2.3612	2.3216	2.2832	2.2459	2.2096	2.1743	2.1399	2.1065
4	3.9020	3.8077	3.7171	3.6299	3.5460	3.4651	3.3872	3.3121	3.2397	3.1699	3.1024	3.0373	2.9745	2.9137	2.8550	2.7982	2.7432	2.6901	2.6386	2.5887
5	4.8534	4.7135	4.5797	4.4518	4.3295	4.2124	4.1002	3.9927	3.8897	3.7908	3.6959	3.6048	3.5172	3.4331	3.3522	3.2743	3.1993	3.1272	3.0576	2.9906
6	5.7955	5.6014	5.4172	5.2421	5.0757	4.9173	4.7665	4.6229	4.4859	4.3553	4.2305	4.1114	3.9975	3.8887	3.7845	3.6847	3.5892	3.4976	3.4098	3.3255
7	6.7282	6.4720	6.2303	6.0021	5.7864	5.5824	5.3893	5.2064	5.0330	4.8684	4.7122	4.5638	4.4226	4.2883	4.1604	4.0386	3.9224	3.8115	3.7057	3.6046
8	7.6517	7.3255	7.0197	6.7327	6.4632	6.2098	5.9713	5.7466	5.5348	5.3349	5.1461	4.9676	4.7988	4.6389	4.4873	4.3436	4.2072	4.0776	3.9544	3.8372
9	8.5660	8.1622	7.7861	7.4353	7.1078	6.8017	6.5152	6.2469	5.9952	5.7590	5.5370	5.3282	5.1317	4.9464	4.7716	4.6065	4.4506	4.3030	4.1633	4.0310
10	9.4713	8.9826	8.5302	8.1109	7.7217	7.3601	7.0236	6.7101	6.4177	6.1446	5.8892	5.6502	5.4262	5.2161	5.0188	4.8332	4.6586	4.4941	4.3389	4.1925
11	10.3676	9.7868	9.2526	8.7605	8.3064	7.8869	7.4987	7.1390	6.8052	6.4951	6.2065	5.9377	5.6869	5.4527	5.2337	5.0286	4.8364	4.6560	4.4865	4.3271
12	11.2551	10.5753	9.9540	9.3851	8.8633	8.3838	7.9427	7.5361	7.1607	6.8137	6.4924	6.1944	5.9176	5.6603	5.4206	5.1971	4.9884	4.7932	4.6105	4.4392
13	12.1337	11.3484	10.6350	9.9856	9.3936	8.8527	8.3577	7.9038	7.4869	7.1034	6.7499	6.4235	6.1218	5.8424	5.5831	5.3423	5.1183	4.9095	4.7147	4.5327
14	13.0037	12.1062	11.2961	10.5631	9.8986	9.2950	8.7455	8.2442	7.7862	7.3667	6.9819	6.6282	6.3025	6.0021	5.7245	5.4675	5.2293	5.0081	4.8023	4.6106
15	13.8651	12.8493	11.9379	11.1184	10.3797	9.7122	9.1079	8.5595	8.0607	7.6061	7.1909	6.8109	6.4624	6.1422	5.8474	5.5755	5.3242	5.0916	4.8759	4.6755
16	14.7179	13.5777	12.5611	11.6523	10.8378	10.1059	9.4466	8.8514	8.3126	7.8237	7.3792	6.9740	6.6039	6.2651	5.9542	5.6685	5.4053	5.1624	4.9377	4.7296
17	15.5623	14.2919	13.1661	12.1657	11.2741	10.4773	9.7632	9.1216	8.5436	8.0216	7.5488	7.1196	6.7291	6.3729	6.0472	5.7487	5.4746	5.2223	4.9897	4.7746
18	16.3983	14.9920	13.7535	12.6593	11.6896	10.8276	10.0591	9.3719	8.7556	8.2014	7.7016	7.2497	6.8399	6.4674	6.1280	5.8178	5.5339	5.2732	5.0333	4.8122
19	17.2260	15.6785	14.3238	13.1339	12.0853	11.1581	10.3356	9.6036	8.9501	8.3649	7.8393	7.3658	6.9380	6.5504	6.1982	5.8775	5.5845	5.3162	5.0700	4.8435
20	18.0456	16.3514	14.8775	13.5903	12.4622	11.4699	10.5940	9.8181	9.1285	8.5136	7.9633	7.4694	7.0248	6.6231	6.2593	5.9288	5.6278	5.3527	5.1009	4.8696
21	18.8570	17.0112	15.4150	14.0292	12.8212	11.7641	10.8355	10.0168	9.2922	8.6487	8.0751	7.5620	7.1016	6.6870	6.3125	5.9731	5.6648	5.3837	5.1268	4.8913
22	19.6604	17.6580	15.9369	14.4511	13.1630	12.0416	11.0612	10.2007	9.4424	8.7715	8.1757	7.6446	7.1695	6.7429	6.3587	6.0113	5.6964	5.4099	5.1486	4.9094
23	20.4558	18.2922	16.4436	14.8568	13.4886	12.3034	11.2722	10.3711	9.5802	8.8832	8.2664	7.7184	7.2297	6.7921	6.3988	6.0442	5.7234	5.4321	5.1668	4.9245
24	21.2434	18.9139	16.9355	15.2470	13.7986	12.5504	11.4693	10.5288	9.7066	8.9847	8.3481	7.7843	7.2829	6.8351	6.4338	6.0726	5.7465	5.4509	5.1822	4.9371
25	22.0232	19.5235	17.4131	15.6221	14.0939	12.7834	11.6536	10.6748	9.8226	9.0770	8.4217	7.8431	7.3300	6.8729	6.4641	6.0971	5.7662	5.4669	5.1951	4.9476
26	22.7952	20.1210	17.8768	15.9828	14.3752	13.0032	11.8258	10.8100	9.9290	9.1609	8.4881	7.8957	7.3717	6.9061	6.4906	6.1182	5.7831	5.4804	5.2060	4.9563
27	23.5596	20.7069	18.3270	16.3296	14.6430	13.2105	11.9867	10.9352	10.0266	9.2372	8.5478	7.9426	7.4086	6.9352	6.5135	6.1364	5.7975	5.4919	5.2151	4.9636
28	24.3164	21.2813	18.7641	16.6631	14.8981	13.4062	12.1371	11.0511	10.1161	9.3066	8.6016	7.9844	7.4412	6.9607	6.5335	6.1520	5.8099	5.5016	5.2228	4.9697
29	25.0658	21.8444	19.1885	16.9837	15.1411	13.5907	12.2777	11.1584	10.1983	9.3696	8.6501	8.0218	7.4701	6.9830	6.5509	6.1656	5.8204	5.5098	5.2292	4.9747
30	25.8077	22.3965	19.6004	17.2920	15.3725	13.7648	12.4090	11.2578	10.2737	9.4269	8.6938	8.0552	7.4957	7.0027	6.5660	6.1772	5.8294	5.5168	5.2347	4.9789
40	32.8347	27.3555	23.1148	19.7928	17.1591	15.0463	13.3317	11.9246	10.7574	9.7791	8.9511	8.2438	7.6344	7.1050	6.6418	6.2335	5.8713	5.5482	5.2582	4.9966
50	39.1961	31.4236	25.7298	21.4822	18.2559	15.7619	13.8007	12.2335	10.9617	9.9148	9.0417	8.3045	7.6752	7.1327	6.6605	6.2463	5.8801	5.5541	5.2623	4.9995

Estimating Social Security Benefits

The Social Security Administration (SSA) provides basic benefits for your retirement, for a period of disability, or for your survivors. To qualify, you must have earned the number of credits required for each benefit program. Once you qualify, the level of benefits received is based on your income in years past that was subject to the Federal Insurance Contributions Act (FICA) taxes, commonly known as Social Security taxes. Benefits increase each year based on a cost of living adjustment (COLA) announced by the SSA each October for the following year. Over the past ten years, COLA adjustments have averaged 2.6 percent. The discussion and Table B.1 provide the authors' estimates of Social Security benefits for 2008 for various income levels using calculators found at http://www.ssa.gov/planners/calculators.htm. The amounts are for a 30-year-old worker but would not differ significantly for workers ten years older or younger.

Social Security Retirement Benefits

To qualify for Social Security retirement benefits, any worker born after 1928 must have earned 40 credits of coverage. As noted in the text, it is possible to receive a maximum of four credits per year. In 2007 a worker would earn one credit for each $1000 of income subject to Social Security taxes (this figure is adjusted upward each year for inflation). Dependent children, spouses caring for dependent children, and retired spouses at age 62 (including former spouses if the marriage lasted at least ten years) may also collect benefits based on the eligibility of the retired worker.

You can use Table B.1 to estimate a person's Social Security retirement benefits in today's dollars, assuming the retiree worked steadily, received average pay raises, and retired at the full-benefit retirement age. If more than one person would receive a benefit under the retiree's account (retiree and spouse, for example), the amount of the second person's benefit would be one-half of the retiree's benefit, giving a couple a total benefit 50 percent higher than the individual figure listed in Table B.1.

Social Security Disability Benefits

Social Security will pay disability benefits to an insured worker, dependent children up to age 18 (or 19 if the child is still in high school), a spouse caring for a dependent child who is younger than age 16 or disabled, and a spouse (even if divorced, but not remarried, provided that the marriage lasted ten years) age 62 or older. The benefit amount depends on two factors. The first factor is the eligibility of the disabled worker. To qualify for disability benefits, workers need at least 40 credits of coverage under Social Security, with at least 20 of the credits attained in the previous ten years (depending on year of birth). A worker younger than age 31 must have attained at least six credits or one more than one-half of the total credits possible after age 21, whichever is greater. (For example, a 26-year-old worker would have five years, or 20 credits, possible and would need ten credits of coverage.) The second factor affecting benefit levels is the predisability income of the covered individual that was subject to the FICA tax.

You can use Table B.1 to estimate an individual's Social Security disability benefits, assuming the disabled person worked steadily and received average pay raises. To obtain figures more specific than those given in Table B.1, contact the Social Security Administration to obtain your Social Security Statement as described in Chapter 17 or log on to http://www.ssa.gov/mystatement/ or http://www.ssa.gov/planners/calculators.htm.

Social Security Survivors Benefits

Social Security will pay benefits to surviving children younger than age 18 (or 19 if the child is still in high school), to a surviving spouse (even if divorced from the deceased, but not remarried) caring for surviving children who are younger than age 16, and to a surviving spouse (even if divorced, if the marriage lasted at least ten years) age 60 or older. Two factors are important in such cases. The first factor is the eligibility of the covered worker. The deceased worker who has accrued at least 40 credits of coverage is considered to be "fully insured." Workers who have earned at least as many credits of coverage as years since turning age 21 will be fully insured as well. Other individuals may be considered "currently insured" if they have earned six credits of coverage out of the previous 13 possible calendar credits. The survivors of currently insured workers receive limited types of benefits compared with those available to fully insured workers. The second factor is the covered worker's level of earnings, as indicated in Table B.1.

You can use Table B.1 to estimate monthly survivors benefits from Social Security in today's dollars for eligible surviving family members. The table assumes that the deceased worker worked steadily and received average pay raises.

Table B.1 Estimates* of Social Security Benefits for the Three Major Social Security Programs

	Current Annual Earnings					
	$25,000	**$35,000**	**$45,000**	**$55,000**	**$70,000**	**$90,000**
Monthly Retirement Benefits at Age 67 in Today's Dollars						
Per month	$ 1,092	$ 1,367	$ 1,642	$ 1,831	$ 2,025	$ 2,282
Per year	$13,104	$16,404	$19,704	$21,972	$24,300	$ 27,284
As a percentage of income	52.4%	46.9%	43.8%	40.0%	34.7%	30.4%
Monthly Retirement Benefits at Age 67 in Future Dollars						
Per month	$ 4,034	$ 5,021	$ 6,007	$6,882	$ 7,576	$ 8,501
Per year	$48,408	$60,252	$72,084	$82,584	$90,912	$102,012
Monthly Disability Benefits If You Became Disabled in 2008						
Individual benefit per month	$ 993	$ 1,234	$ 1,467	$ 1,700	$ 1,896	$ 2,117
Individual benefit per year	$11,916	$14,808	$17,604	$20,400	$22,752	$ 25,404
As a percentage of income	47.7%	42.3%	39.1%	37.1%	32.5%	28.2%
Maximum family benefit per month	$ 1,688	$ 2,091	$ 2,494	$ 2,890	$ 3,223	$ 3,599
Maximum family benefit per year	$20,256	$25,092	$29,928	$34,680	$38,676	$ 43,188
Monthly Survivors Benefits If You Died in 2008						
Individual benefit per month†	$ 766	$ 952	$ 1,136	$ 1,307	$ 1,449	$ 1,623
Individual benefit per year	$ 9,192	$11,424	$13,632	$15,684	$17,388	$ 19,476
As a percentage of income	36.7%	32.6%	30.3%	28.5%	24.8%	21.6%
Maximum family benefit per month	$ 1,687	$ 2,360	$ 2,722	$ 3,081	$ 3,384	$ 3,788
Maximum family benefit per year	$20,244	$28,320	$32,664	$36,972	$40,608	$ 45,456

* Authors' estimates in today's dollars for a 30-year-old worker using Social Security Administration website calculators.
†A surviving spouse age 65 or older would receive a retirement benefit approximately one-third higher than these figures.

Glossary

above-the-line deductions Adjustments subtracted from gross income whether taxpayer itemizes deductions or not.

abstract Detailed written history of the ownership of a piece of property.

acceleration clause Part of a credit contract stating that after a specific number of payments are unpaid (often just one), the loan is considered in default and all remaining installments are due and payable upon demand of the creditor.

accident insurance Pays a specific amount per day—for example, $100 for a hospital stay arising out of an accident—or a specific amount for the loss of certain limbs or body parts.

account reconciliation Comparing your records with your bank's records, checking the accuracy of both sets of records, and identifying any errors.

acquisition fee Pays for a credit report, application fee, and other paperwork, either in cash or included in the gross cap cost.

active investor An investor who wishes to manage her own account by carefully studying the economy, market trends, and investment alternatives; regularly monitoring these factors; and buying and selling three to four times a year, with or without the advice of a professional.

activities of daily living (ADLs) Insurance companies use the inability to perform a certain number of such activities as a criterion for deciding when the insured becomes eligible for long-term care benefits.

actual cash value (of personal property) Represents the purchase price of the property less depreciation.

add-on interest method Interest is calculated by applying an interest rate to the amount borrowed times the number of years to arrive at the total interest to be charged.

add-on loans/flipping Occurs when you refinance or rewrite a loan for a larger amount before it has been completely repaid.

adjustable life insurance Allows the owner of a policy to modify one of the three cornerstones of cash-value policies—the premium, the policy face amount, and the rate of cash-value accumulation—with corresponding changes occurring in the other two.

adjustable-rate mortgage (ARM)/variable-rate mortgage Mortgage in which the borrower's interest rate fluctuates according to some index of interest rates based on the rising or falling cost of credit in the economy—thus transferring interest rate risk to the borrower.

adjusted capitalized cost (adjusted cap cost) Subtracting the capitalized cost reductions from the gross capitalized cost.

adjusted gross income (AGI) Gross income less any exclusions and adjustments.

adjustments to income Allowable subtractions from gross income.

adoption tax credit A nonrefundable income tax credit of up to $11,390 based on qualifying costs of the adoption of a child.

advance medical directive Statement of medical preferences, including designation of surrogate decision maker if patients become unable to make medical decisions for themselves in case of coma, dementia, or brain death.

affinity card Standard bank credit cards with the logo of a sponsoring organization imprinted on the face of the card.

after-tax dollars Money on which employee has already paid taxes.

after-tax money Funds put into regular investment accounts; subject to income taxes.

after-tax profit Money left over after a firm has paid expenses, bondholder interest, and taxes.

after-tax yield Percentage yield on taxable investment after subtracting effects of federal income taxes.

aggressive growth funds Make investments in speculative stocks with volatile price swings, seeking the greatest long-term capital appreciation possible. Also known as maximum capital gains funds and capital appreciation funds.

aggressive investment philosophy Investors with this philosophy primarily seek capital gains, often with a short time horizon.

all-risk (open-perils) policies Cover losses caused by all perils other than those that the policy specifically excludes.

alpha statistic Quantifies the difference between an investment's expected return and its actual recent performance (outperforming or underperforming) given its risk; positive values indicate better-than-market performance.

alternative dispute resolution programs Industry- or government-sponsored programs that provide an avenue to resolve disputes outside the formal court system.

alternative minimum tax (AMT) Tax rate (26 or 28 percent) triggered for people with excessive deductions.

amortization Loan repayment method in which part of the payment goes to pay interest and part goes to repay principal. Extra payments toward principal shorten the life of the loan and decrease total amount of interest paid.

amortization schedule List that shows all the monthly payments, the portions that will go toward interest and principal, and the debt remaining after each payment is made throughout the life of the loan.

annual fees Charges levied against cardholders for the privilege of having an open account but that are not included in the advertised APR.

annual fund operating expenses Normal operating costs of the business that are deducted from fund assets before shareholders receive earnings.

annual limits Specify the maximum payment under a medical care plan for covered expenses occurring within one year.

annual percentage rate (APR) The cost of credit on a yearly basis as a percentage rate.

annual percentage yield (APY) Return on total interest received on $100 deposit for 365-day period, given institution's simple annual interest rate and compounding frequency.

annual report Legally required yearly report about financial performance, activities, and prospects sent to major stockholders and made available to the general public.

annuitant Person covered by an annuity who is to receive the benefits.

annuity A stream of payments to be received in the future.

any-occupation policy Provides full benefits only if you cannot perform any occupation.

appraisal fee Fee charged for a professionally prepared estimate of the fair market value of the real estate property by an objective party.

aptitudes The natural abilities and talents that individuals possess.

arbitration Dispute resolution process in which a neutral third party hears (or reads) claims made and positions taken by the parties to the dispute and then issues a ruling that is binding on one or both parties.

"as is" Way for seller to get around legal requirements for warranties; buyer takes all risk of nonperformance or other problems despite any salesperson's verbal assurances.

ask price Declared lowest price that anyone is willing to accept to sell a security.

assessed value Price that local authorities place on your home as used to calculate property taxes.

asset Property owned by a taxpayer for personal use or as an investment that has monetary value.

asset allocation Form of diversification in which investor decides on proportions of an investment portfolio that will be devoted to various categories of assets.

asset allocation funds Invest in a mix of assets (usually stocks, bonds, and cash equivalents and sometimes international assets, gold, and real estate); they buy and sell regularly to reduce risk while trying to outperform the market.

asset management account (AMA, central asset accounts, or all-in-one account) Multiple-purpose, coordinated package that gathers most monetary asset management vehicles into a unified account and reports activity on a single monthly statement to the client.

asset-to-debt ratio Compares total assets with total liabilities.

assumable mortgage Buyer pays the seller a down payment generally equal to the seller's equity in the home and takes responsibility for the mortgage loan payments for the remaining term of the seller's existing mortgage loan.

ATM cards Allow deposits and withdrawals into an account and transfers among checking and savings accounts using a PIN at an ATM.

ATM transaction fee Payments levied each time an ATM is used.

automatic enrollment plan Plan in which the employer withholds up to 6 percent (and sometimes more) of an employee's salary and places it into a defined-contribution retirement plan account.

automatic funds transfer agreement Agreement whereby the amount necessary to cover a bad check will be transmitted from your savings account to your checking account.

automatic investment program (AIP) Agreement by which a mutual fund is authorized to withdraw money from your checking account, perhaps monthly, to buy mutual fund shares.

automatic overdraft loan agreement Arrangement whereby the amount necessary to cover a bad check will be automatically loaned to you by your bank or charged to your Visa or MasterCard account as a cash advance.

automatic premium loan Life insurance policy provision that allows any premium not paid by the end of the grace period to be paid automatically with a policy loan if sufficient cash value or dividends have accumulated.

automatic reinvestment When investors choose to automatically reinvest any interest, dividends, and capital gains payments to purchase additional fund shares.

automobile bodily injury liability Occurs when a driver or car owner is held legally responsible for bodily injury losses that other people, including pedestrians, suffer.

automobile insurance Combines the liability and property insurance coverages that most car owners and drivers need into a single-package policy.

automobile medical payments insurance Insurance that covers bodily injury losses suffered by the driver of the insured vehicle and any passengers, regardless of who is at fault.

automobile property damage liability Occurs when a driver or car owner is held legally responsible for damage to others' property.

average daily balance Sum of the outstanding balances owed each day during the billing period divided by the number of days in the period.

average share cost Actual cost basis of the investment used for income tax purposes, calculated by dividing the total amount invested by the total shares purchased.

average share price Calculated by dividing the share price total by the number of investment periods.

average-balance account Checking account for which service fees are assessed if the account's average daily balance drops below a certain level during specified time.

average tax rate Proportion of total income paid in income taxes.

back-end ratio Compares the total of all monthly PITI expenditures plus auto loans and other debts with gross monthly income.

balance sheet (or net worth statement) Snapshot of assets, liabilities, and net worth on a particular date.

bad check A check written for which there were insufficient funds in the account.

balance transfer Full or partial payment on the balance of one credit card using a cash advance from another.

balanced funds Keep a set mix of stocks and bonds, often 60 percent stocks and 40 percent bonds, in order to earn a well-balanced return of income and long-term capital gains.

balloon automobile loan A loan that has a low monthly payment similar in amount to that required if the vehicle had been leased and with a large final payment similar in amount to the residual value under a lease.

bank credit card account Open-ended credit account with a financial institution that allows the holder to make purchases almost anywhere.

Bank Insurance Fund (BIF) of the Federal Deposit Insurance Corporation (FDIC) Federal agency that insures deposits in federally chartered banks against loss up to $100,000 per account.

bankruptcy Constitutionally guaranteed right that permits people (and businesses) to ask a court to find them officially unable to meet their debts.

basic (homeowner's insurance) form (HO-1) Named-perils policy that covers 11 property-damage–causing perils and provides three areas of liability-related protection: personal liability, property damage liability, and medical payments.

basic liquidity ratio Number of months you could meet expenses using only monetary assets if all income ceases.

basic retirement benefit/primary insurance amount Amount of Social Security benefits a worker would receive at his or her full-benefit retirement age, which is 67 for those born after 1960.

bear market Market in which securities prices have declined in value by 20 percent or more from previous highs, often over the course of several weeks or months.

below-average costs "Averaging" means that you purchase more shares when the price is down and fewer shares when the price is high, so most of your shares are purchased at below-average cost.

beneficiary A person or organization designated to receive a benefit.

beneficiary designation Legal form signed by the owner of an asset providing that the property goes to a certain person or organization in the event of the owner's death.

benefit amount Long-term care plans are generally written to provide a specific dollar benefit per day of care.

benefit period Length of time that the individual for whom a policy is written would likely need the care.

best buy Product or service that, in the buyer's opinion, represents acceptable quality at a fair or low price for that quality level.

beta/beta value/beta coefficient A measure of stock volatility; that is, how much the stock price varies relative to the rest of the market.

bid price Declared highest price anyone wants to pay for a security.

billing cycle Time from one billing date to the next for a credit account.

billing/closing/statement date The last day for which any transactions are reported on the credit statement.

binder Temporary insurance contract replaced later by written policy.

biweekly mortgage GEM that calls for payments of half of the normal payment to be made every two weeks; the borrower thus makes 26 payments a year and reduces the principal amount by one full payment each year; this reduces the mortgage term to about 20 years on a 30-year mortgage.

blank endorsement Check that shows only the payee's signature on the back, making it a bearer instrument that anyone can cash.

board of directors Individuals who set policy and name the principal officers of the company.

bond A debt instrument issued by an organization that promises repayment at a specific time and the right to receive regular interest payments during the life of the bond; from investor's standpoint, a loan that the investor makes to a government or a corporation.

bond funds These fixed-income funds aim to earn current income higher than a money market fund without incurring undue risk by investing in a portfolio of bonds and other low-risk investments that pay high dividends and offer capital appreciation.

bond rating An impartial outsider's opinion of the quality—or creditworthiness—of the issuing organization.

book value per share Reflects the book value of a company divided by the number of shares of common stock outstanding.

book value/shareholder's equity Net worth of a company, determined by subtracting total liabilities from assets.

book-entry form Bond certificates aren't issued; rather, account is set up in name of the issuing organization or the brokerage firm that sold the bond, and interest is paid to the bondholder when due.

bounce protection agreement Bank will honor checks written against insufficient funds up to a certain limit and charge customer for each check written.

breakeven price Price at which the cost of a contract is negated by a profit (or the cost is reduced by hedging a loss).

breakpoints Investment levels required to obtain a reduced sales load; start at $10,000.

broad (homeowner's insurance) form (HO-2) Named-perils policy that covers 18 property-damage–causing perils and provides protection from three liability-related exposures.

broker/dealer Financial intermediary that not only buys and sells securities but also makes a market in one or more of the stocks listed on the OTC.

broker's commission Largest selling cost in selling a home; these commissions often amount to 6 percent of the selling price of the home.

brokered certificates of deposit CDs purchased through a stock brokerage firm.

budget Paper or electronic document used to record both planned and actual income and expenditures over a period of time.

budget estimates Projected dollar amounts to receive or spend in a budgeting period.

budget exceptions When budget estimates differ from actual expenditures.

budget variance Difference between amount budgeted and actual amount spent or received.

bull market Market in which securities prices have risen 20 percent or more over time.

bump-up CDs Allow savers to bump up interest rate once if rates rise and to add up to 100 percent of initial deposit whenever desired.

bunching deductions For taxpayers who do not meet floor for itemizing deductions every year, strategy of prepaying expenses in one year so that itemizing works every other year.

business cycle/economic cycle Business cycles can be depicted as a wavelike pattern of rising and falling economic activity; the phases of the business cycle include expansion, peak, contraction (which may turn into recession), and trough.

business-cycle risk The chance that an economic downturn will affect an investment's value.

buy and hold/buy to hold Investment strategy in which investors buy a widely diversified mix of stocks and/or mutual funds, reinvest the dividends by buying more stocks and mutual funds, and hold on to those investments almost indefinitely.

buyer's agent Serves as the buyer's representative in the real estate negotiations and transaction.

buyer's orders Written offer that names a specific vehicle and all charges; only sign such offers after the salesperson and sales manager have signed *first*.

buying long Buying a security (especially on margin) with the hope that the stock price will rise.

call option Gives option holder the right to buy the optioned asset from the option writer at the striking price at any time before the expiration date.

canceled check A check that has been paid to the payee and returned to the writer as a record that the check has been paid.

capital accumulation The process of building wealth.

capital gain Increase in the value of an initial investment (less costs) realized upon the sale of the investment.

capital gains distributions Represent the net gains (capital gains minus capital losses) that a fund realizes when it sells securities that were held in the fund's portfolio.

capital improvements Costs incurred in making value-enhancing changes (beyond maintenance and repair) in real property.

capital loss Decrease in paper value of an initial investment; only realized if sold.

capitalized cost reductions (cap cost reductions) Monies paid on the lease at its inception, including any down payments, trade-in values, or rebates.

card registration service Firm that will notify all companies with which you have debit and credit cards if your cards are lost or stolen.

card verification value The three- or four-digit code on the signature strip on the back of credit cards.

career fairs University-, community- and employer-sponsored events for job seekers to meet with many employers quickly to screen potential employers.

career goal Identifying what you want to do for a living, whether a specific job or field of employment.

career planning Finding employment that will use your interests and abilities and that will support you financially.

cash account A brokerage account that requires an initial deposit (perhaps as little as $100) and specifies that full settlement is due to the brokerage firm within three business days after a buy or sell order has been given.

cash advance The use of a credit card to obtain cash rather than to make a purchase.

cash advance (or convenience) checks A check-equivalent way to take a cash advance on a credit card.

cash basis Only transactions involving actual money received or money spent are recorded.

cash dividend Cash profits that a firm distributes to stockholders.

cash flow Amount of rental income you have left after paying all operating expenses.

cash loan Credit situation in which the borrower receives cash and then uses it to make purchases, pay off other loans, or make investments.

cash surrender value Represents the cash value of a life insurance policy minus any surrender charges.

cash value Represents the value of the investment element in a cash-value life insurance policy.

cash-balance plan Defined-benefit plan funded solely by an employer that gives each participant an interest-earning account credited with a percentage of pay on a monthly basis.

cash-flow calendar Budget estimates for monthly income and expenses.

cash-flow statement (or income and expense statement) Summary of all income and expense transactions over a specific time period.

cashier's checks A check made out to a specific party and drawn on the financial institution's account itself; thus, it is backed by the institution's finances.

cash-value life insurance Pays benefits at death and includes a savings/investment element that can provide a reduced level of benefits to the policyholder prior to the death of the insured person.

catch-up provision Permits workers age 50 or older to contribute an additional $5000 to most employer-sponsored plans ($1000 limit on IRA accounts).

certificate of deposit (CD) An interest-earning savings instrument purchased for a fixed period of time.

certificate of insurance Paper or booklet that outlines group health insurance benefits.

certified check Personal check on which your financial institution imprints the word *certified*, signifying that the account has sufficient funds to cover its payment.

Chapter 7 of the Bankruptcy Act—Immediate Liquidation Plan (straight bankruptcy) Provides for the liquidation of assets with proceeds applied to paying off excusable debts to the degree possible.

Chapter 13 of the Bankruptcy Act—(wage earner or regular income plan) Designed for individuals with regular incomes who might be able to pay off some or all of their debts given certain court protections.

chargeback The amount of the transaction is charged back to the business where the transaction originated in the case of a dispute or challenge by the cardholder.

checking accounts At depository institutions, allow depositors to write checks against their deposited funds, which transfer funds to other people and organizations.

chronological format Résumé that provides your information in reverse order, with most recent first.

city indexes Comparing wages and cost of living for various employment locations.

claims adjuster Person designated by the insurance company to assess whether the loss is covered and to determine the dollar amount that the company will pay.

claims/payout ratio Percentage of premiums collected by an insurance company that is subsequently paid out to reimburse the losses of the participants.

classes of insureds Consist of insureds who share similar characteristics.

cleared A check that has been paid by your bank to the entity to which it was written.

cliff vesting Schedule under which employee is fully vested within three years of employment.

closed-end lease/walkaway lease Agreement in which the lessee pays no charge if the end-of-lease market value of the vehicle is lower than the originally projected residual value.

closed-end mutual funds Funds that issue a limited and fixed number of shares at inception and do not buy them back; after purchase, fund shares trade at market prices.

closing Meeting to transfer ownership on a piece of real property.

closing costs Include fees and charges other than the down payment and may vary from 2 to 10 percent of the mortgage loan amount.

COBRA rights (Consolidated Omnibus Budget Reconciliation Act of 1985) Allow you to remain a member of a group health plan for as long as 18 months if you worked for an employer with more than 20 workers.

co-branded credit card Arrangement in which consumer product companies contract with banks or other financial institutions to offer credit cards.

codicil Legal instrument with which one can make minor changes to a will.

coinsurance Method by which the insured and the insurer share proportionately in the payment for a loss.

collateral An asset pledged in a credit account so that the lender may seize the asset should the borrower fail to repay as agreed.

coinsurance clause Requires insured to pay a proportion of any loss suffered.

collectibles Cultural artifacts that have value because of their beauty, age, scarcity, or popularity, such as antiques, stamps, rare coins, art, baseball cards, and so on.

college savings plan Program that allows after-tax contributions to a designated beneficiary to pay college costs; allows tax-free growth and tax-free withdrawals for beneficiary's college costs.

collision insurance Reimburses insureds for losses to their vehicles resulting from a collision with another car or object or from a rollover.

commercial bank Corporation chartered under federal and state regulations to offer consumer financial services.

commissions Fees or percentages of the selling price paid to salespeople, agents, and companies for their services in buying or selling an investment.

common stock Most basic form of ownership of a corporation.

community property Arrangement in which most of the money and property acquired during a marriage are legally considered the joint property of both spouses.

community property laws In cases of divorce, assumes that the surviving spouse owns half of everything that both partners earned during the marriage, no matter how much was actually contributed by either partner and even if only one spouse held legal title to the property.

comparison shopping Process of comparing products or services to find the best buy.

compounding When interest on an investment itself earns interest.

comprehensive automobile insurance Protects against property damage losses to an insured vehicle caused by perils other than collision and rollover.

comprehensive health insurance Insurance that combines protections against various medical perils into a single policy with policy limits of $1 million or more.

conditional sales contracts/financing leases A type of contract used when purchasing goods with an installment loan; title does not pass to buyer until last installment payment has been made.

conditions Impose obligations on both the insured and the insurer by establishing the ground rules of the agreement.

condominium Form of ownership with the owners holding legal title to their own housing unit among many with common grounds and facilities owned by the developer or homeowner's association.

condominium form (HO-6) Named-perils policy protecting condominium owners from the three principal losses they face.

conservative investment philosophy (risk aversion) Investors with this philosophy accept very little risk and are generally rewarded with relatively low rates of return for seeking the twin goals of a moderate amount of current income and preservation of capital.

consumer credit Nonbusiness debt that consumers use for expenditures other than home mortgages.

consumer finance company/small loan company Firm that specializes in making relatively small secured or unsecured loans that require monthly installment payments.

consumer price index (CPI) A broad measure of changes in the prices of all goods and services purchased for consumption by urban households.

consumer statement Your version of a credit issue that shows up on your credit report when the credit bureau refuses to drop a disputed claim.

consumer-driven health care Approach to medical care insurance with high deductibles that assumes that knowledgeable and informed patients/employees will spend their own money more carefully than they would spend an employer's or health plan's funds.

contents replacement-cost protection Option sometimes available in homeowner's insurance policies (including the renter's form) that pays the full replacement cost of any personal property.

contingency clauses Specify that certain conditions must be satisfied before a contract is binding.

contingent beneficiary Person who becomes the beneficiary if the primary beneficiary dies before the insured.

continuous-debt method Approach for determining your debt limit that asks whether you are able to get completely out of debt every four years (except for a mortgage loan).

contraction A period of negligible economic growth or even a decline in economic activity; unemployment rises and both companies and individuals stop spending.

contributory plan The most common type of employee-sponsored defined-contribution retirement plan; accepts employee as well as employer contributions.

conventional mortgage A fixed-rate, fixed-term, fixed-payment mortgage loan.

convertible preferred stock Can be exchanged at the option of the stockholder for a specified number of shares of common stock.

convertible term insurance Offers policyholders option of exchanging a term policy for a cash-value policy without evidence of insurability.

cooperative (co-op) Form of ownership in which owner holds a share of the corporation that owns and manages a group of housing units as well as common grounds and facilities; co-op owners pay a monthly management fee to an independent entity that carries out activities similar to those that homeowner associations do for condo owners.

coordination-of-benefits clause Prevents you from collecting insurance benefits that exceed the loss suffered by noting the order in which plans will pay if you are covered by multiple plans.

copayment A variation of a deductible, requires you to pay a specific dollar amount each time you use your benefits for a specific covered expense item.

corporate bonds Interest-bearing certificates of long-term debt issued by a corporation.

corporate earnings The profits a company makes during a specific time period indicate to many analysts whether to buy or sell a stock.

corporation State-chartered legal entity that can conduct business operations in its own name.

corpus/trust estate/trust fund Assets put into a trust.

cosigner Individual who agrees to pay a debt if the original borrower fails to do so.

cost index A numerical method used to compare the costs of similar plans of life insurance.

countercyclical (defensive) stock Exhibits price changes contrary to movements in the business cycle; performs well even during weak economic activity and sliding interest rates.

counteroffer Legal offer to sell (or buy) a home at a different price and perhaps with different conditions from those outlined in the original offer.

coupon rate/coupon/coupon yield/stated interest rate Interest rate printed on the certificate when the bond is issued.

cover letter A letter of introduction sent to a prospective employer to get an interview.

coverage A—liability insurance Liability insurance for automobiles that covers insureds when they are responsible for others' losses.

coverage B—medical payments insurance Covers bodily injury losses suffered by the driver of the insured vehicle and any passengers regardless of who is at fault.

coverage C—uninsured and underinsured motorist insurance Coverage that an insured can purchase as part of automobile insurance that covers the insured in an accident with an uninsured or underinsured driver at fault.

coverage D—physical damage insurance Provides protection against losses caused by damage to your car from collision, theft, and other perils.

Coverdell education savings account (education savings account or education IRA) After-tax investments made to pay future education costs for a child younger than age 18; growth and withdrawals are tax free.

covered option Option for a security that the writer owns and thus the writer can settle any call options contract with relatively little risk.

covering a position When an investor using a margin account buys back securities sold short or sells securities bought long.

credit A term used to describe an arrangement in which goods, services, or money is received in exchange for a promise to repay at a future date.

credit agreement Contract that stipulates repayment terms for credit cards.

credit application Form or interview that provides information about your ability and willingness to repay debts.

credit bureau Firm that collects and keeps records of many borrowers' credit histories.

credit card blocking Hotels or other service providers use a credit card number to secure reservations and charge the anticipated cost of services.

credit card liability Amount that cardholder must pay in the case of a lost or stolen card; capped at $50.

credit cards Cards that allow repeated use of credit as long as the consumer makes regular monthly payments.

credit counseling agency (CCA) Agency that can arrange payment schedules with unsecured creditors for overly indebted consumers and can provide individuals with credit counseling.

credit disability insurance Repays an outstanding credit balance if the borrower becomes disabled.

credit history Continuing record of a person's credit usage and repayment of debts.

credit investigation Process in which creditor compares information on your application with your credit report as reported by credit agencies.

credit life insurance/credit disability insurance/credit unemployment insurance Grossly overpriced insurance offered to make credit payments in the event that the borrower dies or becomes disabled or unemployed.

credit limit Maximum outstanding debt that a lender will allow on an open-ended credit account.

credit rating Lender's evaluation of the applicant's creditworthiness.

credit receipt Written evidence of any items returned that notes the specific amount and date of the transaction.

credit repair company (credit clinic) Firm that offers to help improve or fix a person's credit history for a (usually hefty) fee.

credit report Information compiled by a credit bureau from merchants, utility companies, banks, court records, and creditors about your payment history.

credit scoring (risk scoring) system Statistical measure used to rate applicants based on various factors deemed relevant to creditworthiness and the likelihood of repayment.

credit statement The monthly bill on a credit card account showing the charges and payments made, minimum payment required and due date among other information; also called a periodic statement.

credit term life insurance Pays the remaining balance of a loan if the insured dies before repaying the debt.

credit union (CU) Member-owned, not-for-profit federally insured financial institutions that provide checking, savings, and loan services to members.

crude annual rate of return A rough measure of the yield on amounts invested (usually in real estate) that assumes that equal portions of the gain are earned each year.

cumulative preferred stock Preferred stock for which dividends must be paid, including any skipped dividends, before dividends go to common stockholders.

current income Money received while you own an investment; usually received regularly as interest, rent, or dividends.

current rate Rate of return a life insurance company has recently paid to policyholders.

current yield Equals the bond's fixed annual interest payment divided by its bond price.

currently insured status Requires workers to earn six credits in the most recent three years; provides for some survivors or disability benefits but no retirement benefits.

custodial account An account opened by an adult in the name of a child younger than age 14 under the provisions of the Uniform Gifts to Minors Act (or Uniform Transfers to Minors Act).

custodial care Suitable for many people who do not need skilled nursing care but who nevertheless require supervision (for example, help with eating or personal hygiene).

cyclical stock Describes the stock of a company whose profits are greatly influenced by changes in the economic business cycle, usually a consumer-oriented stock.

damage deposit Amount given in advance to a landlord to pay for repairing rental space beyond the damage expected from normal wear and tear.

day trading Occurs when an investor buys and sells stocks quickly throughout a day with the hope that prices will move enough to cover transaction costs and earn some profits.

dealer holdback/dealer rebate Dealer incentive in which the manufacturer allows dealers to hold back a percentage of invoice price, thereby providing the dealer with additional profit on the vehicle.

dealer sticker price Includes additional charges tacked on by the dealer as an attempt to generate additional revenue.

death benefit Amount that will be paid to beneficiary when the insured dies.

debit cards A plastic card that, when used with a PIN number, allows you to withdraw funds or transfer funds among accounts as well as make purchases via point-of-sale (POS) terminals at retail outlets.

debit collection agency Firm that specializes in collecting debts that the original lender could not collect.

debt limit Overall maximum you believe you should owe based on your ability to meet repayment obligations.

debt management plan (DMP) Arrangement whereby consumer provides one monthly payment (usually somewhat smaller than the total of previous credit payments) that is distributed to all creditors.

debt payments-to-disposable income method Percentage of disposable personal income available for regular debt repayments aside from set obligations.

debt payments-to-disposable income ratio Divides monthly disposable personal income into monthly debt repayments.

debt service-to-income ratio Compares dollars spent on gross annual debt with gross annual income.

debt-consolidation loan A loan taken out to pay off several smaller debts.

debts (investments) Lending investments that typically offer both a fixed maturity and a fixed income.

debt-to-equity ratio Ratio of your consumer debt to your assets.

declarations Provide the basic descriptive information about the insured person or property, the premium to be paid, the time period of the coverage, and the policy limits.

declining-balance method Interest calculation method in which interest is assessed during each billing period (usually each month) based on the outstanding balance of the installment loan that billing period.

decreasing term insurance Policy with an annually decreasing face amount of coverage but constant premiums.

deductibles Clauses in medical care plans that require you to pay an initial portion of medical expenses annually before receiving reimbursement.

deed Written document used to convey real estate ownership.

deed restrictions Rules placed on the homeowner's use of a property by local government or a homeowner's association.

deeded timesharing Buyer obtains a legal title or deed to limited time periods of use of real estate and becomes a secured creditor who really does own a time period of habitation.

default Situation in which borrower has failed to make a principal or interest payment when due or has failed to meet any other credit contract requirement.

default rate (on credit cards) A high APR that is assessed whenever a borrower fails to uphold certain rules of the account, such as making on-time payments or staying within the specified credit limit.

default rate (on bonds) Percentage of bonds that do not repay principal at maturity and sometimes cease interest payments in the interim.

default risk/credit risk Uncertainty associated with not receiving the promised periodic interest payments and the principal amount on bonds when it becomes due at maturity.

deferred annuity Annuity plan in which annuitants pay premiums during their working lives, then take income payments at some future date, such as retirement.

deferred load/back-end load A sales commission that is imposed only when shares are sold; often charges are on a sliding scale, with the fee dropping 1 percentage point per year that the investor stays in the fund.

deficiency balance Occurs when money raised by sale of repossessed collateral doesn't cover the amount owed on the debt plus any repossession expenses.

deficit/net loss The result on a cash-flow statement when expenditures exceed income.

defined-benefit retirement plan Employer-sponsored retirement plan that pays lifetime monthly annuity payments to retirees based on a predetermined formula.

defined-contribution plan A retirement plan designed to provide a lump-sum at retirement; it is distinguished by its "contributions"—the total amount of money put into each participating employee's individual account. (Also called *salary reduction plan*.)

deflation Involves generally falling prices across business sectors.

deflation risk Chance that the value of an investment will decline when overall prices decline.

demand deposits Another term for checking accounts, demand deposit funds must be always accessible to customers.

dental expense insurance Provides reimbursement for dental care expenses.

Department of Veterans Affairs (VA) Promotes home ownership among military veterans (active-duty, reserve, and National Guard veterans may qualify) by providing insurance against default.

deposit insurance Insures deposits, both principal amounts and accrued interest, up to $100,000 per account for most accounts ($200,000 for retirement accounts).

depository institutions Organizations licensed to take deposits and make loans.

depreciation Decline in value of an asset over time due to normal wear and tear and obsolescence.

derivative/derivative security A financial instrument that people trade in order to more easily manage the underlying asset upon which these instruments are based that can be used to reduce risk or take on additional risk.

direct deposit Having paychecks electronically sent from employer into your bank account.

direct ownership Results when investor holds actual legal title to real estate property.

direct sellers Companies that market insurance policies through salaried employees, mail-order promotions, newspapers, the Internet, and even vending machines.

disability benefits Substantially reduced benefits paid to employees who become disabled prior to retirement.

disability income insurance Replaces a portion of the income lost when you cannot work because of illness or injury.

discharged debts Debts (or portions thereof) that are excused as a result of a bankruptcy.

disclosure statement Government-required written notice of users' rights and responsibilities in using electronic money management, including receipts for ATM transactions.

discount bonds (zeroes) Bonds that pay no interest that are bought below face value which grow to face value at maturity.

discount brokers Charge commissions to execute trades that are often 30 to 80 percent less than the fees charged by full-service brokers, but also offer fewer services.

discount method of calculating interest Interest is calculated based on discount rate multiplied by the amount borrowed and by number of years to repay. Interest is then subtracted from the amount of the loan and the difference is given to the borrower. In this method, interest is paid up-front before the borrower receives the amount borrowed.

discount yield Difference between the original purchase price of a T-bill and what the Treasury pays you at maturity—the gain, or "par," is interest.

discounted cash-flow method Effective way to estimate the value or asking price of a real estate investment based on after-tax cash flow and the return on the invested dollars discounted over time to reflect a discounted yield.

discretionary income Money left over after necessities such as housing and food are paid for.

disposable (personal) income Amount of income remaining after taxes and withholding.

disposition fee Charge assessed when lessee turns in a vehicle at end of lease and lessor must prepare it for resale.

diversification Process of reducing risk by spreading investment money among several investment opportunities.

dividend Portion of a company's earnings that the firm pays out to shareholders.

dividend payout ratio Dividends per share divided by earnings per share; helps judge likelihood of future dividends.

dividend yield Cash dividend to an investor expressed as a percentage of the current market price of a security.

dividends per share Translates the total cash dividends paid out by a company to common stockholders into a per-share figure.

dollar-cost averaging/cost averaging Systematic program of investing equal sums of money at regular intervals regardless of the price of the investment.

domestic-relations order/court order acceptable for processing QDRO for public-sector employees.

down payment Portion of the purchase price of an item or property that is not borrowed.

dread disease insurance Provides reimbursement for medical expenses arising out of the occurrence of a specific disease, such as cancer.

due-on-sale clause Requires that the mortgage loan be fully paid off if the home is sold. It can impose a burden on the seller because it prohibits a buyer from assuming the mortgage loan.

dunning letters Notices that make insistent demands for repayment.

durable power of attorney Document that appoints someone, called an attorney-in-fact, to handle your legal or business matters and sign your name to documents if illness prevents you from doing so yourself.

early termination charge Charge if lessee turns car in before the end of lease period.

early termination payoff Total amount lessee would need to repay if ending the lease agreement early; includes both early termination charge and unpaid lease balance.

earned income Compensation for performing personal services, such as salaries, wages, tips, and net earnings from self-employment.

earned income credit A refundable income tax credit for workers whose income falls below a certain threshold.

earnest money Funds given to a real estate seller as a deposit to hold the property until a purchase contract can be negotiated.

earnings per share (EPS) A firm's profit divided by the number of outstanding shares; analysts follow EPS because it indicates the income that a company has available to pay dividends and reinvest as retained earnings—used to compare stocks across the board.

earnings yield Inverse of the P/E ratio; helps investors more clearly see investment expectations.

economic growth A condition of increasing production (business spending) and consumption (consumer spending) in the economy and hence increasing national income.

effective marginal tax rate The total marginal rate reflects all taxes on a person's income, including federal, state, and local income taxes as well as Social Security and Medicare taxes.

electronic benefits transfer cards (EBTs) Government cards to pay military personnel and provide Social Security and other government payments.

electronic funds transfers (EFTs) Electronic fund transfers among various accounts or to and from other people and businesses.

electronic money management Transactions conducted without using paper documents.

emergency fund Saving enough money to cover living expenses (perhaps 70 percent of gross income) for three to six months in case of financial emergency.

employee benefit Compensation for employment that does not take the form of wages, salaries, commissions, or other cash payments.

Employee Retirement Income Security Act (ERISA) Regulates employer-sponsored plans by calling for proper plan reporting and disclosure to participants in defined-contribution, defined-benefit, and cash-balance plans.

employee stock option (ESO) Gift, like a bonus, from employer to employees that allows employees to benefit from employer's stock appreciation without putting any money down.

employee stock-ownership plan (ESOP) Benefit plan in which employers make tax-deductible gifts of company stock into trusts, which are then allocated into employee accounts.

employment agency Firm that locates employment for certain types of employees.

endorsement Process of writing on the back of a check to legally transfer its ownership.

endorsements/riders Amendments and additions to the basic insurance policy that can both expand and limit coverage to accommodate specific needs.

endowment life insurance Pays the face amount of the policy either upon the death of the insured or at some previously agreed-upon date (the endowment date), whichever occurs first.

envelope system Placing exact amounts into envelopes for each budgetary purpose.

episode limits Specify the maximum payment for health care expenses arising from a single episode of illness or injury, with each episode being considered separately.

equities Ownership equities such as common or preferred stocks, equity mutual funds, real estate, and so on that focus on capital gains more than on income.

equity Amount by which value of personal assets (excluding primary residence) exceeds debts.

equity (real estate) Dollar value of the home in excess of the amount owed on it.

equity-income funds Invest in well-known companies with a long history of paying high dividends as they emphasize income and capital preservation.

escrow account Special reserve account at a financial institution in which funds are held until they are paid to a third party—for example, for home insurance and for property taxes.

estate Consists of your worldly possessions and financial wealth less any debts you owe.

estate planning Definite arrangements made during your lifetime that are consistent with your wishes for the administration, disposition, and transfer of your wealth and worldly possessions to your dependents and others when you die.

estimated taxes Amounts of quarterly tax payments forwarded to the IRS by people who are self-employed or who receive a substantial income from a source that does not withhold payroll taxes.

excess mileage charge Type of end-of-lease charge attached to closed-end lease agreements if vehicle has been driven more miles than specified in the original contract.

exchange fees Small amount charged to move money among funds within a mutual fund family.

exchange privilege Permits mutual fund shareholders to easily swap shares on a dollar-for-dollar basis for shares in another mutual fund within a mutual fund family. Also called switching, conversion, or transfer privilege.

exchange-traded fund (ETF) Basket of passively managed securities structured like an index fund; owns all or a representative set of securities that duplicate the performance of a market segment or index.

exclusion amount The value of assets that may be transferred to heirs without incurring an estate tax.

exclusions Income not subject to federal taxation.

exclusions (insurance) Narrow the focus and eliminate specific coverages broadly stated in the insuring agreements.

exclusive insurance agents Represent only one insurance company for a specific type of insurance.

executor/personal representative Person responsible for carrying out the provisions of a will and managing the assets until the estate is passed on to heirs.

exemption (or personal exemption) Legally permitted amount deducted from AGI based on number of people that taxpayer's income supports.

expansion phase Phase of the business cycle when economic activity is increasing, unemployment is falling, prices may rise, businesses are investing in capital equipment, and consumption is on the upswing.

expense ratio Expense per dollar of assets under management.

expenses Total expenditures made in a specified time.

exposures Sources of pure risk.

express warranty Any verbal or written warranty.

extended warranty/service contract/maintenance agreement/buyer protection plan Agreement between the seller and buyer of product to repair or replace covered product components for some specified time period; purchased separately from product itself.

face amount Dollar value of protection as listed in a life insurance policy and used to calculate the premium.

Fair Credit Billing Act (FCBA) Helps people who wish to dispute billing errors on revolving credit accounts.

Fair Credit Reporting Act (FCRA) Requires that credit reports contain accurate, relevant, and recent information and that only bona fide users be permitted to review a file for approved purposes.

Fair Debt Collection Practices Act (FDCPA) Prohibits third-party debt collection agencies from using abusive, deceptive, or unfair practices to collect past-due debts.

fair market value Amount a willing buyer would pay to a willing seller for a charitable item; also, the price that a buyer would likely pay for a home based on comparisons with other home sales in the area.

family auto policy (FAP) Covers vehicle owners, relatives living in their households, and people who have the owners' permission to drive the vehicle.

FDIC's Savings Association Insurance Fund (SAIF) Insures deposits in savings banks up to $100,000 per account.

federal estate tax Assessed against a deceased person's estate before property (real estate, stocks and bonds, business interests, and so on) is transferred to heirs or assigned according to terms of a will or state intestacy laws.

federal funds rate The rate that banks charge one another for overnight loans; set by the Federal Reserve Board.

Federal Housing Administration (FHA) An arm of the U.S. Department of Housing and Urban Development (HUD) that insures loans that meet its standards to encourage home ownership.

Federal Insurance Contributions Act (FICA) Act that authorizes Social Security and Medicare tax withdrawals from employee paychecks; amounts withheld go into Social Security trust fund accounts, which pay benefits to current retirees.

Federal Reserve Board (Fed) An agency of the federal government commonly referred to as the *Fed*, it regularly reports its decisions and opinions about the direction of monetary policy via setting the federal funds rate.

FICO score Method using complex statistical models that correlate certain borrower characteristics with the likelihood of repayment.

file To report formally to the IRS your income earned and your tax liability for the year.

filing status Description of a taxpayer's marital status on last day of tax year (December 31).

final expenses One-time expenses occurring just prior to or after a death.

finance charge Total dollar amount paid to use credit.

financial goals Specific objectives addressed by planning and managing finances.

financial literacy Knowledge of facts, concepts, principles, and technological tools that are fundamental to being smart about money.

financial loss Any decline in the value of income or assets in the present or future.

financial planner An investment professional who evaluates the personal finances of an individual or family and recommends strategies to set and achieve long-term financial goals.

financial planning The process of developing and implementing a coordinated series of financial plans to help achieve financial success.

financial ratios Calculations designed to simplify evaluation of financial strength and progress.

financial records Documents that evidence financial transactions.

financial responsibility Means that you are accountable for your future financial well-being and that you strive to make wise personal financial decisions.

financial risk Possibility that an investment will fail to pay a return to the investor.

financial services industry Companies that provide monetary asset management and other services.

financial statements Compilations that show financial conditions, including balance sheets and cash-flow statements.

financial strategies Preestablished action plans implemented in specific situations.

first-to-die policies Cover more than one person but pay only when the first insured dies.

fixed expenses Expenses that recur at fixed intervals.

fixed income Specific rate of return that borrower agrees to pay the investor for use of the principal (initial investment).

fixed maturity Specific date on which borrower agrees to repay the principal to the investor.

fixed yield Interest income payment remains the same regardless of bond's price.

fixed-rate loans Loans for which the interest rate will not change over the life of the loan.

fixed-time deposits/CDs Specify a period (usually 6 months to 5 years) that the savings *must* be left on deposit; early withdrawals carry a penalty.

fizbo For sale by owner (FSBO).

flat-fee brokers Charge a flat fee for their services rather than a percentage-based commission.

flexible benefit plan An employer-sponsored plan that gives the employee a choice of selecting either cash or one or more qualifying nontaxable benefits; also known as a cafeteria plan.

flexible spending account (FSA) or expense reimbursement account Allows employees to fund qualified medical or dependent expenses on pretax basis by reducing take-home salary.

flexible spending arrangements Employer-offered programs that allow employees to have money diverted from their IRS-reported income into accounts that pay medical, dental, vision, or other allowable expenses using pretax dollars.

floater policies Provide all-risk protection for accident and theft losses to movable property regardless of where the loss occurs.

floor broker Brokerage firm's contact person at an exchange.

foreclosure Process in which the lender sues the borrower to prove default and asks the court to order the sale of the property to pay the debt.

fortuitous losses Losses that are unexpected in terms of both their timing and their magnitude.

401(k) plan Defined-contribution plan designed for employees of private corporations.

403(b) plan Defined-contribution plan designed for eligible employees of not-for-profit institutions, such as colleges, hospitals, and religious organizations.

457 plans Defined-contribution plan for state and local governments and non-church controlled tax-exempt organizations. Only employees (not employers) make contributions into the plan.

front-end load A sales charge paid when an individual buys an investment, reducing the amount available to purchase fund shares.

front-end ratio Compares the total annual PITI expenditures for housing with the loan applicant's gross annual income to assess the borrower's ability to pay the mortgage.

full warranty Warranty that meets three stringent promises: product must be fixed at no cost to buyer within reasonable time, owner will not have to undertake an unreasonable task to return product for repair, and defective product will be replaced with a new one or the buyer's money will be returned if product cannot be fixed.

full-benefit retirement age Age at which a retiree is entitled to full Social Security benefits; 67 for those born in 1960 or later.

fully insured Social Security status Requires 40 credits and provides workers and their families with benefits under the retirement, survivors, and disability programs; once status is earned, it cannot be taken away even if the eligible worker never works again.

functional format Résumé that emphasizes career-related experiences.

fund investment advisers Have access to the best research; they select, buy, sell, and monitor the performance of the securities purchased; thus, they oversee the portfolio.

fund screener/fund-screening tool Permits investors to screen all of the mutual funds in the market to gauge performance.

fundamental analysis School of thought in market analysis that assumes each stock has an intrinsic (or true) value based on its expected stream of future earnings.

future value The valuation of an asset projected to the end of a particular time period in the future.

futures contract Type of exchange-traded standardized forward contract that specifies the size of the contract, quality of product to be delivered, and delivery date.

"gap" insurance Pays off the remainder of a totaled vehicle after an accident loan if the insurance payment is insufficient to do so.

garnishment Court-sanctioned procedure by which a portion of debtors' wages are set aside by their employers to pay debts.

general (full-service) brokerage firms Offer a full range of services to customers, including investment advice and research.

generic products Goods that carry store brands or are sold under a general commodity name such as "whole-kernel corn" rather than a brand name, such as Del Monte.

gold bullion coins Various world mints issue these coins, which contain 1 troy ounce (31.15 grams) of pure gold.

gold bullion A refined and stamped weight of precious metal.

good-faith estimate Lender's list of all the costs associated with the loan, including the annual percentage rate, application and processing fees, closing costs, and any other charges that must be paid when the deal is legally consummated.

goods and services dispute Asserts that charges were for faulty, damaged, shoddy, defective, or poor-quality goods and services and cardholder made a good-faith effort to try to correct the problem with the merchant.

government securities money market funds Appeal to investor concerns about safety by investing solely in U.S. Treasury bills and other short-term securities backed by the U.S. government.

grace period (on credit accounts) Time period between the posting date of a transaction and the payment due date during which no interest accrues.

grace period (for interest earning accounts) Period (in days) for which deposits or withdrawals can be made without any penalty.

grace period (in life and health insurance) Period of time during which an overdue premium may be paid without a lapse of the policy.

graduated vesting Schedule under which employees must be at least 20 percent vested after two years of service and gain an additional 20 percent of vesting for each subsequent year until, at the end of year six, the account is fully vested.

graduated-payment mortgage Mortgage in which borrower pays smaller-than-normal payments in the early years but payments gradually increase to larger-than-normal payments in later years.

grantor/settler/donor/trustor Creator of a trust.

gross capitalized cost (gross cap cost) Includes vehicle price plus cost of any extra features such as insurance or maintenance agreements.

gross domestic product (GDP) The nation's broadest measure of economic health, it reports how much economic activity (all goods and services) has occurred within the U.S. borders during a given period.

gross income All income in the form of money, goods, services, and/or property.

group health plan Sold collectively to an entire group of people rather than to individuals, such as the group health care policies offered by employers.

group term life insurance Issued to people as members of a group (such as a company's employees) rather than as individuals.

growing-equity mortgage (GEM) Meant for people who design their loan in advance to reduce interest costs by paying off the mortgage loan early.

growth and income funds Invest in companies that have a high likelihood of both dividend income and price appreciation; less risk-oriented than aggressive growth funds or growth funds.

growth funds Seek long-term capital appreciation by investing in common stocks of companies with higher-than-average revenue and earnings growth, often the larger and well-established firms.

guaranteed insurability (guaranteed purchase option) Permits the cash-value policyholder to buy additional stated amounts of cash-value life insurance at stated times in the future without evidence of insurability.

guaranteed minimum rate of return Minimum rate that, by contract, the insurance company is legally obligated to pay.

guaranteed renewable policies Must be continued in force as long as the policyholder pays the required premium.

guaranteed renewable term insurance Protects you against the possibility of becoming uninsurable.

guardian Person responsible for caring for and raising any child under the age of 18 and for managing the child's estate.

habitability Suitability for use as a dwelling.

harassment Illegal bullying, such as rent increases, eviction, or utility shutoff.

hazard Any condition that increases the probability that a peril will occur.

health care plan An employee benefit designed to pay all or part of the employee's medical expenses.

health care proxy Legal document that appoints another person to make health care decisions if the writer of the proxy is rendered medically incapable of making his or her wishes known.

health insurance Provides protection against financial losses resulting from illness and injury.

health maintenance organizations (HMOs) Provide a broad range of health care services for a set monthly fee on a prepaid basis.

health reimbursement account (HRA) Funds that employers set aside to reimburse employees for qualified medical expenses.

health savings account (HSA) Tax-deductible savings accounts into which individuals or employers can deposit tax-sheltered funds to pay future medical bills.

hedge fund Global company beyond the regulations of the U.S. Securities and Exchange Commission that uses unconventional (and sometimes very risky) investment strategies.

heir Person who inherits or is entitled by law or by the terms of a will to inherit some asset.

high-balling Sales tactic in which dealer offers a trade-in allowance that is much higher than the vehicle is worth.

high-deductible health care plan A plan that requires individuals pay a higher deductible to cover medical expenses before insurance plan payments begin; chosen to save money on premiums.

high-risk/speculative investments Present potential for significant fluctuations in return, sometimes over short time periods.

home equity line of credit Use of home equity as collateral for a line of credit.

home inspection Conducted to ensure that the home is physically sound and that all operating systems are in proper order.

home warranty insurance Operates much like a service contract on existing homes.

homeowner's association Organization of condo owners that is responsible for enforcing bylaws, managing common grounds and facilities, and holding insurance on buildings.

homeowner's fee Fee charged to condo owners to provide for association activities and facilities.

homeowner's general liability protection Applies when you are legally liable for another person's losses, other than those that arise out of use of vehicles or your professional duties.

homeowner's insurance Combines liability and property insurance coverages that homeowners and renters typically need into single-package policies.

homeowner's no-fault medical payments protection Pays for bodily injury losses that others suffer regardless of who was at fault.

homeowner's no-fault property damage protection Pays for property losses of others for which a homeowner wishes to assume responsibility.

I bonds Nonmarketable savings bonds backed by the U.S. government that pay an earnings rate that combines two rates: a fixed interest rate set when the investor buys the bond and a semiannual variable interest rate tied to inflation that protects the investor's purchasing power.

identity theft When someone else uses your personal information to run up debt in your name or access your financial accounts.

image statement A type of bank statement for which you receive a photocopy of checks written and deposits you had made rather than the actual document.

immediate annuity Annuity, often funded by a lump sum from the death benefit of a life insurance policy or lump sum from a defined-contribution plan, that begins payments one month after purchase.

implied warranty/warrant of merchantability/warranty of fitness Product sold is warranted to be suitable for sale (warranty of merchantability) and to work effectively (a warranty of fitness) whether or not a written warranty exists.

impulse buying Buying without fully considering priorities and alternatives.

income Total payments received over a specified time period.

income stock A stock that may not grow too quickly, but year after year it pays a cash dividend higher than that offered by most companies.

incontestability clause Places a time limit on the right of the insurance company to deny a claim.

indemnity plan Health insurance based on reimbursement for losses with the type of care chosen by patients based upon their physicians' advice.

indenture Written, legal agreement between bondholders and debtor that describes terms of the debt by setting forth the maturity date, interest rate, and other details.

independent insurance agents Independent businesspeople who act as third-party links between insurers and insureds.

index fund Mutual fund that seeks to achieve the same return as a particular market index by buying and holding all or a representative selection of securities in it.

index of leading economic indicators (LEI) A composite index reported monthly by the Conference Board that collects relevant economic data for business, governments, and individuals' use.

indexed A procedure used by the Social Security Administration to adjust the earnings during one's working years to reflect increases in average wages for all workers over time; used in the process of calculating SSA benefits.

indexing Yearly adjustments to tax brackets that reduce inflation's effects on tax brackets.

individual account Has one owner who is solely responsible for the account and its activity.

individual practice organization (IPO) HMO structure in which the HMO contracts with—rather than hires—groups of physician.

individual retirement account (IRA) Non-employer-based retirement accounts in which earnings off the account are allowed to accumulate tax free.

inflation A steady and sustained rise in general price levels across economic sectors; measured by the changing cost over time of a "market basket" of goods and services that a typical household might purchase.

inflation risk/purchasing power risk Danger that your money will not grow as fast as inflation and therefore not be worth as much in the future as it is today.

in-force illustration Shows the policy's cash-value status and projections for the future given the current rate of return at the time of the illustration (rather than the rate used at the inception of the policy).

inheritance tax Tax assessed by the decedent's state of residence on beneficiaries who receive inherited property (only eight states have this tax).

initial public offerings (IPOs) New issues of stocks or bonds; the primary market for securities.

insolvent Carrying a negative net worth.

installment credit (closed-end credit) Credit arrangement in which the borrower must repay the amount owed plus interest in a specific number of equal payments.

installment purchase agreements/collateral installment loans/chattel mortgage loans A type of contract used when purchasing goods with an installment loan; title of property passes to buyer when contract is signed.

installment-certain annuity Provides monthly payments for the rest of the life of the annuitant with a guarantee that if the person dies before receiving a specific number of payments, the beneficiary will receive a certain number of payments for a particular time period.

insurance Mechanism for transferring and reducing pure risk through which a large number of individuals share in the financial losses suffered by members of the group as a whole.

insurance agent Representative of an insurance company authorized to sell, modify, service, and terminate insurance contracts.

insurance claim Formal request to the insurance company for reimbursement for a covered loss.

insurance companies Financial institutions that provide property, liability, health, life, and other insurance products, as well as monetary asset services.

insurance dividends Surplus earnings of insurance company when the difference between the total premium charged exceeds the cost to the company of providing insurance.

insurance policy Contract between the person buying insurance (the insured) and the insurance company (the insurer).

insurance rate Price charged for each unit of insurance coverage.

insured Individual whose life is insured.

insuring agreements Broadly defined coverages provided under the policy.

interest The price of borrowing money.

interest inventories Scaled surveys that assess career interests and activities.

interest rate risk Risk that interest rates will rise and bond prices will fall, thereby lowering the prices on older bond issues.

interest-adjusted cost index (IACI) Measures the cost of life insurance, taking into account the interest that would have been earned had the premiums been invested rather than used to buy insurance.

interest-adjusted net payment index (IANPI) If a policy will remain in force until death, this method allows you to effectively measure the cost of cash-value insurance. The lower the IANPI, the lower the cost of the policy.

interest-earning checking account Any account on which you can write checks that pays interest.

interest-only mortgage Mortgage in which the borrower pays only the interest on the mortgage in monthly payments for a fixed term, then either refinances the principal, pays off the principal, or starts paying the higher monthly payment with the principal payments added in.

interest-rate caps Limit the amount by which the interest rate can increase in an ARM.

interests Long-standing topics and activities that engage your attention.

intermediate care Appropriate for people who do not require around-the-clock nursing but who are not able to live alone.

intermediate-term goals Financial targets that can be achieved within one to five years.

Internal Revenue Code Laws governing income tax collection in the United States.

Internal Revenue Service (IRS) Government agency charged with collecting income taxes.

intestate When a person dies without a legal will.

investing Putting saved money to work so that it makes you even more money.

investment (capital) assets Tangible and intangible items acquired for their monetary benefits.

investment assets-to-total assets ratio Compares investment asset value with net worth.

investment banking firms Intermediaries between companies issuing new stocks and bonds and the investing public.

investment philosophy Investor's general tolerance for risk in investments, whether it is conservative, moderate, or aggressive, given the investor's financial goals.

investment plan An explanation of your investment philosophy and your logic on investing to reach specific goals.

investment risk The possibility that the yield on an investment will deviate from its expected return.

investment-grade bonds Offer investors a reasonable certainty of regularly receiving periodic income (interest) and retrieving the amount originally invested (principal).

investments Assets purchased with the goal of providing additional income from the asset itself.

invoice price/seller's cost Reflects the price the dealer has been billed from the manufacturer.

irrevocable charitable remainder trust (CRT) Trust that pays you and/or your survivors tax-advantaged income while you are alive, and then the designated charity eventually receives the corpus of the CRT when you (and your spouse, if so arranged) die.

irrevocable living trust Arrangement in which the grantor permanently gives up ownership and the right to control of the property, to change the beneficiaries, and to change the trustees.

IRS 20 percent withholding rule Rollover penalty that applies if a participant in a retirement plan takes direct possession of the funds.

IRS tax table Used to figure income tax for taxable incomes up to $100,000.

item limits Specify the maximum reimbursement for a particular health care expense.

itemized deductions Tax-deductible expenses.

job interview Formal meeting between employer and potential employee to discuss job qualifications and suitability.

joint account Has two or more owners, each of whom has legal rights to the funds in the account.

joint and survivor benefit/survivor's benefit Annuity whose payments continue to a surviving spouse after the participant's death; often equals at least 50 percent of participant's benefit.

joint tenancy with right of survivorship/joint tenancy Most common form of joint ownership, especially for husbands and wives, in which each person owns the whole of the asset, such as a bank account or home, and can dispose of it without the approval of the other owner(s).

joint-and-survivor annuity Provides monthly payments for as long as one of the two people—usually a husband and wife—is alive.

Keogh Tax-deferred retirement account designed for self-employed and small-business owners.

kiddie tax rule Applies the parents' marginal tax rate to unearned income of a child under age 18 who has such income in excess of $1700 for the year.

land contract/contract for deed Brings greater risk for the buyer because all terms in the contract (including payment of the debt) must be satisfied before transfer of title will occur.

lapsed policy Policy that has been terminated because of nonpayment of premiums.

large-loss principle A basic rule of risk management that encourages us to insure the losses that we cannot afford and assume the losses that we can reasonably afford.

law of large numbers As the number of members in a group increases, predictions about the group's behavior become increasingly accurate.

layering term insurance policies Purchasing multiple level-premium term policies so that coverage grows when you need it most and then can be decreased as your needs change.

LEAP Long-term Equity AnticiPation Security; an option with a much longer term than traditional stock or index options.

lease In this context, a contract specifying both tenant and landlord legal responsibilities.

leasing Renting a product while ownership title remains with lease grantor.

lemon laws State laws that provide guidelines for arbitrators to use to order a dealer's buyback of a "lemon" as defined under the law—commonly a car that has been in the shop four or more times to fix the same problem.

lender buy-down mortgage Mortgage in which base interest rate is set for the loan that is perhaps 0.5 percentage points higher than the interest rate for a conventional mortgage. For the first year, the borrower pays a rate 2 percentage points below the base rate. In the second year, the rate is 1 point below the base rate. In the third and future years, the base rate is charged.

letter of last instructions Nonlegal instrument that may contain suggestions and recommendations regarding funeral and burial instructions, organ donation wishes, material to be included in the obituary, contact information for relatives and friends, and other information useful to the survivors, such as the location of important documents.

level-premium term insurance Term policy with long term under which premiums remain constant. Also called guaranteed level-premium term insurance.

leverage Using borrowed funds to invest with the goal of earning a rate of return in excess of the after-tax costs of borrowing.

liabilities What you owe.

liability insurance Protection from financial losses suffered when you are held liable for others' losses.

lien Legal right to take and hold property or to sell it in the event the borrower (mortgagor) defaults on the loan.

life insurance An insurance contract that promises to pay a dollar benefit to a beneficiary upon the death of the insured person.

life insurance application Policyholder's offer to purchase a policy.

life-cycle funds/target retirement funds Asset allocation funds that offer investors premixed portfolios of stocks, bonds, and cash that investors of a certain age and risk tolerance might prefer.

lifeline banking accounts Offer access to minimal financial services that every consumer needs.

lifestyle trade-offs Weighing the demands of particular jobs with your social and cultural preferences.

lifetime/aggregate limit Places an overall maximum on the total amount of reimbursement available under a policy.

limit order Instructs the stockbroker to buy or sell a stock at a specific price.

limited liability Common shareholders' responsibility for business losses is limited to the amount invested in the shares of stock owned.

limited managed account A company that buys and sells an investor's mutual fund assets to adjust the portfolio to specified standards (called rebalancing).

limited warranty Any warranty that offers less than the three conditions for full warranty.

limited/special power of attorney Allows someone to act in your behalf for a single transaction or limited time period, such as a real estate agent signing your name at a closing if you are unable to attend the closing yourself.

limited-pay whole life insurance Whole life insurance that allows premium payments to cease before the insured reaches the age of 100.

liquidity Speed and ease with which an asset can be converted to cash.

listed Refers to housing that is under contract with the seller and the broker.

listing agent The party with whom the seller signs the listing agreement; listing agent advertises the property, shows it to prospective buyers, and assists the seller in negotiations.

listing agreement Agreement that brokers require homeowners to sign that permits the broker to list the property exclusively or with a multiple-listing service.

living benefit clause Allows the payment of all or a portion of the death benefit prior to death if the insured contracts a terminal illness.

living trust A trust that takes effect while the grantor is still alive.

load funds Mutual funds that always charge a "load" or sales charge upon purchase; the load is the commission used to compensate brokers.

loan Consumer credit that is repaid in equal amounts over a set period of time.

loan commitment/loan preapproval Lender's promise to grant a loan.

loan origination fee Fees (often 1 point) that a lender might charge for the paperwork associated with the processing of the mortgage loan application.

loan preapproval Oral commitment from a bank or credit union agreeing to furnish credit for a purchase; lets buyers know how much they can borrow and at what interest rate.

loan-to-value (LTV) ratio Measures the amount of leverage in a real estate purchase or investment project by dividing the total amount of debt by the market price of the property.

long-term care insurance Provides reimbursement for costs associated with intermediate-term and custodial care in a nursing facility or at home.

long-term gain/or loss A profit or loss on the sale of an asset that has been held for more than a year.

long-term goals Financial targets to achieve more than five years in the future.

long-term liability Debt that comes due in more than one year.

loss control Designing specific mechanisms to reduce loss frequency and loss severity.

loss frequency Refers to the likely number of times that a loss might occur over a period of time.

loss severity Describes the potential magnitude of loss due to a peril.

low-balling An attempt to raise an already negotiated price when it comes time to finalize the written contract.

low-load funds Carry sales charges of perhaps 1 to 3 percent; sold by brokers, via mail, and sometimes through mutual fund retailers located in shopping centers.

lump-sum distribution When all of the funds are removed from a retirement account at one time, usually "rolled over" into another qualified plan.

managed care plans Plans that seek to control the conditions under which health care can be obtained.

managed funds Each fund's professional managers constantly evaluate and choose securities to buy or sell, using a specific investment approach.

management Individuals who run the firm's day-to-day operations.

manufactured housing Fully or partially factory-built housing units transported to home site for final assembly.

manufacturer's suggested retail price (MSRP)/ sticker price Suggested initial asking price.

margin account Account at a brokerage firm that requires a substantial deposit of cash or securities and permits the purchase of other securities using credit granted by the brokerage firm.

margin buying Using a margin account to buy securities; allows the investor to apply leverage that magnifies returns—or losses.

margin call If a stock price declines to the point that the investor's equity is less than the required percentage, a representative of the brokerage firm makes a phone call and tells the investor to either put up more money or securities or face having the position bought on margin liquidated.

margin rate Set by the Fed, percentage of the value (or equity) in an investment that is not borrowed—recently 25 to 40 percent.

marginal cost The additional (marginal) cost of one more incremental unit of some item.

marginal tax bracket (MTB)/marginal tax rate One of six income-range segments at which income is taxed at increasing rates.

marginal tax rate The tax rate at which your last dollar earned is taxed.

marginal utility The extra satisfaction derived from gaining one more incremental unit of a product or service.

marital deduction Allows an estate to pass on an unlimited amount of assets to a surviving spouse free of estate taxes.

market interest rates Current long- and short-term interest rates paid on various types of corporate and government debts that carry similar levels of risk.

market making Occurs when a broker/dealer provides a continuous market in a security by maintaining an inventory to sell to other brokerage firms and stands ready to buy reasonable quantities of the same security or securities at market prices.

market order Instructs the stockbroker to execute an order at the prevailing market price—that is, the current selling price of the stock.

market price Current price that a buyer is willing to pay a willing seller for a share of stock.

market risk/systematic risk/undiversifiable risk Risk that the value of an investment may drop due to influences and events that affect all similar investments.

market timers Long-term investors who pull out of stocks or bonds in anticipation of a market decline or hold back from investing until the market "settles down"—that is, when they expect prices to climb.

marketability risk The chance that, if you need to sell your investment quickly, you may not get your full asking price—you might have to sell at a discount.

market-volatility risk The extent to which an asset's returns vary over time.

matching contributions Employer programs that match employees' 401(k) contributions up to a particular percentage.

maturity date Date upon which the principal is returned to the bondholder.

maximum taxable yearly earnings (MTYE) The maximum amount to which the FICA tax is applied.

mediation Procedure in which a neutral third party works with parties involved in a dispute to arrive at a mutually agreeable solution.

Medicaid A government health care program for low-income people funded jointly by the federal and state governments.

medical care plan Generic name for any program that pays or provides reimbursement for direct medical care expenditures.

medical information bureaus Similar to credit bureaus, these sources provide medical information to insurance companies.

Medicare The federal government's medical care program for the elderly.

Medicare Part A Hospitalization portion of the program; it requires no premium.

Medicare Part B Supplementary medical expense insurance portion for outpatient care, doctor office visits, or certain other services.

mentor Experienced person who offers advice to a less experienced person.

minimum payment The lowest amount a borrower may repay in a given month to avoid penalties.

minimum-balance account Checking account that requires customers to keep a certain minimum amount for a specified time period to avoid fees.

mobile homes Fully factory-assembled housing units that are designed to be towed on a frame with a trailer hitch.

moderate investment philosophy Investors with this philosophy accept some risk as they seek capital gains through slow and steady growth in investment value along with current income.

modern portfolio theory (MPT) Goal is to identify the investor's acceptable level of risk tolerance and then find an optimal portfolio of assets that will have the highest expected returns for that level of risk.

modified life insurance Whole life insurance for which the insurer charges smaller premiums in the early years and higher premiums thereafter.

monetary asset (cash) management How you handle your monetary assets.

monetary assets Cash and low-risk, near-cash items that can quickly be converted into cash.

money factor Measures the rent charge portion of lease payment; lessors must disclose true credit (money factor) costs. Also known as lease rate or lease factor.

money market account Interest-earning accounts that pay relatively high interest rates and offer limited check-writing privileges.

money market deposit account (MMDA) Government-insured money market account in a depository institution with minimum-balance requirements and tiered interest rates.

money market mutual fund (MMMF) Money market account in a mutual fund rather than at a depository institution.

money order A checking instrument bought for a particular amount.

Monte Carlo analysis Technique that performs a large number of trial runs of a particular portfolio mix of investments, called simulations, to find an optimal allocation for a particular investor's goals and risk tolerance.

morale hazard Arises when a person is indifferent to a peril, such as being careless about preventing a loss.

mortgage broker Individual or company that acts as an intermediary between borrowers and lenders.

mortgage insurance Insures the difference between the amount of down payment required by an 80 percent LTV ratio and the actual, lower down payment.

mortgage interest tax credit A nonrefundable income tax credit of up to $2000 for persons who borrow money to buy a home under certain state and local government programs.

mortgage loan Loan to purchase real estate in which the property itself serves as collateral.

mortgage lock-in Agreement that includes a lender's promise to hold a certain interest rate for a specified period of time, such as 60 days.

mortgage refinancing New mortgage is obtained to pay off and replace an existing mortgage, usually at a lower interest rate.

multiple Another term for P/E ratio.

multiple indemnity clause Provides for a doubling or tripling of the face amount if death results from certain specified causes.

multiple-listing (open-listing) service An information and referral network among real estate brokers allowing properties listed with a particular broker to be shown by all brokers.

multiple-of-earnings approach Method of estimating the amount of life insurance needed by multiplying income by some number, such as 5, 7, or 10.

municipal government bonds (munis) Long-term debts (bonds) issued by local governments (cities, states, and various districts and political subdivisions) and their agencies. Interest from munis, also known as tax-free bonds or tax-exempt bonds, is exempt from federal income tax.

mutual fund ask price Price at which an investor can purchase a mutual fund's shares; current NAV per share plus sales charges.).

mutual fund bid price Same as NAV (net asset value).

mutual fund dividend Income paid to investors out of profits earned by the mutual fund from its investments.

mutual fund family Investment management company that offers a number of different funds to the investing public, each with its own investment objectives or philosophies of investing.

mutual fund Investment company that pools funds by selling shares to investors and makes diversified investments to achieve financial goals of income or growth, or both.

mutual fund funds Earn a return by investing in other mutual funds, providing extensive diversification and higher-than-average expenses and fees.

mutual savings bank (MSB) Depositors own these financial institutions and share in earnings from deposits and housing and consumer loans.

naked option Speculative option that the writer does not own thus exposing the writer to unlimited risk (if selling a call) or substantial risk (if selling a put).

named-perils policies Cover only losses caused by perils that the policy specifically mentions.

NASDAQ National Association of Securities Dealers Automated Quotations system, which provides instantaneous information on securities offered by more than 3200 domestic and foreign companies.

NCUSIF The credit union checking and savings account program.

need Item thought to be necessary.

needs-based approach A superior method of calculating the amount of insurance needed that considers all of the factors that might potentially affect the level of need.

negative amortization Occurs when monthly payments are actually smaller than necessary to pay interest on the loan, which will result in a rising principal loan balance.

negotiating/haggling Process of discussing actual terms of agreement with a seller, usually on higher-priced items.

net asset value (NAV) Per-share value of a mutual fund.

net cost A misleading way to compare several life insurance policies, the net cost equals the total of all premiums to be paid minus any accumulated cash value and accrued dividends.

net surplus Amount remaining after all budget classification deficits are subtracted from those with surpluses.

net worth What's left when you subtract liabilities from assets.

new-vehicle buying service No-fee organization that arranges discount purchases for new-car buyers who are referred to nearby participating automobile dealers that have agreed to charge specific discount prices.

no-load mutual funds Funds that allow investors to purchase shares directly at the net asset value without the addition of sales charges.

nominal income Also called money income, it is income that has not been adjusted for inflation and decreasing purchasing power.

noncancelable policies Must be continued in force without premium changes up to age 65 as long as the participant pays the required premium.

noncontributory plan An employer-sponsored defined-contribution retirement plan in which only the employer makes contributions.

noncumulative preferred stock Preferred stock that gives stockholders no claim to previously skipped dividends.

nondeeded timesharing Legal right-to-use purchase of a limited, preplanned timesharing period of use of a property; does not grant legal real estate ownership interest to the purchaser.

nonforfeiture values Amounts stipulated in a life insurance policy that protect the cash value, if any, in the event that the policyholder chooses not to pay or fails to pay required premiums or wishes to cash in the policy.

noninstallment credit Single-payment, open-ended credit and service credit arrangements.

nonparticipating policies Policies that don't pay insurance dividends.

nonprobate property Does not go through probate; includes assets transferred to survivors by contract (such as beneficiaries listed on retirement accounts and bank accounts held with another person).

nonrefundable tax credit Credit that can reduce your tax liability only to zero.

notary fees Fees charged by a public official authorized to authenticate signatures for contracts, deeds, affidavits, and so on.

odd lot An amount of a security that is less than the normal unit of trading for that particular security; for stocks, any transaction less than 100 shares is usually considered to be an odd lot.

older home form (HO-8) Named-perils policy that provides actual-cash-value protection on the dwelling, which may be more valuable than a new home.

online brokers Such brokers, also called Internet or electronic brokers, have reduced the cost of executing a trade to perhaps $20 or even $10 because their primary business is online trading.

open-end lease Agreement in which lessee must pay any difference between projected residual value of vehicle and actual market value at the end of the lease period.

open-end mutual funds Issue redeemable shares that investors purchase directly from the fund (or through a broker for the fund).

open-ended (revolving) credit Arrangement in which credit is extended in advance of any transaction so that borrowers do not need to reapply each time they need to use credit.

open-enrollment period Period during which employees can make changes in coverage or switch among alternative health plans.

opportunity cost The opportunity cost of any decision is the value of the next best alternative that must be forgone.

option Contract to buy or sell a financial asset at a specified point in the future at a specified price.

option holder Person who buys and then owns an option contract.

option premium Price of an option contract.

option writer Agrees to sell an option contract that promises either to buy or to sell a specified asset for a fixed striking price.

optionally renewable policies May be canceled or changed by the plan provider, but only at the time of expiration and renewal.

ordinary income dividend distributions Occur when the fund pays out dividend income and interest (monthly, quarterly, or annually) it has received from securities held in the fund.

organized exchanges Actual physical location for a market, at which some securities prices are set by open outcry. Organized exchanges are quickly merging with electronic markets.

overindebted When one's excessive personal debts make repayment difficult and cause financial distress.

over-the-counter (OTC) marketplace Electronic marketplace for securities transactions.

overwithholding Occurs when employees have their employers withhold more in estimated taxes than the tax liability ultimately due the government.

owner/policyholder Retains all rights and privileges granted by the policy, including the right to amend the policy and the right to designate who receives the proceeds.

own-occupation policy Provides benefits if you can no longer perform the occupation you had at the time you became disabled.

paid-up Point at which the owner of a whole life policy can stop paying premiums.

par value/face value Some multiple of $1000 that is printed on a bond when issued and repaid at maturity.

participating policies Policies that pay insurance dividends.

partnership theory of marital rights Presumes that wedded couples intend to share their fortunes equally, thus, property acquired during the marriage and titled in the name of only one partner (other than property acquired by gift or inheritance) becomes the property of both spouses.

passive investor An investor who does not actively engage in trading securities or monitoring his or her investments; seeks to match the market return via mutual funds or other managed investments in the longer term.

pawnshop Lender that offers small single-payment loans for short time periods in return for an item of personal property that serves as collateral.

payable-at-death designation Status granted to individuals who are not joint tenants and who might need to access accounts without going through probate—the deceased signs the designation before death and the designee simply presents a death certificate to access the accounts.

payday lenders Businesses that grant credit by honoring a personal check but agree not to deposit the check for a week or longer (until payday).

payment caps Limit the amount by which the payment can vary on an ARM.

payroll withholding An employer takes a certain amount from an employee,s income as a prepayment of an individual,s tax liability for the year and sends that amount to the IRS

peak Point in the business cycle when economic activity is at its highest.

penny stocks Stocks that sell for less than $1 per share and often are issued by new companies with erratic sales, few profits, and only some hope of success.

Pension Benefit Guaranty Corporation (PBGC) ERISA-established watch-dog organization that insures defined-benefit (but not defined-contribution) pension plans to guarantee certain minimum benefits to eligible workers whose employers' plans are not financially sound enough to pay their obligations.

pension Sum of money paid regularly by a former employer as a retirement benefit.

peril Any event that can cause a financial loss.

periodic rate The APR for a charge account divided by the number of billing cycles per year (usually 12).

periodic statements Consumer-protecting recaps that show all transfers to and from accounts, fees charged, and opening and closing balances.

periodic tenancy Type of lease that provides for residency week to week, month to month, or some other set period and that can be terminated by either party upon advance notice.

permanent insurance Alternate name for cash-value insurance, so named because the insurance remains in effect for the insured's entire life.

personal auto policies (PAPs) Policies that cover all property and bodily injury liability losses resulting from an accident until the limit is reached.

personal finance The study of personal and family resources considered important in achieving financial success; it involves how people spend, save, protect, and invest their financial resources.

personal inflation rate Inflation's effect on a particular person's purchasing power. For example, inflation pushes up the cost of borrowing, so monthly car payments and home mortgage rates increase when the personal inflation rate rises.

personal injury protection (PIP) Medical payments coverage for the driver and any passengers for bodily injury losses as well as possibly lost wages and rehabilitation expenses common in no-fault accident states.

personal line of credit Form of open-ended credit in which the lender allows the borrower access to a prearranged revolving line of credit.

personal losses Losses that specific individuals or organizations suffer rather than society as whole suffering the losses.

personal values The principles, standards, or qualities that you consider desirable.

physical hazard A particular characteristic of the insured person or property that increases the chance of loss.

PITI Elements of a monthly real estate payment consisting of principal, interest, real estate taxes, and homeowner's insurance.

planned buying Thinking through all the details of a purchase from the initial desire to buy to your satisfaction after the purchase.

point/or interest point Fee equal to 1 percent of the total mortgage loan amount.

policy illustration Charts the projected growth in the cash value for given rates of return.

policy limits Specify the maximum dollar amounts that will be paid under the policy.

portability option Allows you to convert your group medical care coverage to individual coverage within 180 days before COBRA ends.

portability Upon termination of employment, employees with portable benefits can keep their savings in tax-sheltered accounts by transferring retirement funds from employer's account directly to another account without penalty.

portfolio diversification Practice of selecting a collection of different asset classes of investments (such as stocks, bonds, mutual funds, real estate, and cash) that are chosen not only for their potential returns but also for their dissimilar risk-return characteristics.

portfolio tracking Automatically updates the value of your portfolio after you enter the symbols of the stocks you own and the number of shares held.

portfolio Collection of investments assembled to meet your investment goals.

posting date The date at which a credit card transaction is actually charged to the card holder's account.

potential rate of return Determined by adding anticipated income (from dividends, interest, rents, or other sources) to future value of investment and then subtracting investment's original cost.

preapproved credit card offers Firms find and send prescreened creditworthy individuals applications that become active accounts upon the individual signing the application.

preemptive right Common stockholders hold this right to purchase additional shares before a firm offers new shares to the public.

preexisting conditions Medical conditions or symptoms that the plan participant knew about or had been diagnosed within a certain time period before the plan effective date.

preferred employer Identifying employers that would suit you best.

preferred provider organization (PPO) Group of medical care providers (doctors, hospitals, and other health care providers) who contract with a health insurance company to provide services at a discount.

preferred stock Type of fixed-income ownership security in a corporation that pays fixed dividends.

premium A sum of money paid in addition to a face amount for a bond; comparatively small, predictable fee for insurance with which individuals or companies can replace an uncertain—and possibly large—financial loss.

premium conversion plans Employees can pay their share of insurance premiums with pretax dollars; such pretax paid expenses come off of total income reported to the IRS.

premium quote service Offers computer-generated comparisons among 20 to 80 different companies.

prepaid educational service plan Type of qualified tuition program that allows purchase of a child's future college education at today's prices, locking in tuition prices.

prepayment fee/penalty (mortgages) Charge set to discourage buyers from continually refinancing their home loans, this is a mortgage contract clause that charges 1 to 3 percent of the original mortgage loan if the mortgage is paid off prematurely.

prepayment penalty Special charge assessed to the borrower for paying off a loan early.

present value The current value of an asset (or stream of assets) that will be received in the future; also known as discounted value.

preservation of capital An investment goal that means the investor does not want to risk any principal or original investment; risk averse.

preshopping research Gathering information before actually beginning to interact with sellers.

prestige cards Bank credit cards whose names are often associated with a precious metal ("gold," "silver," "platinum"); require users to possess higher credit qualifications and offer enhancements such as free traveler's checks and higher credit limits.

pretax dollars Money income that has not been taxed by the government.

pretax income Income before taxes are calculated.

pretax money Investing with pretax money to a tax-sheltered retirement account comes out of your earnings before income taxes are calculated, thus gaining an immediate elimination of part of your income tax liability for the current year.

price/earnings ratio (P/E ratio) Widely followed measure of stock value that is calculated by dividing the current market price of a stock by earnings per share over the past four quarters.

price/sales ratio (P/S ratio) Tells the number of dollars it takes to buy a dollar's worth of a company's annual revenues; calculated by dividing company's total market capitalization by its sales for the past four quarters.

price-to-book ratio (P/B ratio) Current stock price divided by the per-share net value of a firm's plant, equipment, and other assets (book value); helps investors identify stocks that are value rich. Also called market-to-book ratio.

price-to-rent ratio Measures the current income in a real estate market; multiply the monthly rent by 12 and then divide the property price by this figure. The higher the number, the less likely you are to make money.

primary-care physician HMO-assigned doctor who usually must order or approve referrals to specialized health care providers.

prime rate Key measure of interest rates in the economy; its fluctuations drive the changes in rates for all types of variable-rate credit.

principal The original amount invested; or total amount owed on a credit account not including interest.

principle of indemnity Insurance will pay *no more* than the actual financial loss suffered.

private mortgage insurance Mortgage insurance obtained from a private company rather than a government agency.

probate Court-supervised process that allows creditors to present claims against an estate and ensures the transfer of a decedent's assets to the rightful beneficiaries according to a properly executed and valid will or, when no will exists, to the people, agencies, or organizations required by state law.

probate court Special court specifically charged to conduct the distribution of assets of people who have died.

professional abilities Job-related activities that you can perform physically, mentally, artistically, mechanically, and financially.

professional liability insurance/malpractice insurance Protects individuals and organizations that provide professional services when they are held liable for their clients' losses.

professional networking Making and using contacts with individuals, groups, and other firms to exchange career information.

professional shopper In exchange for a fee based on the sticker price, will find the best available price from a nearby dealer and finalize the sale or, for a lower price, will provide easily comparable information to buyer so that buyer can finalize purchase.

profile prospectus/fund profile Describes the mutual fund, its investment objectives, and how it tries to achieve its objectives in lay terms rather than the legal language used in a regular prospectus.

profit Money left over after a firm pays all expenses and interest to bondholders.

profit-sharing plan Employer-sponsored plan that allocates some of the employer profits to employees in the form of end-of-year cash or common stock contributions to employees' 401(k) accounts.

progressive income tax Tax rate increases as taxable income increases.

projected P/E ratio Because investors need to look to the future rather than the past, this measure divides price by projected earnings over the coming four quarters. Also known as forward price/earnings ratio.

promissory note Written installment loan contract that spells out the terms of the loan.

property insurance Protection from financial losses resulting from the damage to or destruction of your property or possessions.

prospectus Highly legalistic information presented by a firm to the SEC and to the public with any new issue of stock; this disclosure statement describes the experience of the corporation's management, the company's financial status, any anticipated legal matters that could affect the company, and potential risks of investing in the firm.

provider-sponsored network (PSN) Group of cooperating physicians and hospitals who have banded together to offer a health insur-ance contract. Also known as provider-sponsored association.

proxy Shareholders' written authorization to allow someone else to represent them and to vote their shares at a stockholder's meeting.

public corporation Corporation that issues stock purchased by individuals and traded in stock markets.

purchase contract/sales contract Formal legal document that outlines the actual agreement that results from the real estate negotiations.

purchase loan/sales credit Credit situation in which the consumer makes a purchase on credit with no cash transferring from the lender to the borrower.

purchase offer/offer to purchase Written offer to purchase real estate.

purchasing power Measure of the goods and services that one's income will buy.

pure risk Exists when there is no potential for gain, only the possibility of loss.

put option Gives option holder the right to sell the optioned asset to the option writer at the striking price at any time before the option expires.

qualified domestic-relations order (QDRO) Establishes the rights of an alternate payee to receive all or a portion of a participant's retirement plan benefits upon divorce or as soon as the participant leaves a private-sector job or reaches retirement age—must be court approved.

qualified retirement accounts IRS-approved retirement savings programs.

qualified tuition (Section 529) program Provides tax-sheltering when saving for a child's education.

quant funds (quantitative funds) In quant funds, computers make the buy and sell decisions based strictly on constant crunching of many numbers according to the criteria they are programmed to monitor.

random/unsystematic risk Risk associated with owning only one investment of a particular type (such as stock in one company) that, by chance, may do very poorly in the future due to uncontrollable or random factors that do not affect the rest of the market.

rate of return/yield Total return on an investment expressed as a percentage of its price.

real estate Property consisting of land, all structures permanently attached to that land, and accompanying rights and privileges, such as crops and mineral rights.

real estate broker (agent) Person licensed by a state to provide advice and assistance, for a fee, to buyers or sellers of real estate. Real estate brokers who are members of the National Association of Realtors often use the registered trademark of Realtor® to describe themselves.

real estate investment trust (REIT) Special kind of closed-end mutual fund that invests in a portfolio of assets, such as properties, like office buildings and shopping centers, or mortgages.

real estate property taxes Taxes assessed by local government agencies on the value of real estate to pay for schools and municipal services.

real estate transfer taxes Community-assessed taxes paid by the seller and also sometimes by the buyer based on the purchase price of the home or the equity the seller has in the home.

real income Income measured in constant prices relative to some base time period. It reflects the actual buying power of the money you have as measured in constant dollars.

real rate of return Return on an investment after subtracting the effects of inflation and income taxes.

rebate A partial refund of a purchase price offered as an inducement to buy.

recession A recurring period of decline in total output, income, employment and trade, usually lasting from six months to a year and marked by widespread contractions in many sectors of the economy.

record date Date that an issuer establishes to determine who is eligible to receive a dividend or distribution.

record keeping Recording sources and amounts of dollars earned and spent.

recurring clause Clarifies conditions under which a recurrence of an illness is considered a continuation of the first episode or a separate episode.

redeems When an investor sells shares.

redemption charge/exit fee Similar to a deferred load but often much lower; used to reduce excessive trading of fund shares.

redress Process of righting a wrong.

reenter provision Clause in a level-premium term policy that requires proof of good health at regular intervals.

refundable tax credit Credit that reduces taxes to below zero and the excess is refunded to taxpayer.

registered bond Bondholder's name is recorded so that checks or electronic funds transfers for payment of interest and principal can be safely forwarded when due.

regressive income tax As income rises, tax rate decreases.

reinvestment risk Risk that the return on a future investment will not be the same as the return earned by the original investment.

release Insurance document affirming that the dollar amount of the loss settlement is accepted as full and complete reimbursement.

remainder beneficiaries Parties named in the trust who are to receive the corpus upon termination of the trust agreement.

rent Payment received in return for allowing someone to use your real estate property, such as land or a building.

rental reimbursement coverage Provides a rental car when the insured's vehicle is being repaired after an accident or has been stolen.

rental yield A computation of how much income the investor might pocket from rent each year (before mortgage payments) as a percentage of the purchase price; divide the annual rent by 2 and then divide by the purchase price.

renter's contents broad form (HO-4) Named-perils policy that protects the insured from losses to the contents of a rented dwelling rather than the dwelling itself.

rent-to-own programs Provide a mechanism for buying an item with little or no down payment by renting it to the borrower for a period of time after which the borrower owns the merchandise.

repairs Usually tax-deductible expenses necessary to maintain property value.

replacement-cost requirement Stipulates that a home *must* be insured for 80 percent of its replacement value (some companies require 100 percent) in order for any loss to be fully covered.

repossession/foreclosure Legal proceeding by which the lender seizes an asset.

residual claim Common stockholders have a right to share in the income and assets of a corporation after higher-priority claims are satisfied.

residual clause of disability income policy Feature of own-occupation policies that allows for some reduced level of disability income benefits when a partial—rather than full—disability strikes.

residual value Projected value of leased asset at end of lease time period.

restrictive endorsement Uses the phrase *For deposit only* written on the back along with signature, authorizing the financial institution to accept the check only as an account deposit.

résumé Summary record of your education, training, experience, and other qualifications.

retail credit cards Allow customers to make purchases on credit at any of the outlets of a particular retailer.

retained earnings Money left over after firm has paid expenses, bondholder interest, taxes, preferred stockholder dividends, and common stockholder dividends.

retirement The time in life when the major sources of income change from earned income (such as salary or wages) to employer-based retirement benefits, private savings and investments, income from Social Security, and perhaps part-time employment.

retirement plan contribution credit/saver's tax credit Program to encourage low-income individuals to save for retirement, this tax credit ranges from 10 to 50 percent of every dollar they contribute to an IRA or employer-sponsored retirement plan up to $2000.

retirement savings goal/retirement nest egg Total amount of accumulated savings and investments needed to support desired retirement lifestyle.

return-of-premium policy Very expensive policy that promises to return all the premiums paid if the insured person maintains the policy and lives past a certain number of years—usually 30.

reverse mortgage/home-equity conversion loan Allows a homeowner older than age 61 to continue living in the home and to borrow against the equity in a home that is fully paid for and to receive the proceeds in a series of monthly payments, often over a period of 5 to 15 years or for life.

revocable living trust Grantor maintains the right to change the trust's terms or cancel it at any time, for any reason, during his or her lifetime.

revolving savings fund Variable budgeting tool that places funds in savings to cover large irregular or higher-than-usual expenses.

right of escheat Law by which, in the absence of a will, an estate transfers to the state if no surviving legal heirs exist.

risk Uncertainty about the outcome of a situation or event.

risk avoidance Refraining from owning items or engaging in activities that expose you to possible financial loss.

risk management Diversifying financial resources and ensuring you can handle large unexpected expenses.

risk management (in insurance) Process of identifying and evaluating purely risky situations to determine and implement appropriate management.

risk premium Amount that risk-averse investors require for taking on a riskier investment rather than a risk-free investment like U.S. government securities. The riskier the investment, the greater the premium demanded.

risk reduction Includes mechanisms, such as insurance, that reduce the overall uncertainty about the magnitude of loss.

risk retention Consciously accepting that some risks simply arise in the course of one's life and consciously retaining that risk.

risk tolerance An investor's ability and willingness to weather changes in security prices, that is, to weather market risk.

risk transfer Paying someone else, such as an insurance company, to accept the risk in your place and to reimburse you for any financial loss.

rollover Action of moving assets from one tax-sheltered account to another tax-sheltered account or to an IRA within 60 days of a distribution.

rollover IRA IRA opened to accept rollover funds.

rollover mortgage Consists of a series of short-term loans for two- to five-year time periods but with total amortization spread over the usual 25 to 30 years. The loan is renewed for each time period at prevailing market interest rates.

rollover penalty Penalty assessed by IRS if owner of qualified retirement plan does not follow IRS rollover regulations.

Roth individual retirement account (IRA) Investments made with after-tax money; the investment returns on such accounts is allowed to grow tax free, and withdrawals are also tax free.

round lots Standard units of trading of 100 shares of stock and $1000 or $5000 par value for bonds.

rule of 72 A formula for figuring the number of years it takes to double the principal using compound interest; simply divide the interest rate that the money will earn *into* the number 72.

rule of 78s method/sum of the digits method for calculating prepayment penalties A common method of calculating the prepayment penalty on a loan.

salary reduction plan Qualified plan in which contributed income is not included in an employee's salary.

sales finance company Seller-related lender whose primary business is financing sales for its parent company.

saver credit A credit of 50 percent of the amount contributed to a qualified retirement plan applies if adjusted gross income does not exceed $31,000 on a joint return or $15,500 for singles.

savings Income not spent on current consumption.

savings account Account that provides an accessible source of emergency cash and a temporary holding place for extra funds that will earn some interest.

savings banks (savings and loan associations—S&Ls) Financial institutions that pay depositors a slightly higher interest rate and focus primarily on savings and providing mortgage and consumer loans.

Savings Incentive Match Plan for Employees IRA (SIMPLE IRA) Defined-contribution retirement plan for employees of firms with fewer than 100 employees.

second mortgage An additional loan on a residence besides the original mortgage, usually at a higher interest rate because in case of default, the first mortgage is paid first.

Section 529 Plan Provides a tax-free way to save for college.

secured bond Pledges specific assets as collateral in indenture or has the principal and interest guaranteed by another corporation or government agency.

secured loan Loan that is backed by collateral or a cosigner.

securities Negotiable instruments of ownership or debt, including common stock, preferred stock, and bonds.

Securities and Exchange Commission (SEC) Federal government agency that ensures full disclosure of securities information to the investing public and approves rules and regulations employed by the organized securities exchanges.

securities exchange/stock market Market where agents of buyers and sellers can find each other easily by providing an orderly, open plan to trade securities.

securities market index Measures the average value of a number of securities chosen as a sample to reflect the behavior of a more general market, for example, the Dow Jones Industrial Average, the S&P 500, and so on.

security deposit Amount, often equal to the last month's rent payment, that landlords usually charge to ensure that tenants do not move without paying their rent.

security's street name Securities certificates kept in the brokerage firm's name instead of the name of the individual investor.

self-directed In defined-contribution plans, employees control the assets in their account—how often to make contributions to the account, how much to contribute, how much risk to take, and how to invest.

seller financing/owner financing When seller self-finances all or a portion of the buyer's purchase by accepting a promissory note from buyer.

selling agent Any real estate agent who seeks out buyers for a home. Listing agents also play this role, but any real estate agent can search for buyers to whom to sell a property.

selling short Investors selling securities they do not own (borrowing them from a broker) and later buying the same number of shares of the security at a lower price (returning them to the broker).

separable property Property wholly owned by one spouse; the property either belonged to one spouse before marriage or was received by that person as a gift or an inheritance during the marriage.

serial bonds Bonds that are retired serially; that is, each bond is numbered consecutively and matures according to a prenumbered schedule at stated intervals.

Series EE savings bonds Nonmarketable, interest-bearing bonds issued by the federal government that are issued at a sharp discount from face value and pay no annual interest, and they may be redeemed at full value upon maturity.

service credit Credit that public utilities, physicians, dentists, and other service providers extend to clients or users.

settlement options Choices from which the life insurance policyholder and/or beneficiary can choose in how the death benefit payment will be structured.

share draft account A checking account at a credit union.

shared-appreciation mortgage The lender offers an interest rate about one-third less than the market rate. In exchange, the lender gains the right to receive perhaps one-third of any appreciation in the home's value when the home is sold or ten years after the time of the loan.

shareholder fees Charged directly to investors for specific transactions, such as purchases, redemptions, or exchanges.

short-term (current) liability Obligation paid off within one year.

short-term gain/loss A profit or loss on the sale of an asset that has been held for one year or less.

signature card Identification used to verify the signatures of the owners of an account.

simplified employee pension—individual retirement account (SEP-IRA) Intended for taxpayers with self-employment income and owners of small businesses, contributions are tax deductible and funds grow tax deferred.

single-family dwelling Housing unit that is detached from other units.

single-payment loans Credit arrangement in which the full principal and interest amount is repaid at a specified future date.

single-premium life insurance Premium is paid once in the form of a lump sum; often used to pay for final expenses.

sinking fund Bond feature through which money is set aside with a trustee each year for repayment of the principal portion of the debt at maturity.

skilled nursing care Intended for people who need intensive care, meaning 24-hour-a-day supervision and treatment by a registered nurse, under the direction of a doctor.

skills format Résumé that emphasizes your aptitudes and qualities.

small-claims court State courts in which civil matters are often resolved without attorney assistance.

Social Security Administration (SSA) U.S. government agency that distributes checks to survivors and disabled workers—our national "safety net" funded by employee and employer contributions.

Social Security blackout period Once the youngest child reaches 18, the surviving spouse cannot collect Social Security survivors' benefits again until age 60.

Social Security credits Accumulated quarterly credits to qualify for Social Security benefits obtained by paying FICA taxes.

Social Security Disability Income Insurance Under this government program, eligible workers can collect some income for up to one year if their disabilities are total and expected to last one year or until death.

Social Security rider Provides an extra dollar amount of protection if you fail to qualify for Social Security disability benefits (70 percent of all applicants are rejected).

Social Security Statement The SSA periodically sends this document to all workers; it includes records of earnings history, records of how much workers and their employers have paid in Social Security taxes, and estimates of current and future benefits.

Social Security survivor's benefits Government program benefits paid to a surviving spouse and children of a deceased worker.

socially conscious funds Invest in companies that meet some predefined standard of moral and ethical behavior.

special (homeowner's insurance) form (HO-3): Provides open-perils protection (except for the commonly excluded perils of war, earthquake, and flood) for four types of property losses.

special endorsement Additional information, such as "Pay to the order of (name)," that creates a two-party check; such checks are very difficult to cash.

special needs trust Provides disabled beneficiary with lifelong access to supplemental and emergency funds to cover expenses that public assistance does not.

specialist Person on floor of an exchange who handles trades of a particular stock in an effort to maintain a fair and orderly market.

speculative risk Exists in situations that offer potential for gain as well as for loss. Investments involve speculative risk.

speculative-grade bonds Long-term, high-risk, high-interest-rate corporate (or municipal) IOUs issued by companies (or municipalities) with poor or no credit ratings. Also called junk bonds or high-yield bonds.

spending Amount of cash flow used in consuming goods and services now.

split-definition policy Provides benefits for rehabilitation and retraining at insurance company expense.

spousal consent requirement Federal law that protects surviving rights of spouse or ex-spouse to retirement or pension benefits unless the person signs a waiver of those rights.

spousal IRA Account set up for spouse who does not work for wages; offers tax-deferred growth and tax deductibility.

spread Represents difference between bid price at which a broker/dealer will buy shares and higher ask price at which the broker/dealer will sell shares.

springing power of attorney "Jumps" into effect when a specified event occurs, usually mental incapacitation or disability.

standard deduction Fixed amount that all taxpayers may subtract from their adjusted gross income if they do not itemize their deductions.

standard deviation A measure of a security's or mutual fund's volatility; also known as beta.

standard of living Material well-being and peace of mind that individuals or groups earnestly desire and seek to attain, to maintain if attained, to preserve if threatened, and to regain if lost.

standardized expense table SEC-required information that describes and illustrates mutual fund charges in an identical manner so that investors can accurately compare the effects of all of a fund's fees and other expenses relative to other funds.

start-up capital Funds initially invested in a business enterprise.

statement savings account (passbook savings account) Savings account that permits frequent deposits or withdrawals of funds without fees as long as client maintains minimum balance.

stay An order in bankruptcy court that temporarily prevents all creditors from recovering claims arising from before the start of the bankruptcy proceeding.

stock brokerage firms Licensed financial institutions that specialize in selling and buying stocks, bonds, and other investments for investors.

stock dividend Dividend paid in the form of stock shares instead of cash.

stock option Security that gives the holder the right to buy or sell a specific number of shares (normally 100) of a certain stock at a specified (striking) price before a specified expiration date.

stock split Occurs when stock shares owned by existing shareholders are divided into a larger number of shares.

stockbroker/account executive Professional who is licensed to buy and sell securities on behalf of the brokerage firm's clients.

stockholder/shareholder Each person who owns a share of a company's stock holds a proportionate interest in firm ownership (a very small slice) and, therefore, in the assets and income of the corporation.

stocks Shares of ownership in a business corporation's assets and earnings.

stock-screening tools Enable you to quickly sift through vast databases of hundreds of companies to find those that best suit your investment objectives.

stop order Instructs a stockbroker to sell your shares of stock at the market price if a stock declines to or goes below a specified price.

stop-payment order Notifying your bank not to honor a check when it's presented for payment.

stored-value card Usually gift cards that have magnetic strips or bar codes that encrypt the amount of money stored via the card.

straight annuity Provides lifetime payments for the life of the annuitant only.

subleasing An arrangement in which the original tenant leases the property to another tenant.

subordinate budget Detailed listing of planned expenses within a single budgeting classification.

subprime market Market that serves higher-risk credit applicants at higher interest rates.

subrogation rights Allow an insurer to take action against a negligent third party (and that party's insurance company) to obtain reimbursement for payments made to an insured.

suicide clause Allows the life insurance company to deny coverage if the insured commits suicide within the first few (usually two) years after the policy is issued.

super NOW account Government-insured money market account offered through depository institutions.

surplus/net gain/net income Income that exceeds total expenditures.

surrender charge A fee assessed if the policyholder withdraws some or all of the cash value accumulated.

survey Professional study undertaken to certify the specific boundaries of a lot.

survivorship joint life policy Pays when the last person covered dies.

sweat equity property Property that needs repairs but that has good underlying value; an investor buys the property at a favorable price and fixes it up to rent or sell at a profit.

sweeps Computer programs that check various subaccounts in an AMA and adjust balances in and out of the MMMF to ensure the highest interest rates.

take-home pay/disposable income Pay received after employer withholdings for taxes, insurance, and union dues.

tangible (use) assets Personal property used to maintain your everyday lifestyle.

tax avoidance Reducing tax liability through legal techniques.

tax balance due Money you must pay to the IRS if withholding and quarterly payments are insufficient to cover tax liability.

tax credit Dollar-for-dollar decrease in tax liability; also known as credit.

tax deferred Interest, dividends, or capital gains that are allowed to grow without taxes until distributions are taken.

tax evasion Deliberately, willfully, and illegally hiding income, falsely claiming deductions, or otherwise cheating the government out of taxes owed.

tax losses Paper losses that may not represent actual losses created when deductions generated from an investment exceed income from the investment.

tax planning Seeking legal ways to reduce, eliminate, or defer income taxes.

tax rate schedules Equations to figure taxes for returns with taxable incomes above $100,000.

tax refund Amount the IRS sends back to taxpayer if withholding and estimated payments exceed tax liability.

taxable income Income upon which income taxes are levied.

tax-deferred compounding Tax-free growth of tax-deferred investments.

taxes Compulsory government-imposed charges levied on citizens and their property.

tax-exempt income Income that is totally and permanently free of taxes.

tax-exempt money market funds Funds that limit their investments to tax-exempt municipal securities with maturities of 90 days or less.

tax-free exchange Arises when a real estate investor trades equity in one property for equity in a similar property and no other forms of property or money change hands.

tax-sheltered income Income exempt from income taxes in the current year but that will be subject to taxation in a later tax year.

tax-sheltered investments Investments that yield returns that are tax advantaged.

tax-sheltered retirement accounts Retirement account for which all earnings from the invested funds are not subject to income taxes.

tax-sheltered retirement plan Employer-sponsored, defined-contribution retirement plans including 401(k) plans and similar 403(b) and 457 plans.

teaser rate Low interest rate that lenders sometimes use to lure buyers; these rates will be low for the first year or so and then will rise to more realistic rates.

technical analysis Method of evaluating securities that uses statistics generated by market activity, such as past prices and volume, over time to determine when to buy or sell a stock.

10-K report A firm's financial statements and activity details for any publicly traded company appear in this mandatory report sent to the SEC annually.

tenancy by the entirety Restricted to property held between a husband and a wife; under this arrangement, no one co-owner can sell or dispose of his or her portion of an asset without the permission of the other.

tenancy for a specific time Type of lease that provides for residency for a specific period of time—usually one year.

tenancy in common A form of joint ownership in which two or more parties own the asset, but each retains control over a separate piece of the property rights.

term life insurance "Pure protection" against early death; pays benefits only if the insured dies within the time period (term) that the policy covers.

testamentary trust Becomes effective upon death of the grantor according to the terms of the grantor's will or a revocable living trust. Such trusts can provide money or asset management after the grantor's death for the heirs' benefit.

testator Writer of a will and owner of the estate.

tiered interest Common feature of NOW accounts that pays lower interest on smaller deposits and higher interest on larger balances.

tiered pricing Lending practice whereby those with best credit scores are offered better terms than those with less-than-perfect scores.

time deposits Savings accounts that financial institutions expect to remain on deposit for an extended period.

time horizon The period of time for which an investor is willing to invest; the longer the term, the higher return investors expect.

time value of money (TVM) A method by which one can compare cash flows across time, either as what a future cash flow is worth today (present value) or what an investment made today will be worth in the future (future value).

timesharing Joint ownership or lease of vacation property through which the principals occupy the property individually for set periods of time.

title Legal right of ownership interest to real property.

title insurance Protects the lender's interest if the title search is later found faulty.

title search An examination of local government records to ensure that the seller of a piece of property is the legal owner and that there are no liens or other claims outstanding.

total income Compensation from all sources.

total return Income an investment generates from current income and capital gains.

towing coverage Pays the cost of having a disabled vehicle transported for repairs.

trade-off Giving up one thing for another.

traditional (regular) IRA Account that offers tax-deferred growth; the initial contribution may be tax deductible for the year that the IRA was funded.

trailing commission Compensation paid to salespeople for months or years in the future.

trailing P/E ratio Calculated using recently reported earnings, usually from the previous four quarters.

transaction date Date on which a credit cardholder makes a purchase (or receives a credit).

transaction fees Charges levied against cardholders per use of the card but that are not included in the APR advertised.

travel and entertainment (T&E) cards Credit cards that allow holders to make purchases at numerous businesses but that require the holder to repay the entire balance charged within 30 days.

traveler's checks Financial instruments issued by extremely large institutions that are accepted virtually anywhere in the world upon countersignature.

Treasury bills Known as T-bills, U.S. government securities with maturities of one year or less.

Treasury Inflation-Protected Securities (TIPS) Marketable Treasury bonds whose value increases with inflation. These inflation-indexed $1000 bonds are the only investment that guarantees that the investor's return will outpace inflation.

Treasury note/Treasury bond Fixed-principal, fixed-interest-rate government security issued for an intermediate term or long term. Notes mature in ten years or less; bonds mature in more than ten years.

Treasury securities Known as Treasuries, securities issued by the U.S. government, including bills, notes, and bonds.

trough The point in the business cycle when economic activity is at its lowest point.

trust Legal arrangement between you as the creator of the trust and the trustee, the person designated to faithfully and wisely manage any assets in the trust to your benefit and to the benefit of your heirs.

trustee Financial institution, bank, or trust company that has fiduciary responsibility for holding plan assets and that invests the money in various securities; person charged with carrying out the trust for the benefit of the grantor(s) and heirs.

trustee-to-trustee rollover Retirement funds go directly from the previous employer's trustee to the trustee of the new account, with no payment to the employee occurring.

Truth in Lending Act (TIL) Requires lenders to disclose to credit applicants both the interest rate expressed as an annual percentage rate (APR) and the finance charge.

12b-1 fees/distribution fees Annual fees that some "no-load" fund companies deduct from a fund's assets to compensate salespeople and pay other expenses; they decrease the amount of money available for investment.

2006 Pension Protection Act Prohibits companies from requiring that employees buy company stock to qualify for matching contributions.

U.S. government savings bonds Nonmarketable, interest-bearing bonds issued by the U.S. Treasury.

umbrella (excess) liability insurance Catastrophic liability policy that covers liability losses in excess of those covered by any underlying homeowner's, automobile, or professional liability policy.

unearned income Investment returns in the form of rents, dividends, capital gains, interest, or royalties.

underwriting Insurer's procedure for deciding which insurance applicants to accept.

unfair discrimination Making distinctions among individuals based on unfair criteria when granting credit.

uniform settlement statement Lists all of the costs and fees to be paid at the closing.

unit investment trust (UIT) Closed-end investment company that makes a one-time public offering of only a specific, fixed number of units; once the UIT closes, it becomes an unmanaged fund that is somewhat illiquid.

universal default Situation in which credit companies assign much higher rates to accounts because credit report rechecks indicate repayment problems in one or more other accounts with any lender.

universal life insurance Provides the pure protection of term insurance and the cash-value buildup of whole life insurance, along with face amount variability, rate of cash-value accumulation, premiums, and rate of return.

unmanaged fund Fund with very low management fees since managers do not evaluate or

select individual securities; ETFs and index funds are examples.

unsecured bond/debenture Does not name collateral as security for debt; backed only by the good faith and reputation of the issuing agency.

unsecured loan/signature loan Loan granted based solely on borrower's good creditworthiness.

"upside down" Situation in which you owe more on the vehicle than its current market value.

use-it-or-lose-it rule An IRS regulation requiring that unspent dollars in a flexible spending account at the end of a calendar year be forfeited, unless the employer allows a three-month grace period for spending the funds.

usury laws/small loan laws Laws that stipulate state-mandated maximum amounts, interest rates, and credit-related fees for different types of loans.

utility A highly personalized concept that expresses how much satisfaction each person will obtain from any particular decision.

value funds Specialize in stocks that are fundamentally sound whose prices appear to be low (low P/E ratios) based on the logic that such stocks are currently out of favor and undervalued by the market.

values Fundamental beliefs about what is important, desirable, and worthwhile.

vanishing-premium life insurance Designed to allow policyholders to cease making premium payments after just a few years.

variable annuity Annuity whose value rises and falls like mutual funds and pays a limited death benefit via an insurance contract. Not as efficient as a mutual fund; costs are high for little return.

variable expenses Expenses over which you have substantial control.

variable interest rate cards Have rates that change monthly or annually according to general changes in the economy as a whole.

variable life insurance Allows you to choose the investments made with your cash-value accumulations and to share in any gains or losses.

variable value Because interest rates change, bonds may trade at a premium (more than face value) or at a discount (less than par) so that the yield equals the current yield for bonds with similar maturities and risk levels.

variable-rate (adjustable-rate) loans Loans for which the interest rate varies with the monthly payment going up or down, allowing the loan to be paid off by the original end date.

variable-rate certificates of deposit (or adjustable-rate CDs) Financial instruments that pay an interest rate that tracks general interest rates in the economy.

variable-universal life insurance Form of universal life insurance that gives the policyholder some choice in the investments made with the cash value accumulated by the policy. Also called flexible-premium variable life insurance.

vesting Ensures that a retirement plan participant has the right to take full possession of all

employer contributions and earnings if employee is dismissed, resigns, or retires.

viatical companies Firms that specialize in buying life insurance policies from insureds for $0.50 to $0.80 per $1 of death benefit in return for being named beneficiary on the policy.

vision care insurance Provides reimbursement for eye examinations and purchase of glasses and contact lenses.

volatility A mutual fund's (or any security's) tendency to rise or fall in price over time.

voting rights Proportionate authority to express an opinion or choice in matters affecting the company.

waiting period Long-term care and disability income policies can pay benefits from the first day of a triggering event or they can include a waiting period. Premiums drop with longer waiting periods.

waiver of premium Sets certain conditions under which an insurance policy would be kept in full force by the company without the payment of premiums.

want Item not necessary but desired.

warranty Sellers' assurances that goods are as promised and that certain steps will be taken to rectify problems if they arise.

whole life insurance Form of cash-value life insurance that provides lifetime life insurance protection and expects the insured to pay premiums for life. Also called straight life insurance.

will Written document in which a person tells how his or her remaining assets should be given away after death; without a will, the property will be distributed according to state probate law.

withdrawal options/systematic withdrawal plans Arrangements with a mutual fund company for shareholders who want to receive income on a regular basis from their mutual fund investments.

workers' compensation insurance Covers employers for liability losses for injury or disease suffered by employees that result from employment-related causes.

work-style personality Your own ways of working with and responding to job requirements, surroundings, and associates.

yield to maturity (YTM) Total annual effective rate of return earned by a bondholder on a bond if the security is held to maturity—takes into consideration both the price at which the bond sold and the coupon interest rate to arrive at effective rate of return.

zero-coupon bonds (zeros or deep discount bonds) Municipal, corporate, and Treasury bonds that are issued at a sharp discount from face value and pay no annual interest but are redeemed at full face value upon maturity.

zero-sum game Situation in which the wealth of all investors remains the same; the trading simply redistributes the wealth among those traders. Each profit must be offset by an equivalent loss; therefore, the average rate of return for all investors in futures is zero.

Index

Note: Boldface type indicates key terms that are defined in text.